INTERNATIONAL MONETARY FUND

Financial Soundness Indicators

Compilation Guide

2006

Cataloging-in-Publication Data

Financial soundness indicators : compilation guide—Washington, D.C. : International Monetary Fund, 2006.
p. cm.

Includes bibliographical references.
ISBN 1-58906-385-6

1. Financial institutions—Auditing. 2. International Monetary Fund.
I. International Monetary Fund.
HF5686.F46F35 2006

Price: $32.00

Please send orders to:
International Monetary Fund, Publication Services
700 19th Street, N.W., Washington, D.C. 20431, U.S.A.
Tel.: (202) 623-7430 Telefax: (202) 623-7201
E-mail: publications@imf.org
Internet: http://www.imf.org

recycled paper

Contents

Abbreviations ix

1 **Introduction** 1
Background 1
Some Key Aspects of the *Guide* 3
Structure of the *Guide* 6
Terminology 7

PART I: CONCEPTUAL FRAMEWORK

2 **Overview of the Financial System** 11
Introduction 11
What Is a Financial System? 11
Financial Corporations 11
Nonfinancial Corporations 13
Households 14
Nonprofit Institutions Serving Households (NPISHs) 14
General Government 14
Public Sector 14
Financial Markets 14
Payment System 15
Real Estate Markets 15

3 **Accounting Principles for Financial Soundness Indicators** 17
Introduction 17
Definition of Flows and Positions 17
Time of Recognition of Flows and Positions 17
Valuation 20
Residence 22
Domestic and Foreign Currencies, Unit of Account, and Exchange Rate Conversion 23
Maturity 24

4 **Accounting Framework and Sectoral Financial Statements** 26
Introduction 26
Accounting Framework 27
Sectoral Financial Statements 27

5 **Aggregation and Consolidation of Data** 54
Introduction 54
Defining Terms 54

The Aggregate Resident-Based Approach 55
The Consolidated-Based Approach 56
Applying Consolidated Group Reporting to the Needs of FSI Data 58
Specific Issues Arising from the Consolidated Approach 60
Compiling Consolidated Sector-Level Data 61
Annex. Detailed Specification of the Sector-Level Adjustments Required 63

PART II: SPECIFICATION OF FINANCIAL SOUNDNESS INDICATORS

6 Specification of Financial Soundness Indicators for Deposit Takers 75
Introduction 75
Financial Soundness Indicators 76

7 Specification of Financial Soundness Indicators for Other Sectors 88
Introduction 88
Calculation of Financial Soundness Indicators 88

8 Financial Markets 91
Introduction 91
Interest Rates 91
Securities Markets 94
Annex. Structural Indicators for Financial Markets 99

9 Real Estate Price Indices 101
Introduction 101
Measuring Real Estate Prices 101
Structural Indicators of Real Estate Markets 103
Constructing Real Estate Price Measures 104

PART III: COMPILATION AND DISSEMINATION OF FINANCIAL SOUNDNESS INDICATORS

10 Strategic and Managerial Issues 111
Introduction 111
Strategic Issues 111
Managerial Issues 114

11 Compilation of FSI Data: Practical Issues 118
Introduction 118
Basic Data Sources 118
Other Data Requirements 121
Availability of Data 132
Breaks in Data Series 132
Seasonal Adjustment 137

12 Dissemination of FSI Ratios and Related Data 138
Introduction 138
Dissemination Practices 138
A Framework for Disseminating FSIs 139

PART IV: ANALYSIS OF FINANCIAL SOUNDNESS INDICATORS

13 Financial Soundness Indicators and Macroprudential Analysis. 147
Introduction 147
Why Are FSI Data Needed? 147
What Is the Financial Stability Framework Within Which FSI Data Can Be Used? 148
What Are Some Other Tools That Can Enhance the Usefulness and Understanding of FSI Data? 151

14 What Use Can Be Made of the Specific FSIs? 155
Introduction 155
Deposit Takers 155
Other Financial Corporations 159
Nonfinancial Corporations 159
Households 160
Real Estate Markets 160

15 Peer Group Analysis and Descriptive Statistics 161
Introduction 161
Peer Group Analysis 161
Descriptive Statistics 162

Appendixes
I. Survey on the Use, Compilation, and Dissemination of Macroprudential Indicators . . 173
II. Summary of Guidance for Each Financial Soundness Indicator 180
III. Additional Definitions of FSIs and Related Data Series 203
IV. Reconciliation Between the *Guide*'s Methodology and National and Commercial Accounting 213
V. Numerical Examples 230
VI. Remaining Issues: Provisioning, Interest Rate Risk, and Stress Testing 256
VII. Glossary of Terms 270

Bibliography 278

Index 282

Boxes
4.1. Measurement Frameworks 28
4.2. The Basel Capital Adequacy Ratio 30
4.3. Islamic Financial Institutions and Financial Soundness 36
4.4. The Approach to Valuation and Provisioning in the *Guide*. 41
5.1. Interbank Flows and Positions 62
5.2. Flows and Positions in the Non-Deposit-Taking Sectors 63
5.3. What Is the Difference Between Data on a Cross-Border and a Domestic Basis? 64
8.1. Converting Bid-Ask Spreads from Yield Quotes into Price Terms 98
10.1. Managing Data Compilation Systems 116
11.1. Relationship Between Monetary and Financial Statistics and FSIs 119
12.1. Illustrative Points for Items to Be Covered in the Metadata 144
13.1. Using Interbank Stress Testing to Assess Systemic Risk 152
A2.1. FSIs: Index of Summaries 181
A3.1. The International Standard Industrial Classification of All Economic Activities (ISIC) 205

A6.1. U.S. Loan Classification System (Commercial Bank Examination Manual) 257
A6.2. Loan Classification System of Japanese Financial Supervisory Agency 257

Tables

1.1. Financial Soundness Indicators: The Core and Encouraged Sets 2
4.1. Deposit Takers 31
4.2. Other Financial Corporations 48
4.3. Nonfinancial Corporations 49
4.4. Households 52
5.1. Schematic Presentation of Levels of Consolidation 57
5.2. Sector-Wide Data: Consolidating Income and Expense as Well as Balance Sheet Items 66
6.1. Deposit Takers: Financial Soundness Indicators 76
6.2. Net Open Position in Foreign Currencies 80
6.3. Example of Measuring the Net Open Position in Foreign Exchange 81
6.4. Future Cash Flows Arising from Financial Derivative Contracts by Maturity 84
8.1. Stage of Development in Domestic Financial Markets for a Hypothetical Country 100
8.2. Example of Data Request During an FSAP 100
9.1. Quantities and Prices of Real Estate 105
11.1. Domestic Deposit Takers: Series Not Covered in National Accounts Methodology 122
11.2. Domestic Deposit Takers: Intrasector Positions and Flows 123
11.3. Domestic Deposit Takers: Other Intragroup Positions and Flows 124
11.4. Domestically Controlled Deposit Takers: Intergroup Positions and Flows (Cross-Border Consolidated Data) 128
11.5. Other Financial Corporations: Additional Data Series 129
11.6. Nonfinancial Corporations: Series Not Covered in National Accounts Methodology 130
11.7. Nonfinancial Corporations: Additional Data Series 131
11.8. Example for Computing Changes in Capital Adequacy Ratio Given the Changes in Population of Reporting Banks 132
11.9. Deposit Takers' Income and Expense Statement and Balance Sheet 133
11.10. Nonfinancial Corporations' Income and Expense Statement and Balance Sheet 135
11.11. Households' Income 136
12.1. Illustrative Presentation of Financial Soundness Indicators 140
12.2. Illustrative Presentation of Structural Indicators for the Domestic Financial Sector 142
13.1. Basel Core Principles Containing Information Relevant to the Interpretation of FSIs... 153
15.1. Example of Computing the Herfindahl Index 163
15.2. Example of Computing the Gini Index 164
15.3. Dispersion Statistics of Capital Asset Ratios (Equal-Weight Approach) 165
15.4. Dispersion Statistics of Capital Asset Ratios (Weighted-by-Contribution Approach) 165
15.5. Extensions of Dispersion Statistics of Capital Asset Ratios (Equal-Weight Approach) 167
15.6. Statistics of Capital Asset Ratios, by Range 167
15.7. Statistics of Capital Asset Ratios, by Percentile 168
15.8. Transition Matrix for One-Year Transitions Among Percentiles of the Distribution of Return on Capital 169
15.9. Analysis of Tails of the Distribution by Industry Classification 170
A1.1. FSIs by Type of Economy 174
A1.2. Group II FSIs by Type of Economy 175
A3.1. Calculating the Hui-Heubel Ratio 207

A3.2. Deposit Takers: Memorandum Series 208
A3.3. Other Financial Corporations: Memorandum Series 211
A3.4. Nonfinancial Corporations: Memorandum Series 211
A5.1. Income and Expense Statements: Deposit Takers—Aggregated Data 231
A5.2. Balance Sheets and Related Material: Deposit Takers—Aggregated Data 232
A5.3. Financial Soundness Indicators: Deposit Takers—Aggregated Data 234
A5.4. Recording Gains and Losses on Traded Instruments: Case 1 236
A5.5. Recording Gains and Losses on Traded Instruments: Case 2 236
A5.6. Recording Gains and Losses on Traded Instruments: Case 3 236
A5.7. Recording Gains and Losses on Traded Instruments: Case 4 237
A5.8. Recording Gains and Losses on Traded Instruments: Case 5 237
A5.9. Treatment of Interest on Nonperforming Loans: Case 1 238
A5.10. Treatment of Interest on Nonperforming Loans: Case 2 238
A5.11. Treatment of Interest on Nonperforming Loans: Case 3 238
A5.12. Interbank Positions and Flows 241
A5.13. Other Intragroup Positions and Flows 242
A5.14. Income and Expense Statements: Deposit Takers—Sector-Level Consolidated Data (Domestic Consolidated Data) 243
A5.15. Balance Sheets: Deposit Takers—Sector-Level Consolidated Data (Domestic Consolidated Data) 244
A5.16. Intergroup Positions and Flows (Cross-Border Consolidated Data) 245
A5.17. Income and Expense Statements: Deposit Takers—Sector-Level Consolidated Data (Cross-Border Consolidated Data) 246
A5.18. Balance Sheets: Deposit Takers—Sector-Level Consolidated Data (Cross-Border Consolidated Data) 247
A5.19. Consolidation of Sector-Wide Capital: Base Case 248
A5.20. Consolidation of Sector-Wide Income and Capital: Unrealized Valuation Gains—Case 1 248
A5.21. Consolidation of Sector-Wide Income and Capital: Unrealized Valuation Gains—Case 2 249
A5.22. Consolidation of Sector-Wide Income and Capital: Realized Valuation Gains—Case 1 249
A5.23. Consolidation of Sector-Wide Income and Capital: Realized Valuation Gains—Case 2 250
A5.24. Goodwill and Sector-Wide Capital: Purchase with Cash 252
A5.25. Goodwill and Sector-Wide Capital: Purchase by Issuing Shares 252
A5.26. Income and Expense Statements: Nonfinancial Corporations—Sector-Level Consolidated Data 253
A5.27. Balance Sheets: Nonfinancial Corporations—Sector-Level Consolidated Data 254
A5.28. Financial Soundness Indicators: Nonfinancial Corporations—Sector-Level Consolidated Data 255
A6.1. Levels of Provisions for Different Loan Classifications 260
A6.2. Interest Rate Risk 261
A6.3. Example of Gap Analysis 262
A6.4. Interest-Rate-Sensitive Assets and Liabilities with a Time to Repricing of One Year or Less 263
A6.5. Duration (*D*) of a Six-Year Eurobond with 8 Percent Coupon and Yield 264
A6.6. Portfolio Duration 264
A6.7. Sector-Level Duration 265
A6.8. Duration (*D**) When the Yield Curve Is Upward Sloping 266

Figures

8.1. Market Depth and Tightness 95
13.1. Analytic Framework for Financial Stability 149
15.1. Distribution of Observations 165
15.2. Distribution of Ratios by Weight 166
15.3. Distribution of Capital Asset Ratios by Number of Institutions and by Weight 166
15.4. Percentiles of Distribution of Return on Equity 169
15.5. Coincidence of Financial Soundness Indicators 170
A1.1. Average Number of FSIs Compiled and Disseminated, by Type of Economy 177

Abbreviations

AAOIFI	Accounting and Auditing Organization for Islamic Financial Institutions
BCBS	Basel Committee on Banking Supervision
BCLP	*Bank Loan Classification and Provisioning Practices in Selected Developed and Emerging Countries* (Laurin and Majnoni, 2003)
BCPs	Basel Core Principles
BIS	Bank for International Settlements
BPM5	*Balance of Payments Manual*, fifth edition (IMF, 1993)
CAMELS	Capital adequacy, asset quality, management soundness, earnings and profitability, liquidity, and sensitivity to market risk
CFC	Consumption of fixed capital
CPLG	Basel Core Principles Liaison Group
DQAF	Data Quality Assessment Framework (IMF)
EBIT	Earnings before interest and tax
ECB	European Central Bank
ERGD	Expected recovery given default (BCBS)
EWS	Early warning system
FC	Funds contributed by owners
FSAP	Financial Sector Assessment Program
FSF	Financial Stability Forum
FSI	Financial Soundness Indicator
FSIM	Financial services indirectly measured
G-10	Group of Ten
GDDS	General Data Dissemination System
GDP	Gross domestic product
GFSM	*Government Finance Statistics Manual* (IMF, 2001a)
GNF	Global note facility
HHR	Hui-Heubel Ratio
IAS	International accounting standard
IASB	International Accounting Standards Board
IBS	International banking statistics (BIS)
IFI	Islamic financial institution
IFRS	International Financial Reporting Standard (IASB)
IFSB	Islamic Financial Services Board
IIF	Institute for International Finance
IMF	International Monetary Fund
IRB	Internal Ratings Based (BCBS)
ISIC	International Standard Industrial Classification of all Economic Activities
LGD	Losses given default
LoCs	Letters of credit
MFSM	*Monetary and Financial Statistics Manual* (IMF, 2000a)
NIF	Note issuance facility

NPISHs	Nonprofit institutions serving households
NPLs	Nonperforming loans
ODC	Other depository corporation
OFC	Other financial corporation
OTC	Over-the-counter
PD	Probabilities of default
PLS	Profit and loss sharing
RAROC	Risk-adjusted return on capital
Repo	Repurchase agreement
ROA	Return on assets
ROE	Return on equity
RTGS	Real Time Gross Settlement
RUF	Revolving underwriting facility
SDDS	Special Data Dissemination Standard (IMF)
SDRs	Special drawing rights
SIC	Standard Industrial Classification
SIR	Spread between the highest and lowest interbank rate
SLDR	Spread between reference lending and deposit rates
1993 SNA	*System of National Accounts 1993* (Commission of the European Communities and others, 1993)
SPE	Special purpose entity
SPV	Special purpose vehicle
WAMU	West African Monetary Union

I. Introduction

1.1 The primary purpose of this *Compilation Guide on Financial Soundness Indicators* (the *Guide*) is to provide guidance on the concepts and definitions, and sources and techniques, for the compilation and dissemination of the financial soundness indicators (FSIs) identified by the IMF's Executive Board (see Table 1.1). The *Guide* is intended to encourage compilation of FSIs and promote cross-country comparability of these data, as well as assist compilers and users of FSI data, for the purpose of supporting national and international surveillance of financial systems.

1.2 FSIs are indicators of the current financial health and soundness of the financial institutions in a country, and of their corporate and household counterparts. They include both aggregated individual institution data and indicators that are representative of the markets in which the financial institutions operate. FSIs are calculated and disseminated for the purpose of supporting macroprudential analysis. This is the assessment and surveillance of the strengths and vulnerabilities of financial systems, with the objective of enhancing financial stability and, in particular, limiting the likelihood of failure of the financial system.

1.3 FSIs are a new body of economic statistics that reflect an amalgam of influences. This is evident from the conceptual framework described below. Some concepts are drawn from prudential and commercial measurement frameworks, which have been developed to monitor individual entities. Other concepts are drawn from macroeconomic measurement frameworks, which have been developed to monitor aggregate activity in the economy. Given the flexibility provided by the *Guide,* these frameworks can be drawn upon to develop the data set out in the *Guide.* Advice is also provided on reconciling the data relevant for the *Guide* with these frameworks. However, some new data sources may need to be developed. In this regard, the *Guide* serves as a benchmark or reference point for future development work and as a reference document for technical assistance to support the compilation efforts.

1.4 While the international community, through the IMF Executive Board, considers that fostering comparability of FSI data is a medium-term objective, in discussions during the preparation of this *Guide* many commentators stressed the need for flexibility in the application of the guidance set out below. So, as experience is gathered on compiling this new set of macrostatistics, users should be aware that data sourced from national prudential and commercial measurement frameworks will vary across countries, thus limiting cross-country comparability of data. Looking ahead, the work of the Basel Committee on Banking Supervision (BCBS) on revising its Capital Accord to be more risk sensitive could affect the calculation of FSIs primarily sourced from supervisory data, and subsequent editions of the *Guide* could accommodate such revisions.

1.5 It is also recognized that the compilation of FSI data is likely to require a relatively high level of technically skilled staff at the compiling agencies.

Background

1.6 By allocating funds for viable investment projects and providing payment services, healthy and robust financial systems help increase economic activity and welfare. However, experience has shown that financial systems are prone to instability and crisis that have the potential to disrupt financial activity and impose huge and widespread costs on the economy. With the liberalization of financial markets and the greater recognition of the importance of systemic effects of financial sector weakness, policymakers and others are paying increasing attention to the stability of national financial systems. Thus the long-established surveillance of individual institutions is

Table 1.1. Financial Soundness Indicators: The Core and Encouraged Sets[1]

	Core Set
Deposit takers	
Capital adequacy	Regulatory capital to risk-weighted assets
	Regulatory Tier 1 capital to risk-weighted assets
	Nonperforming loans net of provisions to capital
Asset quality	Nonperforming loans to total gross loans
	Sectoral distribution of loans to total loans
Earnings and profitability	Return on assets
	Return on equity
	Interest margin to gross income
	Noninterest expenses to gross income
Liquidity	Liquid assets to total assets (liquid asset ratio)
	Liquid assets to short-term liabilities
Sensitivity to market risk	Net open position in foreign exchange to capital
	Encouraged Set
Deposit takers	Capital to assets
	Large exposures to capital
	Geographical distribution of loans to total loans
	Gross asset position in financial derivatives to capital
	Gross liability position in financial derivatives to capital
	Trading income to total income
	Personnel expenses to noninterest expenses
	Spread between reference lending and deposit rates
	Spread between highest and lowest interbank rate
	Customer deposits to total (noninterbank) loans
	Foreign-currency-denominated loans to total loans
	Foreign-currency-denominated liabilities to total liabilities
	Net open position in equities to capital
Other financial corporations	Assets to total financial system assets
	Assets to gross domestic product (GDP)
Nonfinancial corporations sector	Total debt to equity
	Return on equity
	Earnings to interest and principal expenses
	Net foreign exchange exposure to equity
	Number of applications for protection from creditors
Households	Household debt to GDP
	Household debt service and principal payments to income
Market liquidity	Average bid-ask spread in the securities market[2]
	Average daily turnover ratio in the securities market[2]
Real estate markets	Real estate prices
	Residential real estate loans to total loans
	Commercial real estate loans to total loans

[1]A summary of the guidance outlined in the *Guide* for each FSI is provided in Appendix II.
[2]Or in other markets that are most relevant to bank liquidity, such as foreign exchange markets.

being supplemented by the monitoring of risks to the stability of national financial systems arising from the collective behavior of individual institutions. This work is known as macroprudential analysis.

1.7 The traditional focus of prudential data reporting and analysis is on the *microprudential* objective of limiting the likelihood of failure of individual institutions. *Macroprudential* analysis has a somewhat different set of data requirements owing to its focus on identifying risks emerging in the financial system as a whole. For instance, while increased lending to the real estate market, or to the corporate sector, may be profitable to a bank in the short term, if such lending is mirrored in other banks, the resultant sharp expansion of the banking sector's exposure to real estate or the corporate sector's debt to equity ratio might raise concerns from a macroprudential viewpoint. In such instances, risks considered exogenous to any one institution are endogenous to the financial system.[1]

1.8 Further, the magnitude and mobility of international capital flows has made it increasingly important to monitor the strength of financial systems and their resilience to capital flow volatility. The financial sector is often the conduit between global financial markets and domestic borrowers and, as such, is sensitive to external capital markets conditions, as well as domestic developments. Moreover, weaknesses in domestic banks can have a pervasive influence on consumer and investor confidence, capital flows, and public finances, as well as on domestic financial intermediation.

1.9 Attention also needs to be given to balance sheet and profitability indicators of nonfinancial corporations. Financial weaknesses such as a high leverage ratio and/or low profitability of these corporations can directly affect the strength of the financial sector because of their impact on asset quality. Also, financially weak corporations can render an economy more susceptible, and less resilient, to external shocks. Governments also play an important role.[2]

1.10 The recognition of the importance of macroprudential analysis has increased the need for supporting data. This consideration led the IMF to undertake in 2000 a survey of its member countries and of regional and international agencies to identify those indicators considered to be most relevant to the macroprudential work of national and regional authorities, both as compilers and users of data. A summary of the results is presented in Appendix I. Also, in 1999, the IMF and the World Bank launched the Financial Sector Assessment Program (FSAP), designed to identify financial system strengths and vulnerabilities and to help develop appropriate policy responses. This work has involved the use of FSIs, drawing on available data sources in countries.

1.11 Using the results of the survey of member countries, the experience from FSAPs, and discussions with international agencies interested in this work, a list of key FSIs was developed and presented to the IMF's Executive Board in June 2001. From this meeting, the list of core and encouraged FSIs set out in Table 1.1 was agreed (agreed FSIs), based on various selection criteria.[3] The list was modified by the Board in January 2004.[4] To help prioritize future work, the core set is considered relevant for all countries, while the encouraged set might be developed as country circumstances require. At the same time, the Board encouraged the IMF's staff to produce the *Compilation Guide* to help compilers develop the agreed indicators and undertake further development work in this field.

1.12 The *Guide* is a comprehensive document that not only explains how to compile the core and encouraged FSIs but also sets out the conceptual frameworks from which the data series required to calculate the FSIs could be drawn. A summary of the guidance for compiling each FSI is provided in Appendix II. In addition, in the process of consultation, some associated data series have been suggested that assist in the interpretation of FSIs, such as information on the structure of a country's financial system. However, in reading the *Guide* compilers should be aware that in terms of data requirements the priority is the core set of FSIs, followed by the encouraged FSIs. Also, while as far as possible the *Guide* draws on existing data systems, compiling FSIs most likely will add to the statistical burden. The extent of any additional costs will depend on a number of factors, including the amount of data already available, the structure of the financial system, and the time horizon over which the data are developed.

Some Key Aspects of the *Guide*

1.13 From the work undertaken, it is clear that the range and type of FSIs compiled and disseminated differ among countries, but that given their pivotal

[1]Crockett (2000) elaborates on these ideas.

[2]IMF staff is separately developing fiscal indicators for the government sector.

[3]The chosen criteria were (1) focus on the core markets and institutions, (2) analytical significance, (3) revealed usefulness through high scores in the survey results, (4) relevance in most circumstances, and (5) availability. The core set met all the chosen selection criteria and provided data covering all main categories of bank risk, while the encouraged set met some but not all. See Sundararajan and others (2002, p. 66).

[4]As a consequence, the large exposures to capital FSI was moved from the core to the encouraged set, and measures of duration were dropped from the list completely. These changes arose from advice given to the Executive Board by a group of experts that met in October 2003 to discuss the draft *Guide* and primarily reflected the problems in compiling these FSIs on a sector-level basis rather than their relevance to macroprudential analysis.

role in all national economies, FSIs for the deposit takers—particularly the core set—are considered central to any analysis of the current health and soundness of a national financial system. This is reflected in the *Guide.* In addition, because of the importance of the credit quality of deposit takers' assets to the profitability and soundness of these deposit takers, information on their main customers—particularly the corporate and household sectors—is relevant for such analysis. The need for FSIs for other financial corporations will vary depending on their importance within the economy.

1.14 FSIs need to cover several aspects of financial health and soundness. In a financial system, capital strength is important for all types of institutions, especially as a "cushion" against unexpected losses. In monitoring the financial soundness of financial institutions, important considerations are also the quality and composition of their assets, and exposures to financial risk. Information on income and expenses is also critical—without sufficient income generation, no entity is financially healthy or sound. For nonfinancial corporations, the focus is on their liabilities and their ability to meet their financial obligations as they fall due. In short, FSIs are intended for use in monitoring the development of positions (and exposures) and flows that could indicate increased financial sector vulnerability and could help assess the potential resilience of the sector to adverse circumstances.

1.15 Because most FSIs are in the form of ratios, definitions are required for the underlying series used to calculate FSIs. Further, in considering the definitions for these individual series, it is apparent that many are derivable from information contained in balance sheets and income statements. So for all sectors, including deposit takers and nonfinancial corporations, the *Guide* starts from the presumption that, as far as possible, the underlying series should be drawn from internally consistent financial statements that encompass an income and expense statement and a balance sheet. Calculating FSI ratios from data series derived from internally consistent financial statements enhances the analytical usefulness of the indicators and contributes to the quality control of published data owing to the well-established linkages among financial statement items.

1.16 In developing guidance on definitions, the *Guide* draws on the *System of National Accounts 1993* (*1993 SNA*) (Commission of the European Communities and others, 1993) and related manuals (for example, the *Monetary and Financial Statistics Manual* [*MFSM*] [IMF, 2000a]), and the international accounting standards (IASs) and International Financial Reporting Standards (IFRSs) (IASB, 2004), developed by the International Accounting Standards Board (IASB).[5] Both of these international measurement systems have developed their guidance within the context of internally consistent financial statement frameworks. For deposit takers, the work of the BCBS is also drawn upon. While there are many similarities between the international measurement systems, the conceptual approach in the *Guide* allows for flexibility to accommodate differences between them and meet the needs of macroprudential analysis. Further, Appendix IV explains how the guidance in the *1993 SNA* and IASs/IFRSs correspond with the requirements of the *Guide.* The *Guide* also provides methodological guidance on measurement issues that are new at the international or even national level, for example, regarding real estate prices and certain financial market information.

1.17 Despite the reliance to the extent possible on existing measurement systems, the needs of macroprudential analysis are different from those the existing systems are addressing, and this is reflected in the framework developed.

1.18 For deposit takers, macroprudential analysis monitors the profitability, capital strength, quality and composition of assets, and exposures to financial risks faced by the sector as a whole. Supervisors have similar interests but at the level of the individual institution. Further, some supervisors adapt accounting guidance to meet the needs of individual institutions, whereas the consistent application of accounting rules across all entities in the sector is essential to avoid asymmetries in the macro-based data.

1.19 The sector focus and the consistent application of accounting rules are applicable for other macro-based data such as the national accounts, monetary aggregates, and the Bank for International Settlement's (BIS's) international banking statistics

[5]Throughout the *Guide,* information presented within square brackets refers to relevant paragraph numbers in the IFRSs as of March 31, 2004, which were to come into effect on January 1, 2005.

(IBS). However, there are differences in analytical focus. National accounts data are focused on production, income and its distribution and use, and the financial claims and liabilities generated. Compared with these data sets, the FSI framework focuses more on capital strength and profitability, making essential the avoidance of double counting capital, and activity based on that capital, at the sector level. So macroprudential analysis favors consolidation of group accounts, whereas national accounts data focus on the gross output and activity of individual entities within groups. Further, the buildup of claims and liabilities among deposit takers is of macroprudential interest, not least to monitor the potential for contagion, whereas monetary aggregates focus on deposit takers' claims and liabilities vis-à-vis other sectors and so eliminate such intrasectoral positions.

1.20 Furthermore, it is worth noting that compared with other measurement systems, the extent of institutional coverage for macroprudential purposes is not clearly determined. While the *Guide* requires the compilation of FSIs on a consolidated group basis to support soundness analysis, this can involve consolidating the activities of branches and subsidiaries with those of the parent entity regardless of location—more akin to the commercial accounting and supervisory approaches for individual entities. Data on domestically located operations might be separately distinguished if authorities believe the data would contribute materially to their financial stability analysis (for example, to illustrate the linkage with other macroeconomic information). Chapter 5 discusses these approaches in more detail.

1.21 More generally, the *Guide* recognizes that the analysis of FSIs must take into account country-specific circumstances.[6] Most relevant to any assessment is the structure of a country's financial system, for instance, the number of deposit takers, the extent of cross-border ownership, the extent of government ownership, the relative size of other financial institutions, and the extent to which security markets are used to raise capital. All these factors can influence the interpretation of FSIs. Therefore, guidance is provided on the types of information on financial system structure that could be disseminated, both to help provide context for the analysis of FSIs—including through peer group and dispersion analysis—and to provide information relevant for policymakers and other users. Also important is the strength of a country's financial infrastructure, such as the level of development of financial markets and payment systems. The *Guide* provides some advice on the type of information on the structure of the financial system that could be disseminated.

1.22 In developing the framework for use in compiling data, consultations with experts raised some points that go beyond the requirements of the agreed FSIs. First, the framework developed should be flexible to allow for future growth as analytical needs evolve; the idea of developing sectoral financial statements for macroprudential purposes is consistent with this concern. Second, some additional series were recommended to be included that meet specific financial soundness needs, such as information on contingent liabilities and the value of assets transferred to special purpose entities; these ideas are included in Appendix III. Third, as far as possible, the framework should draw on and take account of the related statistical needs of international and regional agencies; IMF staff has consulted with other agencies in the process of producing this *Guide.*

1.23 The *Guide* recognizes the importance of disseminating FSI data for use by market participants, policy analysts, and other users. The dissemination of data on a frequent and timely basis allows new developments to be identified at an early stage and facilitates comparisons and analysis of data over time. Also, it is vital that any dissemination of data be supplemented with the provision of metadata (information about data) so that users can understand the methodology underlying the available information. Chapter 12 discusses these issues in more detail.

1.24 Finally, experience demonstrates that FSIs are only one input into macroprudential analysis. Also relevant are (1) indicators that provide a broader picture of economic and financial circumstances, such as asset prices, credit growth, gross domestic product (GDP) growth (including its components), inflation, and the external position; (2) the institutional and regulatory framework for an economy, in particular through assessments of compliance with international financial sector standards; (3) the outcome of stress

[6]For this reason and owing to the limited experience to date, the *Guide* does not provide numerical benchmarks for each FSI. Moreover, the *Guide* is not the appropriate vehicle for presenting such information.

tests;[7] and, as mentioned above, (4) the structure of the financial system and strength of the financial infrastructure. More generally, FSI data can potentially complement the use of early warning systems and contribute to crisis prevention.

1.25 Stress testing, in particular, is a tool that when used in combination with FSIs can enhance their usefulness in several ways. First, estimated FSIs are typically the output of stress tests and, in some cases, an "intermediate" input also. For example, the impact of a macroeconomic shock is usually measured as the impact on the capital ratio FSIs. Second, stress tests can provide information on the linkages among different FSIs—for instance, in stress tests that make use of banks' credit risk models, the "shock" is worked through nonperforming loans (NPLs), providing a direct measure of the linkage between changes in the NPL-based FSIs and the capital ratio FSIs. Further, stress tests provide a complementary, but more direct, way to assess certain types of risks that are hard to measure precisely using FSIs, including the risk of interbank contagion.

Structure of the *Guide*

1.26 The *Guide* is presented in four parts. They are (1) conceptual framework—covering Chapters 2–5, (2) specification of FSIs—covering Chapters 6–9, (3) compilation and dissemination of FSIs—covering Chapters 10–12, and (4) analysis of FSIs—Chapters 13–15. There are also a number of appendixes.

1.27 The *Guide* is provided to encourage compilation and dissemination of the FSIs agreed by the IMF Executive Board. Part II provides specific guidance on how to calculate the individual FSIs in the list, but before a compiler is in a position to use such guidance, certain definitional issues need to be addressed: the definition of each sector, the accounting principles underlying data compilation, the definitions of the individual series that are used to calculate the ratios, and the scope of coverage within the sector. These are the issues covered in Part I. In Part III, the *Guide* provides advice on practical compilation and dissemination issues that are likely to face compilers as they put together this body of data, while Part IV provides information on the analytical use of FSIs.

1.28 More specifically, chapters of each part address the following issues.

Conceptual Framework

- Chapter 2 identifies and defines the main institutions and markets that typically constitute a financial system.
- Chapter 3 provides accounting principles for FSIs.
- Chapter 4 provides an accounting framework and sectoral financial statements from which the series required to calculate FSIs could be identified and defined.
- Chapter 5 explains how data can be aggregated and consolidated.

Specification of Financial Soundness Indicators

- Chapter 6 defines each of the agreed indicators for deposit takers.
- Chapter 7 defines each of the agreed indicators for other sectors.
- Chapter 8 defines the indicators for financial markets.
- Chapter 9 provides advice on the compilation of data on real estate prices.

Compilation and Dissemination of Financial Soundness Indicators

- Chapters 10 and 11 provide an overview of the compilation of FSIs.
- Chapter 12 presents a framework for the dissemination of FSIs.

Analysis of Financial Soundness Indicators

- Chapter 13 discusses FSIs and macroprudential analysis.
- Chapter 14 looks at the analytical use of specific FSIs.
- Chapter 15 discusses peer group and descriptive statistics.

Appendixes

1.29 Appendix I summarizes the survey of countries conducted in 2000 to understand more about coun-

[7]Stress tests are techniques used to assess the vulnerability of portfolios to major changes in the macroeconomic environment or to exceptional but plausible events.

tries' needs for, and compilation practices relating to, FSIs. Appendix II summarizes in tabular form the detailed information on each agreed FSI contained in the *Guide.* Appendix III provides additional definitions of FSIs and related data series. Appendix IV provides information on how to derive FSI series from both the national accounts and commercial accounting frameworks. Appendix V provides a set of numerical examples. Appendix VI discusses provisioning, interest rate risk, and stress-testing issues on which at the time of drafting there was not an international consensus or best practice to draw upon. Finally, Appendix VII provides a glossary of terms.

Terminology

1.30 Different methodologies can use different terms for the same item or instrument, so it is necessary to note that the terms used in the *Guide* are consistent with those used in the agreed list of FSIs. Thus, where supervisors might use the phrase "allowance," the *Guide* uses the phrase "provision." Other terms are drawn from the *1993 SNA*—particularly for those items in the sector accounts that the *1993 SNA* also covers—and from supervisory sources. In a few instances, the text notes alternative terms for the same item/instrument at the appropriate point in the text.

PART I

Conceptual Framework

2. Overview of the Financial System

Introduction

2.1 As noted in Chapter 1, FSIs are calculated and disseminated for the purpose of assisting in the assessment and monitoring of the strengths and vulnerabilities of financial systems. Such assessments need to take account of country-specific factors, not least the structure of the financial system. Simply stated, whether an economy has a few or many banks, has diverse financial intermediaries, has a deep and liquid securities market, and whether the financial intermediaries have international operations, matters to any assessment. This chapter identifies and defines the main types of players and markets that typically constitute a financial system.

What Is a Financial System?

2.2 A financial system consists of institutional units[1] and markets that interact, typically in a complex manner, for the purpose of mobilizing funds for investment and providing facilities, including payment systems, for the financing of commercial activity. The role of financial institutions within the system is primarily to intermediate between those that provide funds and those that need funds, and typically involves transforming and managing risk. Particularly for a deposit taker, this risk arises from its role in maturity transformation, where liabilities are typically short term (for example, demand deposits), while its assets have a longer maturity and are often illiquid (for example, loans). Financial markets provide a forum within which financial claims can be traded under established rules of conduct and can facilitate the management and transformation of risk. They also play an important role in identifying market prices ("price discovery").

2.3 Within a financial system, the role of deposit takers is central. They often provide a convenient location for the placement and borrowing of funds and, as such, are a source of liquid assets and funds to the rest of the economy. They also provide payments services that are relied upon by all other entities for the conduct of their business. Thus, failures of deposit takers can have a significant impact on the activities of all other financial and nonfinancial entities and on the confidence in, and the functioning of, the financial system as a whole. This makes the analysis of the health and soundness of deposit takers central to any assessment of financial system stability.

Financial Corporations[2]

Deposit Takers[3]

2.4 The term "bank" is widely used to denote those financial institutions whose principal activity is to take deposits and on-lend or otherwise invest these funds on their own account. In many countries, "banks" are defined under banking or similar regu-

[1]An institutional unit is an entity, such as a household, corporation, or government agency, that is capable in its own right of owning assets, incurring liabilities, and engaging in economic activities and transactions with other entities.

[2]The intention is that the definitions of institutional sectors and subsectors in the *Guide* be consistent with the *1993 SNA,* except where explicitly stated otherwise.

[3]As well as accurately portraying the types of institutions covered, the *Guide* uses the term "deposit takers" rather than "other depository corporations" (ODCs) as used in the *MFSM* (IMF, 2000a) because of the possible difference in coverage of institutions. In reflecting analytical interest in broad money, ODCs are defined as including all those entities that issue liabilities included in the national definition of money. This may exclude (include) institutional units that are otherwise included (excluded) within the *Guide*'s definition (for example, certain offshore banks). Notably, money market funds are explicitly excluded from the *Guide*'s coverage of deposit takers (see paragraph 2.10) but can be included in the *MFSM*'s coverage of ODCs. Any institutional unit classified as an ODC that does not meet the *Guide*'s definition of a deposit taker should be classified as an "other financial corporation."

latory legislation for supervisory purposes. In the *Guide,* banks and other deposit takers (other than central banks) are included within an institutional sector that is known as "deposit takers." Deposit takers are defined as those units that engage in financial intermediation as a principal activity—that is, channel funds from lenders to borrowers by intermediating between them through their own account—and

- have liabilities in the form of deposits payable on demand, transferable by check, or otherwise used for making payments; or
- have liabilities in the form of instruments that may not be readily transferable, such as short-term certificates of deposit, but are close substitutes for deposits in mobilizing financial resources and are included in measures of money broadly defined.

2.5 Commercial banks, which typically take deposits and are central to the payment system, fall under the definition of deposit takers. These banks, which participate in a common clearing system, may be known as deposit money corporations. Other types of institutions that may be covered by the definition include institutions described as savings banks (including trustee savings banks, as well as savings and loan associations); development banks; credit unions or cooperatives; investment banks; mortgage banks and building societies (where their particular specialization distinguishes them from commercial banks); and microfinance institutions that take deposits. Government-controlled banks (for example, post office savings banks and rural or housing banks) are also deposit takers if they are institutional units separate from the government and they meet the definition of a deposit taker outlined in paragraph 2.6. This list is not exhaustive, and classification as a deposit taker depends on the function of the corporation, and not on its name.

2.6 Within an economy, the definition of deposit takers should encompass a group of institutions that meet the definition of banks and similar institutions under banking or other legislation, because like the statistical definition for deposit takers, a common legal criterion for a bank is the taking of deposits. If some institutions are banks in a legal sense but not deposit takers as described above, in following the *Guide* they should still be classified as "deposit takers," but in any associated description of the FSI data the status of these institutions should be explained, with some indication of their importance to the data disseminated.

2.7 Conversely, if there are any other groups of institutions that meet the *Guide*'s definition of a deposit taker but are not banks or similar institutions under the legislative approach, they should be separately identified so that their importance to the information disseminated can be judged.

2.8 As noted in Chapter 1 and described in more detail in Chapter 5, to meet analytical needs, deposit takers can be grouped on the basis of common characteristics. Two types of reporting populations are particularly identified in the *Guide:* domestically incorporated and controlled deposit takers, including any foreign branches and subsidiaries, and all domestically located deposit takers.

Special cases

2.9 *Holding corporations* are entities that control a group of subsidiary corporations and whose principal activity is owning and directing the group rather than engaging in deposit taking. As the *Guide*'s focus is the health and soundness of deposit takers as a sector, in principle the *Guide* considers that holding corporations should be excluded from the deposit taking sector, even if the business of the subsidiaries it owns is primarily deposit taking. Rather, such holding corporations should be classified as other financial corporations. It is acknowledged that this approach may not be consistent with *1993 SNA,* but it is consistent with present supervisory guidance.[4] Nonetheless, there may be interest in information on financial conglomerates headed by holding corporations, as discussed in Appendix III.

2.10 In the *Guide,* it is recommended that *money market funds* not be classified as deposit takers but be separately identified as investment funds within other financial corporations (see below), because the nature and regulation of their business are different from that of deposit takers, although their liabilities can be included in broad money. A similar treatment

[4]The revised Basel Accord proposes to extend consolidated reporting to include bank holding companies. In paragraph 4.100 the *1993 SNA* attributes a holding company to the activity carried out mainly by the group it controls, unless no single type of financial activity is predominant within the group, in which instance it is classified as an other financial intermediary. Thus, the attribution of the holding company to the deposit-taking sector, or not, in the *1993 SNA* is dependent upon all the business of all the entities in the group and not just a deposit-taking subsidiary.

is recommended for any other institution that engages primarily in securities activity and issues liabilities that are included in broad money but are not deposits.

2.11 There is little international conformity of law or practice in the area of banking regulation governing the treatment of *banks in distress,* with official efforts to rehabilitate banks differing both in their time horizon and nature, from the enforcement of banking law and the restriction of new business, to the receivership and liquidation of banks (see, for example, Asser, 2001; Garcia, 2000). In the *Guide,* it is recommended that financial institutions in distress that otherwise meet the definition of a deposit taker continue to be included in the deposit-taking reporting population for calculating FSIs. Their assets and liabilities exist in the deposit-taking system, and the costs of resolution may be significant. Accordingly, until a deposit taker is liquidated (that is, all assets and liabilities are written down and/or redeemed and the entity ceases to exist) or all deposit liabilities removed from its balance sheet (through either repayment or transfer to another entity), its balance sheet and income statement continue to be included in the data used for calculating FSIs for the deposit-taking sector.

2.12 If banks in distress hold significant positions, data both including and excluding these deposit takers might be considered, particularly if the liquidation process is very lengthy.[5] In any associated description of the FSI data, the importance of banks in distress to the data disseminated could be indicated.

Central Bank

2.13 The *central bank* is the national financial institution that exercises control over key aspects of the financial system and carries out such activities as issuing currency, managing international reserves, and providing credit to deposit takers. Central banks are excluded from the reporting population for compiling FSIs.

[5]For example, this could be considered if banks that are in distress over a long period of time have large foreign exchange exposures (but "active" deposit takers do not). Also, during a long process of liquidation, it is recognized that there may be difficulties in collecting current information on banks in distress.

Other Financial Corporations

2.14 *Other financial corporations* (OFCs) are those financial corporations that are primarily engaged in financial intermediation or in auxiliary financial activities that are closely related to financial intermediation but are not classified as deposit takers.[6] Their importance within a financial system varies by country. Other financial corporations include insurance corporations, pension funds, other financial intermediaries, and financial auxiliaries. Other financial intermediaries include securities dealers, investment funds (including money market funds), and others, such as finance companies and leasing companies. Moreover, included as other financial intermediaries are special asset management companies created for the purpose of managing nonperforming assets that have been transferred from other financial corporations, typically deposit takers.[7] In addition, acting as agents rather than as principals are other financial auxiliaries, such as market makers. Detailed descriptions of all these types of financial corporations are provided in Appendix VII: Glossary of Terms.

Nonfinancial Corporations

2.15 As customers, *nonfinancial corporations* are important to the health and soundness of financial corporations. Nonfinancial corporations are institutional entities whose principal activity is the production of goods or nonfinancial services for sale at prices that are economically significant.[8] They include nonfinancial corporations, nonfinancial quasi corporations,[9] and nonprofit institutions that are producers of goods or nonfinancial services for sale at prices that are economically significant. They can be controlled by the government sector.

[6]Provided that they do not take deposits, other financial corporations include funds created to invest income received from a specific source, such as from sales of oil, for the benefit of future generations.

[7]If such a corporation records deposits in its balance sheet, it would be classified as a deposit taker. In Appendix III, the idea of collecting additional data on their ownership of NPLs is discussed.

[8]Economically significant prices are those that have a significant influence on the amounts that producers are willing to supply and on the amounts purchasers wish to buy.

[9]A quasi corporation is an unincorporated enterprise that functions as a corporation. Typically it will keep a separate set of accounts from its owner(s) and/or, if owned by a nonresident, be engaged in a significant amount of production in the resident economy over a long or indefinite period of time.

Households

2.16 *Households* are also customers of financial corporations. They are defined as small groups of persons who share the same living accommodation, pool some or all of their income and wealth, and consume certain types of goods and services (for example, housing and food) collectively. Unattached individuals are also considered households. Households may engage in any kind of economic activity, including production.

Nonprofit Institutions Serving Households (NPISHs)

2.17 *NPISHs* are engaged mainly in providing goods and services to households or the community at large free of charge or at prices that are not economically significant (and thus are classified as nonmarket producers), except those that are controlled and financed mainly by government units, which are classified as part of the general government sector (see paragraph 2.18). NPISHs are financed mainly from contributions, subscriptions from members, or earnings on holdings of real or financial assets. They are customers of financial corporations, although experience suggests that their impact on the financial stability of the economy is limited. Examples of NPISHs include consumer associations, trade unions, and charities financed by voluntary transfers.

General Government

2.18 *General government* units exercise legislative, judicial, or executive authority over other institutional units within a specified area. Governments have authority to impose taxes, to borrow, to allocate goods and services to the community at large or to individuals, and to redistribute income. They affect and can be affected by the activities of financial corporations. The general government sector consists of departments, branches, agencies, foundations, institutes, nonmarket nonprofit institutions controlled and financed mainly by government, and other publicly controlled organizations engaging in nonmarket activities. Various units of general government may operate at the central, state, or local government level.

Public Sector

2.19 The *public sector* includes the general government, central bank, and those entities in the deposit-taking and other sectors that are public corporations. A *public corporation* is defined as a nonfinancial or financial corporation that is subject to control by government units, with control over a corporation defined as the ability to determine general corporate policy by choosing appropriate directors, if necessary. A fuller discussion of control is provided in paragraph 5.7.

Financial Markets

2.20 A financial market can be defined as a market in which entities can trade financial claims under some established rules of conduct. There are various types of financial markets, depending on the nature of the claims being traded. They include money markets, bond markets, equity markets, derivatives markets, commodity markets, and the foreign exchange market.

2.21 The *money market* is the market that involves the short-term lending and borrowing of funds among a range of participants. The typical instruments traded in a money market have a short maturity and include treasury bills, central bank bills, certificates of deposit, bankers' acceptances, and commercial paper. They also include borrowing through repurchase agreements and similar arrangements. It is the market that can provide short-term liquidity to governments and financial and nonfinancial corporations. An active money market allows entities to manage their liquidity in an efficient manner, by facilitating investment of excess holdings of cash in interest-bearing assets, which can be drawn upon when needed, and by providing a source of funds for those short of liquidity, or who wish to finance short-term positions in other markets.

2.22 One specific money market is the *interbank market,* which is the market in which banks lend to each other. This market allows banks with excess liquidity to lend these funds to banks with a shortage of funds, often overnight and usually on an unsecured basis. An efficient interbank market improves the functioning of the financial system by enabling the central bank to add or drain liquidity from the system more effectively and banks to redistribute their individual excesses and shortages of liquidity among themselves without causing undue interest rate volatility. If funds do not flow freely among banks in the interbank market, this impedes liquidity management by individual banks, posing a risk to financial stability, and could result in the central bank having to supply liquidity to banks on a case-by-case basis, complicating the management of monetary policy.

2.23 The *bond market* is the market in longer-term debt instruments issued by governments and financial and nonfinancial corporations. The bond market allows a borrower to obtain long-term funds through the issuance of debt securities, while providing investors with an opportunity to purchase and sell these securities. For borrowers, such a market provides an alternative to bank lending as a form of long-term finance and, in the instance of asset-backed securities, whose income payments and principal repayments are dependent upon a pool of assets such as loans, allows a lender to, in effect, convert illiquid assets into tradable securities.[10] An active bond market also allows credit risks to be spread over a wide range of investors, reducing the potential for concentration of credit risk to develop and providing borrowers with up-to-date information on the market views of their creditworthiness. Bonds also provide an investment opportunity for those investors that have a long-term investment horizon, such as pension funds with long-term liabilities.

2.24 The *equity market* is where equity securities are traded. An active equity market can be an important source of capital to the issuer for use in business and allows the investor to benefit from the future growth of the business through dividend payments and/or an increase in the value of the equity claim. However, the market value of the equity security can also fall. Turnover serves as an indicator of liquidity in equity markets.

2.25 *Financial derivatives markets* are different from money, bond, and equity markets in that the instruments—such as swaps and options—are used to trade financial risks such as those arising from foreign exchange and interest rates, to those more able or willing to bear them. Credit risk can also be traded, through credit derivatives. The value of derivative instruments depends on the price of the underlying item—the reference price. These markets can broaden financial market activity in that, for instance, investors can, in a derivatives market, trade away financial risk inherent in a security, such as exchange rate risk, that otherwise would have deterred them from purchasing the security. However, financial derivatives can be used to take on risk and thus can pose a threat to financial stability if significant losses are incurred.

2.26 In financial markets, *liquidity* is important, because it allows investors to manage their portfolios and risks more efficiently, which tends to reduce the cost of borrowing. There are several dimensions to market liquidity, including tightness, depth, immediacy, and resilience. Tightness is a market's ability to match supply and demand efficiently and can be measured by the bid-ask spread. Market depth relates to the ability of a market to absorb large trade volumes without a significant impact on prices and can be approximated by the amounts traded over a period of time (turnover) and quote sizes. Immediacy is the speed with which orders can be executed and settled, and resilience is the speed with which price fluctuations arising from imbalances in trades are dissipated.

Payment System

2.27 A payment system consists of instruments, banking procedures, and (typically) interbank fund transfer systems that ensure the circulation of money. The payment system is a channel through which shocks can be transmitted across financial systems and markets. A robust payment system is a key requirement in maintaining and promoting financial stability. Thus, a broad international consensus has developed on the need to strengthen payment systems by promoting internationally accepted standards and practices for their design and operation (BIS, 2001a; BIS, 2003a).

Real Estate Markets

2.28 Experience has shown that real estate markets can be an important source of financial instability. Real estate markets allow the trading of claims on, and investments in, real estate and can also involve

[10]There are several key features of asset-backed securities: the original lender will usually sell the assets to a trust or other form of intermediary (special purpose vehicle), and so, in the case of a deposit taker, this activity frees "capital" that regulatory guidelines require a deposit taker to hold against the assets. The intermediary will finance the purchase of the assets by issuing securities.

markets associated with the financing of real estate. In the *Guide,* real estate is defined to include both land and buildings (including other structures used as dwellings, for example, houseboats). Because land is a more or less fixed resource, as are buildings in the short term, traditionally real estate has lent itself to speculative activity—when demand and prices significantly increase in a short period—and, often associated with this, large financing flows. In addition, for households, changes in the value of the real estate they own can have a significant effect on their economic behavior.

3. Accounting Principles for Financial Soundness Indicators

Introduction

3.1 To compile both position and flow data for use in calculating FSIs, a consistent set of accounting principles is required. This chapter provides guidance on accounting principles that could be employed, drawing on existing international standards and taking account of the analytical needs of FSI data. But it is recognized that at this time, in practice, there is no full-fledged adherence to internationally agreed prudential, accounting, and statistical standards by all countries. Thus, in disseminating any information, countries are encouraged to disclose the basis of accounting that is used to compile FSI data series, along with the critical assumptions made.

Definition of Flows and Positions

3.2 In the *Guide,* flow data include transactions in goods, services, income, transfers, and nonfinancial and financial assets; holding gains and losses arising from price or exchange rate movements; and other changes in the volume of assets, such as losses from extraordinary events. Under certain circumstances, potential costs can also be included. Position data are the value of outstanding stocks of nonfinancial and financial assets, and liabilities.[1]

Time of Recognition of Flows and Positions

3.3 The guiding principle in the *Guide* is that flows and positions should be recorded using the accrual basis of accounting. On this basis, flows are recognized when economic value is created, transformed, exchanged, transferred, or extinguished. In other words, under accrual accounting, revenue and gains are recognized in the period when they are earned, and expenses and losses when they are incurred, rather than when cash is received or disbursed. Existing actual assets and liabilities are recognized, but contingent positions are not.

3.4 The accrual approach to recording is adopted because by matching the time of recognition with the time of resource flows and the time of gains and losses in value, the economic consequences of transactions and events on the current health and soundness of the reporting entities is best observed. Moreover, this method has the advantage of capturing all types of resource flows, regardless of whether or not cash has been exchanged.

3.5 Whether assets and liabilities exist and are outstanding is determined at any moment in time by the principle of ownership.[2] So for debt instruments, the creditor owns a claim on the debtor, and the debtor has a symmetric obligation to the creditor.[3]

3.6 When a transaction occurs in assets, the position should be recorded on the date of the change of ownership (the value date), when both creditor and debtor have entered the claim and liability, respectively, in their books. If an existing asset is sold by one entity to another, the first entity derecognizes and the second entity recognizes the asset on the date of the change of ownership. The date of recording

[1]A fuller definition of transactions and other flows, and of positions, is provided on pages 72–78 of the *1993 SNA* and on pages 9–12 of the *European System of Accounts 1995* (Eurostat, 1996). However, potential costs cannot be included as flow data within the conceptual framework of the *1993 SNA*.

[2]IASs use the criteria of the probability of future economic benefits that can be measured reliably and of control to recognize assets. In recognizing subsidiaries, the *Guide* also adopts the concept of control (see paragraph 5.7).

[3]So the *Guide* does not recognize any unilateral repudiation of debt by the debtor.

may actually be specified to ensure matching entries in the books of both parties. If no precise date can be fixed on which the change in ownership occurs, the date on which the creditor receives payment in cash or in some other asset is decisive. When a service is rendered, interest accrues, or an event occurs that creates a transfer claim (such as taxation), a financial claim is created and exists until payment is made or forgiven. Service charges, like interest, can accrue continuously. After dividends are declared payable, they are recorded as liabilities/assets until paid.

3.7 The *Guide* recommends that interest costs accrue continuously on debt instruments, matching the cost of funds with the provision of funds and increasing the principal amount outstanding until the interest is paid.[4] The preference of the *Guide* is that interest should accrue at the rate (effective yield) agreed at the time of the issuance of the debt instrument. For example, for a loan this is the contractual rate of interest. Thus, for fixed-rate instruments, the effective yield is the rate of interest that equates the future payments to the issue price. For variable-rate instruments, the yield will vary over time in line with the terms of the contract. No adjustment should be made to interest income for any gains or losses arising from financial derivatives contracts, as these are recognized as gains and losses on financial instruments (see paragraph 4.22). These recommendations for the accrual of interest are largely consistent with the approach in the related international statistical and accounting standards.[5] However, it is recognized that for data compiled under IASs (IAS 18.31), when an instrument is traded, interest accrues for the new creditor at the effective yield at the time of acquisition of the instrument and not the effective yield at the time of issuance of the instrument.[6]

[4]Interest accrual on nonperforming assets is discussed in Chapter 4.

[5]Under some accounting systems, certain fees are treated as an integral part of the effective yield of a financial instrument, and hence affect the rate at which interest accrues. As discussed under "Fees and Commissions Receivable/Payable" in Appendix IV, this approach is followed in IASs.

[6]This opens the possibility that there could be asymmetric reporting of interest income for traded financial instruments by debtor and creditor deposit takers. One possibility is to calculate interest income based on the average current effective yield during the period. Such a yield may be observable by both parties, reducing the possibility of asymmetric reporting. However, a consensus on the merits of adopting such an approach more generally in macroeconomic statistics has not emerged at the time of writing the *Guide*.

3.8 For interest costs that accrue in a recording period, these transactions should be recorded as an expense (income) in that period. For position data, there are three measurement possibilities for interest costs that accrue: (1) they are paid within the reporting period, in which instance there is no impact on end-period positions; (2) they are not paid, because they are not yet payable (for example, interest is paid each six months on a loan or debt security, and the position is measured after the first three months of this period—in which instance, the positions increase by the amount of interest that has accrued during the three-month period); or, (3) they are not paid when due, in which instance, the positions increase by the amount of interest costs that has accrued during the period (excluding any specific provisions against such interest—see also paragraph 4.19). The *Guide* recommends including interest costs that have accrued and are not yet payable as part of the value of the underlying instruments.

3.9 For bonds issued on discount or on a zero coupon basis, the difference between the issue price and the value at maturity is treated as interest and recorded as accruing over the life of the bond. As calculated interest income exceeds any coupon payments for these instruments, the difference is included in the outstanding principal amount of the asset. For instruments issued at a premium, coupon payments will exceed calculated interest income, with the difference reducing the principal amount outstanding.

Arrears

3.10 When principal or interest payments are not made when due, such as on a loan, arrears are created. Arrears should continue to be recorded from their creation, which is when payments are not made,[7] until they are extinguished, such as when they are repaid, rescheduled, or forgiven by the creditor. Arrears should continue to be recorded in the underlying instrument (excluding any provisions for accrual of interest on nonperforming assets—see also paragraph 4.19).

[7]It is recognized that in some instances, arrears arise for operational reasons rather than due to a reluctance or inability to pay. Nonetheless, in principle, such arrears, when outstanding at the reference date, should be recorded as arrears.

3.11 If debt payments are guaranteed by a third party (guarantor) and the debtor defaults, the debtor records an arrear until the creditor invokes the contract conditions permitting the guarantee to be exercised. Once exercised, the debtor no longer records an arrear, as the debt is attributed to the guarantor. In other words, the arrear of the debtor is extinguished as though repaid. Depending on the contractual arrangements, in the event of a guarantee being exercised, the debt is not classified as arrears of the guarantor but instead is classified as a short-term debt liability until any grace period for payment ends.

Contingencies

3.12 Many types of contractual financial arrangements between institutional units give rise to conditional requirements either to make payments or provide items of economic value.[8] In this context, "conditional" means that the claim becomes effective only if a stipulated condition or conditions arise. These arrangements are referred to as *contingent items* and are not recognized as financial assets (or liabilities) in the *Guide,* because they are not actual claims (or obligations). Nonetheless, such arrangements represent potential exposures to risks.

3.13 The types of contingent arrangements for which data could be collected on the basis of the maximum potential exposures[9] are described below.

3.14 *Loan and other payment guarantees* are commitments to make payments to third parties when another party, such as a client of the guarantor, fails to perform some contractual obligations. These are contingent liabilities because payment is required only if the client fails to perform, and until such time no liability is recorded on the balance sheet of the guarantor. The common type of risk assumed by a deposit-taking guarantor is commercial risk or financial performance risk of the borrower.

3.15 Included under payment guarantees are *letters of credit* (LoCs). Irrevocable and stand-by LoCs are guarantees to make payment upon nonperformance by the client, provided all the conditions in the letter have been met. LoCs are an important mechanism for international trade. Revocable LoCs allow the terms of the letter to be changed without prior approval of the beneficiary. Also included are *performance bonds* that normally cover only part of the contract value but in effect guarantee a buyer of goods, such as an importer, that the seller, such as an exporter, will meet the terms of the contract.

3.16 *Lines of credit* and *credit commitments,* including undisbursed loan commitments, are contingencies that provide a guarantee that undrawn funds will be available in the future, but no financial liability/asset exists until such funds are actually advanced.

3.17 Included under credit commitments are unutilized back-up facilities such as *note issuance facilities* (NIFs) that provide guarantees that parties will be able to sell short-term debt securities (notes) that they issue and that the financial corporations providing the facility will purchase any notes not sold in the market. Other note guarantee facilities providing contingent credit or back-up purchase facilities are *revolving underwriting facilities* (RUFs), *multiple options facilities,* and *global note facilities* (GNFs). Both banks and nonbank financial institutions provide such back-up purchase facilities.

3.18 Also, *potential* costs—such as potential losses of deposit takers on financial assets in general or costs of nonfinancial corporations associated with product warranties—are not recognized in the *Guide* as liabilities on the balance sheet because no clear legal claim/liability exists. However, if such potential costs can be valued reliably, they are included as an expense in the income statement (for example, as a provision), as such an approach provides a better measure of current financial health. It is preferred that the amounts so provisioned be included as a general reserve in capital and reserves,[10] consis-

[8]In the *Guide,* financial derivatives instruments, as defined in Chapter 4, including credit derivatives, are actual—not contingent—positions.

[9]The valuation of contingent liabilities is complex and, among other things, depends on the probability of the contingent "event" occurring. Valuation of contingent liabilities is discussed in more detail in Chapter 9 of IMF (2003b).

[10]Consistent with the approach in IASs, such potential costs could arise from future judicial settlements and/or other penalties arising from past actions that contravene existing legislation. For deposit takers, consistent with the approach in IASs, amounts set aside for general banking risks, outside of provisions for losses on assets, should not be provisioned through the income statement but rather be appropriated from retained earnings. See Chapter 4 for a detailed exposition of expenses to be included in the income statement for deposit takers.

tent with prudential regulation but not with IASs (see also Box 4.4).

3.19 If such costs are subsequently realized, there is no impact on net income because the costs have already been recognized,[11] but general reserves (and thus capital and reserves) decline. Also, there is either a decline in the value of assets—through, for example, a settlement of the expense or a decline in the value of an instrument—or a liability is recognized on the balance sheet. Overestimation of potential costs could be reversed in subsequent periods, increasing income, through, for example, a lower amount of provisioning.

Valuation

3.20 The *Guide* prefers valuation methods that can provide the most realistic assessment at any moment in time of the value of an instrument or item.[12] This approach supports macroprudential analysis by facilitating the compilation of more reliable measures of capital strength and profitability than provided by other approaches.

3.21 Crucial in determining which valuation approach to adopt is whether a market exists for the instrument or for similar instruments (or items) that can allow a reliable measure of value to be established.[13] When an instrument is tradable the expectation is that it should be valued at market or fair value (approximation of market value). For nontradable instruments, the *Guide* acknowledges that nominal value[14] (supported by appropriate provisioning policies) may provide a more realistic assessment of value than the application of fair value. For such instruments, application of fair value when a significant degree of subjectivity is involved could diminish the reliability of data for macroprudential analysis. For transactions, the market value is the amount of money that willing buyers pay to acquire something from willing sellers.

3.22 It is recognized that the use of market or fair value can introduce fluctuations into the valuation of assets and liabilities that may prove temporary. Nonetheless, at any moment in time, the opportunity costs facing the creditor and debtor, as reflected in the market or fair value, provide the most relevant, though not perfect, basis for assessing financial soundness. In this light, an institution that owns securities that have fallen significantly in value but that are valued on the balance sheet on a historic cost basis will be overstating its capital strength—and its financial soundness—because the institution cannot realize the value for the assets recorded on the balance sheet. Moreover, an institution that holds assets on a historic cost basis and has a weak capital position and low profitability has an incentive to sell those assets that show a significant gain in the market and hold those that do not, thereby boosting profits and capital while the overall quality of assets held deteriorates.

3.23 Information on the trends in market prices over time is of analytical value in its own right, not least in allowing the price risk associated with the end-period observation to be assessed. Given this, it might be appropriate to monitor period-average and end-period market prices for representative assets and liabilities of the reporting population. Data on average period market prices could also help indicate unusual outlier

[11]If a specific provision is made from the general reserve, then in that period—all other things being equal—in the income statement specific provisions increase and general provisions decrease, with no impact on net income. However, the value of the instrument against which the specific provision has been made declines, as do provisions in capital and reserves, by the amount of the specific provision.

[12]Including real estate and other nonfinancial assets.

[13]IASs 39.95-102 [IAS 39.48–39.49 and AG.69–AG.82] outline fair value measurement considerations and emphasize that fair value is reliably measured if (a) the variability in the range of fair value estimates is not significant for the instrument, and (b) the probabilities of the various estimates within the range can be reasonably assessed and used in estimating fair value. Moreover, this IAS includes the idea that reliability encompasses the ability of the user to rely on the assumption that data presented are fairly representing what they purport to represent.

[14]Nominal value is the amount the debtor owes to the creditor at any moment in time. This value is typically established by reference to the terms of a contract between the debtor and creditor. It reflects the value of the claim/liability at creation and any subsequent economic flows, such as transactions (for example, repayment of principal), valuation changes (including exchange rate and other valuation changes other than market price changes), and any other changes (such as write-offs). Conceptually, the nominal value of a debt instrument can be calculated by discounting future interest and principal payments at the existing contractual interest rate(s) on the instrument; the latter may be fixed-rate or variable-rate. Nominal value is not necessarily face value, which is the undiscounted amount of principal to be repaid. For equity instruments, the nominal value is the amount(s) contributed by shareholders.

observations in end-period market price data. (In the same vein, IASs 30.24–30.25 state that banks should disclose, as a minimum, the fair value of each class of its financial assets and liabilities. The four classes are loans and receivables, held-to-maturity investments, financial assets at fair value through profit and loss, and available-for-sale financial assets.)

Transactions

3.24 Transactions are generally valued at the actual prices agreed by the transactors, including transactions that are sales of instruments classified as nontradable, such as loans. Market price equivalents might be needed when no actual market price is set or when the value is far from the prevailing market value—for instance, for transactions between related entities. In such instances, a customary approach is to construct market prices by analogy with known market prices for the same or similar items, established under conditions that are considered essentially the same. Any difference from such an estimated price and the transaction price could be classified as a subsidy from one party to the other (see also paragraph 4.30).

Positions

3.25 The market value of an asset or liability on the balance sheet is a measure of what the financial and nonfinancial asset or liability is worth in the market at the reference date of the balance sheet.

3.26 The market value for a traded instrument at a reference date should be determined by the market price for that instrument prevailing on the date to which the position relates. Such a price is the best indication of the value that economic agents currently attribute to specific financial claims. The ideal source of a market price for a traded instrument is an organized exchange or other financial market (for example, an over-the-counter, or off-exchange market) in which the instrument is traded in considerable volume and the market price is listed at regular intervals. If the markets are closed on the reference date, the market price that should be used is that prevailing on the closest preceding date when the market was open. In some financial markets, the market price quoted for traded debt securities does not take account of interest costs that have accrued but are not yet payable, but in determining market value, these interest costs need to be included.

3.27 When specific assets are not traded in organized exchanges or other financial markets but are tradable, various approaches can be taken to estimate the market value. The preferred approach in the *Guide* is to estimate the present value of the instrument by discounting the expected stream of future benefits associated with the asset at an appropriate market rate of interest.[15] Both the *1993 SNA* and IASs support this approach.[16]

3.28 The method requires that (1) the future cash flows are known with certainty or can be reliably estimated, and (2) a market interest rate or series of market interest rates are observable (such as through reference to a similar instrument(s) traded in organized markets).

3.29 Other approaches to estimating market or fair value can include (1) using market prices that are observable for similar assets that are traded; (2) using a market-related price reported for accounting or regulatory purposes; and (3) for nonfinancial assets, accumulating and revaluing acquisitions less disposals of the asset in question over its lifetime, including taking account of depreciation (consumption of fixed capital)[17] or amortization costs. If used, these methods should be applied consistently both over time and, where relevant, in debtors' and creditors' financial statements.

3.30 For some financial instruments, such as loans, currency and deposits, and trade credit, because of their nontraded nature and the difficulty of reliably pricing them at fair value, nominal value may provide the most realistic measure of value. Such instruments may be predominant in the balance sheet of

[15]Options and instruments with embedded options are not valued by this method. Instead, pricing could require the use of an appropriate options pricing model.

[16]The formula for calculating the discounted present value is

$$\sum_{t=1}^{n} \frac{(cash\ flow)_t}{(1+i)^t},$$

where $(cash\ flow)_t$ denotes the cash flow in a future period (t), n denotes the number of future periods for which cash flows are expected, and i denotes the interest rate that is applied to discount the future cash flow in period t. A single discount rate, i, is usually used to discount the cash flow in all future periods. In some circumstances, using different discount rates in the various future periods may be warranted.

[17]Depreciation is discussed in Appendix IV (paragraphs 31–34).

deposit takers. Nonetheless, for nontraded instruments, particularly loans, recorded at nominal value, the creditor (but not the debtor) should reduce the balance sheet value of the asset for expected losses by making specific provisions or otherwise writing down the value of the asset. Provisioning is discussed in more detail in Chapter 4 in the section on deposit takers.[18]

3.31 If an instrument that is considered to be nontradable is sold or transferred to another entity, in the absence of market or fair valuation the transaction value should be the basis for any subsequent balance sheet valuation. So, for instance, if a deposit taker sells a portfolio of loans that are not tradable to another deposit taker at a heavily discounted price, the initial balance sheet value for the purchaser should be the purchase price. The seller would record as a loss in the income statement, under gains and losses on financial instruments, the difference between the value on the balance sheet (after deduction of specific provisions) at the end of the previous period and the sale value.

3.32 As markets and valuation techniques develop, the likelihood could increase of estimating fair values for nontraded instruments that provide for a more realistic measure of value than nominal value—such as using information from credit derivatives linked to the credit risk of individual entities. In such instances, compilers are encouraged to compile information on market or fair values of nontraded instruments initially as supplementary information so that the implications of market (fair) valuation for such instruments can be assessed.

3.33 The value of a share and other equity investment in an associate and unconsolidated subsidiary is equal to the investor's proportionate share, in terms of ownership of the equity capital, of the value of the capital and reserves of the associate/subsidiary. Any equity investment by an associate or unconsolidated subsidiary in the parent investor (known as a reverse equity investment) is similarly valued. In practice, balance sheet values of these entities are generally utilized to determine the value of this investment. If the investor sells equity so that it no longer retains an associate stake but still retains some equity in the other entity, the remaining investment is valued in the same manner as any other equity investment. On the other hand, if the investor adds to an equity investment so that an associate or subsidiary stake is created, the whole investment is valued on a proportionate basis.

Residence

3.34 In the *Guide,* residence (or location) is a relevant concept, as the location of a deposit taker, and in some instances that of its parent, determines the extent to which data should be collected. The same holds true for other types of entities. The residence of a parent deposit taker determines the residence of the deposit-taking group. When such deposit takers have international operations, it is essential that account be also taken of the activity of their foreign branches and subsidiaries through consolidation of their domestic and foreign operations. Domestically located deposit takers are those resident in the economy—a host country concept consistent with the approach taken in economic statistics.

3.35 The concept of residence is not based on nationality or legal criteria but rather on whether an institutional unit has a center of economic interest—dwelling, place of production, or other premises—in the economic territory of the country in question, from which it intends to engage (indefinitely or for a year or more) in economic activities and transactions on a significant scale. Thus, corporations (or quasi corporations) are residents of a country in which they are ordinarily located. This concept is central to the compilation of national accounts data.

3.36 The economic territory of a country covers geographic territory administered by a government within which persons, goods, and capital circulate freely, and includes free trade zones, entrepôts, and bonded warehouses or factories that are physically located within a country's boundaries. This territory is not always based strictly on physical or political borders, although there is usually a close correspondence.[19] In recording the geographic distribution of

[18]Depending on national accounting practices, loan values could increase if information exists to make such a revaluation.

[19]A country's economic territory includes (1) airspace; (2) territorial waters; (3) any continental shelf lying in international waters over which the country enjoys exclusive rights or over which it has, or claims to have, jurisdiction with respect to the right to exploit natural resources such as fish, minerals, or fuels; and (4) clearly demarcated territorial enclaves that are located in the rest of the world and are established by formal agreements with the governments of the countries in which the enclaves are physically located.

assets, claims of deposit takers or other lending entities are attributed to economies on the basis of the residence of the entity on which they have a claim.

Some Specific Aspects of Residence

3.37 A *branch* or *subsidiary* is resident in the economy in which it is ordinarily located, because it engages in economic activity and transactions from that location, rather than necessarily in the economy in which its parent is located.

3.38 The residence of an *offshore unit* is in the economy in which it is located. For instance, in some countries, deposit takers, including branches of foreign banks, are licensed to take deposits from and lend primarily, or even only, to residents of other economies and are treated as *offshore banks.* These banks usually face different exchange or other regulatory requirements and may not be required to provide the same amount of information to supervisors as *onshore banks.* Nonetheless, they are resident in the economy in which they are located.

3.39 Similar issues can arise with *brass plate companies, shell companies,* or *special purpose entities* (SPEs). These entities may have little physical presence in the economy in which they are legally incorporated or legally domiciled (for example, registered or licensed), and any substantive work of the entity may be conducted in another economy. In such circumstances, there might be debate as to where the center of economic interest for such entities lies. The *Guide* attributes residence to the economy in which the entity that has the liabilities on its balance sheet—and, therefore, on whom a creditor has a claim—is legally incorporated, or, in the absence of legal incorporation, is legally domiciled.

3.40 However, brass plate companies, shell companies, or SPEs, if deposit takers, should be included in the cross-border consolidated information of the parent deposit-taking entity.

3.41 A *household* is resident in the country in which its members maintain regular residence. The situation differs for military personnel and civil servants (including diplomats) employed abroad in government enclaves such as military bases and embassies, and for students and medical patients abroad, who remain members of households in their home countries.

3.42 The *ownership of land and structures* within the economic territory of a country is not deemed to be sufficient in itself for the owner to have a center of economic interest in that country. When an owner of land or buildings in an economy is a resident of another economy, he/she is classified as a nonresident from the viewpoint of the first economy.

3.43 Unless *agents* take positions between the borrower and the creditor bank onto their own balance sheets, the debtor/creditor relationship is between the lending bank and the borrowing entity, with the agent merely facilitating the transaction by bringing the borrower and lender together.

Domestic and Foreign Currencies, Unit of Account, and Exchange Rate Conversion

3.44 The extent to which assets and liabilities on the balance sheets of corporations are denominated in foreign currencies, and the degree to which currency risks are matched, is important for financial stability analysis because of the potential changes in the domestic currency value of assets and liabilities stemming from movements in foreign exchange rates.

3.45 Domestic currency is the one that is legal tender in the economy and issued by the monetary authority for that economy or for the common currency area to which the economy belongs.[20] Any currencies that do not meet this definition are foreign currencies to that economy. Under this definition, an economy that uses as its legal tender a currency issued by a monetary authority of another economy—such as U.S. dollars—or of a currency area to which it does not belong should classify the currency as a foreign one, even though domestic transactions are settled in it.

3.46 In the *Guide,* the currency composition of assets and liabilities is determined primarily by characteristics of the future payment(s). Foreign currency instruments are those payable in a currency other than the domestic currency. A subcategory of foreign currency instruments comprises those payable in a

[20]In this context, a common currency area is one to which more than one economy belongs and that has a regional central bank with the legal authority to issue the same currency within the area. To belong to this area, the economy must be a member of the regional central bank or be authorized by the regional authority to use the currency.

foreign currency but with the amounts to be paid linked to a domestic currency (domestic-currency-linked instruments). Foreign-currency-linked instruments are those payable in domestic currency but with the amounts to be paid linked to a foreign currency. Domestic currency instruments are those instruments payable in the domestic currency and not linked to a foreign currency. In the unusual instance of debt instruments with interest payments to be paid in a foreign currency but principal payments to be paid in a domestic currency, or vice versa, only the present value of the payments to be paid in a foreign currency should be classified as a foreign currency instrument.

3.47 From the perspective of the national compiler, the domestic currency unit is the obvious choice in which to calculate FSIs. Such data are compatible with the national accounts and most of the economy's other economic and monetary statistics, which are expressed in that unit. However, if the value of the domestic currency is subject to significant fluctuation relative to other currencies, a statement denominated in domestic currency could be of diminished analytical value, because valuation changes could make period-to-period comparisons less meaningful.

3.48 The calculation of FSIs can be complicated by the fact that transactions, other flows, and positions may be expressed initially in a variety of currencies or in other standards of value. Their conversion into a reference unit of account is a requisite for the construction of a consistent and analytically meaningful set of FSI statistics. The most appropriate exchange rate to be used for conversion of position data denominated in foreign currencies into the unit of account is the market (spot) exchange rate prevailing on the reference date to which the position relates. The midpoint between buying and selling rates is preferred to ensure consistency of approach among the reporting population. For conversion of an instrument in a multiple rate system,[21] the rate on the reference date for the actual exchange rate applicable to the specific liabilities or assets should be used. Transactions and other flows in foreign currencies should be converted at the market exchange rate—the midpoint between buying and selling rates is preferred—prevailing at the moment when the transaction occurs. If this information is not available, the average rates for the shortest period applicable should be used. If only information on aggregated transactions over a period is available, then the average exchange rate over this period is a suitable proxy.

Maturity

3.49 Maturity is relevant for financial stability analysis both from a liquidity viewpoint (for example, in calculating the value of liabilities falling due in the short term) and from an asset/liability mismatch perspective (for example, in estimating the effect of changes in interest rates on profitability). In the *Guide,* short-term is defined as a maturity of one year or less[22] and long-term as a maturity of more than one year (or no stated maturity).

3.50 One approach is to determine the maturity classification of financial instruments on the basis of the time until repayments of principal (and interest) are due—known as remaining maturity (and sometimes referred to as residual maturity).[23] Another approach uses the maturity at issuance—known as original maturity—thus indicating whether the funds were raised in the short-term or long-term markets.

3.51 Yet another approach to maturity is to calculate the *duration* of assets and liabilities. Duration is the weighted average term to maturity of a financial instrument and can be used as a measure of the sensitivity of the value of financial assets to changes in interest rates, rather than of maturity as such.

3.52 For a given portfolio of financial assets and liabilities, the magnitude of gains or losses arising from potential interest rate changes can be estimated using duration analysis and compared with capital and reserves.

[21]A multiple exchange rate system is one in which there are schedules of exchange rates, set by the authorities, and where different exchange rates are applied to various categories of transactions/transactors.

[22]For financial instruments, inter alia, this category includes amounts payable on demand and those debt instruments redeemable at short notice.

[23]Strictly defined, the outstanding amount of short-term assets or liabilities on a remaining maturity basis is the present value of payments due in one year or less. In practice, the outstanding amount of short-term assets or liabilities on a remaining maturity basis can be measured by adding the present value of short-term debt (original maturity) to the present value of long-term debt (original maturity) to be paid in one year or less.

3.53 The longer the duration of a portfolio, the greater the gains (or losses) for any given change in interest rates. Therefore, if despite the matching of the maturities of financial assets and liabilities, the timing of the cash flows on assets and liabilities is not perfectly matched—that is, the duration of assets and liabilities differs—corporations can be open to gains (or losses) as interest rates change.[24]

3.54 For fixed-rate instruments, the time period until the receipt/payment of each cash flow, such as six months, is weighted by the present value of that cash flow as a proportion of the present value of total cash flows over the life of the instrument. So the more cash flows are concentrated toward the early part of an instrument's life, the shorter the duration relative to maturity. Duration equals remaining maturity only for zero coupon instruments. In the *Guide,* the preferred approach is that the discount rate used to calculate present value of each payment is the current yield to maturity of the instrument.

3.55 For a floating-rate instrument, its duration is the time until the next interest rate reset date rather than the time until the receipt/payment of each cash flow.

3.56 Depending on the analytical need, the instrument coverage of duration measures can vary. Shares and other equity are typically excluded from the calculation.

[24]A specific measure of duration—Macaulay duration—can be calculated as follows:

$$D_i = \frac{\sum_{t=1}^{N} CF_t \times DF_t \times t}{\sum_{t=1}^{N} CF_t \times DF_t} = \frac{\sum_{t=1}^{N} PV_t \times t}{\sum_{t=1}^{N} PV_t},$$

where

D_i = duration measured in years for instrument i

CF_t = cash flow to be received on the financial instrument at end of period t

N = last period in which the cash flow is received—maturity of instrument

DF_t = discount factor = $1/(1+R)^t$ where R is the yield or current level of interest rates in the market

$\sum_{t=1}^{N}$ = summation sign for addition of all terms for $t = 1$ to $t = N$

PV_t = present value of the cash flow due at the end of the period t, which equals $CF_t \times DF_t$.

The use of a single interest rate as the discount factor implies that changes in interest rates result in a parallel shift in the yield curve. Alternatively, to account for the possibility of changes in the shape of the yield curve as interest rates change, specific discount factors for each cash flow could be employed. However, this approach might be harder to implement in practice.

4. Accounting Framework and Sectoral Financial Statements

Introduction

4.1 Fundamental to understanding the financial condition of deposit takers, other corporations, and households is information from the traditional financial statements on income and expense, and the stock of assets and liabilities—the balance sheet. Data series obtained from such statements can be used to calculate many of the FSI ratios for corporations and households.

4.2 This chapter begins by outlining the traditional accounting framework from which financial statements are drawn, before presenting detailed sectoral financial statements and defining the line-item series. The guidance is provided to assist in the compilation of the component series required to calculate the FSI ratios. It draws on the relevant conceptual advice for other economic statistics, IASs, and supervisory guidance, and takes account of macroprudential requirements.

4.3 In addition to data reported by individual institutions, some data are required to make adjustments at the sector level, primarily to eliminate transactions and positions among institutions within the same sector. While sector-level data are discussed in more detail in Chapter 5, where appropriate the series required for sector-level adjustments are noted in footnotes in this chapter.[1]

4.4 It is recognized that countries have different accounting systems and will rely on national sources of data to compile FSIs. For example, to compile data on a domestically controlled cross-border consolidated basis, compilers may rely on supervisory-based data. Some data series may not be collected, and others may not meet the definitions suggested in the *Guide.* In such circumstances, the data that most closely approximate the principles in the *Guide* should be used. In determining the need to collect new data, with the associated increased resource cost, authorities must make a judgment as to the likely impact and importance of the additional data series for compiling and monitoring FSI data.

4.5 In comments made on an earlier draft of the *Guide,* many compilers urged that flexibility be given to countries to take account of the differences in the readiness to adopt international standards. It was acknowledged that such flexibility may make comparison difficult between countries that have different criteria for recording information, increasing the importance of disseminating metadata (information about data). Such information could potentially give greater transparency.

4.6 Given these concerns, why does the *Guide* provide sectoral accounts and detailed definitions? First, such an approach supports compilation efforts at the national level by specifying how the series required to calculate FSIs are to be defined. Second, by providing a consistent framework that draws on relevant international standards, and takes account of analytical needs, a benchmark is provided for use by national compilers, even if their own national standards differ. Such a benchmark can be used as a reference when disseminating metadata. Third, such an approach helps foster greater comparability of data across countries—a medium-term objective in line with the views of the IMF Executive Board. In this regard, the definitions provided in this chapter can help guide the future development of sectoral financial data to be used to calculate FSIs.

[1] The *Guide* prefers the reporting of financial statement data by individual institutions on a basis that is internally consistent for each institution, with additional information provided by individual institutions to permit appropriate adjustments at the sector level. This approach will not only provide more coherent information from the viewpoint of an individual institution, but it also facilitates identification of intrasector transactions and positions and is consistent with the approach to peer group and dispersion analysis as described in Chapter 15.

Accounting Framework

4.7 Outlined below are the key elements of financial statements.

Income and Expense Statement

4.8 This statement includes income and expenses related to the operations of the entity. After expenses have been deducted along with any dividends paid or payable to shareholders, any remaining income is transferred to the capital and reserves as retained earnings. As noted in Chapter 3, in the *Guide* income and expenses are recorded on an accrual rather than a cash basis. As defined in the *Guide,* net income before dividends measures the increase or decrease in value during the period that arises from the activities of the sector.

Balance Sheet

4.9 The balance sheet is the statement of assets, liabilities, and capital at the end of each accounting period:

- Assets include both financial[2] and nonfinancial assets.
- Liabilities include debt liabilities and financial derivatives.
- The difference between the value of assets and liabilities is known in the *Guide* as capital and reserves.[3] This represents the "cushion" to absorb any losses arising from the income and expense statement, or for other reasons. If liabilities exceed assets, then the entity is technically insolvent.

4.10 Some liabilities and assets of corporations are contingent on a certain event(s) occurring and are recorded off balance sheet (see paragraph 3.12). As noted in Chapter 3, such items require monitoring to assess the full financial risk exposure of the corporation.

4.11 Measures of profitability and capital depend on the accounting definitions and recognition rules adopted. For instance, if valuation gains and losses on assets are recorded in the income and expense statement, they will affect the recorded profitability of corporations. Moreover, if some assets or liabilities are off—rather than on—balance sheet, this will affect measured capital. In developing the guidance on definitions set out below, to a varying extent three sources of accounting definitions are drawn upon. These are described in Box 4.1. The constituents of capital used in calculating the Basel capital adequacy ratio are described in Box 4.2.

4.12 Appendix IV provides a detailed reconciliation of the definitions set out in this chapter with those in both national and commercial accounting—the basic data sources most likely to be drawn upon. This appendix supplements the main text and can be drawn upon for additional guidance.

Sectoral Financial Statements

4.13 Sectoral financial statements are set out below on an institutional sector basis. While the income and expense statements and the balance sheets for the specific sectors have a considerable degree of overlap in terms of line-item series identified (particularly the balance sheets), there are significant differences in presentation between the sectors. These differences have implications for the calculation of FSIs. For instance, the net interest margin is an important FSI series for deposit takers but not for the household sector, for which gross disposable income is a more relevant measure. The deposit-taking sector is presented first, because of its central role in the financial system and the wider range of series from the sectoral financial statements required to calculate FSIs for deposit takers.

4.14 The line-item series in the financial statements for which definitions are provided are those required to calculate the FSIs set out in Chapters 6 and 7, either directly or as important building blocks in calculating the required aggregates. The advantage of defining these series within the framework of a financial statement is the accounting rigor that is imposed—the series are defined to ensure that the integrity of a double-entry recording system is maintained, while promoting a consistency of approach in the classification and coverage of transactions and positions. The conceptual guidance for the calculation of financial market FSIs is provided in Chapter 8.

4.15 Unless stated otherwise, each series presented below is defined only once, even if it appears in other sectoral financial statements. Most of the definitions are provided in the section covering the deposit takers' financial statement. It is recognized that there may need to be a degree of flexibility in interpreting

[2]Including financial derivatives.

[3]"Capital and reserves" is the term used in the IASs (IAS 1.66) and is consistent with the terminology used in the list of FSIs. In the *1993 SNA* the equivalent terms are "shares and other equity" together with "net worth." In the *Guide,* the term "shares and other equity" is used to denote equity assets.

Box 4.1. Measurement Frameworks

In determining those accounting rules most relevant for the compilation of FSIs, three basic measurement frameworks can be drawn upon—national accounting, commercial accounting, as well as banking supervision guidance. This box aims to place these frameworks in context, explain their analytical purposes, describe their key characteristics, and provide references for further reading. It concludes by explaining that the FSI framework draws on these other frameworks but does not coincide with them because its analytical objectives are different.

National accounts data

The System of National Accounts (SNA) consists of a coherent, consistent, and integrated set of macroeconomic accounts, balance sheets, and tables based on a set of internationally agreed concepts, definitions, classifications, and accounting rules. The SNA provides a comprehensive accounting framework within which aggregated economic data can be compiled and presented in a format that is designed for purposes of economic analysis, decision making, and policymaking. Its intention is to provide comprehensive coverage of economic activities within an economy.

Central to the development of national accounts and the related methodologies is the concept of residence. The SNA groups resident institutional units into five resident institutional sectors and nonresident units into the rest of the world sector. It groups the related economic flows and stocks into three broad sets of accounts. The current accounts and the accumulation accounts cover economic flows (transactions and other flows), and the balance sheet accounts cover stocks. These three broad sets of accounts are fully integrated through sequential accounts that range from production accounts to balance sheet accounts.

The main source of information on national accounting is the *System of National Accounts 1993* (*1993 SNA*) (Commission of the European Communities and others, 1993). Other related methodologies include the *Monetary and Financial Statistics Manual* (*MFSM*) (IMF, 2000a); *Balance of Payments Manual*, fifth edition (*BPM5*) (IMF, 1993); *Government Finance Statistics Manual (GFSM)* (IMF, 2001a); and *External Debt Statistics: Guide for Compilers and Users* (IMF, 2003b).

International accounting standards

The International Accounting Standards (IASs) are a series of standards for commercial accounting that provide concepts that underlie the preparation and presentation of financial statements of commercial, industrial, and business reporting enterprises, whether in the public or the private sector. A revised set[1] of IASs, so-called International Financial Reporting Standards (IFRSs), was completed in 2004. It includes significant revisions to the standards for disclosure and treatment of financial instruments. References in this *Guide* to specific IAS provisions include several concordance tables between the current standards and earlier versions.

The objective of financial statements is to provide information (including information on a consolidated basis) about the financial position and performance of an enterprise, as well as changes in its financial position. Consolidated reporting provides information on the group as a whole, which is usually the concern of users of financial statements. A reporting enterprise is an enterprise for which there are users who rely on financial statements as their main source of financial information about the enterprise. Users include investors, employees of the enterprise, lenders, suppliers and other trade creditors, customers, governments and their agencies, and the public.

The financial statements portray the financial effects of transactions and other events by grouping them into broad categories according to their economic characteristics. The elements directly related to the measurement of the financial position in the balance sheet are assets, liabilities, and equity. The elements directly related to performance in the income statement are income and expenses. Like the *1993 SNA*, the presentation of these elements in the balance sheet and income statements involves a process of subclassification. For example, assets and liabilities may be classified by their nature or function in the business of the enterprise to display information in the manner most useful for making economic decisions. But unlike the *1993 SNA* framework, the IAS framework is not designed to produce aggregated statistics.

The IASs are available from the International Accounting Standards Board (IASB), www.iasb.org.

Banking supervision

In 1988, the Basel Committee on Banking Supervision (BCBS) agreed on supervisory regulations governing the capital adequacy of international banks. These regulations, which were amended in 1996, provide a framework (commonly known as Basel I) for the measurement of capital in relation to the perceived credit and market risk of the assets owned by the bank. Two fundamental objectives lie at the heart of the BCBS's work. First, the framework is intended to strengthen the soundness and stability of the international banking system. Second, the framework is intended to be fair and, through a high degree of consistency in its application to banks in different countries, to diminish sources of competitive inequality among international banks.

The agreement reached was applied to banks on a consolidated basis, including subsidiaries undertaking banking and financial business. Consolidated reporting captures the risks within the whole banking group. The constituents of capital are divided into three tiers and are described in more detail in Box 4.2. While banking supervisors rely on commercial accounting standards for financial statements from banks, and thus do not provide a

[1]The effective date of the new IASs and IFRSs is January 1, 2005, which could introduce breaks in series in those countries where it is adopted. The IASs and IFRSs are voluntary standards that are implemented by national legislation. The European Union adopted the IASs and IFRSs beginning in 2005, as have other countries, while other countries may not adopt the IASs and IFRSs, may do so partially, or may introduce them over a period of time. Also, the IASs and IFRSs are not universal sets of standards in that they apply principally to large corporate entities that issue securities that are publicly traded. National commercial accounting standards may differ from IASs and IFRSs in important respects.

Box 4.1 *(concluded)*

separate comprehensive framework comparable to those available from the national and commercial accounting sources, over the years they have developed various guidance rules with regard to capital adequacy for activities that directly affect banks' capital (for example, on provisioning).

In 2004, the BCBS published a revised framework that modified the existing capital adequacy requirements and incorporated new standards for supervisory oversight of banking and for disclosure of banking information. The new framework is commonly known as Basel II.

The main sources of information on the BCBS's capital adequacy requirements are the "International Convergence of Capital Measurement and Capital Standards" (BCBS, 1988) and "Amendment to the Capital Accord to Incorporate Market Risks" (BCBS, 1996). There is also other related documentation in BCBS (2001a).[2] The new framework is published in *Basel II: International Convergence of Capital Measurement and Capital Standards: A Revised Framework* (BCBS, 2004).

Financial soundness indicators

The objective of the *Guide* is to set out a framework of guidelines to underlie the preparation of financial statements for deposit takers, other financial corporations, nonfinancial corporations, and households in order to calculate FSIs for the purpose of assisting in the assessment and monitoring of the strengths and vulnerabilities of financial systems.

The framework draws on existing frameworks and therefore has many similarities of approach with them; for instance, the accrual method of recognition of flows and positions. However, in broad terms there are three significant differences in approach from existing frameworks: sector information, recording of activity, and consolidation.

- Unlike the interest of commercial accounting and supervisory approaches in individual entities, the FSI framework, like the national accounts, focuses on aggregated sector information.
- Whereas the national accounts embrace symmetric recording of flows and positions within and across sectors (because of the economy-wide perspective) and commercial accounting and supervisory approaches do not (because of the focus on the individual entity), the FSI framework favors a symmetric recording of flows and positions within the sector, to avoid distortions in the sector data, but not necessarily among sectors, because the type of data required differs by sector.
- Whereas the national accounts are keen to capture more or less all economic activity, the FSI framework, like commercial and supervisory accounting, favors a consolidated approach to avoid the double counting of capital and activity.

[2]Also available on the BIS website (http://www.bis.org/publ/bcbsc002.htm#pgtop).

this guidance when compiling data. When disseminating data, compilers are encouraged to document any significant differences between national practice and the guidance provided below.

Deposit Takers

Income and expense

4.16 The sectoral financial statement for deposit takers is set out in Table 4.1.

4.17 For deposit takers the main source of revenue and expense is interest. *Interest income* is a form of income that accrues on debt instruments such as deposits, loans, debt securities, and other accounts receivable. For the borrower it is the cost (known as an interest cost) of the use of another entity's funds (Box 4.3).[4] As explained in Chapter 3 (paragraph 3.7) in the *Guide,* interest is recorded as accruing continuously. As can be seen in Table 4.1, the difference between interest expense and interest income is known as *net interest income.*

4.18 A specific issue arises of whether interest should accrue on nonperforming assets, and if so, should this affect the net interest income line. The *Guide* recommends that interest on a nonperforming asset should be recorded on a cash payment, not accrual, basis. Interest income should not include the accrual of interest on nonperforming assets, because otherwise net interest income would be overstated relative to the actual interest-earning capacity of the deposit taker.[5]

[4]Box 4.3 discusses the implications of Islamic principles, such as the prohibition of receipt and payment of interest, for the compilation of FSIs for deposit taker sectors that include Islamic financial institutions (IFIs).

[5]The *Guide* recognizes that while in many countries classification of an asset as nonperforming is strong evidence for it to be placed on a nonaccrual basis, the provision of collateral or other guarantees might lead the deposit taker to consider that the debtor will continue to meet his obligations. While accepting that national practices do vary on this matter, for the purposes of developing international guidance for FSIs, the *Guide* considers classification as nonperforming sufficient evidence to cease accruing interest on the asset and to record interest income only if the debtor subsequently makes an interest payment.

Box 4.2. The Basel Capital Adequacy Ratio

The Basel capital adequacy ratio was adopted in 1988 by the Basel Committee on Banking Supervision (BCBS) as a benchmark to evaluate whether banks operating in the Group of Ten (G-10) countries have sufficient capital to survive likely economic shocks. The ratio calls for minimum levels of capital to (1) provide a cushion against losses due to default arising from both on- and off-balance-sheet exposures, (2) demonstrate that bank owners are willing to put their own funds at risk, (3) provide quickly available resources free of transaction and liquidation costs, (4) provide for normal expansion and business finance, (5) level the playing field by requiring universal application of the standard, and (6) encourage less risky lending.

The original Basel capital ratio, along with subsequent amendments, requires international banks to have a specific measure of capital greater than or equal to 8 percent of a specific measure of assets weighted by their estimated credit risk. The ratio is an analytical construct with complex definitions of the numerator (capital) and the denominator (risk-weighted assets) that cannot be derived directly from standard financial statements. The ratio can be expressed as:

$$\textit{Risk-based capital adequacy ratio} = \frac{\textit{Capital} \times 100}{\textit{Risk-weighted assets}} \geq 8.$$

This formula states that a banking enterprise must have capital on a worldwide consolidated basis equal to 8 percent or more of its risk-weighted assets, which includes an on-balance-sheet equivalent position of off-balance-sheet positions, where capital can be expressed as:

$$\textit{Capital} = (\textit{Tier 1 capital} - \textit{goodwill}) + (\textit{Tier 2 capital}) + (\textit{Tier 3 capital}) - \textit{adjustments}.$$

Tier 1 capital, or "core capital," consists of equity capital and disclosed reserves that are considered freely available to meet claims against the bank.

Tier 2 capital consists of financial instruments and reserves that are available to absorb losses but that might lack permanency, have uncertain values, entail costs if sold, or otherwise lack the full loss-absorption capacity of Tier 1 capital items.

Tier 3 capital consists of subordinated debt with an original maturity of at least two years for use, if needed, against market risk exposures associated with fluctuations in the market value of assets held. Neither interest nor principal on its debt may be paid if such payments mean that the bank falls below or remains below its minimum capital requirement.

Goodwill is subtracted because the value of goodwill may fall during crises, and various *adjustments* are made to capital to prevent possible double counting of value.

Risk-weighted assets, the denominator of the Basel capital ratio, are the weighted total of each class of assets and off-balance-sheet asset exposures, with weights related to the credit risk associated with each type of asset. In the example below, the market value of assets is 940, but the value of risk-weighted assets is 615.

Example of Estimation of Risk-Weighted Assets

Type of Asset	Value of Holdings	Risk Weight	Risk-Weighted Assets
U.S. Treasury bonds	200	0%	0
Mortgage loans	250	50%	125
Corporation bonds	120	100%	120
Consumer loans	370	100%	370
Total	940	—	615

Capital adequacy ratios are often not directly comparable among countries because national supervisors have some leeway in defining weights and adjustments and, even more important, national practice may vary in the valuation of assets, recognition of loan losses, and provisioning, which can significantly affect the ratio. In addition, an aggregate measure of capital adequacy potentially disguises information on individual institutions, and thus for macroprudential analysis, it is useful to supplement the aggregate ratio with information on the dispersion of ratios for individual institutions or subsectors of the banking system.

Recent developments regarding the ratio include attempts to refine the weighting system. In particular, in 2004 the Basel Committee issued a revised framework, known as Basel II, that permits greater differentiation among assets based on their risk, including the possibility of using—under specified conditions—internal model-based measures of risk exposures (BCBS, 2004).

Table 4.1. Deposit Takers

Income and Expense Statement

1. Interest income[1]
   - (i) Gross interest income
   - (ii) Less provisions for accrued interest on nonperforming assets
2. Interest expense[1]
3. *Net interest income* (= 1 minus 2)
4. Noninterest income
   - (i) Fees and commissions receivable[1]
   - (ii) Gains or losses on financial instruments
   - (iii) Prorated earnings
   - (iv) Other income[1]
5. *Gross income* (= 3 + 4)
6. Noninterest expenses
   - (i) Personnel costs
   - (ii) Other expenses
7. Provisions (net)
   - (i) Loan loss provisions
   - (ii) Other financial asset provisions
8. *Net income (before extraordinary items and taxes)* (= 5 minus (6 + 7))
9. Extraordinary items
10. Income tax
11. *Net income after tax* (= 8 minus (9 + 10))
12. Dividends payable
13. *Retained earnings* (= 11 minus 12)

Balance Sheet

14. **Total assets** (= 15 + 16 = 31)
15. *Nonfinancial assets*
16. *Financial assets* (= 17 through 22)
17. Currency and deposits[1]
18. Loans (after specific provisions)
    - (i) Gross loans[1]
      - (i.i) Interbank loans[2]
        - (i.i.i) Resident
        - (i.i.ii) Nonresident
      - (i.ii) Noninterbank loans
        - (i.ii.i) Central bank
        - (i.ii.ii) General government
        - (i.ii.iii) Other financial corporations
        - (i.ii.iv) Nonfinancial corporations
        - (i.ii.v) Other domestic sectors
        - (i.ii.vi) Nonresidents
    - (ii) Specific provisions[3]
19. Debt securities[1]
20. Shares and other equity
21. Financial derivatives[1]
22. Other assets[1]
23. *Liabilities* (= 28 + 29)
24. Currency and deposits
    - (i) Customer deposits
    - (ii) Interbank deposits[2]
      - (ii.i) Resident
      - (ii.ii) Nonresident
    - (iii) Other currency and deposits
25. Loans
26. Debt securities
27. Other liabilities
28. *Debt* (= 24 + 25 + 26 + 27)
29. Financial derivatives
30. Capital and reserves
    - (i) *Of which:* Narrow capital and reserves[4]
31. **Balance sheet total (= 23 + 30 = 14)**

Memorandum series

Other series required to calculate the agreed FSIs

Supervisory series

32. Tier 1 capital
33. Tier 2 capital
34. Tier 3 capital
35. Supervisory deductions
36. *Total regulatory capital* (= 32 through 34 minus 35)
37. Risk-weighted assets
38. Number of large exposures

Series that provide a further analysis of the balance sheet

39. Liquid assets (core)
40. Liquid assets (broad measure)
41. Short-term liabilities
42. Nonperforming loans
43. Residential real estate loans
44. Commercial real estate loans
45. Geographic distribution of loans[5]
46. Foreign currency loans
47. Foreign currency liabilities
48. Net open position in equities
49. Net open position in foreign currency for on-balance-sheet items

Table 4.1 (concluded)

Balance-sheet-related series

50. Total net open position in foreign currency
51. Exposures of largest deposit takers to largest entities in the economy
52. Exposures to affiliated entities and other "connected" counterparties

[1]To understand the interconnections among deposit takers, separate identification of income and claims on other deposit takers in the reporting population is encouraged.

[2]Interbank loans and deposits comprise those loans to or deposits from any other deposit taker (resident or nonresident).

[3]If only gross loans data are available, including the accrual of interest on NPLs, any provisions for accrued interest on NPLs should be included in this line item and, if significant, separately identified.

[4]These are funds contributed by owners plus retained earnings (including appropriations from retained earnings to reserves). Purchased goodwill is excluded. Data are compiled only if Tier 1 data are not available.

[5]While individual country circumstances will vary, data on the distribution of lending by regional groupings of countries are encouraged, with additional country information where relevant (see paragraph 6.63).

4.19 To ensure consistency of approach between debtors and creditors, Table 4.1 includes the line items for *gross interest income,* including interest accrual on nonperforming assets, and *provisions for interest accrual* on nonperforming assets. The latter should be deducted from the former to eliminate the interest accruing on nonperforming assets in the interest income line.[6,7] If the debtor subsequently pays interest on nonperforming assets to the deposit taker, interest income should increase through an adjustment to the provision in the period payments are received and, if significant, should be referred to in any accompanying explanatory documentation.[8] If any interest accrued before an asset was classified as nonperforming, given that such accrual would increase the value of the asset, a specific loan loss provision would be appropriate (see paragraph 4.32). If data are available only on interest income, excluding interest accrual on nonperforming assets, then only the interest income line (line 1 in Table 4.1) should be reported. Appendix V provides numerical examples of how to record interest on NPLs.

4.20 *Noninterest income* is all other income received by the deposit taker. Included are *fees and commissions* from the provision of services, *gains and losses on financial instruments,*[9] and *other income.* Net interest income together with noninterest income is equal to *gross income.*

4.21 *Fees and commissions* are for services such as payment services; intermediary services (for example, those associated with lines of credit and letters of credit); services related to transactions in securities (for example, brokerage, placements and underwriting of new issues, arrangement of swaps and other financial derivatives, security lending); and services related to asset management (for example, portfolio management, safe custody).[10] National practice might require that fees and commissions payable to other deposit takers in the reporting population be included as a negative income item rather than included as an expense.

4.22 *Gains and losses on financial instruments* are those arising during the period under review. The *Guide* encourages the inclusion in this item of realized and unrealized gains and losses arising during each period on all financial instruments (financial

[6]BCBS (1999, p. 29) notes the need for such an approach in countries where, as a result of laws or regulations, banks must accrue interest on impaired loans in accordance with the original terms of the contract. Nonetheless, the general guidance of the BCBS is that for impaired loans a bank should cease accruing interest in accordance with the contract.

[7]The approach of accruing at the contractual rate and including a provision for interest accrual could be adopted for an instrument that is not classified as nonperforming but for which only partial payment of interest is expected in the coming period(s), or has occurred in the current period. Under such circumstances, simply accruing interest at the contractual rate would likely overstate income.

[8]Where interest ceases to accrue on claims on other deposit takers in the reporting population, to avoid asymmetric reporting of net income at the sector level, additional information on the amounts involved should be reported—both the provisions and any amounts subsequently paid.

[9]Such gains and losses are not classified as income in the *1993 SNA*.

[10]Implicit fees and commissions, such as those corresponding to the *1993 SNA* concept of "financial intermediation services indirectly measured" (FSIM), are not included in this item. In other words, interest income is not adjusted for any FSIM estimates.

assets and liabilities, in domestic and foreign currencies) valued at market or fair value on the balance sheet,[11] including investment account securities but excluding equity in associates, subsidiaries, and any reverse equity investments.[12,13] Gains and losses on foreign exchange instruments and on financial derivative instruments, such as interest rate swaps, are also included. Gains and losses on financial instruments exclude any interest included in the net interest income account as accrued for that instrument in the reporting period, as such amounts have been already accounted for in the income account as interest income.

4.23 In contrast, gains and losses in deposit takers' accounts have traditionally covered gains and losses recorded on assets and liabilities held for a short period as deposit takers seek to take advantage of short-term fluctuations in market prices. Coverage varies among the various accounting standards but typically includes realized and unrealized gains and losses during the period on securities and derivatives held in the so-called dealing account.[14] Coverage includes gains and losses arising from on-selling of securities acquired under security repurchase agreements, securities lending, and sell/buyback arrangements (see paragraph 4.48); any gains or losses realized during the period on sales of securities held in the investment account; and gains or losses arising from the holding, sale, and purchase of foreign exchange instruments (except for equity investments in associates and subsidiaries), including foreign exchange derivative contracts.

[11]For data at the sector level, gains and losses on any holdings of equity issued by other deposit takers in the population should be excluded (see Box 5.1).

[12]Associates and subsidiaries are defined in the next chapter.

[13]Changes in the value of equity in associates, unconsolidated subsidiaries, and reverse equity investments are excluded from this income line because income would be double counted: the line *other income* includes the prorated share of profits and losses from associates, unconsolidated subsidiaries, and reverse equity investments. Moreover, if a deposit taker sells a stake in a deposit-taking associate or subsidiary (or there is a disinvestment of a reverse investment) at a value greater than the proportionate value of the capital and reserves, the difference should not be included within income. Instead, it should be added to the seller's capital and reserves, thus ensuring symmetric treatment with that for goodwill, which is deducted from capital and reserves (see paragraph 4.110).

[14]Banks typically distinguish in their accounts between securities held for trading (dealing account or trading book) and those held for long-term investment (investment account or banking book), usually to maturity. IAS 39 further distinguishes the latter category between financial instruments held to maturity and financial instruments available for sale.

4.24 However, the *Guide* encourages the wider coverage of gains and losses on financial instruments outlined in paragraph 4.22 for the following purposes:

(1) ***Net income reflects current health and not past developments.*** In other words, changes in the value of financial instruments that can be reliably measured are recorded in sector income in the period they arise.[15] Experience has demonstrated that the buildup of hidden gains and losses that remain unrecorded in the income statement until they are realized can be misleading for macroprudential analysis.

(2) ***Return on capital is reliably observed.*** Capital is employed by deposit takers to generate income primarily through activity in financial instruments. Excluding unrealized gains and losses in financial instruments, whose value can be reliably measured, obscures in any one period the extent to which capital is efficiently employed. While immediate recognition of gains and losses might generate greater period-to-period volatility in the return on capital data than nonrecognition, understanding the causes of such volatility and observing the trend over time provides a more robust basis for macroprudential analysis.

(3) ***The relative importance of gains and losses on those financial assets and liabilities valued at market or fair value can be monitored.*** Experience has shown that gains and losses on financial instruments can be a more volatile element in deposit takers' earnings than other income items, perhaps reflecting potentially greater risk taking. Identification of the size and sensitivity of deposit takers' income and capital to changes in market conditions is best observed by time-series data that capture the gains and losses on an ongoing basis.

(4) ***Asymmetric reporting of gains and losses at the sector-wide level is avoided.*** If individual deposit takers record gains and losses on the same instrument at different times, this will lead to inconsistent measures of net income at the sector level.[16]

[15]For nontraded instruments, reduction in value recognized by the deposit taker is reflected in provisions.

[16]Unlike the instruments covered by this item, for instruments recorded at nominal value asymmetries can arise when creditors but not debtors make provisions for the credit risk of the debtor. In Chapter 5, the *Guide* discusses sector adjustments for instances where both the debtor and creditor are in the deposit-taking sector.

4.25 Appendix V provides numerical examples of how to record gains and losses on financial instruments.

4.26 It is acknowledged that coverage of gains and losses as set out in paragraph 4.22 may not be feasible for reporters at the time of writing, and that data collection systems may need to be developed.

4.27 For those financial instruments for which gains and losses can be recorded only when realized, the gain or loss should be measured as the difference between the transaction value and the market value recorded on the balance sheet at the end of the previous period. Any unrealized gains or losses that developed over previous periods and that are included in the valuation adjustment should be transferred to retained earnings. In other words, so as not to distort measures of current health, or create adverse selection-type incentives described in paragraph 3.22, net income should not reflect the realization of gains or losses that have developed in the balance sheet valuation of financial instruments and been retained over a number of reporting periods. In addition, all gains or losses in the reporting period—that is, since the previous end-period—that are realized on any other financial assets (except for those related to associate, subsidiary, and reverse equity investments, which are all recorded directly in capital and reserves) should also be included within the gains and losses on the financial instruments line. This includes gains and losses on loan sales. If these gains and losses are significant in any one period, compilers are encouraged to provide additional information so that their importance to the data disseminated can be judged.

4.28 *Prorated earnings* cover the share—on the basis of the share of equity owned—of net income after tax[17] from associates, unconsolidated subsidiaries,[18] and reverse equity investments, and, for domestic-based data, foreign branches.[19]

[17]Unless the taxes on net income are payable by the investor, in which instance this item covers net income before tax.

[18]This item also covers income reflecting the withdrawal of income by the owner from a quasi corporation. Only withdrawal of income from the net income earned by the quasi corporation should be included.

[19]At the sector level, any earnings from deposit-taking associates that are covered in the reporting population should be excluded from this line (see also Box 5.1).

4.29 *Other income* covers (1) dividends declared payable by other corporations or cooperatives in which deposit takers have an equity stake,[20] (2) gains or losses on sales of fixed assets in the current period (measured as the difference between the sale value and the balance sheet value at the previous end-period),[21] (3) rental and royalty income receivable (including income from buildings, other structures, and equipment; from land and subsoil assets; and from other produced and nonproduced assets), and (4) any amounts receivable by deposit takers arising from compensation for damage or injury.

4.30 *Noninterest expenses* cover all expenses other than interest expenses, including *fees and commissions.* They include operating expenses relating to ordinary banking business (other than interest expenses) such as (1) personnel (or staff) costs (see below); (2) expenses for property and equipment (ordinary and regular maintenance and repair);[22] rentals paid on buildings, other structures, and equipment (and related depreciation);[23] and rents paid on land; (3) other expenditures related to the operations, including purchases of goods and services (for example, advertising costs, staff training service expenses, and fees for other services provided), and royalties paid for the use of other produced or nonproduced assets (excluding those expenses classified as per-

[20]To avoid double counting of income before extraordinary items and taxes, in the sector-level data, dividends receivable from other deposit takers in the reporting population should be excluded from this item and instead included (with a negative sign) in the dividends payable line. In this way, the data for dividends payable by, and receivable from, other deposit takers in the reporting population will net out to zero in this line.

[21]At the sector level, any gains or losses realized through a sale of a fixed asset to another deposit taker in the reporting population should, in principle, be excluded from this item and not affect net income. This is because the valuation gain or loss remains unrealized by the sector as a whole. Only when fixed assets are sold to an entity outside the sector should such gains or losses be recorded in the income account. While maintaining records of fixed assets by transactor might raise practical difficulties, it is recommended that at least significant gains and losses for the period under review arising from sales to another deposit taker in the reporting population be identified—subject to confidentiality constraints—and deducted from sector-wide income.

[22]Such expenses are different in nature, and so recorded differently, from expenditures on gross fixed capital formation, which add to nonfinancial assets in the balance sheet.

[23]There are differences between the national accounts and commercial accounts measurements of depreciation. The *Guide* does not make a judgment as to the preferred method. As explained in Appendix IV, the national accounts approach is based on current market prices, whereas the commercial accounts approach is based on historic prices but allows for periodic reviews with adjustments to the schedule of depreciation as necessary.

sonnel costs (see below)); and (4) taxes other than income taxes—such as taxes on the ownership or use of land and buildings or on labor employed (including payroll and other employee-related taxes payable by the employer)—less any subsidies related to operating activity, such as subsidies received from general government. Also included are any fines and penalties imposed on deposit takers, by courts of law or otherwise, and any amounts payable by deposit takers as compensation to other institutional units for injury and damage. For deposit takers, operating expenses also include any premiums paid to a deposit insurance fund.

4.31 *Personnel costs* include the total remuneration, in cash or in kind, payable by the enterprise in return for work done by employees during the accounting period. Included are wages and salaries, including paid annual leave and paid sick leave; profit sharing and bonuses; allowances for housing and cars; as well as free or subsidized goods and services (except those required for employees to carry out their work); and social security contributions, for such items as medical care and pensions.[24] Also included are unfunded employee social insurance benefits such as the continued payment of normal or reduced wages during periods of absence from work as a result of ill health and accidents, redundancy payments, and so on.

4.32 *Loan loss provisions* are net new allowances that deposit takers make in the period against bad or impaired loans, based on their judgment as to the likelihood of losses.[25] General provisions are provisions not attributed to specific assets but to the amount of losses that experience suggests may be in a portfolio of loans. Such provisions are sometimes calculated as a percentage of total assets. Alternatively, they can be calculated by applying progressively higher percentages for lower quality assets, reflecting the increasing probability of losses. Specific provisions are charges against the value of specific loans (including a collectively assessed group of loans) and reflect identifiable losses (see also BCBS, 1999, p. 13).

4.33 The *Guide* relies on national practices in identifying loan loss provisions and distinguishing between specific and general provisions but recommends that such practices be clearly documented. Provisions for the accrual of interest on nonperforming assets should not be included under loan loss provisions, as they are identified within (and excluded from) net interest income.[26] While provisions for losses or future expenses reduce net income, subject to national practice, overprediction of expected losses or expenses in any one period could be reversed in subsequent periods, increasing income in those periods. An explanation of how provisioning affects assets as well as capital and reserves is provided in Box 4.4. In addition, Appendix VI includes a discussion of approaches to the classification of assets and provisioning.

4.34 *Other financial asset provisions* include provisions against any other financial assets (that are neither traded nor recorded at market prices) that can be valued reliably. If it is not feasible at this time to include unrealized gains and losses on securities—such as those in the investment account—within gains and losses on financial instruments (see paragraph 4.22), then the same approach used for loan provisioning should be adopted for these securities, so that losses on these assets are captured within net income.[27] This category also includes any new provisions made for supervisory purposes to take account of changes in the volatility of bid-ask spreads or other factors relating to closing out a position in a less-liquid tradable instrument (see also BCBS, 2001b, para. 579). Gross income less noninterest expenses and provisions[28] equates to *net income (before extraordinary items and tax).*

4.35 *Extraordinary items* cover events that are extraordinary in relation to the business ordinarily carried out by the enterprise. Such events would be rare and include catastrophic losses arising from a natural or other disaster. Extraordinary items can include

[24]International Financial Reporting Standard 2 (IFRS 2), issued in 2004, treats stock options as a personnel expense. Compilers are encouraged to adopt that standard for compiling data for use in calculating FSIs and to describe their approach in any metadata disseminated.

[25]At the sector level, provisions against loans to other deposit takers in the reporting population should be excluded from this item to avoid asymmetric reporting.

[26]As noted in paragraph 4.19, for any interest that has accrued in earlier periods but is subsequently considered to be an expected identifiable loss, the provision for the loss should be included in line item 7, and not as a provision for accrued interest on nonperforming assets.

[27]Specific provisions against the value of a security should reduce the value of the security in the balance sheet, as though it were being marked-to-market.

[28]For provisions and extraordinary items, these items should usually represent a loss. However, in any one period, these items might add to income if they are subsequently recovered, for example.

Box 4.3. Islamic Financial Institutions and Financial Soundness

Islamic financial institutions (IFIs) operate under Islamic principles whereby ex ante interest payments are prohibited, profits and losses of underlying transactions are shared, and lending is based on Islamic ethical principles. They present a unique profile of financial risk and soundness that fundamentally affects the structures of the income accounts and balance sheets, which in turn affect the compilation and meaning of financial soundness indicators. The differences are beginning to be addressed by financial accountants and supervisors of financial institutions, but it may be some time before the full range of issues are identified and appropriate accounting and supervisory standards are developed and adopted.[1] This box describes some of the unique elements of IFIs and how key FSIs might be affected.

Although variations in practice exist, reliance on Islamic principles sets IFIs apart from other institutions in numerous ways. Perhaps the most notable is the prohibition of receipt or payment of interest. For example, loans or deposits with interest rates fixed beforehand are prohibited—a fundamental difference from non-Islamic banks that borrow in exchange for payments of interest and lend in order to acquire assets that can earn interest. Thus, the two core FSIs that focus on the margin between interest receipts and payments apply to non-Islamic banks but not to Islamic banks.

IFIs accept deposits under the Mudarabah concept and invest in permissible and Shariah-compliant investments and financing arrangements. In such a manner, IFIs are undertaking a financial intermediary function. However, in principle depositors are guaranteed neither a pre-fixed return nor the principal amount. Rather depositors act as fund providers, bearing losses alone, as the IFI has incurred a "loss" in the form of entrepreneurial efforts. Profits generated are shared between the IFIs and the depositors based on a preagreed profit-sharing ratio. As for the operation of the accounts, it is similar to deposit operations under conventional banking. Under a second form of depositing, IFIs hold funds for safekeeping with a guarantee of full repayment of principal but no interest.

Also, IFIs can operate through profit and loss sharing (PLS) arrangements that do not guarantee full repayment of principal and do not have fixed profit returns. IFIs earn income by charging fees for services, by engaging in profit sharing, and, most important, from activities such as trade-related financing, hire purchase, and leasing. In some countries, these constitute the primary activities of IFIs.

Under PLS arrangements, the resources of the IFI and investors are often pooled to undertake specific commercial ventures, and the total returns are divided between the IFI and the investors based on a predetermined profit-sharing arrangement. Profits earned could be disbursed during the life of the venture as well as at its conclusion. Depending on the outcome, both may gain or lose on their investments. To this end, IFIs issue securities called PLS certificates that do not provide for either capital certainty or pre-fixed positive returns. Some of these instruments are defined as "unrestricted investment accounts" that give the IFI latitude to make the investments as it sees fit, much as non-Islamic banks invest the funds provided by depositors.

PLS arrangements and unrestricted investment accounts result in a somewhat different role for capital in IFIs from that in other types of banks. For instance, in an IMF Working Paper, Sundararajan and Errico (2002, p. 9) concluded that "it may be reasonable to conclude that the assessment of capital adequacy for Islamic banks should be based not only on a thorough evaluation of the degree of risk in each bank's portfolio, but also an assessment of the mix of PLS and non-PLS assets." In addition, there appears to be ambiguity regarding the identification and valuation of nonperforming loans (NPLs) and provisioning, as well as their disclosure.

In constructing IFI balance sheets, it can be ambiguous whether the contributions of investors in PLS certificates and unrestricted investment accounts are liabilities of the IFI. Often, the IFI will act as a fiduciary or asset manager, placing the funds in off-balance-sheet trust accounts and providing investment advice to receive either fees or a distribution of net profits. Some IFIs are known to handle substantial portions of their business through off-balance-sheet accounts under the assumption that they are performing a fund management role for the investor, which affects leverage ratios and the Basel capital adequacy calculations.[2] At present, national practices in recording such arrangements differ, with both on- and off-balance-sheet treatments used. One opinion, by the Accounting and Auditing Organization for Islamic Financial Institutions (AAOIFI), is that unrestricted investment accounts are part of the balance sheet of the IFI and should be included as a separate type of instrument—between a liability and equity capital. The *Guide* follows the advice of the *Monetary and Financial Statistics Manual (MFSM)*[3] and classifies such instruments as deposits unless they are part of the permanent capital base of the IFI or have the characteristics of a tradable instrument.

The asset structure of IFIs is characterized by a diverse spectrum of Islamic financing structures, ranging from the low-risk lease-based to the higher-risk equity-based modes of finance. As each mode has its own distinct features, different degrees of credit risk, market risk, and operational risk are entailed.

[1] The Accounting and Auditing Organization for Islamic Financial Institutions (AAOIFI) was created in 1991 in Bahrain to set accounting, auditing, and governance standards that are being followed by IFIs in a number of countries. Moreover, in November 2002, the Islamic Financial Services Board (IFSB) was established in Malaysia as an association of central banks, monetary authorities, and other institutions that are responsible for the regulation and supervision of the Islamic financial services industry.

[2] The AAOIFI has stated that its aim is to follow the Basel methodology as closely as possible.

[3] A detailed description of Islamic instruments and their classification is provided on pages 125–127 of the *MFSM* (IMF, 2000a) and this text should be consulted in determining the classification of instruments for the purposes of compiling data for FSIs.

Box 4.3 (concluded)

To date, IFIs have tended to be heavily involved in shorter-term commercial credits and project finance that are normally resolved within a year or two, which permits the redistribution of the net proceeds. This arises in part from the absence of Islamic money markets that permit the ready transfer of short-term liquidity between IFIs and act to establish market-based rates of return for such borrowing. There has been some difficulty in developing instruments, such as interbank instruments, monetary policy instruments, and longer-term instruments such as mortgages, although examples of all these exist. In part, this stems from the greater difficulty, compared with the case of project-type finance, in devising suitable means to measure and distribute net returns on credits to governments, ongoing firms, or noncommercial institutions.

The above pattern has important implications for FSIs—the balance sheets of IFIs differ from those of non-Islamic banks, and estimates of rates of return of IFIs may prove hard to develop and compare.[4] Moreover, instruments are under development, and, in some instances, Islamic banking principles may be mixed with standard banking practices. Against this background, accounting practices for IFIs are still developing. Until this work is further advanced, and standard practices can begin to be identified within markets, the *Guide* considers that it is premature to attempt to link FSIs to specific accounting series used by IFIs.

[4]Bank Negara Malaysia has developed a structured framework in the determination of the rate of return for Islamic banking operations. This framework addresses the issue of uniformity, reducing the potential for distortion in the rate of return.

There is recognition of the need for generally agreed guidance for IFIs on accounting presentations for income statements, balance sheets, fiduciary and trust activity, and other disclosures. Several organizations are working on various aspects, such as the AAOIFI—which has published a revision of the Basel Capital Adequacy Ratios customized for IFIs[5]—the Institute of Islamic Banking and Insurance in London, the International Association of Islamic Banks in Saudi Arabia, and the new Islamic International Rating Agency in Bahrain. Moreover, bank supervisors are seeking effective prudential oversight of IFIs, and international practice is developing: the newly formed Islamic Financial Services Board (IFSB) in Malaysia is intended to help develop an effective system for supervision and regulation of IFIs and to provide guidance on the appropriate monitoring, measuring, and management of risks in Islamic financial products.

Finally, because of their heavy involvement in fiduciary activity, project finance, and profit/loss sharing, many IFIs have characteristics of mutual funds or other nonbank financial institutions. But the prevailing statistical practice is to classify Islamic financial institutions as deposit takers.[6]

[5]See AAOIFI (1999). There is some supervisory opinion that the more flexible risk-weighting algorithms that will be available under Basel II might prove effective in more precisely describing the types of financial risk facing IFIs.

[6]This practice is described in more detail in paragraph 488 of the *MFSM* (IMF, 2000a).

income but will usually be expense items. *Income taxes* are those taxes that accrue in the period under review and are related to the income, profits, and/or capital gains of deposit takers. Once extraordinary items and taxes are deducted from net income, the total is equal to *net income after tax.*

4.36 *Dividends* are amounts declared payable in the period under review to the owners of deposit takers after all other expenses have been met, leaving *retained earnings* to be posted to the retained earnings account of capital and reserves.

Balance sheet

Nonfinancial assets

4.37 Nonfinancial assets are all economic assets other than financial assets. A definition of these assets is provided in the discussion below on the sectoral balance sheet for nonfinancial corporations (paragraph 4.106).

Financial assets and liabilities

4.38 *Financial assets*[29] are those financial claims over which ownership rights are enforced, from which economic benefits may be derived by their owners, and that are a store of value. Financial claims arise out of contractual relationships between pairs of institutional units, and often such claims entitle the owner (that is, the creditor) to receive one or more payments (such as interest payments) from the institutional unit on which the owner has the claim (the debtor). In addition, some financial assets generate

[29]In the *1993 SNA,* financial assets also include monetary gold and special drawing rights (SDRs)—financial assets for which there are no counterpart claims. However, in the *1993 SNA,* by definition, only the official sector, typically the central bank, can be regarded as holding such assets.

holdings gains (and losses) for their owners. When a financial claim is created, a liability of equal value is simultaneously incurred by the debtor as the counterpart to the financial asset.

4.39 The identification and presentation of the different types of financial assets and liabilities can vary depending on analytical needs and national accounting practice. In the list of FSI ratios, the primary focus is on instruments by functional type, such as loans, equities, securities, and derivatives. Thus, in the *Guide,* the primary classifications of financial assets and liabilities are: *currency and deposits, loans, debt securities,*[30] *shares and other equity (assets), financial derivatives,* and *other assets* (or *other liabilities).*

4.40 *Currency* consists of notes and coins in circulation that are commonly used to make payments. It is usually (but not always) issued either by central banks or government units and is a liability of the units that issue it. Currency has a fixed nominal value. Gold and commemorative coins that are not in circulation as legal tender are classified as nonfinancial assets rather than as currency.

4.41 *Deposits* include all nonnegotiable financial claims represented by evidence of deposit. Deposits comprise transferable deposits and other deposits. Transferable deposits comprise all deposits in domestic or foreign currency that are (1) exchangeable, without penalty or restriction, on demand at par and (2) directly usable for making third-party payments by check, draft, giro order, direct debit/credit, or other direct payment facility.[31] Other deposits comprise deposits that have restrictions on the number of third-party payments that can be made per period and/or the minimum size of individual third-party payments and so are considered nontransferable. These include the following:

- Sight deposits that permit immediate cash withdrawals but not direct third-party payments.
- Savings and fixed-term deposits, including nonnegotiable certificates of deposit.
- Nontransferable deposits denominated in foreign currency.
- Shares or similar evidence of deposit issued by savings and loan associations, building societies, credit unions, and the like, which are (legally or in practice) redeemable immediately or at relatively short notice.
- Repurchase agreements (possibly) (see paragraph 4.48).

4.42 *Customer deposits* are those considered to be more "stable" and less volatile types of deposits that can be employed to fund long-term lending. It is a series required to calculate an encouraged FSI.

4.43 Volatility of deposits refers to depositor sensitivity to events that could affect confidence in deposit takers. More specifically, it refers to the likelihood that depositors will, at short notice, withdraw funds in response to a perceived weakness in an individual deposit taker or in the banking system. Determining such a likelihood in advance is difficult, but typically the key factors taken into account are the type of depositor, the existence of insurance coverage, and the maturity of the deposits (remaining maturity). Experience suggests that some types of depositors are less likely to move their funds than others. However, deposits covered by credible insurance schemes are more likely to be a stable form of funding than those not covered. In addition, deposits with a long remaining maturity are likely to be more stable, although the lower the penalties for withdrawal, the less relevant this factor is in determining the likelihood of withdrawal.

4.44 The *Guide* recommends that the type of depositor be the primary factor in defining customer deposits because of both its relevance and its general applicability. Thus, customer deposits include all deposits (resident or nonresident) except those placed by other deposit takers and other financial corporations (resident and nonresident). The depositors in the excluded sectors are more likely to monitor deposit takers' financial information, are less likely to be covered by deposit insurance, and perhaps have a fiduciary responsibility to safeguard their assets. They are, therefore, more prone to shifting deposits as risks increase than other depositors. Perhaps because of deposit insurance, household depositors tend to be less aware of the risks, while commercial depositors may have other relationships with banks that make them more reluctant than institutional

---

[30]Known as "securities other than shares" in the *1993 SNA* and *MFSM.*

[31]Shares of money market funds that offer unrestricted check-writing privileges can be regarded as functionally equivalent to deposits and potentially included in broad money. However, in the *Guide,* such assets and liabilities are classified as shares and other equity, because the nature, and hence regulation, of money market funds is different from that of deposit takers.

investors to move funds.[32] Provided it can be determined that the penalties for withdrawal are high, customer deposits could also include those from the excluded sectors that have a remaining maturity of more than one year.[33]

4.45 *Loans* include those financial assets created through the direct lending of funds by a creditor to a debtor through an arrangement in which the lender either receives no security evidencing the transactions or receives a nonnegotiable document or instrument. Collateral, in the form of either a financial asset (such as a security) or nonfinancial asset (such as land or a building), may be provided under a loan transaction, though it is not an essential feature. Loans include commercial loans, installment loans, hire-purchase credit, loans to finance trade credit and advances, financial leases, repurchase agreements not classified as a deposit (see paragraph 4.48), and overdrafts. Trade credit and similar accounts receivable/payable are not loans. To meet the requirements of the agreed FSI list, in Table 4.1 loans to other deposit takers (resident and nonresident) are distinguished from other loans, which are attributed by sector as defined in Chapter 2 on a residence basis.

4.46 If a loan becomes tradable and is, or has been, traded in the secondary market, the loan is reclassified as a debt security instrument. Given the significance of the reclassification, firm evidence of secondary market trading is needed before a debt instrument is reclassified from a loan to a security. Evidence of trading on secondary markets would include the existence of market makers and bid-offer spreads for the debt instrument. A transfer or one-time sale of a loan would not normally constitute a basis for reclassifying the loan as a security.

[32]In discussions on the definition of customer deposits, the idea was raised that large nonfinancial corporations might manage their liquidity similarly to other financial corporations. Given this, compilers might wish to distinguish deposit liabilities of deposit takers into two categories: those held by publicly listed nonfinancial corporations, and those held by unlisted nonfinancial corporations, excluding the former from the calculation of customer deposits. Any metadata accompanying the dissemination of FSI data should explain the coverage of customer deposits.

[33]Another approach that could yield a similar outcome would be to determine customer deposits by type of deposit—that is, (1) deposits known for their "stability," such as demand deposits, small-scale savings, and time deposits; and/or (2) deposits covered by a (credible) deposit insurance scheme.

4.47 Two forms of loans require further discussion. A *financial lease* is a contract under which a lessee contracts to pay rentals for the use of a good for most or all of its expected economic life. In this case, the risks and rewards of ownership are transferred from the legal owner of the good, the lessor, to the user of the good, the lessee. The lessee is frequently responsible for the maintenance and repair of the good. Under statistical and accounting conventions, the good is treated as having changed ownership, and a loan liability of the lessee is created. The value of the loan at inception is equal to the value of the good. The loan is repaid through the payment of rental fees (which comprise both interest and principal elements) plus any residual payment at the end of the contract (or, alternatively, by the return of the good to the lessor).[34] The assets that have been leased should be removed from the balance sheet of the lessor.

4.48 A *securities repurchase agreement* (repo) is an arrangement involving the sale for cash of securities at a specified price with a commitment to repurchase the same or similar securities at a fixed price either on a specified future date (often a few days later) or with an open maturity.[35] Because the risks and rewards of ownership of the security remain with the original owner, the economic nature of the transaction is that of a collateralized loan (or possibly a deposit).[36] In other words, the funds advanced by the security taker to the security provider are classified as a loan (or deposit) asset of the security taker (and a liability of the security provider), and the underlying securities remain on the balance sheet of the security provider, despite the legal change in ownership. A *gold swap,* under which gold is exchanged for other assets, usually foreign exchange, is similar in nature to a repo and is to be recorded similarly. *Securities lending* is similar to a repo, except that noncash collateral in the form of securities is provided, and so no loan is recorded. If the security taker provides cash as collateral, then the arrangement is treated in the same way as a repo. The securities involved remain on the balance sheet of the security provider.

[34]Consistent with this statistical treatment, IASs regard the stream of payments associated with financial leases as substantially the same as blended payments of principal and interest under loan agreements.

[35]An open maturity exists when both parties agree daily to renew or terminate the agreement.

[36]Sellbacks and buybacks are the same as repos in economic effect but are less sophisticated operationally.

4.49 If securities acquired under a repo or securities-lending arrangement are sold to third parties, the security taker should record on the balance sheet a negative security asset equal to the current market value of the security that was sold.

4.50 *Specific loan provisions* are the outstanding amount of provisions made against the value of individual loans, collectively assessed groups of loans, and loans to other deposit takers[37] (see also paragraph 4.32).[38,39]

4.51 *Debt securities* are negotiable[40] financial instruments serving as evidence that units have obligations to settle by means of providing cash, a financial instrument, or some other item of economic value. The debt security provides evidence that the claim exists, is tradable in financial markets, and gives the holder an unconditional right to receive interest and/or principal payments. Examples of debt securities include the following:

- Bills, such as treasury bills;
- Bonds and debentures, including bonds that are convertible into shares;
- Commercial paper;
- Negotiable certificates of deposit;
- Tradable depository receipts;
- Notes issued through revolving underwriting facilities and note-issuance facilities;
- Negotiable securities backed by loans or other assets;
- Loans that have become de facto tradable;
- Preferred stocks or shares that pay a fixed income but do not provide for participation in the distribution of the residual value of the corporation on dissolution;
- Bankers' acceptances; and
- Mandatorily redeemable shares.

4.52 Some corporate bonds are convertible into shares of the same corporation at the option of the bondholder. If the conversion option is traded separately, then it is recorded as a separate asset and classified as a financial derivative.

4.53 Table 4.1 includes all the above instruments under the heading of debt securities. However, it is recognized that national practice might separately identify certain types of instruments, such as mortgage-backed securities, government securities, and securities considered to be of a liquid nature.

4.54 *Shares and other equity* comprise all instruments and records acknowledging, after the claims of all creditors have been met, claims on the residual value of a corporation. Ownership of equity is usually evidenced by shares, stocks, participation, or similar documents. Preferred stocks or shares, which also provide for participation in the distribution of the residual value on dissolution of an incorporated enterprise, are included.[41] Buybacks by a deposit taker of its own equity securities reduce the number of equity securities outstanding.

4.55 Shares and other equity assets include equity investments in associates, unconsolidated subsidiaries, and reverse equity investments, as well as other equity investments in deposit takers.[42] In the context of domestic data, shares and other equity assets include any share capital provided to foreign branches.

4.56 *Financial derivatives* are financial instruments that are linked to a specific financial instrument, indicator, or commodity and through which specific financial risks can be traded in financial markets in their own right. Their value depends on the price of the underlying item. Unlike debt instruments, no principal is advanced to be repaid, and no investment income accrues. Typical derivative contracts are futures (exchange-traded forward contracts), interest and cross-currency swaps, forward rate agreements, forward foreign exchange contracts, credit derivatives, and various types of options (see also Heath,

[37]Sector-level adjustments for provisions on loans to other deposit takers are discussed in Chapter 5 (paragraph 5.88).

[38]As it is recommended that interest on NPLs should not accrue, specific provisions data should not in principle include specific provisions for interest accrual on NPLs.

[39]If accounting practice is not to accrue interest on NPLs but to include the interest in the value of the loan on the balance sheet offset by an item such as interest in suspense, it is suggested that the interest in suspense be included together with the data for specific provisions on the balance sheet. If this approach is adopted it could be explained in the metadata.

[40]A negotiable financial instrument is one whose ownership is capable of being transferred from one unit to another unit by delivery or endorsement.

[41]Accounting standard setters agree that not everything commonly called equity qualifies as such. For instance, mandatorily redeemable preferred stocks are liabilities, and so are various kinds of puttable stock, where the stocks are being essentially used as currency.

[42]For sector-level data, the value of the investment in any other deposit taker in the reporting population should be excluded from this item, assets in total, and capital and reserves (see also Box 5.1).

Box 4.4. The Approach to Valuation and Provisioning in the *Guide*

This box explains how the various recommendations regarding valuation and provisioning in the detailed line-by-line description of the items in the financial statement fit together.

The *Guide* prefers valuation methods that can provide the most realistic assessment at any point in time of the value of an instrument or item. For tradable instruments, nonrecognition of market value gains, and particularly of losses, can mislead judgments about financial health and soundness of deposit takers. For nontradable instruments, the *Guide* acknowledges that nominal value may provide a more realistic assessment of value than the application of market or fair value, but an appropriate provisioning policy is essential. While the *Guide* relies on national practices in identifying such provisions, nonrecognition of losses when they arise would overstate the health and strength of the deposit taker. A distinction is made between specific provisions for losses that are identifiable and general provisions for potential losses that experience suggests could affect a portfolio.

The rest of this box explains how the approach to market valuation and provisions affects the income and expense statement, assets, and capital and reserves. A short section on arrears is also included.

Income and expense

The income and expense statement is directly affected by the approach taken on valuation and provisioning.[1]

- Interest income should not include the accrual of any interest on nonperforming assets; in other words, interest income should not be overstated relative to the actual circumstances.
- Provisions for loan losses (and other assets) should reduce net income, thus recognizing losses when they become apparent.
- Gains or losses, unrealized and realized, on financial assets and liabilities valued at market or fair value in the balance sheet should be included in income—a rise in value increasing net income and a loss of value reducing net income.[2] To avoid double counting, any accrued interest recorded for the period is excluded from calculations of gains and losses on financial instruments.
- Gains or losses on any other assets or liabilities that arise and are realized in the reporting period should be included in income. Any revaluation gains and losses already included in the valuation adjustment from previous periods should be moved to retained earnings.[3]

The *Guide* considers that capturing interest income and interest expense together with the holding gains and losses on financial assets and liabilities for which market or fair value is established is appropriate for measuring the return on assets and on capital and reserves—two core FSIs. Regarding other financial assets and liabilities, to monitor current health, the *Guide* encourages recording losses through the creation of provisions when these losses become apparent and recording realized gains or losses arising during the current reporting period only in current period income.

Assets

In the *Guide*, changes in the market or fair value of assets (and liabilities) are reflected on balance sheet. For loans and other assets valued at nominal value, their balance sheet value is reduced by specific provisions[4] or by writing down the value of the asset.

It might be considered appropriate to also value loans excluding general provisions, so that probable losses not attributable to specific instruments are recognized as reducing capital and reserves. While the *Guide* recognizes the need to reduce net income to reflect potential losses that experience suggests may take place in a portfolio, it is not evident that the soundness of the deposit taker has been weakened by such general provisioning. So general provisions are included in the capital and reserves (but not in the narrow measure of capital and reserves). This is in line with the Basel Committee on Banking Supervision's (BCBS) Basel I capital adequacy requirements, which recognize in Tier 2 capital general provisions in capital up to a limit of 1.25 percent of (risk-weighted) assets.

Capital and reserves

Changes in market or fair valuation of assets and liabilities affect capital and reserves. Increases in asset values tend to increase capital and reserves, while increases in the value of liabilities tend to decrease capital and reserves. Provisioning can also affect capital and reserves. As noted above, while both specific and general provisions reduce net income, and thus potentially retained earnings, general provisions are posted to capital and reserves.

[1]The treatment of intra-deposit-takers' transactions and positions is discussed in the Text Annex to Chapter 5.

[2]Changes in the market value of equity in associates and unconsolidated subsidiaries, as well as reverse equity investments, are excluded, to avoid the potential for double counting income (see paragraph 4.22).

[3]For unlisted nonfinancial corporations, the same approach can be taken for all financial instruments that relate only peripherally to a firm's primary operating activities.

[4]In Table 4.1, data on loans are presented both before and after adjustment for specific provisions.

1998). Gross market values for financial derivative assets and liabilities should be recorded on the balance sheet and any valuation gains and losses in the income and expense statement.

4.57 Under a forward-type contract, the counterparties agree to exchange an underlying item—real or financial—in a specified quantity, on a specified date, at an agreed contract (strike) price. In the case of a swaps contract, the counterparties agree to exchange cash flows, determined with reference to price(s) of, for example, currencies or interest rates, according to prearranged rules. At the inception of the contract, risk exposures of equal market value are exchanged, and the contract normally has zero value. But as market prices change, asset and liability positions are created, which may change both in magnitude and direction over time.

4.58 Under an option contract, the purchaser of the option, in return for an option premium, acquires from the writer of the option the right but not the obligation to buy (call option) or sell (put option) a specified underlying item—real or financial—at an agreed contract (strike) price on or before a specified date. Throughout the life of the contract the writer of the option has a liability and the buyer an asset, although the option can expire worthless; the option will be exercised only if settling the contract is advantageous for the purchaser.

4.59 The *Guide* prefers that if an instrument such as a security or a loan contains an embedded derivative that is inseparable from the underlying instrument, the instrument is valued and classified according to its primary characteristics, and the embedded derivative is not classified and valued separately.[43] Examples of instruments with embedded derivatives are bonds that are convertible into equity securities, and securities with options for the repayment of principal in currencies that differ from those in which the securities were issued.[44]

[43]If significant amounts of such securities are outstanding, there may be an interest in their separate identification, particularly for securities that can be sold (put) back to the issuer, not least because of the potential impact on the liquidity position of deposit takers.

[44]Under IASs, derivatives embedded in cash instruments are to be accounted for separately unless the entire instrument is fair valued (and the change in fair value is reflected in profit and loss) or the embedded derivative meets the test of being closely related to the underlying cash instrument. This is to prevent such derivatives from escaping "proper" accounting.

4.60 *Other assets* (or *other liabilities* from the debtor perspective) cover trade credits and advances, prepayments of insurance premiums, and miscellaneous other items due to be received or paid. Miscellaneous other items receivable or payable include accrued but unpaid taxes, dividends (including dividends declared but not yet payable), purchases and sales of securities, rent, wages and salaries, social contributions, social benefits, and similar payments. Definitions of trade credit and advances are provided in the discussion below of the sectoral balance sheets for nonfinancial corporations (paragraph 4.112). If significant provisions are made against these assets, particularly trade credit, compilers are encouraged to separately identify these provisions in the same manner as for loans (see above).

4.61 *Debt* is defined as the outstanding amount of those actual current and noncontingent liabilities that require payments of principal and/or interest by the debtor at some point(s) in the future. Thus, debt comprises those financial liabilities that are currency and deposits, loans, debt securities, and other liabilities.

4.62 "*Capital and reserves*" is defined as the equity interest of the owners in an enterprise and is the difference between total assets and liabilities.[45] It represents the amount available to absorb unidentified losses.

4.63 In the *Guide,* total capital and reserves include the following.

- *Funds contributed by owners* comprise the total amount from the initial and any subsequent issuance of shares, stocks, or other forms of ownership of deposit takers. This item is valued as the nominal amount of proceeds from the initial and subsequent issuances. It is not revalued.
- *Retained earnings,* or rather, changes in retained earnings, reflect all after-tax profits that are neither distributed to shareholders nor transferred to or from the reserve and valuation accounts. Deducted (included) is any goodwill arising from the pur-

[45]At the sector level, the proportionate ownership share of a deposit taker in the capital and reserves of an associate deposit taker, as well as equity investments in other deposit takers that are also in the reporting population, should be excluded from capital and reserves (see also Box 5.1).

chase (sale) of a stake in an associate or subsidiary (or reverse equity investment stake).[46] This item is also valued at the nominal amount of earnings that have been retained and is not revalued.

- *General and special reserves* are reserves that reflect appropriations from retained earnings. These reserves are also to be valued at nominal value and are not revalued.
- *Provisions are* included in the income and expense statement (see paragraph 4.32), other than specific provisions. Specific provisions reduce the value of the relevant asset in the balance sheet.[47]
- *Valuation adjustment* is the counterpart to net changes in the market or fair values of assets and liabilities on the balance sheet (excluding any such changes that affect other items within capital and reserves, such as retained earnings). Unrealized gains or losses on assets or liabilities that have been reflected in the valuation adjustment and are now realized should be transferred to retained earnings.[48] The *Guide* recommends that this item include only valuation changes arising from nonfinancial assets, equity investments in associates and unconsolidated subsidiaries, and reverse investments that have not been reflected in retained earnings.

4.64 Tier 1 capital is the core measure of capital (see paragraph 4.70). In the absence of Tier 1 data (as in the case of units not subject to Basel Capital Adequacy guidelines), the data for funds contributed by owners together with retained earnings (including those earnings appropriated to reserves) could be identified.[49]

4.65 Under consolidated reporting, when the parent has less than full ownership of a subsidiary, the capital and reserves attributable to minority shareholders in the subsidiary are included in capital and reserves, because the focus of FSIs is on the total capital and reserves of the deposit takers in the reporting population.

Memorandum series

Other series required to calculate the FSIs

4.66 Some of the series required to calculate the FSIs are not directly available from the financial statements described above. They are included as memorandum items to the financial statement. These series fall into three categories: (1) supervisory-based series, (2) series that provide a further analysis of the balance sheet, and (3) balance-sheet-related series. Series that go beyond those required to calculate these FSIs, but which in the discussions on the *Guide* were considered particularly relevant for macroprudential analysis, are set out in Appendix III.

Supervisory-based series

4.67 These are series to be directly sourced from supervisory information because the definitions conform with supervisory guidance. The *Guide* relies on national practice in calculating regulatory capital and risk-weighted assets data series.

4.68 The Basel Committee on Banking Supervision has developed a specific *regulatory definition of capital* that is used as the numerator in its official regulatory capital adequacy ratio. The definition extends beyond purely capital and reserve account items identified above to include several specified types of subordinated debt instruments that need not be repaid if the funds are needed to maintain minimum capital

---

[46]The deduction of goodwill is consistent with the approach in the Basel Capital Accord. See supervisory deductions discussed below (paragraph 4.73).

[47]If all or part of a loan is considered uncollectible, in some economies this amount is "written (charged) off" against the loan loss provision—rather than being recorded as a specific provision—reducing the value of the loan, with any subsequent recovery being credited to the provision. Practices as to the timing of write-offs vary among countries; for instance, in some countries, a loan cannot be written off until all legal procedures have been completed.

[48]At the sector level, for fixed assets, any gain or loss on sale to another deposit taker in the reporting population should not affect retained earnings in capital and reserves because the gain or loss has not been realized by the sector. However, it is recognized that maintaining records of gains and losses on fixed assets by transactor and only transferring them to retained earnings once the asset is sold to another sector would create considerable practical problems in that chains of sales, perhaps spread over years, would need to be monitored. So it is recommended that no sector-level adjustment be made to the components of capital and reserves for gains and losses on sales of fixed assets to other deposit takers in the reporting population but that—subject to confidentiality constraints—any significant sales be identified. This will permit the impact on sector-level capital and reserves to be assessed.

[49]This is known as the "narrow measure" of capital and reserves in the *Guide*.

levels.[50] All internationally active banks are expected to have regulatory capital of at least 8 percent of *risk-weighted assets.* National supervisors may require a higher ratio and have some leeway in establishing the specific standards for their country.[51]

4.69 There are three tiers of regulatory capital. [52]

4.70 Tier 1 capital comprises paid-up shares and common stock—issued and fully paid ordinary shares/common stock and perpetual noncumulative preference shares—and disclosed reserves created or increased by appropriations of retained earnings or other surplus.[53] The latter include, inter alia, share premiums, retained profit, general reserves, and legal reserves,[54] and are considered to be freely and immediately available to meet claims against the bank.[55]

4.71 Tier 2 capital consists of (1) undisclosed reserves—that part of accumulated retained earnings that banks in some countries may be permitted to maintain as an undisclosed reserve; (2) asset revaluation reserves with regard to fixed assets, and with regard to long-term holdings of equities valued in the balance sheet at historic cost but for which there are "latent" revaluation gains; (3) general provisions/general loan loss reserves (up to 1.25 percent of risk assets);[56,57] (4) hybrid instruments that combine the characteristics of debt and equity and are available to meet losses; and (5) unsecured subordinated debt with a minimum original fixed term of maturity of more than five years and limited-life redeemable preference shares. Tier 2 capital and subordinated debt cannot exceed 100 percent and 50 percent, respectively, of Tier 1 capital.

4.72 Tier 3 capital comprises medium-term debt of two-year or longer original maturity with "lock-in provisions" that stipulate that neither principal nor interest need be paid if the payment reduces the bank's overall capital to less than the minimum capital requirement. Tier 3 capital is intended to cover only market risk and is limited to 250 percent of Tier 1 capital.

4.73 *Supervisory deductions* cover goodwill (see paragraph 4.110), as a deduction from Tier 1 capital. With regard to total capital, supervisory deductions cover investments in unconsolidated banking and financial subsidiaries, and, at the discretion of national authorities, investment in capital of other banks and financial institutions.[58]

4.74 *Risk-weighted assets* include currency and deposits, loans, securities, and other on-balance-sheet assets. Assets are weighted by factors representing their credit riskiness and potential for default. Through the use of credit conversion factors, the credit risk of off-balance-sheet items, such as credit line commitments and letters of credit that serve as financial guarantees, is also taken into account

[50]Basel Core Principle 6 states, "Banking supervisors must set prudent and appropriate minimum capital adequacy requirements for all banks. Such requirements should reflect the risks that the banks undertake, and must define the components of capital, bearing in mind their ability to absorb losses. At least for internationally active banks, these requirements must not be less than those established in the Basel Capital Accord and its amendments."

[51]At the time of writing, a revised Basel Capital Accord was being discussed. Therefore, this section provides an overview of the key aspects of the Accord rather than all the specific details. Information on the latter is available at the BIS website (http://www.bis.org).

[52]The following discussion is drawn from BCBS (2001a, Chapter 1, Annex 1).

[53]In the European Union, the directive on own funds of credit institutions recommends that significant operating losses be included in the Tier 1 capital calculations but that national supervisors have full discretion over the treatment of small operating losses and operating profits of any size. This type of information could be included in any metadata disseminated with FSI information.

[54]They also include general funds, such as funds for general banking risk, subject to four criteria: (1) allocations to the funds must be made out of posttax retained earnings or out of pretax earnings adjusted for all potential tax liabilities, (2) the funds and movements into or out of them must be disclosed separately in the bank's published accounts, (3) the funds must be available to a bank to meet losses for unrestricted and immediate use as soon as they occur, and (4) losses cannot be charged directly to the funds but must be taken through the profit and loss account. See BCBS (2001a).

[55]Tax-deferred assets should be accounted for consistently with the Basel Capital Accord.

[56]Provisions held against specific assets are excluded from being part of capital.

[57]At the time of writing, the BCBS is proposing that under the revised Basel Capital Accord, banks adopting the Internal Rating Based (IRB) approach to measuring risk-weighted assets would treat unexpected and expected losses separately. In particular, the capital requirements under the IRB approach would be based solely on unexpected losses. For expected losses, banks would compare the estimated amount of expected losses with the total amount of provisions made, including both general and specific provisions, and any shortfall in provisions would be deducted 50 percent from Tier 1 and 50 percent from Tier 2 capital. Moreover, any excess in provisions would be eligible for inclusion in Tier 2 capital, up to a maximum of 20 percent of Tier 2 capital. This treatment of excess amounts would replace the current inclusion of general provisions (up to 1.25 percent of risk assets) in Tier 2 capital for those banks that adopt the IRB approach.

[58]In the European Union, holdings of own shares is a common deduction from Tier 1 capital.

in determining regulatory capital requirements.[59] Another component of total risk-weighted assets is used to incorporate a capital charge for market risks.[60]

4.75 How does the total regulatory capital measure of capital compare with the measure of capital and reserves in the sectoral balance sheet provided in Table 4.1 (after the sector-level adjustments described in the next chapter)? Because of the absence of the application of common accounting standards, measures of regulatory capital and measures of sectoral balance sheet capital can differ among countries because of different national practices. In this context, only some general statements can be made.

- Both regulatory capital and the sectoral balance sheet measure of capital cover equity capital, reserves (both disclosed and undisclosed), and general provisions and thus in this sense are the same. Goodwill is deducted from both. However, in the regulatory measure there is a limit on the amount of general provisions (1.25 percent of risk-weighted assets) that can be included. Moreover, the amounts posted to reserves can differ due to different accounting approaches, such as the treatment of gains and losses on financial instruments.
- The regulatory measure covers certain debt instruments, such as subordinated debt, which are excluded from the sectoral balance sheet measure.
- At the sector level, intrasector equity investments in both related and unrelated deposit takers are excluded from the sectoral balance sheet measure. As noted above, at national discretion investments in unrelated deposit takers can be included in regulatory capital calculations.[61]
- Non-deposit-takers can be consolidated for the calculation of regulatory capital (or investments in such entities deducted from regulatory capital), but this is not preferred for the calculation of the sectoral balance sheet measure.

4.76 "*Large exposures*" refers to one or more credit exposures to the same individual or group that exceed a certain percentage of regulatory capital, for example 10 percent (see BCBS, 1991). The number of large exposures of deposit takers is identified under the national supervisory regime.

Series that provide a further analysis of the balance sheet

4.77 To calculate the agreed FSIs there is a need for a number of series that are subtotals of balance sheet totals and that provide a further analysis of the balance sheet beyond that presented in the main table.

4.78 *Liquid assets* are those assets that are readily available to an entity to meet a demand for cash. While it may be possible to raise funds through borrowing, conditions in the market may not always be favorable, and experience has shown the necessity for deposit takers to maintain a prudent level of liquid assets. For a financial asset to be classified as a liquid asset, the holder must have the reasonable certainty that it can be converted into cash with speed and without significant loss under normal business conditions.[62]

4.79 To some extent, whether an instrument is considered liquid or not depends on judgment and is influenced by market conditions. For example, cash, transferable deposits, and deposits that permit immediate cash withdrawals are typically liquid and are included in liquid assets, while nontraded instruments with a long time until maturity are not. Other deposits provide certainty of value but may not be readily convertible into cash because of restrictions on withdrawals prior to maturity. Conversely, tradable securities, particularly those issued by the government or the central bank, might be readily converted into cash through sale on the secondary market, but their realizable value depends on the market price at the time of sale.

4.80 In the *Guide, liquid assets* comprise (1) currency; (2) deposits and other financial assets that are available either on demand or within three months or less (although deposit takers' deposits and other nontraded claims with other deposit takers included in the

[59]As noted above, at the time of writing the Basel Capital Accord is being revised.

[60]In the 1996 Amendment to the Basel Capital Accord to incorporate market risks, the measure of capital charges against market risk as calculated by a deposit taker is multiplied by 12.5 and added to the sum of risk-weighted assets for credit risk purposes.

[61]In addition, supervisors assess the appropriateness of recognizing in consolidated capital the minority interest that arises from the consolidation of less than wholly owned banking (or other financial) entities. No such assessment is undertaken for the sectoral balance sheet data.

[62]In the discussions on the draft *Guide,* the possibility was raised of a deposit taker owning a very short-term asset that, while liquid in nature, might not be liquid in reality. This could come about if the deposit taker failed to renew the credit as it fell due, causing the debtor to face severe business consequences that would also have implications for the deposit taker. In such circumstances, the asset should not be included in liquid assets.

reporting population are excluded);[63] and (3) securities that are traded in liquid markets[64] (including repo markets) that can be readily converted into cash, with insignificant risk of change in value under normal business conditions. Typically, securities issued by the government and/or the central bank in their own currency meet the criteria to be classified as liquid assets, and in a number of markets high credit-quality private securities—both debt and equity securities—also meet the criteria. For instance, if a financial instrument is eligible under normal business conditions for repurchase operations or for rediscount at the central bank, then it can be classified as a liquid asset in that economy. It is recommended that securities issued by private entities with less than an investment grade rating be excluded from the concept of liquid assets, subject to national supervisory guidance.

4.81 Because of the difficulty in defining and measuring liquidity, there is merit in compiling more than one measure. For instance, the instruments in (1) and (2) in the paragraph above can be classified as *core liquid assets,* while the instruments in (3) can be added to provide a *broad measure of liquid assets,* as the latter instruments may lose their liquidity characteristics during times of financial stress. Moreover, distinguishing between foreign- and domestic-currency-denominated liquid assets can be important, particularly in periods of financial stress.

4.82 The availability of foreign exchange in the local market may also be an important consideration in assessing the liquidity of an institutional unit or sector in some countries. For example, a currency mismatch between liquid assets and liabilities, particularly in an environment of restricted access to foreign exchange, can impede the ability to meet foreign-currency-denominated obligations with sales of liquid assets that are denominated in local currency.

4.83 *Short-term liabilities* are the short-term element of deposit takers' debt liabilities (line 28) and the net (short-term, if possible) market value financial derivatives position (liabilities [line 29] less assets [line 21]);[65] the definition excludes such liabilities to other deposit takers in the reporting population. Preferably "short term" should be defined on a remaining maturity basis, although original maturity is a (more limited) alternative.

4.84 To improve the cross-country comparability of data, the *Guide* recommends that loans (and other assets)[66] should be classified as *NPL* when (1) payments of principal and interest are past due by three months (90 days) or more, or (2) interest payments equal to three months (90 days) interest or more have been capitalized (reinvested into the principal amount), refinanced, or rolled over (that is, payment has been delayed by agreement).[67] The 90-day criterion is the time period that is most widely used by countries to determine whether a loan is nonperforming (see Cortavarria and others, 2000, p. 11). In addition, NPLs should also include those loans with payments less than 90 days past due that are recognized as nonperforming under national supervisory guidance—that is, evidence exists to classify a loan as nonperforming even in the absence of a 90-day past due payment, such as when the debtor files for bankruptcy. Indeed, the *Guide* regards the guideline of 90 days past due as an outer bound and does not intend to discourage stricter approaches. The amount of loans (and other assets) recorded as nonperforming should be the gross value of the loan as recorded on the balance sheet, not just the amount that is overdue.

4.85 After a loan is classified as nonperforming, it (and/or any replacement loan(s)) should remain classified as such until written off or payments of interest and/or principal are received on this or subsequent loans that replace the original loan. It is recognized that some national supervisory practices

[63]This is recommended because, while for individual deposit takers such deposits are a form of liquid assets and could be separately identified, for the deposit-taking sector as a whole such deposits are not an "external" source of liquidity.

[64]Market liquidity, discussed further in Chapter 8, can be measured by certain market characteristics: (1) tightness—measured by the difference between prices at which a market participant is willing to buy and sell a security (bid-offer spread); (2) depth—typically proxied by the ratio of average trading volume over a given period of time to the outstanding volume of securities (the *turnover ratio*); (3) immediacy—the speed with which orders can be executed and settled; and (4) resilience—the speed at which price fluctuations resulting from trades are dissipated.

[65]The use of the net position in derivatives is recommended for the reasons explained in paragraph 4.90.

[66]Information on other (than loan) nonperforming assets is not required to calculate any FSI. However, such information allows a complete picture of deposit takers' nonperforming assets and hence supports macroprudential analysis.

[67]It is recommended that a period of time elapse between payments being missed and the loan being classified as nonperforming, because payments might be missed for a number of reasons, and such a lapse of time helps indicate that orderly repayment of the debt is in jeopardy. The *Guide* recognizes that practice as to the time that passes before such classification differs among countries.

might be stricter in that loans are classified as nonperforming until payments are received for specified periods of time. As noted above, the *Guide* does not intend to discourage stricter approaches.

4.86 Replacement loans include loans arising from rescheduling or refinancing the original loan(s) and/or loans provided to make payments on the original loan.[68] While these loans may be granted on easier than normal commercial terms, provided the terms and conditions of the replacement loan are complied with by the debtor, and subject to national supervisory guidance, the loan is no longer classified as an NPL. However, in discussions on the *Guide,* about assessing the credit quality of the loan portfolio, there was strong support among experts about identifying the share of replacement loans within total loans. For this reason, Appendix III provides a memorandum item to Table 4.1 on restructured loans.

4.87 Given the various practices, when disseminating data on NPLs it is essential that metadata describing the practice adopted be disseminated.

4.88 *Residential real estate loans* are those loans that are collateralized by residential real estate. Residential real estate includes houses, apartments, and other dwellings (such as houseboats and mobile homes), and any associated land intended for occupancy by individual households. *Commercial real estate loans* are those loans that are collateralized by commercial real estate, as well as loans to construction companies and loans to companies active in the development of real estate (including those companies involved in the development of multihousehold dwellings). Commercial real estate includes buildings, structures, and associated land used by enterprises for retail, wholesale, manufacturing, or other such purposes.

4.89 The *geographic distribution of loans* refers to an attribution of loans on the basis of the residence of the immediate counterpart—that is, the country of residence of the debtor. While country circumstances will differ, a regional classification of lending is encouraged, with perhaps additional detail on lending to residents of other countries that may be of particular relevance, such as neighboring countries. The regional groupings provided in the dissemination framework in Chapter 12 are based on the IMF's *World Economic Outlook* classification.

4.90 For deposit takers, *foreign currency loans* and *foreign currency liabilities* are those assets and liabilities that are payable in a currency other than the domestic currency and those that are payable in domestic currency but with the amounts to be paid linked to a foreign currency (foreign-currency-linked).[69] For related financial derivative liabilities it is recommended that the net market value position (liabilities less assets) be included in the foreign currency liability measure rather than the gross liability position because of the market practice of creating offsetting contracts, and the possibility of a forward-type instrument switching from an asset to a liability position and vice versa from one period to the next. Domestic currency is defined in paragraph 3.45.

4.91 A deposit taker's *net open position in equities* is described in more detail in Chapter 6 (paragraphs 6.40 to 6.43).

4.92 The *net open position in foreign currency for on-balance-sheet items* and the *total net open position in foreign currency* are calculated by summing the net position for each foreign currency and gold into a single unit of account (the reporting currency). The calculation is described in more detail in Chapter 6 (paragraphs 6.31 to 6.38).

Balance-sheet-related series

4.93 To compile the agreed FSIs there is also a need for a number of series that are derived from the balance sheet but require additional information or calculation.

4.94 *Exposures of the largest deposit takers to the largest entities in the economy* is the total exposure of the five largest deposit takers (the number may vary somewhat depending on national circumstances) to the five largest resident non-deposit-taker entities measured by asset size (including all branches and subsidiaries) in both the other financial corporations sector and nonfinancial corporations sector; this is in addition to the exposure to the general government. Total exposures include all forms of debt assets of the

[68]Types of restructuring include reductions in principal, reductions in the amounts due at maturity, periods of no payments on the loan (grace period), extension of maturity dates, and reductions in interest rates to below market rates or below the deposit taker's cost of funds.

[69]In the *MFSM,* such instruments are classified as domestic-currency-denominated.

deposit taker, equity securities owned, and the net asset position in financial derivatives.[70] Preferably, the value of contingent liabilities of the type described in Chapter 3 (paragraphs 3.12 to 3.19) should also be included, consistent with the supervisory approach. The focus is on gross exposures and the concept of maximum loss, consistent with the supervisory approach. However, deposit takers might take steps to reduce the credit risk (so-called credit risk mitigation), for example through requiring the provision of collateral. Any disseminated data should meet national confidentiality commitments.

4.95 *Exposure to affiliated entities and other connected counterparties* is otherwise known as connected lending. It is to be calculated by summing the total exposures of each deposit taker to its affiliated entities (including its parent entity, such as an insurance corporation) in other sectors, including nonresident entities, and exposures to directors and other employees, as well as exposures to shareholders or owners of the deposit taker. The definition of exposures is the same as in the previous paragraph.

Other Financial Corporations

4.96 The sectoral balance sheet statement for *other financial corporations* (OFCs) is set out in Table 4.2. The definition of balance sheet series presented is the same as for the corresponding series in Table 4.1.

4.97 The sectoral balance sheet for *other financial corporations* includes the separate identification of *insurance technical reserves.* Such reserves include (1) net claims of households on life insurance reserves and pension fund—although held and managed by these entities, these reserves are considered to be owned by households; (2) prepayments of premiums by policyholders; and (3) reserves for outstanding and valid claims—such amounts are considered to be claims of the policyholder.

4.98 *Shares and other equity* assets on the balance sheet include such claims on associates, unconsolidated subsidiaries, and reverse equity investments.[71] In the case of domestic data, shares and other equity assets also include any share capital provided to foreign branches.

Table 4.2. Other Financial Corporations

Balance Sheet[1]
1. **Total assets** (= 2 + 3)
2. *Nonfinancial assets*
3. *Financial assets* (= 4 through 10)
4. Currency and deposits[2]
5. Loans[2]
6. Debt securities[2]
7. Shares and other equity
8. Insurance technical reserves[2]
9. Financial derivatives[2]
10. Other assets[2]
11. *Liabilities* (= 17 + 18)
12. Currency and deposits
13. Loans
14. Debt securities
15. Insurance technical reserves
16. Other liabilities
17. *Debt* (= 12 to 16)
18. Financial derivatives
19. Capital and reserves
20. **Balance sheet total** (= 11 + 19 = 1)

[1]Data on assets are sufficient to calculate the agreed FSIs for other financial corporations. Liabilities as well as capital and reserves are included in the table to illustrate how asset data can be viewed within an internally consistent balance sheet.

[2]To understand the interconnections among *other financial corporations*, separate identification of claims on other *other financial corporations* in the reporting population is encouraged.

Nonfinancial Corporations

4.99 Table 4.3 sets out the sectoral financial statement for nonfinancial corporations.

Income and expense

4.100 *Operating income* of a nonfinancial corporation is the revenue from the *sales of goods and services* (excluding taxes on goods and services) less the *cost of those sales.* The cost of sales includes personnel (staff) costs (defined in paragraph 4.31); costs of materials purchased for the production process; fixed and variable production overheads (including depreciation expense or an allocation thereof); rentals paid on buildings, other structures, and equipment; rents paid on land and subsoil assets; royalties paid for the use of other produced or nonproduced assets; distri-

[70]If significant, the gross asset position could also be monitored because, if the counterparty fails, potential losses on financial derivative contracts may be closer to the gross than the net position.

[71]For sector-level data, the value of the investment in any other other financial corporation in the reporting population should be excluded from this item, assets in total, and capital and reserves (see also Box 5.2).

Table 4.3. Nonfinancial Corporations

Income and Expense Statement	Balance Sheet
1. Revenue from sales of goods and services (excluding indirect sales taxes)	13. **Total assets** (= 14 + 17)
2. Cost of sales	14. *Nonfinancial assets*
3. *Net operating income* (= 1 minus 2)	15. Produced
4. Interest income	Of which: (i) Fixed assets
5. Interest expense	(ii) Inventories
6. Other income (net)	16. Nonproduced
7. *Net income (before extraordinary items and taxes)* (= 3 + 4 minus 5 + 6)	17. *Financial assets*
8. Extraordinary items	18. Currency and deposits
9. Corporate income taxes	19. Debt securities[1]
10. *Net income after taxes* (= 7 minus (8 + 9))	20. Shares and other equity
11. Dividends payable	21. Trade credit[1]
12. *Retained earnings* (= 10 minus 11)	22. Financial derivatives[1]
	23. Other assets[1]
	24. *Liabilities* (= 29 + 30)
	25. Loans
	26. Debt securities
	27. Trade credit
	28. Other liabilities
	29. *Debt* (= 25 through 28)
	30. Financial derivatives
	31. Capital and reserves
	(i) *Of which:* Narrow capital[2]
	32. **Balance sheet total** (= 24 + 31 = 13)

Memorandum series

Other series required to calculate the agreed FSIs

33. Interest income receivable from other nonfinancial corporations
34. Earnings before interest and tax (item 3 + 4 + 6 minus 33)
35. Debt-service payments
36. Corporate net foreign exchange exposure for on-balance-sheet items
37. Total corporate net foreign exchange exposure

[1]To understand the interconnections among nonfinancial corporations, separate identification of claims on other nonfinancial corporations in the reporting population is encouraged.

[2]Funds contributed by owners plus retained earnings (including appropriations from retained earnings to reserves). Purchased goodwill is excluded.

bution costs including all costs to deliver products to customers, including transportation expense, advertising expense, and depreciation and maintenance of any retail shops; any other costs attributed to sales, such as professional fees, insurance, and research and development costs; taxes other than income taxes, such as taxes on the ownership or use of land and buildings or on labor employed; and any fines and penalties imposed, by courts of law or otherwise, and any amounts payable as compensation to other institutional units for injury and damage.

4.101 To provide a better measure of current health and soundness, the *Guide* prefers that provisions for estimated costs related to product warranties, when they can be measured reliably (see paragraph 3.18), be included as a cost of sales and as a general reserve in capital and reserves.[72]

4.102 When inventories are sold, their value is recognized as an expense in the cost of sales line in the period in which the related revenue is recognized (see also paragraph 4.108). All losses on goods held in inventory—whether through normal wastage or exceptional losses—are also recorded as an expense.

4.103 In addition to operating income, other sources of income include net *interest income* (interest income less interest expense) and *other income (net).*

[72]In the *1993 SNA,* potential costs are not recognized as expenses, or in any other item in the system.

Other income (net) encompasses rents, rentals, and royalties receivable (payable); income from holdings of shares and other equity; gains or losses arising during the period on financial instruments and on the sales of fixed assets; and any amounts receivable (payable) by nonfinancial corporations arising from compensation for damage or injury.

4.104 *Rents, rentals, and royalty income receivable (payable)* is income arising from rents received for the use of land and the right to extract (or explore for) subsoil assets; rentals from buildings, other structures, and equipment; and royalties for the use of other produced and nonproduced assets (for example, films and music). *Income from holdings of shares and other equity* includes dividends declared payable in the period by other corporations or cooperatives in which nonfinancial corporations have shares and other equity stakes,[73] and the prorated share—on the basis of the share of equity owned—of net income after tax from associates, unconsolidated subsidiaries, and reverse equity investments, and, for the compilation of domestic data, from foreign branches.[74,75] The term "*gains and losses on financial instruments*" is defined as for deposit takers (see paragraph 4.22); however, for unlisted companies, gains and losses on financial instruments that relate only peripherally to a firm's primary operating activities can be measured as the difference between the sale value and the balance sheet value at the previous end-period. *Gains (or losses) from sales of fixed assets* are measured as the difference between the sale value and the balance sheet value at the previous end-period.

4.105 As with deposit takers, *extraordinary items* cover events that are extraordinary and rare by the nature of the event or transaction in relation to the business ordinarily carried out by the enterprise. *Corporate income taxes* are those taxes payable by the nonfinancial corporations that are related to its income.[76] The amount of income subject to tax is usually less than total income because various deductions are permitted. After taxes are deducted, the total is *net income after tax,* and after dividends payable, *retained earnings* are left to be posted to capital and reserves.

Balance sheet

Nonfinancial assets

4.106 By definition, nonfinancial assets provide benefits to their owners but do not represent claims on other units. Most nonfinancial assets provide benefits either through their use in the production of goods and services or in the form of property income. Nonfinancial assets can come into existence as outputs from a production process (for example, machinery), be naturally occurring (for example, land), or be constructs of society (for example, patented entities). Fixed assets, inventories, and valuables are all forms of *produced assets,* while examples of *nonproduced assets* include land and patented entities.

4.107 *Fixed assets* are produced assets that are used repeatedly or continuously in processes of production for more than one year. Included are tangible fixed assets (dwellings and other buildings and structures, machinery and equipment, and cultivated assets such as livestock and orchards) and intangible fixed assets (such as the "capitalization" of mineral exploration expenses and computer software), whose use in production is restricted to the units that have established ownership rights over them or to other units licensed by the latter.

4.108 *Inventories* are goods held by the institutional unit for sale, use in production, or use at a later date. They can be materials and supplies, works in progress, finished goods, or goods for resale. The *Guide* prefers that inventories be valued at market value (that is, the current purchaser's price) with any valuation gains included in the valuation adjustment and then in retained earnings when the inventories are sold. However, it recognizes the difficulties in implementing such an approach and that in this complex field compilers may need to follow commercial accounting practices when recording inventories as assets or in sales.

[73]To avoid double counting of income before extraordinary items and taxes at the sector level, dividends receivable from other nonfinancial corporations in the reporting population should be excluded from this item and included instead (with a negative sign) in the dividends payable line. Thus, the data for dividends payable to, and receivable from, other nonfinancial corporations in the reporting population will net to zero in this line.

[74]See also Box 5.2, as the treatment of associates in the accounts of nonfinancial corporations is the same as for deposit takers.

[75]Income from holdings of equity and other shares also covers withdrawal of income from a quasi corporation by the owner. Only withdrawal of income from the net income earned by the quasi corporation should be included.

[76]Tax payable is not necessarily the same as tax expense, since the latter includes deferred tax.

4.109 *Valuables* are produced assets that are not used primarily for the purpose of production or consumption but are held as stores of value over time. They can be precious metals and stones, antiques and other art objects, or other valuables, such as collections of jewelry.

4.110 *Nonproduced assets* are assets needed for production that have not been produced, such as land, subsoil assets, water resources, and certain intangible assets such as patented entities, leases, and other transferable contracts relating to nonfinancial assets. Nonpatented know-how is not recognized as an asset in the *Guide* because there is no legal evidence of ownership rights. This treatment may differ from commercial accounting, where know-how that is not patented can be included on the balance sheet if its value can be reliably measured, on the grounds that by keeping that know-how secret, an enterprise controls the benefits that are expected to flow from it. The value of patent protection is amortized over time following commercial accounting standards.[77] Goodwill acquired on purchasing an associate or unconsolidated subsidiary stake (or adding to it)—that is, the excess of the cost of an acquired entity over the market or fair value of the net assets acquired—is deducted from (the narrow measure of) capital and reserves and is not an asset of the acquirer.[78] Therefore, there is no goodwill to be amortized in income in future periods.

Financial assets and liabilities

4.111 The definitions of balance sheet series presented in this table are the same as for the corresponding series in Table 4.1.

4.112 The sectoral balance sheet for nonfinancial corporations separately identifies *trade credit.* Trade credits and advances include (1) trade credit extended directly to purchasers of goods and services and (2) advances for work that is in progress or is to be undertaken, such as progress payments made during construction or for prepayments of goods and services. Trade credit does not include loans, debt securities, or other liabilities that are issued to finance trade credit. So, trade-related loans provided by a third party, such as a deposit taker, to an exporter or importer are not included in this category but are included under *loans.*

4.113 *Shares and other equity* assets include such claims on associates, unconsolidated subsidiaries, and reverse equity investments. For data compiled on a domestic basis, shares and other equity assets also include any share capital provided to foreign branches.[79]

4.114 *Capital and reserves* is otherwise known as equity. As in the case of deposit takers, funds contributed by owners plus retained earnings (including those earnings appropriated to reserves) could be identified as a narrow measure of capital and reserves. However, in many countries there is a paucity of sectoral information on nonfinancial corporations, and in calculating FSI data for this sector, preference is given to total capital and reserves.

Memorandum series

Other series required to calculate the agreed FSIs

4.115 *Interest income receivable from other nonfinancial corporations* is that amount of interest income (line 4) that is receivable from other nonfinancial corporations that are also in the reporting population.

4.116 *Earnings before interest and tax* (EBIT) is defined as operating income (item 3) plus interest income (item 4) plus other income (net) (item 6) less interest receivable from other nonfinancial corporations (item 33). Interest expenses are excluded by definition. Interest receivable from other nonfinancial corporations is deducted from earnings before interest and tax data to ensure that sector earnings are not exaggerated by such intrasector income.

[77]Under the IASB's International Financial Reporting Standards (IFRS), certain acquired intangible assets can be deemed to have an indefinite life; these assets are not amortized but are subject to impairment testing, like goodwill.

[78]Accounting standard setters consider goodwill to be an asset. It is possible that the cost of the acquired entity is less than the market or fair value of the net assets—negative goodwill. If so, it should be determined whether all assets and liabilities being acquired are identified and appropriately valued. If any excess remains after such a determination, the negative goodwill increases (the narrow measure of) capital and reserves. Under the IASB's IFRS, any excess that remains after a rigorous valuation of the net assets acquired is a gain in profit and loss.

[79]For sector-level data, the value of the investment in any other nonfinancial corporation in the reporting population should be excluded from this item, total assets, and capital and reserves (see also Box 5.2).

Table 4.4. Households

Income and Expense Statement	Balance Sheet
Sources of income	7. **Total assets** (= 8 + 11)
1. Wages and salaries from employment	8. *Nonfinancial assets* (= 9 + 10)
2. Property income receivable	9. Residential and commercial real estate
3. Current transfers (e.g., from government)	10. Other
4. Other	11. *Financial assets* (= 12 through 16)
5. Less taxes, including social security contributions, and other current transfers	12. Currency and deposits
6. *Gross disposable income* (= 1 + 2 + 3 + 4 − 5)	13. Debt securities
	14. Shares and other equity
	15. Financial derivatives
	16. Other assets
	17. *Liabilities* (= 20 + 21)
	18. Loans
	19. Other liabilities
	20. *Debt* (= 18 + 19)
	21. Financial derivatives
	22. *Net worth*
	23. **Balance sheet total** (= 17 + 22 = 7)
Memorandum series	
Other series required to calculate the agreed FSIs	
24. Debt-service payments (interest and principal)	
25. Debt collateralized by real estate	

4.117 *Debt-service payments* are interest and principal payments made on outstanding debt liabilities within the specified time period of the statement. Such payments always reduce the amount of debt outstanding. Interest payments are those periodic payments[80] that meet interest costs arising from the use of another entity's funds, and principal payments are all other payments that reduce the amount of principal outstanding.

4.118 The *corporate net foreign exchange exposure for on-balance-sheet items* and the *total corporate net foreign exchange exposure* are calculated by summing the net positions for each foreign currency and gold into a single unit of account (the reporting currency). The calculation is described in more detail in Chapter 6 (paragraphs 6.31 to 6.38).

Households

4.119 The financial statement for households is set out in Table 4.4.

Income and expense

4.120 The main source of *income* for households is *wages and salaries* (gross of any income tax) from employment. These are payable in cash or kind and are a component of compensation for employment (see also paragraph 4.31).[81] Other major sources of income include *property income receivable* (interest, dividends, and rent) and *current transfers,* including those from general government. *Other* income sources include operating income from production activity (gross of consumption of fixed capital).[82] *Gross disposable income* includes these sources of income less current taxes on income and wealth, contributions for social insurance (for example, for old-age insurance paid by households to general government), and other current transfers (such as payments of fines, penalties, and subscriptions to NPISHs).

[80]For long-term debt instruments, interest costs paid periodically are defined as those to be paid by the debtor to the creditor annually or more frequently; for short-term instruments, that is, with an original maturity of one year or less, interest costs paid periodically are defined as those to be paid by the debtor to the creditor before the redemption date of the instrument.

[81]The other component of compensation of employees is the value of social contributions payable by the employer, but such contributions do not affect personal income and so are not included in the sources of income.

[82]Production within the household sector takes place within enterprises that are directly owned and controlled by members of households, either individually or in partnership with others. When members of households work as employees for corporations, quasi corporations, or the government, the production to which they contribute takes place outside the household sector.

Balance sheet

4.121 The financial assets and liabilities series in Table 4.4 are defined in the same way as in Table 4.1.

Memorandum series

4.122 As noted in paragraph 4.117, *debt-service payments* are interest and principal payments made on outstanding debt liabilities within the specified time period of the statement. *Debt collateralized by real estate* covers all debt for which real estate is used as a form of collateral. This includes borrowing for the purchase, refinancing, or construction of buildings and structures (including their alterations and additions), and for equivalent operations regarding land (see paragraph 4.88).

5. Aggregation and Consolidation of Data

Introduction

5.1 The analysis of FSI ratios is affected by the extent to which the data used for their calculation are consolidated. Thus, when constructing FSI ratios, attention needs to be paid to whether the data reported by entities are on a consolidated basis and the method by which the data for the whole of the reporting population[1] are aggregated. This chapter explains what is meant by consolidation and aggregation, and sets out the various approaches. It also sets out the adjustments required to produce sector-level data.

5.2 The FSI data compiled for domestically controlled deposit takers on a cross-border consolidated basis are best suited for financial soundness analysis when the deposit takers have international operations. Data on domestically located operations might be separately distinguished if the authorities believe it would contribute materially to their financial stability analysis (for example, to illustrate the linkage with other macroeconomic information). This chapter will also outline a preferred approach for the other sectors. The data implications of the *Guide*'s preferred approaches are explained in Chapter 11.

Defining Terms

What Is Meant by the Terms "Aggregation" and "Consolidation"?

5.3 *Aggregation* refers to the summation of data on gross positions or flows. Under an aggregation approach, the total positions and flows data for any group of reporting units are equal to the sum of the gross information for all individual units in the group.[2] Thus, the group and subgroup totals equal the sum of their component elements, and the data on claims and liabilities between the members of the group are preserved.

5.4 In contrast, *consolidation* refers to the elimination of positions and flows between units that are grouped together for statistical purposes. Consolidation can arise at various levels of grouping. For an individual institutional unit, all intraunit positions and flows are eliminated. If related institutional units are grouped together to form one individual reporting entity (for example, foreign branches of domestic banks are grouped with their parent bank), then all positions and flows within that reporting entity are eliminated from the reported information—that is, all flows and positions among the branches and with their parent are eliminated. If data for a group of reporting entities are consolidated, such as those in the same institutional sector (or subsector), then intrasector flows and positions are eliminated, leaving data on positions and flows with entities in other sectors (or subsectors).

5.5 Consolidation and aggregation can be combined for the purpose of compiling data series for use in calculating FSIs. For instance, reporting entities might provide consolidated data to the compiling agency, which then aggregates these data to create sector totals. On the other hand, the data provided might be consolidated rather than aggregated at the sector level. In this case, information on positions and flows among the entities covered in the reporting population need to be available to the compiling agency so that such positions and flows be eliminated. The approach

[1]The term "reporting population" refers to all entities included in the sector information. The population can vary depending on the institutional coverage of the sector.

[2]In some instances, data on an economic sector can be compiled using information reported by a sample of reporters, together with estimates for those units in the sector that do not report. Statistically, the more representative the sample is of the total population, the greater the likelihood of estimating reliable information for the nonreporters.

to consolidation and aggregation in compiling series for use in calculating FSIs is discussed below.

What Is Meant by the Terms "Subsidiaries" and "Associates"?

5.6 Before discussing consolidated data in more detail, definitions of subsidiaries and associates are required, as these terms are used throughout the rest of this chapter.

5.7 *Subsidiaries* are corporations over which a parent has established control. While recognizing that national practice on determining control can differ, control is defined in the *Guide* as the ability to determine general corporate policy by choosing (or removing) appropriate directors to obtain benefits from the activities of the corporation. Control is unambiguously established through ownership of more than half of the voting shares or otherwise controlling more than half of the shareholder voting power (including through ownership of a second corporation that in turn has a majority of the voting shares). Control could also be established with ownership of less than half the voting shares,[3] through, for example, special legislation, decree, or regulation.[4]

5.8 An *associate* is a corporation over which the investor has a significant degree of influence and which is not a subsidiary. Significant influence is usually assumed to arise when the investor owns from 10 to 20 percent (depending on national practice) and 50 percent of the equity/voting power of the entity. Typically, if the ownership stake reaches the threshold for classification as an associate but is expected to be of a temporary nature, the investment continues to be classified as a nonassociate equity investment. However, for FSI purposes, if the equity investment has reached the level to be classified as an associate for two successive reporting periods, the implication is that the investment is not temporary.

5.9 Joint ventures are separate entities owned and operated by two or more parties for their mutual benefit. In the *Guide,* such entities are classified either as subsidiaries, as associates, or neither, depending on the criteria set out in the previous two paragraphs. So if there are two or more investing parties, each of which has a significant degree of influence over the joint venture, they should each classify the entity as an associate, consistent with the definition in the previous paragraph.

What Is Meant by the Terms "Domestic Control" and "Foreign Control"?

5.10 When discussing reporting populations in more detail, definitions of domestic and foreign control are required.

5.11 Deposit-taking entities are defined in the *Guide* as *foreign controlled* if they are subsidiaries or branches of a foreign parent deposit taker. Foreign controlled deposit takers, in addition to supervision by the host supervisory authority, are typically subject to supervision by their parent supervisory authority, as recommended in the Basel Concordat of May 1983 (BCBS, 1983). This criterion should be taken into account if there is uncertainty as to the classification of a deposit taker as foreign controlled. All other deposit-taking entities should be classified as *domestically controlled.* If a domestic deposit taker is controlled by a bank holding company in a foreign country that is subject to banking supervision in that foreign economy, then it should be also classified as foreign controlled.[5]

5.12 For corporations in other sectors, they are foreign controlled if they are subsidiaries or branches of a foreign parent. All other resident corporations are to be classified as domestically controlled.

The Aggregate Resident-Based Approach

5.13 In the *Guide,* under an *aggregate resident-based* approach, data are reported at the level of institutional units resident in the economy and aggregated by the compiling agency to provide totals of the sectors. This is the approach adopted in the *1993 SNA,* the sectoral balance sheets in the *MFSM,* and related national accounts methodologies. The *Guide*

[3]There may be instances where a corporation controls another corporation without having any ownership stake, such as instances arising from a loan agreement.

[4]In some instances, governments sell corporate entities but make arrangements so that private investors cannot establish control with a majority stake (the so-called government "golden share").

[5]In some rare instances, the parent might be considered as being located in both the domestic and a foreign economy. In such instances, the compiler is encouraged to classify such entities as domestically controlled.

recommends this approach for the compilation of FSI data for the household sector.

5.14 For corporations in an aggregate resident-based system, the institutional unit within which all transactions and positions are consolidated consists of a headquarters office and any branch offices resident in the economy.[6]

The Consolidated-Based Approach

5.15 In the *Guide,* the consolidated-based approach refers to the consolidation of data at both the group and sector levels. It is the required approach for compiling data on deposit takers and other corporate sectors for use in the calculation of FSIs. The text below discusses both consolidated group reporting and compiling consolidated sector-level data. The deposit-taking sector is used as an illustration, but the principles espoused are also relevant and can be applied to other corporate sectors. Table 5.1 supports the text.

Consolidated Group Reporting

5.16 *Consolidated group reporting* by a resident deposit taker includes coverage not only of its own activities but also those of its branches and subsidiaries, with any transactions and positions among these entities eliminated on consolidation. In essence, consolidation is based on the concept of control by a parent of other operating units. Such an approach is an essential element of banking supervision (BCBS, 1997, No. 20) and is adopted to preserve the integrity of capital in deposit takers by eliminating double counting (gearing) of capital (BCBS, 2001b, para.1). It is for this reason, and also to avoid the double counting of income and assets arising from the intragroup activity of deposit takers—that is, activity that rests on the same pool of capital—that the *Guide* recommends that deposit takers' data be compiled on a consolidated group basis.

Cross-border consolidated data

5.17 *Cross-border consolidated data* are represented by Blocks 1a, 1b, 1c, 2a, 2b, and 2c in Table 5.1. This approach consolidates flows and positions of the domestically incorporated deposit taker with its branches (foreign and domestic) and deposit-taking subsidiaries (foreign and domestic); the approach is described as solo (bank-only) supervision by bank supervisors. The cross-border consolidated approach focuses on domestically incorporated deposit takers and provides an indication of their financial soundness regardless of where the deposit-taking business is undertaken.[7]

Domestically controlled, cross-border consolidated data

5.18 *Domestically controlled, cross-border consolidated data* are represented by Blocks 1a, 1b, and 1c in Table 5.1. This approach consolidates the data of domestically controlled and incorporated deposit takers with their branches (domestic and foreign) and all deposit-taking subsidiaries (domestic and foreign).

5.19 The focus on the health and soundness of domestically controlled deposit takers arises because domestic authorities might ultimately be required to provide financial support. If domestically controlled deposit takers have foreign branches and subsidiaries, they may well be among the larger deposit takers in the domestic economy, so the potential direct financial risk of the failure of these deposit takers could pose a systemic risk.

Domestically controlled, cross-sector consolidated data

5.20 Another option is to consolidate information from all branches and subsidiaries involved in financial intermediation—that is, beyond just deposit-taking business—with that of the domestically controlled and incorporated parent entity. In other words, consolidating information beyond that in 1a, 1b, and 1c. This approach is termed the *domestically controlled cross-sector consolidated* approach in the *Guide.* Most supervisory data rely on this form of consolidation, as it is the approach used in the Basel Capital Accord (although insurance activity is typically excluded).

[6]A separate financial unit within a larger conglomerate might be regarded as an institutional unit if, in its own right, it can own assets, incur liabilities, and engage in economic activities and in transactions with other entities.

[7]A variant of this approach is to cover all domestically incorporated deposit takers and "only" their branches, a so-called legal control approach. This is represented by Blocks 1a, 1b, 2a, and 2b.

Table 5.1. Schematic Presentation of Levels of Consolidation

	Domestic Economy (domestic consolidated data) (1a, 2a, and 3)	Foreign Economies	
Domestically controlled, cross-border consolidated data (1a, 1b, and 1c)	Domestically incorporated, domestically controlled deposit takers *Block 1a*	Foreign branches of Block 1a *Block 1b*	Foreign deposit-taking subsidiaries of Block 1a *Block 1c*
Foreign controlled, cross-border consolidated data (2a, 2b, and 2c)	Domestically incorporated deposit-taking subsidiaries of foreign deposit takers *Block 2a*	Foreign branches of Block 2a *Block 2b*	Foreign deposit-taking subsidiaries of Block 2a *Block 2c*
Foreign deposit-taking parent	Branches of foreign deposit takers *Block 3*		

5.21 The cross-sector consolidated approach can highlight financial strengths and weaknesses of a group in the context of the full range of activities and thus can provide a broader view of soundness than the approach that focuses only on deposit takers. For instance, weak nonbank subsidiaries might trouble the deposit-taking sector. However, there are some drawbacks. At the sector level, the clarity of the institutional sector information is diminished because flows and positions of entities owned by the parent entity—but outside its institutional sector—are included. This could make difficult the early detection of emerging weaknesses in the performance of deposit takers. The coverage of activities is not clear-cut; for instance, should insurance companies in the group be included? Moreover, interpretation of these data might prove problematic, particularly in periods of merger and acquisition activity among units in different institutional sectors. In addition, relationships with other non-deposit-taking members of the group would not be detected, such as connected lending between the deposit takers and their non-deposit-taking affiliates.

Foreign-controlled, cross-border consolidated data

5.22 *Foreign-controlled cross-border consolidated data* are represented by Blocks 2a, 2b, and 2c in Table 5.1. This approach consolidates the data of branches (domestic and foreign) and all deposit-taking subsidiaries (domestic and foreign) with the data of their domestically incorporated foreign-controlled parent. Depending on country circumstances, authorities may consider it necessary to monitor (on a nationality basis) the performance of foreign-controlled deposit takers and their deposit-taking parents.

5.23 As foreign subsidiaries are part of a larger deposit-taking group, their activities in the economy are affected by the policy decisions of their parent, while ultimately foreign banking supervisors are most concerned about the health and soundness of these institutions. To this extent, from the viewpoint of the host authorities, there is a significant prudential difference between foreign-controlled and domestically controlled institutions. However, the host authorities should not be indifferent to the health and soundness of these institutions, as their activities do affect the domestic economy, and financial risks arising from their subsidiaries and branches abroad could ultimately have an impact on the domestic economy.

5.24 The relevance of data on foreign subsidiaries in the economy will vary depending on country circumstances, as will the interest in collecting information on the foreign branches and subsidiaries of such institutions.

Domestic consolidated data

5.25 The *Guide* defines *domestic consolidated* data as data that consolidate flows and positions of the resident deposit takers with those of their branches and deposit-taking subsidiaries (if any) resident in the domestic economy. Domestic consolidated data are represented by Blocks 1a, 2a, and 3 in Table 5.1. The reported data include flows and positions with all nonresidents and residents.

5.26 Data compiled using this approach are of analytical interest because deposit takers resident in a domestic economy provide payment services, offer savings opportunities to the public, and allocate funds for viable investment projects. These institutions are also the agents through which central banks undertake monetary policy actions. In turn, resident deposit takers are affected by domestic conditions.[8] Therefore, their actions both affect and are affected by the domestic economy, and if resident banks fail to undertake, or sharply curtail, their financial intermediation activity, there would be detrimental consequences for the domestic economy.

5.27 Moreover, domestic consolidated data provide a link to other macroeconomic data sets, such as the national accounts and monetary aggregates. Indeed, monitoring the interconnections between domestic consolidated data and macroeconomic data series, such as those on the real economy, credit growth, fiscal positions, and international capital flows, as well as asset price bubbles, could support macroprudential analysis (see, for example, Barton, Newell, and Wilson, 2002, Ch. 3; Crockett, 2000).

5.28 While the net income/loss arising from foreign operations is captured, this approach does not identify the risks to domestic deposit takers incurred through their foreign branches and subsidiaries.

Applying Consolidated Group Reporting to the Needs of FSI Data

5.29 As noted above, for compiling data for use in the calculation of FSIs, consolidated group reporting is preferred for deposit takers and other corporate sectors. However, as already discussed, there are several possibilities for the scope of the reporting population. Should only units located in the domestic economy be covered, or also their foreign offices? Should coverage be distinguished by domestic and foreign control? For deposit takers, should coverage encompass institutional units that do not meet the definition of deposit taker but are subsidiaries of deposit takers?

5.30 On these questions the *Guide* provides the following advice.

Deposit Takers

5.31 First, the *Guide* requires the compilation of data covering *domestically controlled deposit takers* on a cross-border consolidated basis for soundness analysis (see paragraphs 5.18 and 5.19). The data should cover domestically controlled deposit takers with international operations (foreign deposit-taking subsidiaries and branches). For economies that compile BIS consolidated banking data, the *Guide* supports identification of an FSI data set as consistent as possible in coverage with that of the BIS data, as analytical benefits could accrue from comparing the data sets. When foreign deposit takers play a significant role in a financial system, the authorities could compile FSIs on a cross-border consolidated basis for all domestically incorporated deposit takers—that is, domestically controlled deposit takers and the

[8] For instance, the BCBS (1996, p. 3) noted the possibility of legal and procedural difficulties in carrying out the timely management of risks on a consolidated basis. Therefore, while capital requirements for market risk apply on a worldwide-consolidated basis, national authorities retain the right to monitor market risks of individual entities on a non-worldwide-consolidated basis to ensure that significant imbalances within a group do not escape supervision.

local subsidiaries of foreign deposit takers, consolidated with their own branches and deposit-taking subsidiaries (if any).[9] Such data could then be disaggregated into separate FSIs for domestically controlled deposit takers and for the local subsidiaries of foreign deposit takers.[10]

5.32 In some instances, supervisory data on a deposit-takers-only basis may not be available because of the structural features of the banking system. In such circumstances, the inclusion of subsidiaries whose activities are closely related to deposit takers[11] could be justified on soundness grounds.[12]

5.33 The compilation of data covering all *deposit takers resident in the economy* (domestically controlled and foreign controlled) on a domestic consolidated basis might be separately considered if the authorities believe it would contribute materially to their financial stability analysis by promoting understanding of the relationship with the macroeconomy (see paragraphs 5.25 to 5.28).[13,14] Domestic consolidated data (1) can facilitate comparability with other macroeconomic data, (2) can promote cross-country data comparability, and (3) are consistent with the BIS's locational international banking statistics. Providing these data series through the development of sectoral accounts based on national accounts concepts would be an attractive approach, and the *Guide* provides guidance on how this can be achieved. Such an approach might be a medium-term objective in those economies where sectoral accounts are still relatively underdeveloped.[15]

5.34 The purpose of compiling cross-border consolidated data is financial soundness analysis, while that of compiling domestic consolidated data is to illustrate links to the macroeconomy. It is clear from discussions during the preparation of the *Guide* that neither consolidation approach will always satisfy both purposes.

5.35 To undertake meaningful analysis, it is important that the accounting rules and concepts be applied as consistently as possible across all data sets, regardless of the approach to consolidation. When disseminating any data, the institutional coverage and basis of consolidation should be made explicit.

Other Corporate Sectors

5.36 For FSIs covering the other financial and nonfinancial sectors, a consolidated approach is preferred to avoid double counting of assets and capital and, in the case of nonfinancial corporations, to avoid double counting of earnings.

5.37 For *other financial corporations,* the two FSIs currently listed—assets to total financial sector assets and assets to GDP—are intended to provide an indication of the importance of these institutions in the domestic financial system. The first of these two indicators could be compiled on either a cross-border consolidated basis or a domestic consolidated basis, while the second should be compiled on a domestic consolidated basis (for better consistency with GDP). It is important to note that the two currently listed FSIs above could be supplemented by additional FSIs for the sector. Specific proposals for FSIs

[9]Foreign branches may also play a significant role in the domestic economy and compiling separate data on this group might be considered. However, the relevance of some of the FSIs, such as the capital adequacy indicators, would depend on the nature of the funding of the branch—whether it has stand-alone capital or is simply funded from the head office through interbank deposits (see the memorandum item to Table 4.1, "net liabilities of branches of foreign deposit takers to their parents," line 61, Table A3.2, in Appendix III).

[10]On a nationality basis, the authorities could use the FSIs compiled by the countries of the parent deposit takers to further assess the soundness of foreign banks.

[11]Subsidiaries might include financial intermediaries such as, but not limited to, securities dealers. While national practices may differ, the inclusion of any non-deposit-taking subsidiaries should be noted in the metadata disseminated.

[12]If the non-deposit-taking subsidiaries are close to 100 percent owned, the net (but not gross) income and capital positions, if compiled consistently with the *Guide*'s concepts and definitions, will be similar to those of data without such non-deposit-taking subsidiaries. But gross exposure data could differ significantly, because cross-sector group claims are included in the deposit-takers-only data, and the other gross exposures of non-deposit-taking subsidiaries are excluded.

[13]The main difference between this concept and the preceding one is that it excludes foreign branches and subsidiaries of domestic banks, but includes foreign controlled branches and subsidiaries. If the domestic financial system contains only domestically controlled deposit takers with no international operations and no foreign bank operations in the local financial system, the two concepts are the same.

[14]If the domestic financial system contains only subsidiaries of foreign controlled deposit takers that have no foreign deposit-taking subsidiaries or branches, then the foreign-subsidiaries data set is the same as the domestic consolidated deposit takers data set.

[15]Moreover, if the foreign operations of resident deposit takers contribute a relatively small proportion of their total activity, from a practical point of view cross-border consolidated data covering both resident domestically controlled and foreign-controlled deposit takers could be used.

for the insurance sector, in particular, are likely to be forthcoming in the near future to be compiled on a cross-border consolidated basis.

5.38 For *nonfinancial corporations,* as with deposit takers, data might be compiled on both a domestically controlled cross-border consolidated basis and on a domestic consolidated basis. Data on the former basis would capture corporate financial strength and might, for example, be drawn from published corporate financial statements for the larger firms. Where such data are available and cover a substantial part of the sector, their reporting is encouraged. As with any partial coverage of the sector, the potential "survivor bias" should be kept in mind.[16]

5.39 However, the *Guide* acknowledges that in many countries, there is a relative lack of official, sector-level cross-border data and thus accepts, in the first instance, the compilation of domestic consolidated data based on national accounts methodology. Such an approach, through the link to other macroeconomic data sets, would also support the analysis of sectoral behavior in the context of macroeconomic developments, complementing macroprudential analysis. Providing these data series through the development of sectoral accounts would be an attractive approach. In disseminating any data, the institutional coverage and basis of consolidation should be made explicit, along with information on the accounting rules and concepts employed.

Specific Issues Arising from the Consolidated Approach

5.40 While aggregation of data is a simple concept, consolidation is more complex, particularly when deciding when and how to consolidate the activities of a subsidiary with the parent and other affiliated entities when the subsidiary is less than 100 percent owned.

[16]Compilers using sampling techniques based on financial statements need to be aware of the potential "survivor bias." For instance, a sample of large listed nonfinancial corporations might include those with high debt-to-equity ratios, particularly in a period of significant merger and acquisition activity. However, if some of these companies subsequently fail (perhaps due partly to the high gearing), fall out of the sample, and are replaced by other companies, the time series of debt-to-equity data could be noticeably affected. Thus, it is important both to provide information on how the data are constructed and to have as comprehensive a coverage of entities as possible.

5.41 The reason for consolidating activities of a subsidiary with a parent entity and other subsidiaries is that the parent entity has control over its activities and, therefore, directly affects and is affected by the activities of that subsidiary. However, consolidating the activities of minority-owned subsidiaries with a parent entity could potentially result in double counting among reporting entities, and compilers should remain alert to this possibility.

5.42 Furthermore, when consolidating the activities of less than 100 percent owned subsidiaries, the issue arises as to how to account for the minority interest—the other owners. The approach taken in the *Guide* is that full consolidation should be undertaken. Minority interests should not be separately identified in earnings or in the balance sheet as a liability item; they should be included as part of the capital and reserves of the consolidated entity. For deposit takers, such full consolidation is consistent with that of the Basel Capital Accord for the measurement of Tier 1 capital and reflects the focus on the total capital and reserves of the deposit taker in the consolidated group.

5.43 For any unconsolidated subsidiaries[17] and associates, earnings and the value of the equity investment are to be recorded on a proportionate basis in the income statement and in the capital and reserves, respectively, of the owner of the stake. That is, if the owner of the investment has a 50 percent stake in an entity, half of the net earnings after tax should appear as income from the equity investment, and half of the value of the capital and reserves of the entity should be recorded as the value of the equity investment in the balance sheet of the owner. There should be similar treatment for any equity investment by an associate and unconsolidated subsidiary in a parent (reverse equity investment).

5.44 For commercial accounting and bank supervisory data, the full consolidation approach for subsidiaries tends to be preferred, with a prorated approach for profits and capital of associates. A version of the proportionate approach is that adopted in the *1993 SNA* for both foreign subsidiaries and asso-

[17]For data on a domestic consolidated basis, such unconsolidated subsidiaries are those in other non-deposit-taking domestic sectors and all foreign subsidiaries. On a cross-border consolidated basis, such subsidiaries are those in other non-deposit-taking sectors (domestic and foreign).

ciates, whereby proportionate shares of their earnings and capital are attributed to the parent; however, this is not the treatment adopted in the *1993 SNA* for domestic subsidiaries or associates.

Compiling Consolidated Sector-Level Data

5.45 The compilation of consolidated sector-level data for use in FSIs is a two-step process. Given consolidated group reporting for each sector, (1) data reported by the corporations in the reporting population are aggregated, and (2) further sector-level adjustments (consolidations) are made to produce sector-level data.[18] If data are not reported on a consolidated group basis, additional adjustments are required to eliminate intragroup positions and transactions.[19]

5.46 In compiling sector-level data it is important to appreciate that the range of deposit takers whose activities are to be captured in the sector-level data (known in the *Guide* as the reporting population) will vary depending on the consolidated group reporting approach adopted. In other words, each consolidated group reporting approach has its own sector-level reporting population, which will differ from that for other consolidated group reporting approaches. For instance, if foreign branches and deposit-taking subsidiaries are included in the consolidated group data, then the reporting population at the sector level under this approach will be larger than if they were not. The idea that for FSI purposes more than one reporting population can be defined contrasts with other macroeconomic data sets, such as the monetary and financial statistics data sets, for which the reporting population is singly defined based on residence and the nature of the activity undertaken.

5.47 Furthermore, for FSI purposes (and, again, different in approach from other macroeconomic statistics), sector-level adjustments are needed to eliminate double counting of capital and income within the reporting population. These adjustments can be summarized as follows:

- Intrasector equity investments are deducted from the overall capital in the sector, so that capital and reserves held within the sector are not double counted.
- Neither gains and losses from the intrasector claims nor intrasector transactions should affect the sector's net income, or capital and reserves. That is, for deposit takers, value is added or lost through their transactions with and claims on entities that are outside the deposit-taking sector.

5.48 A more detailed specification of the sector-level adjustments required is provided in the text annex below. To aid in carrying out these adjustments, Box 5.1 highlights various recommendations on classification and treatment of interbank flows and positions. Box 5.2 provides similar recommendations for the other (non-deposit-taking) financial corporations sector and the nonfinancial corporations sector. Box 5.3 discusses how consolidated data differ depending on whether the consolidation is on a cross-border or domestic basis.

5.49 It is important to note that sector-level data compiled for FSI purposes should include any intrasector positions in debt and financial derivatives on a gross basis; that is, such positions among groups should not be eliminated. This approach allows the interrelationships among groups in the sector, and hence potential contagion risks, to be identified. This is viewed as particularly relevant for the deposit-taking sector. This is because asset-based FSIs are intended primarily to identify the gross risks faced by the deposit-taking sector, and these risks encompass claims on each other.[20] For instance, to discover whether certain types of deposit takers concentrate on lending in, say, foreign currency, potentially excluding a portion of such lending could be misleading. The same reasoning applies to the other asset-based FSIs. In contrast, in the *MFSM*'s Other Depository Corporations Survey, flows and positions among the reporting population are eliminated.[21]

5.50 More generally, the *Guide* encourages separate identification and monitoring of gross information on interbank positions.

[18]By making adjustments, the sector-level data are not the sum of individual deposit takers' reports. Thus, data on FSIs disseminated by individual deposit takers and those for a sector as a whole will likely differ.

[19]Chapter 11 provides more details on the adjustments required.

[20]In Chapter 13, monitoring interbank exposures on a deposit taker–by–deposit taker basis is discussed.

[21]Box 11.1 sets out how monetary and financial statistics data can be used in the calculation of the agreed indicators.

Box 5.1. Interbank Flows and Positions

Within any financial system, there are likely to be financial relationships among deposit takers. These can be significant and take the form of interbank borrowing and lending, and ownership of equity and other traded instruments issued by deposit takers. How these various interrelationships are captured in the data used for calculating FSIs is important to understanding the data. This box aims to explain how the *Guide*'s various recommendations regarding the classification of interbank flows and positions in the financial statement at the sector level fit together. Chapter 11 sets out the information required to meet these recommendations.

Flows and positions between deposit takers in the same group[1]

In the consolidated approach, all intragroup flows and positions—including capital and reserves—among deposit takers in the reporting population are eliminated from the sector information.

Flows and positions with other deposit takers

For income and expense, and capital and reserves, the approach taken is essentially to exclude from sector data interbank flows and positions with other deposit takers in the reporting population.[2] The objective is to avoid using a gross estimate of the flow of income into, and the measure of total capital in, the sector, which would lead to an overstatement of its financial health and capital strength. In the income and expense statement, intrasector noninterest income and expenses are eliminated; moreover, intrasector dividends are eliminated both in the noninterest income and dividend payable lines. Interbank interest income and expense are presented in gross terms and, in principle, will add up to zero in the net interest income line. Adjustments are made for any provisions on nonperforming claims on other deposit takers in the reporting population. (The text annex to this chapter provides a numerical example of the sector-level adjustments required.)

Following the same approach, liquid assets exclude nontraded interbank claims, thus avoiding the overstatement of the measure of liquidity at the sector level. Such interbank claims are neither "external" sources of liquidity for the sector nor realizable for cash in the market (unlike tradable claims on other banks). Similarly, short-term liabilities used in calculating the FSI *liquid assets to short-term liabilities* should exclude intrasector short-term liabilities.

To monitor risk exposures and the potential for contagion, in the case of gross assets (and liabilities), the *Guide* recommends as a general principle including in the sector data gross interbank claims and liabilities (as with interest flows). This is because asset-based FSIs are intended primarily to identify the gross risks faced by the deposit-taking sector, and these risks encompass claims on each other.

More generally, the *Guide* encourages separate identification and monitoring of the gross amounts of interbank positions.

To avoid asymmetric recording by debtor and creditor deposit takers, adjustments are made to the data for specific provisions on loans (or other assets) on other deposit takers in the reporting population.

[1]A group in this context is a parent deposit taker, its deposit-taking branches, and deposit-taking subsidiaries.

[2]The term "reporting population" includes all deposit takers included in the sector information. It varies depending on the institutional coverage of the sector.

Equity investments

The treatment of equity investments requires special mention.

In all measurement systems, a distinction is made when an equity investment reaches a certain level at which the investor achieves significant influence over management decisions, and hence over the use of the capital resources of the entity. As noted elsewhere in this chapter (paragraph 5.8), depending on national practice, this level may be 10 percent or 20 percent. Consistent with such a distinction, in the *Guide* the value of the investor's equity investment in associates and unconsolidated subsidiaries is to be recorded in the investor's balance sheet, and earnings are to be attributed to the investor's income statement (noninterest income) on the basis of the investor's proportionate share in the capital and reserves of the associate and unconsolidated subsidiary. Any reverse equity investment in a parent by an associate or unconsolidated subsidiary should be similarly recorded in the associate/subsidiary's balance sheet and income statement.

For sector-level data, when both the associate and parent are in the reporting population:

- The value of the earnings attributable to the investing deposit taker should be deducted from noninterest (other) income, so the same net income is not double counted. Moreover, to ensure that dividends payable and retained earnings for the sector are not overstated, the investing deposit taker's share of the dividends payable and of retained earnings (which together should equal the entry in noninterest income) is to be deducted from these items.
- The proportionate share of the investing deposit taker in the capital and reserves of the associate (or parent, in the instance of reverse investment) should be excluded from gross assets and from capital and reserves in the balance sheet for the sector.

Furthermore, if one deposit taker buys an associate or subsidiary stake (or adds to it) in another entity (or there is a reverse investment) and pays above the proportionate value of the capital and reserves of the entity—that is, assets provided are greater in value than those received—the difference is regarded as purchased goodwill.[3] The reporter should deduct the value of goodwill from retained earnings within capital and reserves. Similarly, if a deposit taker sells a stake in an associate or subsidiary (or there is a disinvestment of a reverse investment) at a value greater than the proportionate value of the capital and reserves—that is, assets received are greater in value than those provided—the difference should be added to retained earnings. If own equity is used to purchase a stake in an associate or subsidiary, then the value of assets, as well as capital and reserves of the purchaser, increases by the value of the proportionate share of the capital and reserves of the associate or subsidiary. Appendix V provides two numerical examples of the treatment of goodwill.

For sector-level data, the market value of other equity investments of deposit takers in deposit takers in the reporting population should be excluded from gross assets and from capital and reserves (narrow measure). Moreover, gains and losses realized or unrealized on investments in equity in other deposit takers in the reporting population should be excluded from the income and expense statement.

[3]This will mean that cash will be reduced by more than the value of the equity stake, thus reducing capital and reserves.

Box 5.2. Flows and Positions in the Non-Deposit-Taking Sectors

Within any financial system there are likely to be financial relationships among institutions in the same sector. This box explains how the *Guide*'s various recommendations regarding the classification of intrasectoral flows and positions in the financial statements of the other (non-deposit-taking) financial sector and the nonfinancial sector fit together. Chapter 11 sets out the information required to meet these recommendations.

Other financial corporations

Compared with the deposit-taking and nonfinancial sectors, there is only a short list of FSIs for the other financial corporations. Thus, the sectoral information set out in Chapter 4 is more limited, and hence so are the sector-level adjustments.

In the domestic consolidated approach, all intragroup flows and positions[1]—including capital and reserves—among resident other financial corporations in the reporting population[2] are eliminated from the sector information. This involves excluding any equity holdings from assets and capital and reserves, as well as excluding all intragroup claims and liabilities.

Moreover, at the sector level all equity holdings in other other financial corporations in the reporting population are eliminated from assets and capital and reserves to avoid double leveraging of capital at the sector level.

Nonfinancial corporation

In the domestic consolidated approach, as with deposit takers and other financial corporations, all intragroup flows and positions[3]—including capital and reserves—among nonfinancial corporations in the reporting population are eliminated from the sector information. This involves excluding any equity holdings from assets and capital and reserves, all intragroup claims and liabilities, and all intragroup income and expense items.

Moreover, at the sector level the balance sheet value of all equity holdings in other nonfinancial corporations in the reporting population is eliminated for assets and for (the narrow measure of) capital and reserves, to avoid double leveraging of capital at the sector level. As with the deposit-taking sector, associate investments (and reverse equity investments) by nonfinancial corporations in other nonfinancial corporations are valued on the basis of the investor's proportionate share of the associate's capital and reserves. In principle, if any increase or decrease in the value of equities held in other nonfinancial corporations is recorded by the investing nonfinancial corporation as a valuation adjustment, and not as a gain or loss in income, such valuation changes should be deducted only from total capital and not from the narrow measure of capital and reserves. All these adjustments to data should be made at the sector level.

Intrasector income and expense items should not affect net income. Thus, intrasectoral dividends payable and the parent's share of an associate's retained earnings (and, similarly, in the case of a reverse equity investment, an associate's share of a parent's retained earnings) should be deducted from other (net) income, with counter-entries in dividends payable and retained earnings. Such adjustments ensure that net income, dividends payable, and retained earnings for the entire sector are not overstated. Moreover, any gains and losses on equity holdings in other nonfinancial corporations and on sales of fixed assets to other nonfinancial corporations included in other (net) income should be excluded. All these adjustments to data should be made at the sector level.

Interest income and expenses are presented in gross terms and, in principle, will add up to zero in net income, and thus no adjustment is required. However, to compile the memorandum series of earnings before interest and tax, data are required on interest receivable from other nonfinancial corporations.

[1]A group in this context is a parent other financial corporation, its other financial corporation branches, and other financial corporation subsidiaries.

[2]The term "reporting population" includes all other resident financial corporations (or resident nonfinancial corporations, depending on the sectoral data being compiled).

[3]A group in this context is a parent nonfinancial corporation, its nonfinancial corporation branches, and nonfinancial corporation subsidiaries.

Annex. Detailed Specification of the Sector-Level Adjustments Required

Deposit Takers

5.51 Table 5.2 illustrates the sector-level adjustments required[22] to aggregate individual deposit-taker data to avoid double counting of capital and income. They are explained in the rest of this annex. The table presents data for three deposit takers (1, 2, and 3) resident in the domestic economy. The income and expense and balance sheet statement data of each deposit taker are presented in the first three columns, and the sector-level data are presented in column 4. Deposit taker 3 is an associate of deposit taker 2. Because of the focus on adjustments, not all lines in the full statement of accounts (as set out in Table 4.1) are separately identified. The text notes

[22]It is likely that the authorities will need to collect additional data series beyond their existing basic data sources to make the sector-level adjustments, and this might involve resource costs. Chapter 11 provides some indication of the series required.

Box 5.3. What Is the Difference Between Data on a Cross-Border and a Domestic Basis?

The *Guide* sets out two broad approaches to consolidation: cross-border consolidation and domestic consolidation. In discussions on the draft *Guide,* the question was raised of how the data produced under these approaches differ, not least in the context of helping compilers to comprehend the principles and implications of these consolidation approaches.

This box outlines a set of cases, starting with the most straightforward and continuing through increasing degrees of complexity, to (1) explain how the data produced by these two consolidation approaches differ in principle, if at all, and (2) indicate the potential net effect on the sector-level data series used to compile FSIs. To illustrate the principles involved, the box focuses only on the differences arising from the consolidation approaches and not on the scope of institutional coverage. Clearly, if the scope of institutional coverage differs—such as domestic-controlled-only as opposed to domestic and foreign controlled together—the data sets will differ. While the box focuses on deposit takers, the principles set out are equally applicable to other corporate sectors.

In broad summary, while cross-border consolidated data do not distinguish among banking activities conducted in the domestic and foreign economies, data for the domestic-consolidated banking sector do not capture risks incurred through foreign branches and subsidiaries, and therefore could give a misleading assessment of the soundness of the sector.

1. Domestic deposit takers do not have foreign branches or deposit-taking subsidiaries or associates[1]

In these circumstances the cross-border consolidated and domestic consolidated data are the same.

2. Domestic deposit takers do not have foreign branches, or deposit-taking subsidiaries, but do have foreign deposit-taking associates

In these circumstances, the cross-border consolidated and domestic consolidated data are the same. For both sets of data, the proportionate value of the foreign associates' capital and profits are included in the sectoral income and balance sheet information. In neither instance are these foreign associates included in the reporting population.

3. Domestic deposit takers have foreign branches

In these circumstances, the cross-border consolidated and domestic consolidated data will differ. On a cross-border consolidated basis—but not on a domestic consolidated basis—foreign branches are included in the reporting population.

On a cross-border consolidated basis, unlike a domestic consolidated basis, with some exceptions, gross income and expense flow data and gross balance sheet and off-balance-sheet exposures of the foreign branches will be included in the sector data. The exceptions are that intrasector flows and positions, other than debt positions and associated interest income flows among unrelated deposit takers, are eliminated during consolidation. Therefore, loans extended by a foreign branch to residents of that foreign country and/or to residents in the economy of the parent will be included on a gross basis in the sector balance sheet, unless the borrower is another deposit taker in the same group.

In contrast, on a domestic consolidated basis, all gross income and expense flows and gross claims and liabilities between foreign branches and domestic deposit takers are included in the sector data. Therefore, lending by a domestic parent to its foreign branch will be included in loans to nonresidents in the sector balance sheet.

How do these differences affect the sector-level data series used to compile FSIs? The effect will differ depending on the nature of activity undertaken by foreign branches, but three indications can be provided:

(i) Unless foreign branches are primarily transacting with their parent, data on gross assets and liabilities will be larger in the cross-border consolidated data than in the domestic consolidated data.

(ii) Unless foreign branches are primarily transacting with other deposit takers in the reporting population, gross income and expenses data will also be larger on a cross-border consolidated basis.

(iii) Profits and capital should be more or less the same in both approaches, as all the profits and any capital of the foreign branches are attributable to the parent.

However, some differences might arise because the sector-level adjustments explained in the text annex to this chapter (see paragraphs 5.53 and 5.79) might vary because of differences in the reporting populations—some adjustments might be needed on a cross-border consolidated basis that are not needed on a domestic consolidated basis.

4. Domestic deposit takers have foreign deposit-taking subsidiaries

In these circumstances, the cross-border consolidated and domestic consolidated data will differ. On the cross-border consolidated basis, but not the domestic consolidated basis, foreign subsidiaries are included in the reporting population.

As with foreign branches, on a cross-border consolidated basis, unlike on a domestic consolidated basis, with some exceptions, gross income and expense flow data and gross on-balance-sheet (and off-balance-sheet) exposures of the foreign subsidiaries will be included within the sector data. The exceptions are that intrasector flows and positions, other than debt positions and associated interest income flows among unrelated deposit takers, are eliminated during consolidation.

In contrast, on a domestic consolidated basis, gross income and expense flows and gross claims and liabilities between the foreign subsidiaries and domestic deposit takers are shown in the sector data.

[1]Subsidiaries and associates are defined in paragraphs 5.7 and 5.8.

Box 5.3 *(concluded)*

The impact of the differences on the sector-level data for foreign deposit-taking subsidiaries is the same as for foreign branches as described in items (i) and (ii) in case 3 above, as well as in (iii) above if the foreign subsidiary is 100 percent owned by the domestic parent. However, if the foreign subsidiary is less than 100 percent owned, the impact is not the same as described for foreign branches in (iii) above.

Where foreign subsidiaries are less than 100 percent owned by the parent, profits (or losses) and capital sector-level data on a cross-border consolidated basis are likely to be higher than on a domestic consolidated basis. This is because on the cross-border consolidated basis the full profits (or losses) and capital of foreign subsidiaries are included in the data, but on a domestic consolidated basis the profits and capital of foreign subsidiaries are to be included on a proportionate ownership basis. Therefore, if the subsidiary is 50 percent owned, "only" 50 percent of profits and capital will be included in the domestic consolidated data. In other words, on a cross-border consolidated basis, the minority investors' proportionate ownership of capital and share of the profits is included in the data, which is not the case on a domestic consolidated basis. There is one exception—if the minority investors are other deposit takers in the domestic consolidated reporting population, then the value of their investment and earnings from it are included in the sector data.[2] As described for foreign branches in (iii) above, some other differences might arise at the sector level because of varying sector-level adjustments caused by the difference in reporting populations.

[2]When domestic deposit takers have foreign deposit-taking subsidiaries, if a minority investor in such a subsidiary is in the reporting population, to avoid double counting of income and capital at the sector level on a cross-border consolidated basis, the value of any investment and any earnings on this investment reported by the minority investor should be excluded from the sector data.

5. Domestic deposit takers have subsidiaries and associates in other sectors[3]

In these circumstances, the cross-border consolidated and domestic consolidated data are the same, with one exception: if the parent's investment in the subsidiary or associate is held through a foreign deposit-taking subsidiary in which there are minority investors (see below).

As subsidiaries in other sectors are not consolidated with the deposit-taking parent, gross income and expense flows and gross claims and liabilities between the subsidiaries and the deposit-taking sector are included in both sets of data, as are the parent's proportionate share of the profits and capital and reserves of the subsidiary. The same principles apply for associates in other sectors. If the subsidiary or associate in the other sector is controlled by a foreign deposit-taking subsidiary of the parent that has minority investors, then the proportionate share of profits and capital recorded in the domestic consolidated data is less than in the cross-border consolidated data to the extent of the minority investors' proportionate share of the profits and capital of the subsidiary or associate in the other sector.[4] The reason for this difference is the same as that described in the last paragraph of case 4 above.

[3]These subsidiaries or associates are not included in the reporting population.

[4]The same difference between cross-border consolidated and domestic consolidated data arises when investments in foreign deposit-taking associates are owned by foreign deposit-taking subsidiaries of the domestic parent that has minority investors.

the adjustments that are also required for the other corporate sectors.

5.52 The relevance of each adjustment will depend on national circumstances. Some adjustments, such as for fees and commissions, might be generally applicable, whereas others, such as for provisions on loans to other deposit takers, may not. Compilers should make a judgment on the costs and benefits of the collection of new data. If available evidence suggests that an adjustment is not relevant or would be insignificant, the benefits of collecting such information may not outweigh the potential costs to reporters and the compiling agency.

Adjustments in the income statement

5.53 For the purposes of compiling data for use in calculating FSIs, up to seven adjustments are required to the income statement to eliminate intrasector transactions and gains and losses from the intrasector claims. These adjustments are described below:

- Provisions for accrued interest on nonperforming loans (and other claims) to other deposit takers;
- Fees and commissions receivable and payable from other deposit takers in the reporting population;
- Dividends receivable and payable from other deposit takers in the reporting population;

Table 5.2. Sector-Wide Data: Consolidating Income and Expense as Well as Balance Sheet Items

	Deposit Taker 1	Deposit Taker 2	Deposit Taker 3	**Sector-Wide Data**
Income and expense				
Gross interest income	600	1,300	400	**2,300**
Less provisions for accrued interest on nonperforming assets	0	150	0	**130**
Of which: On loans to other deposit takers[1]	0	20	0	***Eliminated***
Interest income	600	1,150	400	**2,170**
Interest expense	300	500	200	**1,000**
Net interest income	300	650	200	**1,170**
Noninterest income	250	700	400	**1,213.8**
Fees and commissions receivables	110	300	200	**580**
Of which: From other deposit takers	0	30	0	***Eliminated***
Gains/losses on financial instruments	50	100	100	**245**
Of which: On deposit takers' equities	5	0	0	***Eliminated***
Prorated earnings	0	100	0	**20.8**
Of which: From other deposit takers	0	79.2	0	***Eliminated***
Other income	90	200	100	**368**
Of which: Dividends from deposit takers	7	0	0	***Eliminated***
Other income receivable from other deposit takers	0	0	15	***Eliminated***
Gross income	550	1,350	600	**2,383.8**
Operating expenses	500	600	150	**1,215**
Of which: Fees and commissions payable to other deposit takers	15	0	15	***Eliminated***
Other expenses payable to other deposit takers	0	5	0	***Eliminated***
Provisions (net)	50	80	10	**132**
Of which: Provisions on loans to deposit takers	0	8	0	***Eliminated***
Net income (before extraordinary items and taxes)	0	670	440	**1,036.8**
Income tax	0	272	176	**448**
Net income after tax	0	398	264	**588.8**
Dividends payable	0	300	140	**391**
Of which: To other deposit takers	0	0	49	***Eliminated***
Retained earnings	0	98	124	**197.8**
Balance sheet				
Nonfinancial assets	500	500	300	**1,300**
Financial assets	11,250	17,800	7,300	**36,158**
Loans (excluding specific provisions)	8,850	14,100	5,500	**28,458**
Gross loans	9,250	14,400	5,600	**29,250**
Specific provisions	400	300	100	**792**
Of which: Provisions on loans to deposit takers	0	8	0	***Eliminated***
Shares and other equity	100	300	200	**400**
Of which: Investment in deposit-taking associates	0	180	0	***Eliminated***
Investment in other deposit takers	20	0	0	***Eliminated***
Other financial assets	2,300	3,400	1,600	**7,300**
Total assets	11,750	18,300	7,600	**37,458**
Liabilities	11,000	16,700	7,000	**34,700**
Capital and reserves	750	1,600	600	**2,758**
Total liabilities and capital	11,750	18,300	7,600	**37,458**

[1]Deposit takers covered in this and the other "of which" lines are those only in the reporting population.

- The investing deposit taker's prorated share of the earnings of associate deposit takers also in the reporting population;
- Other income receivable and payable from other deposit takers in the reporting population;
- Gains and losses on deposit takers' ownership of equities of other deposit takers in the reporting population; and
- Provisions on loans to other deposit takers in the reporting population.

5.54 A notable exclusion from the list above is data on intra-deposit-takers' interest income and expense. These data are presented gross because they sum to zero in the net interest income line.

Eliminating provisions for accrued interest on intrasector loans[23]

5.55 The *Guide* recommends that, once a loan is classified as nonperforming, interest cease to accrue. If such a loan is to another deposit taker in the reporting population, an asymmetry of approach will arise in that the debtor deposit taker continues to accrue interest, but the creditor deposit taker is not supposed to do so. Therefore, an adjustment is required to eliminate this asymmetry.

5.56 In Table 5.2, of the 1,300 of gross interest income of deposit taker 2, there are provisions of 150 for accrued interest on nonperforming loans, of which 20 relates to an intrasectoral loan. In calculating the sector-wide total (column 4), 20 of the provision is eliminated so that the sector-wide net interest income is greater than the aggregated amount for deposit takers 1, 2, and 3.

5.57 A similar adjustment is required even if interest income is reported as a single figure excluding accrued interest on nonperforming loans. Moreover, if the debtor deposit taker subsequently paid interest, which the *Guide* recommends be recorded in the provisions line, this payment would need to be eliminated in calculating sector-wide data.

Eliminating intra-deposit-takers' fees and commissions

5.58 While intrasector fees and commissions receivable and payable do not affect sector-level net income—since they net out to zero—four FSIs use either the data series "gross income" or "noninterest expense." Therefore, for these gross data series, the *Guide* recommends the exclusion of intrasector fees and commissions.[24]

5.59 In Table 5.2, of the 300 of fees and commissions receivable by deposit taker 2, 30 is receivable from (payable by) the other two deposit takers in the reporting population. These amounts are intrasector transactions, representing neither income from nor payments to other sectors. Therefore, in calculating the sector-wide total (column 4), 30 is eliminated from fees and commissions receivable and payable.

Eliminating intra-deposit-takers' dividends receivable and payable

5.60 For dividends receivable and payable, these amounts net out to zero in the sector-wide retained earnings. However, as with the adjustments required for fees and commissions, including these amounts on a gross basis affects specific series that are used to calculate FSIs. Most notably, the inclusion of dividends receivable from other deposit takers in the reporting population in other income would double count sector-level gross and net income, because the income is already reflected as part of gross and net income of the deposit taker paying the dividend. Therefore, the *Guide* recommends that intrasector dividends receivable and payable be excluded from the gross amounts in which they are included, that is, from other income (dividends receivable) and from dividends payable.

5.61 In Table 5.2, of the 90 of other income of deposit taker 1, 7 corresponds to dividends receivable from deposit taker 3. This intrasector transaction is eliminated by subtracting 7 from sector-level noninterest income and dividends payable.

5.62 The same sector-level adjustments are required for intrasector dividends payable and receivable in the nonfinancial corporations sector.

Eliminating an investing deposit taker's prorated share of an associate's earnings

5.63 For associate (and reverse) investments, the investor recognizes as revenue (expense) each period its proportionate share of the net income (loss) of the associate. For the same reason as given for dividends

[23] The same approach is adopted for provisions for accrued interest on other intrasector claims.

[24] See also paragraph 4.21.

payable and receivable—to eliminate double counting of income—the value of the earnings of a deposit taker that are attributable to an investing deposit taker also in the reporting population is eliminated.

5.64 In Table 5.2, of the 100 of prorated earnings of deposit taker 2, 79.2 corresponds to the proportionate share of the net income of deposit taker 3 (the associate). Of this amount, 42 corresponds to the proportionate share of dividends payable and 37.2 to the proportionate share of retained earnings. These intrasector transactions are eliminated by subtracting 79.2 from sector-level noninterest income (deposit taker 2's proportionate share) and 42 for dividends payable (deposit taker 3's amount payable), thus reducing retained earnings by 37.2.

5.65 The same sector-level adjustments are required for intrasector associate (and reverse investment) earnings in the nonfinancial corporations sector.

Eliminating deposit takers' intrasector other income

5.66 Other income includes all noninterest income other than trading gains and losses, less those items otherwise identified and for which separate adjustments are made—fees and commissions, dividends receivable, and the prorated share of retained earnings. As four FSIs use either the data series "gross income" or "noninterest expense," for these gross data series the *Guide* recommends the exclusion of intrasector other income.

5.67 As other income receivable and payable among deposit takers does not affect sector-level net income (since these amounts net out to zero), in excluding intrasector other income flows two adjustments are made, one in income and the other in expenses. An exception to this symmetric treatment occurs if the income received is a gain or loss on the sale of a fixed asset. In such instances, the gain or loss is deducted from "other income," but there is no adjustment in expenses because such income does not represent an expense of the purchaser. The same sector-level adjustments are required for the nonfinancial corporations sector.

5.68 In Table 5.2, of the 100 of other income receivable by deposit taker 3, 15 is receivable from (payable by) deposit taker 2. This amount is an intrasector transaction, representing neither income from nor expenses paid to other sectors. Of this amount, 10 is a gain on the sale of a fixed asset to another deposit taker. Therefore, in calculating the sector-wide total (column 4), 15 is eliminated from other income receivable and 5 is deducted from operating expenses payable, thus reducing sector-wide retained earnings by 10.

Eliminating gains and losses on ownership of other deposit takers' shares and other equity

5.69 Gains and losses on deposit takers' ownership of other deposit takers' shares and other equity (other than equity investments related to associates and subsidiaries, and reverse investments) should be eliminated from the sector-level gains and losses on financial instruments data, so that gains and losses from the intrasector claims do not affect sector-level income. Unlike debt securities, in the *Guide* equity assets and liabilities of deposit takers are measured differently on the two sides of the balance sheet. While the deposit-taking owner records gains and losses on the shares and other equity assets based on market prices, there is no corresponding change in the issuer's books. Thus, without the exclusion of gains and losses on holdings of the shares and other equity of other deposit takers in the reporting population, sector-level income would be affected.

5.70 Further, at the sector level, the *Guide* considers that transactions in deposit takers' shares and other equity (both intrasector and intersector) are equity financing transactions—that is, transactions that can increase or decrease capital without having to go through the income account. Therefore, at the sector level it is immaterial which deposit taker sells or purchases shares and other equity vis-à-vis an outside sector; all sales and purchases reflect exchanges of equity for capital resources regardless of whether the transactions involve issuance of own equity or secondary purchases in securities markets. The adjustments required at the sector level are further developed below in the discussion on the balance sheet adjustment for intrasector holdings of shares and other equity.

5.71 In Table 5.2, of the 50 of gains on financial instruments of deposit taker 1, 5 corresponds to a gain arising from the ownership of shares and other equity of deposit taker 3. At the sector level, this gain of 5 is eliminated from noninterest income, thus reducing retained earnings by 5.

5.72 When recorded in other income at the entity level, the same sector-level adjustments are required for the gains and losses on intrasector shares and other equity holdings in the nonfinancial corporations sector.

Eliminating specific provisions on loans to other deposit takers

5.73 Specific provisions on loans to other deposit takers in the reporting population need to be eliminated to avoid double recording of losses. A deposit taker will likely make a provision on its loans to another deposit taker if the net income and capital of the borrower deteriorate sharply. The provision decreases the lending deposit taker's net income as the borrower deposit taker's net income and capital resources decrease on account of the same adverse event. At the sector level, the impact of the adverse event would be counted twice unless the specific provisions on intra-deposit-takers' loans were eliminated.

5.74 Moreover, an asymmetry arises if specific provisions reduce the net amount of loans on the lender's books but a similar reduction in the amount of loan liabilities is not made in the borrower's books.

5.75 In Table 5.2, out of 80 in provisions recorded by deposit taker 2, 8 corresponds to provisions on loans to deposit taker 1. At the sector level, the provision of 8 is eliminated from provisions, thus increasing retained earnings by 8.

Calculating sector-wide retained earnings

5.76 In Table 5.2, sector-wide retained earnings (197.8) are not equal to the sum of the retained earnings data of deposit takers 1, 2, and 3 (222). How is the difference reconciled?

5.77 One difference is the prorated share of deposit taker 2 of the retained earnings of deposit taker 3 (37.2), which is eliminated to avoid double counting of retained earnings at the sector level. A second difference arises from adjustments made to gross income data, which are not mirrored elsewhere in the accounts. These adjustments are on account of the provisions for accrued interest on loans to other deposit takers in the reporting population, the gains and losses on other deposit takers' equity, the gains and losses on the sale of fixed assets to other deposit takers, and the provisions on loans to other deposit takers.

5.78 Therefore, sector-wide retained earnings (197.8) are equal to the aggregate retained earnings of deposit takers 1, 2, and 3 (222), less the prorated share of deposit taker 2 of the retained earnings of deposit taker 3 (37.2), less the gain on equity of deposit taker 1 (5), less the gain of deposit taker 3 on the sale of fixed assets (10), plus the provision of deposit taker 2 for accrued interest (20) and for loan losses (8).

Adjustments in the balance sheet

5.79 For the purposes of compiling data for use in calculating FSIs, three adjustments are required to the sector-level balance sheet data, primarily to avoid the double counting (double leveraging) of capital at the sector level. The adjustments concern

- Investments in associates resident in the economy,
- The market value of shares and other equity investments in other deposit takers in the reporting population, and
- Specific provisions on loans to (and other claims on) other deposit takers.

Eliminating the investor's prorated share of an associate's capital and reserves

5.80 In all measurement systems, a distinction is made when an equity investment reaches a level at which the investor achieves significant influence over management decisions and hence over the use of the capital resources of the entity. As noted earlier (paragraph 5.8), depending on national practice, this level may be 10 percent or 20 percent. Consistent with such a distinction, associate investments (and reverse equity investments) by deposit takers in other deposit takers in the reporting population are valued on the basis of the investor's proportionate share of the associate's capital and reserves (for participation in equity below that level, the investment is recorded at market value). If the associate's capital and reserves and the investor's proportionate share of that capital are both included in sector-wide capital and reserves, there will be double counting of capital at the sector level. To avoid this double counting, the value of the intrasector associate (and reverse) investment is eliminated from assets and capital and reserves.

5.81 In Table 5.2, out of 300 of shares and other equity assets of deposit taker 2, 180 corresponds to an investment in deposit taker 3, which is its associate. This investment is valued according to its prorated share in the capital and reserves of the associate.[25] At the sector level, 180 is eliminated from assets and from capital and reserves.

5.82 The same sector-level adjustments are required for intrasector associate (and reverse) investments in the sector-level consolidation for other financial corporations and nonfinancial corporations sectors, respectively.

Eliminating the market value of the shares and other equity investments in other deposit takers in the reporting population

5.83 The market value of the shares and other equity investments of one deposit taker in another deposit taker in the reporting population (except for investments in associates and subsidiaries) should be eliminated from the sector-level data to avoid double counting (double leveraging) of capital; the counter-adjustment is a reduction in sector-level assets.

5.84 If a deposit taker holds the shares and other equity throughout the period and their value increases (decreases) during the period, this increase (decrease) should be deducted from sector-level earnings (as described in paragraphs 5.69 to 5.72). The end-period market value of the shares and other equity should be deducted from sector-level assets and capital and reserves. The reason is that the increase in value does not represent additional capital resources from outside the sector. If a deposit taker sells to a second deposit taker the shares and other equity of a third deposit taker in the reporting population, any gains and losses made by the first deposit taker since the end of the previous period should be deducted from sector-wide income. Such a sale has no impact on capital and reserves, as the equity "merely" switches ownership within the sector, with any subsequent gains and losses deducted from sector-wide income and the market value of the equity deducted from sector-level assets and capital and reserves. Appendix V provides numerical examples of how to record these transactions and positions.

5.85 In Table 5.2, deposit taker 1 has shares and other equity investments in deposit taker 3 with a market value of 20. This amount is eliminated from sector-level data by deducting it from assets and from capital and reserves.

5.86 The same sector-level adjustments are required for intrasector shares and other equity investments in the sector-level consolidation for other financial corporations and nonfinancial corporations, respectively.

Specific provisions on loans to other deposit takers[26]

5.87 Just as in the adjustments to income, adjustments to the balance sheet are required for specific provisions on loans to other deposit takers to avoid asymmetric recording of losses, which arises if the debtor deposit taker records the full value of the loan outstanding while the creditor deposit taker reduces the value of the loan by the amount of the provision.[27] In Table 5.2, at the sector level, the provision of 8 recorded under loan assets of deposit taker 2 is eliminated, thus decreasing specific provisions and increasing capital and reserves.

5.88 Moreover, while not shown in the table, the outstanding amount of any provisions for accrued interest on nonperforming loans (or other assets) to other deposit takers in the reporting population needs to be added to the value of loans outstanding to avoid asymmetric recording, as the debtor deposit taker is accruing interest but the creditor is not.

Calculating sector-wide capital and reserves

5.89 In Table 5.2, sector-wide capital and reserves (2,758) are not equal to the sum of the capital and reserves data of deposit takers 1, 2, and 3 (2,950). How is the difference reconciled?

5.90 The difference is explained by the three adjustments noted above, each of which affects sector-wide capital and reserves. Therefore, sector-wide capital and reserves (2,758) are equal to the aggregate capital and reserves of deposit takers 1, 2, and 3 (2,950) less the equity investments in associates (180) and in other deposit takers in the reporting population (20) plus the specific provisions (8). While not shown in the table, the adjustment to the value of loans for provisions on accrued interest on

[25]This procedure also applies to the valuation of equity investment in unconsolidated subsidiaries. Any reverse equity investment in a parent by an associate or unconsolidated subsidiary should be similarly recorded in the associate's or subsidiary's balance sheet.

[26]The same approach is adopted for specific provisions on other intrasector claims.

[27]For the same reason, a similar adjustment needs to be made if the creditor deposit taker has written off some of the value of the loan, rather than making a specific provision.

nonperforming loans (or other assets) to other deposit takers in the reporting population, discussed in paragraph 5.88, needs to be made to sector-wide capital and reserves (narrow capital and reserves).

Other

Goodwill

5.91 While adjustments for goodwill should be undertaken at the level of the individual entity rather than at the sector level, the treatment of goodwill when a deposit taker buys an associate or subsidiary stake (or adds to it, or there is a reverse investment) in another deposit taker in the reporting population deserves mention. If the investor pays above the value of the capital and reserves of the associate or subsidiary, then the difference is regarded as purchased goodwill. The value of this goodwill should be eliminated from the investor's capital and reserves (and nonfinancial assets), as it reduces capital available to absorb losses, that is, cash is reduced by more than the value of the equity investment acquired. Similarly, if a deposit taker sells a stake in a deposit-taking associate or subsidiary (or there is a disinvestment of a reverse investment) at a price greater than the proportionate value of the capital and reserves, the difference should be added to the selling deposit taker's capital and reserves, thus ensuring symmetrical treatment to that for goodwill. Income is unaffected by such transactions. The same principles apply for the purchase and sale of other entities by deposit takers, and for the sale and purchase of subsidiaries and associates by other corporate sectors.

PART II

Specification of Financial Soundness Indicators

6. Specification of Financial Soundness Indicators for Deposit Takers

Introduction

6.1 This chapter brings together the concepts and definitions set out in Part I of the *Guide* to explain how FSIs for deposit takers are to be calculated. The next two chapters cover the calculation of FSIs for other sectors and for financial market FSIs, respectively. The final chapter in Part II covers real estate price indices.

Accounting Principles

6.2 To summarize the guidance in Chapters 2 and 3:

- The definition of deposit takers is provided in Chapter 2 (paragraphs 2.4 to 2.12).
- Transactions and positions should be recorded on an **accrual** basis, and only existing actual assets and liabilities should be recognized (paragraphs 3.3 to 3.9).
- The *Guide* prefers **valuation methods** that can provide the most realistic assessment at any time of the value of an instrument or item. Market value is the preferred basis of valuation of transactions, as well as for positions in traded securities. For positions in nontradable instruments, the *Guide* acknowledges that nominal value (supported by appropriate provisioning policies) may provide a more realistic assessment of value than the application of fair value (see paragraphs 3.20 to 3.33).
- **Residence** is defined in terms of where an institutional unit has its center of economic interest (see paragraphs 3.34 to 3.36).
- Transactions and positions in **foreign currency** should be converted into a single unit of account based on the market rate of exchange (see paragraphs 3.44 to 3.48).
- Short-term **maturity** is defined as one year or less (or payable on demand), more than one year is defined as long term (see paragraphs 3.49 to 3.50). **Duration** is also defined (see paragraphs 3.51 to 3.56).

6.3 Except where otherwise noted, these are the concepts to be employed in compiling the underlying series used to calculate FSIs.

Underlying Series

6.4 The underlying series to be used in calculating individual FSIs are defined in Chapter 4. In describing the FSIs below, some brief descriptions of the underlying series are provided, together with cross-references to the more detailed definitions provided in earlier chapters. The sector data should be compiled on a consolidated-based approach as described in Chapter 5; that is, it should encompass both consolidated group reporting and consolidation adjustments at the sector level (Box 5.1).

Calculation of FSIs

6.5 Most FSIs are calculated by comparing two underlying series to produce a ratio, as described below. For each ratio, the calculation should use data with the same periodicity for both the numerator and the denominator—either flows recognized during the period, or end-period or average period positions, depending on the ratio being calculated. The *Guide* considers that for the production of time series, the data for the shortest period available should be used (for example, quarterly data). However, even when higher frequency data are available, annual calculations might also be considered, among other things, to reduce the impact of seasonal factors.[1]

6.6 Given that this is a new field of financial and economic statistics, and experience of compiling and using FSIs at both the national and international level is relatively limited, it is recognized that the definitions underlying available data series for use in calculating FSIs might differ among countries, as well as from the guidance set out in the *Guide*. Any dissemination of such FSI data should be accompanied by metadata so that the basis of calculation is transparent.

[1]See also the discussion in Chapter 11 on availability of data, breaks in series, and seasonal factors.

6.7 The *Guide* discusses the compilation of data on a domestically controlled, cross-border consolidated basis and domestic consolidated basis in Chapter 5 (paragraphs 5.31 and 5.33). However, the compilation of FSIs in accordance with the *Guide* requires data on a domestically controlled, cross-border consolidated basis. Additional possibilities arise—for example, separate ratios could be calculated for all domestically incorporated deposit takers, foreign controlled deposit takers, deposit takers that are commercial banks, and deposit takers that are savings banks. For all FSIs, ratios could be calculated for groupings based on these or other structural disaggregations of the financial sector.[2]

6.8 Depending on the analytical needs of users, the guidance provided in the *Guide* is intended to allow compilers the flexibility to calculate additional FSIs that are not specifically described in this *Guide,* using the concepts and definitions provided for the underlying series.

Financial Soundness Indicators

6.9 There are 12 core and 14 encouraged FSIs for deposit takers. Other than the two interest-rate-based indicators, which are described in Chapter 8, the agreed FSIs are set out in Table 6.1 and described in this chapter. The core FSIs are indicated. For exposition purposes, ***capital-based FSIs*** are presented first, followed by ***asset-based FSIs,*** and then by ***income and expense FSIs.***[3] Numerical examples of how to compile and present these data series are provided in Appendix V.[4]

Table 6.1. Deposit Takers: Financial Soundness Indicators

Capital-based

(i) Regulatory capital to risk-weighted assets (core)
(ii) Regulatory Tier 1 capital to risk-weighted assets (core)
(iii) Capital to assets
(iv) Nonperforming loans net of provisions to capital (core)
(v) Return on equity (net income to average capital [equity]) (core)
(vi) Large exposures to capital
(vii) Net open position in foreign exchange to capital (core)
(viii) Gross asset and liability positions in financial derivatives to capital
(ix) Net open position in equities to capital

Asset-based

(x) Liquid assets to total assets (liquid asset ratio) (core)
(xi) Liquid assets to short-term liabilities (core)
(xii) Customer deposits to total (noninterbank) loans
(xiii) Return on assets (net income to average total assets) (core)
(xiv) Nonperforming loans to total gross loans (core)
(xv) Sectoral distribution of loans to total loans (core)
(xvi) Residential real estate loans to total loans
(xvii) Commercial real estate loans to total loans
(xviii) Geographical distribution of loans to total loans
(xix) Foreign-currency-denominated loans to total loans
(xx) Foreign-currency-denominated liabilities to total liabilities

Income- and expense-based

(xxi) Interest margin to gross income (core)
(xxii) Trading income to total income
(xxiii) Noninterest expenses to gross income (core)
(xxiv) Personnel expenses to noninterest expenses

6.10 During the drafting of, and consultation on, the *Guide,* ideas for further developing or redefining some of the FSIs described below were provided. These ideas are set out in Appendix III as examples of additional ratios that go beyond the agreed list but that nonetheless countries might find of relevance to their own national circumstances.

6.11 Monitoring interest rate risk for the deposit-taking sector is important and, in early drafts of the *Guide,* two FSIs—duration of assets and duration of liabilities—were included for this purpose. However, given that the techniques for monitoring system-wide interest rate risk are still being developed, including by the BCBS,[5] it is premature to include at

[2]Chapter 12 describes a range of possible structural indicators that could be disseminated.

[3]This presentation is also adopted in the dissemination tables in Chapter 12. However, it is recognized that alternative presentations are possible, such as grouping return on equity and return on assets together.

[4]In comments on an earlier draft, some experts proposed that setting benchmarks for specific FSIs might be considered. Countries could then judge their own ratios against these international benchmarks. However, given the limited experience with FSIs at the time of writing, the *Guide* does not provide such benchmarks, nor is the *Guide* considered the appropriate vehicle for presenting such information.

[5]See, for instance, BCBS (2003c). This publication outlines both gap and duration models, as well as hybrid models whereby duration-based weights are used in conjunction with a maturity/repricing schedule.

this point specific indicators of interest rate risk in the list of FSIs to be compiled. Research is continuing on the various possible techniques to assess interest rate risk, including duration and gap analysis, as is described in Appendix VI.

6.12 Unless otherwise stated, all the line references in this section refer to Table 4.1.

Capital-Based FSIs

6.13 Capital is defined in terms of the Tier 1 capital (line 32), total regulatory capital (line 36), and capital and reserves (line 30).

6.14 As noted by the Basel Committee in its Capital Accord, *Tier 1 capital* is a common feature in all countries' banking systems, being the basis on which market and supervisory judgments of capital adequacy are made, and having a crucial bearing on profit margins and on a bank's ability to compete. It is less affected than capital and reserves by period-to-period unrealized valuation changes.

6.15 The data for *capital and reserves* (compiled from balance sheet data) are the residual interests of the owners in the assets of the sector after the deduction of liabilities. These data provide a comprehensive measure of the capital resources available to the sector, not least to absorb losses. For instance, when total capital is employed in the "return on equity" FSI ratio, an insight is provided into the extent to which available capital resources are being put to profitable use, while when total capital is employed in the "nonperforming loans net of provisions to capital" ratio, an indication is provided of the extent to which losses can be absorbed before the sector becomes technically insolvent.

6.16 In the absence of Tier 1 data, *funds contributed by owners and retained earnings* (including those earnings appropriated to reserves) could be identified (paragraph 4.64).

(i) Regulatory capital to risk-weighted assets

6.17 This FSI (as well as the second one) measures the capital adequacy of deposit takers and is based on the definitions used in the Basel Capital Accord. The source should be supervisory data. In the metadata provided, the national treatment in Tier 1 of equity investments in other banks and financial institutions should be described, as under the Basel Capital Accord such investments may be excluded from Tier 1 capital at the discretion of the national authorities.

6.18 This FSI is calculated by (1) aggregating data on regulatory capital for the reporting population, (2) aggregating risk-weighted assets for the reporting population, and (3) dividing (1) by (2). Regulatory capital (line 36) and risk-weighted assets (line 37) are defined using regulatory standards and concepts and do not correspond directly to capital and assets as shown in the financial balance sheet. The concept of regulatory capital is described in paragraphs 4.68 to 4.73 and 4.75, and that of risk-weighted assets in paragraph 4.74.

(ii) Regulatory Tier 1 capital to risk-weighted assets

6.19 This FSI is a narrower measure of the previous FSI and is calculated by (1) aggregating data on Tier 1 regulatory capital for the reporting population, (2) aggregating risk-weighted assets for the reporting population as the denominator, and (3) dividing (1) by (2). The concepts of Tier 1 capital (line 32) and risk-weighted assets (line 37) are defined in paragraphs 4.70 and 4.73, and 4.74, respectively. Tier 1 capital can be considered a core measure of capital (for example, BCBS, 1988, p. 3). As noted above, regulatory capital and risk-weighted assets are defined using regulatory standards and concepts and do not correspond directly to capital and assets shown in financial balance sheets.

(iii) Capital to assets

6.20 This FSI provides an indication of the financial leverage—that is, the extent to which assets are funded by other than own funds—and another measure of capital adequacy of the deposit-taking sector.

6.21 The FSI is calculated by taking capital and reserves as the numerator, in addition to, for cross-border consolidated data, Tier 1 capital. In the absence of Tier 1 data, funds contributed by owners and retained earnings (including those earnings appropriated to reserves) could be used. As for the denominator, total assets (line 14) are all nonfinancial and financial assets. Nonfinancial and financial assets are defined in paragraphs 4.37 and 4.38.

(iv) Nonperforming loans net of provisions to capital

6.22 This FSI is intended to compare the potential impact on capital of NPLs, net of provisions. Provided that there is appropriate recognition of NPLs, this ratio can provide an indication of the capacity of bank capital to withstand NPL-related losses. However, the impact of NPL losses on capital is uncertain in most circumstances, as, for various reasons, the lender might expect to recover some of the potential NPL losses; for example, the borrower might have provided the lender with collateral or other forms of credit risk mitigation.[6]

6.23 The FSI is calculated by taking the value of NPLs (line 42) less the value of specific loan provisions (line 18(ii)) as the numerator, and capital as the denominator. Capital is measured as capital and reserves, and for cross-border consolidated data, also total regulatory capital. NPLs and specific provisions are defined in paragraphs 4.84 and 4.50, respectively.[7]

6.24 It is important to understand how provisions affect both the numerator and denominator. Using balance sheet data as described in Chapter 4, specific provisions are deducted in calculating the numerator, while general provisions are included in the denominator. Therefore, if a general rather than a specific provision is made, both the numerator and the denominator are larger than they otherwise would be. Conversely, both are lower if a specific provision is made rather than a general provision. For regulatory capital, the position is more complicated. Under the present Basel Accord, the outcome is similar to that for the balance sheet data, given that total regulatory capital may include general provisions up to 1.25 percent of risk-weighted assets. However, under the proposed Internal Ratings Based approach in the new Basel Accord,[8] if expected losses are not covered, the denominator might be lower than it otherwise would be because of the "shortfall" in the numerator. Put differently, the ratio would give an ex post rather than an ex ante measure of the extent to which capital is covering expected losses, as measured by the NPL less specific provisions. In such circumstances, the authorities could monitor the extent of underprovisioning and how it affects total regulatory capital (see the memorandum items to Table 4.1 and Appendix III [Table A3.2]).

(v) Return on equity (net income to average capital)

6.25 This FSI is intended to measure deposit takers' efficiency in using their capital. Over time it can also provide information on the sustainability of deposit takers' capital position. The ratio needs to be interpreted in combination with FSIs on capital adequacy, because a high ratio could indicate high profitability and/or low capitalization, and a low ratio could indicate low profitability and/or high capitalization.

6.26 Return on equity is calculated by dividing net income (gross income less gross expenses) by the average value of capital over the same period. At a minimum, the denominator can be calculated by taking the average of the beginning- and end-period positions (for example, at the beginning and the end of the month), but compilers are encouraged to use the most frequent observations available to calculate the average. The preferred definition of net income is that before extraordinary items and taxes (line 8), because this provides an indication of net operating income. But net income after extraordinary items and taxes (line 11) might be used in its stead, or used in addition.[9] Net income and its components are defined in paragraphs 4.17 to 4.36. Capital is measured as capital and reserves and, for cross-border consolidated data, also Tier 1 capital.[10] In the absence of Tier 1 data, funds contributed by owners and retained earnings (including those earnings appropriated to reserves) could be identified.

---

[6]In the terminology of the Basel Capital Accord, the expected recovery given default (ERGD) is unlikely to be zero.

[7]The dissemination of data for this indicator could be supplemented with detailed metadata on national supervisory rules for collateral. Appendix III outlines an additional indicator of NPLs net of specific provisions and net of the value of collateral relative to capital.

[8]See paragraph 4.71 for an explanation of provisioning and expected losses under the revised Basel Capital Accord.

[9]In comments and discussions on the *Guide*, views on which income measure to adopt were more or less equally split, although arguably the pretax measure allows for greater cross-country comparability of data in that it is unaffected by different tax policies.

[10]On a cross-border consolidated basis, some countries may prefer to employ total regulatory capital in calculating the remaining capital-based ratios instead of, or in addition to, Tier 1 capital. The measures employed should be outlined in the metadata accompanying any data release, and it is strongly recommended that a consistent approach be employed by a reporting country over time.

(vi) Large exposures to capital

6.27 This FSI is intended to identify vulnerabilities arising from the concentration of credit risk. *Large exposure* refers to one or more credit exposures to the same individual or group that exceed a certain percentage of regulatory capital, such as 10 percent. This supervisory tool is intended to be applicable at the level of the individual deposit taker. The *Guide* sets out three approaches to monitoring large exposures at the sector level.

6.28 One approach is to report the total number of large exposures of deposit takers that are identified under the national supervisory regime (line 38). For such a measure, information on the distribution of the number of large exposures among deposit takers is particularly relevant to highlight whether large exposures are concentrated in a few or many deposit takers. In any metadata, the national supervisory approach to large exposures should be described.[11]

6.29 Another approach is to assess large exposures in the context of lending to the largest entities in other sectors, such as in the other financial corporations and nonfinancial corporations sectors, as failure of the largest entities in the economy could have systemic consequences. One can estimate the total exposure of the five (or about five) largest deposit takers to the five (or about five) largest resident non-deposit-taking entities by asset size (including all branches and subsidiaries) in both the other financial corporations sector and the nonfinancial corporations sector, together with that to the general government (line 51). This figure is then divided by the capital of the five (or about five) largest deposit takers to produce the FSI. Capital is measured as their capital and reserves, and, for cross-border consolidated data, also their Tier 1 capital. In the absence of Tier 1 data, funds contributed by owners and retained earnings (including those earnings appropriated to reserves) could bc identified.

6.30 In addition, it is important to monitor connected lending, as evidence suggests that with such lending credit standards might be relaxed and a significant leveraging of capital within a group of companies might occur, both of which would increase the vulnerability of the deposit-taking sector. Connected lending can be used as a measure of large exposures. It is calculated by taking total exposures to affiliated entities and other "connected" counterparties (line 52) as a percentage of capital. Capital is measured as capital and reserves, and, for cross-border consolidated data, also Tier 1 capital.[12] In the absence of Tier 1 data, funds contributed by owners and retained earnings (including those earnings appropriated to reserves) could be used.

(vii) Net open position in foreign exchange to capital

6.31 This FSI is intended to identify deposit takers' exposure to exchange rate risk compared with capital. It measures the mismatch (open position) of foreign currency asset and liability positions to assess the potential vulnerability of the deposit-taking sector's capital position to exchange rate movements. Even if the sector as a whole does not have an exposed foreign exchange position, this might not be true for individual deposit takers or groups of deposit takers, and thus peer group or dispersion analysis, as described in Chapter 15, might be used to identify risks affecting key segments of the sector.

6.32 A deposit taker's open position in foreign exchange should be calculated by summing the foreign currency positions as set out below into a single unit of account.[13] As described in paragraph 3.46, foreign currency items are both those payable (receivable) in a currency other than the domestic currency (foreign-currency-denominated) and those payable in domestic currency but with the amounts to be paid linked to a foreign currency (foreign-currency-linked). Foreign currency positions should be converted into the unit of account using the mid-market spot exchange rate as of the reporting date.

6.33 The FSI requires a single net position. Table 6.2 provides a disaggregation of the net position by type

[11]Some supervisors also measure the value of large exposures to total regulatory capital. This measure might be additionally considered, but it does not indicate the extent of large exposures in the sector as a whole.

[12]On a cross-border consolidated basis, some countries may prefer to employ the total regulatory capital in calculating the remaining capital-based ratios instead of, or in addition to, Tier 1 capital. The measures employed should be outlined in the metadata accompanying any data release, and it is strongly recommended that a consistent approach be employed by the country over time.

[13]In the special case where an economy uses as its only legal tender a foreign currency, the net open position could be calculated vis-à-vis the legal tender currency.

Table 6.2. Net Open Position in Foreign Currencies[1]
(Unit of accounts)

Financial Instruments	Foreign Currencies				
	US$	Euro	Japanese yen	Other	Total
1. Financial debt assets					
2. Debt liabilities (−)					
3. **Net position on foreign currency debt instruments (1 + 2)**					
4. Principal of financial derivative contracts in a bought position (+)					
Of which: Options in a bought position					
5. Principal of financial derivative contracts in sold position (−)					
Of which: Options in a sold position					
6. **Net position on foreign currency debt unhedged after derivatives (3 + 4 + 5)**					
7. Equity assets					
8. **Net open position in foreign exchange for on-balance-sheet items (6 + 7)**					
9. Net receipts (+) and payments (−) not yet accrued but fully hedged					
10. Guarantees (and similar instruments) that are certain to be called and likely to be irrecoverable (−)					
11. Other exposures					
12. **Total net open position in foreign exchange (8 + 9 + 10 + 11)**					

[1]This table draws on the work of the Australian Bureau of Statistics (2001).

Notes:

(a) This table covers foreign currency items only. Foreign currency items are those payable (receivable) in a currency other than the domestic currency, including foreign-currency-denominated and foreign-currency-linked instruments, as described in paragraph 3.46.

(b) Amounts to be reported should be converted into the unit of account using the midmarket spot exchange rate as of the reporting date.

(c) Specific other currencies could be identified, such as on the basis of those particularly relevant for the economy and/or those currencies in which the deposit takers are in the most overbought or oversold positions.

(d) Line items 1 and 2: Debt instruments comprise currency and deposits, loans, debt securities, and other liabilities, as defined in paragraph 4.61.

(e) Line items 4 and 5: Financial derivatives include futures, swaps, and options, as defined in paragraph 4.56. The nominal (underlying) value of the contract to buy (positive) or sell (negative) foreign currency should be reported. The nominal amount underlying foreign currency options can be reported, or the "delta"-based equivalent, if available.

(f) Line item 7: Equity assets comprise all instruments and records acknowledging, after the claims of all creditors have been met, claims on the residual value of a corporation, such as shares, stocks, and participations, as defined in paragraph 4.54.

(g) Line item 9: Amounts to be reported are those not yet accrued but expected to be received with reasonable certainty and already fully hedged.

(h) Line item 10: Includes guarantees and credit commitments, as defined in paragraphs 3.14 to 3.17, that are certain to be called.

(i) Line item 11: Depending on local accounting conventions, this includes amounts representing a profit or loss in foreign currencies not included elsewhere in the table.

of exposure and by currency that can be used by compilers. This table allows for the identification of significant exposures to particular currencies and any mismatches across currencies (such as for the U.S. dollar and the euro). It also allows for the compilation of partial information on foreign currency positions, such as the net open position for on-balance-sheet items. For these reasons, the *Guide* encourages the use of the table to present data on the net open position. The component elements of the net position, as set out in Table 6.2, are described below and are based on the approach recommended by the

BCBS (1996, p. 23). In line with BCBS guidance, gold is classified as foreign exchange.[14]

- *The net position in on-balance-sheet foreign currency debt instruments.* All foreign currency debt asset items, less all foreign currency debt liability items, including accrued interest. Debt instruments include currency and deposits, loans, debt securities, and other liabilities, as defined in paragraph 4.61.
- *Net notional positions in financial derivatives.* Foreign currency amounts to be received, less all foreign currency amounts to be paid under forward foreign exchange transactions,[15] including (1) currency futures and the principal on currency swaps not included in the spot position, (2) the notional principal amounts for forward and future contracts where the notional amount is not exchanged, and (3) the notional position in foreign currency options. A more accurate measure of the option position is the delta-equivalent as calculated by multiplying the market value of the underlying notional position by the "delta" of the option, which is the first-order or linear approximation of changes in the value of the option with respect to exchange rates.[16] If these data can be compiled, this measure of the option position is preferred. Given the potential measurement uncertainties surrounding options, a separate identification of options positions is encouraged.[17]
- *Equity assets.* On-balance-sheet holdings of foreign currency equity assets as defined in paragraph 4.54 and 4.55 and including investments in associates and unconsolidated subsidiaries (and reverse equity investments).

6.34 The net position of the three items above comprises the *net open position in foreign exchange for on-balance-sheet items.* The remaining items are off balance sheet and for some reporters might be more difficult to compile. These are as follows:

- Net future foreign currency income and expenses not yet accrued but already fully hedged—this element should be applied on a consistent basis. The *Guide* prefers to limit the expected income and expenses to those falling due in the short term, that is, up to a year, as the reliability of the projections is likely to be diminished further into the future. However, it is understood that the Basel Accord applies no such time restriction.
- Foreign currency guarantees and similar instruments that are certain to be called and are likely to be irrecoverable are a subset of guarantees as defined in paragraphs 3.14 to 3.17.

6.35 Depending on national accounting practice, any remaining items representing gain or loss in foreign currencies should be included under the other exposures item.

6.36 To calculate the overall net open position, the net position for each foreign currency and gold is first converted into a single unit of account (the reporting currency) using the spot rate,[18] and then summed, as shown in Table 6.3.[19]

Table 6.3. Example of Measuring the Net Open Position in Foreign Exchange

Yen	Euro	Pound Sterling	U.S. Dollar	Gold	Net Open Position
+50	+100	+150	−180	−35	+85

[14]BCBS guidance regards gold as a foreign exchange rather than a commodity position because its volatility is more in line with foreign currencies and deposit takers manage it in a similar manner to foreign currencies.

[15]Forward positions should be valued at current spot market exchange rates, as using forward exchange rates would result in the measured positions reflecting current interest rate differentials to some extent. However, deposit takers that base their normal management accounting on net present values are expected to use the net present values of each position (discounted using current interest rates and valued at current spot rates) for measuring their forward currency and gold positions.

[16]For deposit takers with large short positions in foreign currency options, a more accurate second-order approximation such as "gamma" may be required instead of the first-order ("delta") approximation.

[17]According to data published semiannually by the BIS, notional values of foreign currency options are typically around 20 percent of the notional amount of foreign currency over-the-counter foreign currency derivatives.

[18]Where a deposit taker is assessing foreign exchange risk on a cross-border consolidated basis, it may be technically impractical in the case of some marginal operations to include the currency positions of a foreign branch or subsidiary of the deposit taker. In line with BCBS guidance, in such cases the internal limit in each currency may be used as a proxy for the positions.

[19]As under the BCBS's so-called "shorthand method," this approach treats all currencies equally. For calculating regulatory capital charges, the sum for all currencies in net short positions or the sum for all currencies in net long positions, whichever is larger, is used, together with the net position in gold.

6.37 For calculating this FSI, the numerator of the ratio is either the net open position in foreign exchange for on-balance-sheet items (line 49 of Table 4.1) or the total net open position in foreign currency (line 50), depending on the availability of data for all deposit takers. If data are available, the total net open position is preferred. In disseminating data, it should be made clear which measure of the net open position is being employed. Capital is measured as capital and reserves, and, for cross-border consolidated data, also Tier 1 capital. In the absence of data on Tier 1 capital, funds contributed by owners and retained earnings (including those earnings appropriated to reserves) could be identified.

6.38 While a matched currency position will protect a deposit taker against loss from movements in exchange rates, it will not necessarily protect its capital adequacy ratio. If a deposit taker has its capital denominated in its domestic currency and has a portfolio of foreign currency assets and liabilities that is completely matched, its capital/asset ratio will fall if the domestic currency depreciates. By running a short position in the domestic currency, the deposit taker can protect its capital adequacy ratio, even though the position would lead to a loss if the domestic currency were to appreciate.

(viii) Gross asset and liability positions in financial derivatives to capital

6.39 These FSIs are intended to provide an indication of the exposure of deposit takers' financial derivative positions relative to capital. While a net matched position might suggest that the exposure is limited, counterparty risk is particularly relevant in the financial derivatives market, and thus it is important to monitor the magnitude of the gross positions.

6.40 There are two FSIs under this heading. The first is calculated by using the market value of financial derivative assets (line 21) as the numerator, and the second is calculated by using the market value of financial derivative liabilities (line 29) as the numerator. Both FSIs take capital as the denominator. Capital is measured as capital and reserves, and for cross-border consolidated data, also Tier 1 capital. In the absence of data on Tier 1 capital, funds contributed by owners and retained earnings (including those earnings appropriated to reserves) could be used. Financial derivatives are defined in paragraphs 4.56 to 4.58.

(ix) Net open position in equities to capital

6.41 This FSI is intended to identify deposit takers' equity risk exposure compared with capital. Even if the sector as a whole does not have an exposed equity position, this might not be true for individual deposit takers or groups of deposit takers.

6.42 Equity risk exposure is the risk that equity price changes will affect the value of a deposit taker's portfolio and, hence, affect the capital position. It has a specific and a general component: a specific one, which is associated with movements in the price of an individual stock; and a general one, which is related to movements of the stock market as a whole. As this FSI takes data on the net position, the focus is on the general market risk.

6.43 This FSI is calculated by taking deposit takers' open position in equities (line 48) as the numerator and capital as the denominator. The open position should be calculated as the sum of on-balance-sheet holdings of equities and notional positions in equity derivatives. The net position is positive if it is a long position and negative if it is a short position. The positions in the market must be calculated on a market value basis. Own equity issued by the deposit taker is excluded from the calculation, as is equity held in associates and unconsolidated subsidiaries (and reverse equity investments). The approach adopted is based on that recommended by the BCBS (1996, p. 19). Capital is measured as capital and reserves, and for cross-border consolidated data, also Tier 1 capital. In the absence of data on Tier 1 capital, funds contributed by owners and retained earnings (including those earnings appropriated to reserves) could be used.

6.44 Regarding the notional positions of equity derivatives (which some reporters may have difficulties compiling) the following should be kept in mind.

- The notional positions for futures and forward contracts relating to individual equities should in principle be reported using the current market prices for the individual equities.
- Futures relating to stock indices should be reported as the marked-to-market value of the notional underlying equity portfolio.
- Equity swaps are to be treated as two notional positions. For example, an equity swap in which a bank is receiving an amount based on the change in value of one particular equity or stock index and paying an amount on the basis of the change in the

value of a different equity index will be treated as a long position in the former and a short position in the latter. If one side of the swap is interest rate based, only the equity side of the swap should be included in the calculation.

- The market value of the equity positions underlying equity options can be employed. However, as with the foreign exchange options discussed above, a more accurate measure of the option position is the "delta" equivalent as calculated by multiplying the market value of the underlying position by the "delta" of the option, which is the first-order or linear approximation of changes in the value of the option with respect to exchange rates.[20] If these data can be compiled, they are preferred (and any associated metadata provided along with the disseminated information should be clear as to which approach was adopted).[21]

Asset-Based FSIs

(x) Liquid assets to total assets (liquid asset ratio)

6.45 This FSI provides an indication of the liquidity available to meet expected and unexpected demands for cash. As noted in Chapter 4, assessing the extent to which an asset is liquid or not involves judgment, and, particularly for securities, it depends on the liquidity of secondary markets. The latter can be monitored using market-based indicators such as bid-ask spreads and turnover figures.

6.46 This FSI is calculated by using the core measure of liquid assets (line 39) as the numerator and total assets (line 14) as the denominator. This ratio can also be calculated by taking the broad measure of liquid assets (line 40). Liquid assets are defined in paragraphs 4.78 to 4.81, and nonfinancial and financial assets are defined in paragraphs 4.37 and 4.38.

(xi) Liquid assets to short-term liabilities

6.47 This FSI is intended to capture the liquidity mismatch of assets and liabilities, and provides an indication of the extent to which deposit takers could meet a short-term withdrawal of funds without facing liquidity problems.

6.48 This FSI is calculated by taking the core measure of liquid assets (line 39) as the numerator and the short-term liabilities (line 41) as the denominator. This ratio can also be calculated by using the broad measure of liquid assets (line 40) as the numerator. Liquid assets are defined in paragraphs 4.78 to 4.81, and short-term liabilities are defined in paragraph 4.83.[22]

6.49 To complement the agreed FSI, Table 6.4 offers a framework for providing information on the expected cash flows underlying financial derivatives and from the settlement of foreign currency spot positions. Increasingly, such positions are important to deposit takers in their liquidity analysis. The table provides three risk categories of derivative instruments: interest rate based, which trade single-currency interest rate risks; currency based, which involve risk exposures to more than one currency; and other, which are primarily those that trade credit, commodity, and equity risks. If reporters are uncertain as to where to classify multirisk exposure derivatives, they are asked to classify them in the following order of precedence: other, currency based, and single currency interest rate based.[23]

(xii) Customer deposits to total (noninterbank) loans

6.50 This FSI is a measure of liquidity, in that it compares the "stable" deposit base with gross loans (excluding interbank activity). When stable deposits are low relative to loans, there is a greater dependence on more volatile funds to cover the illiquid assets in deposit takers' portfolios. In such circumstances, if liquidity stresses arise, there is a greater risk of illiquidity than if a stable deposit base primarily funds the loans.[24]

6.51 The FSI is calculated by taking customer deposits (line 24(i)) as the numerator and noninter-

[20]For deposit takers with large positions in equity options, a more accurate second-order approximation such as "gamma" may be required instead of the first-order ("delta") approximation.

[21]The BCBS also allows equity options, together with the associated hedged underlying position, to be excluded from the calculation.

[22]"Short term" is defined as one year or less, but the denominator could be calculated for liabilities of three months or less. This possibility is discussed in Appendix III.

[23]This ranking is consistent with that used by the BIS in its surveys of over-the-counter derivative markets.

[24]For example, see the discussion in Dziobek, Hobbs, and Marston (2000).

Table 6.4. Future Cash Flows Arising from Financial Derivative Contracts by Maturity[1]

(In thousands of units of account; as at end of xxxx)

			First Month								Second Month								Third Month				Over 3 Months and up to 12 Months			
			1–15 days				16–31 days				1–15 days				16–31 days											
			US$	Euro	Other	Total	US$	Euro	Other	Total	US$	Euro	Other	Total	US$	Euro	Other	Total	US$	Euro	Other	Total	US$	Euro	Other	Total
Derivatives	Interest-rate-based	Receive																								
		Pay																								
	Foreign-currency-based[2]	Receive																								
		Pay																								
	Other types	Receive																								
		Pay																								
	Subtotal	Receive																								
		Pay																								
Unsettled Spot Transaction		Receive																								
		Pay																								
Total		Receive																								
		Pay																								

[1]Amounts to be recorded are those expected to be paid and received in each of the time bucket columns. All the data in this table should be presented in the same unit of account (such as the domestic currency).

[2]These are derivatives that involve the payment and receipt of foreign currency and those on which payments and receipts are linked to a foreign currency.

bank loans (line 18(i.ii)) as the denominator. Customer deposits are defined in paragraphs 4.42 to 4.44, and loans are defined in paragraphs 4.45 to 4.48.

(xiii) Return on assets (net income to average total assets)

6.52 This FSI is intended to measure deposit takers' efficiency in using their assets. It may be interpreted in combination with the FSI on return on equity described above.

6.53 The return on assets is calculated by dividing net income by the average value of total assets (line 14) over the same period. As a minimum, the denominator can be calculated by taking the average of the beginning- and end-period positions (for example, at the beginning and at the end of the month), but compilers are encouraged to use the most frequent observations available to calculate the average. The preferred definition of net income is net income before extraordinary items and taxes (line 8), which is defined in paragraphs 4.17 to 4.34. However, net income after extraordinary items and taxes (line 11, defined in paragraph 4.35) might be used in its stead, or in addition to it.[25] Total assets (nonfinancial and financial) are defined in paragraphs 4.37 and 4.38.

(xiv) Nonperforming loans to total gross loans

6.54 This FSI is intended to identify problems with asset quality in the loan portfolio. It may be interpreted in combination with the NPLs less specific provisions to capital ratio described above. An increasing ratio may signal deterioration in the quality of the credit portfolio, although this is typically a backward-looking indicator in that NPLs are identified when problems emerge. Appropriate recognition of NPLs is essential for this ratio to be meaningful. The indicator can be viewed side by side with those for the nonfinancial corporate sector, as a deteriorating financial position for nonfinancial corporations in particular might well be mirrored in this ratio.

6.55 This FSI is calculated by taking the value of NPLs as the numerator and the total value of the loan portfolio (including NPLs, and before the deduction of specific loan loss provisions) as the denominator. NPLs (line 42) and loans (18(i)) are defined in paragraphs 4.84 and 4.45 to 4.48, respectively.

[25]See also paragraph 6.26.

(xv) Sectoral distribution of loans to total loans

6.56 This FSI provides information on the distribution of loans (including NPLs, and before the deduction of specific loan loss provisions)[26] to resident sectors and to nonresidents. A large concentration of aggregate credit in a specific resident economic sector or activity may signal an important vulnerability of the deposit-taking sector to the level of activity, prices, and profitability in that sector or activity.

6.57 The numerators and denominator for this FSI are, respectively, lending to each of the institutional sectors (line 18(i.i) and 18(i.ii))[27] and gross loans (line 18(i)). As all sectors are covered, the sum of the sectoral ratios should be unity. The resident sectors are defined primarily in Chapter 2: deposit takers (paragraphs 2.4 to 2.7); central bank (2.13); general government (2.18); other financial corporations (2.14); nonfinancial corporations (2.15);[28] other domestic sectors (households (2.16) and NPISHs (2.17)); and nonresidents (3.35–3.36). Loans are defined in paragraphs 4.45 to 4.48.

(xvi) Residential real estate loans to total loans

6.58 This FSI is intended to identify deposit takers' exposure to the residential real estate sector, with the focus on household borrowers. Experience has shown that in many instances, a real estate boom characterized by a rapid rise in real estate prices has been preceded or accompanied by a boom in banking credit to the private sector, perhaps encouraged by expansionary monetary policies. Following a subsequent tightening of these policies, and/or a collapse in market prices, there have been episodes of financial sector problems—usually debtors having difficulty meeting their payments. Moreover, the fall in the value of the residential real estate collateral, especially if it falls beneath the value of the loans, worsens the situation. To determine the exposure of the deposit-taking sector to the residential real estate market, it is important to have information on the size of the credit exposures secured by residential real

[26]It is recognized that for some countries, data are only available on loans after specific provisions.

[27]When compiling data on the sectoral distribution of loans, lending to nonresident deposit takers (line 18(i.i.ii)) should be excluded from interbank lending and included in lending to nonresidents.

[28]As described more fully in Appendix III, the nonfinancial sector could be disaggregated by type of industry.

estate and to monitor the riskiness of the exposure, by, for example, tracking real estate prices.

6.59 The FSI is calculated by taking residential real estate loans as the numerator (line 43 in Table 4.1) and gross loans (line 18(i)) as the denominator. Residential real estate loans are defined in paragraph 4.88 and loans are defined in paragraphs 4.45 to 4.48.

6.60 Household debt collateralized by real estate can be used as the numerator (line 25 in Table 4.4). While not all real estate lending to households is collateralized by residential real estate, such collateralized debt predominates.

(xvii) Commercial real estate loans to total loans

6.61 This FSI measures banks' exposure to the commercial real estate market. Many of the same considerations described above for residential real estate apply for commercial real estate, although the economic impact of booms and busts in commercial real estate can be different in that the range of borrowers is fewer than for households. On the other hand, the conditions that encourage booms in residential real estate borrowing may also encourage excessive commercial real estate borrowing.

6.62 This FSI is calculated by using as the numerator loans that are collateralized by commercial real estate, loans to construction companies, and loans to companies active in the development of real estate (line 44). The amount of gross loans (line 18(i)) is used as the denominator. Commercial real estate includes buildings, structures, and associated land used by enterprises for retail, wholesale, manufacturing, or other such purposes (paragraph 4.88). Lending to those companies involved in the development of multihousehold dwellings is included in the numerator. Loans are defined in paragraphs 4.45 to 4.48.

(xviii) Geographical distribution of loans to total loans

6.63 This FSI provides information on the geographical distribution of gross loans, by regional grouping of countries. It allows the monitoring of credit risk arising from exposures to a group of countries and can help in an assessment of the impact of adverse events in these countries on the domestic financial system. If lending to any individual country or subregion of a country is particularly significant, further disaggregation—and identification of the country or subregion—is welcome.[29] The geographic distribution of claims is defined in paragraph 3.36. Gross loans (line 18(i)) are defined in paragraphs 4.45 to 4.48. The suggested regional grouping of countries in the dissemination tables in Chapter 12 is based on the approach in the IMF's *World Economic Outlook.*

6.64 For cross-border consolidated data, lending is attributed on the basis of the residence of the domestic reporting entity. So, lending by any foreign branches and/or deposit-taking subsidiaries of the reporting entity to residents of the local economy in which they are located (including any local-currency-denominated lending) is classified as lending to nonresidents and allocated to the appropriate region of the world, while lending to residents of the economy for which the FSI data are being compiled is classified as lending to the domestic economy.

(xix) Foreign-currency-denominated loans to total loans

6.65 This FSI measures the relative size of the foreign currency loans within gross loans. Particularly in countries where domestic lending in foreign currency is permitted, it is important to monitor the ratio of foreign-currency-denominated loans to gross loans for residents because of the increased credit risk associated with the ability of the local borrowers to service their foreign-currency-denominated liabilities, particularly in the context of large devaluations or a lack of foreign currency earnings.[30]

6.66 The FSI is calculated by using the foreign currency and foreign-currency-linked[31] element of gross loans (line 46) to residents and nonresidents as the numerator, and gross loans (line 18(i)) as the denominator. Foreign currency, foreign currency instruments, unit of account, and exchange rate conversion are defined in paragraphs 3.44 to 3.48. Foreign cur-

[29]The BIS collects and publishes international banking statistics on both a locational (residence) and consolidated basis from a group of economies with significant international banking activities. The intention is that the definitions and institutional coverage in the *Guide* be consistent with those of the BIS. For countries meeting BIS data needs, such data serve the purpose of this FSI.

[30]In the special case where an economy uses as its only legal tender a foreign currency, this ratio could be compiled excluding borrowing in, and linked to, this currency.

[31]As with foreign-currency-denominated loans, devaluation of the domestic currency will increase the value, in domestic currency terms, of foreign-currency-linked loans.

rency loans are defined in paragraph 4.90. Total loans are defined in paragraphs 4.45 to 4.48. For cross-border consolidated data, the question of whether a currency is a foreign currency is determined by the residence of the domestic reporting entity.

(xx) Foreign-currency-denominated liabilities to total liabilities

6.67 This FSI measures the relative importance of foreign currency funding within total liabilities. The magnitude of this ratio should be considered together with the value of the previous FSI, foreign-currency-denominated loans to total loans. Extensive foreign currency lending funded by foreign currency borrowing in the same currency can help reduce the deposit takers' foreign exchange exposure (although if the lending is to domestic borrowers and they have difficulty servicing the loans, in practice the deposit taker would remain exposed). But a high reliance on foreign currency borrowing (particularly of short-term maturity) may signal that deposit takers are taking greater risks, by increasing their exposure to exchange rate movements and foreign currency funding reversals.[32]

6.68 The FSI is calculated by using the foreign currency liabilities (line 47) as the numerator and total debt (line 28) plus financial derivative liabilities (line 29) less financial derivative assets (line 21)[33] as the denominator. Foreign currency liabilities are defined in paragraph 4.90. Foreign currency, foreign currency instruments, unit of account, and exchange rate conversion are defined in paragraphs 3.44 to 3.48. Total debt is defined in paragraph 4.61, and financial derivatives are defined in paragraphs 4.56 to 4.58.

Income- and Expense-Based FSIs

(xxi) Interest margin to gross income

6.69 This FSI is a measure of the relative share of net interest earnings—interest earned less interest expenses—within gross income. This ratio may be affected by the deposit takers' capital to asset ratio, as for a given level of assets, higher capital results in lower borrowing needs, thus lowering interest expenses and increasing net interest income.

6.70 This FSI is calculated by using net interest income (line 3) as the numerator and gross income (line 5) as the denominator. Net interest income and its components are defined in paragraphs 4.17 to 4.19, while gross income is defined in paragraph 4.20.

(xxii) Trading income to total income

6.71 This FSI is intended to capture the share of deposit takers' income from financial market activities, including currency trading, and thus help in assessing the sustainability of profitability.

6.72 This FSI is calculated by using gains or losses on financial instruments (line 4(ii)) as the numerator and gross income (line 5) as the denominator. Gains and losses on financial instruments are defined in paragraphs 4.22 to 4.27, and gross income is defined in paragraph 4.20.

(xxiii) Noninterest expenses to gross income

6.73 This FSI measures the size of administrative expenses to gross income (interest margin plus non-interest income).

6.74 The FSI is calculated by using noninterest expenses (line 6) as the numerator and gross income (line 5) as the denominator. Noninterest expenses are defined in paragraph 4.30, and gross income is defined in paragraph 4.20.

(xxiv) Personnel expenses to noninterest expenses

6.75 This FSI measures the incidence of personnel costs in total administrative costs.

6.76 This FSI is calculated by using personnel costs (line 6(i)) as the numerator and noninterest expenses (line 6) (that is, not including provisions) as the denominator. Noninterest expenses and personnel costs are defined in paragraphs 4.30 and 4.31.

[32] In the special case where an economy uses as its only legal tender a foreign currency, this ratio could be compiled excluding borrowing in, and linked to, this currency.

[33] For financial derivative liabilities, it is recommended that the net market value position (liabilities less assets) be included rather than the gross liability position, because of the market practice of creating offsetting contracts and the possibility of forward-type instruments switching between asset and liability positions from one period to the next.

7. Specification of Financial Soundness Indicators for Other Sectors

Introduction

7.1 Drawing on the definitions and concepts set out in Part I of the *Guide,* this chapter explains how FSIs for the other financial corporations sector, the nonfinancial corporations sector, and the household sector are to be calculated.

Calculation of Financial Soundness Indicators

7.2 As with the deposit-taking sector, most FSIs for the other sectors are calculated by comparing two underlying series to produce a ratio. For some FSIs, when one or both of the underlying series can be defined in alternative ways, these alternatives are explained. As described in Chapter 5, data for the other financial and nonfinancial sectors should be compiled on a consolidated-based approach, and data for households ought to be compiled on an aggregate residence basis.

7.3 For the corporate sectors, the *Guide* encourages the calculation of FSIs on a consolidated basis to eliminate double counting of income, assets, and capital of entities in the same group. As with deposit takers, data might be compiled on both a domestically controlled cross-border consolidated basis and a domestic consolidated basis. Given the general paucity of information on the non-deposit-taking corporate sectors in many countries, in the first instance compilers may well focus on developing sectoral balance sheet information on a domestic basis. But where domestically controlled cross-border consolidated data are available (such as provided by annual corporate income statements and balance sheets) and cover a substantial part of the sector, their use in compiling the FSI is encouraged.

Other Financial Corporations

7.4 The list of encouraged indicators includes two indicators for other financial corporations to indicate their relative importance to the domestic economy:

- Other financial corporations' assets to total financial system assets, and
- Other financial corporations' assets to GDP.

7.5 These two indicators are described below. Unless otherwise stated, all the line references in this section refer to Table 4.2. The data to be used to calculate FSIs should be adjusted at the sector level, as described in Box 5.2.

(i) Other financial corporations' assets to total financial system assets

7.6 This FSI measures the relative importance of other financial corporations within the domestic financial system. The indicator is calculated by using financial assets owned by other financial corporations (line 3) as the numerator and total financial system assets as the denominator. The latter is the total of financial assets owned by deposit takers (line 16, Table 4.1), other financial corporations, nonfinancial corporations (line 17, Table 4.3), households (line 11, Table 4.4), general government, and the central bank.[1] Financial assets are defined in paragraph 4.38.

(ii) Other financial corporations' assets to gross domestic product

7.7 This FSI measures the size of the other financial corporations subsector relative to the size of the economy. The indicator is calculated by taking financial assets owned by other financial corporations (line 3)

[1]For completeness, financial assets of NPISH could also be included, but in many instances these might be insignificant relative to total financial assets.

as the numerator and GDP as the denominator. Financial assets are defined in paragraph 4.38, and for this indicator, data are compiled on a domestic consolidated basis only. GDP is an aggregate measure of production in the economy, equal to the sum of the gross value added of all resident institutional units engaged in production.

Nonfinancial Corporations

7.8 There are five FSIs covering the nonfinancial corporations sector:

- Total debt to equity,
- Return on equity,
- Earnings to interest and principal expenses,
- Net foreign exchange exposure to equity, and
- Number of applications for protection from creditors.

7.9 Unless otherwise stated, all the line references in this section refer to Table 4.3. The data to be used to calculate FSIs should be adjusted at the sector level, as described in Box 5.2.

(i) Total debt to equity

7.10 This FSI is a measure of corporate leverage—the extent to which activities are financed through liabilities other than own funds. Given the need to make interest and principal payments on debt, high corporate leverage increases the vulnerability of corporate entities in the event of economic or financial market shocks and may impair their repayment capacity. More generally, the extent of corporate leverage considered together with the volatility of the environment in which corporations operate could be important indicators of the probability of corporate financial distress.

7.11 The FSI is calculated by using debt (line 29) as the numerator and capital and reserves (line 31) as the denominator. Debt is defined in paragraph 4.61, and capital and reserves are defined in paragraph 4.62.

(ii) Return on equity

7.12 This FSI is commonly used to capture nonfinancial corporations' efficiency in using their capital. Over time it can also provide information on the sustainability of nonfinancial corporations' capital position.

7.13 Profitability is a critical determinant of corporate strength, affecting capital growth, the ability to withstand adverse events, and, ultimately, repayment capacity. Sharp declines in corporate sector profitability, for example as a result of economic deceleration, may serve as a leading indicator of financial difficulties. However, account should be taken of cyclical movements in corporate sector profitability and of market structure—that is, industry characteristics, competitive environment, and pricing flexibility.

7.14 The FSI is calculated by using earnings before interest and tax (line 34) as the numerator and the average value of capital and reserves (line 31) over the same period as the denominator. At a minimum, the denominator can be calculated by taking the average of the beginning- and end-period positions (for example, at the beginning and the end of the month), but compilers are encouraged to use the most frequent observations available in calculating the average. EBIT is defined in paragraph 4.116 (and see also 4.100 to 4.104). Capital and reserves are defined in paragraph 4.62.[2]

(iii) Earnings to interest and principal expenses

7.15 This FSI measures nonfinancial corporations' capacity to cover their debt-service payments (interest and principal). It serves as an indicator of the risk that a firm may not be able to make the required payments on its debts.

7.16 This FSI is calculated by using earnings (net income) before interest and tax (line 34) plus interest receivable from other nonfinancial corporations (line 33) as the numerator and debt-service payments (line 35) over the same period as the denominator.[3] EBIT is defined in paragraph 4.116, interest receivable from other nonfinancial corporations is defined in paragraph 4.115, and debt-service payments are defined in paragraph 4.117.

[2] If the market value of equities was used instead, the series might be significantly different, and the information available would be limited to quoted companies.

[3] If the numerator excludes interest receivable from other nonfinancial corporations but debt-service payments include those to other nonfinancial corporations, the denominator and numerator would have different coverage.

(iv) Net foreign exchange exposure to equity

7.17 This FSI measures nonfinancial corporations' exposure to foreign currency risk compared with their capital. The more exposed to foreign currency risk, the more a significant currency depreciation could put severe pressure on the financial soundness of nonfinancial corporations and, in turn, on deposit takers. This applies to both borrowing domestically in foreign currency and borrowing in foreign markets (in foreign currency).

7.18 Nonfinancial corporations' net foreign exchange exposure for on-balance-sheet items (line 36) is the numerator, and capital and reserves (line 31) is the denominator. The open position should be calculated as described for deposit takers in paragraphs 6.32 and 6.33. As with deposit takers, by providing more disaggregated information on the net open position for individual major currencies, the *Guide* encourages the use of Table 6.2 to present data on the net open position. Given the potential difficulty in compiling data on off-balance-sheet foreign currency exposures, the *Guide* encourages at least an initial focus on the corporate net foreign exchange exposure for on-balance-sheet items, but the FSI could also be calculated using total corporate net foreign exchange exposure (line 37) as the numerator.[4]

7.19 Capital and reserves are defined in paragraph 4.62.

(v) Number of applications for protection from creditors

7.20 This FSI is a measure of bankruptcy trends and is influenced by the nature of bankruptcy (and related) legislation and the degree of its implementation. It is a simple numerical addition of those resident nonfinancial corporations that have filed for protection from creditors during the period.

Households

7.21 There are two FSIs for households:

- Household debt to GDP, and
- Household debt service and principal payments to income.

7.22 Unless otherwise stated, all the line references in this section refer to Table 4.4. No sector-level adjustments are required.

(i) Household debt to GDP

7.23 This FSI measures the overall level of household indebtedness (commonly related to consumer loans and mortgages) as a share of GDP. As with the nonfinancial corporation sector, high levels of borrowing increase the vulnerability of households to economic and financial market shocks and may impair their repayment capacity. Given the role of households as consumers, as well as depositors of funds to deposit takers and purchasers of other financial liabilities of the corporate sector, changes in household behavior caused by a high debt burden can have significant impact on both real economic activity and financial market developments.

7.24 This FSI is calculated by using household debt (line 20) as the numerator and GDP as the denominator. Debt is defined in paragraph 4.61. GDP is an aggregate measure of production in the economy, equal to the sum of the gross value added of all resident institutional units engaged in production (plus any taxes, and minus any subsidies, on products not included in the value of their outputs).

(ii) Household debt-service and principal payments to income

7.25 This FSI measures the capacity of households to cover their debt payments (interest and principal). It is also a potentially significant predictor of future consumer spending growth: a high debt-service ratio sustained over several quarters can affect the rate of growth of personal consumption.

7.26 This FSI is calculated by using household debt-service payments (line 24) as the numerator and gross disposable income (line 6) over the same period as the denominator. Household debt-service payments are defined in paragraph 4.122 (see also 4.117), and gross disposable income is defined in paragraph 4.120.

[4]If data are provided on a domestic consolidated basis, but open positions on this basis are "hedged" with positions held by related entities in other countries, additional information on the net open position including the foreign-held "hedges" could be provided.

8. Financial Markets

Introduction

8.1 This chapter covers market-based FSIs required for assessing the health of the financial system. The chapter is divided into two sections: interest rate and securities market indicators. The interest rate FSIs provide information on the interest rates charged by and to deposit takers, thus providing an indication of profitability and competitiveness in the banking sector, along with information on the spread in interbank rates that can provide early indications of credit risk concerns among deposit takers. The securities market FSIs provide information on the liquidity of the securities markets in which deposit takers are active and on which they can partially rely to help manage their liquidity.

Interest Rates

Introduction

8.2 To support the monitoring of the financial health and soundness of deposit takers, the *Guide* encourages the compilation of the following two interest-rate-based FSIs: (1) the spread between reference lending and deposit rates (SLDR), and (2) the spread between the highest and lowest interbank rate (SIR).

8.3 Spreads between lending and deposit rates can serve as indicators of trends in deposit takers' net interest income, and hence of *profitability*. The interest rate spread can also provide information on deposit takers' *pricing behavior*. However, further information would be required to understand the causes of behavior: for instance, wide spreads may arise from high risk due to underdeveloped collateral systems or weak protection by the judicial system, while widening spreads over time might reflect increased risk premiums rather than a lessening of competitive pressures.

8.4 Interest rate spreads, such as those between borrowers with different credit risk profiles, can serve to indicate the level of *perceived risk* within the financial system. Therefore, the spread between the highest and lowest interbank rates would help to capture banks' *own* perception of problems and risks facing banks with access to the interbank market.[1]

Measuring the Spread Between Reference Lending and Deposit Rates

8.5 There is no standard definition of reference or representative rates. To measure the SLDR, the *Guide* recommends at a minimum the calculation of the weighted average of all lending and deposit interest rates on loans and deposits (excluding loans and deposits among deposit takers) during a reference period in the portfolio of resident deposit takers. The interest rate spread could also be calculated on a domestically controlled, cross-border consolidated basis, thus providing an indication of profitability, but it would be reflecting activity in different markets. Using loan and deposit amounts as weights, the spread between the weighted average lending and deposit rates gives the *overall interest spread* (in basis points) between loans and deposits.

8.6 Loans and deposits among deposit takers are excluded because the focus of this FSI is on the profitability of the deposit-taking sector as a whole and on its pricing behavior in intermediating the savings of other sectors. While the *Guide* recommends compilation of an aggregate interest rate spread at a minimum, more disaggregated information on spreads

[1]In discussions on the draft *Guide*, it was suggested that other measures of deposit takers' credit risk could be monitored, including spreads of bank paper over sovereign debt and spreads on subordinated debt. See also Gropp, Vesala, and Vulpes (2002). The credit derivatives market is also a potential source of market information on the credit risk of individual entities. Such measures go beyond the agreed FSIs.

could be compiled as needed, such as for nonfinancial corporations and households.

8.7 A method of calculating the weighted average lending rate is to divide the accrued amount of interest income on loans reported by deposit takers for a given period (numerator) by the average position of loans (denominator) for the same period. The weighted average deposit rate can be computed by dividing interest expense on deposits (numerator) by the average position of deposits (denominator) for the same period.[2] Positions should be averaged using the most frequent observations available.

8.8 In principle, using this method, the weighted average interest rate for a portfolio of n loans (types of deposits) can be constructed as follows:[3]

$$\text{Weighted average interest rate} = \sum_{i=1}^{n} R_i L_i \Bigg/ \left(\sum_{t=0}^{T} S_t \Big/ T \right),$$

where R_i = interest rate for Loan i that is outstanding during the period,[4]
L_i = loan i,
S_t = stock of loans observed at time t, and
T = total number of observations during the period.

8.9 This method of calculation could minimize the reporting burden on deposit takers if data on accrued amounts of interest on loans and deposits are readily available from the accounting systems of deposit takers, as typically data on deposit takers' positions in loans and deposits are regularly reported to central banks in balance sheet reports required for the compilation of monetary statistics.[5] Compilers need to ensure that the numerator and the denominator cover the same set of deposit takers.

8.10 Another method of calculating average weighted interest rates for a given reference period is to use contracted interest rates (that is, price data), using the loan (deposit) amounts as weights. The weights are determined by dividing the outstanding value of each loan (type of deposit) at the end of the period by the outstanding value of all loans (deposits) at the end of the period. Two steps are involved: (1) multiply each weight (which can be derived for each loan separately or for a group of loans with the same contracted interest rate) by the contracted rate for each loan (or group of loans), and (2) sum the results to get the overall weighted interest rate. Thus, an overall average weighted interest rate can be constructed as follows:

$$\sum_{n=1}^{N} \left(rate_n \times \frac{Value\ of\ loan_n}{Total\ value\ of\ loan\ book} \right).$$

Key definitions

8.11 Under accrual accounting, interest costs accrue continuously on debt instruments, thus matching the cost of funds with the provision of funds. The rate at which these costs accrue is known as the interest rate, and for deposits and loans it is typically established by contractual arrangement. Interest rates may be fixed or variable. Charges such as fees that reflect payments for the provision of services should be excluded from the interest rate calculation. For compiling the SLDR, annualized interest rates should be calculated.[6] Loans and deposits are defined in Chapter 4. The reporting population is the deposit-taking sector, as defined in Chapter 2, on a resident basis (although data could also be compiled on a domestically controlled, cross-border consolidated deposit taker basis).

End- and average-period interest rates

8.12 Average-period interest rates are more closely related to profitability and pricing behavior than end-period rates and are not subject to the possibility of exceptional daily fluctuations. However, an SLDR

[2]Islamic instruments that are classified as deposits or loans but do not provide capital certainty or a prefixed positive return should be excluded from the denominator.

[3]For example, if during the period of the first quarter there are end-month observations for December (200), January (100), February (200), and March (300), then S_t is the sum of the four observations (800) and T is the number of observations (4), so the denominator in the equation would be 800/4 = 200.

[4]The amount of accrued interest in the numerator depends on the time over which the associated loans are outstanding. For instance, for a loan that is issued midway through the quarter, the numerator should capture accrued interest over one and one-half months only.

[5]The ideal is to have frequent observations of positions, thus matching the data in the numerator. If less frequent observations of positions are available, then the numerator may capture flows unrelated to the amounts in the denominator. If loans and/or deposits in the denominator are valued at fair value, the implicit interest rate will move in line with changes in market rates.

[6]For instance, to produce an annualized rate, interest rates per quarter should be compounded to the power of four. So, an interest rate of 3 percent per quarter is an annualized rate of 12.55 percent, which is the result of $(1.03)^4$.

based on end-period rates, directly measured, with appropriate metadata, provides reliable information. Such a spread between lending and deposit rates would be calculated as the difference between the weighted averages of end-period interest rates for the different types of loans and the different types of deposits (that is, three-month and six-month). The weights for each type of loan and deposit would be calculated using end-period position data (see paragraph 8.10).

Outstanding and new business

8.13 The *Guide* recommends at a minimum the compilation of an SLDR for outstanding business, as this is directly related to profitability. For the purposes of this FSI, *outstanding business* is the stock of deposits placed with deposit takers and the stock of loans extended by deposit takers, excluding deposits from, and loans to, other resident deposit takers. The stock of loans is measured after specific provisions. The interest rate on outstanding business covers all business that has been agreed in all periods prior to the reference date and is still outstanding.

8.14 To reflect more closely current market developments and deposit takers' pricing behavior, rather than outstanding business, countries could also compile an SLDR for new business, particularly if the necessary data are readily available. *New business* is defined as deposits placed with deposit takers and loans extended by deposit takers during the reference period. New business includes "rolled over" or renewed loans and deposits.[7] Interest rates on new business allow for the monitoring of deposit takers' pricing behavior in response to current financial market developments, such as changes in central bank intervention rates.

Nonperforming loans

8.15 In Chapter 4, the *Guide* recommends that interest should no longer accrue on nonperforming loans resulting in an implicit interest rate of zero. While there might be some analytical benefit in excluding NPLs from the SLDR calculation (see below), the *Guide*'s preferred approach is to include such loans in the calculation. In other words, when compiling the interest rate on loans, positions in NPLs (less specific provisions)[8] should be included in the denominator and zero interest included in the numerator. Excluding such positions would give a misleading—an overstated—indication of profitability, as it would significantly widen the spread.[9] Indeed, movements over time in the SLDR could be analyzed with the help of data on outstanding NPLs.

8.16 However, if NPLs are significant in deposit takers' portfolios, to provide additional information on deposit takers' pricing behavior, another SLDR could be calculated that excludes the position in NPLs from the denominator in the compilation of the loan interest rate.

Lending at prescribed interest rates

8.17 In some economies, a certain amount of lending by deposit takers can be directed to priority sectors at prescribed interest rates for the purpose of economic development. As in the discussion above on NPLs, the *Guide* prefers that such loans and the interest that accrues be included in the calculation of an SLDR, because excluding such business could give a misleading indication of profitability. Nonetheless, if significant, another SLDR could be calculated that excludes such prescribed lending and the average interest rate received. In such circumstances, there may be analytical interest in information on the total amount of such lending.

Subcategorization

8.18 As noted above, while the *Guide* recommends at a minimum the compilation of the SLDR on all outstanding business (excluding among deposit takers), this SLDR could be supplemented with information on various subcategories. This is because the SLDR might change for a variety of factors, such as changes in the composition of business and the introduction of new competition, which are not apparent by considering the overall spread alone. For example, the overall interest rate spread might increase if

[7]That is, an existing contract has reached its maturity, and either party could refuse to renew (roll over) the contract.

[8]Specific provisions have already reduced profits, as well as capital and reserves, and thus are deducted from the denominator (that is, from loans).

[9]An alternative approach, although not the preferred one, is to calculate the interest rate on loans excluding NPLs but disseminate the relative size of NPLs in the total loan portfolio. Any metadata provided with disseminated data should specify whether this is the approach taken.

(1) the sectoral concentration of loans becomes more heavily weighted toward the household sector (consumer loans) at the expense of the corporate sector, and the interest rates offered by deposit takers on consumer loans are tending to be higher than those on corporate loans, or (2) the portfolio of loans becomes more weighted toward longer-term loans, in the context of a normal yield curve. Deposit rates can be similarly affected. Indeed, only limited judgments could be drawn about the factors influencing changes in profitability and/or pricing behavior in the financial system solely from the use of the SLDR for all outstanding business.

8.19 In this context, the SLDR for all outstanding business could be supplemented with SLDRs for

- Both the nonfinancial corporations sector and the household sector;
- Both short-term and long-term (original maturity) interest rates;
- Peer groups, to ascertain the pricing behavior of different subgroups within the total resident deposit takers; or
- Both domestic and foreign currency business.

Frequency of compilation

8.20 The *Guide* recommends quarterly compilation and encourages monthly compilation. It is recognized that the accrued interest data on deposits and loans needed to compile information on average interest rates may often be reported in deposit takers' income and expense statements only on a quarterly basis.

Measuring the Spread Between the Highest and Lowest Interbank Rate

8.21 Interbank rates measure the cost of funds to deposit takers in the domestic interbank market—the cost of borrowing the excess reserves of other deposit takers. The source of these data is usually interbank dealers or brokers.

8.22 Deposit takers may be charged different rates depending on their size or financial strength. An increasing spread between the highest and lowest interbank rates could indicate an increasing risk premium being charged on the deposit taker facing the highest rate—that is, deposit takers would themselves be perceiving an increasing risk of lending within the banking system. This may be limited to the weakest deposit taker or may be more systemic in nature.

8.23 However, there can be limitations with this indicator. For instance, in an economy with government-owned deposit takers, such deposit takers might continue to obtain the best interbank rates even if they are close to being insolvent. Moreover, the framework through which central banks provide liquidity to money markets influences the overall liquidity of these markets as well as the extent to which individual banks under stress are able to maintain access to liquidity. Moreover, a single outlier can change the value of the indicator substantially.[10] The specific techniques used by the central bank for market operations can also affect the spread of interbank rates, for example, the timing of interventions and the instruments used. In addition, a perceived increase in risk might also be reflected in informal limits on the quantities (rather than the price) of funds that a deposit taker could borrow in the interbank market.

8.24 Interbank rates are usually short term in nature. Since this FSI provides information on deposit takers' own perceptions of risks facing other banks, and perceptions can change very quickly, the *Guide* encourages weekly compilation of SIRs, using end-period rates for loans of the same maturity (overnight or weekly).[11] While the agreed FSI is a spread, there might also be analytical interest in the dissemination of the highest and lowest interest rates themselves; for instance, these rates could be compared with others in the financial markets.

Securities Markets

Introduction

8.25 Securities markets can support financial stability by diversifying the channels of financial intermediation and allowing perceived risks to be monitored on a continuous basis. For these reasons, although it goes beyond the agreed FSIs, the *Guide* encourages the compilation of securities market data, including information on the total outstanding value of resident securities market issuance, at a minimum, by sector.

8.26 However, conditions in financial markets may not always be favorable to raising funds through bor-

[10]Thus, it might be analytically useful to also look at the spread excluding the highest and lowest rates.

[11]The credit derivatives market is also a potential source of market information on the credit risk of individual entities.

rowing, and experience has shown the necessity for maintaining prudent levels of liquid assets. Moreover, the liquidity of assets depends on how quickly and with what certainty they can be sold in the market. Therefore, to supplement the core indicator on the liquidity of banks' assets,[12] the *Guide* encourages the compilation of indicators on market *depth* and *tightness.*

Market depth and tightness

8.27 While liquidity is difficult to define, two important dimensions of it are market depth and tightness. *Market depth* relates to the ability of a market to absorb large trade volumes without a significant impact on market prices and can be proxied by the average daily turnover ratio—that is, the ratio of the average daily number of trades to the outstanding stock of securities. A higher turnover ratio typically indicates a more liquid market. *Market tightness* indicates the general cost incurred in a transaction irrespective of market price and is measured by the average bid-ask spread—that is, the difference between prices at which market participants are willing to buy (bid) and sell (ask) assets. Bid-ask spreads tend to be narrower in more liquid and efficient markets.[13]

8.28 Figure 8.1 illustrates the concepts of market depth and market tightness. The demand and supply "curves" to the left and right of the price axis represent the price a seller or buyer faces when trading various numbers of shares. A buyer of shares faces a higher price in the market than a seller of shares. Market tightness is graphically depicted by the vertical distance between the buy and sell price. The horizontal distance between the vertical axis and the demand/supply "curve" represents the depth of the market at a particular price.

Figure 8.1. Market Depth and Tightness

Market Reaction Curve

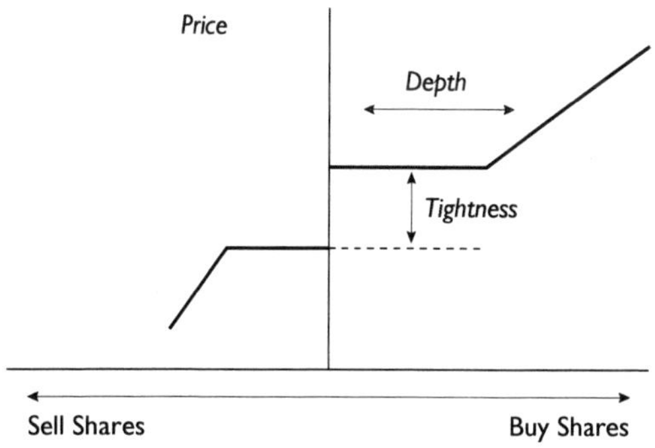

Source: BIS (1999).

Immediacy and resilience

8.29 In addition to market depth and tightness, other important dimensions of market liquidity include immediacy and resiliency.[14] *Immediacy* represents the speed with which orders can be executed and settled, and thus reflects, among other things, the efficiency of trading, clearing, and settlement systems. *Resilience* is the speed with which price fluctuations arising from trades are dissipated or the speed with which imbalances in orders (such as more buy than sell orders, or vice versa) are reversed with new orders. In short, it is a measure of the speed by which "transitory" price movements are corrected. A measure of resilience is described in Appendix III.

Market structure

8.30 Being aware of the institutional microstructure of markets can be important when using liquidity indicators, as different structures can complicate analysis of liquidity indicators across countries, across markets in the same country, and across time.

8.31 Particularly relevant is whether a market is quote or order driven. In a *quote-driven* (dealer) *market,* dealers quote bid and ask prices and may take positions, while in a pure *order-driven* (auction) *market,* potential buyers and sellers submit orders,

[12]To further supplement the analysis of the core indicator, through an analysis of the distribution of option prices, financial derivatives markets can be a source of information on the implied probability distribution of a future asset price—that is, provide an indication of the likelihood that a particular price might be realized. For example, see Bliss and Panigirtzoglou (2002).

[13]Bid-ask spreads may reflect (1) the cost of processing orders, (2) costs arising from asymmetric information among potential transactors, (3) the cost for the dealer of holding the asset (inventory) to meet potential demand (the so-called carrying cost), and (4) oligopolistic market structure. The price volatility of the asset can also be a factor.

[14]See also Sarr and Lybek (2002) for a fuller discussion of market liquidity.

and brokers or an electronic system match them in a central order book. In a quote-driven system, dealers provide immediacy and can even accommodate large orders by holding securities (inventory) to help match temporary imbalances between buyers and sellers. In a pure auction market, liquidity is supplied through limit orders[15]—orders placed with a broker to buy or sell a predetermined number of shares at a specified price or at a better price than the specified price. In practice, many auction markets rely on market makers[16] to supply additional liquidity to the market. Bid-ask spreads and turnover during periods of stress might differ between quote- and order-driven markets.

8.32 Other market structure features that can influence liquidity include the extent of *market transparency,* such as the timing of the disclosure of traded prices and quantities, and the efficiency and cost of *clearing and settlement systems.*[17]

Measuring Market Depth and Tightness

8.33 Indicators of market depth and tightness can be compiled for a wide range of traded financial assets. Because of the link between market-based liquidity indicators and the indicator on deposit takers' liquid assets, turnover ratios and bid-ask spreads should, at a minimum, be compiled for financial instruments included in the wider measure of liquid assets. The natural starting point is to compile indicators for a benchmark domestic government or central bank debt security that is used by the national authorities to influence liquidity conditions in their domestic economy. Depth and tightness indicators for other securities—including equities—may also be useful, particularly if they are within the definition of liquid assets. Similarly, the depth and tightness of the local foreign exchange markets are also relevant if foreign-exchange-denominated securities qualify as liquid assets.

8.34 A breakdown of turnover and bid-ask indicators between on-the-run and off-the-run securities can also be useful in monitoring market liquidity conditions.[18] Empirical evidence suggests that liquidity differentials that typically exist between on-the-run and off-the-run securities may become more acute prior to and during periods of financial stress.[19]

8.35 Major exchanges located in the domestic economy can be used as a source of data for compiling market turnover ratios and bid-ask spreads. Other sources can include dealer associations, central banks, and commercial databases.[20] While high-frequency data on the volume of trades and bid-ask prices are usually available from most exchanges, it is recognized that in some economies data may be infrequently collected centrally, and regularly compiled and consistent data may be limited to certain types of securities.

8.36 To the extent that deposit takers hold securities issued by nonresidents, or hold so-called international securities that are listed on local and overseas exchanges, it is important also to monitor depth and turnover indicators for key foreign financial asset markets, especially if liquidity conditions differ across markets for the same asset.

8.37 Coverage of all market makers may not be necessary to capture trends in turnover ratios and bid-ask spreads, because in highly liquid markets price and size quotes tend to converge across market makers. Nevertheless, market liquidity can vary across assets and over time. The top five market makers, or at least those accounting for a minimum of 75 percent of market turnover, should therefore be covered. Automated electronic market making can also be covered.

8.38 While the transaction price and transaction size might be used to capture realized prices and volumes in the market, bid and ask deals may be undertaken at different times, biasing the resulting "spread." For this reason, quoted bid-ask prices and volume data are preferred.

[15]Limit orders also allow an investor to limit the length of time an order can be outstanding before cancelled.

[16]Market makers are agents that make publicly disclosed quotes for unrelated parties.

[17]Sarr and Lybek (2002, p. 38), provides a list of micro- and macrofactors affecting asset and market liquidity.

[18]On-the-run securities are the most recently issued securities of a given original maturity. All other securities are defined as off the run.

[19]See, for example, Reinhart and Sack (2002) and Furfine and Remolona (2002).

[20]Compilers who approach a commercial database vendor will need to make their own judgments about whether the product being offered meets their needs.

Turnover ratio

8.39 The *Guide* recommends that the turnover ratio for a benchmark domestic government or central bank debt security be calculated as the number of securities traded during a trading period, divided by the average of the number of securities outstanding at the beginning and the end of the trading period:

$$T_t = \frac{N_t}{\left[(S_t + S_{t-1})/2\right]},$$

where N is the number of securities traded during a given period, and S is the number of securities outstanding at the end of a given period.

8.40 The *Guide* encourages the compilation of the turnover ratio on a daily basis or, at a minimum, on a weekly basis.

8.41 While the turnover ratio might also be calculated using the value of securities traded and outstanding in a given period, such a measure could be biased by volatile movements in prices within the period. To gauge market size, information on the total value of securities outstanding on instruments for which turnover data are presented could be collected.

8.42 The number of trades executed during official trading hours of the markets should be captured in the turnover ratio.[21]

8.43 There is a lack of data on foreign exchange market turnover except for the triennial central bank survey of foreign exchange (and derivative market) activity conducted by the BIS.[22] This survey defines foreign exchange turnover as the gross value of all new deals entered into during a given period, both for spot and derivative instruments, measured by the nominal value of the contracts. Information on bid-ask spreads in foreign exchange markets is more readily available.

[21]The increasing prevalence of trading outside official exchange hours, as well as the use of off-hours futures for securities, suggest that there may be an increasing need for supplemental statistics on off-hours trading, especially since liquidity conditions in those markets may differ substantially from conditions during regular trading hours.

[22]The most recent survey collected data on turnover in foreign exchange markets from 48 central banks during 2001 (BIS, 2002). The BIS publication also includes the detailed methodology for the survey.

Bid-ask spread

8.44 The *Guide* is of the view that a natural starting point is the bid-ask spread on a benchmark domestic government or central bank debt security. The simplest measure of the bid-ask spread is the difference between the best (highest) bid and the best (lowest) ask price in the market. Thus, XYZ security with a best bid price of 120.375 and a best ask price of 120.5 has a bid-ask spread of 0.125. It is recommended that both the bid and ask prices be collected. To facilitate comparison of bid-ask spreads across assets of differing value, the *Guide* recommends that bid-ask spreads be expressed as a percentage of the midpoint of the bid and ask price of the asset. For example, ABC security with a bid price of 10.375 and an ask price of 10.5 has a bid-ask spread of 0.125, the same as for XYZ security. But the bid-ask spread for ABC security is larger relative to the value of the security:

- Spread for ABC security as a percentage of midprice = (0.125) / (10.4375)
- = 1.20 percent of midprice.
- Spread for XYZ security as a percentage of midprice = (0.125) / (120.4375)
- = 0.10 percent of midprice.

8.45 More generally, the spread as a percentage of midprice can be calculated as follows:

$$S = \{[AP - BP]/[(AP + BP)/2]\} \times 100,$$

where S is the spread, AP is the ask price, and BP is the bid price.

8.46 For traded debt securities such as bonds and bills, the bid and ask quotes can be in terms of yield rather than in terms of price. In such instances, the *Guide* recommends that the bid and ask yields be separately reported and converted into price terms so that the midpoint and spread in price can be observed. Methods of calculating bid and ask prices from yields can differ depending on the maturity of the instruments and the specific market practices for quoting yields. However, the type of information required for conversion typically includes the par value, the quoted yield, and the maturity (or for longer instruments, the duration) for the instrument. Box 8.1 provides some conversion equations and numerical examples of calculating bid and ask spreads in price terms from yields.

8.47 The number of securities that can be traded at the best bid and best ask price provides an important

Box 8.1. Converting Bid-Ask Spreads from Yield Quotes into Price Terms

For traded debt securities such as bills and bonds, this box provides numerical examples of how to convert bid and offer quotes in yield terms into price terms. These examples are illustrative; national market practices for quoting yields can differ.

Bills

On July 31, 2002, it is assumed that a bill has the following characteristics:

Maturity	Days to Maturity	Bid Yield	Ask Yield
October 26, 2002	86	6.03	6.02

The discount yield on the bill maturing October 26 is 6.03 percent based on the bid price of the bill and 6.02 percent based on the ask price of the bill.[1] If the yields are quoted as *bank discount yields* such that

$$r_{bdy} = \frac{\textit{par value - market price}}{\textit{par value}} \times \frac{360}{n},$$

then rearranging the equation the market price can be computed as follows:[2]

$$\textit{market price} = \textit{par value} \times [1 - r_{bdy} \times (n/360)].$$

Using the bid and ask yields as inputs, and assuming that the par value is $10,000, the bid and ask prices can be derived as follows:

Bid price = $10,000 × {1 – [0.0603 × (86/360)]} = $9,855.95}
Ask price = $10,000 × {1 – [0.0602 × (86/360)]} = $9,856.19}.

The bid-ask spread as a percentage of the midprice can be calculated as (9,856.19 – 9,855.95)/[(9,856.19 + 9,855.95)/2] = 0.002 percent.

If the bid and ask yields on bonds are quoted as *bond equivalent yields* rather than bank discount yields such that

$$r_{bey} = \frac{\textit{par value} - \textit{market price}}{\textit{market price}} \times \frac{365}{n},$$

then the market price can be computed as follows:

$$\textit{market price} = \frac{\textit{par value}}{1 + \left(r_{bey} \times \frac{n}{365}\right)}.$$

[1]The bid price is the price at which a customer can sell the bill to a dealer in the security, whereas the ask price is the price at which the customer can buy a security from a dealer.

[2]The local method used for calculating the bid and ask yield may differ from the discount yield method, for example, the bond equivalent yield might be used; in deriving the bid and ask prices from yields, the formula relevant to local practices should be used.

Using the bid and ask yields as inputs, and assuming that the par value is $10,000, the bid and ask prices can be derived as follows:

Bid price = $10,000/1 + [0.0603 × (86/365)] = 10,000/1.014207
= $9,859.91
Ask price = $10,000/1 + [0.0602 × (86/365)]
= 10,000/1.0141841 = $9,860.14.

The bid-ask spread as a percentage of the midprice is 0.22/9860.03 = 0.002 percent.

Bonds

It is assumed that a bond has the following characteristics:

Coupon	Original Maturity	Remaining Maturity	Par Value	Bid/ Offer
$60 annually	30 years	5 years	$1,000	8.03/7.97

therefore the value of the bond can be written as follows:

$$\textit{price} = \sum_{t=1}^{T} \frac{\textit{coupon}}{(1+r)^t} + \frac{\textit{par value}}{(1+r)^T},$$

or,

$$\textit{price} = \textit{coupon} \times \frac{1}{r}\left(1 - \frac{1}{(1+r)^T}\right) + \textit{par value} \times \frac{1}{(1+r)^T},$$

where T is the number of periods to the maturity, and r is bid/offer interest rate for each period.

Accordingly, the bid and offer prices of the bond in the above example can be derived as follows:

$$\textit{bid price} = 60 \times \frac{1}{0.0803}\left(1 - \frac{1}{(1.0803)^5}\right) + 1,000 \times \frac{1}{(1.0803)^5} = \$919.01$$

$$\textit{ask price} = 60 \times \frac{1}{0.0797}\left(1 - \frac{1}{(1.0797)^5}\right) + 1,000 \times \frac{1}{(1.0797)^5} = \$921.28.$$

The bid-ask spread as a percentage of the midprice is 2.27/920.15 = 0.25 percent.

context for interpreting the bid-ask spread, and the *Guide* encourages the dissemination of this information along with the best bid-ask spread. In particular, any asymmetry in the number of securities that can be bought and sold at the best bid and best ask price should be monitored along with the price quotes. For example, the number of securities that a market maker is willing to sell at 120.5 might be 1,200, while the number of securities that a market maker is willing to buy at 120.375 might be 500, indicating more sell than buy pressure in the market at the quoted price. Sustained over time, such asymmetries convey useful information about the speed and certainty with which deposit takers can dispose of their liquid assets.

8.48 For consistency with the turnover ratio, the bid-ask spread should be compiled on a daily basis or, at a minimum, on a weekly basis. The frequency of price observations can be on a tick-by-tick basis, but preferably at least two quotes per day should be taken (for example at 10:30 a.m. and 2:30 p.m.). If price observations are taken on a less than hourly basis, care is needed to avoid biases related to systematic volatility of intraday price quotes. In particular, empirical work suggests that spreads are typically higher around the opening and the closing of the market, with sharp fluctuations immediately before and after the lunch break. The daily (or weekly) bid-ask spread can be computed as the average of the bid price less ask price observations during the period.

8.49 Beyond the simple measure of the best bid-ask spread described above, there are two additional ways of calculating the bid-ask spread that take into account the quantity of securities that can be traded at the quoted prices.

- A "normalized" version of the simple bid-ask spread can be calculated by taking the difference between bid and ask prices for the same or a similar quantity of securities. For example, suppose that the best sell price for XYZ securities is 120.50 for 1,200 securities. Suppose that on the bid side 1,200 XYZ securities can be sold only in two tranches as follows: 500 at 120.375 and 700 at 120.125. The "normalized" bid-ask spread is 0.271.[23]

[23] 120.50 – {[120.375 × (500/1,200)] + [120.125 × (700/1,200)]} = 0.271

- A weighted average of all bid-ask prices, not just the best in the market, can also be calculated, using the bid-ask size as weights. For example, given the following bid and ask quotes:

Ask quotes Total ask size = 6,700			Bid quotes Total bid size = 2,200		
Size	Percentage	Price	Size	Percentage	Price
1,200	*(18)*	120.50	500	*(23)*	120.375
2,000	*(30)*	120.625	700	*(32)*	120.250
3,500	*(52)*	120.750	1,000	*(45)*	120.125

the weighted average bid-ask spread can be calculated as

$$[(0.18 \times 120.50) + (0.30 \times 120.625) + (0.52 \times 120.750)]$$

$$- [(0.23 \times 120.375) + (0.32 \times 120.250) + (0.45 \times 120.125)]$$

$$= [(21.58 + 36.01 + 63.08) - (27.36 + 38.26 + 54.60)]$$

$$= (120.67 - 120.22)$$

$$= 0.45.$$

More generally, the weighted average bid-ask spread can be calculated as

$$\sum_{n=1}^{N}\left[\left(\frac{AS_n}{TAS} \times AP_n\right) - \left(\frac{BS_n}{TBS} \times BP_n\right)\right],$$

where AP_n and AS_n are, respectively, the nth ask price and nth ask size; BP_n and BS_n are, respectively, the nth bid price and nth bid size; total ask size is given by $TAS = \sum_{n=1}^{N} AS_n$; total bid size is given by $TBS = \sum_{n=1}^{N} BS_n$; and N is the number of observations.

Annex. Structural Indicators for Financial Markets

8.50 In different countries, financial markets are at different stages of development, and this can affect analysis of FSIs, particularly for market-related indicators. While collection systems may not be sufficiently advanced to provide data on activity in the various types of financial markets, it may be beneficial to policymakers and analysts to be provided with some indication of the types of markets that exist and their stage of development.

Table 8.1. Stage of Development in Domestic Financial Markets for a Hypothetical Country

	Overall Evaluation (Entries Are Illustrative)	Comments
Money markets		
Interbank	***	
Treasury bill	**	
Central bank bill	—	
Certificate of deposit	**	
Commercial paper	*	
Bankers' acceptances	*	
Repurchase agreements	**	
Securities markets		
Government bonds	**	
Corporate bonds	*	
Asset-backed securities	*	
Equity	**	
Foreign exchange markets		
Spot	***	
Forward	**	
Swaps	**	
Other derivatives markets		
Futures	*	
Options	*	
Swaps	*	
Other financial markets		
Commodities	—	

***Very important
**Important
*Exists, not important
—Nonexistent

Table 8.2. Example of Data Request During an FSAP[1]

Markets. Describe the number and nature of financial markets (provide copy of pertinent rules and regulations) and list the instruments traded.

Foreign exchange market. Local currency versus U.S. dollar (spot, forwards, and derivatives, if any).

Money market. Provide data for the following:
- — Certificates of deposit with different maturities
- — Repurchase agreements (repos) (including repos for intraday liquidity to support a Real Time Gross Settlement [RTGS] system)
- — Treasury bills with up to one year maturity in local and foreign exchange
- — Central bank bills with up to one year maturity in local and foreign exchange
- — Commercial paper, if any
- — Derivatives, futures, options, forward-rate agreements, and so on

Government securities market. Provide data for the following:
- — Notes (1-, 2-, and 5-year), both benchmarks and off-the-runs, and indexed notes, if available
- — Bonds (10-, 15-, and 30-year), both benchmarks and off-the-runs, and indexed notes, if available
- — Futures and other derivatives, if available

Equities. Provide data for the following:
- — The number of listed companies and total market capitalization
- — Ten most traded equities
- — Derivatives, futures on indexes, and so on

Data. Provide the following data on respective markets for the last three years, if available:

Frequency:	Daily
Price:	Bid and ask prices/interest rates, if available Minimum and maximum prices/interest rates during the day (or period of observation), if relevant Average prices/interest rates, where relevant Closing prices/interest rates, where relevant Market indicators (market index, if available)
Turnover:	Turnover during period (value per day or month) Average number of trades during day
Outstanding value:	Value at market price of pertinent most traded issues Value at market price of total market

[1]Source: Sarr and Lybek (2002).

8.51 For this reason, Table 8.1 can be useful; it also goes beyond the agreed FSIs. The table is intended to provide a summary presentation of the state of development of domestic financial markets, indicating also the extent to which national authorities consider specific markets to be important. Table 8.1 provides a hypothetical example for illustrative purposes. Additional information on whether the market is order- or quote-driven could be added.

8.52 Payment system information is not covered in Table 8.1. However, an example of the type of payment system information that could be made available is provided in the so-called *Red Book* published by the BIS's Committee on Payment and Settlement Systems (BIS, 2003c).[24]

8.53 Table 8.2 provides examples of structural data requested in Financial Sector Assessment Programs (FSAPs) conducted by the IMF and World Bank.

[24]The objective of the *Red Book* is to provide a clear and reasonably comprehensive description of a country's payment systems to a reader who has some familiarity with payment systems in general but who knows little or nothing about the particular arrangements in that country.

9. Real Estate Price Indices

Introduction

9.1 For macroprudential analysis, it is highly desirable to have indices of real estate prices[1] both because deposit takers may have large exposures (both direct and indirect) to real estate and because they may be affected by the potential volatility of price movements. Moreover, real estate assets are a major element of the wealth of the private sector. The direct exposure to risks arising from real-estate-related lending of deposit takers can be monitored through the FSIs related to real estate loans that are described in Chapter 6.

9.2 Deposit takers' exposure to real estate prices can arise because they may

- Own real estate;
- Lend to customers to purchase, construct, or develop real estate;
- Take collateral in the form of real estate;
- Lend to other deposit takers who have real estate exposures or who fund real-estate-related lending;
- Be subject to the risk that real estate loans will be prepaid, which can contribute to balance sheet volatility and asset-liability mismatches;
- Own securities on which the payment of principal and interest is backed by real estate loans;
- Be exposed to the real-estate-related lending exposures of subsidiaries or branches in other economies;
- Be exposed to households and corporations that can be affected by changes in the servicing costs of real-estate-related borrowing and/or price movements in real estate; or
- Be exposed to specific locations (such as tourist facilities or center city offices) that may be subject to more volatile price conditions than in the wider real estate market.

9.3 The reasons why real estate prices are potentially volatile are varied. Real estate markets are illiquid, with sales negotiated with high transactions costs. Supply is inelastic in the short term owing to the time needed to plan projects and complete construction. Development is often subject to many legal or other restrictions, such as a shortage of urban land that can be developed. Under these conditions, the impact of changes in demand on prices is exacerbated. While international capital flows into or out of real estate can rapidly and unpredictably affect market sales and prices, price volatility is also endogenously induced through the provision of domestic credit. During an upswing in real estate prices, real estate may be used as collateral for extensions of credit for further purchases. But once conditions begin to reverse, such exposure can cause the downturns in economic activity, credit, and real estate prices to become mutually reinforcing.

Measuring Real Estate Prices

9.4 Constructing representative real estate price indices is challenging. Difficulties can arise because real estate markets are heterogeneous, both within and across countries, and illiquid. There may be no unambiguous market price. Moreover, such diversity and lack of standardization result in the need to gather a wide range of data to compile indices that are characteristic of the various market segments; this contributes to high data collection costs and may require greater technical sophistication. Representative real estate prices in residential and commercial markets can be hard to measure accurately given the small samples that are often available, as there may be disparate prices for apparently similar properties

[1]In October 2003, a joint IMF/BIS conference was held to explore the relationships between real estate and financial stability, the information needed on real estate, technical aspects of compilation of real estate indicators, and possible avenues for future work. The proceedings of the conference is in BIS and IMF (2005). This chapter reflects some of the discussions at that conference.

and prices may be volatile. Experience has shown that there are particular difficulties in measuring commercial real estate prices across the economy.

9.5 The measurement problem is compounded by the significant differences in price information on real estate transactions, differences that depend on the stage in the transactions process at which the data are collected. It is possible to construct a timeline—which can cover a half-year or more—of the stages in the real estate transactions process:

- Advertisement of the property and its asked price,
- Verbal agreement to purchase at a negotiated price,
- Approval of mortgage financing,
- Agreement on contract,
- Completion of transaction,
- Registration of transaction or deed, and
- Valuation assessment.[2]

9.6 To understand the properties of the price series compiled, it is important to know the stage in the timeline of transactions at which the information is collected. At each stage, different types of coverage, prices, and data sources may be involved. For example, advertised prices available from brokerage firms often exceed the negotiated sales price, which in turn may be different from the amount of the mortgage, as the latter might include fees and exclude cash contributions. Data on advertised prices provide first indications about price trends but are often incomplete and do not reflect actual prices and transactions. Conversely, information provided at the registration of a transaction can be the most complete, as it can also include privately arranged sales, but it may seriously lag behind transactions and turning points in prices. Similarly, mortgage-based information is sometimes highly detailed regarding the characteristics of the property, but it can be proprietary, limited in coverage, or compiled differently by different lenders. The nature of the information derived at different stages of the transaction can also vary depending on the country. Clearly, these differences can affect the analytic uses of the price series compiled.

9.7 Moreover, there is limited international experience in constructing representative real estate price indices. Although compilation of information on real estate prices is a part of the measurement of the national accounts, and such prices are included in many countries' consumer price indices, little attention has been paid to the construction or dissemination of real estate price indices in many countries. Compilation efforts have been constrained by the high cost and technical difficulty involved, the limited demand for such data in the past, and the proprietary control of much of the key detailed data useful for compiling indices. Indeed, in many countries, the compilation and dissemination of real estate indices are undertaken by private corporations or associations involved in the various real estate transactions mentioned above that have good access to data and commercial reasons to compile the indices.

9.8 Given the relative lack of international experience in constructing real estate price indices, the cost of creating real estate price indices, and the diversity of users with needs for different types of real estate information, the *Guide* does not recommend a single set of indices or compilation methods but describes a range of techniques whose application can be based on local needs, conditions, and availability of resources. Nonetheless, the *Guide* does recommend that separate indices be compiled for residential and commercial real estate, because of the very different conditions prevailing in the two markets. To capture changes in real estate price trends, the *Guide* advocates quarterly compilation of data. Metadata describing in detail the content and coverage of, and the conceptual approach underlying, any price index disseminated is essential.

9.9 When developing real estate price indices, the compiler should be aware of the following:

- There is likely to be a wide range of differences among properties. Typically, real estate prices differ widely based on locality, type of real estate, and specific features of each property. It is often difficult to identify a standard real estate unit.
- The mix of transactions by type may vary period by period, complicating the construction of weights to use in indices.
- As noted in paragraphs 9.5 and 9.6, information can differ significantly depending on the stage in the transactions process at which data are collected.
- For subindices in particular, there may be too few observations available within a given period to draw valid statistical conclusions.
- Different approaches may be needed to measure transactions and stocks in real estate. Transactions data, which cover those properties for which transactions are reported in a given period, could be volatile because of the changes in the mix of trans-

[2]This can occur on an ongoing basis.

actions[3] but might provide early signals of price changes. In contrast, stock data can be more representative but cover the large majority of properties for which there are no transactions within the period.

- Real estate exposures of financial institutions may be highly focused and atypical of the broad markets. Moreover, exposures to new real estate ventures may not be well covered by existing statistical data collection systems.

9.10 To the extent that there are a variety of distinct real estate market segments, there may be a demand from users (such as the institutions financing the properties and the regulators of such institutions) for subindices for at least some market segments, in addition to an accurate aggregate index covering the economy. For instance, there may be a demand for subindices that cover large urban centers. Subindices for key types of real estate, combined with information on the most important types of real estate exposures, can help in the analysis of how price changes might affect financial stability conditions within a country. Such analysis can often be useful, provided care is taken to ensure that the price indices used are relevant for the exposures identified. However, as noted above, compiling the necessary information in ways that highlight the specific exposures under investigation may be challenging.

9.11 Finally, real estate price information can be drawn from data used to compile the national accounts, such as balance sheet data on the stock of housing and other real estate, price movements, new construction expenditures, maintenance expenses, and depletion and loss of stock. National statistical offices, which compile sectoral data, could be an important source of information about the condition of the real estate sector and price movements affecting real estate and construction.

Structural Indicators of Real Estate Markets

9.12 To construct real estate price indices that provide a consistent measure of price developments over time, the *Guide* considers it necessary for basic structural information to be collected about the stock of real estate and the factors that affect real estate prices. This involves the preparation of inventories of the stock of residential and commercial properties to provide a baseline for the compilation of price indices. These data could also contribute to the construction of basic statistics on social and economic conditions.

9.13 The inventory could be developed through the use of periodic surveys or censuses of real estate and be updated by information from transactions records or ongoing surveys, or through the use of tax, permit, deed, or other records.[4] For example, transactions records might be obtained from the authority—usually a local or national registry—that is responsible for recording the transfers of property ownership in its locality. When ownership changes hands, these authorities update their records. Related to this can be assessment data used for the determination of any property taxes. While this information may well be updated only infrequently, such records might be detailed to the extent that the level and rate of taxation might vary depending on the characteristics of each property, with the relevant characteristics determined by local circumstances.[5] The availability of transactions data from transactions records held by the local authorities or from real estate agents—that is, entities that bring together buyers and sellers of real estate—could assist in the creation of a price index if such transactions data are available over time for real estate of a similar or common type. Financial institutions active in lending to the real estate market may also be a source of information because they often need detailed descriptions of properties to assess their value for lending purposes, for use as collateral, and/or for any transfer of the mortgage loan to third parties. Valuation assessments are particularly important in the case of commercial property.

9.14 Specifying characteristics (categories) of real estate in any inventory is important. Such categories

[3]Transactions data may be affected by cyclical movements in prices and volumes, as well as by the types of units for which there are transactions. For instance, during periods of price upswings, sales might be more common for higher-priced properties and vice versa in downswings.

[4]One possibility is to undertake a household survey, although obtaining adequate responses from households can be difficult. Such a survey could be incorporated into a broader survey of household income, expenditure, assets, and liabilities that would also support the compilation of other FSIs, and macroeconomic statistics more generally.

[5]These and other data sources are discussed in Pollakowski (1995).

should be sufficiently disaggregated to be able to identify the key features of the real estate that affect its value, but the degree of detail captured will also vary according to needs and resources. The specific categories that are important to determining prices will vary among economies and so should be identified by national authorities, based on local conditions. Set out below are some of the key characteristics that might be captured in such an inventory:

- **Number of units, by major type of unit.** For residential real estate, a unit might be a single-owner dwelling, and the type might be a detached or semidetached town house or apartment.
- **Location.** The address and perhaps neighborhood, census tract, or administrative district.
- **Purpose.** The use of the real estate unit, such as dwelling, shop or retail outlet, factory, or government offices.
- **Type of construction.** Concrete, wood, thatch, and so on.
- **Age of unit.** The number of years since construction or major renovation.
- **Size.** The number of square meters or square feet of the structure and lot.
- **Number of rooms.** The total number of rooms, with possible itemization of specific types of rooms, such as bedrooms or bathrooms.
- **Utilities and amenities.** Whether the property has a water supply connection, sewerage connection, electricity, or other relevant amenity.
- **Physical condition.** Interior and exterior maintenance, evidence of damage, and similar issues.
- **Last sales date and value, current market value,** and **tax valuation.**
- **Vacant units.** Whether the real estate is in use.
- **Tenure.** The status of the occupant, that is, owner-occupied (freehold or leasehold), private rental, or public sector rental.
- **Rental information.** The amounts paid to rent the real estate, in total or in terms of the cost per unit of space, such as per square meter.
- **Building permits, completions, or other measures of current activity.**

9.15 With the above information, data can be compiled on the turnover in, the key structural features of, and the general conditions in the real estate market, which help supplement real estate price information when undertaking financial sector stability analysis.[6] For example, the following basic data, preferably disaggregated between residential and commercial property by city or other geographic location, could be compiled from the information set out in paragraph 9.14:

- Total stock of units and the change in the stock;
- Occupancy rate and vacancy rate;
- Total number of transactions, annually or quarterly; and
- Average rent per residential unit or per unit of business space (such as square meter).

Constructing Real Estate Price Measures

Average (Unit Value) Prices

9.16 An average sales price statistic in each reporting period can be calculated by dividing the sum of sales prices by the number of units for which there were transactions during the period. Unit value indices are probably the most widely available price measures for real estate, in the form of average sales data or average tax assessment data, and sometimes provide useful information about large changes in prices, especially if disaggregated into more homogeneous subindices.[7]

9.17 Such a unit value index is, however, not a true price index. It can be seriously biased by a few transactions with extreme values, changes in the mix of transactions, or changes in the quality of the units being transacted. For example, unit value indices make no adjustment for quality improvements over time and therefore suffer from an upward bias over time. Although broadly useful as a snapshot of overall real estate prices, unit value indices often are less useful than price indices that adjust for changes in the mix of characteristics of properties.

Median and Mode Prices

9.18 To compensate for the biases affecting average prices, some indices are based on median price (the

[6]The inventory of real estate market conditions described here does not provide a complete picture of the financial sector stability implications of real estate, which would also include compilation of data on financial institutions' exposures and the financial conditions of occupants and purchasers.

[7]For instance, subindices for standard two-bedroom apartments in different cities could be compiled, as such types of apartments are usually common.

middle value from among all values in the panel) or mode (the most commonly experienced price). These measures may be useful for specialized purposes, but both methods suffer from the exclusion of significant information.

Price Indices

9.19 Price indices are composite measures that quantify the value of a set of prices for a variety of items. Price indices can be compiled either by standard formulas or regression techniques that estimate the value of a composite or standard unit of real estate.[8] A price index can remove the effects of changes in the composition of transactions or of changes in quality, to arrive at a more accurate measure of prices for comparable units of real estate. Price indices are pure numbers describing a change from a benchmark unit of value (usually 100) in a base period and, as such, can be compared among economies with different types of real estate.

Laspeyres real estate indices

9.20 A Laspeyres price index for real estate calculates the weighted average change in prices over a period for a fixed basket of real estate drawn from some base period. It compares the total cost of purchasing a specific quantity and mix of real estate in the base period with the total cost of purchasing the same quantity and mix in other periods. An index of these costs is then constructed. The intention is to calculate a price index for the outstanding stock of real estate using information from transactions over a period and/or from appraised values of real estate.

9.21 For example, using the information in Table 9.1:

(i) The total cost of purchasing types A, B, and C properties in the base period was (160)(50) + (30)(70) + (10)(100) = 11,100.

(ii) At prices prevailing in the current period, the total cost of purchasing the base period quantities is (160)(60) + (30)(90) + (10)(110) = 13,400.

Table 9.1. Quantities and Prices of Real Estate

Type of Property K_i	Base Period Quantity q_0	Base Period Price p_o	Current Period Price p_t
A ($i = 1$)	160	50	60
B ($i = 2$)	30	70	90
C ($i = 3$)	10	100	110

(iii) The Laspeyres index for the current period is therefore 100(13,400/11,000) = 121.8. This means that prices in the current period are 21.8 percent higher than in the base period.

9.22 Generalizing, the Laspeyres index can be specified as

$$L = \left(\frac{\sum_{i=1}^{K} q_{oi} p_{ti}}{\sum_{i=1}^{K} q_{oi} p_{oi}} \right) \times 100,$$

where

K = the number of property types;
q_{oi} = the quantity of property type i in the base period;
p_{oi} = the price of property type i in the base period; and
p_{ti} = the price of property type i in the current period.

9.23 The following data are needed for calculating a Laspeyres real estate index: (1) the stock of real estate by type in the base period, and (2) the price by type of real estate in the current period relative to the base period price. Ideally, a census of real estate is taken to establish the stock and price for each type of real estate in the base period. Each real estate type i in the base period should be defined to be some common real estate type meaningful for the particular economy (such as two-bedroom apartment, or center-city street-level retail space between 80 and 100 square meters). The index itself is a pure numeric scalar that can be compared between economies without having to directly compare the types of real estate in each economy.

9.24 A Laspeyres index is well suited for constructing broad measures of prices, such as national indices

[8]A standard unit of real estate, separately identified for residential and commercial, is a construct that attempts to take account of all the specific factors that might affect the price of real estate. This construct is associated with hedonic methods of calculating real estate price indices, described below.

of house prices or national accounts estimates of imputed rent for owner-occupied residences.[9] It can also be used for targeted measures of prices, such as housing in the capital city. Problems in Laspeyres indices can arise to the extent that they do not reflect the current mix of transactions, may not capture information on sectors where a standard unit of real estate cannot be defined, and do not adequately capture information on rapidly developing sectors.

Hedonic or quality-adjusted regression price indices

9.25 Hedonic regressions derive the price series for a standard real estate unit by using econometric regressions to remove the influence of specific quality factors that affect actual sales prices. The factors typically include the age of the unit, size, number of rooms, physical location, and facilities such as running water or toilets. The relevant factors differ by country. The use of hedonic regressions is a more advanced approach to calculating real estate price indices. However, this approach requires detailed data on the characteristics of each property and may be challenging to apply.

9.26 In view of the complexity of the defining characteristics of real estate properties, and particularly the effect of the age of structures on prices, hedonic regressions—updated at reasonably frequent intervals—are often used to estimate the evolution of real estate prices. Hedonic models were first defined in the work of Griliches in the 1960s.[10,11] An advantage of hedonic regressions is that they can utilize data from virtually all transactions without having to undertake a base period census. Another advantage is that a variance (disturbance term) not explained by the econometric model is generated, which gives an idea of the dispersion of prices and period-to-period variation after controlling for the mix in property characteristics.[12]

[9]See *1993 SNA*, paragraphs 6.29 and 6.89.

[10]See Griliches (1964).

[11]An example is provided in Case and Szymanoski (1995).

[12]Hedonic estimates can be used in Laspeyres indices. For example, the U.S. Bureau of the Census used this approach for single-family houses until 1996, fixing the house characteristics over the period of the index. Subsequently, indices were constructed that allowed for changes over time in house characteristics as preferences changed.

Liquidity-adjusted price indices

9.27 Liquidity-adjusted price indices adjust price measures to separately account for the influence of changes in the volume of transactions on prices. Market liquidity refers to the speed at which real estate transactions take place, which is a reflection of the relative strength of market demand for real estate relative to supply. Prices are often positively correlated with liquidity, rising during periods of fast turnover, and falling during slowdowns. By factoring in information on the volume of transactions during a given period, it is possible to estimate the separate price effect due to changes in the transactions volume and thus derive a measure of the underlying price movements as if there were no changes in the volume of transactions.

Commercial real estate indices

9.28 The principles described above apply to residential and commercial real estate, but there are some special features of commercial real estate that can either complicate or ease the task of compilation of price indices.

9.29 A complicating factor is the great diversity of types of commercial real estate, which may be highly specialized to serve of the specific business of the occupant. Such specialization means that property price may be closely linked to the success of the occupant's business, or to the need for potential purchasers to make substantial investments in a property to customize it to their needs. Moreover, the number of transactions may be much smaller than in the case of residential transactions, which means that both the mix of transactions and the value of transactions may be quite volatile across reporting periods. Another complicating factor is that statistical reporting systems often do not effectively pick up the relatively small number of commercial transactions—as they may involve privately negotiated sales—and the changing patterns of new construction. Moreover, experience suggests that commercial real estate indices tend to be based on localities, such as big cities, where there are specific concentrations of properties available commercially.

9.30 Facilitating the process of compiling price indices for commercial real estate is the fact that commercial real estate can be characterized as a commodity consisting of square footage or square meters of commercial space for which rental or use values can be estimated. The stock, new construction, rental rates, and vacancy and occupancy rates can all be measured in terms of space. For example, rental rates are often expressed in terms of the annual cost per unit of space, most commonly per square meter. Such measures can also be used for purposes of international comparison of rental costs. Importantly, commercial real estate brokers and lenders often collect current and detailed information on prices, turnover, and demand and supply, all of which can be useful in compiling commercial real estate price indices. Agents and lenders in some countries already compile such indices.

PART III

Compilation and Dissemination of Financial Soundness Indicators

10. Strategic and Managerial Issues

Introduction

10.1 Because of the wide range of data sources that should be drawn on, compiling the full range of FSI data described in this *Guide* is a complex task. Moreover, for many countries such compilation is a new endeavor. In this context, Chapters 10 and 11 aim to help provide a road map for developing FSI data. This chapter covers the strategic and managerial issues that need addressing, while practical data compilation issues are addressed in the next chapter. For countries with an established system of compiling and disseminating FSI data, the need to draw on this chapter in particular may be limited.

Strategic Issues

10.2 Set out below are some of the strategic issues that should be addressed when considering the compilation of FSI data.

Which Agency or Agencies Should Be Responsible for Compiling and Disseminating FSI Data?

10.3 Given the range of data sources that potentially should be drawn on, it is most unlikely that all are available in one agency, and so the job of compiling FSI data will involve more than one agency. Nonetheless, because of the importance of this body of statistics in its own right, and to ensure that there are clear lines of responsibility and accountability, the *Guide* recommends that one agency should be given the primary responsibility for calculating and then disseminating FSIs—the lead agency.[1] The *Guide* does not suggest which agency should be responsible for calculating and disseminating FSIs. National authorities could assign responsibility through a statistical law or other statutory provision, interagency protocols, executive decrees, and so on.

Should a Specific Unit Be Responsible for FSI Data? In Which Department Should It Be Located?

10.4 Once a lead agency has been determined, an additional issue is whether there should be a unit in the lead agency that focuses specifically on the FSI data set, or whether an existing unit should add this task to its work.

10.5 The *Guide* sees benefit in establishing a separate unit because of

- The wide range of data that needs to be handled;
- The need to develop specialist FSI knowledge; and
- The possible pattern of workload peaks: if there is synchronization of peak workloads—the decisions relating to the timing of data release addressed below are relevant in this regard—it may not be possible to add FSI work to the workload of an existing unit.

10.6 If resource constraints dictate that FSI work is to be absorbed into the existing structure, the above points might be considered during the integration process.

10.7 If a decision is made to have a separate unit, in which department should it be located? Again, given the central role of deposit takers' data in the FSI data set, the location of related statistical work on deposit takers should be an important factor in any decision.

What Is the Appropriate Approach to Disseminating Data?

10.8 Decisions relating to the dissemination of data have important implications for a number of the compilation issues mentioned above, because publication deadlines help focus the work processes,

[1]This recommendation does not cover responsibility for the analysis and interpretation of FSI data, which is a separate matter.

which in turn affect resource allocation decisions. An important decision with regard to dissemination concerns periodicity. Also significant are decisions on the range of data to be disseminated, the timeliness of release, and the format of release.

10.9 Owing to the nature of FSIs and their importance for decision making, countries might consider working toward disseminating at least a core FSI data set on a quarterly basis. Release of some key financial market data on a monthly basis could be considered. Chapter 12 discusses in more detail a framework for disseminating FSIs and the periodicity of release. As for the timeliness of release, given the range of data required to compile FSIs, an appropriate release date could be within one quarter after the reference date.

10.10 Regarding the format for the release of data, the *Guide* encourages dissemination on a single centralized website, allowing simultaneous release to all users, general accessibility of the data, and transparency.[2] Nonetheless, careful consideration should be given to the provision of additional information when FSI data are released, given the broad range of source data used in their construction and the complexity of the information they encapsulate. Text commentary on the main trends in the FSI data series could aid interpretation, and detailed metadata would support understanding of the data. Moreover, some countries produce regular publications that include articles and data on financial stability issues, and this can be useful in putting the disseminated FSIs in perspective or in providing extended discussions of relevant methodological issues. Regular statistical publications can also be vehicles for the dissemination of FSI data as well as complementary information.

10.11 General guidance on dissemination practices found in the IMF's Special Data Dissemination Standard (SDDS) and General Data Dissemination System (GDDS) include an emphasis on integrity and the need to avoid nonstatistical interference with the data.

[2]At the June 2003 meeting of the IMF Executive Board to discuss FSIs, as a medium-term objective most Directors supported consideration of the establishment of a Fund Internet gateway to provide a single entry point for accessing FSIs disseminated by IMF member countries.

What Source Data Are Available?

10.12 One of the first tasks in developing systems for compiling FSIs is the identification of available source data. When compared with the information needed to compile FSIs, this inventory of available information will inform decisions on (1) resource needs, (2) the allocation of work across agencies, and (3) the development of work programs. Producing a comprehensive list of existing data will entail close coordination among potential compiling agencies. More generally, it is essential that sources and methods be well documented for use when problems arise, for ensuring continuity of process when there is staff turnover or absence, and to support the development of metadata.

10.13 A related issue is the extent of coverage of entities that fall within the definition of the sector (or subsector). In many instances, a sample of the entities in the sector is surveyed, and the reported data are "grossed up" to estimate data for the entire sector. The coverage of the survey tends to be more comprehensive for the largest entities in the sector. However, especially in the case of the deposit-taking sector, while detection of vulnerabilities in large institutions is important, experience has shown that weaknesses in smaller institutions can also have a disproportionate impact on the health and soundness of the financial system. Clearly, the broader the coverage of institutions, the more resource intensive the work.

Are There Adequate Resources to Compile the Necessary Data?

10.14 National authorities are responsible for the allocation of resources for the compilation of FSIs. They are encouraged to provide at least adequate resources to perform the key tasks for the compilation of the core set of FSIs. These include the identification and assessment of source data and the compilation of the core FSIs. Moreover, authorities should strive to develop and retain over time a core contingent of qualified staff that is knowledgeable in statistical and financial soundness concepts and compilation methods. The allocation of resources among agencies may need to be reconsidered, depending on the function of the lead agency with regard to gathering and calculating FSIs and related data. There may also be costs associated with computer hardware and software that will need to be considered.

10.15 In determining resource allocation, account should be taken of any needed improvements in data. Decisions may need to be made on whether to adapt existing report forms and questionnaires and/or develop new surveys. In setting priorities for improvements, the costs and benefits of existing or new data sources should be considered. As noted in the managerial section ahead, after the initial development work is completed and data are being disseminated, a more detailed development work program can be produced in consultation with other agencies involved in the work.

How Should Agencies Coordinate?

10.16 Regardless of how the statistics are to be collected and compiled, the process will be resource intensive, especially in the initial phase of establishing sources and methods for building an FSI database, and cooperation and coordination among agencies will be essential. Ensuring good cooperation among agencies is likely to form a significant element of the managerial function on a continuing basis—in compiling FSI data, this might often involve cooperation between supervisors and economic statisticians. It is therefore important that the "ground rules" for cooperation among agencies be established at the senior management level. Good practice suggests that, at the outset, written terms and conditions under which agencies are to cooperate should be agreed, and procedures for ongoing cooperation should be established. The type of issues to be covered in a written agreement could be similar to those set out under "Coordination Among Agencies" in the next section, "Managerial Issues." However, at a minimum, such an agreement should cover when and how data are to be supplied, as well as the policies for revising data. In addition, because of the interrelationship between FSIs and other data sets, procedures should be established to ensure that the development of FSI data is consistent with priorities for the development of related statistics.

10.17 Given the increasing presence of foreign controlled deposit takers in emerging markets and the need to report information to their home and host country authorities, cross-border cooperation among compilers might help reduce the cost to these deposit takers of compiling the required data while also supporting the exchange of knowledge and skills between compilers across borders.

What Quality Control Steps Can Be Taken?

10.18 Statistical quality is a multidimensional concept that encompasses the collection, processing, and dissemination of statistical information rather than simply the accuracy of the numbers. At the strategic level, it is important that

- *The principle of objectivity in the collection, processing, and dissemination of statistics be firmly adhered to.* Statistics should be collected and compiled on an impartial basis, with choices of sources and statistical techniques (for example, among surveys and between surveys and administrative records) based solely on statistical considerations. The choice of methodologies should be justified, and information about the choices made should be readily available.
- *A data revisions policy should be set that follows a regular, well-established, and transparent schedule.* Revisions should be analyzed by the compiling agency to allow assessment of the reliability of the preliminary data. Consistency checks within the data set and with other major data sets should be regularly undertaken by the compiling agency.

10.19 The IMF's Data Quality Assessment Framework (DQAF) provides a comprehensive but flexible framework for assessing data quality.[3] Rooted in the United Nations' *Fundamental Principles of Official Statistics,*[4] it is the product of an intensive consultation with national and international statistical authorities and data users inside and outside the IMF. The DQAF covers all aspects of the statistical environment or infrastructure in which data are collected, processed, and disseminated. Some key aspects of the DQAF are reflected in this chapter.[5]

Is There Adequate Legal Backing for the Collection of Data?

10.20 For most FSI-related data series, legal backing for data collection might already be in place. But if new data are required, a first step should be to assess the existing legal support for their collection. Adequate legal backing provides the statistical

[3]See Carson (2001) and IMF (2003c).

[4]Available on the Internet at http://unstats.un.org/unsd/methods/statorg/FP-English.htm.

[5]The DQAF developed for assessing the quality of monetary and financial statistics is available at http://dsbb.imf.org/vgn/images/pdfs/dqrs_MonetaryAcc.pdf (IMF, 2003a) and is relevant for promoting FSI data quality.

agency with the necessary support to encourage the private sector to report the data required, but obtaining such backing for statistical collections could be a complicated and lengthy process that is likely to be undertaken infrequently. This issue should be considered as part of a wider effort to obtain legal support for data collection.

10.21 The terms of legal backing for the collection of statistics vary from country to country, depending on the institutional arrangements and the historical development of the gathering of statistics.[6] There may be a choice between legislation (by parliament) and the issue of other legal acts (by the central bank or the government).

10.22 Some typical dimensions of legal backing for statistical collections are

- Scope. The type of entities the compiling agency can approach for data should be clearly specified (for example, entities in the private business sector), and the rationale for targeting these entities should be explained (for example, to monitor economic activity and financial transactions).
- Flexibility. The legal authority should be clear as to the boundaries of the responsibilities of the compiling agencies, without being so restrictive that the agency lacks the freedom to adapt as new developments emerge.
- Compliance. The compiling agency should have the power to impose penalties on entities that fail to report.
- Confidentiality. The use of information from individual entities for other than statistical compilation purposes should be prohibited,[7] thus establishing independence of the statistical compilation function from other government activity (for example, taxation).
- Integrity. Other government agencies should be prohibited from unduly influencing the content of statistical releases.
- Confidence. Appropriate penalties should be imposed on the compiling agency and (in particular) individual employees who do not respect the confidentiality of data, in accordance with the law.

[6]See also Khawaja and Morrison (2002).

[7]It is recognized that the release of information on individual entities in aggregated form might not always solve the problem of confidentiality if one or two large entities dominate the sector.

10.23 Other important elements of statistical legislation pertain to the release of information on individual entities in aggregated form only and the establishment of an oversight committee of independent experts to ensure the professionalism and objectivity of the compiling agencies.

Managerial Issues

10.24 Having decided on the strategic direction of the work, a number of managerial issues arise concerning the implementation of work on FSIs. Most important are the coordination with other agencies, development of a work schedule, and consultation with both data suppliers and users.

Coordination Among Agencies

10.25 Because data for compiling FSIs are likely to be supplied by different agencies, a number of management challenges arise. First, procedures are needed to ensure that the concepts used and data compiled by the different agencies are consistent, or at least reconcilable. To this end, the lead agency should develop expertise in international practices and benchmarks for the compilation of FSIs and, in a sense, act as their guardian within the country.

10.26 Second, the lead agency should establish key commonalities and differences in the source data and should be aware of any inconsistencies with the core concepts outlined in the *Guide.* The definitions of sectors and instruments should be assessed, as should the accounting and valuation rules. The coverage of the reporting population should be compared for data drawn from different sources and used to calculate FSIs for the same sector. Revision policies for source data should also be established and monitored. In particular, revisions in regulatory data are sometimes restricted by legal mandate, whereas data collected for monetary and national accounts statistics are often revised on an ongoing basis. Such differences in revision policy can affect the comparability of source data.

10.27 Third, the lead agency should be in close contact with the data-supplying agencies so that both sides understand the other's needs and problems. The timing, content, and formats of the data provided by the agencies should be established. Any changes in coverage, definition, or classification should be identified in advance of the provision of data so that there are no surprises during the data compilation process. Breaks in data series should be clearly identified. Data-supplying/producing agencies should also supply information on the shortcomings of the data.

10.28 Most data are collected from individual institutions on a strictly confidential basis and, in accordance with the usual restriction that individual entity data cannot be disseminated, are published on an aggregated basis. These confidentiality considerations could restrict the access of the lead agency to the individual entity data, leaving it to rely on aggregate data to calculate FSIs. In such circumstances, and given the role of the lead agency in ensuring the accuracy and reliability of the published FSIs, the lead agency should work closely and cooperatively with the data-supplying agency to ensure that aggregated data are constructed in accordance with the agreed principles. The lead agency should closely monitor the data supplied and should have the right to require that the data suppliers provide explanations regarding the data. Preferably, the procedures to be followed will be covered in the written terms and conditions under which agencies cooperate.

10.29 Beyond the "official" procedures, it is important that arrangements be put in place to facilitate formal and informal contacts among the staffs of the different agencies to deal with any problems expeditiously and to avoid duplication of data coverage in the different institutions. One approach for encouraging cooperation, developing contacts, and resolving problems is to establish a regular working-level meeting among staffs of the various agencies. The *Guide* recommends this approach. These meetings could facilitate the resolution of problems and provide opportunities to discuss upcoming developments and possible future enhancements or changes to collection systems. Such meetings could also facilitate the assessment of the impact of changes in economic circumstances on the range of data compiled and disseminated. Such cooperation helps ideas to spread, fosters improvements, allows institutions to understand each other's positions, and helps build important personal contacts.

Planning Workloads

10.30 After the release schedule for FSI data is agreed, a compilation work schedule should be established (Box 10.1).[8] The schedule should specify the sequence of tasks including

- The delineation of responsibilities for each task;
- The data inputs and scheduling of the delivery of data, with the supplying agencies' agreement on the scheduling, where appropriate;
- The time frame for compilation and verification;
- The schedule for the flow of data from one production stage to the next; and
- The agreed release schedule.

10.31 The establishment of the compilation work schedule should be a process that occurs over some period of time. If the initial schedule turns out to be too tight, some delay in the release date for data might be necessary. When compilers first start to compile FSIs, much potential for unforeseen problems exists. Therefore, countries might initially provide a longer period before the release of data, with a greater margin for delay, and gradually improve the timeliness as they gain experience. Indeed, a trial period for testing the compilation of FSIs is advisable before deciding to disseminate data to the public in accordance with a prearranged timetable. At a minimum, it is recommended that the compilation procedures be tested for two periods to identify and resolve any compilation problems that might arise. Such an approach would also allow the authorities to gain greater understanding of the nature of these data before providing them to the public.

Consultation with Data Reporters

10.32 Even though legal backing will support compilers' efforts to obtain the necessary information from the primary reporters of data (such as the individual deposit takers), it is essential that a "culture of reporting" be developed. This is not easily or quickly achieved but should be considered as an ongoing aspect of the work. Steps to encourage a culture of reporting include convening meetings with potential respondents and addressing their concerns, developing report forms that fit easily into existing management reporting systems and are not overly complex, and disseminating and promoting the FSIs in a trans-

[8]Moreover, a decision should be made regarding the way data should be stored and managed so that they are best available for various uses. Box 10.1 provides some ideas.

Box 10.1. Managing Data Compilation Systems[1]

The choice of computer system is important for the compilation of FSIs. While it is recognized that data-processing systems are developed to meet the circumstances in each country, this box provides a brief overview of some of the considerations to take into account and outlines a few good practices.

The most straightforward choice of computer system for FSI-based data work is the computer system already standard in the agency. This approach has a number of advantages: staff is already trained on the system, the capabilities are known, and computer support is presumably available if technical difficulties arise. In addition, only limited time and effort need be spent on choosing the appropriate software package. Such an approach should also facilitate the running of the system by compilers, rather than by computer specialists without statistical expertise.

Important considerations in establishing the compilation system are determining how the work on FSI-based data fits into the other tasks of the agency and how existing compilation and information technology systems are to be utilized. For instance, a well-specified naming structure for the data series is essential for the compilation system. If such a structure already exists, a decision might be made to extend the existing structure to accommodate additional FSI data series rather than create a new structure. The naming structure determines organization of the data and the navigation of the database. In principle, any structure should be easy to understand, and the type of data (frequency, value, name) and other attributes should be well documented.

Some countries base their data compilation systems on spreadsheets such as Lotus or Excel. Spreadsheets are useful for small-scale tasks, such as development work. However, as the system moves from the developmental to the operational stage, it is desirable to shift to a compilation system that is built on database software and to use it for the large tasks of data storage and computation. Experience shows that, when dealing with large quantities of numbers, transferring data between spreadsheets can easily result in errors that are difficult to trace. In addition, it can be difficult to keep records of different versions of data.

There are different types of databases. Relational database packages store data in a set of linked two-dimensional tables that facilitate cross-sectional analysis. Common relational database packages include *Access, dBASE, Oracle,* and *Sysbase*. Time-series databases treat all objects (data arrays or vectors) as time series and are particularly suitable when the time dimension is a prominent feature of the data. Common time-series database packages include *Aremos, Dbank,* and *Fame*. None of the database packages currently available is optimal for both types of operations. Given the nature of the FSI data set, a combination of databases—a time-series database for the storage and computation of FSIs, and a relational database for the calculation of the underlying data series—might be used in producing FSIs. The database system should allow for receiving and downloading data in spreadsheet format to assist in data exchange with data reporters and users.

Some good practices in data handling during the compilation process are the following:

- Each figure should be entered only once and subsequently referenced by links so that all consequential changes are made in the event of revisions. This is particularly important for FSI work, so that the system is flexible enough to accommodate requests, such as for ad hoc peer group data. Prerequisites are that the source data are readily available and there are not duplicate versions that could result in errors.
- Documentation of sources, processes, assumptions, and adjustments to assist later compilers should be included in text or notes. Data should have headings that describe the series and its units.
- Standardized formats should be used for all parts of the system (for example, basic sheets for input, checking, and aggregation; either rows or columns for time series, not both; screens that display several years of data; expressions in millions or billions, not both). The formats should be designed for compatibility with input formats required by the central compiling agency.
- Multiple layers of pages should be used to show stages of compilation separately while allowing links to related stages.
- Formulas should be double checked to see that they do what was intended and have not been unintentionally affected by other changes.
- Color and font options should be used to separate inputs, outputs, and edit checks.
- Spreadsheets received should be dated (for example, printed copies can be dated by using the Excel function "=today()"). Backups of previous versions should be stored.
- Any spreadsheet files and worksheets should have meaningful names.
- Backups of data and relevant software should be maintained in separate, but easy to access, facilities.

[1]This section draws on Bloem, Dippelsman, and Mæhle (2001).

parent manner. Indeed, data reporters should see some benefit arising from the provision of data, such as obtaining information on financial sector conditions relevant for their own analysis. If data are collected and compiled in an efficient manner and the FSIs are viewed as important, experience suggests that data reporters are more likely to respond.

10.33 Thus, for example, when new data are to be collected, the compiler is advised to undertake report form testing—that is, obtain feedback from a sample of potential reporters on whether the instructions are clear and workable before they become operational. Moreover, seminars and workshops explaining the reporting requirements are valuable to both reporters and the compiling agency, and are encouraged. The ongoing maintenance of an electronic register of contacts at the data reporting institutions (including the telephone numbers of those who have contacted the agency) provides information that can help ensure a well-run statistical operation. Through such a register, institutional memory at the statistical agency can be developed and maintained.

Consultation with Users

10.34 There should be mechanisms to ensure that the FSIs continue to meet the needs of policymakers and other users. For instance, experience has shown that corporate and household debt tends to increase following financial liberalization, perhaps warranting expansion of the FSIs to these sectors, if data are not already available.

10.35 Meetings with policymakers and other data users should be periodically convened to review the comprehensiveness of the FSIs and to identify emerging data requirements. New initiatives could be discussed with policy departments and statistical advisory groups; such discussions would provide justification for seeking additional resources. As with any new body of statistics, programs that reach out to users can be useful for promoting awareness and understanding of the data, as well as for identifying data quality issues and other user concerns.

Improving Source Data

10.36 While in the short term compilers may rely on existing data sources to compile FSIs, over time plans for improving or developing additional data series for FSIs may well need to be formulated. After the regular dissemination of FSI data is established, if not before, a priority list of improvements and a medium-term timetable for actions should be developed, maintained, and regularly reviewed. This list and timetable should be informed by consultation with both data users and other compiling agencies, so that the lead agency obtains support for the data compilation process. In some instances, it might be possible to absorb FSI development work into existing projects to save resources.

Quality Control

10.37 As noted above, data quality is a multidimensional concept, and many of the steps for ensuring good quality data are inherent in the discussions above. Nonetheless, it is important to recognize that the reliability of FSI data will be enhanced if the managers responsible for the collection and compilation of source data have strategies and procedures in place for monitoring and improving the quality of the collection and compilation of statistics, and for dealing with timeliness/quality trade-offs.

11. Compilation of FSI Data: Practical Issues

Introduction

11.1 The previous chapter discussed strategic and managerial issues that arise in the compilation and dissemination of FSI data. This chapter focuses on practical considerations.

11.2 At the outset, it is worth noting that practical experience in compiling FSI data is still relatively limited, and experience will be gained as the compilation and calculation of FSIs gather momentum. In this context, this chapter focuses on the basic data sources that can be employed in calculating FSI ratios, as well as on other data series required to meet the *Guide*'s requirements. The focus is on FSI ratios derived from financial statements. Data sources for the FSIs covering financial and real estate markets are discussed in Chapters 8 and 9, respectively.

11.3 It is likely that existing data sources for deposit takers can meet many of the data requirements for compiling FSIs. This may be particularly true for domestically controlled cross-border consolidated data, whose source is information available to supervisors (see paragraph 11.8). The compiler should thus see the extent to which existing data sources, including possible adaptations, can meet the requirements of the *Guide* before investigating the possibility of collecting new data series. In determining the need to collect new data, and hence to incur increased cost, authorities must make a judgment as to the likely impact and importance of the additional data series for compiling FSI data. For instance, where an additional series would have an insignificant impact on an FSI ratio, the case for collecting such data would not be strong.

Basic Data Sources

Deposit Takers

11.4 There are typically three main sources of information available for compiling FSIs on deposit takers. They are (1) commercial accounting data, (2) national accounts data, including monetary statistics (see Box 11.1), and (3) supervisory data.[1]

11.5 There are important differences between national accounts and commercial accounting data, arising from the different purposes for which data are compiled. In terms of scope, commercial accounting statements for deposit takers consolidate activities of subsidiaries with the parent to evaluate the performance of the entire group. In contrast, national accounts data include only the flows and positions of deposit takers located in the domestic economy, reflecting the focus of the data on macroeconomic developments in the domestic economy. Therefore, whereas commercial accounting data and supervisory data eliminate intragroup transactions, national accounts data are based on those reported for each individual deposit taker within a group, without netting out transactions and positions with other group members. Another important difference between the data sources is that national accounts data are collected on the basis that the information will be aggregated to compile data for the sector as a whole,[2] unlike commercial accounting and supervisory data that have been designed for the reporting of the activity of individual units.

11.6 In summary, national accounts data are more suited to monitoring developments in the domestic

[1]In many economies, credit registers can provide a wealth of information on loans and other forms of credit advanced by deposit takers. For the geographic distribution of loans, data on cross-border exposures published by the BIS can be utilized. Information on the coverage of BIS data is available in BIS (2003b). There are also private sources of data that provide information derived from published financial statements (as discussed in Bhattacharya [2003] in using such databases).

[2]Not all institutions in the population may report each period for national accounts purposes. For instance, the smallest institutions may report less frequently than other reporters. For periods when some institutions do not report, the aggregated reported data are typically "grossed up" to take account of the "missing" reporting entities.

Box 11.1. Relationship Between Monetary and Financial Statistics and FSIs

Balance sheet data reported to central banks by financial corporations for the compilation of monetary aggregates and financial statistics are a potential source of information for the compilation of data for deposit takers on a domestic consolidation basis. In 2000, the IMF published the *Monetary and Financial Statistics Manual* (*MFSM*).[1] The *MFSM* is harmonized with the *1993 SNA* and addresses specific analytical needs relating to the role of monetary statistics in assisting monetary policy formulation and monitoring. This box explains how data collected using the *MFSM* methodology can be utilized to compile the agreed indicators for deposit takers.

The *MFSM* encourages the collection of balance sheet data from resident financial corporations (including branches of foreign banks). Subject to adjustments (see below), the balance sheet items specified in the *MFSM*[2] can be aggregated to construct the following data series on a domestic consolidated basis:[3]

- Customer deposits
- Noninterbank loans
- Sectoral distribution of loans
- Total loans
- Capital and reserves
- Assets
- Gross asset and liability positions in financial derivatives
- Total liabilities
- Equity and other shares

While a reliable source, monetary statistics might need to be adjusted to bring data series on loans, capital, financial derivatives, and assets and liabilities into accordance with the principles set out in the *Guide*.[4] Moreover, unlike the monetary data, the balance sheet data presented in the *Guide* are explicitly linked to an income and expense account for the financial corporations.

Drawing on the series set out in Tables 11.1–11.3, the following adjustments might be necessary:

- Equity investments in subsidiaries and associates are valued on the basis of the investor's prorated share of these entities' capital and reserves and not at the market price of the equity held. Any difference in the value is reflected in assets and in capital and reserves. Data shown in Table 11.1 could be used.
- To avoid double counting of deposit takers' capital and reserves at the sector level, equity investments among deposit takers in the reporting population should be excluded and counterpart adjustments made to capital and reserves. The adjustments could be implemented by using information collected under item 1 (and perhaps 2) in Table 11.2 to eliminate from assets and capital and reserves (1) the market value of shares and other equity investments in other resident deposit takers and (2) equity investments in deposit-taking subsidiaries and deposit-taking associates.
- Other bilateral claims and liabilities among resident deposit takers that belong to the same group should be eliminated using the information specified in Table 11.3. Thus, loans and positions in financial derivatives among resident deposit takers in the same group should be excluded from the aggregated balance sheet data used to compile the data series listed above.
- In the *Guide*, unlike the *MFSM*, data on loans (and other assets) should exclude accrued interest on nonperforming loans (other assets).
- In contrast to the *MFSM* approach, in the *Guide* the value of total assets excludes specific provisions.[5] Accordingly, total assets in the aggregated balance sheet should be adjusted to exclude specific provisions, with a counteradjustment to capital and reserves (as well as to narrow capital and reserves). In addition, in the *Guide* the value of total assets and of capital and reserves excludes purchased goodwill, unlike in the *MFSM*.
- Moreover, while general provisions are classified as "other receivables/payable" in the *MFSM*,[6] they are classified as part of capital and reserves in the *Guide*.
- Whereas the *Guide* includes unrealized gains/losses on financial assets and liabilities in retained earnings,[7] such gains and losses are included as part of the revaluation account in the *MFSM*. Thus, if compiling a narrow measure of capital and reserves from the aggregated balance sheet data, unrealized gains/losses on financial instruments should be reallocated to retained earnings.

Moreover, although the *MFSM* encourages the collection of balance sheet data from all resident financial corporations, as explained in Chapter 2, coverage of the "other depository corporations" in the *MFSM* might not be identical to that of the deposit-taking sector in the *Guide* (see paragraph 2.4, footnote 3).

Other data sources, such as the BIS locational data on the geographic distribution of bank lending, may be collected from the same reporting population as for monetary and financial statistics, facilitating combination of data sources to compile the agreed FSIs. For example, the indicator on the geographic distribution of loans to total loans can be constructed by using the aforementioned BIS data for the numerator and data on total loans from the monetary statistics for the denominator.

[1]IMF (2000a).

[2]See Table 7.1 on pages 80–86 of the *MFSM*.

[3]The following structural indicators can also be constructed: total assets of the financial system and of subgroups of financial corporations, as well as claims of financial corporations on residents as a share of total assets.

[4]As noted in this chapter, in determining the need to collect new data, and hence to incur the increased resource cost, authorities must make a judgment as to the likely impact and importance of the additional data series for compiling FSI data.

[5]The value of loans after the deduction of specific provisions is a series used in calculating an agreed indicator.

[6]See paragraph 179 of the *MFSM*.

[7]In other words, in the *Guide* unrealized gains and losses on financial assets/liabilities are routed through the income and expense account.

economy on an aggregate basis,[3] while commercial and supervisory data are more suited to monitoring developments of deposit-taking groups on a cross-border consolidated basis.

Commercial and supervisory data

11.7 Balance sheet as well as income and expense data are usually collected by supervisory agencies as an essential element of their supervisory function. Because typically the collection has a statutory basis, these data may be more reliable than those collected for statistical purposes in economies with weak statistical systems. However, while there are internationally agreed supervisory requirements, the methods by which these are implemented vary by country. Moreover, the accounting standards that supervisors regard as a basis for relevant and reliable measures of income and expense and balance sheet items, as well as of capital adequacy, are currently varying across countries, even though the International Accounting Standards Board is working toward common international standards.

11.8 In some countries, data might be collected for supervisory purposes on standardized forms with clear and specific instructions on how and when they should be completed. In other countries, supervisory and national accounts data are collected together on returns that are organized and structured in a single framework, and additional series are collected for supervisory or national accounts purposes as needed. Such reporting approaches might lend themselves to providing data that can be aggregated for FSI purposes. Alternatively, in some countries, supervisors collect data that are separate from national accounts data and are customized to individual institutions, both with respect to content and the reference date for the reports. In such instances, to compile FSIs the *Guide* encourages movement toward greater consistency of approaches, whenever feasible.

11.9 Table 11.9 at the end of this chapter reconciles the income and expense and balance sheet items in Table 4.1 with the relevant international accounting standards to illustrate how commercial accounting data might be utilized to meet the *Guide*'s requirements. However, this table should be regarded as a broad guide, and the reader is advised to consult Appendix IV for more details. Data series that might not be available from regulatory or commercial accounting sources but might be needed for the compilation of FSIs are highlighted below.

National accounts data

11.10 Balance sheet data are usually collected from resident deposit takers by the central bank on a monthly basis to produce monetary aggregates. Moreover, while not normally collected as part of the data for compiling monetary statistics, income data might well be collected on a quarterly basis for use, along with the monthly balance sheet data, in the compilation of national accounts data.

11.11 Table 11.9 at the end of this chapter reconciles the income and expense and balance sheet items in Table 4.1 with those in the *1993 SNA,* illustrating how national accounts data can be used to meet the *Guide*'s requirements. However, Table 11.9 should be regarded as a broad guide, and the reader is advised to consult Appendix IV for more details. Series not covered by national accounts data but that might be needed for the compilation of FSIs are highlighted below.

Other Financial Corporations

11.12 Official data collection on the activities of other financial corporations has traditionally lagged that for the activities of deposit takers both in terms of its scope and frequency. However, the increasing importance of other financial corporations in financial systems has produced a trend toward increased data collection. Central banks and/or national statistical offices might already be collecting information on other financial corporations. Alternatively, it might be necessary to rely initially on information provided in the published accounts of other financial corporations until official data sources are developed.

Nonfinancial Corporations and Households

11.13 The agency responsible for compiling national accounts statistics is likely to collect data on the nonfinancial corporations and household sectors. To meet the data needs for compiling the encouraged list of FSIs, additional data series will need to be developed, such as debt service payments and other data that are not specified in the *1993 SNA* framework. While

[3]As noted in Chapter 5, the *MFSM* (IMF, 2000a) eliminates intra-deposit-takers' positions in the depository corporations' survey.

national accounts data are usually the source of official information on the household sector, in the case of the nonfinancial corporations sector, published accounts are an important alternative source of information. Typically, economic statistics for nonfinancial corporations are based on representative sample surveys or tax records. Tables 11.10 and 11.11 at the end of this chapter provide a reconciliation of the data needs of the *Guide* with the *1993 SNA* framework and IASs, respectively.

11.14 Obtaining data on the household sector is difficult. If the agency calculating FSIs is different from the one that compiles national accounts data on the household sector, coordination between the two agencies is essential.

11.15 While the household sector is likely to borrow from resident financial corporations, with modern forms of communication and the ability to advertise products across borders, borrowing from abroad might become more prevalent. Thus, there may be a need to capture cross-border borrowing activity of households. Some countries set up specific procedures to capture cross-border assets and liabilities of residents with nonresident financial corporations. Under these procedures, all households are obliged to report such positions to the central bank on a regular basis (monthly, quarterly, or annually). However, transactions settled through these accounts abroad are to be reported by households, with the frequency and detail of individual reporting dependent on the scale of the activity undertaken.

11.16 The additional data series on debt service that are required could be included in household surveys of expenditures, income, and financial assets and liabilities. Alternatively, available information on outstanding household debt and interest rates could be used together with some assumptions about possible repayment schedules, perhaps based on remaining maturities data for loan debt and minimum payment amounts for credit card debt, to provide some estimates for debt service.[4] While some approximations may be rough, by using the same methods and data series over time and taking into account market developments, important changes over time can be captured.

[4]For one possible approach, taken by the U.S. Federal Reserve Board, see United States Board of Governors of the Federal Reserve System (2004).

Other Data Requirements

Deposit Takers

11.17 While data from available sources can serve as a basis, other information might be needed to meet the data series requirements of the *Guide* to enable the consolidation and aggregation of data. As can be seen from the tables below, considerably fewer additional data series might be needed to compile the data required by the *Guide* if the sources are commercial accounting and supervisory sources rather than national accounts sources. This is because many of the concepts underlying the list of FSIs for deposit takers are supervisory in nature, including the framework for compiling data on a consolidated group basis.[5]

11.18 As noted above, in determining the need to collect new data, and hence to incur an increased resource cost, the *Guide* recommends that the authorities make a judgment as to the likely impact and importance of the additional data series for compiling FSI data.

Domestic consolidated data

11.19 The additional data series for deposit takers that might be required are shown in Tables 11.1–11.3. These tables are based on an assessment of what information could be available from national accounts sources compared with the *Guide*'s requirements. These tables assume that data are collected on the same basis as for national accounts data—that is, on an institutional unit basis.

11.20 Table 11.1 shows those series that are not covered in national accounts data but are needed to calculate the agreed indicators. Table 11.2 covers those series needed for the aggregation of data at the sector level, and Table 11.3 covers those series needed to present data on a consolidated basis rather than on a separately incorporated entity basis.

Series not covered in national accounts methodology

11.21 Table 11.1 presents those series that, along with those available from the national accounts,

[5]In the *Guide*, a group is defined as the parent deposit taker, its deposit-taking branches, and its deposit-taking subsidiaries. A similar approach is followed in the case of the other financial and nonfinancial corporations sectors.

Table 11.1. Domestic Deposit Takers: Series Not Covered in National Accounts Methodology

Income and expense		
Provisions		
Accrued interest on nonperforming assets	Required	
Loan loss provision	Required	
Other financial asset provisions	Required	
Gains and losses on financial instruments	Required	
Gains and losses on the sale of an associate or subsidiary[1]	Required[2]	
Gains and losses on sale of fixed assets in the period[1]	Required	
Extraordinary items	Required	
Balance-sheet-related		
Liquid assets		
Core	Required	
Broad	Required	
Short-term liabilities (remaining maturity)	Required	
Nonperforming loan assets	Required	
Provisions		
Accrued interest on nonperforming loans[3]	Required	
Specific loan provisions	Required	
Other specific provisions	Required[4]	
Foreign-currency-denominated		
Loan assets	Required	
Liabilities	Required	
Foreign-currency-linked		
Loan assets	Required	
Liabilities	Required	
Real estate loan assets		
Residential	Required	
Commercial	Required	
Large exposures		
Number of large exposures	Required	
Exposures to largest entities in the economy	Required	
Exposures to affiliated entities and other connected entities[5]	Required	
Net open position in foreign currency	Required	
Net open position in equities	Required	
	Subsidiaries[8]	*Associates*[8]
Shares and other equity[6]	Required	Required
Shares and other equity[7]	Required	Required
Prorated share of retained earnings (income)	Required	Required
Purchased goodwill	Required	Required

[1]Measured as the difference between the sale value and the balance sheet value at the previous end period.

[2]Depending on the source of information on gains and losses on financial instruments (see paragraph 11.24).

[3]This item is required if gross loan data are available only on a basis that includes accrued interest on nonperforming loans. If other assets are also recorded inclusive of accrued interest on nonperforming assets, then additional data on accrued interest for such nonperforming assets will be required.

[4]To be identified by type of instrument.

[5]These cover exposures to other group entities and associates of the reporting entity, to directors and other employees, and to shareholders or owners of the deposit taker.

[6]Valued as the proportionate share of the parent deposit taker's stake in the capital and reserves of subsidiaries and associates.

[7]As valued on the balance sheet if different from the previous line.

[8]Including reverse equity investments of subsidiaries and associates in their parent companies. The data for subsidiaries and associates could be provided in one aggregate figure; that is, separate identification is not essential.

allow the compilation of the agreed indicators for deposit takers. Set out below are brief explanations of why these data series are required and information on their possible sources. Only those series required to calculate an agreed indicator are shown in the table. Appendix III discusses some additional series that might be relevant, depending on country circumstances.

Income and expense series

11.22 *Provisions.* Data on provisions are essential for understanding the soundness of a deposit taker,

Table 11.2. Domestic Deposit Takers: Intrasector Positions and Flows

	Total	Of Which: Subsidiaries[1,2]	Associates[1,2]	Other deposit takers
1. Shares and other equity[3]	Required[4]	Required[4]	Required	
2. Shares and other equity		[5]	[5]	Not applicable
3. Noninterest income (excluding trading gains and losses):	Required			
Of which: Fees and commissions	Required			
Dividends receivable	Required			
Prorated share of retained earnings	Required[6]			Not applicable
Gains or losses in the period on sale of fixed assets to other deposit takers	Required			
4. Gains and losses on equity investments in other deposit takers		Not applicable	Not applicable	Required
5. Nonperforming loans to other deposit takers in the reporting population[7]				
Current period				
Provisions for accrued interest	Required			
Specific provisions	Required			
Outstanding position				
Provisions for accrued interest	Required			
Specific provisions	Required			
6. Short-term claims on other deposit takers in the reporting economy (remaining maturity)	Required			

[1]Including deposit-taking branches of separately incorporated subsidiaries and associates.

[2]Resident deposit-taking subsidiaries or associates that have reverse equity investments in their resident parent deposit-taking investor should report the transactions and positions vis-à-vis the parent investor in these columns.

[3]Valued as the proportionate share of the parent deposit takers' stake in subsidiary/associate capital and reserves (and similarly for reverse investments), and as the market value of any equity stake in other resident deposit takers. For subsidiaries and associates, if Tier 1 data are not available, the narrow measure of capital and reserves could also be identified (see paragraph 4.64).

[4]These data series could be reported as one combined figure.

[5]As valued in the balance sheet, if different from line 1. Moreover, if the balance sheet value of subsidiaries and associates is reported in Table 11.1, these data are not required.

[6]Subsidiaries and associates only.

[7]If there are other nonperforming claims on other deposit takers in the reporting population, the data series specified in item 5 are required for these assets.

because of the impact of loan and other potential losses on profits and capital. Data on provisions are not among the *1993 SNA* data series but may be collected for supervisory purposes.

11.23 *Gains and losses on financial instruments, gains on sale of fixed assets, and extraordinary items.* Data on gains and losses on financial instruments are an integral element of profitability. They are directly required for the calculation of one indicator and are indirectly required for the calculation of several others. As explained in Appendix IV, data on gains and losses on financial instruments are potentially available from the revaluation account of the *1993 SNA*, but at the present time collection of these data is relatively limited. Similar reasoning applies to the data on extraordinary items. Gains from the sale of fixed assets, such as property used for branch operations, affect profits but are not identifiable from *1993 SNA* data. Data on gains or losses in a given period are required because they are included in net income for the period.

11.24 *Gains or losses from the sale of a subsidiary or associate.* The *Guide* recommends that such gains or losses (including those on reverse investments) be excluded from income. In the national accounts, such gains or losses are classified as a valuation change if a corporation or quasi corporation is sold. Therefore, if data on gains and losses on financial instruments are sourced from the revaluation account of the *1993 SNA*, data on gains and losses from the sale of subsidiaries and associates should be excluded. Moreover, this latter series may be of analytical interest in its own right.

Table 11.3. Domestic Deposit Takers: Other Intragroup Positions and Flows[1]

Balance sheet	
Liabilities:	
Deposits	Required
Loans	Required
Of which: Foreign-currency-denominated	Required
Foreign-currency-linked	Required
Debt securities	Required
Financial derivatives	Required
Other liabilities	Required
Total foreign-currency-denominated liabilities	Required
Total foreign-currency-linked liabilities	Required
Income and expense statement	
Interest income receivable	Required[2]
Memorandum items relating to claims:	
Liquid assets claims (core)	Required
Liquid assets claims (broad)	Required
Nonperforming loans	Required

[1]A group in this context is a parent deposit taker, its deposit-taking branches, and deposit-taking subsidiaries in the reporting population. Thus, this column covers those entities that are within the same group as the reporting entity but are separately incorporated or are domestic offices of entities that are separately incorporated.

[2]This item is required to ensure that there is consistency in the consolidated balance sheet between the treatment of debt instruments in the balance sheet (intragroup claims excluded) and gross interest income and expense in the income account (intragroup flows also excluded).

Balance-sheet-related series

11.25 *Liquid assets.* Data on liquid assets are used to calculate two indicators. While monetary statistics provide some data, such as deposits at the central bank, the liquid-asset concepts developed in the *Guide* are not available in national accounts data.

11.26 *Short-term liabilities.* While data on short-term liabilities are available on an original maturity basis from national accounts data sources, the preference in the *Guide* is for data on a remaining maturity basis. This is because the indicator for which this series is required is a measure of liquidity, comparing short-term liabilities with liquid assets.

11.27 *Nonperforming loans.* As with provisions, data on nonperforming loans are essential for understanding the financial soundness of the deposit-taking sector and are required for the calculation of two indicators. However, such data are not contained in national accounts data, although they may be collected for supervisory purposes.

11.28 *Provisions.* Data on the outstanding position of specific loan provisions are required to calculate the data series *nonperforming loans net of provisions* that is used to calculate one indicator and to adjust the value of outstanding loans for specific provisions. Information on provisions for the accrual of interest on nonperforming loans is required if data on gross loans (and the sectoral breakdown) are available only inclusive of the accrual of such interest—that is, the procedures must be consistent with the *1993 SNA*. Other specific provisions relate to the outstanding level of specific provisions for other financial assets. Such provisions reduce the value of these assets in the balance sheet and should be separately identified in the same manner as specific provisions for loans. Moreover, the outstanding amounts for specific provisions, and for provisions for accrued interest on nonperforming loans, should be excluded from capital and reserves for data sourced from national accounts information. Data on provisions are not among the *1993 SNA* data series[6] but may be collected for supervisory purposes.

11.29 *Foreign currency loans and liabilities.* Positions in foreign currency raise the potential of vulnerability to exchange rate movements. Two indicators are used to measure this vulnerability. While some national accounts methodologies, in particular the monetary and external debt methodologies, encourage the collection of data on foreign currency positions and could be extended to cover the data required here, the coverage in the *Guide* differs from both. The data for foreign-currency-denominated and foreign-currency-linked loans could be collected as a single series, and similarly for liabilities.

11.30 *Residential and commercial real estate loans.* Experience suggests that exposure to the real estate market can be a source of risk to the deposit-taking sector and is reflected in two indicators. The loan data required in the national accounts methodology do not include the separate identification of data on residential and commercial real estate loans, but such loan data could be collected at a more disaggregated level. The International Standard Industrial Classification (ISIC) identifies real estate at the subcategory level (see Box A3.1 in Appendix III). Commercial real estate lending among deposit takers in the report-

[6]The *MFSM* indistinguishably includes provisions as a liability item under other accounts receivable/payable but encourages separate identification of expected loan losses (paragraph 390).

ing population that are part of the same group should be excluded from the data. As noted in Chapter 6, if available, data on household debt collateralized by real estate could be employed instead of data on residential real estate loans.

11.31 *Large exposures.* Data on large exposures are required to calculate one indicator. Such data are not required for national accounts purposes, but the number of large exposures of deposit takers that are identified under the national supervisory regime should be available to bank supervisors. Data on connected borrowers might also be available from supervisory sources. However, the *Guide*'s other definition of large exposures, that is, those to the largest entities in other sectors, may not be the same as that used for supervisory purposes. Exposures to deposit takers in the reporting population that are part of the same group should be excluded from the data.

11.32 *Net open positions.* Net open positions in equities and foreign exchange are included in the list of FSIs. Such information may be collected and monitored by supervisors.

11.33 *Shares and other equity, and prorated share of retained earnings.* The *Guide* recommends that for all sectors (1) investments in subsidiaries and associates be valued on the balance sheet on the basis of the prorated share of the value of these entities' capital and reserves, and (2) the prorated share of earnings be included in income. This approach is also recommended for the so-called reverse equity investments—that is, if an associate or subsidiary takes an equity stake in its parent. This is not the approach taken for domestic subsidiaries and associates in the national accounts data.[7] So for all corporations, additional data are required to adjust the balance sheet, particularly capital and reserves and income data derived from national accounts data.[8] Any difference between the reported balance sheet value of the equity investments in subsidiaries and associates and the proportionate share should increase (if the latter is greater than the former) or decrease (if the former is greater than the latter) capital and reserves, with the adjustment attributed to the valuation adjustment.

11.34 *Goodwill.* The *Guide* recommends that data on goodwill be deducted from nonfinancial assets and from capital and reserves. National accounts data include goodwill in nonfinancial assets and, implicitly, in net worth.[9]

Data required for the aggregation of deposit takers' data

11.35 Some adjustments are required to avoid double counting of capital and assets, and overstatement of specific income and expense lines when data for individual entities are aggregated to produce information for the entire sector. These sector-level adjustments are explained in Chapter 5. Table 11.2 provides a complete list of the series required to make the adjustments, which are explained below, although, depending on national circumstances, not all may be relevant. Moreover, the total data could be disaggregated by column to gain greater understanding of the relationships with subsidiaries, associates, and other deposit takers.

11.36 Table 11.2 relates to positions and flows among deposit takers in the reporting population and is based on the assumption that the reporting population covers all domestic deposit takers. Additionally, subgroups of the reporting population could be specified to create data on a peer group basis. However, this would increase data collection costs, and the *Guide* considers that such a collection of additional detailed data should be based on the specific analytical needs of each country. Peer group data and their compilation are discussed in Chapter 15; given the costs, peer group data might well be compiled on an approximate best practice basis.

11.37 *Equity investments in deposit-taking subsidiaries, deposit-taking associates, and other deposit takers.* To avoid double counting of deposit takers' capital and reserves for the entire sector, equity investments in other deposit takers need to be excluded.[10] So, for equity investments in deposit-taking subsidiaries and deposit-taking associates (and for reverse equity investments), the value of the proportionate share in the capital and reserves should be

[7]However, it is the approach for nonresident subsidiaries or associates owned by resident corporations.

[8]Because income data are not presented for the other financial corporations sector, no additional information on retained earnings for this sector is needed.

[9]It was noted in Chapter 4 (paragraph 4.110) that negative goodwill is possible.

[10]For the same reason, similar adjustments are needed for the nonfinancial corporations sector because equity is a denominator for three FSIs for that sector (see below).

separately identified.[11] The required data on equity investments are not ordinarily collected as part of the national accounts data. The series in Table 11.2 differ from the similar series in Table 11.1 to the extent that the deposit takers have non-deposit-taking subsidiaries and associates (included in the Table 11.1 series but not in the Table 11.2 series). While the table provides a disaggregated view of the data required, aggregated data will suffice for shares and other equity for deposit takers' subsidiaries and associates in the reporting population.

11.38 For equity investments in other deposit takers, the market value of the equity owned should be identified and deducted from total capital and reserves (a numerical example is provided in Appendix V, Part III). The required data on such equity investments might be available from national accounts sources if the market value of equity investments in resident subsidiaries and associates can be separated from equity investments in other deposit takers in the reporting population.

11.39 Line 2 of Table 11.2—shares and other equity—is not required if captured in data reported under Table 11.1.

11.40 *Certain income items.* The income data series in Table 11.2 (item 3) are required to ensure that specific subtotals are not overstated for the sector as a whole.

11.41 Fees and commissions and any other noninterest income earned by a deposit taker from another deposit taker will not affect net income but will be reflected in gross terms in both the noninterest income and expenses lines (see also paragraph 4.21). It is recommended that any such intra-deposit-taking sector income and expense be excluded from the sector totals for gross income and noninterest expenses. These data might be available from national accounts sources.

11.42 Similarly, as the inclusion of dividend income in the noninterest income line would affect gross and net income for the sector, it is recommended that such income be eliminated from gross income and dividends payable. With regard to the proportionate share of retained earnings from deposit-taking associates and deposit-taking subsidiaries (and from reverse equity investments), these amounts should also be excluded from noninterest income and from retained earnings for the entire sector. Any gain or loss in the period on a sale of fixed assets to another deposit-taker is not a gain or loss for the sector as a whole and thus is deducted from sector-wide income. Data on dividends may be available from national accounts sources, but data on the proportionate share of retained earnings and sales of fixed assets will not be so available.

11.43 *Gains and losses on equity investments in other deposit takers* (item 4) are required so that gains and losses arising from these intrasector claims do not affect sector-wide income.

11.44 Data on *nonperforming loans to other deposit takers in the reporting population* (item 5) are required to eliminate asymmetric reporting at the sector level between debtor and creditor deposit takers.[12] The data on outstanding specific provisions to other deposit takers in the reporting population are required to be added back to capital and reserves and to reduce the total amount of outstanding specific provisions (see paragraph 11.28). Moreover, provisions for accrued interest on nonperforming loans to deposit takers in the reporting population should be added to the outstanding value of loans.

11.45 Data on *short-term claims on other deposit takers in the reporting economy* (item 6) are required to adjust the short-term liabilities data for those to other deposit takers.

Consolidated information

11.46 The *Guide* encourages the compilation of FSI series on a consolidated basis for entities in the same sector and reporting population. Thus, for data compiled using national accounts information, certain additional intragroup data should be eliminated. The series required are set out in Table 11.3.

11.47 The series in Table 11.3 are intended to supplement those in Table 11.2. Whereas the series in Table 11.2 are required to eliminate some positions and transactions when aggregating data at the sector level, the series in Table 11.3 are those needed to consolidate sector-wide data (see Box 5.1). Informa-

[11]If Tier 1 data are not available, the proportionate share of narrow capital and reserves could additionally be identified (paragraph 4.64).

[12]The same approach is adopted for other nonperforming intrasector claims.

tion on intragroup positions might also be of analytical interest in its own right.

11.48 Intragroup positions are those positions with resident entities that are in the same group as the reporter but are separately incorporated or are offices of separately incorporated entities. Therefore, if a parent has positions with its domestic deposit-taking subsidiary, these are included in the table, as are positions of the subsidiary with a domestic deposit-taking branch of the parent or other domestic subsidiaries (or branches of the subsidiary) in the group and the reporting population. It might help the compiler to be informed of the names of group members in the reporting population.

11.49 For the balance sheet items, data are for liabilities only, and for the memorandum items, data refer to claims only. Data on foreign-currency-denominated and foreign-currency-linked loans could be reported as one combined figure. For the balance sheet series at the sector level, gross liabilities and gross assets are reduced; if the parent lends to its subsidiary, gross loan assets and liabilities and the gross interest income and expense are reduced at the sector level by the outstanding amount of loans extended and interest income receivable, respectively, by the parent vis-à-vis the subsidiary as of the reference date.

11.50 The data for the memorandum items are needed to reduce the sector-level totals on account of these items.

Cross-border consolidated data

11.51 To compile data on a domestically controlled cross-border consolidated basis, compilers may need to rely on supervisory data. If these data are reported on a cross-border consolidated basis,[13] Table 11.4 sets out the series needed to avoid overstatement of certain income items, as well as capital and reserves in the sector-wide data. The table relates to positions and flows among deposit takers in the reporting population.

11.52 The extent to which data are required will depend on national circumstances. For example, if supervisory requirements do not permit, or require data to be reported, excluding intra-deposit-taking equity investments, then data on shares and other equity are not additionally required. As noted above, in determining the need to collect new data, and hence incur an increased resource cost, authorities must make a judgment as to the likely impact and importance of the additional data series for compiling FSI data.

11.53 Depending on accounting standards adopted, additional series not included in Table 11.4 might be needed to adjust individual deposit taker's data. These series comprise (1) purchased goodwill, which should be excluded from nonfinancial assets and from capital and reserves; (2) the amount of amortized goodwill each period, which should be excluded from income; and (3) gains and losses on the sale of subsidiaries and associates (including those on reverse investments), which should be excluded from income.

11.54 The data requirements in Table 11.4 mirror those in Table 11.2 and are needed for the same reasons provided in describing that table. They relate to the positions and flows among domestically controlled deposit-taking groups that have parent banks incorporated in the domestic economy.

11.55 The total data could be disaggregated by column to gain a greater understanding of the relationships with associates and other deposit takers.

Compiling cross-border consolidated data from national accounts information

11.56 To compile data on a cross-border consolidated basis, as noted above, compilers might need to rely on supervisory data. However, there is growing interest among compilers and users of macroeconomic statistics to develop foreign affiliate trade data. One focus at the present time is on information on trade in services, as well as on understanding the modes of supply by domestic entities to foreign markets, one of which is through direct investment in a foreign market by establishing local subsidiaries, branches, or associates. The 2001 manual on international trade in services[14] is likely to lead to progress in this field. Beyond production and trade-in-services data, the manual discusses the possibility of compiling data on

[13]If supervisory data are reported on a group consolidated basis, which consolidates information for subsidiaries that are not deposit takers, other adjustments are needed to "deconsolidate" such subsidiaries to compile data on a deposit-takers-only basis.

[14]See United Nations and others (2001).

Table 11.4. Domestically Controlled Deposit Takers: Intergroup Positions and Flows (Cross-Border Consolidated Data)

	Other Domestically Incorporated, Domestically Controlled Deposit Takers, Their Subsidiaries,[1] and Branches		
		Of which:	
	Total	Associates[2]	Other
1. Shares and other equity[3]		Required	Required
2. Shares and other equity[4]		Required	Not applicable
3. Noninterest income (excluding trading gains and losses):	Required		
Of which: Fees and commissions	Required		
Dividends receivable	Required		
Prorated share of retained earnings		Required	Not applicable
Gains or losses on sale of fixed assets to other deposit takers	Required		
4. Gains and losses on equity investments in other deposit takers		Not applicable	Required
5. Nonperforming loans to other deposit takers in the reporting population[5]			
Current period			
Provisions for accrued interest	Required		
Specific provisions	Required		
Outstanding position			
Provisions for accrued interest	Required		
Specific provisions	Required		
6. Short-term claims on other deposit takers in the reporting economy (remaining maturity)	Required		

[1]Including deposit-taking branches of separately incorporated subsidiaries.

[2]Domestically controlled deposit takers that are associates of domestically controlled deposit takers and have reverse equity investments in the latter should report the transactions and positions vis-à-vis the associate investor in this column.

[3]Valued as the proportionate share of the parent deposit takers' stake in associates' capital and reserves (and similarly for reverse investments) and as the market value of any equity stake in other deposit takers in the reporting population.

[4]As valued in the balance sheet, if different from line 1.

[5]If there are other nonperforming asset claims on other deposit takers in the reporting population, the data series specified in item 5 are required for these assets.

assets and net worth for foreign affiliates (paragraphs 4.67–4.68 of the manual) on the basis of the concepts in the *1993 SNA*. Given these developments, there may be mutual benefit in FSI compilers' consulting with those agencies responsible for compiling trade-in-services data to learn more about ongoing or planned compilation of data on trade of foreign affiliates of domestic entities.

Other Financial Corporations

11.57 For other financial corporations, additional data series for the balance sheet only might be required, primarily to exclude intrasectoral equity investments. For data reported on a nonconsolidated basis, information on intragroup positions would be needed.

11.58 The additional data series required are set out below. Unlike the tables for deposit takers above, Table 11.5 can be relevant for both domestic and cross-border consolidated data.

11.59 Shares and other equity in subsidiaries and associates (and reverse investments) should be valued on the balance sheet at the proportionate share of the investor's stake in the capital and reserves of each subsidiary and associate. If these equity investments are reported on the balance sheet at market value, these data need to be replaced by the proportionate value information specified in the required shares and other equity series in columns 1 and 2. Depending on the source, the data for subsidiaries and associates might be reported on a combined basis. For data provided on a consolidated basis, adjustments for subsidiaries may not be required.

11.60 Equity investments of other financial corporations in their other financial corporations subsidiaries

Table 11.5. Other Financial Corporations: Additional Data Series

			Of Which: "Other Financial Corporations" in the Reporting Population		
	Subsidiaries[1] (1)	Associates[1] (2)	Subsidiaries[1,2] (3)	Associates[1] (4)	Other (5)
Balance sheet					
Shares and other equity[3]	Required	Required	Required	Required	Required
Shares and other equity[4]	Required	Required	[5]	[5]	
Purchased goodwill	Required	Required			
Liabilities:[2]					
Deposits			Required		
Loans			Required		
Debt securities			Required		
Insurance technical reserves			Required		
Financial derivatives			Required		
Other liabilities			Required		

[1]Other financial corporations in the reporting population that are subsidiaries/associates and have reverse equity investments should report the positions vis-à-vis their parent investor(s) in columns 1 and 2. If both the reverse investor and the entity in which they are investing are in the reporting population, data should also be reported in column 3 and/or in column 4.

[2]These data are required only if the source data are available only on an unconsolidated basis, such as in the national accounts. This column covers positions with all those entities that are in the same group as the reporting entity and are in the reporting population but are separately incorporated or are offices of entities that are separately incorporated.

[3]Valued as the proportionate share of the investor's stake in subsidiaries' and associates' capital and reserves (similar for reverse investments), and as the market value of any equity stake in other financial corporations in the reporting population.

[4]As valued in the balance sheet, if different from the line above.

[5]These series are required only if the series in columns 1 and 2 are not reported.

and associates in the reporting population (and similarly for reverse investments) as well as in other financial corporations in the reporting population need to be excluded from sector-wide capital to avoid double counting of capital. Hence, the required shares and other equity series in columns 3, 4, and 5. The data for subsidiaries and associates could be combined, depending on the source.

11.61 Data on purchased goodwill are required to deduct the value of goodwill from nonfinancial assets and from capital and reserves. The data for subsidiaries and associates could be combined, depending on the source.

11.62 If source data are on an unconsolidated basis, such as in the national accounts, adjustments will need to be made not only for shares and other equity but also for other intragroup positions that appear on the balance sheet.[15] These balance sheet positions are listed in column 3. As noted in the description of Table 11.3, gross liabilities and gross assets at the sector level are reduced by the amount reported for each series listed.

[15]If source data consolidate information for subsidiaries that are not other financial corporations, other adjustments are needed to "deconsolidate" such subsidiaries to compile data on an other-financial-corporations-only basis.

Nonfinancial Corporations

11.63 For nonfinancial corporations, to calculate the agreed FSIs additional data series might be required. Two sets of data series are presented below: Table 11.6 covers additional data series not available from the national accounts methodology; in Table 11.7, other additional data series are covered. Series marked as "required" are those needed to calculate an agreed indicator. As with other sectors, the importance of specific data series depends on national circumstances, and in determining the need to collect new data, and hence incur increased resource costs, authorities must make a judgment as to the likely impact and importance of the additional data series for compiling FSI data.

11.64 Table 11.6 covers items in the income and expense statement and in the balance sheet. Some data

Table 11.6. Nonfinancial Corporations: Series Not Covered in National Accounts Methodology

Income- and expense-related		
Gains and losses on financial instruments	Required	
Gains and losses on the sale of an associate or subsidiary[1,2]	Required[3]	
Gains and losses on sale of fixed assets in the period[1]	Required	
Extraordinary items	Required	
Balance-sheet-related		
Debt-service payments	Required	
Net open position in foreign currency	Required	
	Subsidiaries[4]	*Associates*[4]
Shares and other equity[5]	Required	Required
Shares and other equity as valued on balance sheet[6]	Required	Required
Prorated share of retained earnings (income)	Required	Required
Purchased goodwill	Required	Required

[1]Measured as the difference between the sale value and the balance sheet value at the previous end period.
[2]Such data are also required if commercial accounting sources are used that include such gains and losses in income.
[3]Depending on the source of information on gains and losses on financial instruments (see paragraph 11.65).
[4]Including reverse equity investments of subsidiaries and associates in their parent investors. The data for subsidiaries and associates for each item could be provided in one aggregate figure; that is, separate identification is not essential.
[5]Valued as the proportionate share of the parent institution's stake in subsidiary/associate capital and reserves.
[6]As valued on the balance sheet, if different from the previous line.

series are required to adjust sector-level income to ensure that it is not unduly increased by intrasector transactions, while other series are those specifically required to compile an FSI ratio.

11.65 Unlike national accounts sources, data on gains and losses on financial instruments are included under income in the *Guide,* as are gains and losses in a given period on the sale of fixed assets. Gains and losses on financial instruments are potentially available from the revaluation account of the *1993 SNA;* if so, data on gains and losses on the sale of subsidiaries and associates need to be excluded (see paragraph 11.24). Data on extraordinary items might also be available from national accounts sources (see Appendix IV).

11.66 Data on debt-service payments and on the net open position in foreign exchange are required to calculate two indicators and are not available from national accounts sources. The need for data on shares and other equity and the prorated share of retained earnings relating to subsidiaries, associates, and other nonfinancial corporations is the same as described for deposit takers in paragraph 11.33. Data on purchased goodwill are required to deduct it from nonfinancial assets and from capital and reserves (and to exclude the amortization of such goodwill from income).

11.67 Additional data series required are set out in Table 11.7, but unlike the tables for deposit takers above, this table can be relevant for both domestic and cross-border consolidated data. The table relates to positions and flows among nonfinancial corporations in the reporting population. Many of the series are required to eliminate (1) intragroup positions to ensure that the sector-level data are compiled on a consolidated basis, (2) intrasector equity investments to avoid double counting of capital and reserves at the sector level, and (3) intrasector income transactions to ensure that sector income is not unduly increased by intrasector transactions.

11.68 For the income items, the need for data on dividends receivable, gains and losses on sale of fixed assets to other nonfinancial corporations, and gains and losses on equity investments in nonfinancial corporations is the same as described for deposit takers for Table 11.2 (see paragraphs 11.41 and 11.42). With regard to the proportionate share of retained earnings, any amounts attributable to nonfinancial associates and subsidiaries (and from reverse equity investments) in the reporting population should be excluded from sector-wide income. However, in the consolidated data at the sector level, interest receivable from nonfinancial subsidiaries should be excluded from interest income and interest expense (see also paragraph

Table 11.7. Nonfinancial Corporations: Additional Data Series

	Nonfinancial Corporations (in the Reporting Population)[1]	Of Which:		
		Subsidiaries[2,3]	Associates[2]	Other
Income- and expense-related[4]				
Dividends receivable	Required			
Interest income receivable		Required	Required[5]	Required[5]
Prorated share of retained earnings	Required[6]			Not applicable
Gains or losses in the period on sale of fixed assets to other nonfinancial corporations	Required			
Gains and losses on equity investments in other nonfinancial corporations				Required
Balance sheet				
Shares and other equity[7]		Required	Required	Required
Shares and other equity		[8]	[8]	
Liabilities				
Of which: Deposits		Required		
Loans		Required		
Debt securities		Required		
Trade credit		Required		
Financial derivatives		Required		
Other liabilities		Required		
Balance-sheet-related				
Debt-service receipts		Required		

[1]If data are provided on a consolidated basis, with subsidiaries in the reporting population included, then the data in this column should exclude transactions with these subsidiaries. The total data could be disaggregated by column to gain greater understanding of the relationships with subsidiaries, associates, and other nonfinancial corporations.

[2]Nonfinancial corporations in the reporting population that are subsidiaries or associates and have reverse equity investments should report the positions vis-à-vis their parent investor(s) in these columns.

[3]These data are required only if the source data are available only on an unconsolidated basis, such as in the national accounts. This column covers positions with all those entities that are in the same group as the reporting entity and are in the reporting population but that are separately incorporated or are offices of entities that are separately incorporated.

[4]If commercial accounts data are the source of information, depending on the accounting practice adopted, data on the amortization of goodwill will also be required so that it can be excluded from income.

[5]Data on interest income receivable from associates and other nonfinancial corporations in the reporting population can be combined into one figure.

[6]Covers only subsidiaries and associates.

[7]Valued as the proportionate share of the investor's stake in subsidiaries' and associates' capital and reserves (similar for reverse investments) and as the market value of any equity stake in other nonfinancial corporations in the reporting population.

[8]As valued in the balance sheet, if different from the line above. Moreover, if the balance sheet value of subsidiaries and associates is reported in Table 11.6, these data are not required.

11.49). In addition, the total data could be disaggregated by column to gain greater understanding of the relationships with subsidiaries, associates, and other nonfinancial corporations.

11.69 Data on shares and other equity relating to subsidiaries, associates, and other nonfinancial corporations are needed to eliminate intersector equity investments to avoid double counting of capital and reserves at the sector level (see also paragraphs 11.37 and 11.38). If source data are on an unconsolidated basis, such as in the national accounts, intragroup positions in the balance sheet items listed in the second column should be deducted from gross liabilities and gross assets to derive positions on a consolidated basis. Moreover, if source data are on an unconsolidated basis, debt-service receipts from subsidiaries are also required to be deducted from debt-service payment data on a consolidated basis.[16]

11.70 Another data series that is required is the number of applications for protection from creditors.

[16]It is proposed that receipts from, rather than payments to, other nonfinancial corporations be collected given that if tradable bonds are issued, the payer might not know the identity of the creditor. But of course, debt-service receipts from the creditor perspective are debt-service payments from the perspective of the debtor.

Table 11.8. Example for Computing Changes in Capital Adequacy Ratio Given the Changes in Population of Reporting Banks

	Period 1	Period 2	Period 3	Period 4
Number of banks in population	10	10	9	9
Joiners (+), leavers (–)	0	0	(+1) (–2)	0
Capital adequacy ratio	0.8	0.7	0.10	0.12
Percentage change	—	–13%	+43%	+20%
Adjusted percentage change	—	—	–5%	—

Availability of Data

11.71 It is unlikely that all data series specified in the *Guide* are readily available to all national authorities. As noted earlier, some data series may not be currently collected, and others may not meet the definitions recommended in the *Guide.* In such circumstances, the data that most closely approximate the principles in the *Guide* should be used, but it is important that, for each data series, differences from the recommendations in the *Guide* be described in the metadata.

11.72 Data series for the numerator and denominator of an FSI ratio may not be available with the same periodicity, restricting the frequency of compilation of the indicator. Depending on the nature of the underlying series, it may be possible to estimate the series that are available less frequently,[17] but the results should be used with caution.

11.73 The assumptions underlying any "grossing-up" procedures for missing reporting entities should be carefully reviewed. For example, they might implicitly assume that the reporting population is representative of the nonreporting population, whereas the nonreporting population might be specialized in certain lines of business.

Breaks in Data Series

11.74 It is particularly important to monitor and document breaks in data series because they can affect the analysis. One of the most frequent types of breaks arises from changes in the reporting population. For instance, new deposit takers can be licensed while others are closed. Moreover, mergers between deposit takers can have significant consequences.

11.75 For data compiled on a domestically controlled cross-border consolidated basis, resident deposit takers' acquisitions of nonresident deposit takers boost the assets and liabilities of the resident deposit-taker sector and increase the exposure of the sector to nonresident markets, while foreign deposit takers' acquisitions of domestically controlled deposit takers have the opposite effect. Furthermore, for domestic consolidated data, if one deposit taker merges with another, the existing positions between these deposit takers will be eliminated, causing a break in the data series for the entire sector; the larger the deposit takers, the more significant such a break in the data series will be. The effect could be even more significant on peer group analysis. For instance, if the merger is between deposit takers in different peer groups, both sets of peer group data (balance sheet as well as income and expense data) will be affected.

11.76 In general, it is important for compilers to document mergers and any changes in underlying accounting rules that affect the continuity of the data series. Such information should be maintained over time.

11.77 In calculating any percentage changes when there are changes in the reporting population, adjustments are required if a consistent time series is to be produced. The example in Table 11.8 illustrates

[17]For instance, for data available only annually, but that are required to compile a quarterly ratio, growth could be projected from the previous annual observation based on past trends or with reference to some relevant index or item, adjusted for any occasional events that would affect the series. For past quarters for which beginning- and end-year data are available, a linear growth rate between the end-year observations could be assumed or the growth rate could reflect movements in a relevant index, adjusted for known occasional events that would have affected the time series. Such estimation methods are used, for example, by the Austrian National Bank in compiling quarterly financial accounts data.

Table 11.9. Deposit Takers' Income and Expense Statement and Balance Sheet

Data Series per Table 4.1	System of National Accounts (1993 SNA) Line item(s)	International Accounting Standards Relevant standard(s)
Income and expense		
1. Interest income	D.41; P.11	IAS 18.29–18.31; 30.10–30.17
2. Interest expense	D.41; P.11	IAS 18.29; 30.10–30.17; 32.30–32.31 [IAS 32.35–32.36]
3. Net interest income	D.41; P.11	IAS 30.10–30.17
4. Noninterest income (net)		
(i) Fees and commissions receivable	P.11	IAS 18.20; 18 App. 10–20
(ii) Gains or losses on financial instruments	AF.2; AF.3; AF.4; AF.5; AF.7; AF.8	IAS 39.103–39.108 [IAS 39.55–39.57]; 30.10–30.15; IAS 21.15; 21.17; 21.19
(iii) Prorated earnings	D.43; part of D.42	IAS 28.3; 28.6; 31.32–31.34
(iv) Other income		
Rental income	D.45; P.11	IAS F.74; IAS 40.66(d)(i)
Dividends and other income from equity holdings	part of D.42	IAS 18.30
Other income	D.75; part of AN.11	IAS 8.16–8.18; 16.56; 40.28
5. Gross income	3 + 4	3 + 4
6. Noninterest expenses		
(i) Personnel costs	D.1; D.623	IAS 19.4
(ii) Other expenses		
Purchases of goods and services	P.2; D.45	IAS 78; 1.80–1.82
Depreciation	K.1; part of K.9	IAS 16.41–16.50
Other operating expenses	D.71; D.75	n.a.; IAS 8.18, F.70 and F.78–F.80; 37.24
Taxes other than income taxes, and subsidies	D.29; D.59; D.39	n.a.; IAS 20.29–20.30
7. Provisions (net)		
(i) Loan loss provisions	K.10	IAS 30.43–30.49; 30.58–30.70
(ii) Other financial asset provisions	K.10	IAS 39.109–39.111 [IAS 39. IG. E.4]
(Bad debt recoveries)		IAS 39.114 [IAS 39.65; 39.66; 39.70]
8. Net income before extraordinary items and taxes	5 minus –6 minus –7	5 minus –6 minus 7
9. Extraordinary items	K.7; K.8	IAS 8.6; 8.11–8.15
10. Income tax expense	D.51	IAS 12.2
11. Net income after tax	8 minus (9 + 10)	8 minus (9 + 10)
12. Dividends payable	D.42; D.43	IAS 18.30; 32.30 [IAS 32.35]
13. Retained earnings	11 minus 12	11 minus 12

	System of National Accounts (1993 SNA)	International Accounting Standards	
	Line item	Disclosure requirements	Relevant standard(s)
Balance sheet			
14. Total assets			
15. Nonfinancial assets	**AN**		**IAS 1.66**
	AN.1	Property, plant, and equipment	IAS 1.66a; 16.6
	AN.2 minus (part of AN.22)	Inventories	IAS 1.66e; 2.4
		Intangible assets	IAS 1.66b; 38.7
16. Financial assets	**AF**		**IAS 30**
17. Currency and deposits	AF.2	Cash and balances with central bank	IAS 30.19; 30.21
		Placements with other banks	IAS 30.21
18. Loans	AF.4		
(i.i) Interbank	AF.4, S.122	Placements with and loans and advances to other banks less placements with other banks	IAS 30.19; 30.21; 39.10 IAS 30.19
(i.ii) Noninterbank	AF.4 minus (AF.4, S.122)	Loans and advances to customers	IAS 14.9
Sectoral distribution of loans	AF.4, S.1–S.2		IAS 14.19; 30.40–30.41 [IAS 32.83–32.85]
Geographical distribution			IAS 30.19

Table 11.9 (concluded)

	System of National Accounts (*1993 SNA*)	International Accounting Standards	
	Line item	Disclosure requirements	Relevant standard(s)
19. Debt securities	AF.3	Treasury bills and other bills eligible for rediscounting with the central bank	IAS 30.19
		Other money market placements	IAS 30.19–32.60 (c); 39.10 [IAS 39.9; 39. AG. 14–15]
		Part of government and other securities for dealing purposes	IAS 30.19–32.60 (c); 39.10 [IAS 39.9; 39. AG. 16–25]
		Part of investment securities	IAS 30.19; 39.10 [IAS 39.9; 39.AG. 14–15]
20. Shares and other equity	AF.5	Part of government and other securities for dealing purposes	IAS 30.19; 1.66d; 28.6
		Part of investment securities	IAS 32.9–32.10; 39.10 [IAS 39.9–39.13; 39. AG. 9–12]
21. Financial derivatives	AF.7	Derivative financial instruments	IAS 1.66f; 39.10 [IAS 39.9]
22. Other assets	AF.6 + AF.8	Trade and other receivables	IAS 1.66i; 12.12
		Tax assets	
23. Liabilities	**AF**		IAS 30
24. Currency and deposits	AF.2		IAS 30.19
(i) Customer deposits	AF.2 minus (AF.2, S.12)	Amounts owed to other depositors	IAS 30.19
(ii) Interbank deposits	AF.2, S.122	Deposits from other banks	IAS 30.19
(iii) Other currency and deposits	AF.2, S.12 minus AF.2, S.122	Other money market deposits	IAS 30.19
25. Loans	AF.4	Part of other borrowed funds	IAS 30.19
26. Debt securities	AF.3	Part of borrowed funds	IAS 30.19
		Certificates of deposit	IAS 30.19
		Promissory notes and other liabilities evidenced by paper	IAS 1.66h
27. Other liabilities	AF.8	Trade and other payables	IAS 1.66i; 12.12
		Tax liabilities	IAS 30.19
28. Debt	AF.2 + AF.3 + AF.4 + AF.8	Deposits from other banks + other money market deposits + amounts owed to other depositors + other borrowed funds + certificates of deposit + promissory notes and other liabilities evidenced by paper + trade and other payables + tax liabilities	
29. Financial derivatives	AF.7	Derivative financial instruments	IAS 32.9–32.10; 39.10 [IAS 39.9–39.13; 39. AG. 9–12]
30. Capital and reserves	AF.5 + B.90 minus (part of AN.22)	Capital and reserves	IAS 1.66m; F.65–F.68
(i) Narrow capital	Funds contributed by owners	Issued capital	IAS 1.74; IAS F.65
	Retained earnings	Accumulated profit/loss	IAS F.65
	General and special reserves	Reserves	IAS F.65–F.66

Note: Information presented within square brackets refers to relevant paragraph numbers in the IFRS as of March 31, 2004, which was to come into effect on January 1, 2005.

Table 11.10. Nonfinancial Corporations' Income and Expense Statement and Balance Sheet

Data Series per Table 4.3	System of National Accounts (*1993 SNA*) Line item(s)	International Accounting Standards Relevant standard(s)
Income and expense		
1. Revenues from sales of goods and services (excluding indirect sales taxes)	P.11 minus (part of P.52)	IAS 18.14; 18.20
2. Cost of sales		
Personnel costs	D.1; D.623	IAS 19.4
Cost of goods and services	P.2; D.45	IAS F.78
Depreciation	K.1; part of K.9	IAS 16.41–16.48; 16.50
Other costs of sales	D.75; n.a. (potential costs)	IAS 8.18; 37.24
Taxes other than income taxes, and subsidies	D.29; D.59; D.39	n.a.; IAS 20.29–20.30
3. Net operating income	1 minus 2	1 minus 2
4. Interest income	D.41	IAS 18.29
5. Interest expense	D.41; P.2	IAS 18.29; IAS 32.30–32.31 [IAS 32.35–32.36]
6. Other income (net)	D.45	n.a.
Rental income	D.45; P.11	IAS F.74; IAS 25.40.66 (d) (i)
Dividends and other income from equity holdings	D.42; D.43	IAS 18.30; 28.3; 31.24–31.34
Net gains/losses on assets and liabilities	part of AN.11; AF.2; AF.3; AF.4; AF.5; AF.7; AF.8	IAS 16.56; 40.28; 21.15; 21.17; 21.19
Other income	D.75	IAS 8.18
7. Net income before extraordinary items and taxes	3 + 4 minus 5 + 6	3 + 4 minus 5 + 6
8. Extraordinary items	K.7; K.8	IAS 8.11–8.15
9. Corporate income taxes	D.51	IAS 12.2
10. Net income after taxes	7 minus (8 + 9)	7 minus (8 + 9)
11. Dividends payable	D.42; D.43	IAS 18.30; IAS 32.30
12. Retained earnings	11 minus 12	11 minus 12

Balance sheet	System of National Accounts (*1993 SNA*) Line item(s)	International Accounting Standards Disclosure requirement(s)	 Relevant standard(s)
13. Total assets			
14. Nonfinancial assets	**AN**	**14 + 15**	**IAS 1.66**
15. Produced	AN.1		
Fixed assets	AN.11	Property, plant, and equipment	IAS 1.66a; 16.6
Inventories	AN.12	Inventories	IAS 1.66e; 2.4
Other	AN.13	Part of intangible assets	IAS 1.66b; 38.7
16. Nonproduced	AN.2 minus (part of AN. 22)	Part of tangible assets Part of intangible assets	IAS 1.66a; 16.6 IAS 1.66b; 38.7
17. Financial assets	**AF**	**17 + 18 + 19 + 20 + 21 + 22**	**IAS 1.66**
18. Currency and deposits	AF.2	Cash and part of cash equivalents	IAS 1.66g; 7.6
19. Debt securities	AF.3	Part of other financial assets	IAS 1.66c
20. Shares and other equity	AF.5	Investments accounted for using the equity method Part of other financial assets	IAS 1.66d; 28.6 IAS 1.66c
21. Trade credit	AF.81	Part of trade and other receivable	IAS 1.66f; 39.10
22. Financial derivatives	AF.7	Derivative financial instruments	IAS 32.9–32.10; 39.10 [IAS 39.9–39.13; 39.AG. 9–12]
23. Other assets	AF.6 + AF.89	Part of trade and other receivables Tax assets	IAS 1.66f; 39.10 IAS 1.66i; 12.12
24. Liabilities	**AF**	**28 + 29**	**IAS 1.66**
25. Loans	AF.4	Part of noncurrent interest-bearing liabilities Part of cash equivalents	IAS 1.66k IAS 1.66g; 7.8
26. Debt securities	AF.3	Part of noncurrent interest-bearing liabilities	IAS 1.66k
27. Trade credit	AF.81	Part of trade and other payables	IAS 1.66h
28. Other liabilities	AF.89	Part of trade and other payables Tax liabilities	IAS 1.66h IAS 1.66i; 12.12

Table 11.10 *(concluded)*

Balance sheet	System of National Accounts (*1993 SNA*) Line item(s)	International Accounting standards: Disclosure requirement(s)	International Accounting standards: Relevant standard(s)
29. Debt	AF.3 + AF.4 + AF.8	Trade and other payables + tax liabilities + noncurrent interest-bearing liabilities + part of cash equivalents	IAS 1.66
30. Financial derivatives	AF.7	Derivative financial instruments	IAS 32.9–32.10; 39.10 [IAS 39.9–39.13; 39.AG. 9–12]
31. Capital and reserves	AF.5 + B.90 minus (part of AN.22)	Capital and reserves	IAS 1.66m; F.65–F.68
(i) Narrow capital		Issued capital	IAS 1.74; F.65
		Accumulated profit/loss	IAS F.65
		Reserves	IAS F.65–F.66

Note: Information presented within square brackets refers to relevant paragraph numbers in the IFRS as of March 31, 2004, which was to come into effect on January 1, 2005.

the adjustments needed. In this example, in period 3, one deposit taker joins the reporting population and two leave. As a result, the sector-level capital adequacy ratio is substantially strengthened. However, the implied increase in the ratio between periods 2 and 3 (+43 percent) does not reflect the change in the underlying performance of the population of reporting deposit takers but rather changes in the composition of the reporting population. To ascertain the underlying trend, the percentage change should be adjusted so that the population base in the current period (period 3) is the same as that in the comparator period (period 2).

Specifically, whereas the percentage change is calculated as follows,

$$\text{Percentage change} = \left\{ \frac{\left[\left(\dfrac{S^{num}_{pop_{t=3}}}{S^{denom}_{pop_{t=3}}} \right) - \left(\dfrac{S^{num}_{pop_{t=2}}}{S^{num}_{pop_{t=2}}} \right) \right]}{\left(\dfrac{S^{num}_{pop_{t=2}}}{S^{num}_{pop_{t=2}}} \right)} \right\} \times 100,$$

the underlying percentage change, adjusted for differences in the reporting population between the two periods being compared, is calculated as

Table 11.11. Households' Income

FSI Lines in the *Guide*	System of National Accounts (*1993 SNA*) Line item(s)
1. Wages and salaries	D.11
2. Property income receivable (net)	D.4
3. Current transfers	D.62; D.7
4. Other	P1 minus (P2 + D.1 + D.29 + D.39 + part of P.52)
5. Less: taxes including social security contributions	D.5; D.612; D.613; D.62; D.7
6. Gross disposable income	B.6

$$\text{Adjusted percentage change} = \left\{ \frac{\left[\left(\frac{S^{num}_{pop_{t=3}} - S^{num}_{joiners_{t=3}} + S^{num}_{leavers_{t=3}}}{S^{denom}_{pop_{t=3}} - S^{denom}_{joiners_{t=3}} + S^{denom}_{leavers_{t=3}}} \right) - \left(\frac{S^{num}_{pop_{t=2}}}{S^{num}_{pop_{t=2}}} \right) \right]}{\left(\frac{S^{num}_{pop_{t=2}}}{S^{num}_{pop_{t=2}}} \right)} \right\} \times 100,$$

where S is the aggregate value of the numerator (denominator) for the population in periods 2 and 3 (that is, the joining or leaving bank(s) in period 3).

Seasonal Adjustment

11.78 As with many economic and financial data series, regularly occurring events or "seasonal factors"—such as public holidays and end-of-year profit taking by financial institutions and other corporations—can influence changes in the level of an FSI for a given period. Various techniques can be used to identify and remove seasonal influences from FSI time-series data, ranging from simple visual inspection of the data series to the application of sophisticated statistical tools.[18] Nevertheless, while the dissemination of seasonally adjusted FSI time series could be considered and can be recommended where large and statistically reliable seasonal influences can be identified, it should be regarded as complementing rather than replacing the dissemination of non-seasonally adjusted time-series data. Seasonal adjustment methods should be documented in metadata, and consideration should be given to disseminating information on the statistical reliability of the seasonal factors.

[18]For a discussion of a range of seasonal adjustment techniques see European Central Bank (2003).

12. Dissemination of FSI Ratios and Related Data

Introduction

12.1 To enhance the transparency of their financial system, countries are encouraged to disseminate the core and other FSIs on a frequent basis. This chapter provides a standard framework for the dissemination of the core and encouraged FSIs. It can be adapted to meet specific country circumstances. The chapter also provides additional frameworks for the dissemination of information that allow analysts to interpret the FSI data in the context of specific country circumstances, including the structural features of the financial system. Dissemination of this additional information can be essential, because disseminating FSIs alone may not provide an adequate basis for their interpretation due to the complexity of information they encapsulate, the range of data sources used in their construction, and the various accounting rules under which the data can be compiled.

12.2 While FSIs provide a variety of information on the health and soundness of the financial system that is essential for macroprudential analysis, they are not sufficient in their own right to provide a comprehensive analysis of the vulnerabilities of a country's financial system. Other factors that are important, but lie outside the scope of the *Guide,* include the quality of supervision and of corporate governance, as well as the incentives facing financial corporations, including the legal framework and the role of government in the financial system. Some of these factors are discussed in the next part of the *Guide.* It should be recognized that coming to a judgment on the strength and vulnerability of any financial system by combining these qualitative factors with the quantitative FSI data is not an exact method of analysis.

Dissemination Practices

12.3 As noted above, it is recommended that FSIs be disseminated on a frequent basis. The availability of information can vary among FSIs—for instance, information on interbank interest rates will be available more frequently than information on the geographic distribution of lending. Nonetheless, countries might work toward releasing at least a basic, rather than the full, FSI data set on a quarterly basis, within one quarter of the reference date. Some FSIs, such as financial market indicators, may be available for dissemination more frequently. Dissemination of a basic data set on a quarterly basis allows new developments to be identified at an early stage and provides time-series data that can be used to assess variations in FSI data across time and in comparison with other key economic data.

12.4 The data covered in a basic data set can vary depending on national circumstances, but as a minimum it should include the core FSIs specified in this *Guide.* Preferably, the data with a quarterly frequency should cover institutions that account for a significant part of the assets of the reporting population; complete coverage should be achieved with at least annual frequency. The need for dissemination of encouraged FSIs depends on national circumstances.

12.5 When data are disseminated, provisional data should be clearly indicated and any major revisions explained by way of notes to the published tables. Breaks in series, for example, due to changes in the reporting population, should be clearly identified and quantified where possible. Such explanations are particularly important given that the entrance or departure of a few institutions from the reporting sample could potentially have a significant impact on the FSIs. More generally, metadata describing in detail the content and coverage of the FSIs, as well as the accounting conventions and other national guidelines reflected in the data, should be made publicly available.

12.6 Given the wide range of source data needed for compiling FSIs, data from various agencies (for example, the central bank, the statistical agency, and the supervisory agency) are likely to be included. Nevertheless, as noted in Chapter 10, it is recommended that one agency take the lead and the responsibility for the dissemination of all the FSIs produced in the country on one centralized website and/or in a paper publication. Such an approach facilitates access by users. The lead agency should be designated as the contact point for user queries on national FSIs.

A Framework for Disseminating FSIs

12.7 Set out below is a dissemination framework based on two modules. These modules organize information into a series of tables aimed at providing a coherent body of information. The two modules and their elements are (1) the FSIs and related data, and (2) metadata required to interpret the FSIs.

Module I

- **The core and encouraged FSIs.** Table 12.1 provides an illustrative presentation of the list of indicators on both a domestic controlled cross-border and domestic consolidated basis. It is recognized that alternative possibilities for the ordering of the list exist. Time-series data are encouraged, as are graphical presentations that can facilitate the identification of trends in FSIs and complement the data series themselves.[1]
- **Financial sector overview.** The *Guide* sets out some structural indicators for deposit takers and other financial corporations (see Table 12.2). These indicators go beyond the core and encouraged sets of FSIs in this *Guide*.
- **Sector-level income and expense and balance sheet statements.** These statements provide the underlying data series used to calculate many FSIs. The *Guide* considers that disseminating these statements would support the analysis of the FSI data sets, although such dissemination goes beyond the agreed FSIs. Such data can help gauge the magnitudes of the underlying amounts, enable interpretation of ratios—especially whether movements in ratios over time are caused by changes in the component elements of the numerator and/or denominator—and allow additional FSIs to be calculated as country circumstances require. The tables for disseminating the sector-level income and expense and balance sheet data are presented in Chapter 4—Table 4.1 (Deposit Takers), Table 4.2 (Other Financial Corporations), Table 4.3 (Nonfinancial Corporations), and Table 4.4 (Households).

[1]Ideally, data series would extend back to cover at least one business cycle to facilitate the interpretation of current FSIs.

The core and encouraged FSIs

12.8 Table 12.1 provides an illustrative presentation of FSI data (1) on a domestically controlled, cross-border consolidated basis and (2) on a domestic basis (with data for deposit takers and other corporations on a domestically consolidated basis). The core FSIs are highlighted in bold italics. For deposit takers, the *Guide* requires the compilation and dissemination of data on a domestic controlled cross-border consolidated basis. Data on a domestically consolidated basis might be separately compiled if the authorities believe such data would contribute materially to their financial stability analysis.

12.9 As noted in Chapter 5, national authorities may see a need to compile separate FSIs on subsidiaries of foreign controlled deposit takers (also consolidated cross-border with their own branches and deposit-taking subsidiaries in other countries, if any); such information could be disseminated as an additional column in the table for deposit-taking FSIs only.

Financial sector overview

12.10 As noted in Chapter 2, each country has its own unique financial structure, and this will affect the range of data available for calculating FSIs and any assessment of FSIs that are disseminated. Thus, Table 12.2 presents structural indicators for the domestic financial sector that might be relevant for any such assessment. This list goes beyond the agreed FSIs.

Deposit takers

12.11 To provide an overview of the size and ownership structure of the deposit-taking sector, thus supporting the interpretation of FSIs, the following key structural indicators could be disseminated on, at least, an annual basis:

- Number of domestically incorporated deposit takers and number of branches of foreign banks.
- Number of domestic employees in all resident deposit takers.
- Number of branch outlets of deposit takers in the economy.
- Total value of assets (domestic and foreign) owned by resident deposit takers, of which
  (1) domestically controlled deposit takers[2]
    (a) government controlled
    (b) privately controlled

[2]In those rare instances where the parent might be considered as being located both in the domestic and a foreign economy and the deposit taker classifies such entities as domestically controlled, separately identifying such entities, when disseminating any data on financial structure, might be considered.

Table 12.1. Illustrative Presentation of Financial Soundness Indicators
(Ratios unless otherwise stated)

	Domestically Controlled, Cross-Border Consolidated Basis (for Soundness Analysis) (Required) (1)	Domestic Consolidated Basis (for Link with Macroeconomy) (2)
Deposit takers[1]		
Capital-based[2]		
Regulatory capital to risk-weighted assets		[3]
Regulatory Tier I capital to risk-weighted assets		[3]
Capital to assets		
Nonperforming loans net of provisions to capital		
Return on equity		
Large exposures to capital		
(number of large exposures)		
(to large resident entities)[4]		
(to connected borrowers)[5]		
Net open position in foreign exchange to capital[6]		
Gross asset position in financial derivatives to capital		
Gross liability position in financial derivatives to capital		
Net open position in equities to capital		
Asset-based		
Liquid assets to total assets		
Liquid assets to short-term liabilities		
Customer deposits to total (noninterbank) loans		
Return on assets		
Nonperforming loans to total gross loans		
Sectoral distribution of loans to total loans (percentages of total)[7]		
Deposit takers		
Central bank		
General government		
Other financial corporations		
Nonfinancial corporations		
Other domestic sectors[8]		
Nonresidents		
Residential real estate loans to total loans		
Commercial real estate loans to total loans		
Geographical distribution of loans to total loans (percentages of total)[9]		
Domestic economy		
Advanced economies		
Regions, excluding advanced economies		
Africa		
Of which: Sub-Sahara		
Asia		
Europe		
Of which: Former Soviet Union, including Russia		
Middle East		
Western Hemisphere		
Foreign-currency-denominated loans to total loans		
Foreign-currency-denominated liabilities to total liabilities		
Income- and expense-based		
Interest margin to gross income		
Trading income to total income		
Noninterest expenses to gross income		
Personnel expenses to noninterest expenses		
Other financial corporations		
Assets to total financial system assets		
Assets to GDP	n.a.	

Table 12.1 *(concluded)*

	Domestically Controlled, Cross-Border Consolidated Basis (for Soundness Analysis) (Required) (1)	Domestic Consolidated Basis (for Link with Macroeconomy) (2)
Nonfinancial corporations		
Total debt to equity		
Return on equity		
Earnings to interest and principal expenses		
Net foreign exchange exposure to equity		
Number of applications for protection from creditors	n.a.	
Households[10]		
Household debt to GDP	n.a.	
Household debt service and principal payments to income	n.a.	
Real estate markets		
Residential real estate prices (annual percentage increase)	n.a.	
Commercial real estate prices (annual percentage increase)	n.a.	
Market liquidity		
Average bid-ask spread in the securities market (percentage of midpoint price) (specify type of instrument)	n.a.	
Average daily turnover ratio in the securities market (specify type of instrument)	n.a.	
Interest rates		
Spread between reference lending and deposit rates (basis points)		
Spread between highest and lowest domestic interbank rate (basis points)	n.a.	

Note: n.a. = not applicable.

[1]All series highlighted in bold and italics are core FSIs.

[2]For all the capital-based indicators, except the regulatory capital-based FSIs, both a narrow and total capital measure can be adopted. Where applicable, Tier 1 capital should be used as the narrow measure.

[3]In most cases, such data might be applicable only to incorporated deposit takers.

[4]Defined as claims of the largest deposit takers on the largest entities in the resident economy, including government, to capital (see paragraph 6.29).

[5]Defined as claims on affiliated entities, including nonresident entities, and other connected counterparties, to capital (paragraph 6.30).

[6]The measure of the net open position employed, whether total or on-balance-sheet items only, should be made explicit when disseminating data.

[7]Supplementary information by type of industry could also be provided.

[8]Consists of households and NPISHs. These sectors could be separately identified.

[9]Supplementary information by jurisdiction could also be provided, if significant.

[10]To be compiled on an aggregate residence basis.

(2) foreign controlled deposit takers
   (a) subsidiaries of nonresident parent entities
   (b) branches of nonresident parent entities.

12.12 As described in Chapter 5, in the *Guide* control is defined as the ability to determine general corporate policy by choosing (or removing) appropriate directors. Any deposit taker that is neither controlled by the government of the economy in which it is located, nor foreign controlled (as defined in paragraph 5.11), is to be classified as private domestically controlled.

12.13 The number, employment, and value of assets owned by the deposit-taking sector provide information on the size of the sector. Additionally, information on the net number of deposit takers entering or leaving the business and information from FSIs, such as the spread between deposit and lending rates, provide some indication of competitive pressures or whether the sector could be under stress. In addition, the number of branch outlets in the economy can be a source of information both on cost pressures and on the size of the deposit-taking industry within the economy.[3]

[3]Although the nature of a branch can vary across countries—from "brick and stone" branches to one-person windows.

Table 12.2. Illustrative Presentation of Structural Indicators for the Domestic Financial Sector

	Number of Institutions	Number of Employees	Number of Branches	Financial Assets			Market Concentration[2]	Claims on Residents (as a percentage of assets)	Total Premium Income
				Billions ($)	Percentage of system assets[1]	Percentage of GDP			
Resident deposit takers[3]									
Domestically controlled									n.a.
Of which:									n.a.
Government									
Private									n.a.
Foreign controlled									
Of which:									n.a.
Subsidiaries									
Branches									n.a.
Memorandum item:									
Cross-border consolidated[4]					n.a.	n.a.			n.a.
Other financial corporations[3]									
Insurance companies[5]			n.a.						
Nonlife insurance			n.a.						
Life insurance			n.a.						
Pension funds[5]			n.a.						n.a.
Securities dealers[5]			n.a.						n.a.
Investment funds[5]			n.a.						n.a.
Other financial entities[5]			n.a.						n.a.

Note: n.a. = not applicable.

[1]Percentage of total financial system assets (see paragraph 7.6).

[2]Number of institutions accounting for 75 percent or more of the financial assets of the sector.

[3]Identifying the names of the top five institutions in the sector (or a number around five that is considered more appropriate to national circumstances) and their combined share of financial assets can identify the important financial corporations in the economy.

[4]Cross-border consolidation of deposit-taking business of domestically incorporated and controlled deposit takers.

[5]If there is significant foreign control of domestic institutions, a distinction by domestically controlled and foreign controlled could be considered.

12.14 Attributing the value of assets between domestically controlled, including government-controlled, deposit takers and subsidiaries and branches of foreign parent entities provides an indication of the ownership structure of the deposit-taking sector. Moreover, the value of assets could be divided into claims on residents and nonresidents, thereby indicating the importance of foreign business to deposit takers. When the value of deposit takers' assets and, in particular, the value of loans to nonfinancial corporations and households are compared with GDP, the importance of deposit takers' financial intermediation to the economy is highlighted. In this regard, compilers could also disseminate information from national accounts data on the value added by domestic deposit takers compared with GDP.

12.15 In many economies, the deposit-taking sector may consist of specialist institutions, as described in Chapter 2. If so, the nature of the banking business undertaken by various types of specialist institutions may differ significantly. To further understand the structure of the financial system, compilers could distinguish structural information on commercial banks and on distinctive types of specialized banks such as savings banks, cooperative banks, and microfinance institutions. Moreover, where appropriate, offshore deposit takers—that is, those licensed to take deposits from and lend primarily, or solely, to residents of other economies—could be distinguished.[4]

12.16 The concentration of deposit takers' assets is also important to understanding the structure of the financial system. Thus, compilers might consider dissemination of the additional indicators as discussed below:

- Names and, in terms of the value of deposit takers' assets, the combined market share of the top five resident deposit takers (or a number around five that is considered more appropriate to national circumstances).
- Number of deposit takers that accounts for 25, 50, and 75 percent of the value of deposit takers' total assets.
- Measures of concentration in the sector. One possibility is the Herfindahl Index, which is calculated as the sum of squares of the market shares of all firms in the sector and is described in more detail, along with other measures of concentration, in Chapter 15.

12.17 Finally, subject to national confidentiality constraints, countries could disseminate information on their deposit insurance schemes, because the level of coverage of depositors' funds can affect economic behavior and thus have implications for financial stability.

Other financial corporations

12.18 Given the different specializations within the other financial corporations sector, to more fully understand the structure of the sector, compilers could disseminate the following subsector information for insurance companies, pension funds, security (including derivative) dealers, investment funds, and other financial entities:

- Number of resident institutions (with separate identification of life insurance and other insurance companies).
- Number of domestic employees.
- Total value of assets (domestic and foreign) owned or, for investment companies, under management,
  - of which
    (1) domestically controlled
    (2) foreign controlled.

12.19 Information on the split of assets of other financial corporations between claims on residents and nonresidents could also be disseminated.

12.20 Compilers could identify the largest corporations in the other financial corporations sector so that it is transparent as to who might be the major players in the financial markets outside the deposit-taking sector. Compilers could disseminate the following information:

- Names and, in terms of the value of assets, market share of the top five companies (or a number around five that is considered more appropriate to national circumstances).

12.21 For insurance companies the following could also be disseminated:

- Total premium income of resident insurance companies,
  - of which
    (1) life
    (2) nonlife.

[4]FSIs could be compiled both including and excluding such deposit takers, depending on national circumstances. While the operations of such deposit takers have implications for the domestic economy—a wide-scale collapse of offshore deposit takers could have systemic consequences—the authorities might consider the nature of the business of offshore deposit takers as different from that of other deposit takers.

12.22 The types of financial institutions mentioned above are likely to be the major owners of financial assets within the other financial corporations sector. However, if other groups of financial institutions are significant owners of financial assets in the economy, for example, finance companies, compilers could disseminate information on the value of their assets by type of activity.

Nonfinancial corporations

12.23 While not covered in Table 12.2, compilers might consider providing the names of, and the value of assets owned by, the top five nonfinancial corporations (or other number appropriate to national circumstances) to facilitate the compilation of data on large exposures and to provide an indication of their importance within the economy.

Module 2

- **Metadata** describing in detail the content and coverage of the FSIs and the accounting conventions and other national guidelines reflected in the data should be publicly available. In particular, deviations from the principles set out in the *Guide* should be clearly explained, and any differences in approaches within and between sectors should be highlighted. At the development stage, some FSIs may be calculated from data drawn from data covering various subgroups that apply different accounting principles. Such situations should be highlighted in the metadata.

12.24 Box 12.1 presents some illustrative points for items that could be covered in such metadata. This module is modeled on the approach in the IMF's Special Data Dissemination Standard and the General Data Dissemination System.

Specific information on FSIs disseminated

12.25 A brief description should be provided of the definitions and the data sources for the numerator and denominator of each FSI, with cross-references to the general information section. Other specific information could include whether the numerator and denominator are available with the same periodicity, and if not, how this affects the use of the data.

Box 12.1. Illustrative Points for Items to Be Covered in the Metadata

Coverage, Periodicity, and Timeliness of Data

Data category
Coverage, such as deposit takers or nonfinancial corporations.

Periodicity and timeliness of release
The frequency with which data are disseminated, and the timeliness of dissemination. If some data series are released more frequently than others, this can be specified.

Access by the Public

Dissemination practices
The mode(s) of disseminating FSIs and the main centralized source for users wanting to access FSIs.

Contacts
Names, addresses, e-mail addresses, and other contact information.

Integrity

Terms and conditions
The terms and conditions under which these data are produced and the agencies involved in the process, and similar information.

Revisions
Information on revisions in the data sets and advance notices of major changes in methodology.

Quality of the Disseminated Data

General information

Accounting framework
Descriptions of the underlying accounting framework(s).

Nature of the basic data
Data sources, consolidation methodology, institutional coverage, and so on.

Compilation practices
Information on samples and surveys, statistical adjustments, methods of verifying data, and so on.

Accounting and classification principles
Time of recognition principles, valuation methods, classification of accounts, netting procedures, and so on. Differences in standards or practices from those recommended in the *Guide* should be described.

Other
Any other relevant information on compilation practices for the data that are disseminated, including information on significant changes in the reporting population.

PART IV

Analysis of Financial Soundness Indicators

13. Financial Soundness Indicators and Macroprudential Analysis

Introduction

13.1 This chapter provides an overview of the use of FSI data in macroprudential analysis. It focuses on three questions:

- Why are FSI data needed?
- What is the financial stability framework within which FSI data can be used?
- What are some other tools that can enhance the usefulness and understanding of FSI data?

13.2 *The collection, compilation, and dissemination of data involve resource costs for suppliers and compilers.* Therefore to justify such work, it is necessary to ask the following question.

Why Are FSI Data Needed?

13.3 The recognition of the need for FSI statistics among the international community arose out of the financial crises of the 1990s.[1] A review of recent decades shows that many IMF member countries experienced financial crises that often resulted in severe disruptions of economic activity. The significant costs of these crises, both direct (such as the cost of recapitalizing the deposit takers) and indirect (such as the loss of real economic activity), have highlighted the need to develop a body of—preferably high-frequency—statistics that could help policymakers in macroprudential analysis, that is, in identifying the strengths and vulnerabilities in their countries' financial systems. Such analysis could form the basis for taking action to prevent crises from occurring.

13.4 Understanding of the nature and causes of financial system crises has developed a great deal in recent years, but analytical work continues.

13.5 Financial system crises can arise from the failure of one or more institutions, whose effects then spread through a variety of contagion mechanisms to affect the whole system. The original shock that caused the failure is likely to be external or *exogenous* to the institution. Indeed, prudential supervision supports efforts to identify potential vulnerabilities in individual institutions before they become severe, and if they do become serious to inform actions that limit their systemic consequences.

13.6 Systemic crises can also arise from the exposure of a financial system to common risk factors. Under these circumstances, systemic stability is determined by behavior internal or *endogenous* to the system. In other words, financial crises arise when the collective actions of individual agents make the system itself vulnerable to shocks. The buildup of these vulnerabilities and risks tends to occur over time, such as during an economic upswing when confidence is high, before materializing in recessions.

13.7 The sources of vulnerability of the financial system can vary: for example, poor asset quality, undue exposures to market and credit risk, and lack of capital. The timing of a crisis and its immediate causes can also vary: for example, the deteriorating condition of private borrowers, excess government borrowing that undermines confidence, concern over a large current account deficit, and/or a sharp swing in the exchange rate. When the financial system is vulnerable, such events can result in a financial system crisis that imposes severe losses on an economy, both directly and indirectly: directly as depositors lose funds as banks fail and as governments incur fiscal costs to rebuild the financial system; indirectly as economic activity is reduced by the disruption of financial intermediation and/or payment systems. Moreover, there can be adverse social consequences from the economic and financial disruptions.

13.8 Experience has shown that actions or policies that seem appropriate from an individual entity's

[1]This section of the chapter draws on Borio (2003) and Crockett (2002).

viewpoint can have unwelcome systemic consequences. For instance, in the face of perceived higher risk caused by financial market developments, or a reduction in capital adequacy caused by weak profitability, individual deposit takers might tighten lending terms. This might impede economic activity over significant periods of time and/or precipitate financial stress and asset price declines, which in turn could increase financial system risk.

13.9 FSIs and the framework provided in this *Guide* have been developed to assist macroprudential analysis. The position at a single moment in time and developments over time, such as through a full business cycle, can be assessed. Indeed, understanding how vulnerabilities build up over time is particularly relevant to this analysis, along with an understanding of the mutually reinforcing dynamic interaction between the financial system and the real economy. The focus of this body of data is somewhat different from, but also complements, that for prudential supervision (which is rationalized in terms of deposit protection). The focus of this body of data is also different from that in the national accounts (which is used to monitor macroeconomic activity). Thus, while necessary, FSI data alone are not sufficient to meet all the needs of macroprudential analysis, as discussed later in this chapter.

13.10 *If the need for the body of data is understood, how does the set of data series fit together?* In short, it is necessary to ask the following question.

What Is the Financial Stability Framework Within Which FSI Data Can Be Used?

13.11 The development of a financial stability framework for the analysis of FSIs and related data is still at a relatively early stage, and, indeed, dissemination of data would support further empirical research.[2] In June 2003, the IMF staff presented to the IMF's Executive Board such a framework (see Figure 13.1). While it is considered a useful tool, it nonetheless requires further development.

13.12 The framework has four different elements:

- Assessment of the risk of a shock to the financial sector. Among the tools available are indicators used in early warning system (EWS) models. These indicators are typically based on country-specific data, developments in the global economy, and political risk.[3,4]
- The use of FSIs to (1) assess the vulnerability of the financial sector to shocks; (2) assess the condition of nonfinancial sectors; (3) monitor financial sector vulnerabilities arising from credit, liquidity, and market risk; and (4) assess the capacity of the financial sector to absorb losses, as measured by capital adequacy, for example.[5]
- Analysis of macrofinancial linkages to obtain an indication of the effect on macroeconomic conditions, debt sustainability, and impairment in the intermediation capacity of the financial sector.
- Surveillance of macroeconomic conditions to assess the effect of shocks on macroeconomic developments and debt sustainability.

13.13 From Figure 13.1 it can be seen that FSIs are part of a larger body of information and tools used to monitor financial stability, and there are interrelationships among the different elements.

13.14 While the financial stability framework indicates how a shock might be transmitted through the financial system, the direction of causality is not set. For example, weakness in banks' capital adequacy could result in a tightening of credit standards that would affect the condition of the nonfinancial sector, and declining productivity and income in the nonfinancial corporations sector that reduce debt-servicing capacity could make the financial system vulnerable. Therefore, widespread compilation and dissemination of FSIs and related data, such as the sectoral financial statements and the structural indicators outlined in the *Guide,* would help in the understanding of linkages among FSIs as well as between FSIs and other economic data.

Analysis of Linkages Among FSIs

13.15 The complexities of the relationships or linkages among FSIs are still far from being fully under-

[2]This section draws on IMF (2003d).

[3]While EWS models offer a systematic, objective, and consistent method for predicting crises, they have a mixed record in terms of forecasting accuracy and are used as only one among many inputs into IMF surveillance.

[4]See also Abiad (2003).

[5]Moreover, these vulnerabilities and capital adequacy should be monitored both for the sector as a whole and for key peer groups that are sources of risk to financial stability.

Figure 13.1. Analytic Framework for Financial Stability

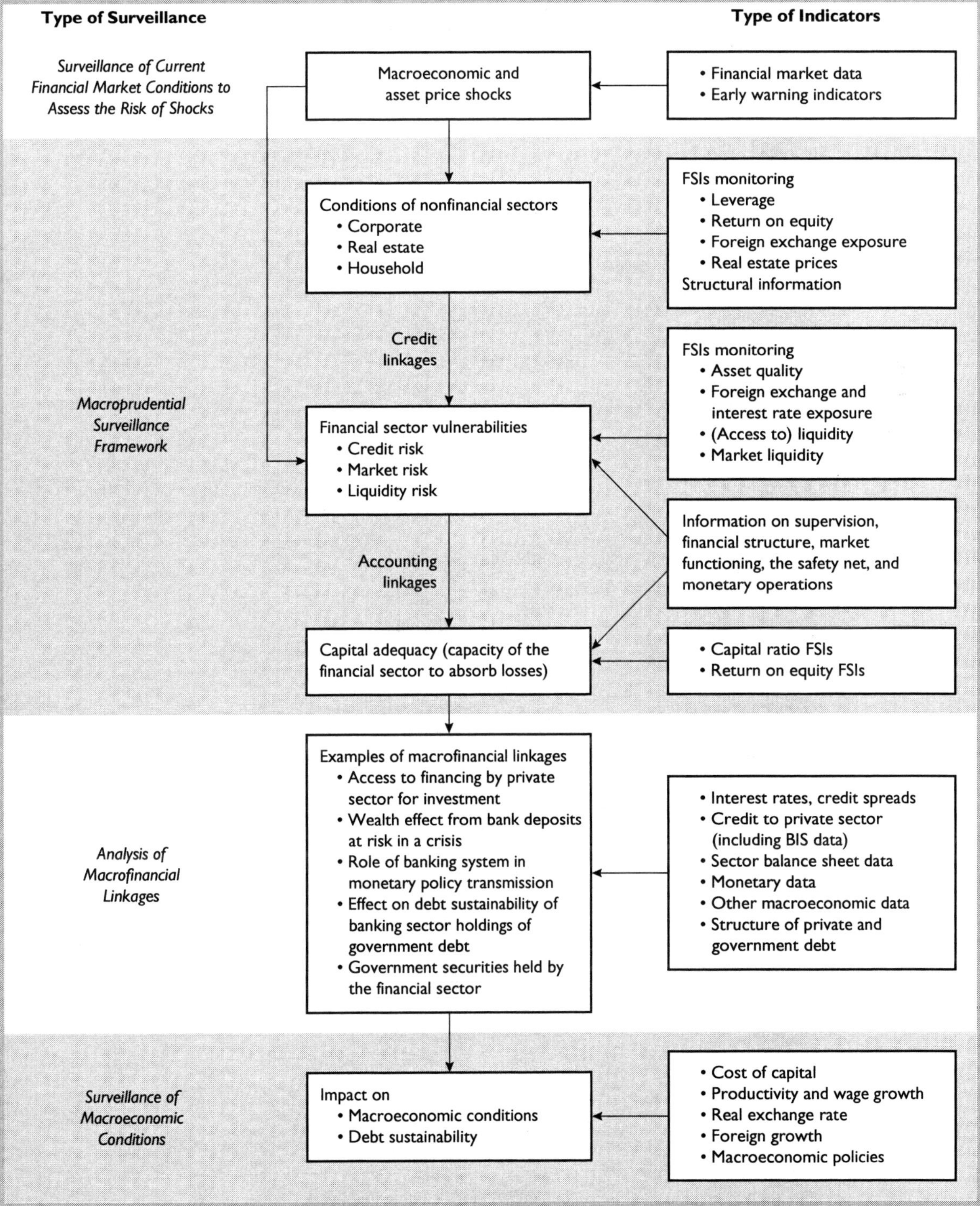

stood. Nonetheless, even in the absence of widespread dissemination of FSI data, some linkages are clear.

Corporate leverage and asset quality

13.16 FSIs monitoring the financial condition of the nonfinancial corporations sector may help in detecting a potential deterioration in asset quality at an early stage, before it is reflected in NPLs. Such FSIs help compensate for the fact that NPLs—the best available measure of asset quality—are a lagging indicator, partly due to the period that a loan needs to be in arrears before it is declared nonperforming. The corporate leverage and debt-service capacity ratios can be used as indicators of the asset quality, as the corporate sector is a key channel through which shocks affect the deposit-taking sector.[6]

Asset quality and capital adequacy

13.17 The linkages between FSIs of asset quality and capital adequacy derive from loan classification and provisioning rules that determine when, and how much, banks provision against nonperforming loans. Thus, these rules influence the size and timing of any reduction in capital that results from a deterioration in asset quality. Since these rules vary across countries, the linkages are likely to be different for each country. Especially when banks have significant discretion in classifying loans or there may be forbearance, close attention needs to be paid to these rules because of the greater scope for banks to underreport the actual deterioration in credit quality. Similarly, inadequate provisioning rules enable banks to delay addressing credit problems, which are likely to become more serious over time as a result.

Taking account of macrofinancial linkages

13.18 The macrofinancial linkages between nonfinancial sectors and the banking sector are important for gauging the possible impact of a financial crisis on macroeconomic developments. These linkages arise from the borrowing and the depositing of funds by other sectors with deposit takers. The importance of these linkages can be measured through a combination of monetary data and, for transactions routed through foreign centers, BIS international banking statistics. Because in most economies deposit takers are at the center of the financial system, these linkages are likely to be very significant.

13.19 Table 12.2 sets out a set of structural indicators that help to understand the importance of deposit takers to the economy and to gauge the possible impact of a financial crisis: the number of institutions and the structure of their ownership, the number of branches and employees, the absolute and relative size of financial assets held, and so on. Moreover, these indicators, through the information they provide on the ownership structure, can indicate the possibility that deposit takers might receive outside support in a crisis, such as in the case of foreign- and government-controlled deposit takers.

13.20 The financial sector's holdings of debt securities issued by the government and the private sector can be important. Specifically, credit or market losses and a sharp fall in the capital ratio can lead to an adjustment in the deposit-taking sector's holdings of this debt. When deposit takers' balance sheets contain a significant share of outstanding government or private debt securities, the debtors' borrowing costs and capacity to roll over their debt could be affected, with possible implications for debt sustainability. To assess the significance of these linkages, it can be useful to monitor FSIs in combination with sectoral financial statement data. Moreover, the sustainability of government debt might also be affected if there were a banking crisis in which the government had to bail out the banking sector.

13.21 Another linkage exists due to the potential impact of banking sector problems on the monetary policy transmission mechanism. Financial system weakness could make it more costly to tighten monetary policy, limiting the policy options of the central bank. In this case, FSI data complement monetary data. Data on financial structure, including the relative importance of market and bank financing, can also be useful in this analysis. Payment systems are also vital links between the financial sector and the rest of the economy. This aspect of financial stability is discussed below.

13.22 *FSI and related data provide quantitative information on the current health and soundness of the financial system, but additional tools can be used.*

[6]See IMF (2003d, p. 24). Work in the Fund described in IMF (2003d) found that the nonfinancial corporations sector's leverage ratio had a significant impact on deposit takers' asset quality with a one-year lag.

What Are Some Other Tools That Can Enhance the Usefulness and Understanding of FSI Data?

13.23 The analysis of FSIs can be strengthened by using stress tests and information on the effectiveness of banking supervision and the robustness of the financial system infrastructure.[7]

Stress Testing and FSIs

13.24 Analytical work has focused on how aggregate stress testing can be used in combination with FSIs to enhance their usefulness. Aggregate stress testing involves applying standardized shocks to deposit takers' balance sheets and then aggregating the results across deposit takers to obtain the impact on the sector as a whole. Stress testing also provides a way to assess certain types of risks that are hard to measure precisely using FSIs, including risks arising from derivatives and off-balance-sheet exposures.

13.25 The relationship between FSIs and stress testing derives from the fact that changes in FSIs are typically outputs of stress tests and also "intermediate" inputs of stress tests in some cases. Specifically, in stress testing the impact of a macroeconomic shock is usually measured by its impact on the capital ratio FSIs. Moreover, some shocks are formulated in terms of changes in the level of NPLs and thus provide a direct measure of the linkage between changes in the NPL-based FSIs and the capital ratio for the deposit-taking sector.

13.26 Stress testing and FSIs are different but complementary approaches to assessing risks to financial stability. FSIs allow more continuous monitoring of specific strengths and vulnerabilities over time, while the stress tests give an estimate of the losses (typically reported as a change in the capital ratio FSI) in the context of vulnerabilities from a one-time, plausible shock to a relevant macroeconomic risk factor. An introduction to stress testing is provided in Appendix VI.

13.27 While a systemic risk arising from interbank exposures can be monitored by aggregated data, such an approach does not take into account the structure of bilateral interbank exposures within the sector. Stress tests can use information on the distribution of interbank exposures within the sector to assess more precisely the risk of a systemic crisis being triggered by the failure of a systemically important bank, as described in Box 13.1.

Basel Core Principles (BCPs) and FSIs

13.28 A wide range of information relevant to assessing the soundness of the banking sector can be found in the assessment of compliance with the BCPs for effective banking supervision.[8] Assessing compliance with the BCPs is an integral part of every FSAP. The assessments are sometimes conducted separately as well.

13.29 The link between compliance with core principles and financial stability remains complex. It involves, for example, lags in the implementation of rules and their ultimate effect on the health of the financial system. The descriptive information contained in the assessments of BCPs can help assess how a lack of compliance with specific core principles may contribute to banking sector vulnerabilities and affect the capacity of the banking sector capital to absorb potential losses.

13.30 Table 13.1 lists specific BCPs that may contain relevant information to assess particular aspects of the stability of the financial system and indicates in which area of macroprudential analysis this information may be useful. The table suggests that many of the core principles contain information potentially relevant to the assessment of risks to the stability of the financial system.[9]

13.31 More broadly, the information provided in the assessments of BCPs can be used to help interpret FSIs in a number of ways:

- To support the metadata that should be provided with the dissemination of FSI data, assessments of BCPs can clarify what is being measured by the FSIs. For example, when assessing capital adequacy FSIs, BCP 6 clarifies the definition of capi-

[7]Comprising payment systems, financial market infrastructure, systemic liquidity arrangements, accounting and disclosure, insolvency regimes, and financial safety nets.

[8]IMF and World Bank (2002) reviews the experience of the IMF and the World Bank in conducting BCP assessments in over 60 countries to identify the extent to which it is possible to use these assessments to investigate the effectiveness of banking supervision.

[9]The assessments of BCPs contain two types of information: descriptive information regarding the way in which specific criteria are met and a rating of the degree of compliance with each core principle.

Box 13.1. Using Interbank Stress Testing to Assess Systemic Risk[1]

Interbank stress testing can be used to assess the systemic risk deriving from the potential of a shock to trigger contagion through interbank exposures. It estimates the potential for the failure of one, or a few banks, triggered by a shock, to cause other banks to fail. This exercise has two stages: first, a standard stress test applied to individual banks is used to identify the bank (or banks) that are at greatest risk of failure. Second, an interbank stress test based on data on bilateral interbank exposures is used to assess whether failure of the vulnerable bank or banks could trigger the failure of other banks in the system (which could have already been weakened directly by the shock) due to the interbank exposures between them. The interbank stress test then identifies those banks (if any) that have a large exposure to the failed bank(s) and thereby could also be forced into insolvency. The interbank exposure data take the form of a matrix with the cells containing the net bilateral interbank exposures between banks, where each row in the matrix gives the interbank exposures of a bank to every other bank in the matrix (see the Figure). In effect, the nonzero cells serve to provide comparisons of these exposures to the banks' capital to ascertain whether the losses incurred due to default on their interbank loans would reduce their capital sufficiently to cause them to also fail. This type of stress test has already been conducted on several FSAPs.

[1]Interbank stress tests are reported in the Luxembourg FSAPs (see IMF, 2002) and in Elsinger, Lehar, and Summer (2002).

Illustrative Matrix of Net Bilateral Interbank Exposures

	Bank 1	Bank 2	...	Bank *n*
Bank 1	—	Interbank exposure of bank 1 to bank 2	...	Interbank exposure of bank 1 to bank *n*
Bank 2	Interbank exposure of bank 2 to bank 1	—	...	Interbank exposure of bank 2 to bank *n*
. . .	. . .	. . .	—	. . .
Bank *n*	**Interbank exposure of bank *n* to bank 1**	**Interbank exposure of bank *n* to bank 2**	...	—

tal by providing information on the types of instruments that supervisors allow banks to include in capital. In addition, BCP 8 helps assess the impact of accounting and provisioning rules on reported banking sector capital used in FSIs.

- Assessments of BCPs can help establish the underlying cause of observed movements in FSIs when there are competing explanations. For example, a decline in the risk-weighted capital adequacy ratio may reflect an FSI deterioration or improvement, depending on whether this change is driven by a rapid growth of assets that are considered more risky or by a remedial action that requires higher loss recognition. The latter interpretation is more likely in a supervisory system where prompt remedial action is usually taken. Assessment of BCP 22 provides information on the extent to which supervisors take prompt remedial action to reduce risk in the financial system.
- Assessments of BCPs can indicate the responsiveness of the supervisory system to emerging financial sector problems, which reveals how quickly vulnerabilities identified by FSIs are likely to be corrected. For example, BCP 7, on the adequacy of banks' credit policies, can help judge when FSIs monitoring asset quality warrant concern. Similarly, BCP 9, covering the restrictions on large exposures and portfolio concentrations set by supervisors, is relevant to the interpretation of FSIs monitoring sectoral loan concentrations. Finally, BCP 12, covering market risk, can help reveal whether the banks have the discretion to build up market exposures large enough to pose a risk to the soundness of the system.
- Assessments of BCPs provide information on the effectiveness of banks' risk management. This indicates how effectively the banking system is responding to the risk associated with particular values for FSIs. For example, BCP 11 provides complementary information on the adequacy of banks' management of country risk. Similarly, information from BCP 12 on limits and capital charges on market exposures and banks' market risk management can help inter-

Table 13.1. Basel Core Principles Containing Information Relevant to the Interpretation of FSIs

Information Relevant to Macroprudential Surveillance	BCPs Providing Information Relevant to Macroprudential Surveillance: BCP number	BCPs Providing Information Relevant to Macroprudential Surveillance: Information content of BCP
I. Robust financial infrastructure		
Sound and stable macroeconomic policies	Precondition 1	Soundness of macroeconomic policies
Well-developed public infrastructure	Precondition 2	Judicial system, accounting principles and auditing systems, payment and clearing system
Efficient bank resolution procedures	Precondition 4	Bank resolution procedures
Appropriate public safety nets	Precondition 5	Bank safety nets
II. Effective supervision		
Autonomy, power, and resources of supervisory authority	BCP 1	Independence
	BCP 1	Enforcement powers
	BCP 1	Legal protection
Capacity to take prompt remedial actions in response to identified weaknesses	BCP 22	Remedial measures
Capacity to collect necessary information	BCP 16–19	On- and off-site supervision
Capacity to verify data provided by banks	BCP 21	Accounting standards
Capacity to collect and verify information on cross-border activities	BCP 1	Information sharing
	BCP 23–25	Cross-border information sharing
III. Macroprudential surveillance		
Surveillance of FSIs of capital adequacy	BCP 6	Capital adequacy
	BCP 8	Loan evaluation and loan loss provisioning
	BCP 20	Consolidated supervision
	BCP 23	Globally consolidated supervision
Surveillance of FSIs of asset quality	BCP 7	Credit policies
	BCP 8	Loan evaluation and loan loss provisioning
	BCP 9	Large exposure limits
	BCP 10	Connected lending
	BCP 20	Consolidated supervision
	BCP 23	Globally consolidated supervision
Surveillance of FSIs of earnings and profitability	—	—
Surveillance of FSIs of liquidity	BCP 11	Country risk
	BCP 13	Other risks
Surveillance of FSIs of sensitivity to market risk	BCP 12	Market risk

pret FSIs of sensitivity to market risk. Finally, BCP 13 gives information on banking sector management of liquidity risk.

- Assessments of BCPs provide information on risks that cannot be captured adequately using FSIs, such as operational and legal risk.

Role of information on financial infrastructure

13.32 Information on the financial system infrastructure can also help interpret FSIs. The financial market infrastructure includes payment and settlement systems and a broad range of different markets that banks rely on as funding sources and for trading. It also includes central bank operations and other systemic liquidity arrangements. The financial system infrastructure affects financial institutions' capacity to access and manage liquidity. Tables 8.1 and 8.2 provide a framework for disseminating some information on the financial system infrastructure and can be used to help interpret the liquidity FSIs.

13.33 Information on the types of markets and their functioning can be useful in assessing how vulnerable the banking sector is to a loss of access to market funding in a crisis. For example, while the interbank market is generally the most important and lowest cost source of funding for banks, banks can lose access to interbank funding if their credit quality deteriorates by even a relatively small amount. In contrast, in repo markets and securities markets, access to liquidity is likely to be more robust to such deterioration, as repo markets lend on a secured basis while securities markets price risk by charging lower quality borrowers a wider interest rate spread.

13.34 Information on market microstructure, such as whether markets are in organized exchanges, are over-the-counter (OTC), or rely on electronic trading systems, can provide insights into the robustness of market liquidity. For OTC markets, information on features affecting the capacity of market makers, such as the number of market makers and the size of the positions they take, could be useful. For exchanges, information on the trading systems, price transparency, margining rules, and capital committed by the exchange to support trading could be used. For electronic trading systems an indicator of liquidity is the standard transaction size. Also relevant is the extent to which closely related assets are traded on the different types of markets, which can substitute for each other if one market loses liquidity (for example, some currencies are traded on OTC markets, exchanges, and electronic trading systems). By reducing credit risk, the liquidity of financial markets can also be affected by the extent to which trades are cleared through a central counterparty.

13.35 The BIS's so-called *Red Book* (see the Text Annex to Chapter 8) provides information on payment systems of individual countries. Specifically, very large, short-term (including intraday) credit exposures can arise in some payment systems, which could make banks less willing to lend to each other in a crisis. Thus, it may be desirable to monitor indicators of payment system functioning, such as on intraday interbank exposures and daylight overdrafts. Moreover, it may be useful to have information on the settlement lags, loss-sharing arrangements, reliance on collateral, and markets that have Real Time Gross Settlement; all this information provides indications of the extent to which banks may have succeeded in controlling this source of credit risk.

13.36 Also relevant to interpreting liquidity FSIs is information on the financial system safety net, including deposit protection schemes and central banks' liquidity support to markets, which influences the extent to which banks can continue to access market liquidity in a crisis.

14. What Use Can Be Made of the Specific FSIs?

Introduction

14.1 The previous chapter explained the need for FSIs and how they fit into the wider concept of macroprudential analysis. This chapter considers the use that can be made of the FSIs that have been agreed by the IMF's Executive Board.[1] These are considered below by sector.

Deposit Takers

14.2 The strengths and vulnerabilities of deposit takers can be analyzed under the headings of capital adequacy, asset quality, earnings and profitability, liquidity, and sensitivity to market risk. This is commonly known as the CAMELS framework used by banking supervisors in their assessment of the soundness of individual institutions, less—for FSI purposes—the "M," which represents the quality of management.[2]

Capital Adequacy

14.3 Capital adequacy and availability ultimately determine the robustness of financial institutions to withstand shocks to their balance sheets. Aggregate risk-based *capital ratios* (for example, the ratio of regulatory capital to risk-weighted assets) are the most common indicators of capital adequacy, based on the methodology agreed to by the BCBS in 1988 (see Box 4.2). Simple leverage ratios, such as the *ratio of capital to assets,* often complement this measure. An adverse trend in these ratios may signal increased exposure to risk and possible capital adequacy problems. In addition to the amount of capital, it may also be useful to monitor indicators of capital quality. In many countries, bank capital consists of different elements that have varying availability and capability to absorb losses, even within the broad categories of Tier 1, Tier 2, and Tier 3 capital. If these elements of capital can be reported separately, they can serve as additional indicators of the ability of banks to withstand losses and help to put overall capital ratios into context.

14.4 The BCBS has recently updated the standard capital ratios to introduce greater sensitivity to risk in the capital requirements by taking into account the rapid development of risk-management techniques and financial innovation.[3] These proposals introduce greater refinement into the existing system of risk weighting to relate its categories more accurately to the economic risks faced by banks. These risks could be measured by banks' own internal ratings systems. Alternatively, they could be measured on the basis of ratings given by external rating agencies. However, improved risk measurement could come at the expense of comparability of information among banks, because under these new proposals each bank's methods of estimating credit risk can differ. The resulting differences among banks in risk-weighted assets and capital ratios would make aggregation of individual banks' data problematic.

14.5 An important indicator of the capacity of bank capital to withstand losses from NPLs is the ratio of *NPLs net of provisions to capital.* This FSI can help detect situations where deposit takers may have delayed addressing asset quality problems, which can become more serious over time as a result.[4] Well-designed loan classification and provisioning rules are key to obtaining a meaningful capital ratio. Loan classification rules are commonly a determinant of the level of provisioning,[5] which in turn affects

[1]This chapter draws on Sundararajan and others (2002).

[2]The quality of management is an important potential source of vulnerability. However, rather than using quantitative indicators on which there is no consensus, financial sector licensing and supervisory authorities usually assess this vulnerability qualitatively.

[3]See BCBS (2004). At the time of writing this *Guide,* Basel II was not yet finalized.

[4]This ratio does not show whether the borrower has provided the lender with collateral or other forms of credit risk mitigation. An alternative version of this FSI including collateral is provided in Appendix III.

[5]This is discussed in more detail in Appendix VI.

capital indirectly (by reducing income) and directly (through the inclusion of general provisions in regulatory capital). Moreover, in the FSI framework banks should deduct specific provisions from loans (that is, credit should be calculated on a *net* basis), which reduces the value of total assets and hence of capital (when the latter is calculated residually).

Asset Quality

14.6 Risks to the solvency of financial institutions most often derive from an impairment of assets, which in turn can arise from a deterioration in the financial health and profitability of the institutions' borrowers, especially the nonfinancial corporations sector (discussed below). The *ratio of NPLs to total gross loans* is often used as a proxy for asset quality. The coverage ratio—the ratio of provisions to NPLs—provides a measure of the share of bad loans for which provisions have already been made.

14.7 Lack of diversification in the loan portfolio signals the existence of an important vulnerability of the financial system. *Loan concentration in a specific economic sector or activity* (measured as a share of total loans) makes banks vulnerable to adverse developments in that sector or activity. This is particularly true for exposures to the *real estate sector.* Country- or region-specific circumstances often determine the particular sectors of the economy that should be monitored for macroprudential purposes.

14.8 Exposure to country risk can also be important in countries that are actively participating in the international financial markets. Data on the *geographical distribution of loans* allow the monitoring of credit risk arising from exposures to particular (groups of) countries and an assessment of the impact of adverse events in these countries on the domestic financial system.

14.9 Concentration of credit risk in a small number of borrowers may also result from *connected lending* and *large exposures.* Monitoring of connected lending, usually measured as the share of capital lent to related parties, is particularly important in the presence of mixed-activity conglomerates in which industrial firms control financial institutions. Credit standards may be relaxed for loans to affiliates, even when loan terms are market based. The definition of what constitutes a connected party is usually set in consideration of the legal and ownership structures prevalent in a particular country, which makes this indicator often difficult to use in cross-country comparisons. The assessment of large exposures, usually calculated as a share of capital, aims at capturing the potential negative effect on a financial institution should a single borrower experience difficulties in servicing its obligations. Identifying the number of such exposures provides an indication of how widespread such large exposures are. In addition, exposures of the largest deposit takers to the largest resident entities provide an indication of concentrated lending among the largest entities in the economy.

14.10 In countries where domestic lending in foreign currency is permitted, it is important to monitor the ratio of *foreign-currency-denominated loans to total loans.*[6] Delgado and others (2002) note that ideally, a measure of risk from domestic lending in foreign currency should identify loans to unhedged domestic borrowers. In these cases, hedging would also include "natural hedges," or borrowings for which an adverse exchange rate impact on foreign currency obligations is compensated by a positive impact on revenue and profitability. The level of the above ratio is related to that of *foreign-currency-denominated liabilities to total liabilities,* although differences may be observed, notably when sources of foreign currency financing are available from foreign lines of credit and other foreign capital inflows. It should be noted that owing to the compound nature of credit and currency risk in foreign-currency-denominated lending, even institutions with a balanced foreign exchange position face risks. For example, an exchange rate depreciation can impose losses directly on the banking sector but also have an indirect effect on asset quality by causing losses in the nonfinancial corporations sector.

14.11 *Derivatives* can be a source of vulnerability. Positions in these instruments should be explicitly monitored and recognized on balance sheets using market value or an equivalent measure of value. In addition, monitoring bank soundness requires tracking the risks involved in *off-balance-sheet operations* (on account of guarantees and contingent lending arrangements). As a general rule, "exposures" should include positions that are both on balance sheet and off balance sheet, rather than merely positions on the balance sheet. However, off-balance-sheet positions

[6]Data on credit—assets for which the counterpart incurs a debt liability—are a more comprehensive concept than loans and could additionally be used.

can present special problems in evaluating the condition of financial institutions, because of the lack of reporting of such positions in some countries.

Earnings and Profitability

14.12 Accounting data on bank margins, income, and expenses are widely used indicators of bank profitability. Common operating ratios used to assess bank profitability include net income to average total assets (also known as *return on assets* [ROA]) and net income to average equity (also known as *return on equity* [ROE]).[7]

14.13 Differences in capital structure and business mix across countries should be considered in analyzing bank performance and highlight the need to look at several operating ratios at the same time.[8] Banks with lower leverage (higher equity) will generally report higher ROAs but lower ROEs. Hence, an analysis of profitability based exclusively on ROEs would tend to disregard the greater risks normally associated with high leverage. Income ratios may also be affected by leverage. In the case of banks with low leverage, the *interest margin* and net income ratios will be higher because banks with higher levels of equity need to borrow less to support a given level of assets and thus have lower interest expenses. The proportion of gross income generated through fees and commissions compared with net interest income should also be monitored, as the employment of capital, the level of operating costs, and the level of assets held can differ.

14.14 Information on the *spread between lending and deposit rates* could provide an indication of the underlying profitability of the sector, while data on *trading income to total income* provide an indication of the reliance on market-related activity to generate profits. The ratios of *personnel expenses to noninterest expenses* and *noninterest expenses to gross income* can provide an indication of efficiency; high and increasing ratios could affect profitability.

14.15 In analyzing the above-mentioned ratios, the differing mix of banking business among banks should be taken into account. For example, retail banking is associated with higher lending rates, lower deposit rates, and higher operating costs than is wholesale corporate banking. Often, high margin business involves high operating costs. Banks that offer a wider range of services, such as investment banks, tend to have higher noninterest income.

14.16 Returns can also be calculated on a risk-adjusted basis, although this is not the approach taken in the *Guide.* The risk-adjusted return is calculated by discounting cash flows according to their volatility: the more volatile the cash flow, the higher the discount rate and the lower the risk-adjusted return. Risk-adjusted return on capital (RAROC) measures the return on capital required to offset losses on the underlying asset should volatility cause its value to decline (by two or more standard deviations). RAROC is particularly useful to banks in evaluating businesses and products according to their place along a risk/return spectrum and thus in correctly pricing a transaction. At the sector level, RAROC can be computed as interest margin to assets multiplied by the potential loss. Estimating the potential loss requires data on historical default and recovery rates and on banks' ability to liquidate assets (liquidity risk).

Liquidity

14.17 The level of liquidity influences the ability of a banking system to withstand shocks. For instance, a large shock, contributing to credit or market losses, could cause a loss of confidence in the banking sector by market participants or depositors. In turn, this could result in a liquidity crisis that has the potential to push solvent banks into insolvency, because if they lose access to funding they could be forced to sell assets at depressed prices to obtain liquidity.

14.18 A common measure of liquidity is *liquid assets to total assets* (liquid asset ratio), which indicates how much balance sheet shrinkage the sector could absorb before being forced to sell illiquid assets. Another measure of liquidity is the ratio of *liquid assets to short-term liabilities,* which indicates the short-term liabilities that would have to be covered by asset sales if access to funding were lost. These indicators can highlight excessive maturity mismatches and a need for more careful liquidity management. The ratio of *customer deposits to total (noninterbank) loans* is also sometimes used to detect liquidity problems—a low ratio might indicate potential liquidity stress in the banking system and perhaps a loss of depositor and

[7]The ratios can be calculated using various income measures: for example, before or after provisions and before or after tax charges and (net) extraordinary items.

[8]Vittas (1991).

investor confidence in the long-term viability of the sector.

14.19 Information on the volatility of bank liabilities can supplement the information provided by liquidity ratios. Bank liabilities that are subject to the risk of reversal of foreign capital flows, such as external credit lines and deposits of nonresidents, should be monitored closely, for example through indicators of the size of this type of funding in total bank liabilities. Such indicators of exposure to international capital movements highlight the relevance of macroprudential analysis to the assessment of external vulnerability.

14.20 As bank liquidity depends on the level of liquidity of the overall system, it is important to monitor measures of *market liquidity.* The focus may be on a benchmark domestic government or central bank debt security, or on other securities that are most relevant to the liquidity of banks. Indicators of the tightness, depth, and resilience of a market can capture market liquidity.[9]

14.21 Tightness indicates the general cost incurred in a transaction irrespective of the level of market prices and can be measured by the *bid-ask spread* (the difference between prices at which a market participant is willing to buy and sell a security); a narrower spread can indicate a more competitive market with a larger number of buyers and sellers providing liquidity. Monitoring spread volatility might also be useful for macroprudential purposes. A financial system might have relatively high but stable spreads, whereas a less stable financial system might have spreads narrower on average but more volatile under stressful conditions.

14.22 *Depth* denotes the volume of trades possible without affecting prevailing market prices and is proxied by the *turnover ratio. Resilience* refers to the speed at which price fluctuations resulting from trades are dissipated and can be measured by the Hui-Heubel Ratio.

14.23 Where foreign currency transactions are relevant, liquidity management can be complicated if the availability of foreign currency is limited and interbank foreign exchange lines are vulnerable to disruption. In these cases, it is also important to measure the liquidity of foreign exchange markets and monitor its determinants. Foreign exchange liquidity also depends on developments in the external sector, where there is the potential for reversals of capital flows and where foreign exchange reserves may become inadequate.

14.24 Standing central bank facilities, which are accessed at the initiative of banks, provide liquidity to banks (usually against collateral) and are an essential component of the liquidity infrastructure. A large increase in central bank credit to banks and other financial institutions—as a proportion of their capital or their liabilities—often reflects severe liquidity (and frequently also solvency) problems in the financial system. Therefore, it is important to monitor through monetary and financial statistics central bank lending to financial institutions.[10]

14.25 The *dispersion in interbank rates* is a very useful indicator of liquidity problems and bank distress. Very often, banks themselves first detect problems in other banks because they are exposed to such institutions in the interbank market. A high dispersion in interbank rates—measured, for instance, by the spread between the highest and lowest rates in that market—may signal that some institutions are perceived by their peers as risky. Moreover, changes in interbank credit limits or an unwillingness of some institutions to lend to other institutions may indicate serious concerns about the liquidity of the latter.

Sensitivity to Market Risk

14.26 As banks become increasingly involved in diversified operations and take positions in financial instruments, they become more exposed to risk of losses arising from changes in market prices—that is, to market risk. The most relevant components of market risk are interest rate and exchange rate risk. Moreover, in some countries, banks are allowed to engage in proprietary trading in stock markets, which results in equity price risk. Financial derivatives may be used to manage such risks.

14.27 A potential indicator of sensitivity to interest rate risk is the *duration of assets and liabilities.* The

[9]In times of particular financial distress, dealers may not be willing to make a market at all in certain securities. Such instances can be captured through surveys of primary security dealers. See Nelson and Passmore (2001).

[10]Such transactions may also have important implications for the conduct of monetary policy and the financial position of the central bank.

greater the mismatch in duration or "average" life between assets and liabilities, the greater the interest rate risk, and the greater the likely impact of changes in interest rates on earnings and capital. Alternatively, gap analysis can be used to assess interest rate risk. For floating-rate nonequity assets and liabilities, gap analysis considers the average time to repricing; for fixed-rate instruments, the focus is on the time remaining until payments are due.

14.28 The most common measure of *foreign exchange exposure* is the net open position, as defined by the BCBS, and a commonly used measure of a bank's equity risk exposure is its *net open position in equities.*

Other Financial Corporations

14.29 FSIs on the other financial corporations sector help monitor, and raise awareness of, potential risks emanating from this sector. Such indicators should provide information on the size of the other financial corporations sector—*other financial corporations assets to total financial system assets*—to gain a sense of its systemic importance. The size threshold in terms of systemic importance would vary from country to country depending on the institutional setting, such as the manner in which other financial corporations raise funds from the public (and segments of the public—small savers or wholesale investors—from which they raise funds). The indicator *other financial corporations assets to GDP* can also provide information on the importance of the sector. Finally, very rapid expansion of credit and accumulation of assets in general may indicate the potential for problems in this sector.

14.30 The development of FSIs for other financial corporations is at an earlier stage than that for deposit takers.

Nonfinancial Corporations

14.31 The quality of financial institutions' loan portfolios is directly dependent on the financial health and profitability of the institutions' borrowers, especially the nonfinancial corporations sector; it is, therefore, important to monitor the financial condition of the sector.

14.32 Excessive corporate leverage increases the vulnerability of corporate entities in the event of a shock and may impair their repayment capacity; a common indicator is *total debt to equity,* also called the gearing (or leverage) ratio.

14.33 Profitability is a critical determinant of corporate strength, affecting capital growth, ability to raise equity, operating capacity, ability to withstand adverse shocks, and, ultimately, repayment capacity and survival. Sharp declines in corporate sector profitability may serve as a leading indicator of financial system distress. The most significant measures of profitability include (1) *return on equity* (EBIT to average equity), (2) *return on assets* (EBIT to average assets), and (3) *income to sales* (EBIT to sales).[11] The absolute levels of these ratios are important, but it is equally important to focus on trends. Information on profitability is particularly affected by market structure—that is, industry characteristics, competitive environment, and pricing flexibility.

14.34 Earnings can also be viewed in relation to a company's burden of fixed charges. Cash flow adequacy is often measured by the ratio of earnings to interest expenses, or by the ratio of *earnings to interest and principal expenses.* Earnings can be measured before interest and taxes (EBIT). These ratios indicate the likelihood of corporate financial distress better than corporate leverage, as low debt-service capacity suggests growing financial fragility. Moreover, corporate liquidity determines the sector's ability to carry out business without endangering credit quality.

14.35 Assessments of corporate sector vulnerability should also measure the *net foreign exchange exposure to equity,* since significant currency depreciation could put severe pressure on those banks whose clients have large foreign currency debt-servicing burdens. This applies both to firms borrowing domestically in foreign currency and firms turning to foreign sources of financing.[12]

14.36 A measure of bankruptcy trends in this sector is provided by the *number of applications for protection*

[11]Pretax measures of profitability provide measures of the income earned through the activities of the enterprise during a given period independent of the tax regime (which can differ widely among countries), and thus, such measures are suitable for international comparisons.

[12]In some cases, strengthened financial sector supervision may create incentives for firms to borrow abroad, thereby shifting to the corporate sector vulnerabilities related to foreign exchange exposure.

from creditors, which is affected by the quality and nature of bankruptcy (and other related) legislation.

Households

14.37 The size of household exposure to the deposit takers can be substantial. Furthermore, household consumption behavior has a strong effect on the corporate sector, while household asset portfolio decisions can affect bank liabilities and bank asset prices.

14.38 The vulnerability of households may be assessed through the use of sectoral balance sheets, flow of funds, and other macro- and microeconomic data. Indicators include the ratios of *debt to GDP,* debt to assets, and *debt service and principal payments to income.* Other indicators that can be used derive from credit risk analysis, such as the ratio of a household's debt to the value of collateral it has pledged.

14.39 Most of the analysis of the vulnerability of the household sector is focused on the direct exposure of deposit takers to households and thus relies heavily on the analysis of households' debt-servicing capacity. Alternatively, indicators of the asset composition of households' portfolios highlight households' exposures to equity and real estate price movements.

Real Estate Markets

14.40 Rapid increases in *real estate prices*—often fueled by expansionary monetary policy or by large capital inflows—followed by a sharp economic downturn can have a detrimental effect on financial sector soundness, by affecting credit quality and the value of collateral.

14.41 Ideally, a range of indicators should be analyzed to get a sense of real estate market developments and to assess financial sector exposure to the real estate sector. To determine the riskiness of this exposure, it is necessary to distinguish among different types of real-estate-related loans that may have very different risk characteristics. For example, it would be useful to distinguish between lending (1) for the purpose of investment in (purchase of) *commercial real estate,* or more generally, to construction companies, and (2) for the purpose of investment in *residential real estate,* including mortgages.

15. Peer Group Analysis and Descriptive Statistics

Introduction

15.1 Both users and compilers of FSIs have recognized the need for peer group analysis and dispersion analysis. This chapter sets out options and ideas in these areas for use by compilers and analysts.

15.2 Sector balance sheets and income and expense data can disguise important information. For example, the sector-wide capital-to-asset ratio for deposit takers is essentially the average capital-to-asset ratio for the system (derived by the summation of all institutions' capital and its division by all institutions' assets) and, if normally distributed, would convey information about the median capital asset ratio as well as the most frequently observed capital asset ratio (the mode). However, the ratio does not indicate whether the individual institution's capital ratios are clustered in a narrow range around the average value or are spread over a wide range. Moreover, if the data for one highly capitalized deposit taker offset the data for several undercapitalized deposit takers, the aggregate ratio may appear robust, masking significant vulnerabilities from weak deposit takers whose failure could lead to contagion throughout the system.

15.3 A wide variety of meaningful peer groups can be created for comparison purposes, and descriptive statistics can be compiled to examine the dispersion and concentration of the institutions within the peer group or sector. This chapter describes some types of peer groups and discusses measures of concentration and of dispersion. Issues in developing these data are set out, such as weighting the contribution of the individual institutions, and some guidance in analyzing the data is provided.

Peer Group Analysis

15.4 A peer group is a set of individual institutions that are grouped on the basis of analytically relevant criteria. Peer groups can be used to compare FSI ratios: (1) individual deposit takers with similar institutions, (2) peer groups with other domestic peer groups, and (3) peer groups across countries. Peer group analysis can be undertaken using either cross-border or domestic consolidated data.

Types of Peer Groups

15.5 Depending on analytical needs and data availability, different types of peer groups may be constructed. Some might be constructed on an ad hoc basis. For example, ad hoc peer groups might cover recent entrants into the market, deposit takers with low capital ratios or low return on equity, deposit takers with high levels of nonperforming loans, and deposit takers that concentrate on lending to particular types of borrowers. Other peer groups might be created to facilitate ongoing analysis, such as groups of similarly sized deposit takers (based on their total assets).

15.6 By way of example, peer group data could be constructed for groupings of deposit takers based on the following major characteristics:

- **Size of assets or revenues.** The size of institutions might affect market competitiveness or market power. Moreover, the condition of the peer group composed of the largest deposit takers—such as the three to five largest deposit takers, based on total assets—is often important for understanding overall stability, because these deposit takers are the most likely to be systemically important and may exercise the greatest market power. Such a group has a small enough number of institutions that it can be constructed for most economies and can facilitate international comparison.
- **Line of business.** For example, regular retail banks might be distinguished from mortgage banks.
- **Type of ownership.** For example, publicly controlled deposit takers might be distinguished from privately controlled deposit takers.

- **Offshore or onshore.** Deposit takers that are offshore can have transactions with only nonresidents and thus might be an important group to identify.
- **Region of the country.**

15.7 From the above list, the *Guide* encourages, at a minimum, the compilation of core FSIs for peer groups based on the relative size of assets. The *Guide* discourages the dissemination of peer group data that might reveal information on specific institutions, unless the country normally requires deposit takers to publicly disclose such information.

Compilation of Peer Group Data

15.8 A key consideration in constructing peer group data is determining how such data are to be compiled. Regardless of the approach taken, constructing peer group data depends critically on the cost of compiling these data and on the ease with which they can be reorganized to serve various analytical needs. To allow construction of peer group data, the *Guide* encourages compilers to maintain individual institution data in a database that allows quick, flexible, and low-cost data aggregation. Under such an approach, peer group data can potentially be compiled using the same principles as sector-level data. For example, intragroup income and expense items and, depending on data availability, intragroup equity holdings could be eliminated in constructing peer group data.

15.9 In constructing the data, a decision needs to be made on whether the peer group should be treated as a subgroup of the total population (that is, the data are the peer group's contribution to the total for the population) or as a *stand-alone* grouping (that is, the group is self-contained, with all institutions outside the group treated as external to the group). There are advantages in adopting either approach, but data compilation considerations may be decisive, particularly if ad hoc groups are created.

15.10 The stand-alone approach is likely to require less additional data than the subgroup approach. For instance, under either approach, intra-peer-group interest income and expense will be eliminated in the net interest income line. However, under the subgroup approach, the elimination of interest income and expense vis-à-vis institutions within the sector but outside the peer group requires the collection of additional data.

15.11 However, even the stand-alone approach will require additional data if the peer group data are to be compiled in line with the sector-level approach. Some of this information might be obtainable from the data reported in Tables 11.2 and 11.4, depending on the consolidation approach adopted. For instance, intra-peer-group holdings of equity could be eliminated to the extent that individual deposit takers identify their holdings of equity issued by other deposit takers. As a practical matter, peer group data might be compiled on an approximate best practice basis; this would still allow the identification of trends but—depending on the degree of approximation and the scope of analysis—could potentially mask relevant interrelationships. In such circumstances, it is encouraged that any relevant potential limitations of the data be identified for the user, such as capital and reserves' not being fully adjusted for intra-peer-group holdings.

Descriptive Statistics

15.12 In many ways, concentration and dispersion analysis uses specific techniques depending on the nature of the issue under review, the types of data available and the ease of using them, and any limitations on revealing information on specific institutions. Flexibility in selecting techniques should be maintained. This section provides a menu of techniques that are useful in a variety of situations. However, in disseminating information to the public, some types of descriptive statistics may prove particularly useful, because they can describe concentration and dispersion without revealing information on individual institutions.

Measures of Concentration

15.13 The **Herfindahl Index,** *H,* is the sum of squares of the market shares of all firms in a sector, that is,

$$H = \sum_{i=1}^{N} \left(share_i\right)^2 .$$

By using market shares, this index stresses the importance of the larger firms in the population. Higher values indicate greater concentration. In a situation with no concentration, where each of the 100 firms has an identical 1 percent share of the market, the value of $H = 100$. In contrast, with perfect concentration, where one firm has a 100 percent market share, $H = 10{,}000$;

Table 15.1. Example of Computing the Herfindahl Index

Deposit Taker	Assets	Percentage Share	Share[2]
1	300	30	900.0
2	200	20	400.0
3	130	13	169.0
4	90	9	81.0
5	80	8	64.0
6	50	5	25.0
7	50	5	25.0
8	40	4	16.0
9	20	2	4.0
10	20	2	4.0
11	20	2	4.0
Total	1,000	100	**1,692.0 Herfindahl Index** (Top 5 = 1,614)

that is, the contribution of the monopoly firm is 100 × 100 = 10,000. A rule of thumb sometimes used is that *H* below 1,000 indicates relatively limited concentration, and *H* above 1,800 points to significant concentration. Table 15.1 illustrates how to compute *H* for a country consisting of 11 deposit takers.

15.14 As noted in Chapter 12, the *Guide* encourages dissemination of the Herfindahl Index. For ease of compilation, it is also possible to compile partial Herfindahl indices, such as the one based on the shares of the total sector assets of the largest five deposit takers.

15.15 The **Gini Index** estimates the degree of inequality, indicating how equally a variable is distributed among participants. It captures the information shown in a Lorenz curve, which is the difference between the actual distribution of a variable and the hypothetical state in which the distribution of the variable is uniform. In the hypothetical state every unit has the same endowment (of income, market share, volume of market trading, and so on), which generates a Gini index of zero. If only one unit is endowed with all income, assets, and so on, and no other unit has any, there is perfect concentration and the Gini index is one. Gini indices are especially useful to track changes in inequality over time. Table 15.2 illustrates an example of computation of Gini index.

15.16 For example, for *N* deposit takers, arrayed by the size of assets, from smallest to largest:

$$\text{Gini} = \sum_{i=1}^{N} 2\left(X_i - Y_i\right)\Delta X_i,$$

where $X_i = \frac{i}{N} \times 100$

Y_i = cumulative percentage share

$\Delta X_i = X_i - X_{i-1}$.

Measures of Dispersion

15.17 The four main categories of these statistics are measures of (1) central tendency, (2) variability, (3) skewness, and (4) kurtosis. They can be useful for data analysis, for comparing multiple data sets and for reporting final results of a survey.[1] In disseminating information, graphical presentations, such as simple scatter diagrams, can also be useful in providing users with information on the dispersion of data.

15.18 Measures of central tendency include:

- *Mean* (first moment of the distribution), or

$$\bar{X} = \sum_{i=1}^{N} \frac{x_i}{N} = \sum\left(x_i \times \frac{n_i}{N}\right).$$

This is the arithmetic average of the data. Generalizing,

$$\bar{X} = \sum\left(x_i \times weight_i\right),$$

where

x_i = value of observation i

n_i = number of observations with value x_i

N = total number of observations

$\frac{n_i}{N}$ = weight

$\bar{X}$ = population mean.

15.19 As the mean can be affected by extreme observations, other measures of central tendency might also be calculated:

- *Median* is the middle observation in a data set. It is often used when a data set is not symmetrical, or when there are outlying observations.

[1]An issue arises as to whether dispersion analysis should be undertaken on a stand-alone basis or on a subgroup basis. As noted elsewhere in this chapter, there are advantages to both approaches. To help in the understanding of any data disseminated, it is important to know the approach taken, as (for example) the mean and variance for FSI ratios for peer groups can vary depending on which basis the data are compiled.

Table 15.2. Example of Computing the Gini Index

Deposit Taker	Assets	Percentage Share	Cumulative Actual Share Y_i	Cumulative Equal Share X_i	Difference $X_i - Y_i$	Difference × 2 $(X_i - Y_i) \times 2$	((Difference × 2) × .091[1]): $((X_i - Y_i) \times 2) \times (X_i - X_{i-1})$
11	20	2	2	9.1	7.1	14.2	1.291
10	20	2	4	18.2	14.2	28.4	2.583
9	20	2	6	27.3	21.3	42.6	3.875
8	40	4	10	36.4	26.4	52.8	4.803
7	50	5	15	45.5	30.5	61.0	5.549
6	50	5	20	54.6	34.6	69.2	6.296
5	80	8	28	63.7	35.7	71.4	6.496
4	90	9	37	72.8	35.8	71.6	6.514
3	130	13	50	81.9	31.9	63.8	5.804
2	200	20	70	91.0	21.0	42.0	3.820
1	300	30	100	100.0	0.0	0.0	0.000
							47.030[2] **Gini Index**

[1]The "equal share" percentage of the total.
[2]This index is scaled by a factor of 100.

- *Mode* is the value around which the greatest number of observations are concentrated, or the value of the most common observation.

15.20 Measures of variability describe the dispersion (or spread) of the data set:

- *Range* is the difference between the largest and the smallest observations in the data set. It has limitations because it depends on only two observations in the data set.
- *Variance* (the second moment of the distribution), or

$$\sigma^2 = \sum_{i=1}^{N} \frac{(x_i - \bar{X})^2}{N} = \sum_{i=1}^{N} \left[\frac{n_i}{N} \times (x_i - \bar{X})^2 \right]$$

measures the dispersion of the data around the mean, taking into account all data points. Generalizing,

$$\sigma^2 = \sum \left[(x_i - \bar{X})^2 \times weight_i \right].$$

- *Standard Deviation* (or $\sigma = \sqrt{\sigma^2}$) is the positive square root of the variance and is the most common measure of variability. Standard deviation indicates how close observations are to the mean.

15.21 Skewness (the third moment of the distribution, or μ_3) indicates the extent to which data are asymmetrically distributed about the mean. Positive skewness indicates a longer right-hand side (tail) of the distribution; negative skewness indicates a longer left tail. One measure of skewness is based on the difference between the mean and the median, standardized by dividing by the standard deviation:

$$\text{Skewness} = \frac{\sum_{i=1}^{N} \left[(x_i - \bar{X})^3 \times weight_i \right]}{\sigma^3}.$$

15.22 Kurtosis (the fourth moment of the distribution, or μ_4) indicates whether the data are more or less concentrated toward the center; that is, it indicates the degree of flatness of the distribution near its center. As the kurtosis of a normal distribution equals 3, it is common to subtract 3 from the measure of kurtosis to estimate "excess kurtosis." Positive excess kurtosis indicates that the distribution is more peaked than the normal distribution; negative excess kurtosis indicates a relatively flat distribution.

$$\text{Kurtosis} = \left(\frac{\sum_{i=1}^{N} \left[(x_i - \bar{X})^4 \times weight_i \right]}{\sigma^4} \right) - 3.$$

Weighting options

15.23 In compiling dispersion data, an issue to address is whether data should be compiled so that each observation has the same weight (equal-weight approach) or is weighted by its relative contribution to the numerator and denominator (weighted-by-contribution approach). As noted above, the *Guide,* at the sector level, uses the weighted-by-contribution approach.

15.24 The equal-weight approach facilitates identification of whether weaknesses are concentrated in one or two deposit takers or spread across a larger number of institutions and helps identify emerging weaknesses regardless of the size of the institution.

15.25 Variance, skewness, and kurtosis can be calculated using the weight of the contribution from each observation. For variance, the distance of each observation to the mean should be scaled by its weight in the overall average; for skewness and kurtosis, the weight measures the contribution of each observation to the mean, relative to a normal distribution. Compilation (and dissemination) of descriptive statistics on a weighted-by-contribution basis might reveal whether outliers are small or large relative to the sector.

15.26 Because of their analytical usefulness, dispersion statistics could be compiled using both weighting approaches, depending on data availability. However, if the equal-weight approach is adopted, users should be made aware that the mean calculated under this approach might well be different from the FSI itself.

Interpretation of descriptive statistics

15.27 Figure 15.1 sets out an example of an economy that has 100 deposit takers with capital asset ratios distributed as shown in the figure. Table 15.3 provides dispersion statistics on an equal-weight basis, and Table 15.4 provides the equivalent statistics calculated on a weighted-by-contribution basis.

Figure 15.1. Distribution of Observations

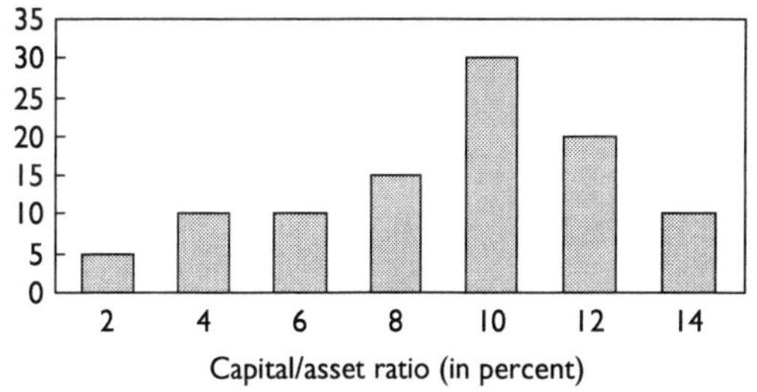

15.28 The statistics in Table 15.3 could be interpreted as follows: because the value of the mean is smaller than both the median and mode, the distribution is asymmetric with a leftward skew (that is, a longer tail toward smaller values). This is confirmed by the negative value for the measure of skewness. In addition, the standard deviation indicates some significant dispersion around the mean. The flat distribution (relative to a normal distribution) is confirmed by the negative kurtosis.[2]

15.29 The weighted-by-contribution approach produces different results from that of the equal-weight approach. As seen in Table 15.4, the mean is lower and standard deviation higher, respectively, than those shown in Table 15.3 due to the large weights for

[2]The standard deviation for the population can be used to estimate the percentage of the population members that lies within a specified distance of the mean. Tcehbychev's rule is commonly used for forming such estimates.

Table 15.3. Dispersion Statistics of Capital Asset Ratios (Equal-Weight Approach)

Mean	Median	Mode	Variance	Standard Deviation	Skewness	Kurtosis
9.1	10.0	10.0	10.7	3.3	–0.5	–0.5

Table 15.4. Dispersion Statistics of Capital Asset Ratios (Weighted-by-Contribution Approach)

Weighted Mean	Standard Deviation	Median	Mode	Skewness	Kurtosis
7.4	4.7	10.0	10.0	0.17	–1.51

Figure 15.2. Distribution of Ratios by Weight

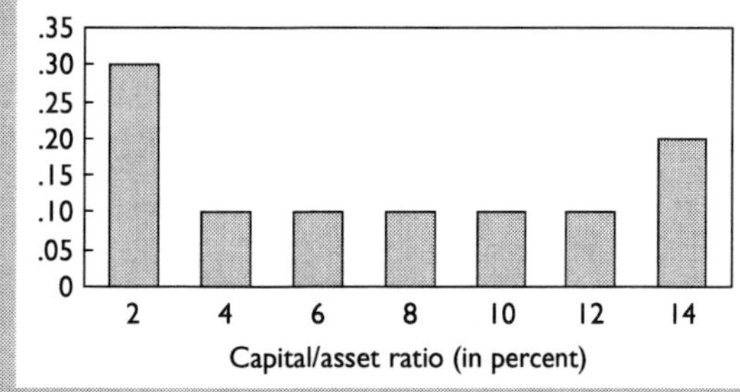

the observations at the end of the tails. The large negative kurtosis also reflects low peakedness (that is, "fat" tails).

15.30 Figures 15.2 and 15.3 add to this analysis. The height of the columns in Figure 15.2 shows the distribution of the individual institution's ratios by weight, that is, the contribution of those deposit takers to the sector-level FSI. The weights are presented in percentage terms. Figure 15.3 indicates both the weight (through the size of the bubble) and the number (through the bubble's height) of institutions at each ratio. These figures show that the outlying observations in the equally weighted distribution take on increased significance in the weighted-by-contribution distribution. In this example, of the 100 deposit takers in the system, there are only 5 deposit takers with ratios of 2 percent and 10 deposit takers at 14 percent, but together they account for half the weight—in other words, the outliers are relatively important.

Figure 15.3. Distribution of Capital Asset Ratios by Number of Institutions and by Weight

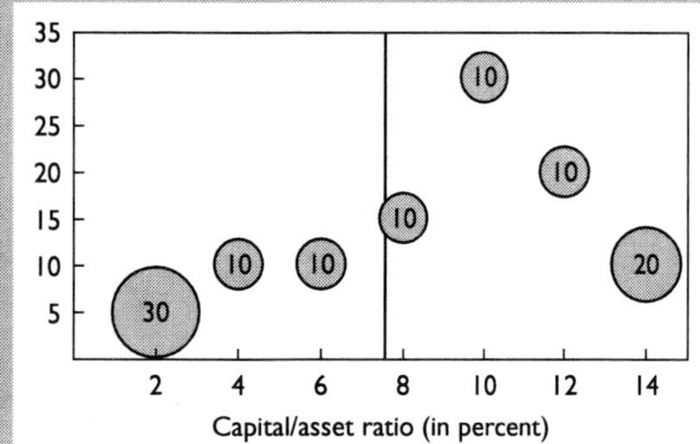

15.31 Another approach is to compare individual deposit takers' (or peer groups') contribution to specific FSIs with their relative contribution to sector assets. For example, a deposit taker generating large income flows through transactions in the financial market could make a significantly bigger contribution to the sector's income-based FSIs than its asset size would suggest. Such divergence over a period of time might indicate that the deposit taker is taking large risks to generate large income flows. Such comparisons might also be used to check the reliability of data submitted.

15.32 Divergence between the relative balance sheet size of a deposit taker and its contribution by weight to specific FSIs can be identified by constructing the following comparison ratio:

$$\textit{Comparison ratio}_{i,j} = \frac{\textit{Weight-by-contribution}_{i,j}}{\textit{Weight-by-asset size}_j},$$

where $\textit{Weight-by-asset size}_j = \dfrac{\textit{Asset size}_j}{\sum_{j=1}^{N} \textit{Asset size}_j}$,

and i is the ith FSI, j is the jth reporting institution, and N is the number of reporting institutions.

15.33 A comparison ratio for a given deposit taker and a given FSI larger (smaller) than unity indicates that, compared with the rest of the deposit-taking sector, that deposit taker makes a larger contribution to the specific FSI than its balance sheet size suggests. A summary matrix of comparison ratios (for deposit takers and FSIs) can be constructed.

Extensions of Dispersion Measures

15.34 Although the above set of descriptive statistics provides a useful overview of the distribution of data, it does not adequately illuminate weak (strong) conditions—that is, those in the left tail of the distribution.[3] Specifically, no information is provided on how many deposit takers populate the left tail and

[3]The terms "weak" and "strong" are relative concepts in this context. That is, they are used to convey weakness or strength relative to the mean, which itself may be weak or strong vis-à-vis a predetermined norm or benchmark (such as 8 percent for the capital adequacy ratio).

Table 15.5. Extensions of Dispersion Statistics of Capital Asset Ratios (Equal-Weight Approach)

	Mean	Median	Mode	Variance	Standard Deviation	Skewness	Kurtosis
Total	9.1	10.0	10.0	10.7	3.3	–0.5	–0.5
Left tail	5.8	6.0	8.0	4.6	2.1		
Right tail	11.3	11.0	10.0	2.3	1.5		

how they are distributed therein. In this context, some possible extensions to the descriptive statistics in the *Guide* are explored below.

Option 1: Right- and left-tail attributes

15.35 The measures of central tendency and variance set out in the *Guide* can be applied to the left and right tails of the distribution, as shown in Table 15.5. This provides some additional insight into the size of the skewness, especially if the size of the standard deviation for the left and right tails relative to their respective means are compared; the relatively large standard deviation for the left tail reveals there are a number of institutions with ratios significantly below 5.8. Nevertheless, further disaggregation of the data is needed to arrive at how many institutions are involved and how far to the left the distribution is skewed.

Option 2: Ranges

15.36 One way of conveying additional information about the distribution is to show the number of institutions falling within specified ranges or intervals (Table 15.6). This can be supplemented with mean and variance information for each interval. While providing additional insight into the shape of the distribution, the usefulness of this approach is dependent on the size of the intervals. Moreover, cross-country and cross-FSI comparisons may not be useful because the appropriate intervals will likely differ across countries and FSIs.

Table 15.6. Statistics of Capital Asset Ratios, by Range

Range	2–4	5–8	9–11	12–14
Number	15.0	25.0	45.0	30.0
Mean	3.3	7.2	10.0	12.7
Standard deviation	1.0	1.0	0.0	1.0

15.37 Nevertheless, this approach might be well suited to indicators that have an accepted norm or benchmark, such as the Basel Capital Adequacy Ratio, for which the analysis could focus on the distribution of ratios to the left of the benchmark. This approach may become more widely applicable as countries gain experience with FSIs and the calibration of benchmarks to local circumstances.

Option 3: Percentiles

15.38 The percentile distribution of individual deposit takers' ratios goes some way toward addressing concerns about cross-country comparison of ranges. Percentile analysis involves arranging observations in ascending order and dividing the data into groups with equal numbers of observations. The values that serve as the dividing lines among groups are called percentiles. For example, Table 15.7 shows that the 10th percentile corresponds to an observation of 4, and that the 20th percentile corresponds to an observation of 6.[4]

15.39 Combined with the mean and standard deviation for each percentile range (for example, 0–10 percent, 10–20 percent, and 20–30 percent), these statistics can reveal areas of financial weakness.[5] For instance, from Table 15.7, the large standard deviation relative to the mean for the bottom percentile indicates that the tail extends below 4 percent for a number of institutions. By contrast, the standard deviation of zero for other percentile ranges indicates that within each range all observations are equal to the mean for the range.

[4]It is important to note this does *not* imply that all deposit takers with ratios of 4 percent are in the bottom percentile; some deposit takers with ratios of 4 percent may also populate the next percentile.

[5]The mean and standard deviation can also be calculated for each percentile range on a cumulative basis (for example, 0–10 percent, 0–20 percent, and 0–30 percent).

Table 15.7. Statistics of Capital Asset Ratios, by Percentile

Percentile	10	20	30	40	50	60	70	80	90	100
FSI ratio ≤	4.0	6.0	8.0	9.2	10.0	10.0	10.6	12.0	12.2	14.0
Mean for percentile range	3.0	5.0	7.0	8.0	10.0	10.0	10.0	12.0	12.0	14.0
Standard deviation for percentile range	1.1	1.0	1.1	0.0	0.0	0.0	0.0	0.0	0.0	0.0

15.40 An interquartile range involves arranging the observations in ascending order and dividing them into four groups of equal size. The values that serve as dividing lines among the groups are called quartiles.

15.41 As with any system that involves decomposition of aggregated data, the choice of approach can be constrained by confidentiality issues. For example, it is a common statistical practice not to disclose data from cells containing fewer than three institutions. Moreover, the usefulness of this approach depends on the number of percentiles used.

Further Extensions of Dispersion Measures

15.42 To extend the data analysis, it is often useful to observe the variation in the distribution of FSI ratios and the persistence of individual deposit takers' FSI values over time.

Variation in the distribution[6]

15.43 At different percentiles, the variation in the distribution of deposit takers' rates of return over time can facilitate an understanding of trends within sector-level data.

15.44 Figure 15.4 provides an example using data on profitability. An interpretation of the figure might be as follows: until period 4, the rates of return at all percentiles tended to move in the same direction, but thereafter there was a noticeable variation in the distribution. While the path of profitability of the median deposit taker (that is, the return on equity at the 50th percentile) was broadly unchanged, deposit takers in the top percentile recorded an increasing rate of return (notably, from 31 percent in period 10 to 47 percent in period 12), while those in the bottom percentile recorded falling profitability (notably from –3.0 percent in period 10 to –24.9 percent in period 12).

Persistence

15.45 Inspection of particular percentiles is not informative about the "persistence" of an individual deposit taker's performance from one year to the next. One way of capturing this information is by constructing a transition matrix (Table 15.8) that shows the movement of deposit takers among percentile groups over a period of time.

15.46 The principal diagonal (shaded, top left to bottom right) in a transition matrix gives the proportion of deposit takers that persist in the same percentile over time. For example, Table 15.8 shows that 65.2 percent of the deposit takers that populated the top percentile in period 1 also populated that percentile in period 2. The remaining 34.8 percent of deposit takers that populated the first percentile in period 1 populate lower percentiles in period 2.

15.47 An interpretation of the example provided in Table 15.8 might be as follows: there is a relatively high degree of persistence, with typically about half to two-thirds of the deposit takers in a particular percentile remaining in that percentile the following period. Moreover, persistence among the very profitable deposit takers (in the top percentile) and very unprofitable deposit takers (in the bottom percentile) is greater than that for the deposit takers in the three middle percentiles. Moreover, mobility from one percentile to the neighboring percentiles is greater than mobility to the more distant percentiles.

Explaining the distribution of financial performance

15.48 Whereas describing the patterns observed in measures of financial health is relatively straightforward, explaining the patterns can be more diffi-

[6]Based on Benito and Vlieghe (2000).

Figure 15.4. Percentiles of Distribution of Return on Equity

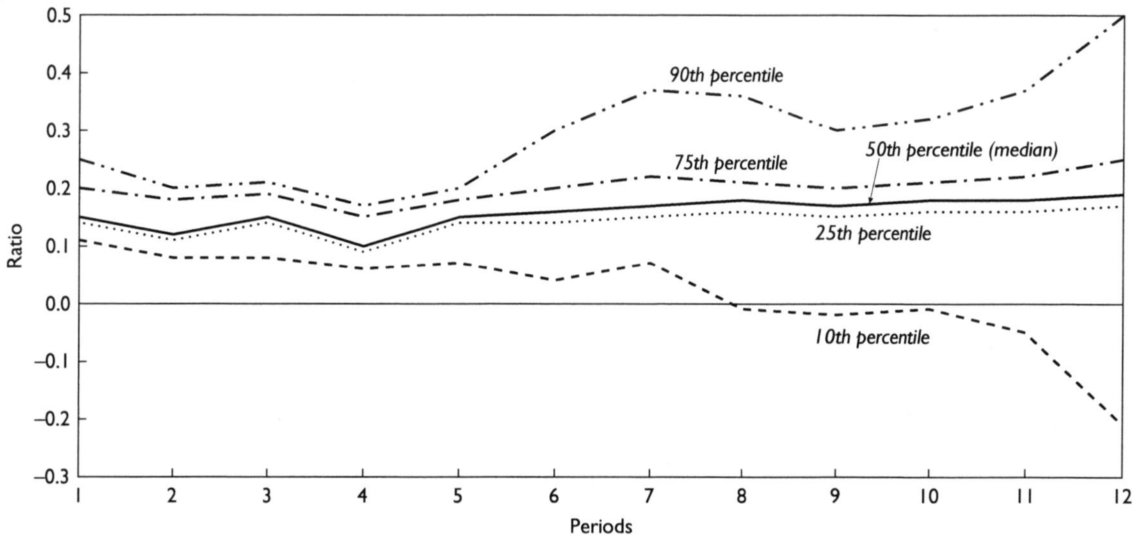

cult. Nevertheless, some insights can be provided by examining the characteristics of those entities in the tails of the distributions of these indicators, in effect, by combining peer group and percentile analysis.

15.49 For example, Table 15.9 considers the composition by industry of those nonfinancial companies that in the current period have the lowest level of profitability and the highest levels of capital gearing (debt-to-equity ratio). For illustrative purposes, low profitability refers to levels below those in the 10th percentile, while high capital gearing refers to levels above those in the 90th percentile. The table, based on the number of firms in each industry group expressed as a percentage of the total number of firms, compares the industrial distribution at the tails (rows 2 and 3) with that of the whole sector (row 1). An interpretation of the data in Table 15.9 might be as follows: while firms with the lowest profitability are to be found within each of the industry groups, the extraction and transport and communications industries have more such firms relative to their presence in the sector as a whole. Among the companies with high capital gearing, again the transport and communications industries are overrepresented.

Interactions among indicators of financial health

15.50 From a financial soundness perspective, it may matter whether, for example, the companies with high

Table 15.8. Transition Matrix for One-Year Transitions Among Percentiles of the Distribution of Return on Capital

Percentile	Percentile $1_{t=2}$	Percentile $2_{t=2}$	Percentile $3_{t=2}$	Percentile $4_{t=2}$	Percentile $5_{t=2}$
Percentile $1_{t=1}$	65.2	21.1	6.4	3.1	4.2
Percentile $2_{t=1}$	20.0	50.5	22.6	5.4	1.5
Percentile $3_{t=1}$	7.9	21.6	46.9	20.7	2.8
Percentile $4_{t=1}$	4.1	7.4	21.7	52.3	14.5
Percentile $5_{t=1}$	4.7	2.5	3.9	18.7	70.1

Table 15.9. Analysis of Tails of the Distribution by Industry Classification
(In percent)

	Percentage Represented in Each Industry Classification (SIC)								Total
Industry Group	SIC 1	SIC 2	SIC 3	SIC 4	SIC 5	SIC 6	SIC 7	SIC 8	Percentage of Firms
1. All firms in sample	5	6	15	12	10	18	20	14	100
2. Firms with low profitability (ROE)	2	16	10	10	4	9	37	13	100
3. Firms with high capital gearing	3	6	8	16	7	11	34	15	100

Note: Industry groups are one-digit nonfinancial, Standard Industrial Classification (SIC-1980) groups.
1. Energy and water supplies; 2. Extraction of minerals and ores other than fuels; manufacture of metals, mineral products, and chemicals; 3. Metal goods, engineering, and vehicles industry; 4. Other manufacturing; 5. Construction; 6. Distribution, hotels, and catering; 7. Transportation and communication; and 8. Other services.

debt levels are also suffering losses and/or have low liquidity. The overlaps among indicators can therefore be important to the analysis, not least because the interactions among indicators can amplify vulnerability to shocks. One approach to monitoring interactions among FSIs is through regression analysis, while another is presented in Figure 15.5.

15.51 Figure 15.5 provides a stylized example of the overlaps among indicators for companies. One-third of the companies (that is, 32 percent) with the highest gearing also had the lowest profitability. In addition, nearly one-third of companies (that is, 29 percent) with the highest gearing had the lowest liquidity. A small group comprising 9 percent of the sector had all three of these characteristics.

Figure 15.5. Coincidence of Financial Soundness Indicators

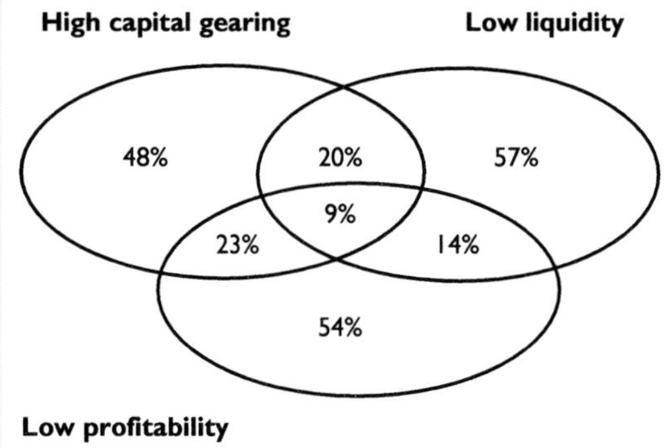

Appendixes

Appendix I. Survey on the Use, Compilation, and Dissemination of Macroprudential Indicators

1. The *Survey on the Use, Compilation, and Dissemination of Macroprudential Indicators* was conducted by the IMF in 2000. It was an important step in the IMF's program to develop a common set of FSIs.[1]

Background

2. The objective of the survey was to obtain information on national needs and practices related to FSIs to (1) gauge the usefulness of specific indicators, (2) assess compilation and dissemination practices to help identify international best practices where possible, (3) evaluate whether the SDDS or other vehicles would be appropriate to encourage the public dissemination of FSIs, and (4) explore the analytical frameworks used by member countries in macroprudential analysis.

3. The survey had two parts. The first part, the *User Questionnaire,* gathered information from financial supervisors, financial policymakers, and the private sector on the usefulness of the FSIs and methods of macroprudential analysis. The second part, the *Compilation and Dissemination Questionnaire,* inquired about national practices in compiling and disseminating FSIs.

4. The FSIs included in the survey largely focused on information about depository corporations (banks) but included some key information on their corporate and household counterparties. This focus was determined in light of the importance of banking institutions and the greater availability of information for banks compared with other types of institutions.

5. Central banks in each economy received the survey, with a request that they coordinate its distribution, completion, and return to the IMF. They were asked to distribute the survey within their economy to whichever parties they judged could best provide representative information on needs and practices relating to FSIs, such as the supervisory agency, the central government, and private sector participants.

6. A total of 122 responses (74 percent of those receiving the survey), covering 142 countries and other jurisdictions, was received. The first part of the survey (*User Questionnaire*) was completed by all 122 respondents, while 93 respondents completed the second part (the *Compilation and Dissemination Questionnaire*). The high response rate to the survey is an indication of the importance being attached worldwide to issues relating to macroprudential analysis and the possible role of FSIs in such analysis. This view is bolstered by the evident effort made by respondents to thoroughly answer the survey and provide detailed comments.

Results

The Most Useful FSIs

7. Respondents judged all major categories of FSIs to be broadly useful. Indicators of *capital adequacy, asset quality (lending institutions),* and *profitability* were deemed the most useful, followed by indicators of *liquidity* and *sensitivity to market risk.* Users in industrial countries in particular deemed the *liquidity* and *sensitivity to market risk* indicators less useful than the others. Several respondents from industrial countries commented that the *liquidity* and *sensitivity to market risk* indicators were sophisticated and possibly difficult to construct with precision.

8. With the highest score possible being 4, Table A1.1 presents the 13 FSIs with an average usefulness score of 3.5 or over. These FSIs include central elements of bank soundness. Two of them—the Basel capital adequacy ratio and one of its components—

[1]A more detailed discussion of the survey and its results is provided in Sundararajan and others (2002).

Table A1.1. FSIs by Type of Economy
(Most useful FSIs, with average usefulness scores of 3.5 and higher)

FSI #	FSI	All Countries	Industrial Countries	Emerging Countries	Developing Countries
1.1	Basel Capital Adequacy Ratio	3.8	3.7	3.9	3.6
1.1a	Ratio of Basel Tier 1 capital to risk-weighted assets	3.6	3.6	3.6	3.5
2.4	Distribution of loans, by sector	3.6	3.5	3.6	3.5
2.5	Distribution of credit extended, by sector	3.5	3.3	3.6	3.6
2.8	Ratio of total large loans to own funds	3.5	3.2	3.6	3.6
2.9	Ratio of gross nonperforming loans to total assets	3.9	3.9	3.9	3.8
2.10	Ratio of gross nonperforming loans net of provisions to total assets	3.8	3.8	3.8	3.8
3.2	Ratio of profits to period-average assets (ROA)	3.6	3.5	3.8	3.6
3.3	Ratio of profits to period-average equity (ROE)	3.6	3.5	3.8	3.6
3.4	Ratio of net interest income to total income	3.5	3.3	3.6	3.6
3.8	Spread between reference lending and deposit rates	3.5	3.4	3.6	3.5
4.3	Ratio of liquid assets to total assets	3.5	3.2	3.6	3.5
4.4	Ratio of liquid assets to liquid liabilities	3.6	3.2	3.7	3.7

relate to the capital base, which serves as a buffer to withstand shocks; four of them measure profitability, which serves to sustain the capital base. The remaining FSIs assessed to be most useful relate to the quality of banks' assets—as covered by data on nonperforming loans, the distribution of assets, and asset liquidity. This list is the basis of the core indicators provided in Chapter 1.

9. Table A1.2 presents the FSIs with an average usefulness score of 3.0 to 3.4. These FSIs form the basis of the list of encouraged indicators set out in Chapter 1. They cover some of the elements of capital adequacy, the distribution of bank credit by risk weight category and by country, the financial condition of the corporate and household sectors, some of the elements of operating income and expenses of banks, the maturity and duration of assets and liabilities, and other market risks.

Additional Indicators

10. The *User Questionnaire* also asked respondents to identify FSIs they considered useful but that were not covered in the survey. The most frequently identified useful additional FSIs were asset prices. Among the asset prices suggested were the prices of real estate, both commercial and residential, and equity prices, including the stock prices of the depository corporations subsector relative to the overall stock price index and stock prices disaggregated by industry. Moreover, to prevent the masking of relevant information through the aggregation process and to help in the identification of outliers, clustering of problem cases, or tiering in markets, there were calls for more information on the distribution or dispersion of observations. Several respondents identified the ratio of gross nonperforming loans to total loans as useful, in lieu of the FSI in the survey that used total assets as the denominator.

Importance of Nondepository Financial Institutions

11. About 80 percent of the respondents reported that information on nondepository financial institutions, markets, and activities was important to the overall analysis of financial sector soundness. On nondepository financial institutions,[2] the majority of the respondents were most interested in information on insurance corporations and pension funds, followed by information on other financial intermediaries. Many of these institutions were viewed by respondents as playing an important role in financial intermediation and possibly in contagion. Several respondents mentioned the importance of specialized financial intermediaries, such as venture capital funds for advanced economies, and microcredit insti-

[2]Defined, in line with the *MFSM* (IMF, 2000a), as insurance corporations and pension funds, other financial intermediaries, and financial auxiliaries.

Table A1.2. Group II FSIs by Type of Economy
(Useful FSIs, with average usefulness scores of 3.0 to 3.4)

FSI #	FSI	All Countries	Industrial Countries	Emerging Countries	Developing Countries
1.1b	Ratio of Basel Tier 1 + 2 capital to risk-weighted assets	3.4	3.2	3.6	3.4
1.1c	Ratio of Basel Tier 1 + 2 + 3 capital to risk-weighted assets	3.0	2.9	3.1	3.1
1.2	Distribution of capital adequacy ratios (number of institutions within specified capital adequacy ratio ranges)	3.3	3.3	3.4	3.1
1.3	Leverage ratio (ratio of total on-balance-sheet assets to own funds)	3.2	2.9	3.3	3.3
2.1	Distribution of on-balance-sheet assets, by Basel risk weight category	3.4	3.2	3.5	3.4
2.4a	Loans for investment in commercial real estate	3.2	3.3	3.3	3.1
2.4b	Loans for investment in residential real estate	3.2	3.3	3.2	3.2
2.6	Distribution of credit extended, by country or region	3.1	3.2	3.2	2.8
2.7	Ratio of credit to related entities to total credit	3.4	3.0	3.6	3.5
2.11	Ratio of corporate debt to own funds ("debt-equity ratio")	3.4	3.4	3.5	3.3
2.12	Ratio of corporate profits to equity	3.3	3.1	3.4	3.2
2.13	Ratio of corporate debt-service costs to total corporate income	3.2	3.2	3.4	3.0
2.14	Corporate net foreign currency exposure	3.2	3.2	3.4	2.9
2.15	Ratio of household total debt to GDP	3.0	3.2	3.0	2.8
3.5	Ratio of trading and foreign exchange gains/losses to total income	3.3	3.2	3.4	3.3
3.6	Ratio of operating costs to net interest income	3.4	3.0	3.6	3.6
3.7	Ratio of staff costs to operating costs	3.2	2.8	3.4	3.4
4.5	Average maturity of assets	3.4	3.0	3.4	3.6
4.6	Average maturity of liabilities	3.4	3.0	3.4	3.6
4.10	Ratio of customer deposits to total (noninterbank) loans	3.2	2.9	3.3	3.3
5.1	Ratio of gross foreign currency assets to own funds	3.1	2.7	3.2	3.2
5.2	Ratio of net foreign currency position to own funds	3.4	3.1	3.6	3.5
5.3	Average interest rate repricing period for assets	3.0	2.8	3.3	3.0
5.4	Average interest rate repricing period for liabilities	3.0	2.8	3.2	3.0
5.5	Duration of assets	3.2	3.0	3.4	3.0
5.6	Duration of liabilities	3.2	3.0	3.3	3.0
5.8	Ratio of net equity position to own funds	3.0	2.8	3.0	3.1

tutions and development banks or funds for developing countries. Some respondents noted the importance of information on financial conglomerates, especially those that included insurance companies.

12. On financial markets, about 90 percent of those responding on the issue indicated that data on the securities markets (public and private debt and equity markets) were important.[3] A few thought that information on foreign exchange markets (16 percent) and derivatives markets (6 percent) was also important.

13. Several respondents noted that borrower information (indebtedness and asset-liability mismatches) was useful, as it provided some indication on emerging credit quality trends and risks in the corporate, household, or foreign sectors. Some respondents said that they paid particular attention to large corporations, while a few others mentioned the importance of monitoring other financial activity, such as the functioning of payment, settlement, and clearing systems. In addition, some respondents emphasized that qualitative information—such as the thoroughness of supervision and the transparency of financial policies—was important to the overall assessment of financial sector stability.

Disaggregation of "Depository Corporations" into Subsectors

14. Almost 60 percent of the respondents thought that more disaggregated information on depository corporations was needed, particularly breakdowns by ownership, function, exposure to risk (for example, geographical, asset type, borrower type), and size. A few respondents felt that disaggregated data that highlighted distributions among banks or allowed for peer group analysis were also useful. One respondent

[3]The types of data mentioned included trading volumes, bid-ask spreads, and credit spreads.

felt that the disaggregation of banks' data should be as fine as possible to enable distinctive activity patterns to be identified. Several respondents, however, stressed that the type of disaggregation would depend on the issue being analyzed.

15. Almost 30 percent of all respondents (about half of those who felt that more disaggregation was useful) mentioned that they analyzed or would like to analyze institutions by ownership characteristics (for example, domestic versus foreign, private versus state-owned, and publicly held stock versus privately held equity). Of these respondents, almost all stated that a breakdown between domestic and foreign institutions was useful, with some emphasizing that the domestic/foreign distinction was important because foreign institutions might operate under different regulatory and supervisory regimes. At the same time, one-fourth of the respondents stated that a breakdown between private and state-owned institutions was important.

16. About 20 percent of the respondents said that disaggregation by function or exposure was useful. The functions most often mentioned were commercial banking, universal banking, and specialized banking (especially mortgage lending and, to a lesser extent, development lending). About 80 percent of the respondents interested in disaggregation by exposure indicated that they would like information on internationally active banks. Sixteen percent wanted disaggregated information on offshore banks, while another 16 percent wanted information on banks disaggregated by their geographical market.

Systemically Important Institutions

17. Almost 60 percent of the respondents reported doing some evaluation of systemically important institutions. Supervisors tended to be more concerned about such institutions—two-thirds of them reported that they evaluated the condition of these institutions, as opposed to less than half of market participants and about half of the government policy or research analysts.

18. Most respondents reported using a measure of size (of assets and/or deposits) to ascertain the importance of an institution. Sometimes size was coupled with other criteria, for instance, exposure to certain risks (such as foreign exchange risk), complexity of transactions, or complexity of ownership structure. However, some respondents mentioned only risk exposure, or used legal or prudential definitions, while others evaluated all institutions by sector or a particular category. This had as a result that all institutions within a particular classification (for example, problem banks, deposit-taking institutions, institutions with insured deposits, commercial banks, international banks) ended up sometimes being considered systemically important. This was often the case in countries with small, developing, or concentrated markets.

19. Many respondents said that the techniques used to evaluate the condition of systemically important institutions were similar to those used to evaluate other institutions. Most mentioned using the CAMELS framework or ratio analysis. Among the variables stressed by the respondents as important in their evaluations were interbank activity, liquidity, large exposures, foreign exchange exposure, consolidated positions for institutions that are part of a financial group, and risk management practices (including assessment by internal models).

Benchmarks

20. Many respondents reported that specific norms, benchmarks, or thresholds were not used in macroprudential analysis. While some of them were considering using norms and benchmarks in the future, others preferred using comparisons with peer group countries to establish relative rankings.

21. Among those who reported using norms and benchmarks for FSIs, some highlighted their critical role in guiding interpretation of the indicators. For this purpose, benchmarks were constructed in a number of ways, including (1) historical averages, (2) bank supervisors' prudential thresholds applied at the aggregate level, (3) trigger points, (4) cross-country comparisons, and (5) criteria constructed from econometric studies.

Business Surveys

22. Overall, about half of all respondents reported that they made use of business survey results—qualitative or quantitative measures of business expectations and potential leading indicators of instability—to supplement macroprudential analysis.

Compilation and Dissemination Practice[4]

23. Country practices on the compilation and dissemination of FSIs and their components were mixed. With only a few exceptions, compilation of FSIs themselves was quite limited, and dissemination of FSIs—especially outside the industrial countries—was scanty. However, compilation and dissemination of components of FSIs were more extensive.

24. The average number of FSIs compiled and disseminated by industrial countries, emerging countries, and developing countries is shown in Figure A1.1. Industrial countries compiled and disseminated the largest number of FSIs, and emerging countries compiled and disseminated the second largest number of FSIs. Industrial and emerging countries compile on average more than half of the indicators specified in the survey.

25. For almost all FSIs, users in countries subscribing to the SDDS rated the usefulness of FSIs nearly identically with users in industrial and emerging countries. Although subscribers' performance in the dissemination of components of FSIs was somewhat better than nonsubscribers' performance, the overall results were broadly similar to those for the total population of respondents—that is, SDDS subscribers had somewhat limited compilation and dissemination of FSIs but relatively extensive compilation and dissemination of the component data series used to compile the FSIs.

26. The survey also inquired about country practices regarding the periodicity of compilation and dissemination as well as users' needs in those areas. The periodicity of dissemination of FSIs varied considerably among the different categories of FSIs. No general pattern could be ascertained, and the number of responses was too low to draw valid conclusions.

Concepts Employed

27. The *Compilation and Dissemination Questionnaire* asked a series of quantitative and open-ended questions about accounting and statistical issues to assess the state of existing practices, possibly identify best practices that might be used as a basis for development of international standards, and help identify strategies for improving the comparability of FSIs.

Figure A1.1. Average Number of FSIs Compiled and Disseminated, by Type of Economy

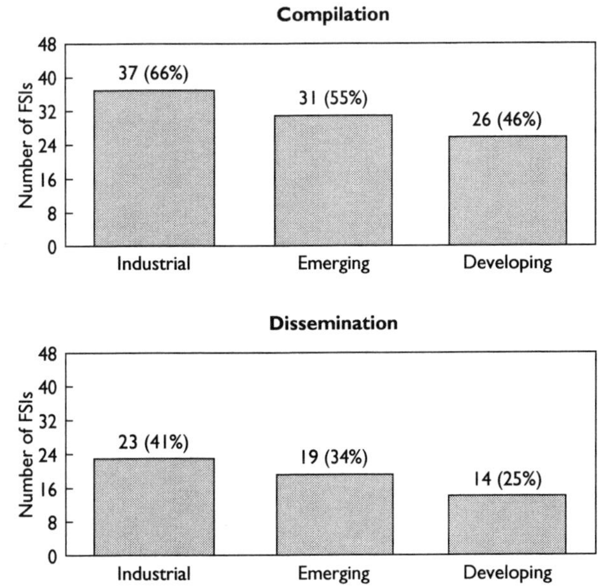

Note: Comparison of the number of FSIs compiled and disseminated indicates that around 60 percent of compiled FSIs were disseminated; this percentage was broadly the same for each type of economy. Divergence between the number of FSIs compiled and disseminated indicated that the private sector had access to a narrower range of FSIs than is available to national authorities. It also indicates that there is scope for increasing the number of publicly available indicators of financial sector soundness in all types of economies.

28. The responses highlighted a diversity of national practices and revealed many reasons why FSIs might not be comparable across economies:

- Different, and often complex, standards exist for recognition of substandard claims and provisioning.
- National definitions of regulatory capital differ: for instance, as regards deductions and components of each tier of capital. Moreover, numerous countries indicated that they had not approved the inclusion of Tier 3 capital within the base.
- Consolidation practices for foreign branches and subsidiaries differ (see section below). Within each country, some FSIs use global (cross-border) consolidations drawn from supervisory data, while other FSIs use domestic (national residence basis) consolidations drawn from statistical sources. Overall, however, some degree of international

[4]For a detailed discussion of compilation and dissemination practices, see Slack (2003).

conformity exists in consolidation practices because of the rather widespread use of domestic consolidation.

- Valuation practices for financial instruments differ (see section below). Key issues include the limited use of market valuations for debt securities and shares, and the diverse practices for on-balance-sheet recognition of derivatives, repurchase agreements, and securities lending.
- Different rules exist across countries for revaluing foreign currency positions. Although there appears to be convergence in industrial countries toward use of market exchange rates in revaluing foreign-currency-denominated positions, continued use of official rates in a number of emerging and developing countries might hinder the comparability of FSIs.

29. The list of issues above indicated that practices were diverse and that cross-country comparison of FSIs was challenging.

Consolidation

30. The survey sought information on country practices for consolidating information on foreign branches and subsidiaries of financial institutions into single accounting statements or statistical reports. A key issue was whether data were compiled on a domestic or global consolidation basis.

31. Strong differences in practices by type of economy were found. Respondents in developing countries adhered overwhelmingly to a national residence basis for most FSIs. This possibly reflects the fact that banks with headquarters in developing countries may often have few or no nonresident branches or subsidiaries. It might also reflect limited supervisory infrastructures in developing countries that may not always effectively monitor and supervise nonresident operations. To some extent, adherence to domestic consolidation was also reported by respondents in emerging countries. In industrial countries, supervisors used global consolidation most often but also reported that data using both approaches to consolidation were available for numerous FSIs.[5]

[5]The availability of FSI data on both bases could have some important advantages. For example, one respondent noted, "The survey does not address the main statistical aspect, which is reconciliation between the home and host country approach, which will be viable if both supervisory and macroeconomic statistical data sources are used."

32. Differences in practices by category of FSI were also found. These differences often reflected whether the primary source data are supervisory or statistical in nature. A summary of the practices by category of FSI is provided below.

Capital adequacy. In industrial countries and emerging countries, data were primarily from supervisory sources and generally on a global consolidation basis, although data using both consolidation approaches were often available. In a number of emerging countries and many developing countries, only data on a national residence basis were used. In terms of worldwide totals, the two approaches were used about equally, and in the case of some FSIs up to one-fourth of respondents used both. A small number of countries reported nonstandard consolidations in their data, such as including nonresident branches but not nonresident subsidiaries.

Asset quality (lending institutions). FSIs derived from monetary statistics were overwhelmingly on a national residence basis. FSIs derived from supervisory sources were most often on a global consolidation basis, but in many cases they were available on a national residence basis or on both bases.

Asset quality (borrowing institutions). FSIs were almost exclusively on a national residence basis because the underlying data were drawn from national macroeconomic statistical series.

Profitability and competitiveness. Data were most often on a national residence basis or were available on both bases. However, a number of countries had data only on a global basis. Within the profitability category, nonstandard consolidations were used by a number of countries.

Liquidity. Consolidation on a national residence basis was most common, but the FSIs on liquid assets and average maturities of assets and liabilities were often consolidated on a global basis. Global consolidation is not relevant for some of the liquidity FSIs that refer solely to national conditions.

Sensitivity to market risks. Consolidation on a national residence basis was most common. Consolidation on a cross-border basis was used to some extent in supervisory data in industrial and emerging countries.

Valuation

33. For deposits and loans, historical valuations were most commonly used—in supervisory data, in at least three-fourths of all responses, and in statistical data, in about 9 out of 10 cases. In contrast, for securities (other than shares), as well as for shares and other equity, no valuation method clearly predominated, although use of market values was more common than other valuation approaches. For financial derivatives, market valuations were used most often, with supervisors also reporting fairly common use of "other" valuation methods, such as hedge valuations. Historical valuations predominated in miscellaneous receivables and payables and in nonfinancial assets, but use of the other types of valuations was not uncommon.

34. On the translation of the value of foreign-currency-denominated instruments into domestic currency equivalents, end-of-period exchange rates were used most often for all types of financial instruments. A large minority of emerging countries and developing countries reported that they used official exchange rates. Foreign currency positions were revalued most often at the rate applying on the balance sheet closing date. However, revaluations of foreign currency positions at other frequencies were not uncommon for securities (other than shares), shares and other equities, and financial derivatives.

Presentation

35. The majority of respondents preferred the use of ratios and growth rates in presenting their FSIs. However, many respondents also felt that the preferred mode of presentation depended on the particular FSI in question and the type of analysis being conducted. For example, for sectoral aggregates, it was useful to have weighted averages as well as simple averages, accompanied by the frequency distribution of institutions according to the range of values of the indicators.

36. Some respondents noted that measures of dispersion (standard deviations, histograms, Gini indices, and so forth) could be particularly useful in presenting FSIs because they allowed the analyst to identify, among other things, outliers, trends in concentration, and tiering in markets, which could be relevant for the analysis of financial stability.

Appendix II. Summary of Guidance for Each Financial Soundness Indicator

1. This appendix brings together in summary form the guidance outlined in the *Guide* for each agreed FSI. The main purpose of this appendix is to support the work of compilers by bringing together in one place the various elements of guidance relating to each FSI, not least to help compilers locate the relevant detailed advice in the main text. The summaries are of one page length or less, and there is some cross-referencing among them. In addition, for ease of reference, an index of the FSI summaries is provided (Box A2.1).

2. For many of the agreed FSIs, the *Guide* recommends that the data series be drawn from sectoral financial statements; therefore, even though FSIs are described individually below, the compiler needs to remain aware of the broader context. In other words, the FSIs are a body of data with interrelationships that may not be apparent in the short summaries. Where relevant, the appropriate lines in the sectoral financial statements (Tables 4.1, 4.2, 4.3, and 4.4 in Chapter 4) are referenced.

3. Each summary below has the following three subheadings.

- Definition: provides the definition of the FSI and, where appropriate, guidance on where the component series are defined in the *Guide.*
- Issues for compilers: draws out specific issues of which compilers should be aware.
- Data sources: provides information on where the information can be obtained. Relevant to this subheading is Chapter 11, which provides a detailed discussion of sources of information and additional data series that might be required. Also relevant is Appendix IV, which reconciles the *Guide*'s methodology with the national accounts and commercial accounting frameworks. As outlined in Chapter 11, it is not possible to generalize as to what information is available from supervisory sources, but some of the key differences in methodology between national accounts and supervisory information should be explored in compiling cross-border consolidated data for deposit takers.

4. For deposit takers, it is assumed that data from supervisory sources are available on a consolidated basis, but the nature of the consolidation should be compared with the *Guide*'s recommendations (see Chapter 5). If countries decide that domestic consolidated data (see paragraph 5.25) can also be derived from supervisory sources, then the references under cross-border consolidated information also apply to domestic data, but in general the summaries assume that the national accounts will be the source for domestic based data.

5. In reviewing the summaries below and determining the need to collect new data (and incur increased resource costs), authorities must make a judgment as to the importance of the additional data series for compiling and monitoring FSI data.

6. To summarize the guidance in Chapters 2 and 3:

- The definitions of deposit takers and other sectors are provided in Chapter 2 (paragraphs 2.4 to 2.19).
- Transactions and positions should be recorded on an **accrual** basis, and only existing, actual assets and liabilities should be recognized (paragraphs 3.3 to 3.9).
- The *Guide* prefers **valuation methods** that can provide the most realistic assessment at any moment in time of the value of an instrument or item. Market value is the preferred basis of valuation of transactions as well as of positions in traded securities. For positions in nontradable instruments, the *Guide* acknowledges that nominal value (supported by appropriate provisioning policies) may provide a more realistic assessment of value than the application of fair value (see paragraphs 3.20 to 3.33).
- **Residence** is defined in terms of where an institutional unit has its center of economic interest (see paragraphs 3.34 to 3.36).
- Transactions and positions in **foreign currency** should be converted into a single unit of account based on the market rate of exchange (see paragraphs 3.44 to 3.48).

Box A2.1. FSIs: Index of Summaries

Core FSIs

Deposit takers

Regulatory capital to risk-weighted assets
Regulatory Tier 1 capital to risk-weighted assets
Nonperforming loans net of provisions to capital
Nonperforming loans to total gross loans
Sectoral distribution of loans to total loans
Return on assets
Return on equity
Interest margin to gross income
Noninterest expenses to gross income
Liquid assets to total assets (liquid asset ratio)
Liquid assets to short-term liabilities
Net open position in foreign exchange to capital

Encouraged FSIs

Deposit takers

Capital to assets ratio
Large exposures to capital
Geographical distribution of loans to total loans
Gross asset and liability position in financial derivatives to capital
Trading income to total income
Personnel expenses to noninterest expenses
Spread between reference lending and deposit rates
Spread between highest and lowest interbank rate
Customer deposits to total (noninterbank) loans
Foreign-currency-denominated loans to total loans
Foreign-currency-denominated liabilities to total liabilities
Net open position in equities to capital

Other financial corporations

Assets to total financial system assets
Assets to GDP

Nonfinancial corporations

Total debt to equity
Return on equity
Earnings to interest and principal expenses
Net foreign exchange exposure to equity
Number of applications for protection from creditors

Households

Household debt to GDP
Household debt service and principal payments to income

Market liquidity

Average bid-ask spread in the securities market
Average daily turnover ratio in the securities market

Real estate markets

Real estate prices
Residential real estate loans to total loans
Commercial real estate loans to total loans

- Short-term **maturity** is defined as one year or less (or payable on demand), with maturities over one year defined as long term (see paragraphs 3.49 and 3.50).

7. Moreover, as the *Guide* recommends that for each corporate sector—deposit takers, other financial corporations, and nonfinancial corporations—data be compiled on a consolidated basis, the word "group" is used on a number of occasions in the summaries. For deposit takers, as well as for other corporate entities, a group in this context includes the parent deposit taker, its deposit-taking branches, and its deposit-taking subsidiaries.

8. For deposit takers, the *Guide* requires the compilation of data covering ***domestically controlled deposit takers*** on a cross-border consolidated basis (domestically controlled, cross-border consolidated data). Data on a domestic consolidated basis might be separately compiled if the authorities believe that such data would contribute materially to financial stability analysis (for example, to illustrate the linkage with other macroeconomic information).

Core FSIs

Deposit Takers

Regulatory capital to risk-weighted assets

Definition

9. This FSI measures the capital adequacy of deposit takers using the definitions of regulatory capital and risk-weighted assets of the BCBS. Sector-wide regulatory capital is the numerator and is defined in paragraphs 4.68 to 4.73. Sector-wide risk-weighted assets is the denominator and is defined in paragraph 4.74. The FSI is defined in paragraphs 6.17 and 6.18.

Issues for compilers

10. Data are based on supervisory concepts. To derive sector-wide regulatory capital, the consolidated regulatory capital of the deposit-taking groups in the reporting population is aggregated. To derive sector-wide risk-weighted assets, the consolidated risk-weighted assets of the deposit-taking groups in the reporting population are also aggregated.

Sources of data

11. *Domestically controlled, cross-border consolidated and domestic consolidated data:* The availability of data reported to supervisory agencies will determine the scope of the data that can be disseminated. Consolidated regulatory capital and consolidated risk-weighted assets of each domestically controlled deposit-taking group in the reporting population should be available to supervisors.

Regulatory Tier 1 capital to risk-weighted assets

Definition

12. This FSI measures the capital adequacy of deposit takers based on the core capital concept of the BCBS. Sector-wide Tier 1 capital is the numerator and is defined in paragraphs 4.70 and 4.73. Sector-wide risk-weighted assets is the denominator and is defined in paragraph 4.74. The FSI is defined in paragraph 6.19.

Issues for compilers

13. Data are based on supervisory concepts. To derive sector-wide Tier 1 capital, the consolidated Tier 1 capital of the deposit-taking groups in the reporting population is aggregated. To derive sector-wide risk-weighted assets, the consolidated risk-weighted assets of the deposit-taking groups in the reporting population are also aggregated.

Sources of data

14. *Domestically controlled, cross-border consolidated and domestic consolidated data:* The availability of data reported to supervisory agencies will determine the scope of the data that can be disseminated. Consolidated Tier 1 capital and consolidated risk-weighted assets of each domestically controlled deposit-taking group in the reporting population should be available to supervisors.

Nonperforming loans net of provisions to capital

Definition

15. This FSI is intended to compare the potential impact on capital of NPLs, net of provisions. The impact of NPL losses on capital is uncertain in most circumstances, because for various reasons the lender might expect to recover some of the potential NPL losses. This FSI is calculated by taking the value of NPLs less the value of specific loan provisions (lines 42 and 18(ii), respectively, in Table 4.1) as the numerator and capital as the denominator. The FSI is defined in paragraphs 6.22 and 6.23.

Issues for compilers

16. The guidance for NPLs is the same as that provided for the ratio of NPLs to gross loans. Provisions are defined as specific provisions, which are the outstanding amount of provisions made against the value of individual loans (including a collectively assessed group of loans) (see paragraph 4.50). Provisions on intrasectoral loans are deducted from the specific provisions data. The *Guide* relies on national practices in identifying specific provisions but recommends that such practices be clearly documented. In calculating this ratio, it is important to understand how provisions data affect both the numerator and the denominator (see paragraph 6.24).

17. Capital is measured as total capital and reserves (line 30 in the sectoral balance sheet and defined in paragraph 4.62) and, for cross-border consolidated data, also as total regulatory capital (line 36 and defined in paragraphs 4.70 to 4.73). In measuring sector-wide capital, intrasector equity investments are deducted from the overall capital in the sector so that capital and reserves held within the sector are not double counted. Also, in line with supervisory guidance, capital excludes purchased goodwill. See the text annex to Chapter 5 for information on these adjustments to capital and reserves and those relating to intrasector provisions.

Sources of data

18. *Domestically controlled, cross-border consolidated data:* Information on NPLs and specific provisions (adjusted for provisions on intrasectoral loans) for the reporting population are typically available from supervisory sources, although national definitions of a NPL can vary. Similarly, capital and reserves data might be available from supervisory sources, although for total capital and reserves, the definition would need to be investigated to ensure compatibility with the approach of the *Guide*. See Table 11.4 for possible adjustments required. Supervisory data should already be on a consolidated basis—although coverage would require investigation—but data may need to be aggregated to calculate the numerator and denominator for this ratio.

19. *Domestic consolidated data:* National accounts sources do not provide information on NPLs, so additional data would need to be collected. NPLs on account of lending among deposit takers in the reporting population that are part of the same group (if any) are excluded. Data on specific provisions would also need to be collected (adjusted for provisions on intrasectoral loans, if any (paragraph 5.87)). For capital, data are available from national accounts sources, such as monetary and financial statistics, but are subject to adjustment (see Box 11.1 and the capital and reserves entry in Appendix IV). In addition to the deductions mentioned under issues for compilers, NPLs should be reduced by the amount of any specific provisions (adjusted for provisions on intrasectoral claims). Moreover, in the balance sheet, equity investments in subsidiaries and associates (and reverse investments) should be valued at the proportionate share in the subsidiary's or associate's capital and reserves, and this could affect total capital and reserves measured on a national accounts basis. The treatment of equity investments is discussed in Box 5.1, and the text annex to Chapter 5 provides numerical examples of the adjustments at the sector level (see in particular paragraphs 5.89 and 5.90). Information on the funds contributed by owners and retained earnings (including those earnings appropriated to reserves) may be collected separately, or perhaps from monetary and financial statistics sources if data are collected by component of capital and reserves as set out in the *MFSM* (paragraph 214), subject to the deductions and other adjustments mentioned above. See also Box 11.1 and Tables 11.1–11.3.

Nonperforming loans to total gross loans

Definition

20. This FSI is intended to identify problems with asset quality in the loan portfolio. It is calculated by using the value of NPLs as the numerator and the total value of the loan portfolio (including NPLs and before the deduction of specific loan loss provisions) as the denominator. NPLs and loans (lines 42 and 18(i) in Table 4.1) are described in paragraphs 4.84 to 4.86 and 4.45 to 4.48, respectively. The FSI is defined in paragraphs 6.54 and 6.55.

Issues for compilers

21. The *Guide* provides guidance for identifying NPLs. Loans are nonperforming when payments of principal and interest are past due by three months (90 days) or more, or interest payments corresponding to three months (90 days) or more have been capitalized (reinvested into the principal amount), refinanced, or rolled over (that is, payment has been delayed by agreement). In addition, NPLs should also include those loans with payments less than 90 days past due that are recognized as nonperforming under national supervisory guidance—that is, evidence exists to classify a loan as nonperforming even in the absence of a 90-day past due payment, such as if the debtor files for bankruptcy. After a loan is classified as nonperforming, it (and/or any replacement loan(s)) should remain so classified until written off or payments of interest and/or principal are received on this or subsequent loans that replace the original loan. Replacement loans include loans arising from rescheduling or refinancing the original loan(s) and/or loans provided to make payments on the original loan.

22. Data on loans should exclude accrued interest on nonperforming loans and lending among deposit takers in the reporting population that are part of the same group.

Sources of data

23. *Domestically controlled, cross-border consolidated data:* Information on NPLs for the reporting population is typically available from supervisory sources, although national definitions of an NPL can vary. Similarly, information on loans might be available from supervisory sources and is likely to be subject to the exclusions mentioned under issues for compilers. Also, the *Guide*'s definition of deposit takers should be compared with the definition used for supervisory purposes. Supervisory data may need to be aggregated to calculate the numerator and denominator for this ratio.

24. *Domestic consolidated data:* National accounts data do not provide information on NPLs; additional data on NPLs would need to be collected for domestic consolidated data. Data on loans should be available from monetary and financial statistics but perhaps not subject to the exclusions mentioned above. Also, the *Guide*'s definition of a deposit taker should be compared with the definition of "other depository corporations" used for monetary and financial statistics. Box 11.1 explains how data collected using *MFSM* methodology can be utilized in compiling FSIs for deposit takers.

Sectoral distribution of loans to total loans

Definition

25. This FSI provides information on the distribution of loans (including NPLs and before the deduction of specific loan loss provisions) to resident sectors and to nonresidents. The numerators and denominator for this FSI are *lending to each of the institutional sectors* (lines 18(i.i) and 18(i.ii) in Table 4.1) and *gross loans* (line 18(i)), respectively. The resident sectors are deposit takers (see paragraphs 2.4 to 2.7), the central bank (2.13), the general government (2.18), other financial corporations (2.14), nonfinancial corporations (2.15), other domestic sectors (households (2.16) and nonprofit institutions serving households (2.17)). Nonresidents are defined in paragraphs 3.35 and 3.36. Loans are defined in paragraphs 4.45 to 4.48. This FSI is defined in paragraphs 6.56 and 6.57.

Issues for compilers

26. Sectoral analysis is a concept used in the national accounts that classifies entities by the nature of their economic activity. Lending is attributed on the basis of the residence of the reporting entity.

27. Data on loans should exclude accrued interest on nonperforming loans as well as lending among deposit takers in the reporting population that are part of the same group. Because all sectors are covered, the sum of the sectoral ratios should be unity.

Sources of data

28. *Domestically controlled, cross-border consolidated data:* The availability of data on loans by sector might vary depending on supervisory practices. Lending by any foreign branches and/or deposit-taking subsidiaries of the reporting entity to residents of the economy for which the FSI data are being compiled is classified as lending to the relevant resident sector. In contrast, lending to residents of the local economy in which the foreign subsidiary/branch is located is classified as lending to nonresidents. To derive sector-wide data on deposit takers' lending by institutional sector, the consolidated data may need to be aggregated to derive both the numerators and the denominator of this FSI.

29. *Domestic consolidated data:* Data on loans to the various sectors are available from monetary and financial statistics, subject to the adjustments mentioned above. Loans to deposit-taking branches and subsidiaries abroad are included in the data as lending to nonresidents.

Return on assets

Definition

30. This FSI is intended to measure deposit takers' efficiency in using their assets. It is calculated by dividing net income before extraordinary items and taxes (although net income after extraordinary items and taxes (line 11 of Table 4.1) might instead, or additionally, be used) by the average value of total assets (financial and nonfinancial) over the same period. At a minimum, the denominator can be calculated by using the average of the beginning- and end-period positions, but compilers are encouraged to use the most frequent observations available to calculate the average. Net income before and after extraordinary items and taxes (lines 8 and 11, respectively, in Table 4.1) and its components are defined in paragraphs 4.17 to 4.35; total assets (nonfinancial and financial assets) (line 14) are defined in paragraphs 4.37 and 4.38. The FSI is defined in paragraphs 6.52 and 6.53.

Issues for compilers

31. Net income is calculated on a basis closer to commercial accounting and supervisory approaches than to national accounting. Unlike the national accounts, in the *Guide* net income includes gains and losses on financial instruments, and gains and losses from the sales of fixed assets, which are measured as the difference between the sale value and the balance sheet value at the previous end period (see Table 4.1).

32. Notably, compilers should be aware that the *Guide* recommends that interest income not include the accrual of interest on nonperforming assets (paragraph 4.18). It also encourages the inclusion of realized and unrealized gains and losses arising during each period on all financial instruments (financial assets and liabilities, in domestic and foreign currencies) valued at market or fair value in the balance sheet, excluding equity in associates, subsidiaries, and any reverse equity investments (paragraph 4.22).

33. At the sector level, a number of adjustments are specified to eliminate the impact of intrasector transactions on sectoral net income. These include the elimination of the following income items arising from claims on deposit takers in the reporting population: the investing deposit taker's prorated share of the earnings of associate deposit takers, dividends receivable from other deposit takers, provisions for accrued interest on nonperforming claims, and specific provisions on claims on other deposit takers. A full list of adjustments is provided in Chapter 5 (paragraph 5.53).

34. In line with supervisory guidance, goodwill is deducted from capital and reserves. Thus, goodwill is not classified as an asset (see paragraph 4.110) and, given this, not amortized in the income account. Consistent with this, gains and losses on the sale of an associate or subsidiary (and disinvestment of a reverse investment) are also excluded from income (paragraph 5.91).

Sources of data

35. *Domestically controlled, cross-border consolidated data:* The data for net income available to supervisory sources may depend on the national commercial accounting practice, as might the extent to which they meet the definitions in the *Guide.* It is likely that there will be a need for the sector-wide adjustments set out above (see Table 11.4 and paragraph 11.51). The available information may need to be aggregated to calculate both the numerator and denominator.

36. *Domestic consolidated data:* For national accounts-based data, there is a need to include within net income those items classified as income items in the *Guide* but not in the national accounts. These adjustments include, most notably, gains and losses on financial instruments and provisions on nonperforming assets (see Table 11.1). Moreover, the sector-wide adjustments described above for net income and total assets, including those transactions and positions with other deposit takers in the reporting population that are part of the same group (see Tables 11.2 and 11.3), should be considered. Information on goodwill may also be needed (Table 11.1).

Return on equity

Definition

37. This FSI is intended to measure deposit takers' efficiency in using their capital. It is calculated by dividing net income before extraordinary items and taxes (although net income after extraordinary items and taxes (line 11 of Table 4.1) might instead, or additionally, be used) by the average value of capital over the same period. As a minimum, the denominator can be calculated by taking the average of the beginning- and end-period positions (for example, at the beginning and the end of the month), but compilers are encouraged to use the most frequent observations available in calculating the average. Net income before and after extraordinary items and taxes (lines 8 and 11, respectively, in Table 4.1) and its components are defined in paragraphs 4.17 to 4.36. The FSI is defined in paragraphs 6.25 and 6.26.

Issues for compilers and sources of data

38. Regarding net income, issues for compilers and sources of data are discussed in the *return on assets* summary.

39. Capital is measured as total capital and reserves (line 30 in the sectoral balance sheet and defined in paragraph 4.62) and, for cross-border consolidated data, also Tier 1 capital (line 32 of Table 4.1 and defined in paragraphs 4.70 and 4.73). In the absence of Tier 1 data, funds contributed by owners and retained earnings (including those earnings appropriated to reserves) could be used (line 30(i) of Table 4.1 and defined in paragraph 4.64). In measuring sector-wide capital, intrasector equity investments are deducted from the overall capital in the sector so that capital and reserves held within the sector are not double counted. Moreover, in line with supervisory guidance, capital excludes purchased goodwill. See the text annex to Chapter 5 for information on these adjustments to capital and reserves and those relating to intrasector provisions.

40. Sources of data for capital are discussed in the *nonperforming loans net of provisions to capital* summary.

Interest margin to gross income

Definition

41. This FSI is a measure of the relative share of net interest earnings—interest earned less interest expenses—within gross income. It is calculated by using net interest income (line 3 in Table 4.1) as the numerator and gross income (line 5) as the denominator. Net interest income and its components are defined in paragraphs 4.17 to 4.19, while gross income is defined in paragraph 4.20. The FSI is defined in paragraphs 6.68 and 6.69.

Issues for compilers

42. In the *Guide,* interest income should not include the accrual of interest on nonperforming assets (see paragraph 4.18). However, to avoid asymmetric reporting at the sector level, an adjustment should be made so that interest does accrue on nonperforming claims on other deposit takers in the reporting population (paragraphs 5.55 to 5.57).

43. Gross income includes both net interest income and other gross income. Among other gross income items, the *Guide* encourages the inclusion of realized and unrealized gains and losses arising during each period on all financial instruments (financial assets and liabilities, in domestic and foreign currencies) valued at market or fair value in the balance sheet, excluding equity in associates, subsidiaries, and any reverse equity investments (paragraph 4.22). Moreover, at the sector level, a number of adjustments are specified to eliminate the impact of intrasector transactions on sectoral gross income. These are the elimination of the following income items arising from positions and transactions with other deposit takers in the reporting population: fees and commissions receivable; the investing deposit taker's prorated share of the earnings of associate deposit takers, dividends receivable from other deposit takers, other income receivable from other deposit takers, and gains and losses on deposit takers' ownership of equities of other deposit takers. A description of these adjustments is provided in Chapter 5, starting at paragraph 5.53 and in Box 5.1.

44. Gains and losses on the sale of an associate or subsidiary (and disinvestment, of a reverse investment) are excluded from gross income (paragraph 5.92).

Sources of data

45. *Domestically controlled, cross-border consolidated data:* Consolidated data for net interest income and gross income should be available from supervisory sources, but the extent to which they meet the definitions in the *Guide* could depend on national commercial accounting practice. It is likely that there will be a need for the sector-wide adjustments set out above (see Table 11.4 and paragraph 11.51). The available information may need to be aggregated to calculate both the numerator and denominator.

46. *Domestic consolidated data:* From national accounts-based sources, data on deposit takers' net interest income should be available—Table 11.9 identifies the relevant line items in the *1993 SNA* accounts—although to make adjustments for the nonaccrual of interest on nonperforming loans, additional data may be needed. For gross income data, there may be a need for additional information to include within gross income those items classified as income items in the *Guide* but not in the national accounts (see Table 11.1), and also to make the sector-wide adjustments described above (see Table 11.2).

Noninterest expenses to gross income

Definition

47. This FSI measures the size of administrative expenses to gross income. The FSI is calculated by using noninterest expenses (line 6 in Table 4.1) as the numerator and gross income (line 5) as the denominator. Noninterest expenses are defined in paragraph 4.30 and gross income in paragraph 4.20. This FSI is defined in paragraphs 6.73 and 6.74.

Issues for compilers

48. Noninterest expenses cover all expenses other than interest expenses. Provisions are not included in noninterest expenses but are separately identified in the sectoral income and expense statement (line 7). To derive the sector-wide total, all noninterest expenses paid to other deposit takers are deducted (see Table 11.2). These comprise fees and commissions payable and other expenses payable. Moreover, no goodwill is amortized in the income and expense statement (paragraph 4.110).

49. Regarding gross income, issues for compilers are discussed in the *interest margin to gross income* summary.

Sources of data

50. *Domestically controlled, cross-border consolidated data:* The data for noninterest expenses and gross income available to supervisory sources may depend on national commercial accounting practice. Nonetheless, it is likely that there will be a need for the sector-wide adjustments set out above (see Table 11.4 and paragraph 11.51). Regarding gross income, sources of data are discussed in the *interest margin to gross income* summary. The available information may need to be aggregated to calculate both the numerator and the denominator of this FSI.

51. *Domestic consolidated data:* From national accounts-based sources, data on deposit takers' noninterest expenses should be available—Table 11.9 identifies the relevant line items in the *1993 SNA* accounts. The sector-wide adjustments for noninterest expenses need to be considered (see Table 11.2). Regarding gross income, sources of data are discussed in the *interest margin to gross income* summary.

Liquid assets to total assets (liquid asset ratio)

Definition

52. This FSI provides an indication of the liquidity available to meet expected and unexpected demands for cash. It is calculated by using the core measure of liquid assets (line 39 in Table 4.1) as the numerator and total assets (line 14) as the denominator. This ratio can also be calculated using the broad measure of liquid assets (line 40). Liquid assets are defined in paragraphs 4.78 to 4.81, and nonfinancial and financial assets (total assets) are defined in paragraphs 4.37 and 4.38. The FSI is defined in paragraphs 6.45 and 6.46.

Issues for compilers

53. Assessing the extent to which an asset is liquid or not involves judgment and, particularly for securities, depends on the liquidity of secondary markets. The *Guide* distinguishes between core and broad liquid assets.

54. Core liquid assets comprise currency and deposits and other financial assets that are available either on demand or within three months or less, but deposit takers' deposits (and other nontraded claims) with other deposit takers in the reporting population are excluded.

55. Broad liquid assets include those in the core measure plus securities that are traded in liquid markets (including repo markets) that can be readily converted into cash with insignificant risk of change in value under normal business conditions. Such securities include those issued by the government and/or the central bank in their own currency and high credit-quality private securities—both debt and equity securities. For instance, if a financial instrument is eligible under normal business conditions for repurchase operations at the central bank, then it can be classified as a liquid asset. Private sector securities of less than investment grade should be excluded from liquid assets.

56. The issues for compilers for total assets are the same as in the *return on assets* summary.

Sources of data

57. *Domestically controlled, cross-border consolidated data:* Data on liquidity should be available from supervisory sources. The BCBS (2000b) stresses the need for good liquidity management by banks, including the need for effective measurement processes. The extent to which national approaches to measuring liquidity meet the concepts in the *Guide* would require consideration. In particular, for sector-wide total liquid assets, deposit takers' nontraded claims on other deposit takers in the reporting population need to be deducted before aggregation. The available information may need to be aggregated to calculate both the numerator and denominator of this FSI.

58. *Domestic consolidated data:* While monetary statistics provide some data, such as deposits at the central bank, the liquid-asset concepts developed in the *Guide* are not covered in national accounts-based data, and additional data may need to be requested. Some approximation of the core measure might be available from the *1993 SNA*'s full sequence of accounts, and this is discussed in more detail in Appendix IV under the entry for *liquid assets.*

Liquid assets to short-term liabilities

Definition

59. This FSI is intended to capture the liquidity mismatch of assets and liabilities, and provides an indication of the extent to which deposit takers could meet the short-term withdrawal of funds without facing liquidity problems. This FSI is calculated by using the core measure of liquid assets (line 39 in Table 4.1) as the numerator and the short-term liabilities (line 41) as the denominator. This ratio can also be calculated by taking the broad measure of liquid assets (line 40). Liquid assets are defined in paragraphs 4.78 to 4.81, and short-term liabilities are defined in paragraph 4.83. The FSI is defined in paragraphs 6.47 to 6.48.

Issues for compilers

60. Short-term liabilities are the short-term element of deposit takers' debt liabilities (line 28) plus the net (short-term, if possible) market value of the financial derivatives position (liabilities (line 29) less assets (line 21)); it excludes such liabilities to other deposit takers in the reporting population. Preferably, "short term" should be defined on a remaining maturity basis, but original maturity is an alternative (defined in paragraphs 3.49 and 3.50).

61. It is recommended that the net (short-term) market value position (liabilities less assets) of financial derivative liabilities be included rather than the gross liability position because of the market practice of creating offsetting contracts and the possibility of forward-type instruments switching between asset and liability positions from one period to the next. Moreover, because of the potential importance to deposit takers of financial derivatives in their liquidity analysis, the *Guide* provides a table (Table 6.4) that could be used to provide information on the expected cash flows underlying financial derivatives and from the settlement of foreign currency spot positions. The FSI could also be calculated excluding financial derivative positions—that is, calculating the ratio using short-term debt only—particularly if a net financial derivative asset position were significantly affecting the ratio.

62. The issues for compilers for liquid assets are the same as in the *liquid assets to total assets* summary.

Sources of data

63. *Domestically controlled, cross-border consolidated data:* Data on short-term liabilities on a remaining maturity basis might be available from supervisory sources. The extent to which the data meet the concepts in the *Guide,* particularly with regard to financial derivatives, would require consideration. Sources of data on liquid assets are discussed in the *liquid assets to total assets* summary.

64. *Domestic consolidated data:* Data on short-term liabilities for all debt instruments are generally not available in national accounts-based data on a remaining maturity basis, but they are often available on an original maturity basis. The IMF (2003b) outlines the presentation of remaining maturity data for banks, on an external debt basis only. Any data should exclude short-term liabilities among deposit takers in the reporting population that are part of the same group. Data on financial derivatives positions are available in national accounts-based data (see Box 11.1) but not on a short term basis. Data sources on liquid assets are discussed in the *liquid assets to total assets* summary.

Net open position in foreign exchange to capital

Definition

65. This FSI is intended to show deposit takers' exposure to exchange rate risk compared with capital. A deposit taker's open position in foreign exchange should be calculated by summing the foreign currency positions into a single unit of account as the numerator. Capital is the denominator. The FSI is defined in paragraphs 6.31 to 6.38. These paragraphs provide a detailed explanation as to how to measure the net open position in foreign exchange.

Issues for compilers

66. The guidance in the *Guide* for measuring the net open position in foreign exchange is based on that recommended by the BCBS. Therefore, deposit takers' net open position is the sum of the net position in on-balance-sheet foreign currency debt instruments; net notional positions in financial derivatives; on-balance-sheet holdings of foreign currency equity assets; net future foreign currency income and expenses not yet accrued but already fully hedged; foreign currency guarantees and similar instruments that are certain to be called and are likely to be irrecoverable; and, depending on the national commercial accounting practice, any other item representing a profit/loss in foreign currencies of the foreign currency positions set out in a single unit of account. The *Guide* describes the sum of the first three items listed above as the "net open position in foreign exchange for on-balance-sheet items."

67. Included among foreign exchange instruments for this FSI are foreign-currency-linked instruments: that is, instruments where the amounts payable are linked to a foreign currency, although the payments are made in domestic currency (paragraph 3.46).

68. Regarding capital, issues for compilers are discussed in the *return on equity* summary.

Sources of data

69. *Domestically controlled, cross-border consolidated data:* Data on the net open position in foreign exchange are likely to be available from supervisory sources because of the supervisory interest in banks' exposure to foreign currency. The extent to which the national approach to measuring the net open position meets the concepts in the *Guide* would require consideration. Regarding capital, sources of data are discussed in the *nonperforming loans net of provisions to capital* summary.

70. *Domestic consolidated data:* The net open position in foreign exchange is not available from national accounts-based data but might be obtained from supervisory sources or could be additionally requested (see Table 11.1). Regarding capital, sources of data are discussed in the *nonperforming loans net of provisions to capital* summary.

Encouraged FSIs

Deposit Takers

Capital to assets

Definition

71. This is the ratio of capital to total assets, without the latter being risk weighted. It measures the extent to which assets are funded by other than own funds and is a measure of the capital adequacy of the deposit-taking sector. The FSI is calculated by using capital as the numerator and assets (line 14 in Table 4.1) as the denominator. Total assets (nonfinancial and financial assets) are defined in paragraphs 4.37 to 4.38. The FSI is defined in paragraphs 6.20 and 6.21.

Issues for compilers and sources of data

72. Regarding capital, issues for compilers, including the definitions of capital, are discussed in the *return on equity* summary, and sources of data are discussed in the *nonperforming loans net of provisions to capital* summary.

73. Regarding total assets, issues for compilers and sources of data are discussed in the *return on assets* summary.

Large exposures to capital

Definition

74. This FSI is intended to identify vulnerabilities arising from the concentration of credit risk. The *Guide* sets out three approaches to defining this FSI at the sector level:

- The total number of large exposures of deposit takers that are identified under the national supervisory regime (line 38 in Table 4.1).
- Total exposure of the five largest deposit takers (or about five, depending on national circumstances) to the five largest, by asset size, resident entities (including all branches and subsidiaries) in both the other financial corporations sector and nonfinancial corporations sector, in addition to the exposure to the general government (line 51), as a percentage of the five largest deposit takers' capital.
- Total exposures of deposit takers to affiliated entities and connected counterparties (line 52) as a percentage of capital.

75. The FSI is defined in paragraphs 6.27 to 6.30.

Issues for compilers

76. From a supervisory point of view, large exposures are defined as one or more credit exposures to the same individual or group that exceed a certain percentage of regulatory capital, such as 10 percent. It is intended to be applicable at the level of the individual deposit taker. The number of large exposures of deposit takers is that identified under the national supervisory regime (see paragraph 4.76).

77. However, at the sector level, lending by the largest deposit takers to the largest entities in other sectors, such as the other financial corporations and nonfinancial corporations sectors, could have systemic consequences in the event of failure of the largest entities in the economy (paragraph 4.94). Moreover, experience has shown the potential significance of connected lending (paragraph 4.95).

78. Indications of a buildup of concentrated positions within sectoral or geographic distribution data could allow compilers to identify sectors and/or countries for which more detailed information might be required.

79. Regarding capital, issues for compilers are discussed in the *return on equity* summary.

Sources of data

80. *Domestically controlled, cross-border consolidated data:* Data on large exposures should be available from supervisory sources. The BCBS (1991) stresses the need for a satisfactory regime for the measurement and control of large exposures, including the need for appropriate levels of large exposure limits (to capital), with special attention paid to connected lending. Moreover, the BCBS (1991) notes the need to closely monitor risks arising from exposures to particular sectors and/or geographic areas. The extent to which national approaches to measuring large exposures meet the concepts in the *Guide* would require consideration. Regarding capital, data sources are discussed in the *nonperforming loans net of provisions to capital* summary.

81. *Domestic consolidated data:* Data on large exposures are not available from national accounts-based data but might be obtained from supervisory sources or additionally requested (see Table 11.1). Regarding capital, sources of data are discussed in the *nonperforming loans net of provisions to capital* summary.

Geographical distribution of loans to total loans

Definition

82. This FSI provides information on the geographic distribution of gross loans, by region. It allows the monitoring of credit risk arising from exposures to a group of countries. The approach by which claims are distributed geographically is defined in paragraph 3.36, and gross loans (line 18(i) of Table 4.1) are defined in paragraphs 4.45 to 4.48. The FSI is defined in paragraphs 6.63 and 6.64. The suggested regional classification follows that used in the IMF's *World Economic Outlook* and is illustrated in Table 12.1.

Issues for compilers

83. Lending is classified geographically on the basis of the residence of the domestic reporting entity. Therefore, lending by any foreign branches and/or deposit-taking subsidiaries of the reporting entity to residents of the local economy in which they are located is classified as lending to nonresidents and allocated to the appropriate region of the world, while lending to residents of the economy for which the FSI data are being compiled is classified as lending to the domestic economy. If lending to any subregion or countries is particularly significant, further disaggregation—and identification of the country or subregion—is encouraged.

84. Regarding total loans, issues for compilers are the same as in the *nonperforming loans to total gross loans* summary.

Sources of data

85. *Domestically controlled, cross-border consolidated data:* Supervisory sources might have available information on the geographic distribution of loans (see the sources of data entry in the *large exposures to capital* summary). The data prepared for BIS's consolidated international banking statistics can be used. Otherwise, additional data might be requested. Regarding total loans, the sources of data are the same as described in the *nonperforming loans to total gross loans* summary.

86. *Domestic consolidated data:* Information on the geographic distribution of loans might not be available from national accounts or supervisory sources, but the BIS's locational international banking statistics are a source for those countries that compile these BIS data. Otherwise, additional data might be requested. Any lending among deposit takers in the reporting population that are part of the same group should be excluded, but loans to deposit-taking branches and subsidiaries abroad are included in the data as lending to nonresidents. Regarding total loans, sources of data are the same as in the *nonperforming loans to total gross loans* summary.

Gross asset and liability positions in financial derivatives to capital

Definition

87. These FSIs are intended to provide an indication of the exposure of deposit takers' financial derivative positions relative to capital. There are two FSIs under this heading. The first is calculated by using the market value of financial derivative assets (line 21 in Table 4.1) as the numerator, and the second is calculated by using the market value of financial derivative liabilities (line 29) as the numerator. Both FSIs use capital as the denominator. Financial derivatives are defined in paragraphs 4.56 to 4.58. The FSIs are defined in paragraphs 6.39 and 6.40.

Issues for compilers

88. The coverage of financial derivatives includes forwards (including swaps) and options.

89. Regarding capital, issues for compilers, including the definitions of capital, are discussed in the *return on equity* summary.

Sources of data

90. *Domestically controlled, cross-border consolidated data:* Data on the market value position of financial derivative assets and liabilities should be available from supervisory sources. Regarding capital, sources of data are discussed in the *nonperforming loans net of provisions to capital* summary.

91. *Domestic consolidated data:* The gross asset and liability positions in financial derivatives can be obtained from national accounts-based data (monetary and financial statistics), in the sectoral balance sheet. However, national accounts data are not on a consolidated basis, and any data should exclude financial derivatives positions among deposit takers in the reporting population that are part of the same group. Therefore, additional data might need to be separately requested (see Table 11.3). Regarding capital, sources of data are discussed in the *nonperforming loans net of provisions to capital* summary.

Trading income to total income

Definition

92. This FSI is intended to capture the share of deposit takers' income from financial market activities, including currency trading. This FSI is calculated by using gains or losses on financial instruments (line 4(ii) of Table 4.1) as the numerator and gross income (line 5) as the denominator. Gains and losses on financial instruments are defined in paragraphs 4.22 to 4.27, and gross income is defined in paragraph 4.20. The FSI is defined in paragraphs 6.71 and 6.72.

Issues for compilers

93. Compilers should be aware that the *Guide* encourages the inclusion of realized and unrealized gains and losses arising during each period on all financial instruments (financial assets and liabilities, in domestic and foreign currencies) valued at market or fair value in the balance sheet, excluding equity in associates, subsidiaries, and any reverse equity investments (paragraph 4.22). Traditionally, in deposit takers' accounts this item has covered gains and losses recorded on assets and liabilities held for a short period as deposit takers seek to take advantage of short-term fluctuations in market prices. The *Guide*'s reasoning for its approach is set out in paragraph 4.24. The *Guide* acknowledges that the proposed coverage of gains and losses may not be feasible in the short run and that data collection systems may need to be developed.

94. Moreover, at the sector level, gains and losses on deposit takers' ownership of equities of other deposit takers in the reporting population should be deducted (paragraph 5.69).

95. Regarding gross income, issues for compilers are discussed in the *interest margin to gross income* summary.

Sources of data

96. *Domestically controlled, cross-border consolidated data:* Data on gains and losses on financial instruments should be available to supervisory sources, but the extent to which they meet the definitions in the *Guide* could depend on national commercial accounting practice. It is likely that there will be a need for the sector-wide adjustments set out above (see Table 11.4). Regarding gross income, sources of data are discussed in the *interest margin to gross income* summary. The available information may need to be aggregated to calculate both the numerator and the denominator for this FSI.

97. *Domestic consolidated data:* Data on gains and losses on financial instruments could be available from the revaluation account of the *1993 SNA,* but at the present time collection of these data is relatively limited, and thus additional data may need to be separately requested (Table 11.1). If revaluation data are used, data on gains and losses on sales of subsidiaries and associates need to be excluded (see Table 11.1). It is likely that the need for the sector-wide adjustments set out above will require consideration (see Table 11.2). Regarding gross income, sources of data are discussed in the *interest margin to gross income* summary.

Personnel expenses to noninterest expenses

Definition

98. This FSI compares personnel costs with total noninterest costs. It is calculated by using personnel costs (line 6(i) in Table 4.1) as the numerator and noninterest expenses (line 6 of Table 4.1) as the denominator. Personnel costs and noninterest expenses are defined in paragraphs 4.30 and 4.31. The FSI is defined in paragraphs 6.75 and 6.76.

Issues for compilers

99. No recommendations are made at this time regarding the possible inclusion of stock options. Methodological work on the treatment of stock options is ongoing.

100. Regarding noninterest costs, issues for compilers are discussed in the *noninterest expenses to gross income* summary.

Sources of data

101. *Domestically controlled, cross-border consolidated data:* The data for personnel costs available to supervisory sources may depend on national commercial accounting practice. National practice will also determine the extent to which the data meet the definitions in the *Guide.* Regarding noninterest costs, sources of data are discussed in the *noninterest expenses to gross income* summary. The available information may need to be aggregated to calculate both the numerator and the denominator for this FSI.

102. *Domestic consolidated data:* Data on personnel costs should be available from national accounts-based sources—Table 11.9 identifies the relevant line items in the *1993 SNA.* See also the entry for *personnel costs including wage and salaries* in Appendix IV. Regarding noninterest costs, sources of data are discussed in the *noninterest expenses to gross income* summary.

Spread between reference lending and deposit rates

Definition

103. This FSI is the difference (expressed in basis points) between the weighted average loan rate and the weighted average deposit rate, excluding rates on loans and deposits between deposit takers. To measure the spread, the *Guide* recommends at a minimum the calculation of the weighted average of all lending and deposit interest rates (excluding intrasector loans and deposits) during a reference period in the portfolio of resident deposit takers. The interest rate spread could also be calculated on a domestically controlled, cross-border consolidated basis, thus providing an indication of overall profitability but combining activity in different markets. The FSI is defined in paragraphs 8.5 to 8.10.

Issues for compilers

104. A method of calculating the weighted average lending rate is to divide the accrued amount of interest income on loans reported by deposit takers for a given period (numerator) by the average position of loans (denominator) for the same period. The weighted average deposit rate can be computed by dividing interest expense on deposits (numerator) by the average position of deposits (denominator) for the same period. Positions should be averaged using the most frequent observations available.

105. Contracted interest rates (that is, price data) can also be used to calculate weighted average interest rates for a given reference period, using the loan amounts as weights. Chapter 8 discusses these approaches and considers the merits of using end- and average-period interest rates and of calculating interest rates on outstanding and new business. The treatment of interest on nonperforming loans and on lending at officially prescribed rates is also discussed in Chapter 8.

Sources of data

106. For the first method mentioned above, data on accrued amounts of interest on loans and deposits should be readily available from the accounting systems of deposit takers, while typically data on deposit takers' positions in loans and deposits are regularly reported to central banks in balance sheet reports required for the compilation of monetary statistics.

107. Compiling information on contracted interest rates by type of loan and deposit may require that separate information be requested.

Spread between highest and lowest interbank rate

Definition

108. This FSI measures the spread between the highest and lowest interbank rates charged to deposit takers in the domestic interbank market. It is defined in paragraphs 8.21 to 8.24.

Issues for compilers

109. There can be limitations with this indicator. The framework through which central banks provide liquidity to money markets influences the overall liquidity of these markets, while one outlier can change the value of the indicator substantially. In addition, a perceived increase in risk might also be reflected in informal limits on the quantities (rather than the price) of funds that a deposit taker could borrow in the interbank market. While the agreed FSI is a spread, there might also be analytical interest in the dissemination of the highest and lowest interest rates so that they can be compared with other rates in the financial markets.

Sources of data

110. The source of these data is usually interbank dealers or brokers. The data might be available to supervisory authorities or the statistical departments of central banks.

Customer deposits to total (noninterbank) loans

Definition

111. This FSI is a measure of liquidity, in that it compares a stable deposit base with gross loans (excluding interbank activity). The FSI is calculated by using customer deposits (line 24(i) in Table 4.1) as the numerator and noninterbank loans (line 18(i.ii)) as the denominator. Customer deposits are defined in paragraphs 4.42 to 4.44, and loans are defined in paragraphs 4.45 to 4.48. The FSI is defined in paragraphs 6.50 and 6.51.

Issues for compilers

112. Assessing the extent to which a deposit is stable involves judgment, although experience suggests that some types of depositors are less likely to move their funds than others in response to a perceived weakness in an individual deposit taker or in the banking system. The key factors that can be taken into account are the type of depositor, the extent to which deposits are covered by credible insurance schemes, and remaining maturity.

113. The *Guide* recommends that the type of depositor be the primary factor in defining customer deposits, both because of its relevance and general applicability. Thus, customer deposits include all deposits (resident or nonresident) except those placed by other deposit takers and other financial corporations (resident or nonresident).

114. However, it is recognized that there can be variations to this approach. Large nonfinancial corporations might well manage their liquidity similarly to other financial corporations, and, thus, compilers might wish to exclude these deposits from the measure of customer deposits. Alternatively, customer deposits could also include those that have a remaining maturity of more than one year, regardless of the sector of the depositor.

115. In another approach, customer deposits could be determined by type of deposit—that is, deposits known for their "stability," such as demand deposits, small-scale savings, time deposits, and/or those covered by a (credible) deposit insurance scheme.

116. Regarding total loans, issues for compilers are discussed in the *nonperforming loans to total gross loans* summary. Additionally, loans to other deposit takers in the reporting population are excluded from this measure of loans.

Sources of data

117. *Domestically controlled, cross-border consolidated data:* Supervisory sources might provide information that allows the compilation of a measure of customer deposits consistent with the approach of the *Guide.* Regarding total loans, sources of data are the same as in the *nonperforming loans to total gross loans* summary, while loans to other deposit takers in the reporting population should be available to supervisors.

118. *Domestic consolidated data:* Data on customer deposits based on the sector approach and data on interbank loans are available from monetary and financial statistics sources (subject to ensuring the appropriate sectoral coverage, see paragraph 2.4). Regarding total loans, data sources are discussed in the *nonperforming loans to total gross loans* summary.

Foreign-currency-denominated loans to total loans

Definition

119. This FSI measures the relative size of foreign currency loans within gross loans. It is calculated by using the foreign currency and foreign-currency-linked part of gross loans (line 46 in Table 4.1) to residents and nonresidents as the numerator, and gross loans (line 18(i)) as the denominator. Foreign currency loans are defined in paragraph 4.90. Loans are defined in paragraphs 4.45 to 4.48. For cross-border consolidated data, the determination of what is and what is not a foreign currency is determined by the residence of the parent entity of that specific consolidated group. The FSI is defined in paragraphs 6.65 and 6.66.

Issues for compilers

120. In the *Guide,* domestic currency is that which is legal tender in the economy and issued by the monetary authority for that economy or the common currency area. Any currencies that do not meet this definition are foreign currencies to that economy (paragraph 3.45).

121. The currency composition of assets (and liabilities) is primarily determined by the characteristics of future payment(s). Foreign currency instruments are those payable in a currency other than the domestic currency. A subcategory of foreign currency instruments are domestic-currency-linked instruments that are payable in a foreign currency but with the amounts to be paid linked to the domestic currency. Foreign-currency-linked instruments are those payable in domestic currency but with the amounts to be paid linked to a foreign currency. Foreign-currency-linked loans are included in the numerator, as movements in the domestic exchange rate will affect their value in domestic currency terms (paragraph 3.46).

122. In the special case where an economy uses as its only legal tender a foreign currency, this FSI could be compiled excluding borrowing in, and linked to, that foreign currency.

123. The most appropriate exchange rate to be used for conversion of a position into the unit of account is the market (spot) exchange rate prevailing on the reference date to which the position relates. The midpoint between buying and selling rates is preferred (paragraph 3.48).

Sources of data

124. *Domestically controlled, cross-border consolidated data:* Data on foreign-currency-denominated and foreign-currency-linked loans might be available from supervisory sources because of the supervisory interest in banks' exposure to foreign currency. If such data are not available, they may need to be additionally requested. Regarding total loans, the sources of data are the same as described in the *nonperforming loans to total gross loans* summary. The available information may need to be aggregated to calculate both the numerator and the denominator of the FSI.

125. *Domestic consolidated data:* While some national accounts-based sources, in particular the monetary and financial statistics, may include data on foreign currency assets, data on foreign-currency-denominated and foreign-currency-linked loans may need to be additionally requested (see Table 11.1). If the data source is on an institutional unit basis, then foreign-currency-denominated and foreign-currency-linked loans among deposit takers in the reporting population that are part of the same group should be excluded. Regarding total loans, sources of data are the same as in the *nonperforming loans to total gross loans* summary.

Foreign-currency-denominated liabilities to total liabilities

Definition

126. This FSI measures the relative importance of foreign currency funding within total liabilities. The level of this ratio should be viewed along with the previous FSI: foreign-currency-denominated loans to total loans. The FSI is calculated using the foreign currency liabilities (line 47 in Table 4.1) as the numerator and total debt (line 28) plus financial derivative liabilities (line 29) less financial derivative assets (line 21) as the denominator. Foreign currency liabilities are defined in paragraph 4.90, while total debt is defined in paragraph 4.61, and financial derivatives are defined in paragraphs 4.56 to 4.58. The FSI is defined in paragraphs 6.67 and 6.68.

Issues for compilers

127. The definitions of foreign currency, foreign-currency-denominated and foreign-currency-linked instruments, as well as exchange rate conversion, are the same as those set out in the issues for compilers in the *foreign-currency-denominated loans to total loans* summary.

128. For total liabilities, it is recommended that the net market value position (liabilities less assets) of financial derivatives be included, rather than the gross liability position, because of the market practice of creating offsetting contracts and the possibility of forward-type instruments switching between asset and liability positions from one period to the next.

129. In the special case where an economy uses as its only legal tender a foreign currency, this ratio could be compiled excluding positions in, and linked to, this currency.

Sources of data

130. *Domestically controlled, cross-border consolidated data:* Data on foreign currency and total liabilities might well be available from supervisory sources. The extent to which the data meet the concepts in the *Guide,* particularly with regard to financial derivatives, would require consideration. The available information may need to be aggregated to calculate both the numerator and the denominator of this FSI.

131. *Domestic consolidated data:* While some national accounts-based sources, in particular the monetary and financial statistics and external debt data, may include data on foreign currency liabilities, data on foreign-currency-denominated and foreign-currency-linked liabilities may need to be additionally requested (see Table 11.1). Data on total liabilities should be available from national accounts sources, such as monetary and financial statistics (see paragraph 2.4). If the data are compiled on an institutional unit basis, then foreign-currency-denominated and foreign-currency-linked loans among deposit takers in the reporting population that are part of the same group should be deducted.

Net open position in equities to capital

Definition

132. This FSI is intended to identify deposit takers' equity risk exposure compared with capital. It is calculated by using a deposit takers' open position in equities (line 48 in Table 4.1) as the numerator and capital as the denominator. The FSI is defined in paragraphs 6.41 to 6.44. These paragraphs provide a detailed explanation as to how to measure the net open position in equities.

Issues for compilers

133. The guidance in the *Guide* for measuring the net open position in equity is based on that recommended by the BCBS. Therefore, deposit takers' net open position (positive if a long position is held and negative if a short position is held) is the sum of on-balance-sheet holdings of equities and notional positions in equity derivatives.

134. The long and short positions in the market must be calculated on a market-value basis. Own equity issued by the deposit taker is excluded from the calculation, as is equity held in associates and unconsolidated subsidiaries (as well as reverse equity investments).

135. The notional positions in equity derivatives comprise the notional positions for futures and forward contracts relating to individual equities, futures relating to stock indices, equity swaps, and the market value of equity positions underlying options.

136. Regarding capital, issues for compilers, including the definitions of capital, are discussed in the *return on equity* summary.

Sources of data

137. *Domestically controlled, cross-border consolidated data:* Data on the net open position in equities are likely to be available from supervisory sources. The extent to which national approaches to measuring the net open position meet the concepts in the *Guide* would require consideration. Regarding capital, sources of data are discussed in the *nonperforming loans net of provisions to capital* summary.

138. *Domestic consolidated data:* The net open position in equities is not available from national accounts-based data but might be obtained from supervisory sources or additionally requested (see Table 11.1). Regarding capital, sources of data are discussed in the *nonperforming loans net of provisions to capital* summary.

Other Financial Corporations

Assets to total financial system assets

Definition

139. This FSI measures the relative importance of other financial corporations within the domestic financial system. The numerator is other financial corporations' financial assets (line 3 in Table 4.2) and the denominator is total financial system assets. The latter is the total of financial assets owned by deposit takers (line 16, Table 4.1), other financial corporations, nonfinancial corporations (line 17, Table 4.3), households (line 11, Table 4.4), the general government, and the central bank. Financial assets are defined in paragraph 4.38. The FSI is defined in paragraph 7.6.

Issues for compilers

140. For total financial system assets, the coverage includes all entities resident in the domestic economy. Moreover, the *Guide* recommends that for each corporate sector—deposit takers, other financial corporations, and nonfinancial corporations—data be compiled on a consolidated basis; therefore, claims on other resident entities classified in the same sector should be eliminated. Cross-sector claims should not be eliminated.

141. For completeness, financial assets of NPISHs (see paragraph 2.17) could also be included within total financial system assets, but in many instances these might be relatively insignificant.

Sources of data

142. *Domestic consolidated data:* Data for total financial assets of other financial corporations and of the other sectors in the economy can be drawn from national accounts-based data, subject to the adjustments needed to exclude intragroup claims (see Tables 11.3, 11.5, and 11.7). To be able to make the adjustments, additional data might need to be requested.

143. *Domestically controlled, cross-border consolidated data:* For the larger entities, data might be drawn from published corporate financial statements and aggregated to derive the numerator of the FSI. However, the extent to which the resulting data would be consistent with the concepts in the *Guide* would require consideration.

Assets to gross domestic product

Definition

144. This FSI measures the importance of other financial corporations compared with the size of the economy. Other financial corporations' financial assets (line 3 in Table 4.2) is the numerator and GDP is the denominator. Financial assets are defined in paragraph 4.38. The FSI is defined in paragraph 7.7.

Issues for compilers

145. For other financial corporations' assets, issues for compilers are the same as in the *other financial corporations' assets to total financial system assets* summary.

Sources of data

146. GDP data are available from the national accounts sources.

147. For other financial corporations' assets, sources of data are the same as in the *other financial corporations' assets to total financial system assets* summary. For this indicator, data are compiled on a domestic consolidated basis only.

Nonfinancial Corporations

Total debt to equity

Definition

148. This FSI is a measure of corporate leverage—the extent to which activities are financed out of own funds. The FSI is calculated by using debt (line 29 in Table 4.3) as the numerator and capital and reserves (line 31 of Table 4.3) as the denominator. Debt is defined in paragraph 4.61, and capital and reserves are defined in paragraph 4.62. The FSI is defined in paragraphs 7.10 and 7.11.

Issues for compilers

149. Debt claims among nonfinancial corporations in the reporting population that are part of the same group should be excluded.

150. Equity investments in associates and unconsolidated subsidiaries (and reverse investments) are to be recorded in the investor's balance sheet (see paragraph 3.33) on the basis of the investor's proportionate share in the capital and reserves of the associate and unconsolidated subsidiary, and not using the market value of the traded equity.

151. In measuring sector-wide capital, all intrasector equity investments are deducted from the overall capital in the sector so that capital and reserves held within the sector are not double counted (see Box 5.2). Moreover, in line with the approach for deposit takers, goodwill is deducted.

Sources of data

152. *Domestic consolidated data:* Nonfinancial corporations' debt and capital can be drawn from national accounts-based data. However, additional data may be needed to make the adjustments noted above in the issues for compilers (see Tables 11.6 and 11.7).

153. *Cross-border consolidated data:* For the larger entities, data might be drawn from published corporate financial statements and aggregated to get both the numerator and the denominator of the FSI. However, the extent to which the resulting data would be consistent with the concepts in the *Guide* would require consideration, and there may be a need to make sector-wide adjustments.

Return on equity

Definition

154. This FSI is commonly used to capture nonfinancial corporations' efficiency in using their capital. It is calculated by using EBIT (line 34 in Table 4.3) as the numerator and average value of capital and reserves (line 31) over the same period as the denominator. At a minimum, the denominator can be calculated by taking the average of the beginning- and end-period positions (for example, at the beginning and the end of the month), but compilers are encouraged to use the most frequent observations available in calculating the average. EBIT is defined in paragraph 4.116 (and see also 4.100 to 4.104). Capital and reserves are defined in paragraph 4.62. The FSI is defined in paragraphs 7.12 to 7.14.

Issues for compilers

155. As with deposit takers, income is calculated on a basis closer to commercial accounting and supervisory approaches than to national accounting. Therefore, the *Guide* encourages the inclusion of realized and unrealized gains and losses arising during each period on all financial instruments (financial assets and liabilities, in domestic and foreign currencies) valued at market or fair value in the balance sheet, excluding equity in associates, subsidiaries, reverse equity investments (paragraph 4.22), and gains and losses from the sales of fixed assets, which are measured as the difference between the sale value and the balance sheet value at the previous end period.

156. Sector-wide adjustments are also specified to prevent intrasectoral income from affecting the EBIT measure. Notably, dividends received and the parent's share of an associate's retained earnings (and similarly, arising from a reverse equity investment, an associate's share of a parent's retained earnings) are to be deducted from other income (net). Also excluded are any gains and losses on equity holdings in other nonfinancial corporations and sales of fixed assets to other nonfinancial corporations included in other income (net). Since goodwill is not classified as an asset, it is not amortized in the income account (see paragraph 4.110).

157. Because data are on a consolidated basis, transactions and positions among nonfinancial corporations in the reporting population that are part of the same group are excluded.

158. Regarding capital, issues for compilers, including the definitions of capital, are discussed in the *total debt to equity* summary.

Sources of data

159. *Domestic consolidated data:* Data can be drawn from national accounts-based data. However, additional data may be needed to make the adjustments noted above in the issues for compilers (see Tables 11.6 and 11.7).

160. *Cross-border consolidated data:* For the larger entities, data might be drawn from published corporate financial statements and aggregated to get both the numerator and the denominator in this FSI. The concept of earnings before tax and interest is one used in the analysis of corporate accounts. However, the extent to which the resulting data would be consistent with the concepts in the *Guide* would require consideration, and there may be a need to make sector-wide adjustments.

Earnings to interest and principal expenses

Definition

161. This FSI measures nonfinancial corporations' capacity to cover their debt-service payments (interest and principal). It serves as an indicator of the risk that a firm may not be able to make the required payments on its debts. The FSI is calculated by using earnings (net income) before interest and tax (EBIT) (line 34 in Table 4.3) plus interest receivable from other nonfinancial corporations (line 33) as the numerator and debt-service payments (line 35) over the same period as the denominator. EBIT is defined in paragraph 4.116, interest receivable from other nonfinancial corporations is defined in paragraph 4.115, and debt-service payments are defined in paragraph 4.117. The FSI is defined in paragraphs 7.15 and 7.16.

Issues for compilers

162. The denominator, debt-service payments, includes payments to other nonfinancial corporations (excluding payments among nonfinancial corporations in the reporting population that are part of the same group). The numerator includes interest payments receivable (excluding those among nonfinancial corporations in the reporting population that are part of the same group) from other nonfinancial corporations. Therefore, the denominator and numerator have the same coverage.

163. Regarding EBIT, issues for compilers are discussed in the *return on equity* summary.

Sources of data

164. *Domestic consolidated data:* While the external debt statistics methodology requires collection of data on debt-service payments on external debt, it is likely that additional data on debt-service payments may need to be separately requested, including on payments among nonfinancial corporations in the reporting population that are part of the same group (see Tables 11.6 and 11.7).

165. *Cross-border consolidated data:* For the larger entities, data might be drawn from published corporate financial statements and aggregated to calculate both the numerator and the denominator in this FSI. Debt service coverage (particularly interest coverage) is a concept used in the analysis of corporate accounts. However, the extent to which the resulting data would be consistent with the concepts in the *Guide* would require consideration, and there may be a need to make sector-wide adjustments.

Net foreign exchange exposure to equity

Definition

166. This FSI measures nonfinancial corporations' exposure to foreign currency risk compared with their capital. The larger the exposure to foreign currency risk, the greater the stress on the financial soundness of nonfinancial corporations from a significant currency depreciation and, as a consequence, the greater the stress on deposit takers. Nonfinancial corporations' net foreign exchange exposure for on-balance-sheet items (line 36 in Table 4.3) is the numerator, and capital and reserves (line 31) is the denominator. The open position should be calculated as described for deposit takers in paragraphs 6.32 and 6.33. The FSI is defined in paragraphs 7.17 to 7.19.

Issues for compilers

167. The net foreign exchange position is to be measured using the same methodology as that described for deposit takers in the *net open position in foreign exchange to capital* summary.

168. Given the potential difficulty in compiling data on off-balance-sheet foreign currency exposures, the *Guide* encourages at least an initial focus on the *corporate net foreign exchange exposure for on-balance-sheet items,* but the FSI could also be calculated using total corporate net foreign exchange exposure (line 37) as the numerator.

169. Regarding capital, issues for compilers, including the definitions of capital, are discussed in the *total debt to equity* summary.

Sources of data

170. *Domestic consolidated data:* It is likely that additional data on the corporate net foreign exchange exposure may need to be separately requested, as it is not available from national accounts sources (see Table 11.6). Regarding capital, data sources are discussed in the *total debt to equity* summary.

171. *Cross-border consolidated data:* For the larger entities, data on the corporate net foreign exchange exposure might be available from published corporate financial statements for the larger firms and aggregated to get both the numerator and denominator, but the extent to which the resulting data would be consistent with the concepts in the *Guide* would require consideration. Regarding capital, data sources are discussed in the *total debt to equity* summary.

Number of applications for protection from creditors

Definition

172. This FSI is a measure of bankruptcy trends, but it is influenced by the quality and nature of bankruptcy and related legislation. It is a simple numerical addition of those nonfinancial corporations that have filed for protection from bankruptcy during the period. The FSI is defined in paragraph 7.20.

Issues for compilers

173. For sector-wide data, the data provided should be the total number of nonfinancial corporations resident in the economy that have filed for protection in a particular period. Filings by foreign subsidiaries of resident entities should not be included.

Sources of data

174. These data might be available from the national statistical office or the Department/Ministry of Commerce/Industry.

Households

Household debt to GDP

Definition

175. This FSI measures the overall level of household indebtedness (commonly related to consumer loans and mortgages) as a share of GDP. This FSI is calculated by taking household debt (line 20 in Table 4.4) as the numerator and GDP as the denominator. Debt is defined in paragraph 4.61. The FSI is defined in paragraphs 7.23 and 7.24.

Issues for compilers

176. The data for household debt comprise debt incurred by resident households of the economy only.

Sources of data

177. *Domestic data:* Information on household debt and GDP should be available from national accounts sources (see paragraph 11.15).

Household debt service and principal payments to income

Definition

178. This FSI measures the capacity of households to cover their debt payments (interest and principal). It is calculated by using household debt-service payments (line 24 in Table 4.4) as the numerator and gross disposable income (line 6) over the same period as the denominator. Household debt-service payments are defined in paragraph 4.122 (see also 4.117), and gross disposable income is defined in paragraph 4.120. The FSI is defined in paragraphs 7.25 and 7.26.

Issues for compilers

179. Obtaining data on the household sector is difficult. Coordination with the agency compiling data on the household sector for inclusion in national accounts statistics is essential.

Sources of data

180. *Domestic data:* Information on household disposable income should be available from national accounts sources. However, data on debt-service payments might not be available from national accounts sources, so additional data may need to be separately requested (see paragraph 11.16).

Market Liquidity

Average bid-ask spread in the securities market

Definition

181. This FSI is the difference between the prices at which market participants are willing to buy (bid) and sell (ask) assets; it is a measure of market tightness—the relative cost of engaging in a transaction irrespective of the absolute level of the market price of the items being sold. It is calculated as the difference between the best (highest) bid and the best (lowest) ask price in the market, expressed as a percentage of the midpoint of the buy and sell price of an asset—a benchmark domestic government or central bank debt security in the first instance. Bid-ask spreads tend to be narrower in more liquid and efficient markets. The FSI is defined in paragraphs 8.27 and 8.44 to 8.46.

Issues for compilers

182. Because of the link between market-based liquidity indicators and the indicator on deposit takers' liquid assets, bid-ask spreads should be compiled, at a minimum, for financial instruments included in the wider measure of liquid assets. The natural starting point is to compile indicators (1) for domestic government or central bank bills that are used by the national authorities to influence liquidity conditions in their domestic economy, and (2) for corporate securities if they are included in the definition of liquid assets.

183. Similarly, the tightness of the local foreign exchange markets may also be relevant if foreign-exchange-denominated securities qualify as liquid assets.

184. The quantities of securities that can be traded at the best bid price and at the best ask price, respectively, provide important information for interpreting the bid-ask spread, and the *Guide* encourages the dissemination of this information along with the bid-ask spread (paragraph 8.47).

185. The bid-ask spread should be compiled on a daily basis or, at a minimum, on a weekly basis. The frequency of price observations can be on a tick-by-tick basis, but preferably at least two quotes per day should be taken (for example at 10:30 a.m. and at 2:30 p.m.). If price observations are taken on a less than hourly basis, care is needed to avoid biases related to systematic volatility of intraday price quotes (paragraph 8.48).

186. The *Guide* provides other advice, on how to calculate the spread if the bid and ask quotes are in terms of yield rather than in terms of price (paragraph 8.46 and Box 8.1), and provides an additional way of calculating the bid-ask spread that takes into account the quantity of securities that can be traded at the quoted prices (paragraph 8.49).

Sources of data

187. Major exchanges located in the domestic economy can be used as a source of data for compiling bid-ask spreads. Other sources can include dealer associations, central banks, and commercial databases, although compilers who approach a commercial database vendor will need to make their own judgments about whether the product being offered meets their needs. Coverage of all market makers, the likely primary source of the information, may not be necessary. It is recommended that the top five market makers or at least those accounting for a minimum of 75 percent of market turnover should be covered. Automated electronic market making can also be covered.

Average daily turnover ratio in the securities market

Definition

188. This FSI is the ratio of average daily trades to the outstanding stock of securities; it is a measure of market depth—the ability of a market to absorb large trade volumes without a significant impact on market prices. It is calculated as the number of securities bought and sold during a trading period divided by the average number of securities outstanding at the beginning and the end of the trading period. The volume of all trades executed during official trading hours of the markets should be captured. The *Guide* recommends that turnover be calculated in the first instance for a benchmark domestic government or central bank debt security. The FSI is defined in paragraph 8.39.

Issues for compilers

189. As regards other types of securities to cover and the periodicity of compilation, the same considerations apply as described in the issues for compilers in the *average bid-ask spread in the securities market* summary.

190. There is a lack of data on foreign exchange market turnover outside of the triennial central bank survey of foreign exchange (and derivative market activity) conducted by the BIS.

Sources of data

191. Sources of data are the same as described in the *average bid-ask spread in the securities market* summary.

Real Estate Markets

Real estate prices

Definition

192. This FSI covers residential and commercial real estate price indices separately. Currently, there is limited international experience in constructing representative real estate price indices, reflecting the difficulty of the task: real estate markets are heterogeneous, both within and across countries, and illiquid. Therefore, the *Guide* describes a range of techniques whose application can be based on local needs, conditions, and resources rather than recommending a single set of indices or compilation methods. The need to prepare inventories of residential and commercial properties to provide a baseline for compilation of price indices is noted (paragraph 9.12).

193. The *Guide* discusses two major methods for constructing real estate price indices: the Laspeyres real estate price index (see paragraphs 9.20 to 9.24) and the hedonic or quality-adjusted regression price index (see paragraphs 9.25 and 9.26). Among other price measures discussed are average price (unit value) indices (paragraphs 9.16 and 9.17) and liquidity-adjusted price indices (paragraph 9.27).

Issues for compilers

194. The Laspeyres index calculates the weighted average change in prices over a period for a fixed basket of real estate in some base period. The hedonic regression price index derives the price series for a standard real estate unit by regressing and removing the price influence of multiple specific quality factors that affect actual sales prices. However, hedonic approaches can be complex and expensive in terms of data demands and require professional knowledge of compiling such measures.

195. The *Guide* also describes the "unit-value index" which, although not a price index, is probably the most widely available price measure for real estate and sometimes provides useful information about large changes in prices. However, this index can be seriously biased by a few transactions with extreme values, changes in the mix of transactions, or changes in the quality of the units being sold (paragraphs 9.16 and 9.17).

196. Commercial real estate has specific features that can influence the task of compilation, including the great diversity of types of commercial real estate, which may be specialized because of the specific business of the occupant. On the other hand, the commercialized nature of the product permits many properties to be characterized as a commodity, consisting of a square footage of commercial space (see paragraphs 9.28 to 9.31).

Sources of data

197. Transactions data for real estate may be available from official registries of such information. These registries are responsible for recording the transfers of property ownership in their locality; when ownership changes hands, they update their records. Another source of transactions data is real estate agents, who bring together buyers and sellers of real estate. Data from these two sources may assist in the construction of a price index, particularly if the data are available over time for real estate of a similar or common type. Financial institutions active in lending to the real estate market may also be a source of information.

Residential real estate loans to total loans

Definition

198. This FSI is intended to identify deposit takers' exposure to the residential real estate sector, with the focus on household borrowers. It is calculated by using residential real estate loans as the numerator (line 43 in Table 4.1) and gross loans (line 18(i)) as the denominator. Residential real estate loans are defined in paragraph 4.88, and loans are defined in paragraphs 4.45 to 4.48. The FSI is defined in paragraphs 6.58 to 6.60.

Issues for compilers

199. For the compilation of this FSI, the consistent application by deposit takers of a definition of residential real estate is central: houses, apartments, and other dwellings (such as houseboats and mobile homes), and any associated land intended for occupancy by individual households.

200. Household borrowing collateralized by real estate can be used as the numerator (line 25 in Table 4.4). While not all real estate lending to households is collateralized by residential real estate, it is often the prevailing practice.

201. Regarding total loans, issues for compilers are the same as in the *nonperforming loans to total gross loans* summary.

Sources of data

202. *Domestically controlled, cross-border consolidated data:* Data on residential real estate loans may need to be additionally requested if they are not available from supervisory sources. The available information may need to be aggregated. Regarding total loans, the sources of data are the same as in the *nonperforming loans to total gross loans* summary.

203. *Domestic consolidated data:* Residential real estate loans may be available from monetary and financial statistics sources that provide an industrial classification of lending by type of economic activity (Box A3.1 in Appendix III). Otherwise, additional data may need to be separately requested (see Table 11.1). Regarding total loans, the sources of data are the same as in the *nonperforming loans to total gross loans* summary.

Commercial real estate loans to total loans

Definition

204. This FSI measures banks' exposure to the commercial real estate market. It is calculated by using as the numerator loans collateralized by commercial real estate, loans to construction companies, and loans to companies active in the development of real estate (line 44 of Table 4.1), and by using gross loans (line 18(i)) as the denominator. Commercial real estate loans are defined in paragraph 4.88, and loans are defined in paragraphs 4.45 to 4.48. The FSI is defined in paragraphs 6.61 and 6.62.

Issues for compilers

205. As with residential real estate loans, the consistent application by deposit takers of a definition of what constitutes commercial real estate lending is central. Commercial real estate lending among deposit takers in the reporting population that are part of the same group is deducted.

206. Regarding total loans, issues for compilers are the same as in the *nonperforming loans to total gross loans* summary.

Sources of data

207. *Domestically controlled, cross-border consolidated data:* Data on commercial real estate loans may need to be additionally requested if they are not available from supervisory sources. The available information may need to be aggregated. Regarding total loans, sources of data are the same as in the *nonperforming loans to total gross loans* summary.

208. *Domestic consolidated data:* Commercial real estate loans may be available from monetary and financial statistics sources that provide an industrial classification of lending by type of economic activity (Box A3.1 in Appendix III). If so, lending among resident deposit takers that are part of the same group should be deducted. Otherwise, additional data may need to be separately requested (see Table 11.1). Regarding total loans, sources of data are the same as in the *nonperforming loans to total gross loans* summary.

Appendix III. Additional Definitions of FSIs and Related Data Series

1. The main text discusses the set of core and encouraged FSIs. This appendix sets out ideas that arose during the drafting of, and consultation on, the *Guide* for additional definitions of the FSIs and for related data series. Issues relevant for the monitoring of financial conglomerates are also discussed. Information provided in this appendix may be useful to compilers when developing FSIs for use in their own national context.

Extensions to FSIs as Specified in the *Guide*

Deposit Takers

2. Chapter 6 brings together the concepts and definitions set out in Part I of the *Guide* to explain how each FSI for deposit takers is to be calculated. Additional definitions of some FSIs were proposed during discussions on the preparation of the *Guide,* which are set out below. In some instances, more disaggregated data series would be needed to compile these FSIs.

3. The *Guide* recommends that sector-level data compiled to calculate FSI ratios include any intrasector positions in debt and financial derivatives on a gross basis (paragraph 5.49). This approach allows the interrelationships among groups in the sector, and hence potential contagion risks, to be identified. However, for FSI ratios where gross assets or liabilities are either the denominator or the numerator—for example, return on assets and the capital-to-assets ratio—they could also be calculated excluding intrasector positions in debt and financial derivatives, so that both the numerator and the denominator of the ratio exclude intrasector transactions and positions.

Capital-to-assets ratio

4. The *debt-to-capital ratio* is another measure of financial leverage that could be considered in addition to the capital-to-assets ratio.

Return on equity (net income to average capital)

5. *Return on equity* could be calculated including purchased goodwill in the denominator, which would amount to using a measure of capital and reserves closer to that used in commercial accounting.

Nonperforming loans net of provisions to capital

6. With a view to providing a broader measure of nonperforming assets, this FSI could be calculated using total debt claims in the numerator and not just loans.

7. This FSI could also be calculated for resident and nonresident borrowers separately. The approach might be relevant in the context of differing economic circumstances prevailing in the domestic and foreign markets.

8. In economies where collateral is widely used, *nonperforming loans net of provisions and collateral to capital* is an alternative FSI that might give a more realistic picture of the potential for losses by deposit takers than the FSI ratio, which is calculated by excluding collateral.[1] Any dissemination of this ratio would need to be supplemented with detailed metadata on collateral rules in use, including the valuation approach adopted by national supervisors.

Large exposures to capital

9. The number of large exposures at various percentages of regulatory capital could be considered, such as the total number of individual large exposures above 10 percent but below 20 percent of regulatory capital, between 20 percent and 40 percent of

[1]In addition to or instead of collateral, account could be taken of credit risk transfer instruments. However, at the time of writing there is little to no experience with measuring the credit risk offset at the sector level arising from the use of these instruments.

regulatory capital, and above 40 percent of regulatory capital.

10. To identify the location of the counterparties, the number of large exposures could be divided between resident and nonresident counterparties.

11. To monitor concentrated lending by deposit takers, as peer groups or as for the sector as a whole, FSIs could be constructed that relate to the sectoral—particularly by industry—and geographic distribution of loans. Indications of a buildup of concentrated positions derived from these data could allow compilers to specify sectors and/or countries for which more detailed information might be required.

12. Other approaches to monitoring concentrated lending include (1) specifying a minimum exposure amount in nominal terms at which any search for concentrated lending by deposit takers could begin, and (2) developing a credit concentration ratio (for example, the ratio of the total exposures to the largest 20 borrowers by each bank to the total exposures of banks).

13. Some economies rely on credit registers to monitor large exposures. Through such registers, the total exposure of the deposit-taking sector (and indeed of the financial system) to each individual borrower can be measured, and reports could, for example, be generated each quarter on the exposures to the 100 largest borrowers. An identification code attributed to each borrower would allow consistency of recording. However, the exposures of the foreign branches and subsidiaries of resident deposit takers might not be covered by such registers.

Net open position in equities to capital

14. There may be analytical interest in presenting the net open position in equities by country to identify any large exposures to equity holding in particular economies.

Liquid assets to short-term liabilities

15. This FSI could be calculated using very short-term liabilities—three months or less—as the denominator. Such liabilities would be closer to the liquidity concept used for liquid assets. Moreover, this FSI could be calculated excluding short-term customer deposits from short-term liabilities; that is, excluding those short-term liabilities considered to be a more stable, less volatile form of funding. This FSI could also be calculated excluding financial derivatives positions—that is, calculating the ratio taking short-term debt only into consideration—particularly if a net derivative asset position is significantly affecting the ratio.

Nonperforming loans to total gross loans

16. To identify the sectoral concentration of NPLs, this FSI could be calculated for each sector (using the same sectors as in calculation of the sectoral distribution of loans to total loans).

Sectoral distribution of loans to total loans

17. A more disaggregated view of lending to the other financial corporations sector could be provided through dissemination of the ratios for loans to the five subsectors,[2] defined in Appendix VII, the Glossary of Terms.

18. An additional possibility is to classify loans by type of borrower using the International Standard Industrial Classification of all Economic Activities (ISIC). This approach might be particularly relevant when an economy has systemically important industries, such as petroleum and agriculture. The ISIC has 17 major categories of economic activity in the resident economy and places more emphasis on the type of activity undertaken than on the economic nature of the business, which is the basis of the sector distribution described in Chapter 2. The categories and short definitions of the activities covered in each category are set out in Box A3.1 of this appendix. An alternative approach is to classify loans by type, such as retail, commercial, and industrial.

19. If this FSI is compiled on a cross-border consolidated basis to also capture loans by deposit takers' branches and subsidiaries abroad, a complementary, but far more ambitious, approach would be to attribute loans by sector regardless of the residence of the borrower. For instance, total lending to nonfinancial entities worldwide, regardless of residence, could be compiled. In this way, exposures of deposit takers in

[2]These subsectors are insurance and pension funds, security dealers, investment funds, other financial intermediaries, and financial auxiliaries.

Box A3.1. The International Standard Industrial Classification of All Economic Activities (ISIC)

The ISIC is an industrial classification developed by the United Nations that groups establishments that have the same principal activity by industry. An establishment is defined as an enterprise, or part of an enterprise, that is situated in a single location and in which only a single productive activity is carried out or in which the principal productive activity accounts for most of the value added.

The industries identified in the ISIC are as follows:

- *Agriculture, hunting, and forestry,* including related service activities
- *Fishing,* including fish farming and service activities incidental to fishing
- *Mining and quarrying,* including service activities incidental to oil and gas extraction, excluding surveying
- *Manufacturing*
- *Electricity, gas, and water supply*
- *Construction*
- *Wholesale and retail trade, repair of motor vehicles, motorcycles, and personal and household goods*
- *Hotels and restaurants*
- *Transport, storage, and communications*
- *Financial intermediation*
- *Real estate, renting, and business activities*—such as computer and related activities, and research and development
- *Public administration*
- *Education*
- *Health and social work*
- *Other community, social, and personal service activities*
- *Private households with employed persons*
- *Extraterritorial organizations and bodies*

the reporting population to similar activities worldwide could be monitored.

Residential and commercial real estate loans to total loans

20. To identify the residence of the counterparty, these FSIs could be compiled for real estate lending to residents and to nonresidents separately.

Geographical distribution of loans to total loans

21. In the case where loans to nonresidents are significant, when compiling data on a cross-border consolidated basis, such loans to nonresidents could be categorized as either (1) local currency loans of the foreign branch or subsidiary in the local economy or (2) other loans. The risks arising from lending funded primarily from local deposits are considered to be different from those arising in the context of cross-border lending.

22. This FSI could be expanded to a geographic distribution of deposit takers' total debt claims on nonresidents; that is, covering claims defined in paragraph 4.61 (lines 17 to 19, and 22 of Table 4.1).

Foreign-currency-denominated loans to total loans

23. Various disaggregations of the data in the numerator could be considered: by resident/nonresident, by sector, by major currencies (for example, U.S. dollar, yen, and euro), and by maturity (remaining maturity measure). Loans to nonresidents in foreign currency could be categorized as either (1) local currency loans of the foreign branch or foreign subsidiary in the local economy or (2) other foreign currency loans. This FSI could also be calculated using total debt claims and not just loans.

Foreign-currency-denominated liabilities to total liabilities

24. To identify the residence of the counterparties, the data in the numerator could be categorized as either liabilities to residents or liabilities to nonresidents. Liabilities to nonresidents in foreign currency could be categorized as either (1) local currency liabilities of the foreign branch or foreign subsidiary in the local economy or (2) other foreign currency liabilities.

25. This FSI could be calculated excluding financial derivatives positions—that is, including only debt positions—particularly if a net financial derivative asset position (foreign currency and/or total position) significantly affects the FSI ratio. In addition, short-term (remaining maturity) foreign-currency-denominated liabilities could be compared with total liabilities.

Interest margin to gross income

26. Since a major source of gross income of deposit takers typically comes from interest income, *interest margin to total assets* could be compiled in addition to the return on assets.

Noninterest expenses to gross income

27. The ratio *noninterest expense to interest margin* could be calculated to assess whether interest income covers noninterest expenses.

Other Financial Corporations

Assets to total financial system assets

28. To identify the relative importance of other financial corporations among financial corporations, this FSI could be calculated by including in the denominator only those financial assets owned by other financial corporations, deposit takers, and the central bank. Financial assets are defined in paragraph 4.38.

Nonfinancial Corporations

Total debt to equity

29. This FSI could be calculated by excluding from the numerator debt owed to other nonfinancial corporations. The resulting FSI would indicate the amounts owed to other sectors as a percentage of capital and reserves in the nonfinancial sector. In addition, the ratio could be calculated using the narrow measure of capital and reserves (line 31(i) of Table 4.3 defined in paragraph 4.114) as the denominator.

30. This FSI could be extended to include liquid assets along with capital and reserves in the denominator, as such assets are available to meet liabilities.

31. It could be useful to identify the type of activity undertaken by those nonfinancial corporate borrowers that have high debt-to-equity ratios to discover whether corporate indebtedness is concentrated in sectors that are particularly vulnerable to shifts in economic activity. Corporate activities could be classified using the ISIC (see Box A3.1).

Return on equity

32. This FSI could be calculated using the narrow measure of capital and reserves (line 31(i) of Table 4.3, defined in paragraph 4.114) as the denominator. Another approach would be to calculate the return on equity by including purchased goodwill in the denominator; that is, using a measure of capital and reserves closer to that used in commercial accounting.

33. As with the previous indicator on corporate leverage, monitoring could also be undertaken at the subsector level, using the ISIC (see Box A3.1).

34. As for deposit takers, information on the return on equity could be supplemented with information on the *return on assets.*

Debt-service coverage

35. This FSI could be defined to include interest only (see line 38 of Table A3.4), as this is the standard ratio often reported in corporate press releases and corporate sector databases.

36. This FSI could be calculated by excluding interest receivable from other nonfinancial corporations (line 33 of Table 4.3) from the numerator and debt-service payments to other nonfinancial corporations (see line 39 of Table A3.4) from the denominator. The resulting FSI would provide a measure of debt-service coverage of nonfinancial corporations to other sectors.

37. Payments on operating leases could be included in the denominator, as such payments can be significant, and the items leased can be important for ongoing operations.

Net foreign exchange exposure to equity

38. This FSI could be calculated using the narrow measure of capital and reserves (line 31(i) of Table 4.3, defined in paragraph 4.114) as the denominator.

Households

Debt to GDP

39. *Debt to total assets* might be compiled to provide an overall measure of the balance sheet position of households.

Financial Market FSIs

Spread between reference lending and deposit rates

40. As other forms of lending become more important, an SLDR could be calculated that covers total debt claims and liabilities.

Measuring resilience in securities markets

41. Resilience and depth of markets can be measured by the Hui-Heubel Ratio (HHR). This ratio relates the volume of trades as a proportion of the outstanding stock of the given instrument to their impact on prices. Thus, the larger the volume of trades relative to the percentage price change—that is, the lower the HHR—the more resilient and deep the market is. The HHR is specified as follows:

$$HHR = \frac{\left[\left(P_{max} - P_{min}\right) / P_{min}\right]}{\left[V / \left(S \times \bar{P}\right)\right]},$$

where P_{max} = highest price over the period
P_{min} = lowest price over the period
V = total value traded over the period
S = average number of instruments outstanding during the period
$\bar{P}$ = average daily closing price of the instrument during the period.

42. Subject to data availability, the ratio could be calculated on a daily basis for a benchmark domestic government or central bank debt security to capture very short-term price movements. Alternatively, it could be calculated as the average of five-day period measures in a specified period of time (such as three months) to smooth volatility.

43. If there is a lack of data, the numerator in the HHR can be measured as the percentage change in the price of the asset over the period chosen. Other measures of trading volume could also be used, such as the number of securities traded.

44. Table A3.1 below provides an example of how the HHR can be calculated for a benchmark security over a three-month period. The highest and lowest daily prices observed in each week are shown in the first two columns. The value of securities traded and the number of securities outstanding are shown in the next two columns, and the average closing price of the instrument is shown in the fifth column. The HHR, calculated on a weekly basis, is shown in the last column; the monthly average HHR is also shown in that column. The average HHR for the month shown in Table A3.1 indicates that the resilience and depth of the market improved over the three-month period; the HHR declined from 0.9 in month 1 to 0.6 in month 3.

Table A3.1. Calculating the Hui-Heubel Ratio

	P_{max}	P_{min}	V	S	$\bar{P}$	HHR[1]
Month 1						
Week 1	10	8	120,000	30,000	8.6	0.5
Week 2	12	9	60,000	30,000	10.2	1.7
Week 3	12	9	150,000	30,000	8.2	0.5
Week 4	10	7	150,000	30,000	9.7	0.8
Monthly Average						0.9
Month 2						
Week 1	12	8	120,000	30,000	9.2	1.2
Week 2	13	9	80,000	30,000	10.2	1.7
Week 3	14	12	70,000	30,000	13.0	0.9
Week 4	14	13	130,000	30,000	13.4	0.2
Monthly Average						1.0
Month 3						
Week 1	10	8	120,000	30,000	8.6	0.5
Week 2	12	9	170,000	30,000	10.2	0.6
Week 3	9	8	120,000	30,000	8.2	0.3
Week 4	10	7	120,000	30,000	9.7	1.0
Monthly Average						0.6

[1]For instance, for week 1 of month 1, the HHR is calculated as follows:
[(10 – 8) / 8] / [120,000 / (30,000 × 8.6)] = 0.25 / 0.465 = 0.5.

Stock market indices

45. As equities can serve as collateral for deposit takers' loans and can constitute a significant element of their assets, a representative stock market index could be monitored.

Additional Data Series

46. In developing the sectoral financial accounts for calculating FSIs, several additional data series could be considered. These series are provided below as elaborations of the tables in Chapter 4.

Deposit Takers

47. *Realized gains and losses on financial instruments* could be distinguished from unrealized gains and losses. (This series and those below are set out in Table A3.2, which is a continuation of Table 4.1.)

48. *Very short-term deposits* (one month or less on a remaining maturity basis) are those very liquid liabilities that customers can convert into cash or for-

Table A3.2. Deposit Takers: Memorandum Series[1]

Additional series
53. Duration of assets
54. Duration of liabilities
55. Realized gains and losses on financial instruments
56. Total gains and losses on the sale of fixed assets
57. Very short-term deposits
58. Gross new deposits during the period
59. Gross withdrawal of deposits during the period
60. Shares and other equity investments in deposit takers in the reporting population
 (i) Associates
 (ii) Other deposit takers
61. Net liabilities of branches of foreign deposit takers to their parents[2]
62. Gross loans to the public sector
63. Domestic government securities owned (market value)
64. Sectoral distribution of nonperforming loans
65. Percentage of replacement loans in total loans
66. Other nonperforming assets
67. Loan loss reserves
68. Specific provisions against total debt claims
69. Shortfall in provisions under the revised Basel Capital Accord
70. Arrears
71. Arrears of deposit takers
72. Assets transferred to special purpose entities
73. Guarantees
 (i) Resident
 (ii) Nonresident
74. Credit commitments
 Resident
 Nonresident
75. Assets managed but not owned by deposit takers

[1]This table is a continuation of Table 4.1.
[2]For domestic consolidated data only, if branches of foreign deposit takers are located in the economy. Gross liabilities could also be identified.

eign currencies at very short notice. These liabilities can be compared with total deposits to assess the liquidity of deposit takers.

49. *Gross new deposits during the period* and *gross withdrawal of deposits during the period* provide information on the turnover of deposits.

50. *Shares and other equity investments in deposit takers in the reporting population* are the balance sheet value of such investments in associates (including reverse equity investments by associates) and other deposit takers that are also in the reporting population. These data are excluded from shares and other equity investments (assets) as well as from capital and reserves at the sector level (see Box 5.1). Such information indicates ownership links within the sector.

51. *Net liabilities of branches of foreign deposit takers to their parents* provide information on the funding of branches from their parents in the domestic consolidated data. Typically, such branches are funded by interbank deposits from their parent rather than having their own capital—their capital requirements being indistinguishable from that of the parent deposit taker. Some host countries require resident branches of foreign banks to have "donation" capital as a sign of the bank's commitment to the country and to help equalize competitive conditions between these branches and domestically incorporated deposit takers. Amounts of donation capital could be separately identified. However, in practice, donation capital might be in a form that can be moved abroad quickly. Data for such a series might be available from those responsible for compiling data on foreign direct investment.

52. *Gross loans to the public sector* are those made to the general government, the central bank, and entities that are public corporations (see paragraph 2.19). Information on lending to the public sector is identified in the BIS's consolidated IBS data.

53. *Domestic government securities owned (market value)* provides an indication of the importance of domestic government securities in the deposit-taking sector's balance sheet.

54. Within the total for NPLs (line 42 in Table 4.1), the sectoral distribution of NPLs could be identified to highlight in which sectors or industries (see Box A3.1) NPLs are concentrated.

55. The percentage of replacement (restructured) loans within gross loans (line 18(i) in Table 4.1) is a measure that helps in assessing the credit quality of a loan portfolio. Replacement loans are defined in paragraph 4.86.

56. Using the same criteria as for loans, the value of *other nonperforming assets,* including securities, could be identified; a rising level might suggest increased financial system vulnerability.

57. *Loan loss reserves* are the outstanding amount of reserves intended to absorb potential but unidentified losses arising from the deposit takers' loan portfolio. Additions, or reductions, to the amount of loan loss reserves (other than any net write-offs) are made through the general loan loss provisions included in the income and expense account. The size of such reserves in relation to nonperforming loans can be an indication of the adequacy of provisioning policy.

58. *Specific provisions against total debt claims* provides an indication of the adequacy of provisions vis-à-vis a broader measure of assets at risk than the ratio of specific provisions to loans.

59. As described in Chapter 4 (paragraph 4.71), using the IRB approach under the revised Basel Capital Accord, any shortfall in provisions for expected losses would be deducted 50 percent from Tier 1 and 50 percent from Tier 2 capital. If there are significant shortfalls in such provisioning, the nonperforming loans net of specific provisions-to-capital ratio (measured using total regulatory capital) will be affected (see paragraph 6.24). This series monitors the extent of underprovisioning against expected losses.

60. *Arrears* are amounts past due for payment on loans or other assets. Arrears can arise through the late payment of principal and/or interest on debt instruments as well as through the failure to meet the terms of other types of transactions, such as for goods and services provided. This statistic provides the actual amounts owed to deposit takers that have not been paid or written off. If time-series data are disseminated, this statistic provides the user with an indication of any difficulties on the asset side of the balance sheet and their development over time, irrespective of valuation or provisioning policies. If arrears are significant, distinguishing them by different types of instrument—loans and securities in particular—might be useful. Principal and interest arrears could also be identified separately.

61. *Arrears of deposit takers* are arrears on deposit takers' own liabilities. Rising amounts might suggest increased financial system vulnerability.

62. *Assets transferred to special purpose entities* are those assets that are still outstanding and that the originating deposit-taker has removed from its balance sheet by transferring them to an SPE or, as it is often called, a Special Purpose Vehicle (SPV). A change of ownership should have occurred before assets are removed from a deposit taker's balance sheet.

63. To highlight potential vulnerabilities, disaggregating the data in this item between those assets transferred to SPEs where a clean break has occurred and those where such a break has not occurred might be considered. Such a distinction is made in the revised Basel Capital Accord to help determine capital adequacy requirements. A clean break is defined as arising when (1) the transferred assets have been legally isolated from the transferring institution (transferor), and (2) the transferor does not maintain effective or indirect control over the transferred assets. A transferor is deemed to have maintained effective control over the transferred assets if it is able to repurchase the assets from the transferee to realize their benefits and is obligated to retain the risk of the assets. The retention of servicing rights to the asset does not necessarily constitute indirect control.

64. *Guarantees* are contingent liabilities arising from an irrevocable obligation to pay a third-party beneficiary when another party, such as a client of the guarantor, fails to perform some contractual obligation. Guarantees represent a potential liability for deposit takers. They include loan and other payment guarantees, letters of credit, and performance bonds. These are described in Chapter 3 (paragraphs 3.14 and 3.15). The intention of this item is to be consistent with the definition of guarantees used in the BIS's IBS data and so should include contingent liabilities of deposit takers as protection sellers of credit derivatives—that is, payments that would need to be made in the event of a default of the credit on which the derivative is written. If the guarantee data include such information on credit derivatives, it is suggested that they be separately identified and that separate data on deposit takers' purchases of protection through credit derivatives also be collected. Such information would allow the net and gross positions on protection bought and sold through credit derivatives to be identified. Guarantees (and credit derivatives) should be valued in terms of the maximum potential loss—that is, assuming 100 percent of the amount guaranteed (protected) will need to be paid.[3] A resident/nonresident disaggregation is useful to allow reconciliation with the BIS's IBS data.

[3]Valuing at the maximum potential loss has an obvious limitation: there is no information on the likelihood of the contingency occurring. However, calculating the likelihood of losses can be difficult, and international standards are still evolving.

65. *Credit commitments* irrevocably oblige a deposit taker to extend credit and hence could affect its liquidity position. They include lines of credit, other types of loan commitments, NIFs, and commitments to purchase securities (under NIFs, for example). These are described in Chapter 3 (paragraphs 3.16 and 3.17). The intention is to be consistent with the definition of credit commitments used in the BIS's IBS data. Credit commitments should be valued in terms of the maximum amount that could be advanced under the commitment. A resident/nonresident disaggregation is useful to allow reconciliation with the BIS's IBS data.

66. *Assets managed but not owned by deposit takers.* These assets represent a form of savings by other sectors that supplements savings captured in the deposit takers' information.

67. *Duration* measures the weighted average life of assets and liabilities, with the weights being the present value of each cash flow as a percentage of the value of the assets or liabilities. In other words, duration adjusts maturity to take account of the size and timing of payments between the current period and maturity, or (for floating-rate instruments) between the current period and the date of the next repricing (see paragraphs 3.51 to 3.56)

68. Duration is intended to identify the sensitivity of the value of deposit takers' portfolios of financial assets and liabilities to changes in interest rates.[4] The greater the duration, the greater is the risk of loss/gain of value, with the corresponding impact on capital, if interest rates rise/fall. Duration is measured for tradable debt assets and liabilities, that is, those debt instruments for which the expectation is that they are valued at market or fair value. If there is a lack of data, duration might be compiled only for domestic currency debt instruments, or for debt instruments denominated in other units of account if the debt instruments are not denominated in the domestic currency.[5]

[4]Duration is "accurate" for only small changes in interest rates, because duration itself changes as interest rates change. Convexity, which is the second derivative of an asset's price, indicates how duration changes in response to changes in interest rates and permits a more accurate estimate of interest rate sensitivity.

[5]Foreign-currency-linked instruments should be classified as foreign currency instruments, if changes in their value arise primarily through changes in foreign interest rates and exchange rates rather than domestic interest rates.

69. Appendix VI provides detail on measuring duration at the sector level and also introduces "gap" analysis, which is an alternative approach to assessing interest rate risk of a portfolio of assets and liabilities.

Other Financial Corporations

70. As in the case of deposit takers, the memorandum series *shares and other equity investments in other financial corporations in the reporting population* provide information on the ownership links within the sector. (This series and those below are set out in Table A3.3, which is a continuation of Table 4.2.)

71. *Nonperforming loans owned by special asset management companies* is the nominal value of the loans owned by those entities that are usually created by the authorities for the purpose of managing NPLs and recovering assets. Even though the NPLs have been sold by deposit takers to the special asset management companies, these loans still exist in the economy, and the cost of their resolution may be considerable. Without monitoring these loans, the amount of NPLs in the financial system would be underestimated. However, caution should be exercised in interpreting these data, as it is also important to know the institutional arrangements under which NPLs are transferred and whether the value of the assets transferred are covered by the value of collateral (see also paragraph 6.22).

72. *Assets managed but not owned by other financial corporations.* These are assets managed by fund managers and other similar financial corporations. These assets represent a form of savings by other sectors that supplements savings captured in the deposit takers' information.

Nonfinancial Corporations

73. *Debt-service interest payments* are defined in Chapter 4; interest payments are those periodic payments that meet interest costs arising from the use of another entity's funds. The use of this series in calculating the debt service coverage ratio was described earlier in this appendix. (This series and those below are set out in Table A3.4, which is a continuation of Table 4.3.)

Table A3.3. Other Financial Corporations: Memorandum Series[1]

Additional series

21. Shares and other equity investments in other financial corporations in the reporting population
    (i) Associates
    (ii) Other other financial corporations
22. Nonperforming loans owned by special asset management companies
23. Assets managed but not owned by other financial corporations

[1]This table is a continuation of Table 4.2.

Table A3.4. Nonfinancial Corporations: Memorandum Series[1]

Additional series

38. Debt-service interest payments
39. Debt-service receipts (interest and principal) from other nonfinancial corporations
    (i) Interest
    (ii) Principal
40. Shares and other equity investments in nonfinancial corporations in the reporting population
    (i) Associates
    (ii) Other nonfinancial corporations
41. Liquid assets (core measure)
42. Liquid assets (broad measure)
43. Variable-rate debt

[1]This table is a continuation of Table 4.3.

74. *Debt-service receipts from other nonfinancial corporations*[6] are a subset of the total debt-service payments (line 35 of Table 4.3); with these two series, both intrasector debt-service payments and those to other sectors can be identified. The use of this series in calculating the debt-service coverage ratio was described earlier in this appendix. Separately identifying interest allows the debt-service coverage ratio calculated using interest only in the numerator to also be calculated excluding intrasector interest payments.

75. As with deposit takers and other financial corporations, *shares and other equity investments in other nonfinancial corporations in the reporting population* provide information on the ownership links within the sector.

76. For nonfinancial corporations, the core and broad measures of liquid assets are defined as for deposit takers; however, for nonfinancial corporations, deposits at deposit takers available on demand or within three months or less are included in the core measure, whereas such deposits are excluded for deposit takers because they are intrasectoral claims.

77. *Variable-rate debt* is the total value of debt instruments on which interest costs are linked to a reference index, such as London Interbank Offered Rate (LIBOR); the price of a specific commodity; or the price of a specific financial instrument that normally changes over time in a continuous manner in response to market pressures. All other debt instruments should be classified as fixed-rate instruments. When the value of the principal is indexed, the change in value resulting from indexation—periodically and at maturity—is classified as interest. Therefore, if principal only is indexed, such debt is to be classified as variable-rate debt regardless of whether interest is fixed or variable, provided the reference index meets the criterion above: that is, it normally changes over time in a continuous manner in response to market pressures. An attribution of debt by type of interest provides an indication of the exposure of nonfinancial corporations to interest rate movements. Nonetheless, interest rate derivative contracts, which are widely employed, can modify these risk characteristics. Thus, information on the notional amounts of such contracts and whether they receive fixed or variable-rate interest flows would also be useful.

Financial Conglomerates

78. In many economies, financial conglomerates are important to domestic markets. Financial conglomerates are defined in the *Guide* as enterprises that have controlling interest in a range of entities that straddle the different types of financial activity described above. This could include bank holding companies. In other words, a holding company might own a de-

[6]It is proposed that receipts from, rather than payments to, other nonfinancial corporations be presented, given that if tradable bonds are issued, the payer might not know the identification of the creditor. But, of course, debt-service receipts from the creditor perspective are debt-service payments from the debtor perspective.

posit taker and an insurance company, and/or other entities. The *Guide* recommends that data be presented separately for each financial sector (deposit takers, other financial corporations, and so forth) because the nature of their financial activities differs; nonetheless, if financial conglomerates are significant within the economy,[7] subject to national confidentiality commitments, compilers could disseminate the information specified below:

- Names of large financial conglomerates.
- The value of assets owned on a basis that allows the information to be disaggregated by type of financial activity in which the conglomerate is involved, for example, deposit takers, insurance corporations, and security dealers.
- The balance sheet value of equity investments of non-deposit-taking conglomerate entities (resident and nonresident) in deposit takers in the reporting population. Such data would highlight cross-sector ownership patterns of conglomerate entities with relation to the deposit-taking sector.
- Return on equity and capital-to-assets ratios for the largest conglomerates.

[7]What is meant by "significant" can differ depending on country circumstances. Nonetheless, while it may be difficult to measure, a conglomerate might be considered "significant" if it either owns one of the top five (or about the top five) entities in any of the types of financial activities mentioned in Chapters 6 or 7 or, in broad terms, has a total value of assets (calculated on an aggregate basis) greater than any of the top five entities (or about the top five entities) in any of the types of financial activities in which the conglomerate is involved.

Appendix IV. Reconciliation Between the *Guide*'s Methodology and National and Commercial Accounting

1. This appendix explains how the concepts outlined in Chapter 3 and the line-item series defined in Chapter 4 can be reconciled with similar concepts developed in the *1993 SNA* (national accounts) and the IASs.[1]

Overview

2. The framework of national accounts in the *1993 SNA* provides for the construction of a range of tables that begin with production, income, and accumulation accounts, as well as balance sheets showing the stock of financial and nonfinancial assets and liabilities for the financial, nonfinancial, household, and general government sectors of an economy. The full sequence of accounts is set out in pages 601–674 of the *1993 SNA*.

3. For each group of assets and liabilities, and for net worth, changes between the opening and closing balance sheets that result from transactions and other flows are recorded in the so-called accumulation accounts. As explained below, many of the data series used in constructing FSIs for the other depository corporations (deposit takers in the terminology of the *Guide*), other financial corporations (OFC), nonfinancial corporations, and the household sector can be obtained from the national accounts framework or related frameworks such as monetary statistics. The derivation of FSI data series from the *1993 SNA* framework are set out in Tables 11.9–11.11.

4. Business accounting is designed to assess the financial condition of individual productive units, measure their economic result, and determine interested parties' (mainly the shareholders' and tax authorities') entitlement to that result. There is a focus on two concepts: solvency (the value of net assets (or equity) held by an entity) and profitability (a component of the value added by the entity during the reporting period).[2] It relies on specific norms and standards (for example, as set out in IASs) to achieve its objectives with understandability, relevance, reliability, and comparability.[3] The *International Accounting Standards 2002* prepared by the IASB (IASB, 2002) are utilized in drafting this appendix.

5. At the time of writing, the IASs consist of 39 separate standards, numbered IAS 1 to IAS 41 (IAS 25 has been withdrawn and IAS 15 is no longer binding). The references below are to those standards and to the relevant paragraph numbers within the quoted standard. In contrast to the *1993 SNA,* there is no standardized set of tables for the presentation of commercial accounts. Moreover, while financial statements prepared in accordance with IASs should, at a minimum, present line items in accordance with IAS 1, for banks and similar financial institutions there is a more detailed specific standard (IAS 30).

Income and Expense Account

Interest Income and Expense

6. In both the *1993 SNA* and the IASs, it is recommended that interest accrue continuously on debt instruments, consistent with the approach in the *Guide.*

7. In the *1993 SNA,* as in the *Guide,* interest accrues at the contractual rate of interest—the effective rate on issuance. In the *Guide,* lines 1(i) and 2 in Table 4.1, lines 4 and 5 in Table 4.3, and part of line 2 in

[1]IASs of 2002 (IASB, 2002). The information presented within square brackets refers to relevant paragraph numbers in the International Financial Reporting Standards (IFRS) as of March 31, 2004, which will come into effect on January 1, 2005 (IASB, 2004). The IFRS also contains revisions affecting the treatment of financial instruments, which are found mostly in IAS 32 and IAS 39.

[2]The *1993 SNA* also has a concept of value added that is related to the production process.

[3]As in "Framework for the Preparation and Presentation of Financial Statements" of IASB (2002).

Table 4.4 in principle correspond to the *1993 SNA*'s full sequence of accounts to line D.41 in the Primary Income Account. Moreover, if FSIM[4] are calculated for deposit takers, they correspond in part to line P.11 of the Production Account for deposit takers, in part to line P.2 of intermediate consumption in the Production Account for enterprises and in part to line P.31 of final consumption in the Use of Income Account for households.

8. In IASs, interest income is defined as one type of revenue (besides royalties and dividends) arising from the use by others of an enterprise's financial assets (IASs 18.29–18.31) (also IASs 32.30–32.31) [IASs 32.35–32.36]. Interest income is recognized on an accrual basis over time, based on the effective yield on the asset, which is defined as the rate of interest required to discount the stream of future cash receipts expected over the life of the asset to equate to the *initial* carrying amount of the asset. Interest income includes the amount of amortization of any discount or premium arising from a difference between the issue price and the par value.[5] If debt instruments are traded and market prices are established, then for creditors there is a difference of approach between the *Guide* and the IASs in that the effective rate of interest on acquisition may be different from that on issuance. The greater the variability of market prices, the more significant this difference could be.

9. For creditors, interest on nonperforming assets is treated differently in the *1993 SNA* and in IASs. In the *1993 SNA,* creditors (and debtors) should continue to accrue interest on nonperforming assets unless the asset is written off. In contrast, IAS 39.116 [IAS 39. AG.93] states that impaired assets should be written down to their estimated recoverable amount and creditors should base the calculation of interest income on the rate of interest that was used to discount the future cash flows for the purpose of measuring the recoverable amount.

10. In "Sound Practices for Loan Accounting and Disclosure," the BCBS (1999) recommends in standard 11 that when a loan is identified as impaired, a bank should cease accruing interest in accordance with the terms of the contract. Interest on impaired loans should not contribute to net income if doubts exist concerning the collectability of loan interest or principal. However, in some countries, when impaired loans are carried at the present value of expected future cash flows, interest may accrue at the effective rate implicit in the present value calculation.

11. The *Guide* follows BCBS in that interest on nonperforming assets should not contribute to net interest income.

Fees and Commissions Receivable/Payable

12. In the *1993 SNA,* fees and commissions receivable reflect the value of services provided (for deposit takers, *1993 SNA,* paragraph 6.123). In the *1993 SNA*'s full sequence of accounts, line 4(i) in Table 4.1 in principle corresponds to the fees and commissions included in line P.11 in the Production Account.

13. In IASs, financial fees and commissions are a form of revenue, and they are defined in IAS 18.20 and in its Appendix paragraph 14. The latter distinguishes fees that are an integral part of the effective yield of an instrument from those that are earned on services provided (such as for servicing a loan) and from those that are earned on the execution of a significant act (such as commission on the allotment of shares to a client). Fees that are an integral part of the effective yield of a financial instrument—and hence affect the rate at which interest accrues—include commitment fees to originate or purchase a loan where it is probable that the enterprise will enter into a specific lending arrangement, and origination fees relating to the creation or acquisition of a financial instrument that is held by the enterprise as an investment. Such fees are regarded as an integral part of generating an ongoing involvement with the financial instrument, and as such are deferred and recognized as an adjustment to the effective yield. The *Guide* differs from IASs in that it does not adjust the effective yield of an instrument for these fees but prefers to record them under fees and commissions.

Gains/Losses on Financial Instruments (Including Foreign Exchange)

14. In contrast to what appears in the *Guide,* in the *1993 SNA* trading gains or losses do not appear in the

[4]FSIM measures the output of the deposit-taking sector arising from the margins earned from the borrowing and lending of funds. See *1993 SNA,* paragraphs 6.124 to 6.131.

[5]Since loans are issued at par, the effective rate for loans is the same as the contractual rate. If the issue price of the asset is different from par, the effective yield would be different from the stated interest (coupon) rate.

distribution and use of income accounts. In the *1993 SNA* full sequence of accounts, such trading gains and losses in principle correspond within the Revaluation Account to lines AF.2 (currency and deposits—partial coverage of foreign currency gains and losses), AF.3 (securities other than shares), AF.5 (shares and other equity—excluding equity investments in associates and subsidiaries), and AF.7 (financial derivatives; see IMF, 2000b). Holding gains and losses in the *1993 SNA* include changes in the value of financial assets and liabilities due to changes in market prices and exchange rate movements. The change in value is measured as the difference in the unit of account between the value of an asset or liability at the end of the accounting period and its value at the start of the accounting period. Moreover, if the instruments were acquired during the period, the value at which they were first entered in the balance sheet is to be used. If they were sold during the period, their value at the start of the accounting period would have to be used. If, however, they were purchased during the period and sold during the period, then the value when they were purchased should be used. Thus, within an accounting period, the *1993 SNA* concept of holding gains/losses encompasses both realized and unrealized gains/losses. As line 4(ii) in Table 4.1 excludes some, and line 6 in Table 4.3 excludes all, unrealized gains and losses, additional data would need to be requested to extract the required information from the *1993 SNA* data. Line 6 in Table 4.3 includes the equivalent to the foreign exchange component of line AF in the Revaluation Account.

15. For banks and similar financial institutions, IAS 30.15 states that gains and losses from the following items are normally reported on a net basis: (1) disposals and changes in the carrying amount of dealing securities, (2) disposals of investment securities, and (3) dealings in foreign exchange. These items are consistent with the *Guide* (although, unlike the *Guide,* IAS 30.15 makes no reference to financial derivative instruments). Moreover, IASs 39.103–39.107 [IASs 39.55–39.57] state that a gain or loss on a financial asset or liability classified as at fair value that is not part of a hedging relationship should be included in net profit or loss; a gain or loss on an available-for-sale financial asset can be treated similarly, or it can be recognized in equity through the statement of changes in equity until the financial asset is sold, collected, or otherwise disposed of, or until it is determined to be impaired, at which point the cumulative gain or loss should be included in net profit and loss for the period. For financial assets and liabilities carried at amortized cost, a gain or loss is recognized in net profit or loss when the financial asset or liability is derecognized or impaired [IAS 39.56]. The IASs 39.121–39.165 [IASs 39.85–39.102] provide separate guidance for hedging instruments. Clearly, while the different treatment in IASs of gains and losses according to the purpose for holding the instrument differs from the approach in the *Guide,* within the IASs the treatment of instruments held for trading and one of the alternative treatments for available-for-sale financial assets are in line with the *Guide*'s recommendations.

16. IAS 21.15 explains the treatment of foreign exchange differences related to "monetary items," which are in turn defined as money held and assets and liabilities to be received or paid in fixed or determinable amounts of money. It states that foreign exchange differences arising from the settlement of monetary items at rates different from those at which they were initially recorded during the period or reported in previous financial statements should be recognized as income or expenses in the period in which they arise, with two exceptions.

17. The first exception, set out in IAS 21.17, covers exchange-rate-related changes in the value of a monetary item that in substance forms part of an enterprise's net investment in a foreign entity. Such differences should be classified as part of equity in the enterprise's financial statements until the disposal of the net investment, at which time they should be recognized as income or expenses (depending on whether the cumulative amount of the exchange-rate-related differences that have been deferred and that relate to the foreign entity reflects a gain or a loss [IAS 21.37]).

18. The second exception, set out in IAS 21.19, covers exchange-rate-related changes in the value of a foreign currency liability accounted for as a hedge of an enterprise's net investment in a foreign entity. Such differences should also be classified as part of equity in the enterprise's financial statements until the disposal of the net investment, at which time they should be recognized as income or expenses (depending on whether the cumulative amount of the exchange-rate-related differences that have been deferred and that relate to the foreign entity reflects a gain or a loss [IAS 21.37]).

19. Both of these exceptions are consistent with the *Guide*'s approach of excluding gains and losses on those foreign exchange instruments related to equity holdings in subsidiaries, although the *Guide* does not recommend inclusion of gains and losses of earlier periods in present period earnings, when these instruments are disposed of.

Rent, Rental, and Royalty Income Receivable

20. In the *1993 SNA,* as in this *Guide,* this item covers income from rents on land or subsoil assets; rentals from buildings, other structures, and equipment; and royalty income from other produced and nonproduced assets. Therefore, part of line 4(iv) in Table 4.1, line 6 in Table 4.3, and part of line 2 in Table 4.4 of the *Guide* in principle most closely correspond to line D.45 in the Allocation of Primary Income Account (rents) and line P.11 in the Production Account (rental and royalty income—classified as services)[6] in the *1993 SNA*. In concept, line D.45 covers only rent on land and subsoil, but the *1993 SNA* does acknowledge (paragraph 7.131) that in practice a single payment may cover rent on land and rentals on buildings. If a split can be made, rentals receivable should be classified as a provision of services (line P.11 in the Production Account). There is no specific standard for rent in IASs except insofar as it is mentioned generally in the IASB Framework, paragraph 74, that rent is part of the revenues of an enterprise. In accordance with IAS 40.66 (d)(i), rental income from investment property should be included in the income statement.

Prorated Share of Income from Associates and Subsidiaries

21. For foreign affiliates, the reinvested earnings element within the "prorated earnings" line (4(iii) in Table 4.1 and line 6 in Table 4.3) of the *Guide* correspond to line D.43 in the *1993 SNA*. There is no equivalent concept for resident affiliates. The dividends element of the prorated share of income is covered below.

22. In IAS 28.3, under accounting by the equity method, the income statement reflects the investor's share of the results of the operations of the investee. This is applicable to associates, the subject of IAS 28, and is one of the three approaches that can be adopted for unconsolidated subsidiaries (IAS 27.30). IASs permit the use of the equity method for jointly controlled ventures, if the assets and liabilities of the joint venture are not proportionately consolidated with the venturer's financial statement (IASs 31.32–31.34).

[6]A corporation consuming these services would record them as intermediate consumption (P2) in the Production Account.

Dividends Declared

23. The standard in the *Guide* is the same as in the *1993 SNA* and in IAS 18.30 in recommending that property income to be distributed to shareholders in the entity be recognized as income when the shareholder's right to receive payment is established. Dividends within the "other income" line (4(iv) in Table 4.1; line 6 in Table 4.3) and dividends within "property income receivable" (line 2 in Table 4.4) of the *Guide* in principle correspond to lines D.421 and D.422 (resources) in the Allocation of Primary Income Account in the *1993 SNA*'s full sequence of accounts. Dividends paid or payable in Table 4.1 (line 12) and in Table 4.3 (line 11) also correspond to D.421 and D.422 (uses).

Net Gains/Losses from Sales of Fixed Assets

24. In the *1993 SNA,* net gains or losses from the sale of fixed assets are defined as the change in the value of fixed assets due to changes in their market price. These gains and losses are included in line AN.11 (holding gains and losses in respect of fixed assets) in the Revaluation Account in the *1993 SNA*'s full sequence of accounts. The change in price is measured as the difference between the value of the fixed asset at the end of the accounting period and its value at the start of the accounting period or, if acquired during the period, its value on the date on which it was first entered in the balance sheet. This *1993 SNA* concept thus encompasses both realized and unrealized gains/losses. Since net gains/losses on fixed assets within line 4(iv) in Table 4.1 and line 6 in Table 4.3 of the *Guide* cover only realized gains during the period, additional data would need to be requested to extract the required information from the *1993 SNA* data.

25. IAS 16.56 states that gains or losses "from the retirement or disposal of an item of property, plant, and equipment should be determined as the difference between the estimated net disposal proceeds and the carrying amount of the asset and should be recognized as income or expense in the income statement." This concept is the same as in the *Guide,* although the *Guide* recommends market valuation of fixed assets, while IAS 16 favors valuation on the basis of historic value. IAS 40 permits enterprises to use either the model in IAS 16 or a fair value model for investment property (but not for owner-occupied property). Under IAS 40, if an enterprise chooses the fair value model, all changes in fair value should be recognized in the income statement (IAS 40.28).

Other Income

26. In the *1993 SNA,* miscellaneous current transfers, such as compensation payments received, are included in D.75. IAS 8.18 covers income from litigation settlements.

Personnel Costs Including Wages and Salaries

27. The concept of personnel costs (line 6(i) of Table 4.1 and implicit in line 2 of Table 4.3) in the *Guide* corresponds in the *1993 SNA*'s full sequence of accounts to D.1, Compensation of Employees in the Generation of Income Account, and D.623, Unfunded Employee Social Insurance Benefits in the Secondary Distribution of Income Account. Wages and salaries from employment (line 1 in Table 4.4) correspond to line D.11. In the *1993 SNA* (paragraphs 7.21 to 7.47), compensation of employees is defined as the total remuneration, in cash or in kind, payable by an employer to an employee in return for work done during the accounting period. Included is remuneration payable to workers away from work for short periods. Compensation of employees can be broken down into the following: (1) wages and salaries in cash and in kind, and (2) employers' social contributions, actual and imputed, for such items as postemployment benefits.

28. The *1993 SNA* does not explicitly cover compensation in the form of options to buy the shares of the entity at some future time at an agreed price (stock options).

29. IAS 19.4 has a similar concept to the *1993 SNA,* defining employee benefits as including the following:

- Short-term employee benefits, such as wages and salaries and social security contributions. These benefits cover paid annual leave and paid sick leave, profit sharing and bonuses, and nonmonetary benefits (such as medical care, housing, cars, and free or subsidized goods or services).
- Postemployment benefits, such as pensions, other retirement benefits, postemployment life insurance, and postemployment medical care.
- Other long-term employee benefits, including long service leave or sabbatical leave, and long-term disability benefits.
- Termination benefits.
- Equity compensation benefits, including stock options (although no guidance is provided on recognition or measurement).

30. The first bullet above is close to the concept of wages and salaries in cash and in kind in the *1993 SNA,* except for social security contributions, which are included in employers' social contributions in the *1993 SNA.*

Depreciation

31. Depreciation within line 6(ii) of Table 4.1 and line 2 of Table 4.3 of the *Guide* corresponds in the *1993 SNA*'s full sequence of accounts to line K.1 (consumption of fixed capital (CFC)). CFC is defined (paragraphs 6.179–6.180) as the amount of fixed assets consumed during the period under consideration as a result of normal wear and tear and foreseeable obsolescence. CFC should be estimated on the basis of the stock of fixed assets, valued at purchasers' prices as of the current period, and the probable average economic life of the different categories of assets. CFC can be calculated according to the straight-line method by which the value of a fixed asset is written off at a constant rate over the whole lifetime of the asset or, depending on the pattern of decline in the efficiency of a fixed asset, according to a geometric depreciation method (*1993 SNA,* paragraphs 6.193–6.197).

32. IASs 16.41–16.48 describe a similar treatment for depreciation. They state that the depreciable amount of an item of property, plant, and equipment should be allocated on a systematic basis over its useful life. The depreciation method used should reflect the pattern in which the asset's economic value is consumed by the enterprise. These methods could include the straight-line method, the diminishing-balance method, and the sum-of-the-units method. Straight-line depreciation, as noted above, results in a constant charge over the useful life of the asset. The diminishing-balance method results in a decreasing charge over the useful life of the asset. The sum-of-the-units method results in a charge based on the expected output of the asset. IAS 16.43 states that the useful life of a depreciable asset should be estimated after considering (1) the expected physical wear and tear, (2) obsolescence, (3) legal or other limits on the use of the asset, and (4) expected usage by the enterprise.

33. The main difference between CFC and the IASs' treatment of depreciation is in the valuation of the fixed assets, which is required to be the current purchasers' prices for CFC but tends to be at historical cost under IASs. CFC should also be distinguished from business accounting of depreciation for tax purposes. However, IASs also state that the depreciation method should be reviewed periodically and, if there has been significant change in the expected pattern of economic benefits, there should be a change in the depreciation charge for the current and future periods (IAS 16.52), which may narrow the difference between CFC and IASs valuations.

34. Losses due to unforeseen obsolescence, such as through the introduction of new technology or unforeseen damage (other than events covered under extraordinary items), are recorded as depreciation. This is consistent with IAS 16.50, and such losses correspond to K.9 in the *1993 SNA* (excluding exceptional losses in inventories, which like depreciation is covered in the line *cost of sales* in Table 4.3).

Other Noninterest Expenses (Such as Plant and Equipment Expenses Including Rentals, Advertising Costs, and Premiums Paid for Deposit Insurance)

35. These expenses are related to the ordinary operations of the entity other than those identified elsewhere in this appendix. The ongoing expenses of operating an enterprise, covered within line 6(ii) in Table 4.1 and line 2 in Table 4.3 of the *Guide,* correspond in the *1993 SNA*'s full sequence of accounts to line P.2 (intermediate consumption), together with D.71 (net nonlife insurance premiums) and D.75 (miscellaneous current transfers). However, unlike the *Guide,* the series in the *1993 SNA* do not include estimated costs related to product warranties.

36. In the IASB Framework paragraphs 70 and 78–80, expenses are defined to encompass those that arise in the course of the ordinary activities of the enterprise, although they are not defined in detail. Expenses arising from product warranties are described in IASB Framework paragraph 98 and more fully in IAS 37.24. In principle, the IAS approach is consistent with the approach taken in the *Guide* for these expenses. IAS 8.18 covers expenses arising from litigation settlements.

37. Rentals payable on buildings, other structures, and equipment are included under this item, along with rents paid on land and subsoil assets, and royalties payable on the use of other produced and nonproduced assets. Receipts for rents, rental, and royalty income were discussed earlier, in a separate section in this appendix.

Taxes Other Than Income Taxes

38. Taxes included in line 6(ii) of Table 4.1 and line 2 in Table 4.3 of the *Guide* correspond in the *1993 SNA*'s full sequence of accounts to line D.29 (taxes on production) and line D.59 (other current taxes). These taxes are compulsory, unrequited payments in cash and in kind levied in respect of the production (such as taxes on payroll or the workforce), as well as on the ownership or use of land or buildings and on other assets and net wealth (described in paragraphs 7.70 and 8.53–8.54 of the *1993 SNA*).

39. The IASs have no specific definitions for taxes that are not levied on income.

40. Operating subsidies from general government included in line 6(ii) of Table 4.1 of the *Guide* correspond in the *1993 SNA*'s full sequence of accounts to subsidies on production (line D.39). IAS 20.29 explains that government grants related to income could be presented as a credit in the income statement or deducted in reporting of the related expenses. The IAS regards either method as acceptable. These grants are defined in IAS 20.3 as assistance by government in the form of a transfer of resources.

Loan Loss Provisions

41. The *1993 SNA* does not have a concept of provisions for loan losses. However, the writing off of bad debts by creditors (K.10) provides some coverage of loan losses (and losses on other claims). The distinctions made in the *Guide* for loan loss provisions follow the IASs. The *Guide,* however, relies on national practice in identifying provisions.

42. IAS 30.45 states that for banks, provisions for specific loans (specific provisions—that is, losses that have been specifically identified) and provisions for losses not specifically identified (general provisions—which experience indicates are present in the portfolio of loans and advances) should both be recognized as expenses. Under IAS 30.51, local circumstances or legislation may require or allow a bank to set aside amounts for general banking risks, including future losses or other unforeseeable risks. However, such amounts set aside should be accounted for as appropriations of retained earnings and not expenses in determining net profit or loss for the period. A bank may also be required or allowed to set aside amounts for contingencies (IAS 37). Such amounts also do not qualify for recognition as provisions but should be recognized as appropriations of retained earnings (IAS 30.51) so as not to distort net income and equity.

Other Financial Assets Provisions

43. As with loans, the *1993 SNA* does not address the concept of provisions for securities or other financial assets.[7] IASs discuss provisions for losses on financial assets in IASs 39.109–39.111 [IASs 30.43–30.49, 39.58–39.70, and 39. IG.E.4], where it is stated that when the carrying amount of the impaired asset is greater than its recoverable amount—estimated by discounting the expected future cash flows using the financial instrument's original effective interest rate—the carrying amount of the asset should be reduced to its estimated recoverable amount either directly or through use of an allowance account, with the loss included in net profit or loss for the period. This concept is not identical to the *Guide's* recommendation that the market value of investment securities be recorded on the balance sheet. If the securities are not recorded at market value, provisions for securities may be greater or smaller than the change in the market value, depending on the deposit takers' views on recoverable amounts on the securities.

Bad Debt Recoveries

44. The IASs recommend that if there is an improvement in the standing of a debtor so that the amount of impairment or bad debt loss decreases, such a reversal should be included in net profits or loss for the period.[8] One approach would be to make adjustments to an Allowance Account. This approach is consistent with that for line 7 of Table 4.1 of the *Guide,* which allows for provisions to be reduced if there was an overprediction of expected losses in an earlier period.

Extraordinary Items

45. The extraordinary items in line 9 in Table 4.1 and line 8 in Table 4.3 of the *Guide* correspond in the *1993 SNA*'s full sequence of accounts to line K.7 (catastrophic losses) and line K.8 (uncompensated seizures). The IAS 8.6 defines an extraordinary item as an event or transaction that is clearly *distinct from the ordinary activities* of an enterprise and is unlikely to recur frequently or regularly. The IAS 1.75 requires the separate disclosure of extraordinary items in the income statement for the period. Such items are determined by the nature of the event or transaction in relation to the business ordinarily carried out by the enterprise rather than by the frequency with which such events are expected to occur. For example, losses sustained as a result of an earthquake may qualify as an extraordinary item for many enterprises but not for insurance enterprises that insure against such risks. The IASs suggest that extraordinary items for most enterprises include an earthquake or other natural disaster and the expropriation of assets (IASs 8.11–8.15). The concept in the *Guide* is consistent with that in the IASs.

Income Tax Expense

46. Income tax expense, line 10 in Table 4.1 and line 9 in Table 4.3, corresponds in the *1993 SNA*'s full sequence of accounts to line D.51. Consistent with the *Guide,* the *1993 SNA* defines these taxes as those assessed on the incomes, profits, and capital gains of individuals, households, corporations, and nonprofit institutions (paragraph 8.52). IAS 12.2 states that

---

[7]Both the *Guide* and the *1993 SNA* recommend that securities be valued at market value and that gains and losses be reported under gains and losses on financial instruments, thus eliminating the need for provisions on securities.

[8]The revised version of IAS 39 provides for several methods to deal with decreases in the amount of impairment or bad debt loss depending on the valuation basis used to carry the instrument on the balance sheet [IASs 39.65, 39.66, and 39.70]. For some instruments, increased value as a result of reductions in impairment will be taken directly to income, but others are handled through adjustments to an allowance account.

"income taxes include all domestic and foreign taxes which are based on taxable profits."

Revenues from Sales of Goods and Services (Nonfinancial Corporations)

47. Line 1 in Table 4.3 of the *Guide* corresponds in the *1993 SNA*'s full sequence of accounts to line P.11 (market output for nonfinancial corporations), which in turn equals line P.1 (gross output) less line P.12 (output for own use) less the value of changes in the inventories of goods produced as outputs (finished goods element of line P.52). However, as noted in the *1993 SNA* (paragraph 6.43), under normal circumstances the available data are accounting data on sales, and thus the national accountant is required to adjust sales for changes in inventories to arrive at the data for production. Moreover, in the *1993 SNA,* the system for recording transactions by retailers and wholesalers is not to record purchases of goods for resale but rather to measure the margin on goods purchased for resale (paragraph 3.30).

48. IASs 18.14 and 18.20 recognize the sale of goods when an enterprise has transferred to the buyer the significant risks and rewards of ownership of the goods and the amount of revenue can be reliably estimated. They also recognize the rendering of services when the amount of revenue can be reliably estimated and the stage of completion of the transaction at the balance sheet date can be measured reliably. This is consistent with the change-of-ownership concept in the *Guide.*

Current Transfers (Households)

49. Line 3 in Table 4.4 of the *Guide* corresponds in the *1993 SNA*'s full sequence of accounts to lines D.62 (social benefits) and D.7 (other current transfers) in the Secondary Distribution of Income Account. Social benefits include pensions and unemployment benefits (*1993 SNA,* 8.75–8.83) and other current transfers (*1993 SNA,* 8.84). The concept in the *Guide* is the same as in the *1993 SNA*. IASs do not have a specific definition of current transfers.

Other Income (Households)

50. Line 4 in Table 4.4 of the *Guide* corresponds in the *1993 SNA*'s full sequence of accounts to lines B.2 (operating surplus) and B.3 (mixed income) in the Generation of Income Account for households.

Taxes, Social Contributions, and Other Current Transfers Made (Households)

51. Line 5 in Table 4.4 of the *Guide* includes social security taxes. In the *1993 SNA*'s full sequence of accounts, these taxes correspond to lines D.6112 and D.6113 (social contributions). IAS 12 defines income tax expense, but IASs do not have a specific definition for social security taxes. (Income taxes were discussed in a separate section, above.) *Other current transfers made* corresponds in the *1993 SNA*'s full sequence of accounts to line D.7 (uses) and to line D.62 (social benefits other than social benefits in kind). As these transfers relate to households, they are not covered in the IASs.

Gross Disposable Income (Households)

52. The concept in the *Guide* is intended to correspond in the *1993 SNA*'s full sequence of accounts to line B.6 in the Secondary Distribution of Income Account (gross of any consumption of fixed capital).

Balance Sheet

Assets, Liabilities, and Net Worth

53. In the *1993 SNA,* economic assets are stores of value over which ownership rights are enforced by institutional units, individually or collectively, and from which economic benefits[9] may be derived by their owners by holding or using them over a period of time. In the *1993 SNA,* financial assets differ from other assets in that there is nearly always a counterpart liability on the part of another institutional unit.[10] Assets and counterpart liabilities that meet the definition are recognized on balance sheet.

54. In terms of specific assets and liabilities identified, the *Guide* is very close to the *1993 SNA,* differing only in the presentation of capital. The concept of capital and reserves in the *Guide* is the residual after taking account of all assets and liabilities, and thus is a wider concept than equity and other shares in the *1993 SNA,* as it also includes the *1993 SNA*'s concept of net worth (total assets less total liabilities).

---

[9]The economic benefits of financial assets can include primary incomes derived from the use of the asset and the possibility of holding gains.

[10]In the *1993 SNA,* by convention, monetary gold and SDRs are financial assets, although there is no counterpart liability.

55. IASB Framework, paragraph 49 defines an asset as a resource controlled by an enterprise as a result of past events and from which future economic benefits are expected to flow to the enterprise. It defines a liability as a present obligation of the enterprise arising from past events, the settlement of which is expected to result in an outflow from the enterprise of resources embodying economic benefits. The definition of financial assets and liabilities in IAS 32.5 [IAS 32.11] provides an overview of the categorization of financial assets and liabilities. Financial assets comprise (1) cash; (2) a contractual right to receive cash or other financial instruments from another enterprise, or to exchange financial instruments with another enterprise under conditions that are potentially favorable; (3) a contract that may be settled in the entity's own equity instruments; and (4) an equity instrument of another enterprise. Financial liabilities comprise contractual obligations (1) to deliver cash or another financial asset to another enterprise or (2) to exchange financial instruments with another enterprise under conditions that are potentially unfavorable. Equity is defined as the residual interest in the assets of the enterprise after deducting all of its liabilities.

56. There are potential differences between the *Guide* and the IASs as to what is deemed to be an asset or a liability. For example, unlike the *Guide,* IASs consider that unpatented know-how may meet the definition of an asset if, by keeping such knowledge secret, the enterprise controls the benefits that are expected to flow from it (IASB Framework, paragraph 57). Similarly, if an enterprise as a matter of policy rectifies products after the warranty period has expired, the expected costs are liabilities (IASB Framework, paragraph 60). However, under IASs, on-balance-sheet recognition also depends on whether the value of the asset or liability can be measured reliably (IASB Framework, paragraphs 89 and 91). This requirement for reliable valuation brings the IASs definitions of on-balance-sheet recognition of assets and liabilities close to the *Guide*'s.

57. In the IASs, the presentation of assets and liabilities is less prescriptive and more dependent on the activity of the individual enterprise than in the *Guide,* and it is different from that in the *1993 SNA.* Moreover, the IASs' presentation of instruments varies between the asset and liability sides of the balance sheet, and the focus is more on the liquidity of the enterprise, which differs from the emphasis in the *Guide* and in the *1993 SNA.*

Nonfinancial Assets

58. Line 15 in Table 4.1, line 2 in Table 4.2, line 14 in Table 4.3, and line 8 in Table 4.4 of the *Guide* correspond in the *1993 SNA*'s full sequence of accounts to nonfinancial assets (AN) in the balance sheet (excluding purchased goodwill, which is part of AN.22).

59. These lines from the *Guide* are closely equivalent to the sum of items identified in IAS 1.66 as (1) property, plant, and equipment; (2) inventories; and (3) intangible assets.

60. The definition of nonfinancial produced assets adopted in the *Guide* is in line with that in IAS 16.6, which defines property, plant, and equipment to include tangible assets that (1) are held by an enterprise for use in the production or supply of goods or services, for rental to others, or for administration purposes; and (2) are expected to be used during more than one period. Excluded from the scope of the IASs are (1) forests and similar regenerative natural resources, which are only classified as an asset in the *Guide* if they are cultivated assets; and (2) mineral rights, the exploration for and the extraction of minerals, oil, natural gas, and similar nonregenerative resources (IAS 16.2), because these activities are so specialized that they give rise to accounting issues that may need to be dealt with in different ways (IAS 38.6).

61. Inventories in the *Guide* are defined consistently with IAS 2, where they include assets that are (1) held for sale in the ordinary course of business, (2) in the process of production for such sale, or (3) in the form of materials or supplies to be consumed in the production process or in the rendering of services (IAS 2.4).

62. Intangibles are defined in IAS 38 as identifiable nonmonetary assets without physical substance held for use in the production or supply of goods or services for rental to others or for administrative purposes (IAS 38.7). This definition is broadly consistent with the one used in the *Guide* but, as noted above, could be interpreted more widely to include "assets," such as unpatented know-how, when the value of the benefits arising from these "assets" can be reliably measured. Intangibles do not include goodwill (IAS 38.10), which is recognized as an asset in IASs when the cost of acquisition exceeds the acquirer's interest in the fair value of the assets and liabilities acquired as of the date of transaction (IAS 22.41). The *Guide* does not recognize goodwill as an asset.

Nonfinancial Produced Assets

63. Line 15 in Table 4.3 of the *Guide* corresponds in the *1993 SNA*'s full sequence of accounts to nonfinancial produced assets (AN.1) in the balance sheet. This line also corresponds to the sum of items identified in IAS 1.66 as property, plant, and equipment that is produced (that is, excluding land (IAS 2)), such as inventories (IAS 16) and that part of intangible assets (IAS 38) that is produced, such as computer software and valuables.

Nonfinancial Produced Fixed Assets

64. Line 15(i) in Table 4.3 of the *Guide* corresponds in the *1993 SNA*'s full sequence of accounts to nonfinancial produced fixed assets (AN.11) in the balance sheet.

65. In the IASs, produced fixed assets are recorded under item (a) identified in IAS 1.66 as property, plant, and equipment that is produced (that is, excluding land), as well as that part of item (b) intangible assets that are produced, such as computer software.

Inventories

66. Line 15(ii) in Table 4.3 of the *Guide* corresponds in the *1993 SNA*'s full sequence of accounts to inventories (AN.12). In the IASs, this line corresponds to the item (e) identified in IAS 2, paragraph 4 as inventories in the balance sheet.

Nonfinancial Nonproduced Assets

67. Line 16 in Table 4.3 of the *Guide* corresponds in the *1993 SNA*'s full sequence of accounts to nonfinancial nonproduced assets (AN.2) in the balance sheet. In the IASs, this line closely corresponds to that nonproduced part of the item (a) identified in IAS 1.66 as property, plant, and equipment—that is, land—and intangible assets that are nonproduced, such as goodwill, patents, leases, and other transferable contracts relating to nonfinancial assets (IAS 38). In the IASs, the value of nonpatented know-how can also be included, if it can be measured reliably.

Residential and Commercial Real Estate

68. Residential and commercial real estate, which is reflected in line 9 in Table 4.4 of the *Guide,* is not explicitly identified either in the *1993 SNA* or in the IASs. Nonetheless, in the *1993 SNA,* dwellings and other buildings and structures are described in paragraphs 10.69–10.71 and included within nonfinancial produced assets (AN.1), while land is described in paragraphs 10.59 and 10.60 and included within nonfinancial nonproduced assets (AN.2) in the balance sheet. In the IASs, real estate is included within the item (a) identified in IAS 1.66 as property, plant, and equipment (IAS 16.35).

Financial Assets

69. Line 16 in Table 4.1, line 3 in Table 4.2, line 17 in Table 4.3, and line 11 in Table 4.4 of the *Guide* correspond in the *1993 SNA*'s full sequence of accounts to financial assets (AF) in the balance sheet.[11]

70. In the IASs, there is a need to distinguish between deposit takers and other corporate entities. For deposit takers, IAS 30 sets out the assets that should be separately disclosed in their financial statements. These include cash and balances with the central bank; treasury bills and other bills eligible for rediscounting with the central bank; government and other securities held for dealing purposes; placements with, and loans and advances to, other banks; other money market placements; loans and advances to customers; government and other securities held for dealing purposes; and investment securities (IAS 30.19). IASs are clear that financial statements should include, but not be limited to, these items. For instance, in the list of instruments in IAS 30 no reference is made to financial derivatives, which under IAS 39 should be recognized on balance sheet at fair value (IASs 39.10 and 39.27) [IAS 39.9], except for derivatives that are designated and effective hedging

[11]To strictly conform with the *Guide,* interest should not accrue on nonperforming assets. However, it is proposed in Chapter 4 that if loan data are available for deposit takers only inclusive of such interest, the amount of accrued interest on nonperforming loans be reported and included together with specific provisions for loan losses. In principle, the same approach should be taken for other assets.

instruments. Moreover, in some instances IAS 1 is relevant for the presentation of the accounts of deposit takers, such as in the case of tax assets (see immediately below). With these exceptions, although presented differently, the definition of the items and the coverage of financial assets in the IASs are close to the *Guide.*

71. With regard to nonbank entities, IAS 1.66 presets assets on a liquidity basis, in the same manner as for deposit takers. While IASs do not prescribe the order or format in which items are to be presented, these standards do regard each of the items presented as sufficiently different in nature or function so as to deserve separate presentation on the balance sheet, along with subtotals necessary to present fairly the enterprise's financial position. The coverage of assets is again close to that of the *Guide,* but the classification and definition of items used are quite different. The financial assets identified by IAS 1.66 are item (g) cash and cash equivalents—cash on hand, demand deposits, and short-term, highly liquid investments that are readily convertible to cash and that are subject to an insignificant risk of change in value (IAS 7.6); item (f) trade and other receivables—assets created by the entity providing money, goods, or services directly to a debtor; item (d) investments accounted for using the equity method—investments in associates (IAS 28) and unconsolidated subsidiaries (IAS 27.30); related tax assets (IAS 12.5), which are not considered assets in the *Guide* except to the extent that taxes have been overpaid and a refund is owed; and item (c) other financial assets, which include securities.

Liabilities

72. Line 23 in Table 4.1, line 11 in Table 4.2, line 24 in Table 4.3, and line 17 in Table 4.4 of the *Guide* correspond in the *1993 SNA*'s full sequence of accounts to liabilities (AF) in the balance sheet.

73. As with assets, in the IASs it is necessary to distinguish deposit takers from other corporate entities. IAS 30.19 sets out the liabilities that should be reported by deposit takers in their financial statements as follows: (1) deposits from other banks, (2) other money market deposits, (3) amounts owed to other depositors, (4) certificates of deposit, (5) promissory notes and other liabilities evidenced by paper, and (6) other borrowed funds. As with assets, the list should include, but not be limited to, these items.

74. In regard to other corporate entries, IAS 1.66 presents liabilities as follows: item (h) trade and other payables (short-term liabilities); item (i) tax liabilities, which are recognized in the *Guide* if unpaid tax amounts are actually owed to the general government; item (j) provisions; and item (k) noncurrent interest-bearing liabilities (long-term liabilities). The latter are recognized when an enterprise has a present obligation as a result of a past event, it is probable that an outflow of resources will be required to settle the obligation, and a reliable estimate can be made of the amount of the obligation. These provisions include such items as product warranties and cleanup costs for environmental damage (IAS 37.19). The *Guide* prefers that provisions for estimated costs related to product warranties be included as a cost of sales and as a general reserve in capital. As with assets, the IASs do not prescribe the order or format in which items are to be presented but regard the items listed as sufficiently different in nature or function so as to deserve separate presentation on the balance sheet, along with subtotals as necessary, to present fairly the enterprise's financial position.

Currency and Deposits

75. On the asset side, line 17 in Table 4.1, line 4 in Table 4.2, line 18 in Table 4.3, and line 12 in Table 4.4 of the *Guide* correspond in the *1993 SNA*'s full sequence of accounts to financial assets (AF.2) in the balance sheet. On the liability side, line 24 in Table 4.1 and line 12 in Table 4.2 of the *Guide* correspond in the *1993 SNA*'s full sequence of accounts to liabilities (AF.2) in the balance sheet.

76. In the IASs, for deposit takers, the closest equivalent to assets is the sum of items identified as cash and balances with the central bank and placements with other banks (IASs 30.19 and 30.21). For other sectors, the closest equivalent is cash (cash on hand and demand deposits) and, perhaps, some element of cash equivalents (short-term highly liquid investments (IAS 7.6)). In IAS 7.8, overdrafts can be recorded as part of cash and cash equivalents rather than as loans, as recommended in the *Guide.*

77. In the IASs, deposit takers' currency and deposits liabilities are equal to the sum of deposits from other banks and amounts owed to other depositors (IAS 30.19).

Loans

78. On the asset side, line 18(i) in Table 4.1 and line 5 in Table 4.2 of the *Guide* correspond in the *1993 SNA*'s full sequence of accounts to loans (AF.4) in the balance sheet. Similarly, on the liability side, line 25 in Table 4.1, line 13 in Table 4.2, line 25 in Table 4.3, and line 18 in Table 4.4 of the *Guide* correspond in the *1993 SNA*'s full sequence of accounts to loans (AF.4) in the balance sheet.

79. In the IASs, for deposit takers, on the asset side, loans most closely equate to the sum of loans and advances to customers and loans and advances to other banks (other than the central bank) (IAS 30.19). The latter item can be easily identified as placements with other banks should be separately identified (IAS 30.21) and excluded from the item "placements with, and loans and advances to, other banks" to provide information on loans. On the liability side, loans would be a subitem within other borrowed funds. In the IASs, specific and general provisions for loan losses can be deducted from the carrying amount of the appropriate category of loans (IAS 30.45). However, deposit takers should disclose the aggregate amount of provisions for loan losses at the balance sheet date (IAS 30.43c). Loans are defined in IAS 39.10 [39.9].

80. For other corporate entities, on the asset side, loans will be a subitem of other financial assets. On the liability side, overdrafts can be included within cash and cash equivalents (IAS 7.8), while loans are also to be included within noncurrent interest-bearing liabilities (IAS 1.66).

81. On two specific issues, the treatment of securities repurchase agreements (repos) in the IASs is consistent with the collateralized loan approach in the *Guide* (IAS 39.10 and IASs 39.35–39.39) [IAS 39. AG.51]. Moreover, the IASs' treatment of financial leases is substantially the same as for loans (IAS 17) and is consistent with the classification of loans in the *Guide.*

Interbank Loans

82. Line 18(i.i) in Table 4.1 of the *Guide* corresponds in the *1993 SNA*'s full sequence of accounts to loans to deposit takers (AF.4 S.122) in the balance sheet.

83. In the IASs, this line is equal to loans and advances to other banks and excludes placements with other banks (IAS 30.19 and 30.21). In other words, compared with the item in IAS 30.19, placements with other banks should be separately identified (IAS 30.21) and excluded from the item "placements with, and loans and advances to, other banks" to provide information on loans.

Noninterbank Loans

84. Line 18(i.ii) in Table 4.1 of the *Guide* corresponds in the *1993 SNA*'s full sequence of accounts to loans (AF.4) less loans to deposit takers (AF.4 S.122) in the balance sheet. In the IASs, this line is equal to loans and advances to customers (IAS 30.19).

Sectoral and Geographical Distribution of Loans

85. Line 18(i) in Table 4.1 of the *Guide* can be attributed by institutional sector. In the *1993 SNA*'s full sequence of accounts, this sectoral detail corresponds to items AF.4 S.1–AF.4 S.2.

86. The *1993 SNA* does not specify the geographical location of the debtor, except for the resident and nonresident distinction.

87. IAS 14 establishes principles for reporting financial information by business and geographic segment. Business segments are determined by the type of products or services produced (IAS 14.9) and so could be considered broadly similar to the industrial classification of lending—one of the possibilities provided in the *Guide.* The geographic segment is based on providing goods and services within a particular economic environment and could be a single country, a group of two or more countries, or a region within a country (IAS 14.9). A country attribution would facilitate the regional attribution of lending described in the *Guide.* Moreover, sectoral and geographic analyses of concentrations of credit risk should be disclosed in accordance with IAS 30.40–30.41 and IASs 32.74–32.76 [IAS 32.83–32.85]. IAS 30.41 suggests that geographical areas may comprise individual countries or groups of countries, or regions within a country; customer disclosures may deal with sectors such as governments, public authorities, and commercial and business enterprises.

Specific Provisions for Loan Losses

88. As with nonperforming loans (NPLs), the *1993 SNA* does not have a concept equivalent to specific provisions (line 18(ii) in Table 4.1) of the *Guide.* Loan values are not adjusted for provisions in the *1993 SNA*. Therefore, until the loans are written off, provisions for impaired assets are implicitly and indistinguishably included as part of net worth (B.90) in the *1993 SNA*'s full sequence of accounts.

89. In IAS 30.43c, the aggregate amount of the provision for losses on loans and advances by banks at the balance sheet date should be disclosed, so that users of financial statements know the impact that losses on loans and advances have on deposit takers' financial positions (IAS 30.47). In contrast to the *Guide,* both specific and general loan loss provisions are included in the disclosure (IAS 30.45). (The difference arises because in the *Guide,* the FSI of *loans less provisions* nets specific provisions only, whereas in the IASs both specific and general provisions are netted against the value of loans.)

Debt Securities

90. On the asset side, line 19 in Table 4.1, line 6 in Table 4.2, line 19 in Table 4.3, and line 13 in Table 4.4 of the *Guide* correspond in the *1993 SNA*'s full sequence of accounts to securities other than shares (AF.3) in the balance sheet. Similarly, on the liability side, line 26 in Table 4.1, line 14 in Table 4.2, and line 26 in Table 4.3 of the *Guide* correspond to securities other than shares (AF.3) in the balance sheet in the *1993 SNA.*

91. For deposit takers, on the asset side, line 19 in Table 4.1 of the *Guide* corresponds to the sum of treasury bills and other bills eligible for discount at the central bank, other money market placements, the debt securities element of government and other securities for dealing purposes, and investment securities (IAS 30.19).[12] Separate identification of debt securities from within these latter two items may not be provided in the main financial statements, but in accordance with IAS 32.60(c) [IAS 32.71(c)], supplementary information should indicate which of the enterprise's financial assets are not exposed to interest rate risk, such as some investments in equity securities. This supplementary information, used in conjunction with items on government and other securities for dealing purposes as well as investment securities, may permit the identification of holdings of debt securities, depending on the level of detail provided in the published accounts (see also IAS 32.64) [IAS 32.74].

92. For deposit takers, on the liability side, line 26 in Table 4.1 of the *Guide* corresponds to the sum of certificates of deposit, other money market deposits, promissory notes, and other liabilities evidenced by paper (IAS 30.19), and the debt securities element of "other borrowed funds."

93. For other corporate entities, on the asset side, debt securities correspond to the debt securities element of cash equivalents and financial assets not otherwise identified. Unless further subclassification is required, debt securities might not be identifiable in the IASs.

Insurance Technical Reserves

94. On the assets side, line 8 in Table 4.2 of the *Guide* corresponds in the *1993 SNA*'s full sequence of accounts to AF.6 in the balance sheet. Similarly, on the liability side, line 15 in Table 4.2 of the *Guide* corresponds to AF.6 in the balance sheet in the *1993 SNA.* IASs do not have disclosure requirements specific to insurance technical reserves. However, in accordance with IAS 1.67, additional items should be presented on the balance sheet, when such a presentation is necessary to fairly represent the enterprise's financial position. IFRS 4 concerns accounting for rights and obligations arising under insurance contracts.

Trade Credit

95. On the asset side, line 21 in Table 4.3 of the *Guide* corresponds in the *1993 SNA*'s full sequence of accounts to trade credit and advances (AF.81) in the balance sheet. Similarly, on the liability side, line 27 in Table 4.3 of the *Guide* corresponds to AF.81 in the balance sheet in the *1993 SNA.*

[12]In accordance with IAS 32. A20–21 [IAS 32.18a], a preferred share that provides for redemption for a fixed or determinable amount on a fixed or determinable future date or at the option of the holder meets the definition of a debt security if the issuer has an obligation to transfer financial assets to the holder of the preferred share. This is consistent with the *Guide*'s definition of a debt instrument as being one on which future payments of interest and/or principal are required.

96. In the IASs, on the asset side, line 21 in Table 4.3 of the *Guide* corresponds most closely to trade and other receivables and, line 27 on the liabilities side, to trade and other payables (IAS 1.66).

Shares and Other Equity

97. On the asset side, line 20 in Table 4.1, line 7 in Table 4.2, line 20 in Table 4.3, and line 14 in Table 4.4 of the *Guide* correspond in the *1993 SNA*'s full sequence of accounts to AF.5 in the balance sheet. However, in practice there may be a difference, depending on how equity investments in associates and unconsolidated subsidiaries are valued. This issue is briefly discussed in terms of foreign affiliates in paragraph 13.74 of the *1993 SNA*.

98. In the IASs, for deposit takers, line 20 in Table 4.1 of the *Guide* corresponds to the equity securities element of government and other securities held for dealing purposes and to investment securities (IAS 30.19). Separate identification of equity securities from within these two items may not be provided in the main financial statements, but in accordance with IAS 32.60(c) [IAS 32.71(c)], supplementary information should indicate which of the enterprise's financial assets are not [directly] exposed to interest rate risk, such as some investments in equity securities. For nonbank corporations, equity securities are included within investments accounted for using the equity method and other financial assets (IAS 1.66). Accounting by the equity method refers to investments in associates (IAS 28.6) and unconsolidated subsidiaries (IAS 27.30), essentially valuing such investments initially at cost and thereafter at the investor's share of net assets of the investee (IAS 28.3).

Financial Derivatives

99. On the asset side, line 21 in Table 4.1, line 9 in Table 4.2, line 22 in Table 4.3, and line 15 in Table 4.4 of the *Guide* correspond in the *1993 SNA*'s full sequence of accounts to financial derivatives (AF.7) in the balance sheet. On the liabilities side, line 29 in Table 4.1, line 18 in Table 4.2, line 30 in Table 4.3, and line 21 in Table 4.4 of the *Guide* correspond to AF.7 in the balance sheet in the *1993 SNA*.[13]

100. In IAS 39.10 [IAS 39.9], financial derivatives are defined, and with the exception of commodity derivatives (see below), this definition is consistent with that in the *Guide* (see also IASs 32.9–32.11). IAS 39.10 [IAS 39.9] makes it clear that financial derivatives are to be recognized as financial instruments and recorded at fair value in profit and loss, except when they are designated and effective hedging instruments. While the IASs do not make specific recommendations for the separate identification of positions in financial derivatives, in accordance with IAS 39.27 [IAS 39.14], financial derivatives are recognized on the balance sheet.[14] Regarding commodity derivatives, whereas the *Guide* includes such derivative contracts within its definition, in the IASs there is some flexibility in that contracts specifically settled in cash according to a formula are classified as financial derivatives, but not otherwise. This is because the IASs do not recognize as financial instruments contracts to deliver goods and services (IASs 32 A9–17) [IASs 32 AG.20–24].

Other Assets

101. Line 22 in Table 4.1, line 10 in Table 4.2, line 23 in Table 4.3, and line 16 in Table 4.4 of the *Guide* correspond in the *1993 SNA*'s full sequence of accounts to the sum of insurance technical reserves (AF.6) and other accounts receivable (AF.8) (excluding trade credits (AF.81) for nonfinancial corporations, as it is separately identified in the *Guide*) in the balance sheet.

102. In the IASs, these lines most closely correspond to the trade and other receivables (IASs 1.66 and 39.10) [IAS 39 AG.26]—although the trade credit element for nonfinancial corporations is separately identified in the *Guide*—and to tax assets (IAS 1.66). However, in contrast to the *Guide,* when the future economic benefit is the receipt of goods or services rather than the right to receive cash or another financial asset, such benefits are not recognized as a financial asset (IAS 32.12) [IAS 32 AG.11]. Nonetheless, if taxes paid exceed the amounts due for the period, the excess should be regarded as an asset (IAS 12.12). Under certain circumstances, in contrast to the *Guide,* the IASs recognize deferred tax assets (IAS 12.24)—essentially

[13]IMF (2001b).

[14]Under IAS 39.23, among other things, if an instrument with an embedded derivative is not valued at fair value and changes in that value are reported in net profit and loss, the embedded derivative should be separately recognized. In the *Guide,* there are no circumstances under which an embedded derivative is separately identified.

when it is probable that taxable profits will be available against which tax benefits arising from past losses can be utilized. With regard to obligations under insurance contracts, IAS 32 explicitly excludes them from financial instruments (IAS 32.1) except for certain reinsurance and investment contracts issued by insurance companies (IAS 32.3). IAS 38 notes that contracts involving insurance companies are specialized and give rise to accounting issues that need to be dealt with in a different way (IAS 38.6).[15]

Other Liabilities

103. Line 27 in Table 4.1, line 16 in Table 4.2, line 28 in Table 4.3, and line 19 in Table 4.4 of the *Guide* correspond in the *1993 SNA*'s full sequence of accounts to other accounts payable (AF.8) (excluding trade credits (AF.81) for nonfinancial corporations as they are separately identified elsewhere) and possibly insurance technical reserves (AF.6) (except for such liabilities of other financial institutions, which are separately identified elsewhere) in the balance sheet. In the IASs, these lines most closely correspond with the trade credit and other payables (excluding those elements included under other items) and with tax liabilities to the extent that they are amounts owed on profits already earned (IAS 12.5).

Debt

104. Line 28 in Table 4.1, line 17 in Table 4.2, line 29 in Table 4.3, and line 20 in Table 4.4 of the *Guide* correspond in the *1993 SNA*'s full sequence of accounts to the sum of liabilities in the form of deposits (AF.2), securities other than shares (AF.3), loans (AF.4), liabilities for insurance technical reserves (AF.6), and other accounts payable (AF.8; see also IMF, 2000b) in the balance sheet.

105. In the IASs, for deposit takers, debt is the sum of deposits from other banks, other money market deposits, amounts owed to other depositors, certificates of deposit, promissory notes and other liabilities evidenced by paper, other borrowed funds (IAS 30.19), and tax liabilities (IAS 1.66), to the extent that they are amounts accrued and unpaid on profits already earned. For other corporate entities, debt is the sum of trade and other payables, noncurrent interest-bearing liabilities, and tax liabilities, to the extent that they are amounts accrued and unpaid on profits already earned (IAS 1.66).

Capital and Reserves

106. Line 30 in Table 4.1, line 19 in Table 4.2, line 31 in Table 4.3, and line 22 in Table 4.4 of the *Guide* closely correspond in the *1993 SNA*'s full sequence of accounts to the sum of shares and other equity (AF.5) and net worth (B.90) in the balance sheet. There is a difference in that in the *Guide,* unlike in the *1993 SNA,* the level of capital and reserves is affected by specific provisions against loans and, where applicable, other assets and by the exclusion of purchased goodwill. Moreover, to avoid double counting of deposit takers' capital and reserves at the sector level, intrasector equity investments are excluded. In addition, a difference may arise from the different valuation approaches used to value equity investments in domestic associates and subsidiaries between the *Guide* and the *1993 SNA.* In the *Guide,* the subcategorization of capital and reserves for deposit takers and nonfinancial corporations is derived from the IMF's *MFSM* (IMF, 2000a, p. 34), and not the *1993 SNA.* However, beyond the differences with the *1993 SNA* mentioned above, there are differences in coverage between the *Guide* and the *MFSM* at the subcategorization level. For example, in contrast to the *MFSM,* the *Guide* excludes general provisions from net income (and thus potentially from retained earnings) and includes them in capital and reserves.

107. In the IASs, capital and reserves most closely correspond in concept to total equity, which is the difference between assets and liabilities (and, as seen above, there are some differences in coverage of these instruments between the *Guide* and the IASs). Equity is the sum of issued capital, retained earnings, reserves representing appropriations of retained earnings, and reserves representing capital maintenance adjustments (IASB Framework, paragraph 65). Under IAS 1.74, information on issued capital should be disclosed. Capital maintenance adjustments are distinguished between financial and physical capital maintenance and are equivalent to holdings gains and losses on financial instruments that are not recorded in the income statement. The minority interest that may arise from consolidating a subsidiary is that part of the net assets of a subsidiary

[15]IFRS 4, which amends IAS 32 and IAS 38, concerns financial reporting for insurance contracts by any entity that issues such contracts. It allows the continuation of existing accounting practices until the IASB completes the second phase of its project on insurance contracts.

attributable to interests that are not owned directly or indirectly through subsidiaries by the parent (IAS 27.6). In accordance with IAS 27, Consolidated Financial Statements and Accounting for Investments in Subsidiaries, a financial instrument classified as an equity instrument by a subsidiary is eliminated on consolidation when held by the parent or presented by the parent in the consolidated balance sheet as a minority interest separate from the equity of its own shareholders. Hence, minority interest is part of capital and reserves.

Selected Memorandum Series

Liquid Assets

108. The *Guide*'s concept of liquid assets—as assets that are readily available to an entity to meet a demand for cash—does not have an equivalent in the *1993 SNA*. Therefore, lines 39 and 40 in Table 4.1, and lines 41 and 42 in Table A3.4 of the *Guide* do not conceptually correspond to any *1993 SNA* lines. Nonetheless, from the *1993 SNA*'s full sequence of accounts, an approximation of the core measure of liquid assets is possible by summing currency (AF.21), transferable deposits (AF.22), (very) short-term loans (AF.41), and other accounts receivable (AF.8). Adding holdings of short-term (less than one year maturity) securities other than shares (AF.31) and perhaps holdings for shares and other equity (AF.5) provides an approximation of the wider measure. These measures of liquid assets will differ from the *Guide* in that certain assets are not covered (nontransferable deposits of less than three months' maturity and long-term holdings of securities traded on liquid markets) and in that several assets that are covered should be excluded (nontradable short-term securities other than shares and other nontradable assets of more than three months' maturity). For deposit takers, the *Guide* excludes from liquid assets any nontraded claims on other deposit takers.

109. The IASs focus more closely on liquidity than does the *1993 SNA*. For deposit takers, from IAS 30.19 the following items equate most closely to liquid assets in line 40 in Table 4.1 of the *Guide:* cash and balances at the central bank, treasury bills and other bills eligible for rediscounting with the central bank, government and other securities held for dealing purposes, and market placements excluding those with other banks. However, any money market placements of more than three months' maturity that cannot readily be converted into cash should be excluded. On the other hand, investment securities that are traded on liquid markets should be included. Moreover, IASs 30.30–30.39 require the disclosure of a breakdown of assets (and liabilities) into relevant maturity groupings based on the remaining period at the balance sheet date until the contractual maturity date—five maturity bands are suggested, the first two of which include assets with remaining maturities of three months or less.

110. For nonfinancial corporations, the closest equivalent to the concept of liquid assets used in the *Guide* is cash and cash equivalents—assets held for the purpose of meeting short-term cash commitments rather than for investment or other purposes (IAS 7.7). For an investment to qualify as a cash equivalent it must be readily convertible to a known amount of cash and be subject to an insignificant risk of change in value. Therefore, an investment normally qualifies as a cash equivalent only when it has a short maturity of, say, three months or less from the date of acquisition (IASs 7.6 and 7.7). Equity investments are excluded unless they are in substance cash equivalents (IAS 7.7). However, bank borrowings in the form of overdrafts that are repayable on demand can be included (deducted) as a component of cash and cash equivalents (IAS 7.8)—in contrast with the *Guide,* which classifies overdrafts as a liability item. Cash and cash equivalents, together with trade receivables with three months or less to maturity, are close in concept to the core measure of liquid assets in the *Guide.* Such instruments are covered within other financial assets (IAS 1.66).

Short-Term Liabilities

111. The *Guide*'s definition of what is short term and its definition of liabilities are the same as in the *1993 SNA*. However, while in the *1993 SNA*'s full sequence of accounts, short-term liabilities in the form of securities other than shares (AF.31) and loans (AF.41) are identified, this is not the case for deposits, other accounts payable, and financial derivatives.

112. The IASs have a similar, but not identical, over- and under-one year maturity distinction to that used in the *Guide* (IAS 1.60 and the glossary in IASB [2002]), unless the enterprise's operating cycle is different from a one year—in which case the boundary with long term is different. Disclosure of information on current liabilities in accordance with IAS 1.60 provides a measure of short-term liabilities that is broadly consistent with the *Guide*'s definition. Moreover, a bank should disclose a breakdown of liabilities (and assets) into relevant maturity groupings based on the remaining maturity at the balance sheet date until the contractual maturity date, in accordance with IAS 30.30. As for assets, IAS 30.33 suggests distinguishing financial liabilities into five maturity groupings.

Nonperforming Loans

113. As with liquid assets, the *1993 SNA* does not have a concept corresponding to nonperforming loans. In the *1993 SNA*'s full sequence of accounts, such loans are indistinguishably included as part of loans (AF.4). Thus, the stock of NPLs cannot be derived from the *1993 SNA*.

114. IAS 39.110 [IAS 39.58–39.70] provides guidance on identifying assets that may be impaired that is broadly consistent with the approach in the *Guide*. Whereas the *Guide* places more emphasis on past due payments exceeding a time limit, guidance on impairment in IAS 39 covers both actual breaches of contract (although no overdue date is recommended) and other evidence of impairment. In addition, IAS 30.43 states that a bank should disclose (a) the accounting basis used to determine the carrying amount of uncollectible loans and advances, (b) details of changes in any allowance account for impairment allowances, (c) the aggregate amount of any allowance account for impairment losses at the balance sheet date, and (d) the aggregate amount included in the balance sheet for loans and advances on which interest is not being accrued.[16] The basis used to determine when to stop accruing interest may vary across enterprises and may differ from the 90-day guidelines suggested in the *Guide*.

Foreign-Currency-Denominated Assets and Liabilities

115. The *1993 SNA* does not define foreign currency assets and liabilities (although this information may be available to economic statisticians from the source data used to construct the national accounts).

116. IAS 32.43(i) [IAS 32.52(a)(i)] requires disclosure of information that assists users of financial statements in assessing the extent of risks associated with, among other things, currency risk—the risk that the value of financial instruments will fluctuate due to changes in foreign exchange rates. However, the standards do not prescribe either the format or level of detail of the information to be disclosed (IASs 32.44–32.45) [32.51–32.52].

Net Open Position in Foreign Exchange

117. The *1993 SNA* does not provide any equivalent concept. Under IAS 30.40, a bank should disclose the amount of any significant net foreign currency exposures.

Large Exposures

118. The *1993 SNA* does not have a concept of large exposures because it is concerned with aggregate economic statistics rather than with the credit risks faced by individual institutional units. Under IAS 30.40, a bank should disclose any significant concentration of its assets, liabilities, and off-balance-sheet items. Such disclosures should be made using breakdowns by geographical areas, customer or industry groups, or other concentration of risk that are appropriate in the circumstances of the bank. IAS 32.74 [IAS 32.83] notes that identification of significant concentrations is a matter of judgment by management, taking into account the circumstances of the enterprise and its debtors. Disclosure of concentrations of credit risk includes a description of the shared characteristic that identifies each concentration and the amount of the maximum credit risk exposure associated with all recognized and unrecognized financial assets sharing that characteristic (IAS 32.76) [IAS 32.85].

Arrears

119. In the *1993 SNA*'s full sequence of accounts, there is no separate identification of arrears (line 70 in Table A3.2), although such an item can be included as memorandum item (*1993 SNA*, 11.101). Arrears are not discussed in the IASs.

[16]The IAS 39 recommends continuing accrual of interest on impaired loans at the discount rate used to revalue an impaired asset (IAS 39.116) [IAS 39.63], whereas IAS 30 discusses loans on which interest has stopped accruing.

Appendix V. Numerical Examples

Introduction

1. This appendix provides a series of numerical examples to illustrate key compilation and methodological concepts described in the *Guide* and to provide guidance on how to calculate FSIs. The examples are grouped together in the following three sections.

Part 1: A **base data set** of examples consisting of income and expense and balance sheet statements, as an illustration of how the agreed FSIs can be calculated.

Part 2: Examples illustrating the **accounting rules** for (1) gains and losses on financial instruments and (2) interest income on nonperforming loans.

Part 3: Examples illustrating **consolidation and associated sector-level issues,** including (1) an extended base data set, (2) examples illustrating the sector-wide consolidation of capital, and (3) examples illustrating accounting for goodwill in sector-wide capital.

While the focus of these examples is on the deposit-taking sector, they can also apply to other corporate sectors. This appendix therefore includes in addition the following section:

Part 4: A discussion of **calculating FSIs for nonfinancial corporations.**

Part 1. Base Data Set

Background

2. To illustrate the principles involved, a base data set for income and expense, balance sheet, and associated memorandum items is provided below, which is used to calculate FSIs. The data set provided is consistent with the guidance in Chapter 4 and Chapter 6. Nonetheless, some simplifying assumptions are made to put aside the consolidation issues (and the additional data needs) relating to the interbank positions and flows that are described in Chapter 5. These simplifying assumptions are relaxed in the later examples on consolidation in Part 3.

The Basic Data Set of Financial Accounts

3. In this example, the economy has three deposit takers. There are no financial relations among them, nor do they have foreign branches or investments in foreign subsidiaries and associates.[1] End-period financial statements (income and balance sheet accounts) for the three resident deposit takers are presented in Tables A5.1 and A5.2, together with the aggregated income and balance sheet statements.

4. All three deposit takers extend loans to residents of the local economy, but the sectoral allocation differs. Each deposit taker also extends some loans to nonresidents; a geographical distribution is reported as an addendum to the balance sheet. Deposits from (nonbank) residents in the local economy are the main form of funding, but deposit takers 2 and 3 have also raised some significant amounts through the issuance of debt securities. Financial derivative instruments are used by all three deposit takers but are limited to interest rate swaps. On the income and expense side, deposit taker 1's performance is weaker than the other deposit takers', reporting zero net income for the period.

Computation of a Base Data Set of FSIs

5. Using the guidance in Chapter 6 and the base data set of financial accounts, Table A5.3 presents the agreed FSIs at the sector level and, for illustrative

[1] As noted earlier, these assumptions are unlikely to hold in practice as deposit takers are expected to have financial relations with other deposit takers in the reporting population.

Table A5.1. Income and Expense Statements: Deposit Takers—Aggregated Data[1]
(In millions of U.S. dollars; unless otherwise stated)

	Deposit Taker 1 A	Deposit Taker 2 B	Deposit Taker 3 C	Aggregation A + B + C
1. Interest income	400	800	300	1,500
(i) Gross interest income	400	800	300	1,500
(ii) Less provisions for accrued interest on nonperforming assets	—	—	—	—
2. Interest expense	100	140	100	340
3. *Net interest income (= 1 minus 2)*	*300*	*660*	*200*	*1,160*
4. Noninterest income	250	700	400	1,350
(i) Fees and commissions receivable	110	300	200	610
(ii) Gains or losses on financial instruments	50	100	100	250
(iii) Prorated earnings	50	140	20	210
(iv) Other income	40	160	80	280
5. *Gross income (= 3 plus 4)*	*550*	*1,360*	*600*	*2,510*
6. Noninterest expenses	500	600	150	1,250
(i) Personnel costs	300	300	100	700
(ii) Other expenses	200	300	50	550
7. Provisions (net)	50	80	10	140
(i) Loan loss provisions	50	80	10	140
(ii) Other financial asset provisions	—	—	—	—
8. *Net income (before extraordinary items and taxes) (= 5 minus (6 + 7))*	—	*680*	*440*	*1,120*
9. Extraordinary items	—	—	—	—
10. Income tax	—	272	176	448
11. *Net income after tax (= 8 minus (9 + 10))*	—	*408*	*264*	*672*
12. Dividends payable	—	300	140	440
13. *Retained earnings (= 11 minus 12)*	—	*108*	*124*	*232*

[1]For a description of the line items, refer to Chapter 4.

purposes, for each bank individually. Moreover, where relevant, the value of the numerator and denominator for each FSI is shown. Because of the lack of financial relations among the three resident deposit takers, the sector-level FSIs can be calculated using the aggregated balance sheet and income statement data shown in Tables A5.1 and A5.2, without the need for sector-level consolidation adjustments discussed in Chapter 5. Furthermore, since the deposit takers have no foreign operations, the construction of FSIs on a domestic basis is sufficient for this economy.

Part 2. Accounting Rules

Treatment of Gains and Losses on Financial Instruments in the Income and Expense Statement

6. In the *Guide,* it is recommended that gains and losses on financial instruments that are valued at market or fair value in the balance sheet be included in the income and expense statement in the period in which they arise. Numerical examples are provided below to illustrate the application of the *Guide*'s recommendation and highlight the asymmetries that can arise at the sector level in the absence of consistent reporting of such gains and losses.

Example 1

7. This example, set out in Tables A5.4 and A5.5, illustrates the *Guide*'s approach to recording unrealized gains and losses on traded instruments and highlights the impact over time of adopting a different approach.

8. In this example, deposit takers 1 and 2 purchase a traded financial asset during period 1 at a purchase price of 100. Deposit taker 1 revalues the asset at its market price at the end of each period and records unrealized losses during periods 2 and 3 in the income statement. The asset is sold during period 4, and deposit taker 1 records a gain of 5 during this period. This approach is in line with the *Guide*'s recommendations.

Table A5.2. Balance Sheets: Deposit Takers—Aggregated Data[1]

(In millions of U.S. dollars, unless otherwise stated)

	Deposit Taker 1 A	Deposit Taker 2 B	Deposit Taker 3 C	Aggregation A + B + C
Balance Sheet				
14. **Total assets** (= 15 + 16 = 31)	12,450	18,201	7,450	38,101
15. *Nonfinancial assets*	*500*	*500*	*300*	*1,300*
16. *Financial assets (= 17 through 22)*	*11,950*	*17,701*	*7,150*	*36,801*
17. Currency and deposits	200	200	100	500
18. Loans (after specific provisions)	9,200	13,900	5,350	28,450
(i) Gross loans	9,250	14,400	5,600	29,250
(i.i) Interbank loans	1,000	900	600	2,500
(i.i.i) Resident	—	—	—	—
(i.i.ii) Nonresident	1,000	900	600	2,500
(i.ii) Noninterbank loans	8,250	13,500	5,000	26,750
(i.ii.i) Central bank	—	—	—	—
(i.ii.ii) General government	400	5,000	2,000	7,400
(i.ii.iii) Other financial corporations	500	2,000	—	2,500
(i.ii.iv) Nonfinancial corporations	7,000	2,000	—	9,000
(i.ii.v) Other domestic sectors	350	2,500	2,500	5,350
(i.ii.vi) Nonresidents	—	2,000	500	2,500
(ii) Specific provisions	50	500	250	800
19. Debt securities	2,250	3,000	1,300	6,550
20. Shares and other equity	100	301	200	601
21. Financial derivatives	200	200	200	600
22. Other assets	—	100	—	100
23. *Liabilities (= 28 + 29)*	*11,050*	*16,501*	*6,850*	*34,401*
24. Currency and deposits	10,200	11,700	5,150	27,050
(i) Customer deposits	10,200	11,200	3,650	25,050
(ii) Interbank deposits	—	500	1,500	2,000
(ii.i) Resident	—	—	—	—
(ii.ii) Nonresident	—	500	1,500	2,000
(iii) Other currency and deposits	—	—	—	—
25. Loans	200	300	150	650
26. Debt securities	400	3,000	1,500	4,900
27. Other liabilities	250	801	50	1,101
28. *Debt (= 24 + 25 + 26 + 27)*	*11,050*	*15,801*	*6,850*	*33,701*
29. Financial derivatives	—	700	—	700
30. Capital and reserves	1,400	1,700	600	3,700
(i) Narrow capital	1,160	1,160	500	2,820
31. **Balance sheet total (= 23 + 30 = 14)**	12,450	18,201	7,450	38,101
Memorandum Series				
Other series needed to calculate the agreed FSIs				
Supervisory series				
32. Tier 1 capital	900	1,200	500	2,600
33. Tier 2 capital	300	604	316	1,220
34. Tier 3 capital	—	—	—	—
35. Supervisory deductions	—	—	—	—
36. Total net capital resources (item 32 through item 34 minus item 35)	1,200	1,804	816	3,820
37. Risk-weighted assets	8,500	12,800	4,220	25,520
38. Number of large exposures	3	2	1	6
Series that provide a further analysis of the balance sheet				
39. Liquid assets (core)	1,000	2,500	500	4,000
40. Liquid assets (broad measure)	1,750	2,700	700	5,150
41. Short-term liabilities	6,000	10,050	2,000	18,050
42. Nonperforming loans	93	660	340	1,093
43. Residential real estate loans	350	1,000	2,000	3,350
44. Commercial real estate loans	—	2,000	—	2,000
45. Geographic distribution of loans	See addendum	See addendum	See addendum	See addendum
46. Foreign currency loans	1,000	3,000	600	4,600

Table A5.2 *(concluded)*

	Deposit Taker 1 A	Deposit Taker 2 B	Deposit Taker 3 C	Aggregation A + B + C
47. Foreign currency liabilities	1,200	2,500	1,500	5,200
48. Net open position in equities	100	301	200	601
49. Net open position in foreign currency for on-balance-sheet items	(200)	500	(900)	(600)
Balance-sheet-related series				
50. Total net open position in foreign currency	(200)	500	(900)	(600)
51. Exposures of largest deposit takers to largest entities in the economy	700	500	—	1,200
52. Exposures to affiliated entities and other "connected" counterparties	—	—	—	—
Addendum				
Geographic distribution of loans				
Total loans to nonresidents	1,000	2,900	1,100	5,000
Advanced economies	500	2,000	600	3,100
Regions excluding advanced economies	—	—	—	—
Africa	250	200	—	450
Of which: Sub-Sahara	—	—	—	—
Asia	250	700	500	1,450
Europe	—	—	—	—
Of which: Former Soviet Union, including Russia	—	—	—	—
Middle East	—	—	—	—
Western Hemisphere	—	—	—	—

[1]For a description of the line items, refer to Chapter 4.

Therefore, as can be seen in Table A5.4, lower retained earnings are recorded in the periods 2 and 3 when unrealized losses arise, and a small gain is recorded in period 4, when the asset is sold.

9. In contrast, while deposit taker 2 also revalues the asset at market prices at the end of each period, it records only realized gains (losses) in the income statement. Unrealized gains (losses) are recorded in a valuation adjustment in the capital and reserves account—the counter-entry to the increase in the value of the instrument in the balance sheet. The asset is sold during period 4 at a (cumulative) loss of 25, which lowers retained earnings in that period. As can be seen in Table A5.4, the loss that accumulated over several periods is recognized only by deposit taker 2 in period 4, a period when the value of the instrument actually rose. The losses in the preceding periods were not reflected in income.

10. For deposit taker 2, Table A5.5 describes the impact on selected FSIs of not recording unrealized gains (losses) in the income statement compared with following the *Guide*'s recommendation, as is done by deposit taker 1. For example, in period 2 the return on assets for deposit taker 2 is higher because income is higher than it would have been if an unrealized loss had been recorded in its income.

Example 2

11. Table A5.6 illustrates how the exclusion of unrealized gains and losses on traded instruments from the income statement disguises the nature of a deposit taker's activity.

12. Deposit takers 1 and 2 both purchase a traded instrument. Both revalue the instrument at its market price; deposit taker 1 records unrealized gains and losses in the income statement as recommended by the *Guide,* but deposit taker 2 does not. As both deposit takers have other income of 5 each period, the result is that deposit taker 1 has net income that is both higher and more volatile than that of deposit taker 2. The relative importance of the business in traded instruments to the earnings of deposit taker 1 and the

Table A5.3. Financial Soundness Indicators: Deposit Takers—Aggregated Data[1]
(FSIs are expressed in percentages; the underlying calculations are in millions of U.S. dollars, except as noted)

	Deposit Taker 1		Deposit Taker 2		Deposit Taker 3		Sector Level	
Capital-based[2] FSIs								
Regulatory capital to risk-weighted assets*	**14%**		**14%**		**19%**		**15%**	
Numerator [line 36][3]	1,200		1,804		816		3,820	
Denominator [line 37]	8,500		12,800		4,220		25,520	
Regulatory Tier 1 capital to risk-weighted assets*	**11%**		**9%**		**12%**		**10%**	
Numerator [line 32]	900		1,200		500		2,600	
Denominator [line 37]	8,500		12,800		4,220		25,520	
Capital to assets	**7%**	**11%**	**7%**	**9%**	**7%**	**8%**	**7%**	**10%**
Numerator [line 32, line 30]	900	1,400	1,200	1,700	500	600	2,600	3,700
Denominator [line 14]	12,450	12,450	18,201	18,201	7,450	7,450	38,101	38,101
Nonperforming loans net of provisions to capital*	**5%**	**3%**	**9%**	**9%**	**13%**	**15%**	**8%**	**8%**
Numerator [line 42 *minus* line 18(ii)]	43	43	160	160	90	90	293	293
Denominator [line 36, line 30]	1,200	1,400	1,804	1,700	816	600	3,820	3,700
Return on equity*	—	—	**57%**	**40%**	**88%**	**73%**	**43%**	**30%**
Numerator[4] [line 8]	—	—	680	680	440	440	1,120	1,120
Denominator[5] [line 32, line 30]	900	1,400	1,200	1,700	500	600	2,600	3,700
Large exposures to capital Number [line 38]	3		2		1		6	
–(to large resident entities)	**78%**	**50%**	**42%**	**29%**	—	—	**46%**	**32%**
Numerator [line 51]	700	700	500	500	—	—	1,200	1,200
Denominator [line 32, line 30]	900	1,400	1,200	1,700	500	600	2,600	3,700
–(to connected borrowers)	—	—	—	—	—	—	—	—
Numerator [line 52]	—	—	—	—	—	—	—	—
Denominator [line 32, line 30]	900	1,400	1,200	1,700	500	600	2,600	3,700
Net open position in foreign exchange to capital*	**−22%**	**−14%**	**42%**	**29%**	**−180%**	**−150%**	**−23%**	**−16%**
Numerator [line 50]	(200)	(200)	500	500	(900)	(900)	(600)	(600)
Denominator [line 32, line 30]	900	1,400	1,200	1,700	500	600	2,600	3,700
Gross asset position in financial derivatives to capital	**22%**	**14%**	**17%**	**12%**	**40%**	**33%**	**23%**	**16%**
Numerator [line 21]	200	200	200	200	200	200	600	600
Denominator [line 32, line 30]	900	1,400	1,200	1,700	500	600	2,600	3,700
Gross liability position in financial derivatives to capital	—	—	**58%**	**41%**	—	—	**27%**	**19%**
Numerator [line 29]	—	—	700	700	—	—	700	700
Denominator [line 32, line 30]	900	1,400	1,200	1,700	500	600	2,600	3,700
Net open position in equities to capital	**11%**	**7%**	**25%**	**18%**	**40%**	**33%**	**23%**	**16%**
Numerator [line 48]	100	100	301	301	200	200	601	601
Denominator [line 32, line 30]	900	1,400	1,200	1,700	500	600	2,600	3,700
Asset-based FSIs								
Liquid assets (core) to total assets*	**8%**		**14%**		**7%**		**10%**	
Numerator [line 39]	1,000		2,500		500		4,000	
Denominator [line 14]	12,450		18,201		7,450		38,101	
Liquid assets (core) to short-term liabilities*	**17%**		**25%**		**25%**		**22%**	
Numerator [line 39]	1,000		2,500		500		4,000	
Denominator [line 41]	6,000		10,050		2,000		18,050	
Customer deposits to total (noninterbank) loans	**124%**		**83%**		**73%**		**94%**	
Numerator [line 24(i))]	10,200		11,200		3,650		25,050	
Denominator [line 18(i.ii)]	8,250		13,500		5,000		26,750	
Return on assets*	—		**4%**		**6%**		**3%**	
Numerator[4] [line 8]	—		680		440		1,120	
Denominator[6] [line 31]	12,450		18,201		7,450		38,101	
Nonperforming loans to total gross loans*	**1%**		**3%**		**3%**		**2%**	
Numerator [line 42]	93		360		140		593	
Denominator [line 18(i)]	9,250		14,400		5,600		29,250	
Sectoral distribution of loans to total loans (percentages of total)*								
Deposit takers [line 18(i.i.i) *divided by* line 18(i)]	—		—		—		—	

Table A5.3 (*concluded*)

	Deposit Taker 1	Deposit Taker 2	Deposit Taker 3	Sector Level
Central bank [line 18(i.ii.i) *divided by* line 18(i)]	—	—	—	—
Other financial corporations [line 18(i.ii.iii) *divided by* line 18(i)]	5%	14%	—	9%
Nonfinancial corporations [line 18(i.ii.iv) *divided by* line 18(i)]	76%	14%	—	31%
Other domestic sectors [line 18(i.ii.v) *divided by* line 18(i)]	4%	17%	45%	18%
Government [line 18(i.ii.ii) *divided by* line 18(i)]	4%	35%	36%	25%
Nonresident [(line 18(i.i.ii) *plus* 18(i.ii.vi)) *divided by* 18(i)]	11%	20%	20%	17%
Residential real estate loans to total loans	**4%**	**7%**	**36%**	**11%**
Numerator [line 43]	350	1,000	2,000	3,350
Denominator [line 18(i)]	9,250	14,400	5,600	29,250
Commercial real estate loans to total loans	—	**14%**	—	**7%**
Numerator [line 44]	—	2,000	—	2,000
Denominator [line 18(i)]	9,250	14,400	5,600	29,250
Geographical distribution of loans to total loans (percentages of total) [addendum items *divided by* line 18(i)]				
Domestic economy	89%	80%	80%	83%
Advanced economies	5%	14%	11%	11%
Regions, excluding advanced economies	—	—	—	—
Africa	3%	1%	0%	2%
Of which: Sub-Sahara	—	—	—	—
Asia	3%	5%	9%	5%
Europe	—	—	—	—
Of which: Former Soviet Union, including Russia	—	—	—	—
Middle East	—	—	—	—
Western Hemisphere	—	—	—	—
Foreign-currency-denominated loans to total loans	**11%**	**21%**	**11%**	**16%**
Numerator [line 46]	1,000	3,000	600	4,600
Denominator [line 18(i)]	9,250	14,400	5,600	29,250
Foreign-currency-denominated liabilities to total liabilities	**11%**	**15%**	**23%**	**15%**
Numerator [line 47]	1,200	2,500	1,500	5,200
Denominator [line 23 *minus* line 21]	10,850	16,301	6,650	33,801
Income- and expense-based FSIs				
Interest margin to gross income*	**55%**	**49%**	**33%**	**46%**
Numerator [line 3]	300	660	200	1,160
Denominator [line 5]	550	1,360	600	2,510
Trading income to total income	**9%**	**7%**	**17%**	**10%**
Numerator [line 4(ii)]	50	100	100	250
Denominator [line 5]	550	1,360	600	2,510
Noninterest expenses to gross income*	**91%**	**44%**	**25%**	**50%**
Numerator [line 6]	500	600	150	1,250
Denominator [line 5]	550	1,360	600	2,510
Personnel expenses to noninterest expenses	**60%**	**50%**	**67%**	**56%**
Numerator [line 6(i)]	300	300	100	700
Denominator [line 6]	500	600	150	1,250

*Core FSIs.

[1]For the specification of the FSIs, refer to Chapter 6.

[2]Two sets of capital ratios are shown. The first set uses Tier 1 capital (except for the nonperforming loans net of provisions to capital FSI, which uses total regulatory capital). The second set uses total capital and reserves.

[3]All line and addendum references are to Table A5.2.

[4]The data entries shown for the numerator are net income before extraordinary items and taxes. As described in Chapter 6, net income after extraordinary items and taxes (line 11) might instead, or additionally, be used as the numerator.

[5]The denominator should be the average value of capital over the period, rather than the end-period value.

[6]The denominator should be the average value of assets over the period, rather than the end-period value.

Table A5.4. Recording Gains and Losses on Traded Instruments: Case 1

		Deposit Taker 1		Deposit Taker 2	
	Price	Δ Net income	Capital position (total)	Δ Net income	Capital position (total)
End period 1	100	—	1,700	—	1,700
End period 2	90	–10	1,690	—	1,690
End period 3	70	–20	1,670	—	1,670
End period 4	75	5	1,675	–25	1,675

Table A5.6. Recording Gains and Losses on Traded Instruments: Case 3

	Deposit Taker 1		Deposit Taker 2
	Δ Net income	*Of which: Trading gains (losses)*	Δ Net income
End period 1	—	—	—
End period 2	30	25	5
End period 3	40	35	5
End period 4	–15	–20	5

potential for greater volatility can be monitored each period. In contrast, the net income of deposit taker 2 disguises the extent to which that deposit taker has invested in a potentially volatile instrument, increasing the potential for surprises when the instrument is sold and the entire holding gain or loss on the instrument is realized at once.

Example 3

13. Table A5.7 illustrates the problems of intrasectoral consistency if deposit takers adopt different approaches to recording realized and unrealized gains and losses on traded instruments.

14. In the example, both deposit taker 1 and 2 purchase a traded financial asset during period 1 at a price of 100. In the first two columns of Table A5.7 the two deposit takers record gains (losses) on the asset in accordance with the recommendations of the *Guide.*

Table A5.5. Recording Gains and Losses on Traded Instruments: Case 2

	Level of FSI of Deposit Taker 2 Relative to Deposit Taker 1		
FSIs	Period 2	Period 3	Period 4
Return on equity	Higher	Higher	Lower
Return on assets	Higher	Higher	Lower
Interest margin to gross income	Lower	Lower	Higher
Trading gains (losses) to gross income	Higher	Higher	Lower
Noninterest expenses to gross income	Lower	Lower	Higher

Therefore, both deposit takers record the same entries in their respective income statements and balance sheets, regardless of whether the asset is sold (as deposit taker 2 does in period 4) or retained (as deposit taker 1 does), and regardless of whether the asset is held in the trading or investment book. At the sector level, changes in net income reflect unrealized losses (gains) of both deposit takers in the period in which they occur, as well as a weakening capital position for the sector.

15. Now, assume deposit taker 2 records only realized gains (losses) in the income statement (shown as 2* in the fourth column of Table A5.7). On selling the asset in period 4, deposit taker 2* records a loss of 25 in its income statement for that period. However, deposit taker 1 reflected such losses in earlier periods, when they arose, causing asymmetries to arise when aggregating data to produce sector-level data on net income and undermining the coherence of the sector-level data in the fifth column of Table A5.7.

16. Further, assume that deposit taker 1, like deposit taker 2*, also records only realized gains (losses) in the income statement but does not sell the asset (shown as 1* in the sixth column in Table A5.7). Even though both deposit taker 1* and 2* are using the same recording approach, there are asymmetries in the measurement of net income—one deposit taker reflects a loss, the other records nothing—between the two deposit takers, again undermining the coherence of the sector-level data (seventh column of Table A5.7).

17. The impact on the sector-level data, and thus on any analysis, of these different approaches is clear. For instance, when both deposit takers follow the

Table A5.7. Recording Gains and Losses on Traded Instruments: Case 4

	Price	Deposit Taker 1	Deposit Taker 2	Subsector Total (Deposit Takers 1 + 2)	Deposit Taker 2*	Subsector Total (Deposit Takers 1 + 2*)	Deposit Taker 1*	Subsector Total (Deposit Takers 1* + 2*)
		Column 1	Column 2	Column 3	Column 4	Column 5	Column 6	Column 7
		Δ Net income	Δ Net income	Δ Net income	Δ Net income	Δ Net income	Δ Net income	Δ Net income
End period 1	100	—	—	—	—	—	—	—
End period 2	90	−10	−10	−20	—	−10	—	—
End period 3	70	−20	−20	−40	—	−20	—	—
End period 4	75	5	5	10	−25	−20	—	−25
End period 5	70	−5	—	−5	—	−5	—	—

Guide's recommendations, losses cease in the fourth period, and a small recovery in income takes place as market prices rebound. In contrast, in the case where one deposit taker records only gains and losses when realized, the losses recorded in the fourth period remain of the same magnitude as in the third, despite the small rebound in market prices. When both deposit takers record gains and losses only when they are realized, there is no evidence of any worsening performance until the fourth quarter, increasing the possibility of a surprise when the losses are taken.

Example 4

18. Table A5.8 illustrates the problems that can arise for sector-level data if a deposit taker records gains and losses on its own traded debt differently from another deposit taker that owns the debt.

19. Deposit taker 2 purchases a traded debt instrument issued by deposit taker 1 in period 1. Both deposit takers revalue the instrument at its market price and record unrealized gains and losses in the income statement each period, in line with the recommendations of the *Guide.* Consequently, both deposit takers record equal and opposite entries in their respective income statements, ensuring that net income (and capital) at the sector level is unaffected by the claims of one deposit taker in the reporting population on another.

20. Now, assume that deposit taker 1 does not record unrealized gains (losses) on its debt liability (deposit taker 1* in the fourth column of Table A5.8). Consequently, asymmetric recording approaches are followed, and the sector's net income is boosted because the sector has recorded a gain in value arising from claims on itself, as shown in the fifth column of Table A5.8.

Table A5.8. Recording Gains and Losses on Traded Instruments: Case 5

	Price	Deposit Taker 1	Deposit Taker 2	Subsector Total (Deposit Takers 1 and 2)	Deposit Taker 1*	Subsector Total (Deposit Takers 1* and 2)
		Column 1	Column 2	Column 3	Column 4	Column 5
		Δ Net income	Δ Net income	Δ Net income	Δ Net income	Δ Net income
End period 1	90	—	—	—	—	—
End period 2	100	−10	10	0	0	10
End period 3	110	−10	10	0	0	10
End period 4	115	−5	5	0	0	5

Treatment of Interest on Nonperforming Loans

21. The *Guide* recommends that interest accrue continuously on loans, unless the loan is nonperforming. Numerical examples are provided below that illustrate the application of the *Guide*'s recommendations on interest accrual on loans, particularly on those loans that are nonperforming.

Example 1: Loan performs through to maturity as envisaged by the contract (base case)

22. As a reference point, Table A5.9 sets out the entries under interest income in the income statement and loans in the balance sheet statement of a creditor deposit taker when a loan performs through to maturity as envisaged by the contract. Each month, the amount of interest that has accrued is recorded as interest income in the income statement, with the counter-entry increasing the outstanding value of the loan recorded in the balance sheet. As a payment of interest is made—quarterly in this example—the cash balances of the deposit taker increase by 3, and the outstanding loan amount decreases by 3 to 100. If the deposit taker compiles data on only a quarterly basis, the only entries would be the accrual of interest of 3 and an increase in cash balances of 3.

Example 2: Loan is classified as nonperforming, but interest is subsequently received

23. Table A5.10 sets out the entries under interest income and loan loss provisions in the income statement and under loans in the balance sheet statement when a deposit taker classifies a loan as nonperforming but subsequently receives payments on the loan. The contractual arrangements for the loan are the same as in example 1 above.

24. In this example, the first-quarter interest payment is missed by the debtor, so the end-first-quarter outstanding loan amount in the balance sheet is 103. The loan continues to accrue interest in the second quarter, but again the second-quarter interest payment is missed, resulting in an end-second-quarter loan amount outstanding of 106. At the start of the third quarter, with payment of interest more than 90 days overdue, the loan is classified as nonperforming. On reviewing the loan, the deposit taker considers that neither the amount of interest that has accrued in the first two quarters (6) nor all the amount originally advanced will be paid. Thus a loan loss (specific) provision of 66 is made in July, reducing the loan amount outstanding (after specific provisions).

25. As the loan is nonperforming, accrual of interest ceases, and the loan is placed on a cash basis—that is, no interest income is recorded until payment is made. Nevertheless, for consistency of recording between the debtor and the creditor, gross interest income continues to be recorded at the contractual rate of interest, although it is offset in the creditor's income statement by a provision for accrued interest on nonperforming assets.

26. At the end of the third quarter, the overdue interest for the six months January–June is paid together with the interest of 3 for the third quarter. The payment increases the deposit taker's cash balances by 9,

Table A5.9. Treatment of Interest on Nonperforming Loans: Case 1

	Jan	Feb	Mar	Apr	May	Jun	Jul	Aug	Sep	Oct	Nov	Dec
Income and expense												
Interest income	1	1	1	1	1	1	1	1	1	1	1	1
(i) Gross interest income	1	1	1	1	1	1	1	1	1	1	1	1
(ii) Less provisions for accrued interest on nonperforming assets	—	—	—	—	—	—	—	—	—	—	—	—
Loan loss provisions	—	—	—	—	—	—	—	—	—	—	—	—
Balance sheet (assets)												
Loans (after specific provisions)	101	102	100	101	102	100	101	102	100	101	102	100
(i) Gross loans	101	102	100	101	102	100	101	102	100	101	102	100
(ii) Specific provisions	—	—	—	—	—	—	—	—	—	—	—	—
Memorandum:												
Cash interest payments by debtor	—	—	3	—	—	3	—	—	3	—	—	3

Table A5.10. Treatment of Interest on Nonperforming Loans: Case 2

	Jan	Feb	Mar	Apr	May	Jun	Jul	Aug	Sep	Oct	Nov	Dec
Income and expense												
Interest income	1	1	1	1	1	1	0	0	3	1	1	1
(i) Gross interest income	1	1	1	1	1	1	1	1	1	1	1	1
(ii) Less provisions for accrued interest on nonperforming assets	—	—	—	—	—	—	1	1	–2	—	—	—
Loan loss provisions	—	—	—	—	—	—	66	—	–6	—	—	—
Balance sheet												
Loans (after specific provisions)	101	102	103	104	105	106	40	40	40	41	42	40
(i) Gross loans	101	102	103	104	105	106	106	106	100	101	102	100
(ii) Specific provisions	—	—	—	—	—	—	66	—	60	—	—	—
Memorandum:												
Cash interest payments by debtor	—	—	0	—	—	0	—	—	9	—	—	3

with the following counter-entries: a negative loan loss provision of 6, partially reversing the provision made in July; a negative provision for accrued interest on nonperforming loans of 2 in the income statement, reversing the provision against interest accrued that was recorded in the first two months of the third quarter; and a recording of gross interest income in September of 1.

27. Once the interest payments are caught up, the expectation is that the debtor will continue to make interest payments according to the loan contract, so the accrual of interest resumes in the fourth quarter. Nonetheless, the deposit taker remains doubtful that all the amount advanced will be repaid, and so a specific provision of 60 remains.

Example 3: Loan is classified as nonperforming, but partial payment of interest is expected

28. Table A5.11 sets out the entries under interest income and loan loss provisions in the income statement and under loans in the balance sheet when a deposit taker identifies a loan as nonperforming but expects partial payment of interest on the loan.

29. In the first quarter, interest accrues and is paid in accordance with the loan contract. At the end of that

Table A5.11. Treatment of Interest on Nonperforming Loans: Case 3

	Jan	Feb	Mar	Apr	May	Jun	Jul	Aug	Sep	Oct	Nov	Dec
Income and expense												
Interest income	1	1	1	0.5	0.5	2	0.5	0.5	0.5	0	0	4.5
(i) Gross interest income	1	1	1	1	1	1	1	1	1	1	1	1
(ii) Less provisions for accrued interest on nonperforming assets	—	—	—	0.5	0.5	–1	0.5	0.5	0.5	1	1	–3.5
Loan loss provisions	—	—	—	—	—	—	—	—	—	—	—	—
Balance sheet												
Loans (after specific provisions)	101	102	100	100.5	101.0	100	100	101	100	100	100	100
(i) Gross loans	101	102	100	100.5	101.0	100	100	101	100	100	100	100
(ii) Specific provisions	—	—	—	—	—	—	—	—	—	—	—	—
Memorandum:												
Cash interest payments by debtor	—	—	3	—	—	3	—	—	1.5	—	—	4.5

quarter, the outstanding loan value is 100. The deposit taker reviews the loan and determines that there is evidence that the loan will not fully perform in the future and expects that only partial payments of interest of 1.5 per quarter will be forthcoming. Therefore, 0.5 is recorded in provisions for accrued interest on nonperforming assets in both April and May. The balance sheet value of the loan at the end of each month includes the accrual of interest income less the provision for accrued interest on nonperforming assets. In this example, unexpectedly at the end of the second quarter interest is paid in accordance with the loan contract. Therefore, the entries in April and May for provisions for accrued interest income on nonperforming assets are reversed in June. At the end of the second quarter, the outstanding loan value is 100.

30. Despite the payment made at the end of the second quarter, the deposit taker continues to expect payment of 1.5 per quarter and so continues to include 0.5 every month in provisions for accrued interest on nonperforming assets. The deposit taker proves to be correct in its expectation, and at the end of the third quarter the debtor pays 1.5. The balance sheet value of the loan at the end of each month continues to include the accrual of interest income less the provision for accrued interest on nonperforming assets. During the third quarter, interest of 1.5 accrues and is actually paid, rendering the outstanding loan amount at the end of the quarter again 100.

31. In the fourth quarter, the deposit taker decides that the loan interest payments are expected to cease, and so accrual of interest ceases—the loan is placed on a cash basis in October. Entries are made in provisions for accrued interest on nonperforming loans to the full amount of the contracted rate of accrual per month. The balance sheet value of the loan at the end of each month is unchanged at 100 because no interest is accrued. However, full payment of interest, including past due interest, is made by the debtor in December. Therefore, the accumulated provisions of 3.5 for accrued interest on nonperforming loans are reversed, and 4.5 is recorded for interest income in the quarter. The outstanding loan amount at the end of the quarter remains at 100.

Part 3. Consolidation and Associated Sector-Level Issues

32. Unlike the base case, within a financial system deposit takers are likely to have interrelations. Therefore, the examples below illustrate the derivation of sector-level consolidated data when such interrelations exist.

Extended Base Data Set

Domestic consolidated data

33. The base case is extended to include interrelations among the three deposit takers. These transactions and positions are reflected in Tables A5.12 and A5.13, which follow the same format as Tables 11.2 and 11.3 of the *Guide.* Tables A5.14 and A5.15 present the income and expense statements and balance sheets for the three domestic deposit takers specified in the base case. The first three columns are similar to those in the base case,[2] while the remaining columns illustrate the derivation of sector-level data when interrelations exist. The derivation is shown in two steps to demonstrate that, consistent with the *Guide*'s recommendations, all intragroup flows and positions are eliminated, but intergroup debt and financial derivatives positions are not eliminated (see Box 5.1). For clarity, an intermediate step that aggregates the group consolidated data for banks in the population is also shown in the table.

(i) Consolidated group data

34. The derivation of consolidated group data involves the elimination of *all* intragroup transactions and positions. The fourth column in Tables A5.14 and A5.15 shows the consolidated group data for deposit taker 2 and its subsidiary, deposit taker 3. The adjustments made to eliminate intragroup transactions and positions are described below. The data that have been adjusted are shaded.

- Income and expense statement (Table A5.14)
  - **Fees and commissions** of 15 that are receivable/payable between deposit taker 2 and deposit taker 3 are eliminated from the group's income and expenses, as such fees and commissions are intragroup transactions.
  - Deposit taker 2 recognizes 134.6 of noninterest income as its **share of the net income** of deposit taker 3. This amount is recorded as 71.4 of dividends payable and 63.2 of retained earnings by deposit taker 3. To eliminate double counting in the group data, the following amounts are eliminated: 134.6 from noninterest

[2]This example differs somewhat from the base case because the balance sheets of deposit takers 1 and 2 incorporate interbank loans and deposits with resident deposit takers (see shaded cells in Table A5.15).

Table A5.12. Interbank Positions and Flows

	Domestic Deposit Takers		
	Bank 1	Bank 2	
	Bank 1's positions with other deposit takers	*Bank 2's positions with its subsidiary*	*Bank 2's position with other deposit takers*
1. Shares and other equity[1]	20	301	—
2. Shares and other equity[2]	—	—	—
3. Noninterest income (excluding trading gains and losses)	—	—	—
Of which: Fees and commissions	—	15	15
Dividends receivable	7	71.4	—
Prorated share of retained earnings	—	63.2	—
Gains or losses on sale of fixed assets to other deposit takers	—	—	—
4. Gains and losses on equity investments in other deposit takers	5	—	—
5. Nonperforming loans to deposit takers in the reporting population[3]	—	—	—
Current period	—	—	—
Provisions for accrued interest	—	—	—
Specific provisions	—	—	8
Outstanding position	—	—	—
Provisions for accrued interest	—	—	—
Specific provisions	—	—	8
6. Short-term claims on other deposit takers in the reporting economy (remaining maturity)	—	—	—

[1]Valued as the proportionate share of the parent deposit taker's stake in subsidiaries'/associates' capital and reserves (and similarly for reverse investments) or as the market value of any equity stake in other deposit takers. The associate investment is attributed to funds contributed by owners together with retained earnings (including those earnings appropriated to reserves)—a measure of narrow capital.

[2]As valued in the balance sheet, if different from line 1.

[3]These items might not be significant in some economies. If there are other nonperforming asset claims on other deposit takers in the reporting population, the data series specified in item 5 are required for these assets.

income, and 71.4 from dividends payable, and 63.2 from retained earnings.

- Balance sheet (Table A5.15)
  - Deposit taker 2 has **deposit liabilities** of 10 to deposit taker 3. These deposits are eliminated on consolidation from the group's currency and deposit liabilities to resident banks and claims on resident banks.
  - Deposit taker 3 has **loan liabilities** of 100 to deposit taker 2. These loans are eliminated on consolidation from the group's loans to and from resident banks.
  - Deposit taker 3 also has liabilities of 1,000 to deposit taker 2 in the form of **debt securities** issued. These are eliminated on consolidation from the group's assets and liabilities.
  - Deposit taker 2 has an **equity investment** of 301 in deposit taker 3, valued according to the prorated share in the capital and reserves of the associate. On consolidation, 301 is eliminated from shares and other equity on the asset side and from capital and reserves on the liability side of the group's balance sheet. If the capital and reserves for deposit takers 2 and 3 were simply aggregated, there would be double counting of capital.
  - Deposit takers 2 has liabilities of 100 to deposit taker 3 in the form of **financial derivatives.** These derivatives are eliminated on consolidation from the group's assets and liabilities.

(ii) Sector-level consolidated data

35. The sixth column in Tables A5.14 and A5.15 presents the sector-level consolidated income and balance sheet data for the banking system. These data are derived by aggregating the data of deposit taker 1 with the group consolidated data (covering the activities of deposit takers 2 and 3) and eliminating certain transactions and positions between deposit taker 1 and the group; as noted earlier, positions in debt instruments and financial derivatives among unrelated deposit takers are not eliminated (see Chapter 5) in the sector-level data. The data eliminated at the sector level on

Table A5.13. Other Intragroup Positions and Flows

	Domestic Deposit Taker Other Group Entities	
	Deposit taker 2	Deposit taker 3
Balance Sheet		
Liabilities to:	—	—
Deposits	10	—
Loans	—	100
Of which: Foreign-currency-denominated		
Foreign-currency-linked	—	—
Debt securities	—	1,000
Financial derivatives	100	—
Other liabilities	—	—
Foreign-currency-denominated liabilities		
Foreign-currency-linked liabilities	—	—
Income and Expense Statements	—	—
Interest income receivable	—	—
Memorandum Items Relating	—	—
to Claims		
Liquid assets claims (core)	—	—
Liquid assets claims (broad)	—	—
Nonperforming loans	—	—

consolidation are described below. The data that have been adjusted are shaded.

- Income and expense statement (Table A5.14)
  - **Fees and commissions** of 15 receivable/payable between deposit taker 2 and deposit taker 1 are eliminated in the sector-level consolidated data. If this adjustment were not made, gross income of the sector would be overstated.
  - Deposit taker 1 made a gain of 5 on holdings of **equity investments** in other resident deposit takers. Because of the asymmetric valuation of capital on the two sides of the balance sheet, these gains are not offset by counterpart losses for the issuing bank. Thus, to avoid overstating net income for the sector, these gains are eliminated from gains and losses on financial instruments and retained earnings at the sector level. Examples that illustrate the *Guide*'s recommendation for the measurement of sector-wide capital are provided below.
  - Deposit taker 1 has **dividends** of 7 receivable from other resident deposit takers, which are eliminated from noninterest income (other income) and dividends payable in the sector-level consolidated data.
  - Deposit taker 2 has expensed 8 in **specific provisions** against loans to deposit taker 1. This provision is eliminated from sector-level provisions and retained earnings data.
- Balance sheet (Table A5.15)
  - The group consolidated data of deposit takers 2 and 3 show **loans to other resident deposit takers** of 50. These and any other intergroup positions in debt instruments and financial derivatives are *not* eliminated in the sector-level data.
  - Deposit taker 2 has a stock of 8 in specific **provisions** against loans to deposit taker 1. Following the elimination of such provisions in the income statement, these provisions are also eliminated from the stock of specific provisions in the sector-level balance sheet. The counteradjustment is higher retained earnings in capital and reserves.
  - Deposit taker 1 has a **portfolio equity investment** of 20 in other resident deposit takers. To avoid double counting of capital, the market value of this equity investment is deducted from shares and other equity on the assets side and from capital and reserves in the sector-level consolidated data. This adjustment is illustrated in the examples below covering the *Guide*'s recommendation for the measurement of sector-wide capital.

Cross-border consolidated data

36. In addition to the interrelations among resident banks discussed above, it is further assumed that deposit taker 2 has a foreign deposit-taking subsidiary and that deposit taker 1 has a foreign branch. Moreover, the foreign subsidiary of deposit taker 2 has a portfolio equity investment in deposit taker 1.

37. The intergroup positions and flows are set out in Table A5.16, which follows the same format as Table 11.4. The cross-border group consolidated income and balance sheet statements for deposit takers 1 and 2 are shown in the first and second columns of Tables A5.17 and A5.18. The financial statements of deposit taker 3 are subsumed within the group-consolidated financial statement of deposit taker 2.

38. The adjustments made to eliminate intergroup transactions and positions to derive sector-level cross-border consolidated data are described below. The data that have been adjusted are shaded.

- Income and expense statement (Table A5.17)
  - Deposit taker 2's group receives 15 in **fees and commissions** from deposit taker 1's group. These intergroup fees and commissions receivable/payable are eliminated from the sector-level data.

Table A5.14. Income and Expense Statements: Deposit Takers—Sector-Level Consolidated Data (Domestic Consolidated Data)[1]

	Deposit Taker 1 A	Deposit Taker 2 B	Deposit Taker 3 C	Step 1: Group Consolidated Data D (= B + C +/– [Group Consolidated Adjustment])	Aggregated Group Consolidated Data E (= D + A)	Step 2: Sector Level Consolidated Data F (= E +/– [Sector Consolidated Adjustment])
1. Interest income	400	800	300	1,100	1,500	1,500
(i) Gross interest income	400	800	300	1,100	1,500	1,500
(ii) Less provisions for accrued interest on nonperforming assets	—	—	—	—	—	—
2. Interest expense	100	140	100	240	340	340
3. *Net interest income (= 1 minus 2)*	*300*	*660*	*200*	*860*	*1,160*	*1,160*
4. Noninterest income	250	700	400	950	1,200	1,173
(i) Fees and commissions receivable	110	300	200	485	595	580
(ii) Gains or losses on financial instruments	50	100	100	200	250	245
(iii) Prorated earnings	50	140	20	25	75	75
(iv) Other income	40	160	80	240	280	273
5. *Gross income (= 3 + 4)*	*550*	*1,360*	*600*	*1,810*	*2,360*	*2,333*
6. Noninterest expenses	500	600	150	735	1,235	1,220
(i) Personnel costs	300	300	100	400	700	700
(ii) Other expenses	200	300	50	335	535	520
7. Provisions (net)	50	80	10	90	140	132
(i) Loan loss provisions	50	80	10	90	140	132
(ii) Other financial asset provisions	—	—	—	—	—	—
8. *Net income (before extraordinary item and taxes) (= 5 minus (6 + 7))*	—	*680*	*440*	*985*	*985*	*981*
9. Extraordinary items	—	—	—	—	—	—
10. Income tax	—	272	176	448	448	448
11. *Net income after tax and extraordinary items (= 8 minus (9 + 10))*	*408*	*264*	*537*	*537*	*533*	
12. Dividends payable	—	300	140	369	369	362
13. *Retained earnings (= 11 minus 12)*	—	*108*	*124*	*169*	*169*	*172*

[1]For a description of the line items, refer to Chapter 4.

- Deposit taker 1 made **gains of 5 on equity investments** in deposit taker 2's group, while deposit taker 2's group made losses of 10 on equity investments in deposit taker 1's group. These intergroup gains and losses are eliminated from gains and losses on financial instruments and retained earnings in the sector-level consolidated data.
- Deposit taker 1's group received 7 in **dividends** from deposit taker 2's group. These intergroup payments are eliminated from other income, as well as from dividends payable, in the sector-level data.
- Deposit taker 2's group has expensed 8 in **specific provisions** on loans to deposit taker 1's group. These expenses are eliminated from loan loss provisions and retained earnings in the sector-level data.

• Balance sheet (Table A5.18)
- The group of deposit taker 2 has accumulated a stock of **specific provisions** of 8 against loans to the group of deposit taker 1. Following the elimination of such provisions in the income statement, this stock of specific provisions is eliminated from the sector-level balance sheet data, resulting in a higher level of loans after specific provisions. The counteradjustment is higher sector-level retained earnings in capital and reserves.
- The group of deposit taker 1 has **portfolio equity investments** of 20 in the group of deposit taker 2, and, conversely, the group of deposit taker 2 has

Table A5.15. Balance Sheets: Deposit Takers—Sector-Level Consolidated Data (Domestic Consolidated Data)[1]

	Deposit Taker 1 A	Deposit Taker 2 B	Deposit Taker 3 C	Step 1: Group Consolidated Data D (= B + C +/– [Group Consolidated Adjustment])	Aggregated Group Consolidated Data E (= D + A)	Step 2: Sector Level Consolidated Data F (= E +/– [Sector Consolidated Adjustment])
14. Total assets (= 15 + 16 = 31)	**12,450**	**18,201**	**7,450**	**24,140**	**36,590**	**36,578**
15. *Nonfinancial assets*	*500*	*500*	*300*	*800*	*1,300*	*1,300*
16. *Financial assets (= 17 through 22)*	*11,950*	*17,701*	*7,150*	*23,340*	*35,290*	*35,278*
17. Currency and deposits	200	200	100	290	490	490
18. Loans (after specific provisions)	9,200	13,900	5,350	19,150	28,350	28,358
(i) Gross loans	9,250	14,400	5,600	19,900	29,150	29,150
(i.i) Interbank loans	1,000	900	600	1,400	2,400	2,400
(i.i.i) Resident	300	150	—	50	350	350
(i.i.ii) Nonresident	700	750	600	1,350	2,050	2,050
(i.ii) Noninterbank loans	8,250	13,500	5,000	18,500	26,750	26,750
(i.ii.i) Central bank	—	—	—	—	—	—
(i.ii.ii) General government	400	5,000	2,000	7,000	7,400	7,400
(i.ii.iii) Other financial corporations	500	2,000	—	2,000	2,500	2,500
(i.ii.iv) Nonfinancial corporations	7,000	2,000	—	2,000	9,000	9,000
(i.ii.v) Other domestic sectors	350	2,500	2,500	5,000	5,350	5,350
(i.ii.vi) Nonresidents	—	2,000	500	2,500	2,500	2,500
(ii) Specific provisions	50	500	250	750	800	792
19. Debt securities	2,250	3,000	1,300	3,300	5,550	5,550
20. Shares and other equity	100	301	200	200	300	280
21. Financial derivatives	200	200	200	300	500	500
22. Other assets	—	100	—	100	100	100
23. *Liabilities (= 28 + 29)*	*11,050*	*16,501*	*6,850*	*22,141*	*33,191*	*33,191*
24. Currency and deposits	10,200	11,700	5,150	16,840	27,040	27,040
(i) Customer deposits	10,200	11,200	3,650	14,850	25,050	25,050
(ii) Interbank deposits	—	500	1,500	1,990	1,990	1,990
(ii.i) Resident	—	10	—	—	—	—
(ii.ii) Nonresident	—	490	1,500	1,990	1,990	1,990
(iii) Other currency and deposits	—	—	—	—	—	—
25. Loans	200	300	150	350	550	550
26. Debt securities	400	3,000	1,500	3,500	3,900	3,900
27. Other liabilities	250	801	50	851	1,101	1,101
28. *Debt (= 24 + 25 + 26 + 27)*	*11,050*	*15,801*	*6,850*	*21,541*	*32,591*	*32,591*
29. Financial derivatives	—	700	—	600	600	600
30. Capital and reserves	1,400	1,700	600	1,999	3,399	3,387
(i) Narrow capital	1,160	1,160	500	1,359	2,519	2,507
31. Balance sheet total (= 23 + 30 = 14)	**12,450**	**18,201**	**7,450**	**24,140**	**36,590**	**36,578**

[1]For a description of the line items, refer to Chapter 4.

portfolio equity investments of 50 in the group of deposit taker 1. To avoid double counting of capital, the market value of these equity investments is deducted from shares and other equity on the asset side and from capital and reserves in the sector-level consolidated data. This adjustment is shown in the examples below, which illustrate the *Guide*'s recommendation for the measurement of sector-wide capital.

Deriving Sector-Wide Capital

39. Accurately measuring sector-wide capital is central to monitoring the soundness of deposit-taking institutions. Therefore, it is important not to overestimate or underestimate the actual amount of capital resources available to the deposit-taking sector. In particular, the *Guide* recommends that any double counting of capital arising from intra-deposit-taking

Table A5.16. Intergroup Positions and Flows (Cross-Border Consolidated Data)

	Other Domestically Incorporated, Domestically Controlled Deposit Takers, Their Subsidiaries,[1] and Branches	
	Deposit taker 1 group	Deposit taker 2 group
1. Shares and other equity[2]	20	50
2. Shares and other equity as valued on balance sheet[3]	—	—
3. Noninterest income (excluding trading gains and losses):	—	—
Of which:		
Fees and commissions	—	15
Dividends receivable	7	—
Prorated share of retained earnings	—	—
Gains or losses on sale of fixed assets to other deposit takers	—	—
4. Gains and losses on equity investments in other deposit takers	5	–10
5. Nonperforming loans to deposit takers in the reporting population[4]	—	—
Current period	—	—
Provisions for accrued interest	—	—
Specific provisions	—	8
Outstanding position	—	—
Provisions for accrued interest	—	—
Specific provisions	—	8
6. Short-term claims on other deposit takers in the reporting economy (remaining maturity)	—	—

[1]Including deposit takers' branches of separately incorporated subsidiaries.

[2]Valued as the proportionate share of the parent deposit taker's stake in subsidiaries'/associates' capital and reserves (similar for reverse investments), or as the market value of any equity stake in other deposit takers.

[3]As valued in the balance sheet, if different from line 1.

[4]These items might not be significant in some economies. If there are other nonperforming asset claims on other deposit takers in the reporting population, the data series specified in item 5 are required for these assets.

sector equity investments be eliminated. The numerical examples below illustrate how such elimination is undertaken for equity investments other than in subsidiaries and associates under different scenarios.

40. As in the other examples, it is assumed that there are three deposit takers. Moreover, in the first period (1) deposit taker 1 owns 5 of 60 outstanding shares of deposit taker 2, and (2) the shares of deposit taker 2 have a stated or par value of 2 per share, which is also their market value. So, at end period 1, the equity holdings of deposit taker 1 are valued at 10, and the capital of deposit taker 2 is valued at 120, all "funds contributed by owners" (*FC*). To facilitate exposition, in the examples below, the holdings of deposit taker 1 are explicitly shown in the accounts of deposit taker 2 as "Funds Contributed by Deposit taker 1," ($FC_{(DT\ 1)}$), while funds contributed by owners outside the sector are shown as $FC_{(Other)}$.

Example 1: Consolidation of sector-wide capital (base case)

41. Following the guidance in the *Guide,* Table A5.19 illustrates that sector-wide capital is not the aggregation of the capital of each of the three deposit takers, because some of their respective capital is obtained from within the sector: deposit taker 1 owns 5 shares of the capital of deposit taker 2 with a value of 10. This capital contribution by deposit taker 1 to deposit taker 2 must be eliminated by subtracting its market value from aggregated total capital (with the counter-entry being the elimination from sector-wide assets of the equity investment of deposit taker 1 in deposit taker 2). Therefore in this instance for period 1, where *DT* equals the deposit taker's capital,

Sector-wide capital (Period 1) =

$$\underset{(DT\ 1)}{40} + \underset{(DT\ 2)}{120} + \underset{(DT\ 3)}{40} - \underset{\substack{(FC_{(DT\ 1)})\\ [\textit{market value}]}}{10} = 190.$$

Table A5.17. Income and Expense Statements: Deposit Takers—Sector-Level Consolidated Data (Cross-Border Consolidated Data)[1]

	Deposit Taker 1 Group Consolidated Data A	Deposit Taker 2 Group Consolidated Data B	Sector-Level Consolidated Data C (=A + B +/– [Intergroup Consolidated Adjustment])
1. Interest income	500	1,200	1,700
(i) Gross interest income	500	1,200	1,700
(ii) Less provisions for accrued interest on nonperforming assets	—	—	—
2. Interest expense	100	440	540
3. *Net interest income (= 1 minus 2)*	*400*	*760*	*1,160*
4. Noninterest income	250	700	933
(i) Fees and commissions receivable	110	535	630
(ii) Gains or losses on financial instruments	50	–100	–45
(iii) Prorated earnings	50	25	75
(iv) Other income	40	240	273
5. *Gross income (= 3 + 4)*	*650*	*1,460*	*2,093*
6. Noninterest expenses	525	935	1,445
(i) Personnel costs	320	600	920
(ii) Other expenses	205	335	525
7. Provisions (net)	125	90	207
(i) Loan loss provisions	125	90	207
(ii) Other financial asset provisions	—	—	—
8. *Net income (before extraordinary items and taxes) (= 5 minus (6 + 7))*	—	*435*	*441*
9. Extraordinary items	—	—	—
10. Income tax	—	448	448
11. *Net income after tax (= 8 minus (9 + 10))*	—	*–13*	*–7*
12. Dividends payable	—	377	370
13. *Retained earnings (= 11 minus 12)*	—	*–389*	*–376*

[1]For a description of the line items, refer to Chapter 4.

42. Note that the equity of deposit taker 1 in deposit taker 2 is eliminated from funds contributed by deposit taker 1, $FC_{(DT\ 1)}$, and the consolidated sector-wide balance sheet reflects only capital resources from outside the sector.

Example 2: Consolidation of equity among deposit takers: unrealized valuation gains—case 1

43. In period 2, the net income and retained earnings of deposit taker 2 are 120. The capital resources (net assets) of deposit taker 2 thus double, and the market bids up the share price to 4 per share, doubling the market price of period 1 and reflecting retained earnings. On its equity investment, deposit taker 1 experiences an unrealized valuation gain of 10, increasing net income and retained earnings; deposit taker 1 also marks up the value of its equity investment in the balance sheet to 20. In the example, neither deposit taker 1 nor deposit taker 3 generates any other net income.

44. Sector-wide capital in period 2 is calculated excluding the market value of the equity investment of deposit taker 1 in deposit taker 2. From the perspective of deposit taker 1, the market value is composed of 10 in purchase value and 10 in valuation gain (and is deducted from narrow capital).[3] By com-

[3]When Tier 1 data are not available, funds contributed by owners together with retained earnings (including those earnings appropriated to reserves) could be identified as a narrow measure.

Table A5.18. Balance Sheets: Deposit Takers—Sector-Level Consolidated Data (Cross-Border Consolidated Data)[1]

	Deposit Taker 1 Group Cross-Border Consolidated Data A	Deposit Taker 2 Group Cross-Border Consolidated Data B	Sector-Level Cross-Border Consolidated Data C (=A + B +/– [Intergroup Consolidated Adjustment])
14. **Total assets** (= 15 + 16 = 31)	13,300	35,469	48,707
15. *Nonfinancial assets*	*500*	*1,300*	*1,800*
16. *Financial assets (= 17 through 22)*	*12,800*	*34,169*	*46,907*
17. Currency and deposits	200	540	740
18. Loans (after specific provisions)	10,050	27,670	37,728
(i) Gross loans	10,250	28,070	38,320
(i.i) Interbank loans	1,000	1,550	2,550
(i.i.i) Resident	300	50	350
(i.i.ii) Nonresident	700	1,500	2,200
(i.ii) Noninterbank loans	9,250	26,520	35,770
(i.ii.i) Central bank	—	20	20
(i.ii.ii) General government	400	11,000	11,400
(i.ii.iii) Other financial corporations	500	5,000	5,500
(i.ii.iv) Nonfinancial corporations	7,000	2,000	9,000
(i.ii.v) Other domestic sectors	1,350	6,000	7,350
(i.ii.vi) Nonresidents	—	2,500	2,500
(ii) Specific provisions	200	400	592
19. Debt securities	2,250	5,300	7,550
20. Shares and other equity	100	259	289
21. Financial derivatives	200	300	500
22. Other assets	—	100	100
23. *Liabilities (= 28 + 29)*	*11,900*	*32,700*	*44,600*
24. Currency and deposits	11,200	26,940	38,140
(i) Customer deposits	11,200	24,850	36,050
(ii) Interbank deposits	—	2,000	2,000
(ii.i) Resident	—	—	—
(ii.ii) Nonresident	—	2,000	2,000
(iii) Other currency and deposits	—	90	90
25. Loans	200	350	550
26. Debt securities	400	3,500	3,900
27. Other liabilities	100	1,310	1,410
28. *Debt (= 24 + 25 + 26 + 27)*	*11,900*	*32,100*	*44,000*
29. Financial derivatives	—	600	600
30. Capital and reserves	1,400	2,769	4,107
(i) Narrow capital	1,160	1,890	2,988
31. **Balance sheet total (= 23 + 30 = 14)**	13,300	35,469	48,707

[1]For a description of the line items, refer to Chapter 4.

ponent, 10 is deducted from funds contributed, and 10 is subtracted from retained earnings of deposit taker 1 ($RE_{(DT\ 1)}$):

Sector-wide capital (Period 2) =

$$\underset{(DT\ 1)}{50} + \underset{(DT\ 2)}{240} + \underset{(DT\ 3)}{40} - \underset{(FC_{(DT\ 1)})}{10} - \underset{\substack{(RE_{(DT\ 1)})\\ [market\ value]}}{10} = 310.$$

45. Similar to sector-wide capital, an adjustment is required to sector-wide income. Aggregating the net income of the three deposit takers results in net income in period 2 of 70 (consisting of 10 as unrealized gains of deposit taker 1 and 60 as net income of deposit taker 2). However, 10 of the net income represents a valuation gain of the sector on itself. The *Guide* recommends that all unrealized gains/losses

Table A5.19. Consolidation of Sector-Wide Capital: Base Case

Period 1

Deposit Taker 1

Cash	40	Deposits	20
Loans	10	Capital	40
DT 2 Equity	10	*Of which: $FC_{(Other)}$*[1]	40
Purchase Value	10		

Deposit Taker 2

Loans	220	Deposits	100
		Capital	120
		Of which: $FC_{(Other)}$[1]	110
		Of which: $FC_{(DT\ 1)}$[1]	10

Deposit Taker 3

Cash	40	Deposits	20
Loans	20	Capital	40
		Of which: $FC_{(Other)}$[1]	40

Consolidated Sector-Wide Balance Sheet

Cash	80	Deposits	140
Loans	250	Capital	190
		Of which: $FC_{(Other)}$[1]	190

[1]FC = Funds contributed by owners.
$FC_{(Other)}$ = Funds contributed by non-deposit-takers.
$FC_{(DT\ 1)}$ = Funds contributed by deposit taker 1.

on intrasectoral equity investments be excluded from the income account (which constitutes an exception to the *Guide's* general guidelines on the treatment of valuation changes on financial instruments).

46. Compared with end period 1, sector-wide capital has increased by 120, reflecting the retained earnings of deposit taker 2. The valuation gain experienced by deposit taker 1 adds to its retained earnings and capital but does not contribute any additional capital resources to the sector as a whole, because it represents a valuation gain of the sector on itself. Table A5.20 sets out the entries in the sector accounts.

Example 3: Consolidation of equity among deposit takers: unrealized valuation gains—case 2

47. In Table A5.20, the increase in price of the shares of deposit taker 2 reflected higher retained earnings. In contrast, Table A5.21 covers the treatment of a rise

Table A5.20. Consolidation of Sector-Wide Income and Capital: Unrealized Valuation Gains—Case 1

Period 2

Deposit Taker 1

Cash	40	Deposits	20
Loans	10	Capital	50
DT 2 Equity	20	*Of which: $FC_{(Other)}$*[1]	40
Purchase Value	10	RE[2]	10
Unrealized Gain	10		

Deposit Taker 2

Cash	120	Deposits	100
Loans	220	Capital	240
		Of which: $FC_{(Other)}$[1]	110
		$FC_{(DT\ 1)}$	10
		RE[2]	120

Deposit Taker 3

Cash	40	Deposits	20
Loans	20	Capital	40
		Of which: $FC_{(Other)}$	40

Consolidated Sector-Wide Position

Cash	200	Deposits	140
Loans	250	Capital	310
		Of which: $FC_{(Other)}$[1]	190
		RE[2]	120

[1]FC = Funds contributed by owners.
$FC_{(Other)}$ = Funds contributed by non-deposit takers.
$FC_{(DT\ 1)}$ = Funds contributed by deposit taker 1.
[2]RE = Retained earnings.

Table A5.21. Consolidation of Sector-Wide Income and Capital: Unrealized Valuation Gains—Case 2

Period 2

Deposit Taker 1

Assets		Liabilities	
Cash	40	Deposits	20
Loans	10	Capital	130
DT 2 Equity	100	*Of which:* $FC_{(Other)}$	40
Purchase Value	10	RE	90
Unrealized Gain	90		

Deposit Taker 2

Assets		Liabilities	
Cash	120	Deposits	100
Loans	220	Capital	240
		Of which: $FC_{(Other)}$	110
		$FC_{(DT\ 1)}$	10
		RE	120

Deposit Taker 3

Assets		Liabilities	
Cash	40	Deposits	20
Loans	20	Capital	40
		Of which: $FC_{(Other)}$	40

Consolidated Sector-Wide Position

Assets		Liabilities	
Cash	200	Deposits	140
Loans	250	Capital	310
		Of which: $FC_{(Other)}$	190
		RE	120

in the value of the share price due to market movements unconnected with an increase in retained earnings. In Table A5.21, as in Table A5.20, the retained earnings of deposit taker 2 are 120 in period 2, but in this example the price of the shares of deposit taker 2 rises to 20 per share. This increase in share price results in a valuation gain and higher retained earnings of 90 for deposit taker 1 (see Table A5.21). However, as the unrealized gain arises from the sector's claim on itself, there are no new capital resources for the sector as a whole. Thus, the sector-wide adjustments are the same as in the previous example: the market value of the equity investment of deposit taker 1 in deposit taker 2 is deducted from sector-wide capital, and the associated valuation gains are subtracted from sector-wide net income.

Example 4: Consolidation of equity among deposit takers: realized valuation gains—case 1

48. In this example, in period 2, deposit taker 1 realizes the valuation gains on its equity investment in deposit taker 2 through a sale to another sector (Table A5.22). Otherwise, the assumptions are the same as in the first valuation example above (Table A5.20). At end period 2, the cash position of deposit taker 1 has increased by 20, while its retained earnings have increased by 10. Because of the sale of the shares of deposit taker 1 in deposit taker 2 to an entity outside the sector, the capital resources of all the deposit takers now come from outside the sector. Therefore,

$$\text{Sector-wide capital (Period 2)} = \underset{(DT\ 1)}{50} + \underset{(DT\ 2)}{240} + \underset{(DT\ 3)}{40} = 330.$$

Table A5.22. Consolidation of Sector-Wide Income and Capital: Realized Valuation Gains—Case 1

Period 2A

Deposit Taker 1

Assets		Liabilities	
Cash	60	Deposits	20
Loans	10	Capital	50
		Of which: $FC_{(Other)}$	40
		RE	10

Deposit Taker 2

Assets		Liabilities	
Cash	120	Deposits	100
Loans	220	Capital	240
		Of which: $FC_{(Other)}$	110
		$FC_{(DT\ 1)}$	10
		RE	120

Deposit Taker 3

Assets		Liabilities	
Cash	40	Deposits	20
Loans	20	Capital	40
		Of which: $FC_{(Other)}$	40

Consolidated Sector-Wide Position

Assets		Liabilities	
Cash	220	Deposits	140
Loans	250	Capital	330
		Of which: $FC_{(Other)}$	210
		RE	120

49. In other words, sector-wide capital in period 2 is now simply an aggregation of the capital of the three deposit takers, since there are no intrasectoral equity investments.

50. However, with respect to income, an adjustment is required for sector-level data. If the income data for the three deposit takers were aggregated, sector-wide net income would be 130 (net income of 120 of deposit taker 2 plus realized gain of 10 of deposit taker 1). At the same time, sector-wide capital has increased by 140, consisting of the net income of 120 of deposit taker 2 plus 20 arising from the sale of the equity investment of deposit taker 1 to another sector. Because the *Guide* treats all such transactions in deposit takers' equity as equity financing transactions—transactions that can increase/decrease capital without having to go through the income account—the realized gains/losses of deposit taker 1 on the equity it owns in deposit taker 2 must be excluded from the income account. Consequently, sector-wide net income and retained earnings is 120, equal to the net income of deposit taker 2, while sector-wide capital increases by 140, reflecting 20 in financing from outside the sector, achieving consistency in the relationship between net income and capital.

51. Why does the *Guide* treat transactions in deposit takers' equity as financing transactions? It is because from a *sector-wide perspective,* it is immaterial whether the deposit taker transacting in a deposit taker's equity is the original issuer of the equity operating in the primary market (in which case, the transaction would clearly be classified as financing) or is a deposit taker buying or selling in the secondary market. All sales/purchases of deposit takers' equity vis-à-vis other sectors are exchanges of sector equity for capital resources with another sector. It follows that, if the transaction has occurred at a price higher than that initially recorded in the deposit taker's books (for example, a sale price of 4 per share as opposed to 2 per share in the books of deposit taker 2), the gain to deposit taker 1 has the nature of additional paid-in capital, which should be classified under funds contributed by owners.

52. In Table A5.22, the realized gain is recorded as an increase of 10 in the retained earnings of deposit taker 1, because that is the accounting treatment from the individual deposit taker's perspective. But from a sector-wide perspective, there is a deduction of 10 from sector-wide retained earnings for the reasons explained above.

Example 5: Consolidation of equity among deposit takers: realized valuation gains—case 2

53. In this example, in period 2, deposit taker 1 realizes the valuation gains on its equity investment in deposit taker 2 through a sale to deposit taker 3 (Table A5.23). The remaining assumptions are the same as in the first valuation example above (Table A5.20). At end period 2, the cash position of deposit taker 1 has increased by 20, while its retained earnings have increased by 10. In contrast to the previous example, the sale has not resulted in ownership of deposit takers' equity leaving the sector; ownership of the shares of deposit taker 2 remains within the deposit-taking

Table A5.23. Consolidation of Sector-Wide Income and Capital: Realized Valuation Gains—Case 2

Period 2

Deposit Taker 1				Deposit Taker 2			
Cash	60	Deposits	20	Cash	120	Deposits	100
Loans	10	Capital	50	Loans	220	Capital	240
		Of which: $FC_{(Other)}$	40			*Of which:* $FC_{(Other)}$	110
		RE	10			$FC_{(DT\ 3)}$	10
						RE	120
Deposit Taker 3				**Consolidated Sector-Wide Position**			
Cash	20	Deposits	20	Cash	200	Deposits	140
Loans	20	Capital	40	Loans	250	Capital	310
DT 2 Equity	20	*Of which:* $FC_{(Other)}$	40			*Of which:* $FC_{(Other)}$	190
Purchase Value	20					*RE*	120

sector, with the shares now owned by deposit taker 3 rather than deposit taker 1.[4] Deposit taker 3 records the share value at 20:5 shares at 4 per share.

54. Sector-wide capital in period 2 is calculated excluding the market value of the equity investment of deposit taker 3 in deposit taker 2. From the point of view of the sector, in period 2, 10 is deducted from funds contributed and 10 is subtracted from retained earnings, as shown below. However, as funds contributed and retained earnings are not presented separately in the *Guide,* only 20 should be deducted from sector-wide total (and narrow) capital and reserves.

Sector-wide capital (Period 2) =

$$\underset{(DT\ 1)}{50} + \underset{(DT\ 2)}{240} + \underset{(DT\ 3)}{40} - \underset{(FC_{(DT\ 3)})}{10} - \underset{\substack{(RE_{(DT\ 1)})\\ [market\ value]}}{10} = 310.$$

55. Sector-wide capital is the same as in period 2 in the unrealized valuation gain examples above. The realization of the valuation gain by a sale to another deposit taker has not changed total sector-wide capital, because no additional capital has been obtained from outside sectors. In essence, the deposit-taking sector has "gained" from selling its equity at a price higher than purchased (deposit taker 1 has a realized gain of 10) but has similarly "lost," because as a sector it has bought equity at a price higher than originally recorded in its books (deposit taker 3 has purchased the equity at 4 per share rather than the initial sale price of 2 per share).

56. An adjustment is required for sector-level income data. If the income data for the three deposit takers were aggregated, sector-wide net income would be 130 (net income of 120 of deposit taker 2 plus a realized gain of 10 of deposit taker 1), but sector-wide capital has increased by only 120 (the net income of deposit taker 2). Because the *Guide* treats all transactions in deposit takers' equity as equity financing transactions—transactions that can increase/decrease capital without having to go through the income account—the realized gains/losses of deposit taker 1 from holding the equity of deposit taker 2 must be excluded from the income account. Consistency is achieved in the relationship between net income and capital: sector-wide net income is 120, which is reflected in an increase of 120 in sector-wide capital as compared with period 1 (see example in Table A5.19).

57. In summary, from the four valuation examples above, it can be seen that:

- The market value of equity investments among deposit takers should be eliminated from the asset side of the deposit-taking sector's balance sheet and from total (and narrow) capital and reserves.
- All realized and unrealized gains/losses from deposit takers' ownership of and transactions in equity of other deposit takers must be excluded from sector-wide income.

Accounting for Goodwill in Sector-Wide Capital

Example 1: Purchase with cash

58. In this example, there are three deposit takers in the economy. Deposit taker 1 has 1,000 shares outstanding at a market value of 10 per share, deposit taker 2 has 400 shares outstanding at 5 per share, and deposit taker 3 has 500 shares outstanding at 5 per share, Deposit taker 1 then buys all of the shares of deposit taker 2 with cash at a market price of 5 per share (total cost 2,000), becoming a 100 percent owner of deposit taker 2. The net asset value of deposit taker 2 is 1,500. The difference between the net asset value and the price paid is goodwill (500). This amount is not recorded as an asset by deposit taker 1.

59. Table A5.24 presents the balance sheets of deposit takers 1 and 2 prior to the purchase, the balance sheet of deposit taker 1 after the purchase, the balance sheet of deposit taker 3, and the sector-wide balance sheet. In line with *Guide* recommendations, the balance sheets are all assumed to be marked-to-market, including for fixed assets.

60. After the purchase, cash declines by 2,000 in the balance sheet of deposit taker 1, offset by a prorated claim on a subsidiary (1,500) and 500 of goodwill, which is deducted from assets and from capital and reserves. On consolidation at the sector level, the prorated claim of deposit taker 1 on the subsidiary is eliminated from assets, with the counteradjustment made in the capital of the subsidiary (deposit taker 2).

Example 2: Purchase by issuing new shares

61. In this example, the assumptions are the same as in example 1 above, except that deposit taker 1 purchases the 400 of shares of deposit taker 2 by issuing

[4]Strictly speaking, the sale means that deposit taker 3, rather than deposit taker 1, has the claim on the 10 of funds contributed to deposit taker 2 by its owners.

Table A5.24. Goodwill and Sector-Wide Capital: Purchase with Cash

	Positions Prior to Purchase (at market value)					Sector-Wide Position
	Deposit taker 1	Deposit taker 2	Deposit Taker 1 (after purchase)	Deposit Taker 3	Amounts Eliminated in Consolidation	*DT 1* (after purchase) + *DT 2* + *DT 3*
Balance sheet						
Assets						
Cash	4,000	500	2,000	400	—	2,900
Other assets	8,000	1,500	8,000	3,200	—	12,700
Prorated claim on subsidiary	n.a.	n.a.	1,500	n.a.	−1,500	0
Total assets	12,000	2,000	11,500	3,600	—	15,600
Liabilities and capital						
Liabilities	2,000	500	2,000	600	—	3,100
Capital	10,000	1,500	9,500	3,000	−1,500	12,500
Total liabilities and capital	12,000	2,000	11,500	3,600	—	15,600

200 of its own shares to the owners of deposit taker 1 at the market price of 10 per share.

62. In this example (Table A5.25), the cash on the balance sheet of deposit taker 1 does not decrease following purchase, and the prorated claim of deposit taker 1 on deposit taker 2 (1,500) increases assets. There is a corresponding increase in capital, reflected in the 2,000 of equity issued less the 500 of goodwill deducted. The rationale is that while deposit taker 1 has issued 2,000 of equity, it has purchased "only" 1,500 in assets (net). On consolidation at the sector level, the prorated claim on the subsidiary is eliminated from assets. On the debit side of the sector-level balance sheet, there is a counteradjustment in the capital of the subsidiary (*DT 2*). Goodwill is eliminated from the debit side of the balance sheet of deposit taker 1, with the counteradjustment made in capital. However, because equity rather than cash was used for the purchase, the overall balance sheet (and capital) is 2,000 greater than in the example in Table A5.24.

Table A5.25. Goodwill and Sector-Wide Capital: Purchase by Issuing Shares

	Positions Prior to Purchase (at market value)					Sector-Wide Position
	Deposit taker 1	Deposit taker 2	Deposit Taker 1 (after purchase)	Deposit Taker 3	Amounts Eliminated in Consolidation	*DT 1* (after purchase) + *DT 2* + *DT 3*
Balance sheet						
Assets						
Cash	4,000	500	4,000	400	—	4,900
Other assets	8,000	1,500	8,000	3,200	—	12,700
Prorated claim on subsidiary	n.a.	n.a.	1,500	n.a.	−1,500	0
Total assets	12,000	2,000	13,500	3,600	—	17,600
Liabilities and capital						
Liabilities	2,000	500	2,000	600	—	3,100
Capital	10,000	1,500	11,500	3,000	−1,500	14,500
Total liabilities and capital	12,000	2,000	13,500	3,600	—	17,600

Table A5.26. Income and Expense Statements: Nonfinancial Corporations—Sector-Level Consolidated Data[1]

	Nonfinancial Corporation 1 A	Nonfinancial Corporation 2 B	Nonfinancial Corporation 3 C	Aggregation A + B + C	Sector-Level Consolidated Data A + B + C +/– (Sector Consolidation Adjustment)
1. Revenue from sales of goods and services (excluding indirect sales taxes)	80.0	400.0	1,700.0	2,180.0	2,180.0
2. Cost of sales	90.0	200.0	1,500.0	1,790.0	1,790.0
3. *Operating income (= 1 minus 2)*	*–10.0*	*200.0*	*200.0*	*390.0*	*390.0*
4. Interest income	0.4	2.2	9.3	11.9	11.9
5. Interest expense	12.6	14.0	20.0	46.6	46.6
6. Other income (net)	1.0	10.0	5.0	16.0	9.0
7. *Net income (before extraordinary items and taxes) (= 3 + 4 minus 5 + 6)*	*–21.2*	*198.2*	*194.3*	*371.3*	*364.3*
8. Extraordinary items	—	—	—	—	—
9. Corporate income taxes	—	40.0	38.9	78.9	78.9
10. Net income after taxes (= 7 minus (8 + 9))	–21.2	158.2	155.4	292.4	285.4
11. Dividends payable	—	108.0	105.0	213.0	211.0
12. *Retained earnings (= 10 minus 11)*	*–21.2*	*50.2*	*50.4*	*79.4*	*74.4*

[1]For a description of the line items, refer to Chapter 4.

Part 4. Calculating FSIs for Nonfinancial Corporations

63. The following examples illustrate the application of the principles involved in deriving sector-level data and FSIs for nonfinancial corporations.

The Data Set

64. A set of data for income and expense, balance sheet, and associated memorandum items is provided below and is used to calculate FSIs. The data set provided is consistent with the guidelines in Chapters 4 and 7.

65. In this example, the economy has three resident nonfinancial corporations.[5] There are financial relations among them in the form of cross-holdings of debt and equity securities, but none of the equity holdings qualify as an associate investment. End-period financial statements (income and balance sheet accounts) for the three resident corporations are presented in Tables A5.26 and A5.27, together with aggregated and sector-level income and balance sheet statements.

66. Among the corporations, it can be seen that corporation 3 is the largest in terms of total assets, followed by corporation 2. All three corporations have substantial holdings of nonfinancial produced assets (fixed assets and inventories) and nonproduced assets (for example, land) employed in the production of nonfinancial goods and services. Corporations 2 and 3 also have large holdings of financial assets and strong capital positions. By contrast, corporation 1 has minimal holdings of financial assets and a modest capital position. On the income and expense side, corporation 1 had a loss in the current period. Corporations 2 and 3 had profits for the period that exceeded dividends payable.

Computation of Sector-Level Data and FSIs

67. Using the guidance in Chapter 7 and the financial statements of the three nonfinancial corporations, Table A5.28 presents the agreed FSIs at the

[5]As noted in Chapter 5, data might be compiled on both domestically controlled cross-border consolidated and domestic consolidated bases. The extended data set for deposit takers illustrates the issues involved in compiling domestically controlled cross-border consolidated data.

Table 5A.27. Balance Sheets: Nonfinancial Corporations—Sector-Level Consolidated Data[1]

	Nonfinancial Corporation 1 A	Nonfinancial Corporation 2 B	Nonfinancial Corporation 3 C	Aggregation A + B + C	Sector-Level Consolidated Data A + B + C +/– (Sector Consolidation Adjustment)
13. Total assets (= 14 + 17)	126.0	761.0	837.0	1,724.0	1,709.0
14. *Nonfinancial assets*	*125.0*	*650.0*	*560.0*	*1,335.0*	*1,335.0*
15. Produced	95.0	570.0	470.0	1,135.0	1,135.0
Of which: (i) Fixed assets	90.0	500.0	410.0	1,000.0	1,000.0
(ii) Inventories	5.0	70.0	60.0	135.0	135.0
16. Nonproduced	30.0	80.0	90.0	200.0	200.0
17. *Financial assets*	*1.0*	*111.0*	*277.0*	*389.0*	*374.0*
18. Currency and deposits	0.6	40.0	150.0	190.6	190.6
19. Debt securities	0.2	40.0	70.0	110.2	110.2
Of which: Issued by other nonfinancial corporations in reporting population	—	20.0	40.0	60.0	60.0
20. Shares and other equity	—	25.0	50.0	75.0	60.0
21. Trade credit	—	2.0	3.0	5.0	5.0
22. Financial derivatives	0.1	3.0	2.0	5.1	5.1
23. Other assets	0.1	1.0	2.0	3.1	3.1
24. *Total liabilities (= 29 + 30)*	*104.0*	*201.0*	*400.0*	*705.0*	*705.0*
25. Loans	20.0	—	—	20.0	20.0
26. Debt securities	84.0	200.0	400.0	684.0	684.0
27. Trade credit	—	—	—	—	—
28. Other liabilities	—	—	—	—	—
29. *Debt (= 25 through 28)*	*104.0*	*200.0*	*400.0*	*704.0*	*704.0*
30. Financial derivatives	—	1.0	—	1.0	1.0
31. Capital and reserves	22.0	560.0	437.0	1,019.0	1,004.0
(i) Narrow capital[2]	20.0	300.0	110.0	430.0	415.0
32. **Balance sheet total = (24 + 31 = 13)**	126.0	761.0	837.0	1,724.0	1,709.0
Memorandum series[2]					
Other series required to calculate the agreed FSIs					
33. Interest income receivable from other nonfinancial corporations	—	2.0	4.0	6.0	
34. Earnings before interest and tax (items 3 + 4 + 6 minus 33)	–8.6	210.2	210.3	411.9	
35. Debt service payments	16.6	24.0	48.0	88.6	
36. Corporate net foreign exchange exposure for on-balance-sheet items	—	–4.0	40.0	36.0	
37. Total corporate net foreign exchange exposure	—	–2.0	22.0	20.0	
Intrasector positions and flows					
Dividends receivable from other nonfinancial corporations[2]	—	1.0	1.0	2.0	
Gains/losses on equity investments in other nonfinancial corporations[2]	—	2.0	3.0	5.0	

[1]For a description of the line items, refer to Chapter 4.
[2]Included in Table 11.7 of the *Guide*.

Table A5.28. Financial Soundness Indicators: Nonfinancial Corporations—Sector-Level Consolidated Data[1,2]

	Nonfinancial Corporation 1		Nonfinancial Corporation 2		Nonfinancial Corporation 3		Sector Level	
Total debt to equity	**473%**	**520%**	**36%**	**67%**	**92%**	**364%**	**70%**	**170%**
Numerator (line 29)	104.0	104.0	200.0	200.0	400.0	400.0	704.0	704.0
Denominator (line 31 and 31(i))	22.0	20.0	560.0	300.0	437.0	110.0	1,004.0	415.0
Return on equity	**–39%**	**–43%**	**38%**	**70%**	**48%**	**191%**	**41%**	**99%**
Numerator (line 34)	–8.60	–8.60	210.20	210.20	210.30	210.30	411.90	411.90
Denominator (line 31 and 31(i))	22.00	20.00	560.00	300.00	437.00	110.00	1,004.00	415.00
Debt-service coverage	**–52%**		**884%**		**446%**		**472%**	
Numerator (line 34 plus line 33)	–8.6		212.2		214.3		417.9	
Denominator (line 35)	16.6		24.0		48.0		88.6	
Net foreign exchange exposure to equity (on balance sheet)	**—**	**—**	**–1%**	**–1%**	**9%**	**36%**	**4%**	**9%**
Numerator (line 36)	—	—	–4.0	–4.0	40.0	40.0	36.0	36.0
Denominator (line 31 and 31(i))	22.0	20.0	560.0	300.0	437.0	110.0	1,004.0	415.0
Total net foreign exchange exposure to equity	**—**	**—**	**0%**	**–1%**	**5%**	**20%**	**2%**	**5%**
Numerator (line 37)	—	—	–2.0	–2.0	22.0	22.0	20.0	20.0
Denominator (line 31 and 31(i))	22.0	20.0	560.0	300.0	437.0	110.0	1,004.0	415.0
Number of applications for protection from creditors							**10**	

[1]For the specification of the FSIs, refer to Chapter 7.

[2]Two sets of ratios are shown for those using capital: the first set uses total capital, consistent with the definition of the FSI; the second set uses narrow capital, an additional approach (see Appendix III).

sector level and, for illustrative purposes, for each corporation individually. Moreover, where relevant, the numerator and denominator for each FSI are shown. The last columns in Tables A5.26 and A5.27 show the sector-level consolidated data that are used to calculate FSIs and incorporate the sector-level consolidation adjustments discussed in Chapter 5. The data series that have been adjusted are highlighted. The adjustments are described below.

- Income and expense statement (Table A5.26)
  - Corporation 2 and corporation 3 have valuation gains of 5 on their holdings of equity investments in other nonfinancial corporations in the reporting population (see the second item under *intrasector positions and flows in Table A5.27*), which are eliminated from other income (net) and from retained earnings in the sector-level consolidated data.
  - Corporation 2 and corporation 3 have dividends receivable of 2 from corporations in the reporting population (see the first item under *intrasector positions and flows in Table A5.27*), which are eliminated from other income (net) and dividends payable in the sector-level consolidated data.
  - Corporation 2 and corporation 3 also receive interest income from corporations in the reporting population (see memorandum item 33), but these intrasector payments net out in the net income line and are therefore *not* eliminated from the gross interest income and interest expense lines (lines 4 and 5) in the sector-level consolidated income and expense statement.
- Balance sheet (Table A5.27)
  - Corporation 2 and corporation 3 have portfolio equity investments of 15 in corporations in the reporting population. To avoid double counting of capital, the market value of these equity investments is deducted from shares and other equity on the asset side and from capital and reserves in the sector-level data.
  - Corporation 2 and corporation 3 also hold debt instruments issued by corporations in the reporting population (see item 19 in the balance sheet statements), but these intrasector holdings are *not* eliminated in the sector-level data, thus enabling the monitoring of risk exposure and potential contagion.

Appendix VI. Remaining Issues: Provisioning, Interest Rate Risk, and Stress Testing

1. The *Guide* provides guidance for the purpose of compiling and disseminating FSIs. Nonetheless, in the course of the discussions preparing the *Guide,* it became clear that on some issues related to the development of data for use in supporting macroprudential analysis, there was no international consensus or best practice to draw on. This appendix describes current practices and concepts on three such issues, (1) provisioning, (2) measuring interest rate risk, and (3) stress testing, with the objective of supporting national efforts to further develop this work.

Part I. Approaches to the Classification of Assets and Provisioning

Introduction

2. There is no international consensus on best provisioning practices, resulting in significant differences among countries in the reported financial statements of deposit takers. This undermines meaningful cross-country comparisons of FSI data. The BCBS and the IMF have published several papers to encourage best practices.[1] In this section, various approaches to provisioning are reviewed to help indicate a possible framework within which key decisions on provisioning policy could be addressed.[2] These approaches do not necessarily constitute international best practice. The *Guide* relies on national practice in identifying loan loss provisions.

3. In 2003, the World Bank undertook a study titled "Bank Loan Classification and Provisioning Practices in Selected Developed and Emerging Countries" (hereafter referred to as BLCP) that provides the best overall information on current practices.[3] This text is largely based on that study.

Loan Classification and Review

4. The BLCP found that authorities in all 29 countries surveyed require banks to establish loan review procedures to examine the quality of individual loans or portfolios of loans for classification and provisioning purposes. However, the practices adopted are diverse as is the frequency of review.

Loan classification

5. While the BLCP found a very wide range of philosophies and practices, in almost all the countries surveyed, the supervisor has the authority to issue prudential regulations regarding classification of loans. These classifications vary across countries, but an example is provided in the loan classification scheme proposed by the Institute for International Finance (IIF).[4] It has five categories:

- *Standard.* Credit is sound and all principal and interest payments are current. Repayment difficulties are not foreseen under current circumstances, and full repayment is expected.
- *Watch (special mention).* The credit is subject to conditions that, if left uncorrected, could raise concerns

[1]These include BCBS (1999); Cortavarria and others (2000); and Song (2002).

[2]At the IMF Executive Board meeting on FSIs in July 2001, in developing harmonized standards and practices for compiling FSIs, in consultation with relevant international standard-setting organizations, the Directors stated, "Special attention should be given to improving the international comparability of data for nonperforming assets and provisions, and the valuation of liabilities as well as assets."

[3]See Laurin and Majnoni (2003). The study drew on data collected by the Basel Core Principles Liaison Group (CPLG) on practices of its 29 members. Countries surveyed included France, Germany, Italy, Japan, the Netherlands, the United Kingdom, and the United States, among the G-10 countries. Non-G-10 countries were Argentina, Australia, Brazil, Chile, China, the Czech Republic, Hong Kong SAR, India, the Republic of Korea, Mexico, Russia, Saudi Arabia, Singapore, South Africa, Spain, and the West African Monetary Union (WAMU).

[4]The IIF is a private sector association of financial institutions that analyzes risks in emerging market economies, serves as forum for members to discuss key policy issues in emerging markets' finance and regulation, and promotes collaboration between members and multilateral institutions.

about full repayment. Such credit requires more than normal attention by credit officers.
- *Substandard.* Full repayment is in doubt due to inadequate protection (for example, on account of diminished obligor net worth or collateral), and/or interest or principal or both are more than 90 days overdue. These assets show underlying, well-defined weaknesses that could lead to probable loss if not corrected.
- *Doubtful.* Assets for which collection/liquidation in full is determined by bank management to be improbable due to current conditions, and/or interest or principal or both are overdue more than 180 days. Assets in this category are considered impaired[5] but are not yet considered total losses because some pending factors may strengthen the asset's quality (merger, new financing, or capital injection).
- *Loss (write-off).* An asset is downgraded to loss when management considers it to be virtually uncollectible, and/or principal or interest or both are overdue more than one year.

6. As further examples, the loan classification schemes of the United States and Japan are provided in Boxes A6.1 and A6.2.

Review practices

7. Country practices differ on whether ex post or ex ante information should be used to assess loan classification. Ex post methods rely on specific observable evidence from past behavior (such as 90-day nonpayment of interest and/or principal) or from the current condition of the debtor. Ex ante methods assess future losses by considering forward-looking information and a wide range of factors that could affect the ability of the debtor to meet the loan conditions. Reliance on ex ante methods has been increasing with the shift toward more risk-focused supervision and the use of internal models to evaluate risk.

8. In addition, other differences among country practices are evident:
- Some countries follow standard regulatory prescriptions; others allow internal bank evaluations.
- Some countries evaluate the portfolio on an asset-by-asset basis; others require creditors to treat the entire portfolio of loans to a single borrower as

[5]*Impaired* is a supervisory term that implies that there are doubts over whether all the amounts due under a contract will be paid.

Box A6.1. U.S. Loan Classification System (Commercial Bank Examination Manual)

- ***Standard assets.*** Loans in this category are performing and have sound fundamentals. (Fundamentals include the borrower's overall financial condition, resources and cash flow, credit history, and character. They also include the purpose of the loan and types of secondary sources of repayment.)
- ***Specially mentioned loans.*** Loans in this category are performing but have potential weaknesses that, if not corrected, may weaken the loan and the bank's asset quality. Examples are credit that the lending officer is unable to properly supervise, an inadequate loan agreement, uncertainty of the condition of collateral, or other deviations from prudent lending practices.
- ***Substandard loans.*** Loans in this category have well-defined weaknesses, where the current sound worth and paying capacity of the borrower is not assured. Orderly repayment of debt is in jeopardy.
- ***Doubtful loans.*** Doubtful loans exhibit all the characteristics of substandard loans, with the added characteristics that collection in full is highly questionable and improbable. Classification of "loss" is deferred because of specific pending factors that may strengthen the asset. Such factors include merger, acquisition, or liquidation procedures; capital injection; perfecting liens on additional collateral; and refinancing plans.
- ***Loss loans.*** These loans are considered uncollectible and of such little value that their continuance as bankable assets is not warranted. This classification does not mean that the asset has absolutely no recovery or salvage value but rather that it is not practical or desirable to defer full provision or writing off this basically worthless loan. Partial recovery may be effected in the future.

Box A6.2. Loan Classification System of Japanese Financial Supervisory Agency

- ***Category I.*** Assets with no problems in terms of collectability.
- ***Category II.*** Assets with higher collectability risk than normal because of difficulties in fulfilling contracted conditions, or due to concerns about the credit risk of the borrower (15% provisioning required).
- ***Category III.*** Assets with concerns over final collection of value. Losses are likely to be incurred, but it is difficult to make estimates of the timing and scale of losses (70% provisioning required).
- ***Category IV.*** Assets that are assessed as uncollectible or of no value.

impaired if any of the loans to that borrower are impaired.
- The degree to which collateral, guarantees, or other mitigating factors can be taken into consideration varies.
- The definition of *restructured troubled assets* and whether they are treated as impaired varies across countries.

Standard regulatory prescriptions versus allowing internal bank evaluations

9. Some countries have prescriptive systems that specify definitions for classifying loans into different categories based on the likelihood of default. The BLCP suggests that countries with less sophisticated supervisory systems often opt for these more explicit systems because they can be easier to monitor, provide for greater comparability, create a more even playing field among banks, promote better public understanding, and facilitate the compiling of statistical measures for off-site supervision and dissemination. Although there seems to be some convergence among these prescriptive systems toward the use of the five categories of loan quality outlined above, numerous exceptions were found.

10. Some other countries have systems that stress management responsibility in classifying loans and setting the size of provisions, with supervisors and auditors focusing on the oversight of the adequacy of the banks' own internal evaluations and procedures and how well they are implemented. Depending on the country, banks may either be required to establish a classification system or be provided with a basic definition of what constitutes impaired assets, with little or no guidance regarding the appropriate size of provisions.

Classification of multiple loans

11. The BLCP shows that although just over half of the countries in its sample require the downgrading of all loans to a common debtor if any of these loans are classified as impaired, other countries permit a debtor's loans to be evaluated separately or leave the decision to the discretion of individual banks. Moreover, an important related issue is whether the standards apply to the specific debtor that issued the impaired asset or to broader groups of related enterprises, under the presumption that weaknesses within one part of a group suggest weakness throughout the group.

Collateral and guarantees

12. Collateral and guarantees are off-balance-sheet instruments that can reduce the ultimate loss on impaired credits; however, the BLCP found wide differences in supervisory practice. In some jurisdictions the type and amount of collateral and guarantees may be taken into consideration in determining (1) whether the credit is impaired, (2) the recoverable amount and thereby the classification of the credit, and (3) the size of provisions needed. Often, the types of acceptable collateral and their valuation are regulated, and real estate collateral often receives special attention.

13. The liquidity of collateral and the enforceability of claims on collateral and guarantees were found to sometimes affect classification and provisioning. For example, a more creditworthy classification of an asset may be permitted if liquid securities are used as collateral instead of real estate. Where real estate is used as collateral, several countries require reductions in its value (including down to zero) the longer the period of nonrepayment of the credit. Nonetheless, fewer than one-third of respondents considered the condition of collateral in classifying loans, giving weight to the view that the quality of a loan should be judged in its own right independent of collateral and guarantees. Moreover, collateral may involve different debtors, payment conditions and flows, and maturities; it may also be characterized by a different probability of payment than the original loan.[6] Indeed, there is some prevalence of the practice not to consider declines in the value of loan collateral or guarantees as a basis for classifying the loan as impaired, although in such circumstances special mention status could be justified.

14. Disclosures of the treatment of collateral would permit a more ready comparison of data from countries that follow different practices regarding provisions.

Classification of restructured troubled loans

15. Restructured troubled loans are those for which the lender grants concessions it would not otherwise grant because of the debtor's financial difficulty. Restructuring and the lending of new funds to cover

[6]Pillar II of the revised Basel Capital Accord (Basel II) recommends a general disclosure by all bank of total gross credit exposures, by major type of credit exposure (such as loans, securities, and OTC derivatives) without taking into account the effects of credit mitigation such as collateral. (See BCBS, 2003a, Table 4, p. 160.)

the nonpayment of older debts can disguise weakness in credits, and therefore some regulators have rules to define restructured troubled loans to prevent such practices.[7] Although payments on restructured troubled loans may continue, they often are treated identically with impaired assets for provisioning purposes until a record of payment is established, after which they can be upgraded.

16. The BLCP found that 15 of 23 countries define restructured troubled loans by regulation; explicit definitions were much more common outside the G-10 countries.

Frequency of review

17. The BLCP data indicate that 16 of 23 countries require loan review for classification purposes at least every quarter. Often, more frequent review is required for large exposures or for assets deemed less creditworthy.

Provisioning

18. Given the classification of an asset, what size of provision should be applied? Do provisions relate to specific and identifiable events resulting in loss, or to probable losses? When is specific and general provisioning used? How should collateral be treated? Are there specific levels of provisioning for each asset classification, or is this the prerogative of individual banks, or case by case? Different philosophies and practices exist on these matters.

Do provisions relate to specific and identifiable events resulting in loss, or to probable losses?

19. In practice, this issue appears to be closely related to whether classification standards are prescribed by regulation covering readily observable factors or whether they are based on more comprehensive and diffuse reviews of the condition of the borrower. The BLCP found that countries, especially emerging market economies, that prescribe classification rules also frequently prescribe provisioning levels so that they are simple, verifiable, and enforceable. In contrast, countries that emphasize general guidance on classification tend to base provisioning more on estimates of probable losses, which sometimes are based on internal models and estimates of probabilities of default (PD) and of losses given default (LGD). These latter countries might permit provisions to be set within ranges.

When are specific and general provisioning used?

20. A specific provision is a current charge reflecting the loss in value of impaired assets. In contrast, a general provision is a reserve within the capital account that reflects the amount of losses that a portfolio may experience. A dynamic provision is a form of general provision that is adjusted over the course of the economic cycle—being built up during good economic times and drawn down in downturns—to provide for sufficient reserves over the entire life of the financial instrument. Dynamic provisioning is a new concept practiced only in Spain among the countries covered in the BLCP study.[8]

How should collateral be treated?

21. The discussion above on collateral and guarantees describes some of the ways in which collateral can reduce the ultimate loss on impaired credits. The BLCP found that 12 of the 23 countries permitted the use of collateral to reduce the size of provisions, with its use most common among the G-10 countries in the sample.[9] Where use of collateral was permitted in setting provision levels, wide variation was found in the types of collateral permitted in different situations and its valuation.

Are there specific levels of provisioning for each asset classification, or is this the prerogative of individual banks?

22. As noted above, different countries follow different philosophies. The BLCP provided data on the level of provisions set for different asset classifications in

[7] When general improvements in market borrowing conditions occur, banks may renegotiate loan conditions with their clients that are unrelated to any weaknesses in the loan. Such restructuring does not result in adverse classification of the loan or in provisioning. Thus, regulations must be able to distinguish between restructurings of troubled assets and beneficial restructuring of strong assets.

[8] See de Lis, Pagés, and Saurina (2000).

[9] The BLCP does not deal with possible reasons for this pattern, but if it stems from the greater recoverability of collateral in G-10 countries because of the depth of their markets and efficiency of their legal systems, then the use of collateral for setting provisions may be a special case rather than a general pattern. In any event, no simple one-to-one relationship exists between the market value of the collateral and the offset it can provide for provisioning purposes.

Table A6.1. Levels of Provisions for Different Loan Classifications

Classification	Number of Countries Specifying Provisions	Months of Nonpayment	Most Common Level of Provisions (In percent)	Typical Range of Provisions (In percent)
Standard	7/23	—	1	0.25–1
Special mention	6/23	Up to 3	3 or 5	2–5
Substandard	10/23	Over 3 or up to 6	20	10–25
Doubtful	12/23	Over 6	50	50–75
Write-off	10/23	No guidance	100	100

each country based on a classification system in line with that of the IIF, as summarized in Table A6.1.

- The column "Number of Countries Specifying Provisions" indicates the number out of the 23 countries at each classification level that requires specific levels of provisioning. It appears that only about one-half of the respondents require specific provisioning levels, which means that common international patterns have not yet been established, and that in many countries banks probably have substantial leeway in setting provisions.
  The column "Months of Nonpayment" provides the number of months of nonpayment of principal or interest on the loan that is considered evidence of specific levels of impairment. There appears to be some convergence on three months as evidence of basic impairment, and six months as evidence of more severe impairment among those countries that provide such guidelines.
- The remaining columns provide information on the most common levels of provisioning for each loan category and a typical range for provisions, expressed as a percentage of the value of the asset. Although there are hints of convergence around certain values, there are too few cases among the 23 respondents to conclude that there are general international practices.

Tax Treatment of Loan Loss Provisions

23. The tax deduction of specific provisions, which the BLCP found to be nearly universal, affects the reported income, balance sheet, and the capital adequacy ratio. However, variations in tax deductibility exist; fewer than one-third of respondents permit tax deductibility of general provisions, and various caps or special conditions apply to tax deductibility in some cases. The timing of tax deductibility for provisions varies, which affects the reported income: the study showed that a small number of respondents permit tax deductions only in write-off or near write-off situations.

Disclosure

24. In general, deposit takers are currently not expected to provide detailed information on the classification of loans. In contrast, the BLCP found that disclosure of aggregate information on total provisions in the current period is more common. Finally, the BLCP found that in practice, most G-10 and non-G-10 supervisors do not impose penalties on banks that breach disclosure requirements. In summary, with a few exceptions, the disclosure requirements of loan classification and provisioning are not strong.

Conclusions

25. While there is increased awareness of the need for good classification and provisioning systems, the evidence also suggests that little convergence has occurred to date among countries. There are, however, a number of methods and approaches that are in practice in a large number of countries: carrying out loan review on a quarterly or more frequent basis, adopting a multistage classification system, and classifying loans independently of the condition of collateral and guarantees. Future movement in these areas could considerably contribute to improvements in the usefulness and comparability of FSIs, but they are the responsibility of international and regional standard setters in accounting, supervision, valuation, and auditing.

Part 2. Measuring Interest Rate Risk

26. Because of their role in financial intermediation and the nature of their assets and liabilities, deposit takers need to manage interest rate risk—that is, the

Table A6.2. Interest Rate Risk[1]
(In thousands of units of account, as of the end of period)

	0–3 Months	4–6 Months	7–12 Months	1–2 Years	2–5 Years	5–10 Years	10–15 Years	15–20 Years	20 Years and Above
Assets Debt instruments									
Liabilities Debt instruments									
Interest-rate-based financial derivatives									
Difference									
Cumulative									

[1]For fixed-rate instruments to receive/pay fixed-rate-linked payments, expected amounts to be paid/received are recorded according to their remaining maturity. Thus, for a bond with just under two years to maturity and annual coupon payments, the amount of the annual coupon payment will be included in the time bucket column of 7–12 months and the remainder of the payments in the one to two years time bucket column.

For variable-rate instruments contracts to receive/pay variable-rate-linked payments, amounts expected to be paid or received are recorded in the time period at which the next repricing of interest rates is scheduled to occur. Thus, a bond on which the interest is due to be repriced every six months will include the redemption amount of the bond and the next scheduled interest payment under either the first or second time bucket columns, depending on how recently the repricing occurred.

For interest-rate-based financial derivatives, the net amounts expected to be received (+) or paid (–) are to be recorded in each time period, as appropriate.

exposure of capital to interest rate changes. However, standard practices do not exist for monitoring this risk at the sector level.[10,11] The techniques for monitoring interest rate risk are still being developed, by the BCBS and other institutions. Drawing on those approaches used by individual institutions, this appendix describes two common approaches—the "gap" model and duration. Measuring the effects of interest rate changes on interest income and expense using the "interest rate repricing gap" model is also described.

The Gap Model

Price effects

27. One approach to assessing interest rate changes on the market price of a portfolio of assets and liabilities is to use *gap analysis*. Under this approach, expected payments on assets and liabilities are sorted into various time "buckets" according to the time to repricing for floating-rate instruments and the time until payments are due for fixed-rate instruments.[12] As with duration, debt assets and liabilities that are market or fair valued could be covered. The net amounts (receipts minus payments) expected under single-currency interest-rate-based financial derivatives are also included. Table A6.2 provides an illustration of the time buckets that could be set.

28. The net difference (gap) or the gross positions in each time bucket can be multiplied by some assumed change in interest rates and discounted, to gain an indication of the interest rate sensitivity of deposit takers' portfolio of financial assets and liabilities. For instance, one approach could be to consider the impact of the largest interest rate change observed in recent history or some multiple of the standard deviation of interest rates in recent times.

[10]Changes in interest rates change the present value of future cash flows and in some cases the cash flows themselves.

[11]Sources of interest rate risk are discussed in BCBS (2003c).

[12]Amounts payable on demand are included in the first bucket—zero to three months.

29. The gap approach has the advantage of simplicity and intuitive appeal. But by grouping different assets together under broad time buckets, it can mask mismatches in maturities among assets in the same time bucket. For example, liabilities may tend to be repriced toward the end of the range of maturities in a bucket, while assets may tend to be repriced toward the beginning. To avoid this problem, the measure of duration provides a more accurate measure of exposure to interest rate risk; it is described later in this appendix.

Implementing the gap model

30. The use of the gap model can be demonstrated with reference to the first two columns of Table A6.3 showing the annual cash flow payments on two financial instruments. If instrument 1 is assumed to be an asset and instrument 2 a liability, the gain or loss associated with a change in the shape of the yield curve can be estimated as shown in Table A6.3:

31. The difference between NPV_1 and NPV_2 provides the capital gain or loss associated with the assumed change in interest rates. Thus, in Table A6.3, the steepening of the yield curve results in a capital loss of 32 (= 9 + 23). For a portfolio of assets and liabilities with cash flows occurring at different times within each bucket, a weighted average discount factor for each bucket can be used, with the weights given by the proportional size of the individual cash flows occurring in each bucket.

32. Positions in financial derivatives can be incorporated into the gap analysis by estimating changes in the net present value of expected future payments/receipts as interest rates change. For instance, if the expected payment on a bond futures contract in five years' time changed from 0 to 10, the change in the present value of the expected payment of 6.1 would partially offset (hedge) the capital loss expected when the yield curve becomes more steep.[13]

Table A6.3. Example of Gap Analysis

Time	Asset	Liabilities	Gaps (Assets minus Liabilities)	NPV_1^1	NPV_2^2
0–1 years	80	70	10	9	9
1–2 years	80	70	10	8	9
2–3 years	80	70	10	8	8
3–4 years	80	70	10	7	7
4–5 years	80	1,070	–990	–609	–601
5–6 years	1,080	—	1,080	600	559
				23	–9

[1]NPV_1 = Net present $value_1$ = Gap × Discount factor specified in the first row of Table A6.8.

[2]NPV_2 = Net present $value_2$ = Gap × Discount factor specified in the second row of Table A6.8.

Net interest income effects

33. By considering the time to repricing of assets and liabilities, the effect of an interest rate change on interest income and expense can be estimated. The so-called repricing gap model allocates interest-bearing assets and liabilities into buckets according to their time to repricing, and the gap between assets and liabilities in each bucket is then used to estimate the net interest income exposure to interest rate changes.[14] For example, interest-rate-sensitive assets and liabilities with a time to repricing of one year or less are shown in Table A6.4.[15]

34. The one-day gap indicates a difference of minus 10 million between assets and liabilities being repriced in one day. A proportionate rise in interest rates on these assets and liabilities would therefore lower net interest income because there are more interest-rate-sensitive liabilities than assets in this bucket.

35. More generally, for a given change in interest rates (ΔR_i), the repricing gap can be used to calculate the changes in income in each bucket *i:*

$$\Delta Net\ interest\ income_i = GAP_i \times \Delta R_i.^{16}$$

36. For the first bucket, the impact of a 1 percent rate increase ($\Delta R_i = 0.01$) on future income is –100,000.[17] By repeating the calculation for each bucket, the overall effect on net interest income for a one-year horizon

[13]Calculated by multiplying 10 by the discount factor of 0.6070.

[14]Measuring the effect of interest rate changes on interest income and expense should include all interest-bearing instruments, whether they are fair valued or not.

[15]Alternatively, cash flows associated with expected future interest income and interest expenses can be specified and discounted to the current period.

[16]If different interest rates are used for assets and liabilities, the assumed change in rates will need to be applied to assets and liabilities separately in each bucket, rather than to the gap between assets and liabilities in each bucket.

[17](–10 million) × 0.01.

Table A6.4. Interest-Rate-Sensitive Assets and Liabilities with a Time to Repricing of One Year or Less
(In millions)

Time to Repricing	Assets	Liabilities	Gaps (Assets Minus Liabilities)	Cumulative Gap
1 day	20	30	–10	–10
More than 1 day to 3 months	30	40	–10	–20
More than 3 months to 6 months	70	85	–15	–35
More than 6 months to 12 months	90	70	20	–15

(if annualized interest rates are applied to each time bucket) can be estimated. Depending on the time horizon used, it may be necessary to discount the impact on the gaps to the current period.

37. Positions in interest-rate-based financial derivatives can be incorporated into this analysis by recalculating the expected future receipts and payments as interest rates change. For instance, if following the interest rate shock the change in expected net receipts/payments on an interest rate swap contract maturing in 12 months is +150,000, this partially offsets (hedges) the net interest income loss on nonderivative positions associated with the rate change.

Duration

38. Duration[18] measures the maturity of an instrument by taking account of the size and timing of payments between now and maturity. Even if the maturities of financial assets and liabilities are matched, a difference in the timing of the cash flows on those assets and liabilities can expose institutions to gains (or losses) as interest rates change. Thus, the longer the duration of the portfolio of assets or liabilities, the greater the gains (or losses) for any given change in interest rates.[19]

39. A simple measure of duration (Macaulay Duration) can be calculated for any fixed-income security by using the general formula set out below:

$$D_i = \frac{\sum_{t=1}^{N} CF_t \times DF_t \times t}{\sum_{t=1}^{N} CF_t \times DF_t} = \frac{\sum_{t=1}^{N} PV_t \times t}{\sum_{t=1}^{N} PV_t},$$

where

D_i = Duration measured in years for instrument i;
CF_t = Cash flow to be received on the financial instrument at end of period t;
N = Last period in which the cash flow is received (maturity of instrument);
DF_t = Discount factor = $1/(1 + R)^t$, where R is the yield or current level of interest rates in the market (the discount rates on government bonds are commonly used as the discount factor, R, to reflect the time value of money);
$\sum_{t=1}^{N}$ = Summation sign for addition of all terms for $t = 1$ to $t = N$; and
PV_t = Present value of the cash flow due at the end of the period t, which equals $CF_t \times DF_t$.

Duration of a single instrument

40. To illustrate how duration can be measured for a single debt security, suppose the annual coupon on a eurobond is 8 percent, the face value of the bond is $1,000, and the current yield to maturity (R) is also 8 percent. The calculation of duration (D) is shown in Table A6.5.

41. Many bonds carry floating interest rates linked to market rates. The duration of such floating-rate instruments is the time interval to when the next coupon or interest payment is readjusted to reflect current interest rate conditions, referred to as the time to repricing of the instrument. For instance, if a floating-rate note with a coupon rate set at the beginning of each year is bought in the middle of the first year, it has duration of a half-year.

[18]This section is based on Saunders (1999) and Jorion (1997).

[19]Duration is a direct measure of the interest rate sensitivity or elasticity of an asset or liability. The larger the numerical value of duration (D), the more sensitive the price of that asset or liability is to changes in interest rates. For instance, for small changes in interest rates, bond prices move in an inversely proportional fashion according the size of D: $dP/P = -D[dR/(1 + R)]$.

Table A6.5. Duration (D) of a Six-Year Eurobond with 8 Percent Coupon and Yield

Time	CF_t	DF_t	$CF_t \times DF_t$	$CF_t \times DF_t \times t$	Calculation of Duration (D)
1	80	0.9259	74.07	74.07	$D = \frac{4,992.71}{1,000.00} = 4.993$ years
2	80	0.8573	68.59	137.17	
3	80	0.7938	63.51	190.52	
4	80	0.7350	58.80	235.21	
5	80	0.6806	54.45	272.23	
6	1,080	0.6302	680.58	4,083.50	
			1,000.00	4,992.71	

Duration of a portfolio

42. The duration of a portfolio of financial instruments can be calculated as a simple weighted average of individual durations. This is the measure of duration specified in the memoranda items to the deposit taker's balance sheet (Table A3.2). For example, if x_i represents the share of the portfolio invested in bond i, the portfolio duration is

$$D_P = \sum_{i=1}^{M} x_i D_i,$$

where D_i is the duration of bond i.

43. Thus a portfolio with \$100 million, equally invested in five-year bonds and one-year bonds with respective durations of 4.465 years and 1 year, has duration of $(0.5 \times 4.465) + (0.5 \times 1) = 2.733$ years.

44. Table A6.6 provides an illustration for a portfolio of two asset and two liability interest-rate-sensitive instruments, where the portfolio duration for assets (D^A) is 4.41 years and for liabilities (D^L) is 6.25 years.

45. All traded debt instruments that are marked to market or fair valued on the balance sheet can be included in the calculation of portfolio duration.[20] Relevant positions in financial derivatives and off-balance-sheet instruments should also be included in the analysis of interest rate risk (see below).

[20]While demand deposits are not usually included in measures of duration used to assess price revaluation effects, at the end of this section there is a discussion of measuring duration for these instruments in the event that they are fair valued.

Duration at the sector level

46. Measures of duration at the *sector level* can be calculated as a simple weighted average of the individual deposit taker's asset and liability durations, using as weights the market value of the instruments included in the institution's measure of duration. The market values used as weights may be derived from the instrument analysis shown in Table 4.1 or may be obtained directly from the reporting institutions. To illustrate, Table A6.7 shows the derivation of sector-wide duration data.

47. While the concept is simple to express, experience has shown that there are practical difficulties in compiling sector-level duration data. For instance, there is a need to ensure consistency among reporting institutions in terms of instrument coverage and discount rate(s) applied to cash flows.

48. Once measures of duration for positions in the assets and liabilities included in the analysis are com-

Table A6.6. Portfolio Duration

	Duration D_i	Market Value	Weight x_i	Portfolio Duration x_iD_i
Assets				
D^{A1}	5	72	0.71	3.53
D^{A2}	3	30	0.29	0.88
D^A		102	1.00	**4.41**
Liabilities				
D^{L1}	4	20	0.25	1.00
D^{L2}	7	60	0.75	5.25
D^L		80	1.00	**6.25**

Table A6.7. Sector-Level Duration

	Duration D_i	Market Value	Weight x_i	Portfolio Duration x_iD_i
Assets				
Institution 1	2.6	200	0.51	1.33
Institution 2	3.7	72	0.18	0.68
Institution 3	4.6	120	0.31	1.41
		392	1.00	**3.41**
Liabilities				
Institution 1	2	180	0.49	0.97
Institution 2	7	60	0.16	1.14
Institution 3	3	130	0.35	1.05
		370	1.00	**3.16**

piled, assumed changes in interest rates can be measured in terms of their impact on the market values of those assets and liabilities and thus on the capital (E) of an institution (sector), as follows:

$$\Delta E = -\left[D^A - kD^L\right] \times A \times \frac{\Delta R}{(1+R)},$$

where

$[D^A - kD^L]$ = Adjusted duration gap;
A = Asset size; and
$\dfrac{\Delta R}{1+R}$ = Interest rate change.

49. In other words, the total effect of interest rate changes on the value of institutions' (the sector's) capital is composed of three effects:

- *The leverage-adjusted duration gap* = $[D^A - kD^L]$, where D^A = duration of assets; D^L = duration of liabilities; and k = the leverage ratio, which is equal to liabilities/assets. This gap is measured in years and reflects the degree of duration mismatch for the assets and liabilities included in the analysis. Specifically, the larger this gap is in absolute terms, the more exposed institutions are to interest rate changes.
- *The size of the institutions* = A, where the term A measures the size of institutions' assets included in the analysis. The larger the assets, the larger the potential capital exposure from any given interest rate changes.
- *The size of the interest rate shock* = $\Delta R/(1 + R)$. The larger the interest rate change, the greater the impact on capital.

Weaknesses in using duration measures

Large interest rate changes and convexity

50. While duration accurately measures the price sensitivity of fixed-income instruments for small changes in interest rates,[21] for large interest rate increases, duration overpredicts the fall in bond prices, and for large interest rate decreases, duration underpredicts the increase in bond prices. This arises because the bond price-yield relationship is convex rather than linear, as assumed by the basic duration model. Further precision can be obtained by recognizing the second derivative of yield changes (convexity) by measuring the change in the slope of the price-yield curve around a given point. Just as duration (D) measures the slope effect (dP/dR), a new parameter can be specified (CX) to measure the curvature effect (d^2P/dR^2) of the price-yield curve so that the estimated price change for a fixed-income bond, for example, is given by

$$\frac{\Delta P}{P} = D\frac{\Delta R}{(1+R)} + \frac{1}{2}CX(\Delta R)^2.$$

51. The first term in the equation is simple duration (D), and the second term is the second-order effect of an interest rate change, that is, the convexity or curvature adjustment.

52. As in the case of duration, the convexity of a portfolio of fixed-income instruments can be derived from a simple weighted average of the components of the portfolio convexity. Thus, if x_i is the proportion invested in bond i with convexity CX_i, portfolio convexity (CX_p) can be approximated by

$$CX_p = \sum_{i=1}^{N} x_i CX_i.$$

53. A similar approach can be used to derive the convexity of portfolios at the sector level, where CX_i represents the convexity of institution i's portfolio, and x_i represents the amount invested by institution i in the portfolio as a proportion of the aggregate investment by all reporting institutions.

The term structure of interest rates

54. A key assumption of the simple duration model outlined above is that the yield curve or the term struc-

[21] Saunders (1999) suggests that duration provides an accurate measure of sensitivity to interest rate changes when such changes are of the order of one basis point.

ture of interest rates is flat (that is, R is the same across all maturities). This assumption is unlikely to hold in practice—the yield curve is often upward or downward sloping across maturities, depending on the expected future path of interest rates. For more precision, alternative measures of duration can account for the possibility of changes in the shape of the yield curve by using specific discount factors for each maturity:

$$D^* = \sum_{t=1}^{N} t \times \frac{CF_t / (1+R_t)^t}{\sum_{t=1}^{N} CF_t (1+R_t)^t}.$$

55. To illustrate, the example in Table A6.8 calculates duration for a two-instrument portfolio when the yield curve is not flat. The first row of Table A6.8 uses an upward-sloping yield curve, and the second row repeats the calculation using a yield curve with a steeper slope.

Financial derivative positions

56. To assess the extent to which the interest rate duration gap is covered (hedged) by financial derivative positions, the expected gain (loss) on derivative positions for the sector needs to be estimated for the assumed change in interest rates. Such information may be difficult to compile, even if the data are available. While for forwards the change in value arising from changes in interest rates is of a linear nature, this is not true for options, which are complex instruments to price and reprice.

57. The interplay of factors in determining the impact of interest rate changes on deposit takers' capital is a reason for the growing interest in the use of stress tests. These are described in the next section of this appendix.

Measuring duration for mortgages, mortgage-backed securities, and demand deposits

58. The duration of some instruments can be difficult to calculate, notably mortgages, mortgage-backed securities, and demand deposits.

59. The difficulty with mortgages and mortgage-backed securities arises from the risk of prepayment of principal (prepayment risk). As the level of interest rates falls, mortgage debtors have an incentive to prepay their existing fixed-rate mortgage and refinance with a new mortgage at a lower rate of interest, making the projection of future cash flows uncertain. Most probably, the prepayment behavior of mortgage debtors should be modeled on past behavior.

Table A6.8. Duration (D^*) When the Yield Curve Is Upward Sloping

Time (t)	Instrument 1 CF_t	Instrument 2 CF_t	ΣCF	Upward Sloping Yield Curve	DF_t	$\Sigma CF \times DF_t$	$\Sigma CF \times DF_t \times t$	Calculation of Duration
1	80	70	150	8.0%	$1/1.08 = 0.9259$	138.89	138.89	$D^* = \frac{8,285.33}{1,790.72} = 4.62681$ years
2	80	70	150	8.8%	$1/(1.088)^2 = 0.8448$	126.72	253.43	
3	80	70	150	9.4%	$1/(1.094)^3 = 0.7637$	114.56	343.68	
4	80	70	150	9.8%	$1/(1.098)^4 = 0.6880$	103.20	412.80	
5	80	1,070	1,150	10.2%	$1/(1.102)^5 = 0.6153$	707.60	3,538.02	
6	1,080	—	1,080	10.3%	$1/(1.103)^6 = 0.5553$	599.75	3,598.50	
						1,790.72	8,285.33	
				Steepening of Yield Curve	DF_t	$\Sigma CF \times DF_t$	$\Sigma CF \times DF_t \times t$	
				6.8%	$1/1.068 = 0.9363$	140.45	140.45	$D^* = \frac{8,003.98}{1,745.36} = 4.58586$ years
				8.1%	$1/(1.081)^2 = 0.8558$	128.36	256.73	
				9.1%	$1/(1.091)^3 = 0.7701$	115.51	346.53	
				9.6%	$1/(1.096)^4 = 0.6930$	103.96	415.82	
				10.5%	$1/(1.105)^5 = 0.6070$	698.05	3,490.25	
				11.6%	$1/(1.116)^6 = 0.5176$	559.03	3,354.21	
						1,745.36	8,003.98	

60. The difficulty with demand deposit accounts arises because, while payable on demand, the actual timing of repayment is uncertain. There are several possible approaches to defining the duration for such deposits.

- Demand deposits can be considered as bonds that are instantly repayable. Under this assumption, the duration of demand deposits is approximately zero.
- More directly, the net withdrawal sensitivity of demand deposits ($\Delta DD/DD$) to interest rate changes (ΔR) can be examined. Because demand deposits pay either low explicit or implicit interest—where implicit interest takes forms such as subsidized checking fees—there tend to be increased withdrawals and switching into higher yielding instruments as interest rates rise. Regression analysis can be used to estimate this sensitivity.
- Simulations, based on forecasts of future interest rates and the net withdrawals of depositors over some future time period, can be used to estimate cash flows. Taking the discounted present values of these cash flows, a duration measure can be calculated.

61. In addition, banks may choose not to move rates paid on deposits in line with market rates, further complicating the measurement of interest rate risk exposure.

Part 3. FSIs and Stress Testing

62. FSIs can be used in conjunction with stress testing to enhance the quality of financial stability analysis. This section of the appendix outlines how this can be done, while highlighting their different roles and the limits this places on their comparability. It briefly describes what a stress test is but does not discuss how to conduct one. Rather, it references relevant analytical work that provides an overview of this complex topic.[22]

63. Stress testing aims to assess the impact of potential shocks on the soundness of a financial system by applying them to a model of the system. The type of shock is chosen to represent identifiable risks, while the model is customized to reflect the structure of the financial system. For many countries, the model can be quite simple—a spreadsheet of the balance sheets and income statements of banks in the system—while in complex financial systems, institutions' risk management models can be used.[23] Typically, stress tests will evaluate the change in the capital of the financial sector stemming from a particular macroeconomic event, such as an exchange rate depreciation or a recession-induced deterioration in asset quality. The size of stress test shocks should be "large but plausible," since the results of a shock that is regarded as too extreme may not be credible. Stress tests are used to represent macroeconomic scenarios that can involve several simultaneous ("correlated") shocks. They are also used for sensitivity analysis where the shock's impact is evaluated separately to assess the vulnerability of the financial system to specific risk factors.

64. Stress testing and FSIs play different but complementary roles in surveillance. Stress testing is a tool for analyzing the financial system that is forward looking in the sense that it seeks to assess the impact of possible macroeconomic events whose probability is uncertain. In contrast, FSIs are data showing the current condition of the system. Each surveillance tool can contribute to the effectiveness of the other in several ways.

- An analysis of FSIs can be used prior to a stress-testing exercise to help identify the vulnerabilities that need to be analyzed further through stress testing. For example, if FSIs show that the net open position in foreign currency is significant in either the banking or corporate sectors, this would suggest that stress testing using an exchange rate shock is needed.
- The output of simple stress tests is often shown as a change in an FSI—the regulatory capital ratio. In some stress tests, changes in other FSIs are also reported, in which case they can provide information on (or "benchmark") the relationship among the FSIs, allowing them to be used together more effectively.[24] For example, shocks to assess credit risk could reveal how much the NPL to gross loans FSI would need to increase to push the capital ratio FSI below 8 percent. This relationship would be based on an assumption built into the stress test about how banks provision against NPLs derived from supervisory guidelines. This information

[22]An overview of stress-testing methods is provided in Jones, Hilbers, and Slack (2004) and in Blaschke and others (2001).

[23]For a description of how a stress test was implemented in a complex financial system, see Hoggarth and Whitley (2003).

[24]This point is developed in IMF (2003d).

would help users of FSIs judge how concerned they should be when they observe a deterioration in asset-quality FSIs.

- Stress tests can shed light on the sensitivity of FSIs to institutional or regulatory changes. For example, they could reveal how a change in loan classification or provisioning rules would affect the capital ratio FSI.
- Stress tests can shed light on vulnerabilities in areas where data for the FSIs are lacking by relying on informed assumptions, which could be based on analogous situations in other countries or qualitative information. For example, if data on the foreign currency liabilities of the corporate sector are lacking, partial data from a few banks could be used as the basis for an assumption about this exposure in a stress test. Of course, the limitations that these assumptions impose on the analysis must be taken into account.

65. The scope for exploiting the complementarity between stress testing and FSIs is probably greatest in the area of market risk, because of the relatively advanced state of market risk modeling and stress testing. This can be an attractive option, because market risk FSIs for interest rate risk (that is, duration) and foreign exchange risk can be technically difficult to compile.[25,26] It is most likely to be feasible in more sophisticated financial systems where financial institutions that face significant market risk conduct frequent market risk stress tests as an integral part of their risk management. In principle, the output of these stress tests could be used to generate a measure of potential loss arising from market risk that could serve as a soundness indicator. Since the cost of implementing additional stress tests is low, the authorities may be able to work with these institutions to implement standardized shocks at regular intervals that can then be aggregated (which protects confidentiality) to produce it. The results from these stress tests could be presented in a form comparable to a market risk FSI (for example, as a measure of loss relative to capital for a shock of a given size). However, in implementing such an approach, a number of technical issues would need to be addressed, such as how to accommodate differences in risk management models across institutions.[27]

66. In using FSIs and stress testing together, however, due attention needs to be paid to their different roles in surveillance and the limits this places on their comparability.

- Experience has shown that stress testing can play a valuable role in focusing discussions on financial soundness. Specifically, it often helps develop a consensus on the risks a financial system faces and the possible policy responses by highlighting the potential effect and cost of shocks. To serve this purpose, each stress-testing exercise must be tailored to the features of a financial system and needs of the country. Thus, there can be no "standard" method for conducting stress tests comparable to the statistical methodology developed for compiling FSIs and presented in this *Guide.*
- Stress tests rely on judgments and assumptions with respect to the size of the shocks and the structure of the models used. They are also subject to the limitation that the probability of a shock is not known with any degree of precision. Thus, stress test output should not be reported or used outside the context of the stress test exercise. This implies that stress test output cannot be regarded as equivalent in any sense to FSIs, which are based on data and measure the actual condition of a financial system. In particular, FSIs can be used on a stand-alone basis and are subject to rigorous standards of data quality.

67. A final consideration when using stress tests and FSIs together is that, to the extent possible, they should rely on the same data sources, as well as methods of aggregation and consolidation. The bank balance sheets and income statements to which shocks are applied in simple stress tests should also be the data on which the FSIs are based. From this perspective, such stress tests can be viewed as a tool for analyzing these data that complements the analysis of FSIs.

68. The output of these stress tests is typically subjected to peer group analysis (for example, domesti-

[25]Market interest rate risk should be distinguished from the liquidity risk arising from the maturity mismatch on banks' balance sheets, deriving from their maturity transformation role, that is captured by other FSIs such as the ratio of liquid assets to short-term liabilities.

[26]The section on interest rate risk in this appendix highlights how difficult it is to measure this risk.

[27]This complementarity with respect to market risk reflects the close relationship between FSIs and stress testing at the analytic level. For example, the estimated direct loss from a stress test of an exchange rate shock can be approximated by the change in the exchange rate (that is the shock) multiplied by the net open foreign exchange position FSI. This is explained in IMF (2003e).

cally owned banks and foreign bank subsidiaries) to analyze the distribution of the impact of shocks across different parts of a financial system. To effectively integrate the analysis of FSIs and stress testing, they would need to use the same peer groups (which would be natural since they are focusing on the same risks). Similarly, for stress tests applied to individual bank balance sheets—which usually are cross-border consolidated and could alternatively be cross-sector consolidated—attention should to be paid to whether FSIs are based on the same data consolidation approach. Finally, in the case of more sophisticated approaches to stress testing that rely on macroeconomic models and banks' risk management models, it may be difficult to achieve a high degree of comparability, and close attention may need to be paid to the specification of the models when using FSIs and stress tests together.

Appendix VII. Glossary of Terms

Part 1. Financial Corporations

1. This appendix provides more detailed definitions of certain types of institutions in the financial corporations sector than is provided in Chapter 2.[1]

Insurance Corporations and Pension Funds

2. *Insurance corporations* consist of incorporated, mutual, and other entities whose principal function is to provide life, accident, sickness, fire, and other types of insurance to individual units or groups of units through the pooling of risk. Because of the different risks to be managed, insurance companies can be subdivided into nonlife (casualty) insurance companies and life insurance companies, which include commercially provided pension and annuity services. For nonlife insurance companies, payment to a policyholder depends on an event occurring that triggers a claim. In contrast, for life insurance companies there is a certainty that a claim will occur, and the payment of premiums may be viewed as savings that are withdrawn when claims are made. Usually the expectation is that there is a considerable lapse of time between the initiation of a life insurance policy and the payment of a claim.

3. *Pension funds* are constituted in such a way that they are separate institutional units from the units that create them. They are established for the purpose of providing benefits on retirement for specific groups of employees and, perhaps, their dependents. These funds have their own assets and liabilities, and engage in financial transactions on the market on their own account. As with life insurance policies, pension fund liabilities tend to be long term in nature.

4. Pension funds are organized and directed by private or government employers, or jointly by individual employers and their employees. They are funded by the employees and/or employers through regular contributions and from income earned from financial assets. In the *Guide,* pension funds do not include pension arrangements for the employees of private or government entities that do not maintain a separately organized fund, nor do they include arrangements organized by nongovernmental employees and for which the reserves of the fund are simply added to that employer's own reserves or invested in securities issued by that employer.

5. While maintaining a pool of liquid assets, because of the long-term nature of their liabilities, pension funds and insurance companies (particularly life insurance companies) usually invest in longer-term security market instruments, both bonds and equities, or in real estate. This investment behavior helps support the development of capital markets, both in terms of breadth and depth, and thus contributes to the broadening of the financing base for borrowers.

Securities Dealers

6. *Securities dealers* include individuals or firms that specialize in security market transactions by (1) assisting firms in issuing new securities through the underwriting and market placement of new security issues and (2) trading in new or outstanding securities on their own account. Only underwriters and dealers that act as financial intermediaries are classified within this category. Security brokers and other units that arrange trades between security buyers and sellers but do not purchase and hold securities on their own account are classified as financial auxiliaries.

7. By their nature, securities dealers facilitate both primary and secondary market activity in securities. In particular, these institutions can help provide liquidity to markets, both by encouraging borrower and investor activity—not least through the provision of

[1]These definitions are drawn from national accounts sources. For instance, see paragraphs 96 to 101 of the *Monetary and Financial Statistics Manual* (*MFSM*) (IMF, 2000a).

information on market conditions—and through their own trading activity.

Investment Funds

8. *Investment funds* are institutional units, excluding pension funds, that consolidate investor funds for the purpose of acquiring financial assets. Examples are mutual funds, including money market funds; investment trusts; unit trusts; and other collective investment units. Investors usually purchase shares in the fund that represent a fixed proportion of the fund.

9. In investment funds, professional fund managers make the selection of assets, thereby providing individual investors with an opportunity to invest in a diversified and professionally managed portfolio of securities without the need for detailed knowledge of the individual companies issuing the stocks and bonds. Usually, the type(s) of investment undertaken are specified, and the investment funds' managers must adequately inform investors about the risks and expenses associated with investment in specific funds, not least because the value of some types of funds can be highly variable.

10. The liquidity of investment funds can vary considerably. Some types of funds are illiquid or have limited liquidity. Such funds are more likely to be investing in longer-term securities. In other cases, shares issued by investment funds are as (or nearly as) liquid as deposits and other liabilities issued by depository corporations. Money market funds are included in this latter category. Because of the liquidity of their liabilities, they tend to invest in short-term debt instruments, such as certificates of deposit and commercial paper.

Other Financial Intermediaries

11. *Finance companies* are primarily engaged in the extension of credit to nonfinancial corporations and households. Many finance companies are captive subsidiaries that raise funds to be used by the parent corporations. Captive finance companies that are separate institutional units and that do not issue deposits or close substitutes for deposits should be classified as other financial intermediaries. Finance companies that are not separate should be included as part of the parent corporations in the appropriate subsector.

12. *Financial leasing companies* engage in financing the purchase of tangible assets. The leasing company is the legal owner of the goods, but ownership is effectively conveyed de facto to the lessee, who incurs all benefits, costs, and risks associated with ownership of the assets.

13. *Vehicle companies* are financial entities created to be holders of securitized assets or assets that have been removed from the balance sheets of corporations or government units as part of the restructuring of these units. Many are organized as trusts or special purpose vehicles created solely to hold specific portfolios of assets or liabilities.

14. *Specialized financial intermediaries* include financial holding corporations, companies that provide short-term financing for corporate mergers and takeovers (but do not take deposits), export/import finance firms, factors or factoring companies, venture capital and development capital firms, and pawnshops that predominantly engage in lending rather than retailing.

Financial Auxiliaries

15. *Financial auxiliaries* consist of those resident corporations and quasi corporations that engage primarily in activities closely related to financial intermediation but that do not themselves perform an intermediation role.

16. *Public exchanges and securities markets* are organized exchanges and entities such as security depository companies, accounting and clearinghouses, and other companies providing exchange-related services. Depositories and electronic clearing systems operated by financial corporations fall into this category, as do national self-regulatory organizations that regulate or supervise exchanges and related units.

17. *Brokers and agents* are individuals or firms that arrange, execute, or otherwise facilitate client transactions in financial assets. Included are brokers and agents handling the purchase and sale of securities or other financial contracts for clients, and financial advisory services that provide specialized services to brokers and their customers. Because many brokerage firms also trade in financial securities or financial derivatives on the firm's own account, it can be difficult to distinguish the brokers and agents from the underwriters and dealers (who are classified as financial intermediaries). By convention, this grouping includes only brokers and agents that clearly specialize in brokerage and related activities rather than the intermediation activities generally undertaken by underwriters and dealers.

18. *Foreign exchange companies* comprise units that buy and sell foreign exchange in retail or wholesale markets.

19. *Financial guarantee corporations* insure customers against losses to specified financial corporations or against financial loss on specific contracts. Guarantors must have the financial capability to fulfill potential obligations. They also typically agree—usually for a fee—to ensure that investors receive payment on securities or other financial contracts. In addition, the financial guarantee corporations grouping includes specialized corporations that protect depositors and investors against the failure of individual financial corporations. Distinguishing precisely between financial guarantee corporations and insurance corporations is difficult. Guarantee corporations

- Do not have a definable pool of assets constituting insurance technical reserves,
- Do not carry positions off balance sheet,
- May not be regulated as insurance corporations, and
- May be limited to specific types of financial transactions.

In borderline cases, these units should be classified as insurance corporations.

20. *Insurance and pension auxiliaries* include agents, adjusters, and salvage administrators. The unique nature and, in some countries, the large scale of activity of these units justify their separate identification.

21. *Other financial auxiliaries* comprise all other auxiliaries not classified elsewhere. The grouping includes independent units affiliated with the government and established to regulate financial institutions. The *System of National Accounts 1993 (1993 SNA)* recommends classifying these units as part of the central bank subsector. However, these units are not intermediaries, and the activities of some units (such as securities commissioners or insurance regulators) have little relationship to well-recognized central bank activities. Therefore, the *Guide* recommends classification of these units in the financial auxiliaries subsector. Also classified in this category are financial units that facilitate issuance and trading in financial derivatives but do not actually issue derivatives, and representative offices of foreign depository corporations that do not accept deposits or extend credit, even though they promote and facilitate transactions of the nonresident parent company.

Part 2. Selected Financial Stability Terms

Basel Capital Accord

Adopted by the Basel Committee on Banking Supervision (BCBS) in 1988 and amended in 1996, the Basel Capital Accord is an internationally agreed set of supervisory regulations governing the capital adequacy of international banks—capital is measured in relation to the perceived credit and market risk of the assets owned by the banks. The objectives behind the Accord are to strengthen the soundness and stability of the international banking system and to diminish sources of competitive inequality among international banks. At the time of writing, a new Accord is being developed.

Basel Committee on Banking Supervision

Established by the Central Bank Governors of the Group of Ten (G–10) countries at the end of 1974, the BCBS formulates broad supervisory standards and guidelines. It also recommends statements of best practice in the expectation that individual authorities will take steps to implement them through detailed arrangements—statutory or otherwise—that are best suited to their own national systems. It encourages convergence toward common approaches and common standards without attempting detailed harmonization of member countries' supervisory techniques. One of its major objectives is to close gaps in international supervisory coverage in pursuit of the two following basic principles: (1) no foreign banking establishment should escape supervision, and (2) supervision should be adequate.

Basel Concordat

The Basel Concordat refers to the document, "Principles for the Supervision of Banks' Foreign Establishments" prepared by the Basel Committee in 1983. The Basel Concordat sets out the principles for sharing supervisory responsibility for banks' foreign branches, subsidiaries, and joint ventures between host and parent (or home) supervisory authorities.

Basel II

The BCBS's *International Convergence of Capital Measurement and Capital Standards: A Revised Framework,* released in June 2004, is a comprehensive revision of the Basel capital adequacy standards. It includes three "pillars" for ensuring the strength of banking institutions. The first pillar covers the minimum capital requirements for banks, including changes in the risk weights for assets of banks in order that they better reflect the underlying risk incurred, and it includes alternative methodologies for assessing risk, based on banks' internal risk assessment procedures. The second pillar focuses on enhancing the supervisory review process. The third pillar focuses on enhancing market discipline over banking institutions through increased disclosures.

Bid-Ask Spread

The bid-ask spread is an indicator of market tightness, a dimension of market liquidity. It is calculated as the difference between the bid and ask (offer) prices of a financial instrument. *Bid* is the highest price a prospective buyer is prepared to pay at a particular time, and *ask* is the lowest price acceptable to a prospective seller for trading a unit of a given security.

CAMELS Framework

CAMELS is a commonly used supervisory framework that groups indicators of bank soundness into six categories. The categories are (1) *c*apital adequacy, (2) *a*sset quality, (3) *m*anagement soundness, (4) *e*arnings, (5) *l*iquidity, and (6) *s*ensitivity to market risk.

Capital Adequacy Ratio

The capital adequacy ratio is the central feature of the Basel Capital Accord. It is an analytical construct in which regulatory capital is the numerator and risk-weighted assets are the denominator. The minimum ratio of regulatory capital to risk-weighted assets is set at 8 percent (the core regulatory capital element should be at least 4 percent). These ratios are considered the minimum necessary to achieve the objective of securing over time soundly based and consistent capital ratios for all international banks.

Capital and Reserves

Capital and reserves is the difference between total assets and total liabilities in the balance sheet. It represents the equity interest of the owners in an entity and is the amount available to absorb unidentified losses.

Committee on Payment and Settlement Systems

Created in 1990, this Committee originally served as a forum for the central banks of the G-10 countries to monitor and analyze developments in domestic payment, settlement, and clearing systems, as well as in cross-border and multicurrency settlement schemes. In recent years, it has extended its work by developing relationships with non-G-10 central banks, particularly those of emerging market economies. The Bank for International Settlements (BIS) hosts the secretariat.

Consolidation

Consolidation is the elimination of positions and flows that occur among institutional units that are grouped together for statistical purposes. For Financial Soundness Indicator (FSI) purposes, reporting on a consolidated group basis preserves the integrity of capital by eliminating its double counting.

Contagion

Contagion refers to the transmission or spillover of financial shocks or crises across institutions, countries, and/or asset classes.

Contingencies

These are contractual financial arrangements whose principal characteristic is that one or more conditions must be fulfilled before a financial transaction takes place. Contingencies are not recognized as financial assets (liabilities) on balance sheet because they are not actual claims (or obligations). However, these arrangements can potentially affect financial soundness.

Convexity

Convexity is a measure of the sensitivity of prices of fixed-rate instruments (for example, bonds) to interest rate changes. It is the second derivative of a bond's price with respect to interest rates—duration is the first derivative. The longer the maturity of an instrument, the greater the convexity; for instruments with the same duration, the more dispersed the cash flows, the greater the convexity. The higher the convexity, the greater the price gain or price loss for a given change in interest rates. Used together with duration, convexity provides a more accurate approximation of the gains and losses on a fixed-rate instrument portfolio from a given change in interest rates than does duration alone.

Credit Risk

This is the risk that one party to a financial contract will fail to discharge an obligation and thus cause the other party to incur a financial loss. Because of deposit takers' role as financial intermediaries, monitoring the credit risk of their assets through FSIs (such as nonperforming loans to total loans) is central to any assessment of financial soundness.

Deposit Insurance Scheme

This refers to a formal scheme normally established by law that is designed to limit the losses of depositors in the event of bank failure(s). Typically, the scheme is intended to support the confidence in the financial system of small-scale depositors and thus reduce the risk of systemic crises being caused by panic withdrawals of deposits. The scheme can be privately or government operated and funded.

Double Leveraging of Capital

These are situations where related entities share capital. For example, if a deposit taker owns equity in another deposit taker in the group, capital is said to be double leveraged because both entities are resting activity on the same pool of capital. When capital is double leveraged, the capital actually available to the group to meet unanticipated losses is less than the data imply.

Financial Sector Assessment Program (FSAP)

A joint IMF and World Bank program introduced in May 1999, the FSAP aims to increase the effectiveness of efforts to promote the soundness of financial systems in member countries. Supported by experts from a range of national agencies and standard-setting bodies, work under the program seeks to identify the strengths and vulnerabilities of a country's financial system, to determine how key sources of risk are being managed, to ascertain the sector's developmental and technical assistance needs, and to help prioritize policy responses. It also forms the basis of Financial System Stability Assessments, in which IMF staff address financial sector issues of relevance to IMF surveillance, including risks to macroeconomic stability stemming from the capacity of the financial sector to absorb macroeconomic shocks.

Financial Stability Forum (FSF)

The FSF was created in February 1999 to promote international financial stability through enhanced information exchange and international cooperation in financial market supervision and surveillance. The FSF brings together, on a regular basis, national authorities responsible for financial stability in significant international financial centers, international financial institutions, sector-specific international groupings of regulators and supervisors, and committees of central bank experts. The FSF is serviced by a secretariat housed at the BIS.

Global Financial Stability Report

Launched in March 2002, this semiannual IMF publication focuses on current conditions in global financial markets, highlighting issues of financial imbalances and structural problems that could pose risks to financial market stability and sustained market access by emerging market borrowers.

Hedonic Price Indices

Hedonic price indices are quality-adjusted price indices. Using regression analysis, a hedonic price index measures the underlying price changes of goods and/or other assets, unaffected by changes in price due to quality changes. In the *Guide,* the hedonic regression method is one approach to compiling real estate price indices.

Herfindahl Index

This index is a measure of industry concentration. The value of the index is the sum of the squares of the market shares of all firms in an industry. Higher values indicate greater concentration.

Hui-Heubel Ratio

This ratio is a measure of resilience and depth in financial markets. The ratio relates the volume of trades (as a proportion of the outstanding stock of the instrument) to its impact on prices. The larger the volume of trades relative to the price changes, the deeper and more resilient the market is.

Internal Ratings Based (IRB) Approach

The IRB approach of the Basel Capital Accord provides a single framework by which a given set of risk components or "inputs" are translated into minimum capital requirements. The framework allows for both a foundation method and more advanced methodologies. In the foundation method, banks estimate the probability of default associated with each borrower, and the bank supervisors supply the other inputs. In the advanced methodology, a bank with a sufficiently developed internal capital allocation process is permitted to supply other necessary inputs as well.

International Accounting Standards (IASs)

These are a series of standards, developed by the London-based International Accounting Standards Board, that provide the underlying conceptual framework and specific standards for the preparation and presentation of financial statements of commercial, industrial, and business reporting enterprises, whether in the public or the private sector.

International Banking Statistics (IBS)

These data cover international banking business and are compiled and disseminated by the BIS on a quarterly basis. The IBS system has two main data sets: locational banking statistics, which provide data on a residence basis, and consolidated banking statistics, for which reporting banking institutions provide data on a worldwide consolidated basis.

International Financial Reporting Standards 2004 (IFRS)

The IFRS is the new title for the International Accounts Standards, indicating the body of standards in effect as of March 31, 2004 and applicable beginning on January 1, 2005. The IFRS incorporate many changes to the standards, but among the most important are those relating to the recognition, measurement, and disclosure of financial instruments.

Islamic Financial Services Board

Established in Malaysia in November 2002, the Board is an association of central banks and monetary authorities, as well as other institutions, that are responsible for the regulation and supervision of the Islamic financial services industry.

Kurtosis

This is a measure of dispersion that can be used in peer group analysis. It measures the extent to which observed data fall near the center of a distribution or toward its tails. The kurtosis of a normal distribution equals three; a kurtosis value greater than three indicates a high peak, a thin midrange, and fat tails; and a value less than three denotes a distribution with a fat midrange on either side of the mean and a low peak. An alternative formulation subtracts three from the calculated value, so that the normal distribution has a value of zero; positive values indicate a high peak and negative values a low peak.

Laspeyres Index

This index is a method of calculating a price index using fixed weights drawn from a specified base period. One common use for the Laspeyres method is to compile real estate price indices for the assessment of the soundness of the financial system.

Leverage

Leverage refers to having access to the full benefits arising from holding a position in a financial asset without having to fully fund the position with own funds. Leverage can magnify the rate of return (positive and negative) on a position or investment beyond the rate obtained by direct investment of own funds. It can be built up by borrowing (on-balance-sheet leverage, commonly measured by debt-to-equity ratios) and/or by using financial derivatives. The buildup of leverage positions can be associated with rising asset prices and risk exposures.

Liquidity

In terms of markets, liquidity generally refers to the ability to buy and sell assets quickly and in large volume without substantially affecting the asset's price. In terms of instruments, liquidity generally refers to those assets that can be converted into cash quickly without a significant loss in value.

Liquidity Risk

This is the risk that assets may not be readily available to meet a demand for cash. Because deposit takers' assets are typically of longer maturity than their liabilities, monitoring deposit takers' liquidity risk through FSIs (such as liquid assets to total assets and liquid assets to short-term liabilities) is important for financial soundness analysis.

Loan Loss Provisions

These are net allowances that deposit takers make against bad or impaired loans, based on their judgment as to the likelihood of losses occurring. Loan loss provisioning affects both income and, depending on the type of provisions made, capital.

Macroprudential Analysis

This is the assessment and monitoring of the strengths and vulnerabilities of financial systems. It encompasses quantitative information from both FSIs and macroeconomic indicators that provide (1) a broader picture of economic and financial circumstances such as GDP growth and inflation, along with information on the structure of the financial system, and (2) qualitative information on the institutional and regulatory framework—particularly through assessments of compliance with international financial sector standards and codes—and the outcome of stress tests.

Market Depth

Market depth is a dimension of market liquidity and refers to the ability of a market to handle large trade volumes without a significant impact on prices.

Market Risk

This is the risk of losses on financial instruments arising from changes in market prices. Market risk covers interest rate, foreign exchange, equity price, and commodity price risk. As financial intermediaries that take positions in financial instruments, such losses in value affect the income and capital of deposit takers. The duration of assets and liabilities can be used to estimate potential losses arising from changes in market interest rates. Another approach is through the use of stress tests.

Market Tightness

Market tightness is a dimension of market liquidity. It is measured by the general cost incurred in a transaction irrespective of market price.

Notional Amount

Sometimes described as the nominal amount, the notional amount is the amount underlying a financial derivative contract that is used for calculating payments or receipts on the contract. It provides an indication of the potential risk exposure associated with the financial derivative contact. For instance, if a bond is issued and the amount raised is swapped into another currency, the notional value of the derivative is equal to the amount swapped.

Price Discovery

Price discovery is the process of establishing a market price at which demand and supply for an item are matched. By bringing buyers and sellers together and making the process transparent, financial markets facilitate price discovery.

Red Book (Committee on Payment and Settlement Systems)

The *Red Book* is a publication on payment systems, produced by the BIS's Committee on Payment and Settlement Systems. Its objective is to provide a comprehensive description of a country's payment systems. The *Red Book* is revised periodically.

Regulatory Capital

Regulatory capital refers to a specific definition of capital developed by the BCBS and used as the numerator in the BCBS's capital adequacy ratio. The definition includes, beyond the traditional capital and reserve account items, several specified types of subordinated debt instruments that need not be repaid if the funds are needed to maintain minimum capital levels.

Resilience

Resilience is a dimension of financial market liquidity and is the speed with which price fluctuations arising from trades are dissipated or the speed with which imbalances in orders (such as more buy than sell orders) are reversed with new orders. It can be measured using the Hui-Heubel Ratio.

Risk Exposures

In terms of financial stability analysis, among the types of risk exposures faced by a deposit taker that require monitoring are included credit risk, market risk, liquidity risk, foreign exchange risk, large exposures risk, equity price risk, and real estate price risk.

Risk-Weighted Assets

In the *Guide,* risk-weighted assets refer to a concept developed by the BCBS for the capital adequacy ratio. Assets are weighted by factors representing their riskiness and potential for default.

Skewness

Skewness is a measure of dispersion that can be used in peer group analysis. It indicates the extent to which data are asymmetrically distributed around the mean. Symmetrical distributions have a skewness value of zero. A distribution with negative skewness has more observations in the left tail (left of the peak), and a distribution with positive skewness has more observations in the right tail.

Triennial Central Bank Survey

The Triennial Central Bank Survey is a survey of foreign exchange and derivatives markets coordinated by the BIS. The objective is to obtain reasonably comprehensive and internationally consistent information on the size and structure of foreign exchange and over-the-counter derivatives markets.[2] The purpose of these statistics is to increase market transparency and thereby help central banks, other authorities, and market participants to better monitor activity in the global financial system.

Turnover Ratio

The turnover ratio is an indicator of market depth, a dimension of market liquidity. It is calculated as the number of securities bought and sold during a trading period, divided by the average of the number of securities outstanding at the beginning and the end of the trading period.

Variance

Variance is a measure of dispersion around the mean calculated as the sum of squared deviations of each observation from the mean, divided by the number of observations (for population variance) or the number of observations minus one (for sample variance).

Volatility

Volatility is the tendency of quantities or prices to vary over time. Usually measured by the variance or annualized standard deviation of changes, volatility is said to be high if quantities or prices move significantly both up and down. The higher the volatility, usually the higher the risk, as the ability to convert an asset into cash quickly without a significant loss in value is less certain.

[2]The BIS also produces semi-annual data on the over-the-counter (off-exchange) derivatives market. These data are collected on a global consolidated basis from major banks and dealers in G-10 countries and cover notional and market values (see http://www.bis.org/press/p021108.thm).

Bibliography

Abiad, Abdul, 2003, "Early Warning Systems: A Survey and a Regime-Switching Approach," IMF Working Paper 03/32 (Washington: International Monetary Fund).

Accounting and Auditing Organization for Islamic Financial Institutions (AAOIFI), 1999, "Statement on the Purpose and Calculation of Capital Adequacy Ratio for Islamic Banks" (Bahrain).

Asser, Tobias M. C., 2001, *Legal Aspects of Regulatory Treatment of Banks in Distress* (Washington: International Monetary Fund).

Australian Bureau of Statistics, 2001, "Measuring Australia's Foreign Currency Exposure," 2001, in *Balance of Payments and International Investment Position* (Australian Bureau of Statistics) (December), pp. 11–16.

Bank for International Settlements, 1999, "Market Liquidity: Research Findings and Selected Policy Implications," Committee on the Global Financial System Publication No. 11 (Basel).

———, 2000, "Stress Testing by Large Financial Institutions: Current Practice and Aggregations Issues," Committee on the Global Financial System Publication No. 14 (Basel).

———, 2001a, *Core Principles for Systemically Important Payment Systems,* Committee on Payment and Settlement Systems Publication No. 43 (Basel).

———, 2001b, *Statistics on Payment Systems in the Group of Ten Countries,* Committee on Payment and Settlement Systems Publication No. 44 (Basel).

———, 2002, *Triennial Central Bank Survey: Foreign Exchange and Derivative Market Activity in 2001* (Basel).

———, 2003a, *A Glossary of Terms Used in Payment and Settlement Systems,* Committee on Payment and Settlement Systems (Basel).

———, 2003b, "Guide to International Banking Statistics," BIS Paper No. 16 (Basel).

———, 2003c, *Payment and Settlement Systems in Selected Countries,* Committee on Payment and Settlement Systems Publication No. 53 (Basel) (known informally as the *Red Book,* fifth edition).

———, and International Monetary Fund, 2005, "Real Estate Indicators and Financial Stability: Proceedings of a Joint Conference Organized by the BIS and the IMF in Washington on October 27–28, 2003," BIS Paper No. 21 (Basel).

Barton, Dominic, Roberto Newell, and Gregory Wilson, 2002, *Dangerous Markets: Managing in Financial Crises* (New York: Wiley).

Basel Committee on Banking Supervision (BCBS), 1983, "Principles for the Supervision of Banks' Foreign Establishments" (Basel: Bank for International Settlements).

———, 1988, "International Convergence of Capital Measurement and Capital Standards," Basel Committee Publication No. 4 (Basel: Bank for International Settlements).

———, 1991, "Measuring and Controlling Large Credit Exposures" (Basel: Bank for International Settlements).

———, 1996, "Amendment to the Capital Accord to Incorporate Market Risks" (Basel: Bank for International Settlements).

———, 1997, "Core Principles for Effective Banking Supervision" (Basel: Bank for International Settlements).

———, 1999, "Sound Practices for Loan Accounting and Disclosure" (Basel: Bank for International Settlements).

———, 2000a, "Principles for the Management of Credit Risk" (Basel: Bank for International Settlements).

———, 2000b, "Sound Practices for Managing Liquidity in Banking Organisations" (Basel: Bank for International Settlements).

———, 2001a, "Compendium of Documents, Volume One: Basic Supervisory Methods" (Basel: Bank for International Settlements).

———, 2001b, "Consultative Document: The New Basel Capital Accord" (Basel: Bank for International Settlements).

———, 2001c, "Consultative Document: Overview of the New Basel Capital Accord" (Basel: Bank for International Settlements).

———, 2003a, "Consultative Document: Overview of the New Basel Capital Accord" (Basel: Bank for International Settlements).

———, 2003b, "New Basel Capital Accord: Third Consultative Paper" (Basel: Bank for International Settlements).

———, 2003c, "Principles for the Management and Supervision of Interest Rate Risk," Basel Committee

Publication No. 102 (Basel: Bank for International Settlements).

———, 2004, *Basel II: International Convergence of Capital Measurement and Capital Standards: A Revised Framework* (Basel: Bank for International Settlements).

Benito, Andrew, and Gertjan Vlieghe, 2000, "Stylised Facts on U.K. Corporate Financial Health: Evidence from Micro-data," *Financial Stability Review* (Bank of England), Issue 8 (June), pp. 83–93.

Bhattacharya, Kaushik, 2003, "How Good Is the BankScope Database? A Cross-Validation Exercise with Correction Factors for Market Concentration Measures," BIS Working Paper No. 133 (Basel: Bank for International Settlements).

Blaschke, Winfrid J., Matthew T. Jones, Giovanni Majnoni, and Soledad Martinez Peria, 2001, "Stress Testing of Financial Systems: An Overview of Issues, Methodologies, and FSAP Experiences," IMF Working Paper 01/88 (Washington: International Monetary Fund).

Bliss, Robert R., and Nikolaos Panigirtzoglou, 2002, "Testing the Stability of Implied Probability Density Functions," *Journal of Banking & Finance,* Vol. 26 (March), pp. 381–422.

Bloem, Adriaan M., Robert J. Dippelsman, and Nils Ø. Mæhle, 2001, *Quarterly National Accounts Manual: Concepts, Data Sources, and Compilation* (Washington: International Monetary Fund).

Borio, Claudio, 2003, "Towards a Macroprudential Framework for Financial Supervision and Regulation," BIS Working Paper No. 128 (Basel: Bank for International Settlements).

Carson, Carol S., 2001, "Toward a Framework for Assessing Data Quality," IMF Working Paper 01/25 (Washington: International Monetary Fund).

Case, Bradford, and Edward J. Szymanoski, 1995, "Precision in House Price Indices: Findings of a Comparative Study of House Price Index Methods," *Journal of Housing Research,* Vol. 6, Issue 3, pp. 483–96.

Commission of the European Communities, 2000, *Commission Recommendations,* C(2000) 1372 final-EN (Brussels).

———, International Monetary Fund, Organization for Economic Cooperation and Development, United Nations, and the World Bank, 1993, *System of National Accounts 1993* (Brussels/Luxembourg, New York, Paris, Washington).

Cortavarria, Luis, Claudia Dziobek, Akihiro Kanaya, and Inwon Song, 2000, "Loan Review, Provisioning, and Macroeconomic Linkages," IMF Working Paper 00/195 (Washington: International Monetary Fund).

Crockett, Andrew, 2000, "Marrying the Micro- and Macro-Prudential Dimensions of Financial Stability," paper presented at the Eleventh International Conference of Banking Supervisors, Basel, September.

———, 2002, "Introductory Speech," at the Third Joint Central Bank Research Conference on Risk Measurement and Systemic Risk, Basel, March.

Danmarks Nationalbank, 2003, *Financial Stability 2003* (Copenhagen).

de Lis, Santiago Fernández, Jorge Martínez Pagés, and Jesús Saurina, 2000, "Credit Growth, Problem Loans, and Credit Risk Provisioning in Spain," Bank of Spain Working Paper 18 (Madrid: Bank of Spain).

Delgado, Fernando L., Daniel S. Kanda, Greta Mitchell Casselle, and R. Armando Morales, 2002, "Domestic Lending in Foreign Currency," in *Building Strong Banks: Surveillance and Resolution,* ed. by Charles Enoch, David Marston, and Michael Taylor (Washington: International Monetary Fund).

Derivatives Policy Group, 1995, "Framework for Voluntary Oversight of the OTC Derivatives Activities of Securities Firm Affiliates to Promote Confidence and Stability in Financial Markets" (New York).

Dziobek, Claudia, J. Kim Hobbs, and David Marston, 2000, "Toward a Framework for Systemic Liquidity Policy," IMF Working Paper 00/34 (Washington: International Monetary Fund).

Elsinger, Helmut, Alfred Lehar, and Martin Summer, 2002, "Risk Assessment for Banking Systems," Austrian Central Bank Working Paper No. 79 (Vienna: Austrian National Bank).

European Central Bank, 2000, *EU Banks' Income Statements* (Frankfurt).

———, 2003, *Seasonal Adjustment* (Frankfurt).

Eurostat, 1996, *European System of Accounts: ESA 1995* (Luxembourg: Office for Official Publications of the European Communities).

Frécaut, Olivier, 2002, "Banking System Losses in Indonesia: Looking out for Fifty Billion U.S. Dollars—Can the SNA Help?," presented at the Twenty Seventh General Conference of the International Association for Research in Income and Wealth, Stockholm, August.

Furfine, Craig H., and Eli M. Remolona, 2002, "What's Behind the Liquidity Spread? On-the-Run and Off-the-Run U.S. Treasuries in Autumn 1998," *BIS Quarterly Review* (June), pp. 51–58.

Garcia, Gillian G. H., 2000, "Deposit Insurance and Crisis Management," IMF Working Paper 00/57 (Washington: International Monetary Fund).

Griliches, Zvi, 1964, "Notes on the Measurement of Price and Quality Changes" in *Models of Income Determination: NBER Studies in Income and Wealth,* Vol. 28 (Princeton: Princeton University Press).

Gropp, Reint, Jukka Vesala, and Giuseppe Vulpes, 2002, "Equity and Bond Market Signals as Leading Indicators of Bank Fragility," ECB Working Paper No. 150 (Frankfurt: European Central Bank).

Heath, Robert M., 1998, "The Statistical Measurement of Financial Derivatives," IMF Working Paper 98/24 (Washington: International Monetary Fund).

Hoggarth, Glenn, and John Whitley, 2003, "Assessing the Strength of UK Banks through Macroeconomic Stress

Tests," *Financial Stability Review* (Bank of England), Issue 14 (June), pp. 91–103.

International Accounting Standards Board (IASB), 2002, *International Accounting Standards 2002* (London).

———, 2004, *2004 International Financial Reporting Standards (Bound Volume)* (London).

International Monetary Fund, 1993, *Balance of Payments Manual* (Washington, 5th ed.).

———, 2000a, *Monetary and Financial Statistics Manual* (Washington).

———, 2000b, *The New International Standards for the Statistical Measurement of Financial Derivatives: Changes to the Text of the 1993 SNA* (Washington: Statistics Department).

———, 2001a, *Government Finance Statistics Manual* (Washington).

———, 2001b, *The New International Standards for the Statistical Measurement of Financial Derivatives: Changes to the Text of the 1993 SNA* (Washington).

———, 2002, *Luxembourg: Financial System Stability Assessment, Including Reports on the Observance of Standards and Codes on the Following Topics: Monetary and Financial Stability Transparency, Banking Supervision, Securities Regulation, Insurance Regulation, and Payment Systems,* IMF Country Report No. 02/116 (Washington).

———, 2003a, "Data Quality Assessment Framework for Monetary Statistics" (Washington). Available via the Internet: http://dsbb.imf.org/vgn/images/pdfs/dqrs_MonetaryAcc.pdf

———, 2003b, *External Debt Statistics: Guide for Compilers and Users* (Washington).

———, 2003c, "Fifth Review of the Fund's Data Standards Initiative: Data Quality Assessment Framework and Data Quality Program" (Washington). Available via the Internet: http://www.imf.org/external/np/sta/dsbb/2003/eng/dqaf.htm#II

———, 2003d, "Financial Soundness Indicators" (Washington). Available via the Internet: http://www.imf.org/external/np/sta/fsi/eng/2003/051403.htm

———, 2003e, "Financial Soundness Indicators—Background Paper" (Washington). Available via the Internet: http://www.imf.org/external/np/sta/fsi/eng/2003/051403b.htm

———, and World Bank, 2002, "Implementation of the Basel Core Principles for Effective Banking Supervision, Experiences, Influences, and Perspectives" (Washington). Available via the Internet: http://www.imf.org/external/np/mae/bcore/2002/092302.pdf

———, 2003, *Analytical Tools of the FSAP* (Washington). Available via the Internet: http://www.imf.org/external/np/fsap/2003/022403a.pdf

Jones, Matthew T., Paul Hilbers, and Graham Slack, 2004, "Stress Testing of Financial Systems: What to Do When the Governor Calls," IMF Working Paper 04/127 (Washington: International Monetary Fund).

Jorion, Philippe, 1997, *Value at Risk: The New Benchmark for Controlling Derivatives Risk* (Chicago: Irwin Professional Publications).

Khawaja, Sarmad, and Thomas K. Morrison, 2002, "Statistical Legislation: Toward a More General Framework," IMF Working Paper 02/179 (Washington: International Monetary Fund).

Latter, Tony, 2001, "Derivatives from a Central Bank Perspective," presented at the seminar program of the FOW Derivatives Expo, Hong Kong, November.

Laurin, Alain, and Giovanni Majnoni, 2003, "Bank Loan Classification and Provisioning Practices in Selected Developed and Emerging Countries," World Bank Working Paper No. 1 (Washington: World Bank).

Mori, Atutoshi, Makoto Ohsawa, and Tokiko Shimizu, 1996, "A Framework for More Effective Stress Testing," Discussion Paper 96-E-2 (Tokyo: Bank of Japan, Institute for Monetary Economic Studies).

Nelson, William, and Wayne Passmore, 2001, "Pragmatic Monitoring of Financial Stability," in *Marrying the Macro- and Micro-Prudential Dimensions of Financial Stability,* BIS Paper No. 1 (Basel: Bank for International Settlements), pp. 367–84.

Pollakowski, Henry O., 1995, "Data Sources for Measuring House Price Changes," *Journal of Housing Research,* Vol. 6, Issue 3, pp. 377–87.

Reinhart, Vincent, and Brian Sack, 2002, "The Changing Information Content of Market Interest Rates," *BIS Quarterly Review* (June), pp. 40–50.

Sarr, Abdourahmane, and Tonny Lybek, 2002, "Measuring Liquidity in Financial Markets," IMF Working Paper 02/232 (Washington: International Monetary Fund).

Saunders, Anthony, 1999, *Financial Institutions Management: A Modern Perspective* (Boston: Irwin/McGraw-Hill, 3rd ed.).

Schachter, Barry, 1998, "The Value of Stress Testing in Market Risk Management" in *Derivatives Risk Management Service,* ed. by G. Timothy Haight (Boston: Warren Gorham & Lamont).

Slack, Graham L., 2003, "Availability of Financial Soundness Indicators," IMF Working Paper 03/58 (Washington: International Monetary Fund).

Song, Inwon, 2002, "Collateral in Loan Classification and Provisioning," IMF Working Paper 02/122 (Washington: International Monetary Fund).

Sundararajan, Vasudevan, Charles Enoch, Armida San José, Paul Hilbers, Russell Krueger, Marina Moretti, and Graham Slack, 2002, *Financial Soundness Indicators: Analytical Aspects and Country Practices,* IMF Occasional Paper No. 212 (Washington: International Monetary Fund).

Sundararajan, Vasudevan, and Luca Errico, 2002, "Islamic Financial Institutions and Products in the Global Financial System: Key Issues in Risk Management and Challenges Ahead," IMF Working Paper 02/192 (Washington: International Monetary Fund).

Taylor, John B., 1993, "Discretion Versus Policy Rules in Practice," *Carnegie-Rochester Conference Series on Public Policy,* Vol. 39 (December), pp. 195–214.

United Nations, European Commission, International Monetary Fund, Organization for Economic Cooperation and Development, United Nations Conference on Trade and Development, and the World Trade Organization, 2001, *Manual on Statistics of International Trade in Services* (Geneva: United Nations).

United States Board of Governors of the Federal Reserve System, 2004, *Commercial Bank Examination Manual* (Washington: Division of Banking Supervision and Regulation). Available via the Internet: http://www.federalreserve.gov/releases/housedebt/about.htm

Vittas, Dimitri, 1991, "Measuring Commercial Bank Efficiency: Use and Misuse of Bank Operating Ratios," Policy Research Working Paper No. 806 (Washington: World Bank).

Index

Numbers in references refer to paragraphs in chapters, boxes, or appendixes.

AAOIFI. *See* Accounting and Auditing Organization for Islamic Financial Institutions
Accounting and Auditing Organization for Islamic Financial Institutions, Box 4.3
Accounting framework, Box 4.1. *See also* Financial statements
Accrual accounting
  time of recognition of flows and positions, 3.3–3.4
Agents
  defined, App. VII
  residence and, 3.43
Aggregate resident-based approach, 5.13–5.14
Aggregation
  combined with consolidation, 5.5
  data requirements, 11.35–11.45
  defined, 5.3
  overview, 5.1
Arrears, 3.10–3.11, App. IV
Asset-based financial soundness indicators, 6.45–6.68
Asset quality, 14.6–14.11
Assets. *See* Financial assets and liabilities
Associates, 5.8–5.9
Average-period interest rates, 8.12
Average real estate prices, 9.16–9.17

Bad debt recoveries, App. IV
Balance of Payments Manual, fifth edition, Box 4.1
Balance-sheet-related series, 4.93–4.95, 11.25–11.34
Balance sheets
  compiling consolidated data, 5.51–5.92
  for deposit takers, 4.37–4.65
  for households, 4.121
  for nonfinancial corporations, 4.106–4.114, App. V
  for other financial corporations, 4.96–4.98
  overview, 4.9–4.12
  reconciliation and the *Guide*'s methodology, App. IV
Bank for International Settlements, 1.19, 8.52, 13.35
"Bank Loan Classification and Provisioning Practices in Selected Developed and Emerging Countries," App. V
Banking supervision. *See* Basel Committee on Banking Supervision
Bankruptcy protection, 7.20, 14.36, App. II
Banks. *See* Deposit takers
Banks in distress, 2.11–2.12
Basel Capital Accord
  defined, App. VII
Basel capital adequacy ratio
  function of, 14.3–14.4
  requirements of, Box 4.2
Basel Committee on Banking Supervision
  capital adequacy ratio, Box 4.2
  defined, App. VII
  objectives of, Box 4.1
Basel Concordat
  defined, App. VII
Basel core principles, 13.28–13.36
BCBS. *See* Basel Committee on Banking Supervision
BCP. *See* Basel core principles
Bid-ask spread
  calculation of, 8.44–8.49
  converting from yield quotes into price terms, Box 8.1
  defined, App. VII
  monitoring, 14.21
BIS. *See* Bank for International Settlements
BLCP. *See* "Bank Loan Classification and Provisioning Practices in Selected Developed and Emerging Countries"
Bond market
  overview, 2.23
BPM5. See Balance of Payments Manual, fifth edition
Branches, 3.37
Brass plate companies, 3.39–3.40
Brokers
  defined, App. VII
Buy-backs, 4.54

CAMELS framework
  defined, 14.2, App. VII
Capital. *See also* Regulatory capital
  regulatory definition, 4.68
Capital adequacy, 14.3–14.5
Capital adequacy ratio
  defined, App. VII
  requirements of, Box 4.2
Capital and reserves
  compared with regulatory capital, 4.75
  compiling consolidated data, 5.89–5.90
  defined, 4.62, App. VII
  for deposit takers, 4.9, 4.63–4.65
  for nonfinancial corporations, 4.114
  reconciliation and the *Guide*'s methodology, App. IV
  valuation and provisioning, Box 4.4

Capital-based financial soundness indicators, 6.13–6.44
Capital ratios, 14.3–14.4
Capital to assets, 6.20–6.21
Central bank
  overview, 2.13
Central tendency, 15.18–15.19
Collateral, 4.45, 4.122, App. V
Commercial banks. *See* Deposit takers
Commercial real estate indices, 9.28–9.30
Commercial real estate loans, 4.88, 6.61–6.62, App. II, App. III, App. IV
Commissions. *See* Fees and commissions
Committee on Payment and Settlement Systems
  defined, App. VII
  Red Book, 8.52, App. VII
Comparison ratios, 15.31–15.33
Computer systems, Box 10.1
Connected lending, 4.95, 14.9
Consolidated-based approach
  compiling sector-level data, 5.45–5.50
  data requirements, 11.46–11.50
  deposit takers, 5.51–5.92
  flows and positions in the non-deposit-taking sectors, Box 5.2
  interbank flows and positions, Box 5.1
  issues, 5.40–5.44
  overview, 5.15
Consolidated group reporting
  applying to FSI data, 5.29–5.39
  overview, 5.16
Consolidation
  combined with aggregation, 5.5
  defined, 5.4, App. VII
  overview, 5.1–5.2
  of sectorwide capital, App. V
  survey of practices, App. I
Contagion
  defined, App. VII
Contingencies
  defined, App. VII
  overview, 3.12–3.19
Contingent items, 3.12
Convexity
  defined, App. VII
Core capital, Box 4.2
Core financial soundness indicators, 1.1, 1.11, App. II
Corporate income taxes, 4.105
Corporate net foreign exchange exposure, 4.118, 7.17–7.18
Credit commitments, 3.16
Credit risk
  defined, App. VII
  mitigation, 4.94
Cross-border consolidated data, 5.17, 11.51–11.56, Box 5.3
Currency
  domestic, 3.44–3.47
  foreign, 3.44–3.46, 3.48, App. IV
  overview, 4.40
Current transfers, 4.120, App. IV
Customer deposits, 4.42, 4.44, 6.50–6.51, 14.18, App. II

Data compilation systems, Box 10.1
Data requirements
  deposit takers, 11.17–11.56
  nonfinancial corporations, 11.63–11.70
  other financial corporations, 11.57–11.62
Data series
  availability of data, 11.71–11.73
  breaks in, 11.74–11.77
Data sources
  deposit takers, 11.4–11.11
  households, 11.13–11.16
  nonfinancial corporations, 11.13–11.16
  other financial corporations, 11.12
Databases, Box 10.1
Dealing accounts, 4.23
Debt
  bad debt recoveries, App. IV
  defined, 4.61
  household, 7.23–7.26, 14.38, App. II, App. III
  reconciliation and the *Guide*'s methodology, App. IV
Debt collateralized by real estate, 4.122
Debt securities, 4.46, 4.51–4.53, App. IV
Debt service payments, 4.117, 4.122, 7.15–7.16
Debt to capital ratio, App. III
Demand deposits, App. V
Deposit insurance scheme
  defined, App. VII
Deposit money corporations, 2.5
Deposit takers
  accounting principles for calculating FSIs, 6.1–6.3
  calculation of FSIs, 6.5–6.8, App. V
  compiling consolidated data, 5.51–5.92
  consolidated group reporting, 5.31–5.35
  data requirements, 11.17–11.56
  data sources, 11.4–11.11
  definitions of FSIs, App. III
  dissemination of FSI data, 12.11–12.17
  financial soundness indicators, 6.9–6.76, App. II
  financial statements, 4.16–4.95
  memorandum series, 4.66–4.95, App. III
  overview, 2.4–2.12
  underlying series for calculating FSIs, 6.4
  uses of FSIs, 14.2–14.28
Depository corporations, App. I
Deposits
  for deposit takers, 4.41–4.44
  reconciliation and the *Guide*'s methodology, App. IV
  volatility, 4.43
Depreciation, App. IV
Derivatives, 14.11. *See also* Financial derivatives
Descriptive statistics, 15.12–15.51
Disclosure, App. V
Dispersion in interbank rates, 14.25
Dispersion measures, 15.17–15.51

Dividends
for deposit takers, 4.36
reconciliation and the *Guide*'s methodology, App. IV
Domestic consolidated data, 5.25–5.28, 11.19–11.20, App. V, Box 5.3
Domestic control, 5.10–5.12
Domestic currencies, 3.44–3.47
Domestically controlled cross-border consolidated data, 5.18–5.19, 5.31–5.35
Domestically controlled cross-sector consolidated data, 5.20–5.21
Double leveraging of capital
defined, App. VII
Duration analysis, 3.51–3.56, 14.27, App. III, App. V

Early warning system, 13.12
Earnings, 14.12–14.16
Earnings before interest and tax, 4.116, 14.33–14.34
EBIT. *See* Earnings before interest and tax
Electronic trading systems, 13.34
Embedded derivatives, 4.59
Encouraged financial soundness indicators, 1.1, 1.11, App. II
End-period interest rates, 8.12
Equity. *See* Capital and reserves; Shares and other equity
Equity investments, Box 5.1
Equity market
overview, 2.24
EWS. *See* Early warning system
Exchange rate conversion, 3.44, 3.48
Exchanges, 13.34, App. VII
Expenses. *See* Income and expense statements
External Debt Statistics: Guide for Compilers and Users, Box 4.1
Extraordinary items
for deposit takers, 4.35
for nonfinancial corporations, 4.105
reconciliation and the *Guide*'s methodology, App. IV

Fees and commissions
expenses, 4.30
income from, 4.20–4.21
reconciliation and the *Guide*'s methodology, App. IV
Finance companies
defined, App. VII
overview, 2.14
Financial assets and liabilities
for deposit takers, 4.38–4.65
gross positions in financial derivatives to capital, 6.39–6.40, App. II
for nonfinancial corporations, 4.111–4.114
reconciliation and the *Guide*'s methodology, App. IV
valuation and provisioning, Box 4.4
Financial auxiliaries
defined, App. VII
overview, 2.14
Financial conglomerates, App. III
Financial corporations
central bank, 2.13
deposit takers, 2.4–2.12
other financial corporations, 2.14
Financial derivatives
classification of, 4.52
embedded derivatives, 4.59
forward-type contracts, 4.57
option contracts, 4.58
overview, 2.25
reconciliation and the *Guide*'s methodology, App. IV
types of, 4.56
Financial guarantee corporations
defined, App. VII
Financial intermediaries
overview, 2.14
Financial lease, 4.47
Financial leasing companies
defined, App. VII
overview, 2.14
Financial markets
bond market, 2.23
converting bid-ask spreads from yield quotes into price terms, Box 8.1
defined, 2.20
equity market, 2.24
financial derivatives, 2.25
financial soundness indicators, App. III
interbank market, 2.22
interest rates, 8.2–8.24
liquidity, 2.26
money market, 2.21
overview, 8.1
securities markets, 8.25–8.49
structural indicators, 8.50–8.53
Financial Sector Assessment Program
defined, App. VII
function of, 1.10
Financial soundness indicators
accounting principles for, 3.1–3.56
asset-based, 6.45–6.68
availability of data, 11.71–11.73
Basel core principles and, 13.28–13.36
breaks in data series, 11.74–11.77
calculating, App. V
calculating ratios, 1.15
capital-based, 6.13–6.44
comparability, 1.4
compilation issues, 11.1–11.3
compilation of, 1.20–1.22, 10.1–10.37, Box 10.1
core and encouraged sets, 1.11
data requirements, 11.17–11.70
data sources, 11.4–11.16
differences in approach from existing frameworks, Box 4.1
dissemination of data, 1.23, 10.1–10.37, 12.1–12.25
financial stability framework, 13.11–13.14

Financial soundness indicators *(continued)*
function of, 1.2–1.3, 13.3–13.10
importance of, 1.13–1.14
income- and expense-based, 6.69–6.76
linkages among FSIs, 13.15–13.22
for nonfinancial corporations, App. V
numerical examples, App. V
relationship with monetary and financial statistics, Box 11.1
seasonal adjustment, 11.78
stress testing, 13.23–13.27, Box 13.1
structure of *Guide,* 1.26–1.29
terminology, 1.30
uses of, 14.1–14.41, App. I
Financial Stability Forum
defined, App. VII
Financial statements
balance sheet, 4.9–4.12
for deposit takers, 4.16–4.95
for households, 4.119–4.122
income and expense statement, 4.8
for nonfinancial corporations, 4.99–4.118
for other financial corporations, 4.96–4.98
overview, 4.1–4.7
sectoral, 4.13–4.15
Financial systems
financial corporations, 2.4–2.14
financial markets, 2.20–2.26
general government, 2.18
households, 2.16
monitoring strength of, 1.6–1.12
nonfinancial corporations, 2.15
nonprofit institutional serving households, 2.17
overview, 2.1–2.3
payment system, 2.27
public sector, 2.19
real estate markets, 2.28
Fixed assets
for nonfinancial corporations, 4.107
Flows and positions. *See also* Positions
defined, 3.2
interbank, App. V, Box 5.1
intragroup, App. V
in the non-deposit-taking sectors, Box 5.2
time of recognition, 3.3–3.9
Foreign control, 5.10–5.12
Foreign-controlled cross-border consolidated data, 5.22–5.24
Foreign currencies, 3.44–3.46, 3.48, App. IV
Foreign currency liabilities, 4.90, 6.67–6.68, App. II, App. III
Foreign currency loans, 4.90, 6.65–6.66, 14.10, App. II, App. III
Foreign exchange companies
defined, App. VII
Foreign exchange exposure, 14.28, 14.35
Foreign exchange gains, 6.71–6.72, App. II
Forward-type contracts, 4.57
FSAP. *See* Financial Sector Assessment Program
FSF. *See* Financial Stability Forum
FSIs. *See* Financial soundness indicators
Funds contributed by owners, 4.63

G-10. *See* Group of Ten countries
Gains on financial instruments
for deposit takers, 4.20, 4.22–4.27
for nonfinancial corporations, 4.104, App. V
reconciliation and the *Guide*'s methodology, App. IV
Gap model, App. V
GDP. *See* Gross domestic product
General government, 2.18
General provisions, 4.32–4.33
General reserves, 4.63
Geographic distribution of loans, 4.89, 6.63–6.64, 14.8, App. II, App. III, App. IV
Gini Index, 15.15–15.16
Global Financial Stability Report
defined, App. VII
Global note facilities, 3.17
Glossary of terms, App. VII
GNFs. *See* Global note facilities
Gold swap, 4.48
Goods and services
sales of, App. IV
Goodwill
capital adequacy ratio calculation, Box 4.2
compiling consolidated data, 5.91–5.92
nonfinancial corporations and, 4.110
in sector-wide capital, App. V
Government, general, 2.18
Government Finance Statistics Manual, Box 4.1
Gross disposable income, 4.120, App. IV
Gross domestic product, 7.7, 7.23
Gross income, 4.20
Group of Ten countries, App. VII, Box 4.2
Guarantees, App. V

Hedonic price indices
advantages of, 9.25–9.26
defined, App. VII
Herfindahl Index
calculation of, 15.13–15.14
defined, App. VII
Holding corporations, 2.9
Households
calculation of FSIs, 7.1–7.3, 7.21–7.26
data sources, 11.13–11.16
debt, 7.23–7.26, App. II, App. III
financial soundness indicators, App. II
financial statements, 4.119–4.122
overview, 2.16
reconciliation and the *Guide*'s methodology, App. IV
residence, 3.41
uses of FSIs, 14.37–14.39

Hui-Heubel Ratio
calculation of, 14.22, App. III
defined, App. VII

IASB. *See* International Accounting Standards Board
IASs. *See* International accounting standards
IBS. *See* International banking statistics
IFIs. *See* Islamic financial institutions
IFRS. *See* International Financial Reporting Standard
IFSB. *See* Islamic Financial Services Board
Immediacy, 8.29
Income
interest income, 4.17–4.19, 4.103
net income, 4.34, 4.103
net income after tax, 4.35, 4.105
noninterest income, 4.20–4.27
operating income, 4.100
other income, 4.29
prorated earnings, 4.28
reconciliation and the *Guide*'s methodology, App. IV
sources, 4.120
Income- and expense-based financial soundness indicators, 6.69–6.76
Income and expense series, 11.22–11.24
Income and expense statements
compiling consolidated data, 5.51–5.92
for deposit takers, 4.16–4.36
for households, 4.120
for nonfinancial corporations, 4.100–4.105, App. V
overview, 4.8
reconciliation and the *Guide*'s methodology, App. IV
valuation and provisioning, Box 4.4
Income taxes
corporate, 4.105
for deposit takers, 4.35
reconciliation and the *Guide*'s methodology, App. IV
Institutional units
overview, 2.2
Insurance auxiliaries
defined, App. VII
Insurance corporations
defined, App. VII
overview, 2.14
Insurance technical reserves, 4.97, App. IV
Interbank flows and positions, Box 5.1
Interbank loans
reconciliation and the *Guide*'s methodology, App. IV
Interbank market
overview, 2.22
Interbank stress testing, Box 13.1
Interest cost, 4.17
Interest income
for deposit takers, 4.17–4.19
interest margin to gross income, 6.69–6.70, App. II, App. III
for nonfinancial corporations, 4.103, 4.115
Interest rates
average-period, 8.12
end-period, 8.12
overview, 8.2–8.4
risk, App. V
spread between reference lending and deposit rates, 8.5–8.20
spread between the highest and lowest interbank rates, 8.21–8.24
Internal Ratings Based approach
defined, App. VII
International accounting standards
defined, App. VII
objectives of, Box 4.1
overview, 1.16
reconciliation and the *Guide*'s methodology, App. IV
International Accounting Standards Board, 1.16, App. IV, Box 4.1
International banking statistics
defined, App. VII
overview, 1.19
International Financial Reporting Standards, 1.16, 3.7, 3.23, Box 4.1, Tables 11.9 and 11.10, App. IV
International Standard Industrial Classification, App. III
Inventories
for nonfinancial corporations, 4.108
reconciliation and the *Guide*'s methodology, App. IV
Investment funds
defined, App. VII
overview, 2.14
IRB. *See* Internal Ratings Based approach
ISIC. *See* International Standard Industrial Classification
Islamic financial institutions, Box 4.3
Islamic Financial Services Board
defined, App. VII
function of, Box 4.3

Joint ventures, 5.9

Kurtosis
calculation of, 15.22
defined, App. VII

Large exposures, 4.76, 6.27–6.30, App. II, App. III, App. IV
Laspeyres index
defined, App. VII
Laspeyres real estate indices, 9.20–9.24
Leasing companies. *See* Financial leasing companies
Legal issues, 10.20–10.23
Letters of credits, 3.15
Leverage
defined, App. VII
Liabilities. *See also* Financial assets and liabilities
foreign currency, 4.90, 6.67–6.68, App. II, App. III
short-term, 4.83
Lines of credit, 3.16

Liquid asset ratio, 6.45–6.46
Liquid assets, 4.78–4.82, 14.18, App. II, App. IV
Liquid assets to short-term liabilities, 6.47–6.49, 14.18, App. II, App. III
Liquidity
  defined, App. VII
  importance of, 2.26, 14.17–14.25
Liquidity-adjusted real estate indices, 9.27
Liquidity risk
  defined, App. VII
Loan guarantees, 3.14
Loan-loss provisions
  defined, App. VII
  for deposit takers, 4.32–4.33
  reconciliation and the *Guide*'s methodology, App. IV
  tax treatment, App. V
Loans
  classification, App. V
  concentration in specific economic sector, 14.7
  for deposit takers, 4.45–4.50
  foreign currency, 4.90, 6.65–6.66, 14.10, App. II, App. III
  geographic distribution, 4.89, 6.63–6.64, 14.8, App. II, App. III, App. IV
  nonperforming, 1.25, 4.84–4.87
  real estate, 4.88, 6.58–6.62, App. II, App. III, App. IV
  reconciliation and the *Guide*'s methodology, App. IV
  replacement, 4.86
  review practices, App. V
  sectoral distribution to total loans, 6.56–6.57, App. II, App. III
LoC. *See* Letters of credits
Lock-in provisions, 4.72
Long-term maturity, 3.49
Lorenz curve, 15.15
Losses on financial instruments
  for deposit takers, 4.20, 4.22–4.27
  for nonfinancial corporations, 4.104, App. V
  reconciliation and the *Guide*'s methodology, App. IV

Macroprudential analysis
  defined, App. VII
  financial soundness indicators and, 13.1–13.36
  importance of, 1.10
  overview, 1.6–1.7, 1.17–1.20, 1.24
Managerial issues, 10.24–10.37, Box 10.1
Market depth
  defined, 8.27, App. VII
  depiction of, 8.28
  measuring, 8.33–8.38
Market exchange rate, 3.48
Market liquidity, 14.20, App. II
Market risk
  defined, App. VII
  sensitivity to, 14.26–14.28
Market tightness
  defined, 8.27–8.28, App. VII
  measuring, 8.33–8.38
Market transparency, 8.32
Market valuation. *See* Valuation methods
Maturity, 3.49–3.55
  original, 3.50
  remaining, 3.50
  residual, 3.50
Mean, 15.18
Median, 15.19
Median real estate prices, 9.18
Memorandum series
  for deposit takers, 4.66–4.95, App. III
  for households, 4.122
  for nonfinancial corporations, 4.115–4.118, App. III
Metadata, 12.23
MFSM. See Monetary and Financial Statistics Manual
Microprudential analysis
  overview, 1.7
Mode, 15.19
Mode real estate prices, 9.18
Monetary and Financial Statistics Manual, Box 4.1, Box 4.3, Box 11.1
Money market
  overview, 2.21
Money market funds
  overview, 2.10, 2.14
Mortgage-backed securities, App. V
Mortgages, App. V
Mudarabah concept, Box 4.3
Multiple exchange rate system, 3.48
Multiple options facilities, 3.17

National accounts. *See* System of national accounts
Net income after tax, 4.35, 4.105
Net interest income, 4.17–4.18
Net open position
  in equity, 4.91, 6.41–6.44, 14.28, App. II, App. III
  in foreign currencies, 4.92, 6.31–6.38, App. II, App. IV
Net worth, App. IV
New business, 8.13–8.14
NIFs. *See* Note issuance facilities
1993 SNA. See System of National Accounts, 1993
Nondepository financial institutions, App. I
Nonfinancial assets
  for deposit takers, 4.37
  for nonfinancial corporations, 4.106–4.110
  reconciliation and the *Guide*'s methodology, App. IV
Nonfinancial corporations
  calculation of FSIs, 7.1–7.3, 7.8–7.20, App. V
  consolidated group reporting, 5.38–5.39
  data requirements, 11.63–11.70
  data sources, 11.13–11.16
  debt service, App. III
  dissemination of FSI data, 12.23–12.25

Nonfinancial corporations *(continued)*
earnings to interest and principal expenses, 4.99–4.118, App. II
financial soundness indicators, App. II
financial statements, 4.99–4.118
flows and positions, Box 5.2
memorandum series, 4.115–4.118, App. III
net foreign exchange exposure to equity, 4.99–4.118, App. II, App. III
overview, 2.15
return on equity, 4.99–4.118, App. II, App. III
total debt to equity, 4.99–4.118, App. II, App. III
uses of FSIs, 14.31–14.36
Noninterbank loans
reconciliation and the *Guide*'s methodology, App. IV
Noninterest expenses, 4.30–4.31, 6.73–6.74, App. II, App. III, App. IV
Noninterest income, 4.20–4.27
Nonperforming loans
classification of, 4.84–4.87
interest, App. V
interest rates, 8.15–8.16
net of specific provisions to capital, 6.22–6.24, 14.5, App. II, App. III
ratio to total gross loans, 6.54–6.55, 14.6, App. II, App. III
reconciliation and the *Guide*'s methodology, App. IV
stress testing, 1.25
Nonproduced assets, App. IV
for nonfinancial corporations, 4.106, 4.110
Nonprofit institutional serving households
overview, 2.17
Nontransferable deposits, 4.41
Note issuance facilities, 3.17
Notional amount
defined, App. VII
NPISHs. *See* Nonprofit institutional serving households
NPLs. *See* Nonperforming loans
Numerical examples, App. V

OFCs. *See* Other financial corporations
Off-balance-sheet operations, 14.11
Offshore units, 3.38
Operating income, 4.100, 4.120
Option contracts, 4.58
Order-driven markets, 8.31
OTCs. *See* Over-the-counter markets
Other depository corporations. *See* Deposit takers
Other financial corporations
assets to gross domestic product, 4.96–4.98, App. II
assets to total financial system assets, 4.96–4.98, App. II, App. III
calculation of FSIs, 7.1–7.7
consolidated group reporting, 5.36–5.37
data requirements, 11.57–11.62
data sources, 11.12
dissemination of FSI data, 12.18–12.22
financial soundness indicators, App. II
financial statements, 4.96–4.98
flows and positions, Box 5.2
memorandum series, App. III
overview, 2.14
uses of FSIs, 14.29–14.30
Outstanding business, 8.13–8.14
Over-the-counter markets, 13.34
Overall interest spread, 8.5
Ownership of land and structures
residence, 3.42

Payment guarantees, 3.14
Payment system
overview, 2.27
Peer group analysis, 15.1–15.11
Pension auxiliaries
defined, App. VII
Pension funds
defined, App. VII
overview, 2.14
Percentiles, 15.38–15.41
Performance bonds, 3.15
Persistence, 15.45–15.47
Personnel costs, 4.31, 6.75–6.76, App. II, App. IV
PLS. *See* Profit and loss sharing
Positions. *See also* Flows and positions
market value, 3.25–3.33
Price discovery
defined, App. VII
Prorated earnings, 4.28, App. IV
Produced assets, 4.106–4.109, App. IV
Profit and loss sharing, Box 4.3
Profitability, 14.12–14.16
Property income receivable, 4.120
Protection from creditors applications, 7.20, 14.36, App. II
Provisioning, App. V, Box 4.4
Provisions, 4.63
Public corporation
defined, 2.19
Public exchanges
defined, App. VII
Public sector
overview, 2.19

Quality-adjusted regression price indices, 9.25–9.26
Quality control, 10.18–10.19, 10.37
Quote-driven markets, 8.31

Range, 15.20, 15.36–15.37
RAROC. *See* Risk-adjusted return on capital
Ratio of capital to assets, 14.3, App. II
Real estate loans, 4.88, 6.58–6.62, App. II, App. III, App. IV

Real estate markets
constructing price measures, 9.16–9.30
financial soundness indicators, App. II
measuring prices, 9.4–9.11
overview, 2.28
price indices, 9.1–9.30, App. II
structural indicators, 9.12–9.15
uses of FSIs, 14.40–14.41
Red Book
objectives of, 8.52, 13.35, App. VII
Regulatory capital
compared with capital and reserves, 4.75
defined, App. VII
requirements, 4.68
risk-weighted assets, 4.68, 4.74, 6.17–6.18, App. II
supervisory deductions, 4.73
tiers of, 4.69–4.72
Rentals
for nonfinancial corporations, 4.104
reconciliation and the *Guide*'s methodology, App. IV
Rents
for nonfinancial corporations, 4.104
reconciliation and the *Guide*'s methodology, App. IV
Replacement loans, 4.86
Repo. *See* Repurchase agreements
Repurchase agreements, 4.48–4.49
Reserves. *See* Capital and reserves
Residence
aspects of, 3.37–3.43
concept of, 3.34–3.36
geographic distribution of loans, 4.89
Residential real estate loans, 4.88, 6.58–6.60, App. II, App. III, App. IV
Resilience
defined, 8.29, App. VII
measuring, App. III
Retained earnings
compiling consolidated data, 5.76–5.79
for deposit takers, 4.36, 4.63
for nonfinancial corporations, 4.105
Return on assets, 6.52–6.53, 14.12–14.13, App. II
Return on equity, 6.25–6.26, 7.12–7.14, 14.12–14.13, App. III
Revenues from sales of goods and services, App. IV
Revolving underwriting facilities, 3.17
Risk-adjusted return on capital, 14.16
Risk exposures
defined, App. VII
Risk-weighted assets
capital adequacy ratio calculation, Box 4.2
defined, App. VII
regulatory capital requirements, 4.68, 4.74, 6.17–6.18, App. II
ROA. *See* Return on assets
ROE. *See* Return on equity
Royalty income receivable, 4.104, App. IV
RUFs. *See* Revolving underwriting facilities
Salaries, 4.120
Sales of goods and services, App. IV
SDDS. *See* Special Data Dissemination Standard
Seasonal factors, 11.78
Securities dealers
defined, App. VII
overview, 2.14
Securities lending, 4.48–4.49
Securities markets
bid-ask spread, 8.44–8.49
defined, App. VII
immediacy and resilience, 8.29
market depth and tightness, 8.27–8.28, 8.33–8.38
market structure, 8.30–8.32
overview, 8.25–8.26
turnover ratio, 8.39–8.43
Securities repurchase agreements, 4.48–4.49
Series providing analysis of balance sheet, 4.77–4.92
Shares and other equity
for deposit takers, 4.54–4.55
for nonfinancial corporations, 4.104, 4.113
for other financial corporations, 4.98
reconciliation and the *Guide*'s methodology, App. IV
Shell companies, 3.39–3.40
Short-term liabilities, 4.83, App. IV
Short-term maturity, 3.49
SIR. *See* Spread between the highest and lowest interbank rates
Skewness
calculation of, 15.21
defined, App. VII
SLDR. *See* Spread between reference lending and deposit rates
SNA. *See* System of National Accounts
Special Data Dissemination Standard, App. I
Special purpose entities, 3.39–3.40
Special reserves, 4.63
Specialized financial intermediaries
defined, App. VII
Specific loan provisions, 4.50
SPEs. *See* Special purpose entities
Spot exchange rate, 3.48
Spread between reference lending and deposit rates, 8.5–8.20, 14.14, App. II, App. III
Spread between the highest and lowest interbank rates, 8.21–8.24, App. II
Standard deviation, 15.20
Stock market indices, App. III
Strategic issues, 10.2–10.23
Stress testing, 1.25, 13.23–13.27, App. V, Box 13.1
Subsidiaries, 3.37, 5.6–5.7, 5.9
Supervisory-based series, 4.67–4.76
Supervisory deductions, 4.73
Survey on the Use, Compilation, and Dissemination of Macroprudential Indicators, App. I
Survivor bias, 5.38

System of National Accounts, Box 4.1
System of National Accounts, 1993, 1.16, App. IV, Box 4.1

Tails of distribution, 15.35
Taxes, App. IV. *See also* Income taxes
Terminology, 1.30
Tier-1 capital, 4.64, 4.70, 6.19, App. II, Box 4.2
Tier-2 capital, 4.71, Box 4.2
Tier-3 capital, 4.72, Box 4.2
Total debt to equity, 7.10–7.11, 14.32
Trade credits
  for deposit takers, 4.60
  for nonfinancial corporations, 4.112
  reconciliation and the *Guide*'s methodology, App. IV
Trading gains, 6.71–6.72, App. II
Transactions, 3.24
Transferable deposits, 4.41
Triennial Central Bank Survey
  defined, App. VII
Turnover ratio
  average daily trade in securities markets, App. II
  calculation of, 8.39–8.43, 14.22
  defined, App. VII

Unconsolidated subsidiaries, 5.43
Unit of account, 3.48
Unit value real estate prices, 9.16–9.17
Unrestricted investment accounts, Box 4.3

Valuables
  for nonfinancial corporations, 4.109
Valuation adjustment, 4.63
Valuation methods, 3.20–3.23, Box 4.4
Variability, 15.20
Variance
  calculation of, 15.20
  defined, App. VII
Variation in distribution, 15.43–15.44
Vehicle companies
  defined, App. VII
Volatility
  defined, App. VII
  of deposits, 4.43
  monitoring resilience to, 1.8

Wages, 4.120
Weighting, 15.23–15.33